Drugs, Behavior, and Modern Society

Charles F. Levinthal

HOFSTRA UNIVERSITY

Allyn and Bacon

BOSTON
LONDON
TORONTO
SYDNEY
TOKYO
SINGAPORE

Vice President, Publisher: Social Studies: *Susan Badger*
Executive Editor: *Laura Pearson*
Editorial Assistant: *Jennifer Normandin*
Executive Marketing Manager: *Joyce Nilsen*
Editorial-Production Administrator: *Marjorie Payne*
Editorial-Production Service: *Woodstock Publishers' Services*
Composition/Prepress Buyer: *Linda Cox*
Manufacturing Buyer: *Megan Cochran*
Cover Administrator: *Linda Knowles*
Cover Designer: *Studio Nine*
Text Design & Illustration: *Seventeenth Street Studios*

Copyright © 1996 by Allyn & Bacon
A Simon & Schuster Company
Needham Heights, MA 02194

Library of Congress Cataloging-in-Publication Data

Levinthal, Charles F., 1945—
    Drugs, behavior, and modern society / Charles F. Levinthal.
        p.   cm.
    Includes bibliographical references and index.
    ISBN 0–205–14580–9
    1. Drugs.   2. Drug abuse.   3. Drugs—Physiological effect.
  4. Psychotropic drugs.   5. Psychopharmacology.   I. Title.
HV5801.L49   1996
362.29'0973—dc20   95–32753
                                                 CIP

Printed in the United States of America

10 9 8 7 6 5 4 3 2 1   00 99 98 97 96 95

PHOTO CREDITS: Page 3, Ellis Herwig/Stock, Boston; page 9, The Bettmann Archive; page 10, Dennis Stock/Magnum Photos; page 11, Henry Diltz; page 17, Grapes/Michaud/Photo Researchers; page 21, Martin Rogers/Stock, Boston; page 33, Chuck Nacke/Woodfin Camp & Associates; page 37, Eugene Richards/ Magnum Photos; page 42, Robert McElroy/Woodfin Camp & Associates;

Photo credits are continued on page 431, which should be considered an extension of the copyright page.

For
Beth,
David and Brian,
Milt and Selma

Contents

11 Chronic Alcohol Abuse and Alcoholism — 253

12 Nicotine and Tobacco — 283

Preface

n today's world, drugs and their use present a social paradox, combining the potential for good and for bad. As a society and as individuals, Americans can be the beneficiaries of drugs or their victims. This is the essential message of *Drugs, Behavior, and Modern Society*. You will be presented with the basic facts and the major issues concerning drug-taking behavior in U.S. society, in a straightforward, comprehensive, and understandable manner. No background in biology, sociology, psychology, or chemistry is required, only your curiosity about the range of chemical substances that affect our minds and our bodies and your concern about the challenges these substances bring to our daily lives.

As you begin this book, you will embark upon a journey that began thousands of years ago and has been continuing ever since. Some of the problems that we tend to view as belonging to the present time are really problems that society has had to confront for quite a while. In an important way, drugs can be seen as a mirror reflecting ourselves. As humans we are an intensely curious species; we have discovered substances that make us feel stronger, more alert, calmer, more distant from our surroundings, or simply good. It is the misuse and abuse of these substances that has resulted in massive problems in the United States and around the world.

As a first step toward understanding the complex issues surrounding drugs in U.S. society, we need to recognize the enormous diversity that exists among drugs that affect the mind and the body. We must educate ourselves not only about the illicit street drugs such as heroin and cocaine but also about legally available drugs such as nicotine, alcohol, and caffeine. *Drugs, Behavior, and Modern Society* is designed to be the most comprehensive review of psychoactive drugs of any undergraduate college textbook on the market today. It is particularly notable for the attention given to two aspects of drug-taking behavior that have been underreported in previously written texts: inhalant abuse and steroid abuse. They have deserved chapters of their own, Chapters 6 and 14 respectively.

We also need to recognize that the problems surrounding drug misuse and abuse are not someone else's concern but rather everyone's concern. Like it or not, the decision to use drugs today is one of life's choices—regardless of our racial or ethnic background, how much money we have, where we live, how much education we have acquired, whether we are male or female, or whether we are young or old. The potential for misuse and abuse is a problem facing all of us.

Features of This Book

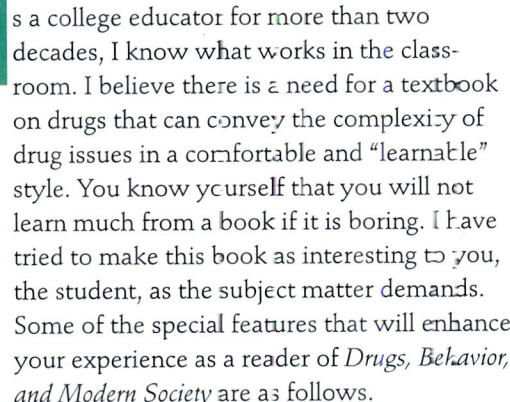

s a college educator for more than two decades, I know what works in the classroom. I believe there is a need for a textbook on drugs that can convey the complexity of drug issues in a comfortable and "learnable" style. You know yourself that you will not learn much from a book if it is boring. I have tried to make this book as interesting to you, the student, as the subject matter demands. Some of the special features that will enhance your experience as a reader of *Drugs, Behavior, and Modern Society* are as follows.

Quick Concept Checks

Sometimes, when the material gets complicated, you may want to have a quick way of finding out if you understand the basic concepts being explained. I have included from time to time a Quick Concept Check, where you can see in a minute or two where you stand. Some of the Checks will be in a matching format; others will be an interpretation of a graph or a diagram. I hope you will enjoy them and the reinforcement they can give you.

Point/Counterpoint Debates

Drug issues are never black or white, right or wrong. Some of the most controversial questions of our day involve the use, misuse, and abuse of drugs, all of which require some critical thinking. This is the reason why I have written a Point/Counterpoint Debate at the end of selected chapters. I have taken some fundamental controversies concerning drugs, collected the primary viewpoints pro and con, and simulated a debate that two hypothetical people might have on that question. I invite you to read these debates carefully and try to come to your own position, as an exercise in critical thinking. You may even wish to continue the debate in your class.

Drug Abuse Alerts

In this book, two features will bring you into the subject matter in a personalized way. The first is the series of Drug Abuse Alerts among the Focus features throughout the text. In some Alerts, they will involve the practical knowledge you might need to deal with emergency situations involving drugs; in other Alerts you may be informed of ways to recognize the behavioral symptoms or bodily signs that drug abuse may be going on among people you know. This information, needless to say, is important; it may even save a life someday.

Portraits

A second personalized feature of this book is the Portraits, which appear in each chapter. They consist of short biographical stories of real people, some who are known to the public at large and others who are not. In each Portrait, there is an important message that I hope will add a human touch to the discussion of drugs in our society. We have to remember that we are dealing with issues that affect real people in all walks of life, now and in the past. These Portraits take you into the lives of people who have influenced and been influenced by social policies regarding drug use and abuse.

Other Features

Other aids to your reading enjoyment and learning experience are a glossary and a pronunciation guide for drug names and other difficult terms, positioned on the page where they are first introduced. At the end of chapters, a summary presented in a "bulleted" fashion allows an easy review of the chapter's main points. An alphabetized list of key terms helps you to review the principal terminology. Video excerpts from Cable News Network (CNN) are also available to help make the connection between material in the text and real-life events. These excerpts have been selected to enhance your classroom experience and to make this book enriching for you as a student.

An invitation to readers

want to invite all of you to tell me your reactions to *Drugs, Behavior, and Modern Society*. Please send your comments and questions to me at the following address: Dr. Charles F. Levinthal, Department of Psychology, Hofstra University, Hempstead NY 11550. You can also FAX them to me at (516) 463–6052 or E-mail them to me at PSYCFL@vaxc.hofstra.edu. I hope to be hearing from you.

Acknowledgments

n the course of writing this book, I have received much encouragement, assistance, and expert advice from a number of wonderful people. I have benefited from their generous sharing of materials, knowledge, and insights. Two of my colleagues at Hofstra, Mitchell Schare and Paul Meller, were indispensable resources for information during my research, particularly in the areas of drug treatment and prevention. Meredith Poulten, director of the Walk-in Center in Medway, Massachusetts, provided me with a unique and personal insight into the real-world challenges that face professionals who are working with young people on a daily basis.

Several others deserve my thanks and appreciation:

Police Sergeant Enrico J. Annichiarico, Director of Community Relations, Suffolk County Police Department, New York

F. Michler Bishop, Institute for Rational-Emotive Therapy, New York

David A. Cohen, Family Treatment Program, Long Island—Jewish Medical Center, New York

Howard Dorfman, Senior Associate Counsel, Bristol-Myers Squibb Company, New York

Royal Brown, Director, Film Studies Program, Queens College, City University of New York

Robert M. Julien, Professor of Anesthesiology, St. Vincent Hospital and Medical Center, Portland, Oregon

Candace Lightner, founder of Mothers Against Drunk Driving (MADD), now residing in Washington D.C.

Louis Macolino, Vice President, On-premise Sales, Charmer Industries, New York

Norweeta Milburn, Assistant Professor, Department of Psychology, Hofstra University

Patrick O'Malley, coauthor of the Monitoring the Future Project, Institute for Social Research, University of Michigan, Ann Arbor

Junko Tanaka-Matsumi, Associate Professor, Department of Psychology, Hofstra University

Sergei Tsystarev, Adjunct Assistant Professor, Department of Psychology, Hofstra University

Elizabeth M. Whalen, President of the American Council on Science and Health, New York

In addition, the following Hofstra students and personal friends were extremely helpful in the process of researching this book: Sonia Azevedo, Marla Cantor, Per Hoegh, and Esther Tonnesen.

I am very fortunate to have worked with a superb team at Allyn and Bacon. Their genuine love for the written word and their standards of excellence have made my association with them a pleasure. I am especially indebted to my editor Laura Pearson, her assistant Jennifer Normandin, and Susan Badger, vice president and publisher at Allyn and Bacon. From our first meeting and throughout the entire project, they have given me their complete faith and support. Their unerring professionalism and friendship are greatly appreciated. I also want to acknowledge the efforts of those individuals whose talents and expertise contributed so much to the production quality of this book: Marjorie Payne, Barbara Gracia, Susan Winslow, Laurie Frankenthaler, and Yoram Mizrahi.

A number of manuscript reviewers, whose identities had been kept secret from me up to now, were invaluable for their suggestions as I modified and improved earlier drafts of this book. Now I know their names, and I thank each of them for their help:

David M. White, East Carolina University; Gerald Garrett, University of Massachusetts/Boston; Molly Laflin, Bowling Green State University; Jack Benson, Eastern Washington University; Frank Wong, Boston University;

Fred Beauvais, Colorado State University; Jeffrey Nevid, St. John's University; Charles W. Sharp, National Institute on Drug Abuse; Elizabeth M. Whalen, American Council on Science and Health; Roland Griffiths, Behavioral Biology Research Center; Pedro Garrido, Cambridge Hospital; Jim MacDonall, Fordham University; Nolan Ashman, Dixie College; Kent Pierce, Purdue University/Calumet; George Taylor, University of Missouri; Donna Procopio, Springfield College; Linda Olasov, Northern Kentucky University; Richard Hurley, Brigham Young University; Dale Evans, California State University/Long Beach; Lloyd Goodwin, East Carolina University; Marc Gellman, University of Miami; and Russell Smiley, Normandale Community College.

On a more personal note, there are others who have given me their support over the years and to whom my appreciation is more difficult to convey accurately or adequately. As always, I thank my mother, Mildred Levinthal. My parents-in-law, Milton and Selma Kuby, not only gave me encouragement throughout this project but also provided valuable resources during its initial stages. I thank them both.

Above all, my family has been a continuing source of strength and support. I will always be grateful for the patience and understanding of my sons, David and Brian, as well as their valuable critiques of early chapters. I am especially grateful to my wife, Beth, for her love and complete faith in my ability to undertake this project. I could not have done it without them.

1

Drugs and Behavior Today

> "Kids . . . do it to fit in with the cool people, and to try to act older."

> A 19-year-old high school graduate, 1994

n the United States today, more than ever, drugs affect our daily lives. It is difficult to pick up a newspaper or to watch television without finding a report or program that concerns drug use or some issue associated with it. In your personal life, you have had to confront the reality of drugs around you. In school, you have probably been taught the risks involved in drug use, and very likely you have had to contend with the possibility of drugs being sold to you. Many high school students on a Monday morning boast about how much beer they consumed at a keg party over the weekend. For some students, alcohol consumption begins in junior high school or earlier. Experimentation with marijuana and mind-altering pills of all sorts seems commonplace. Whether we like it or not, the decision to use drugs has become one of life's choices in American society.

At the same time, we live in a world of mixed messages. On the one hand, advertising images of Joe Camel, the Marlboro Man, and the Virginia Slims Woman convey the desirability of smoking; on the other, warning labels on cigarette packs and billboards tell us about the serious hazards of smoking. Television commercials associate the drinking of beer with a sex life beyond your fondest dreams and then imply that you should know "when to say when." Prominent political figures, including President Bill Clinton and Vice President Al Gore, admit their experience with marijuana earlier in their lives. And yet, marijuana remains an illegal substance that has been classified since 1970, as will be noted in Chapter 2, in the same category as heroin and cocaine.[1] Antidrug campaigns in the media attempt to discourage young people from

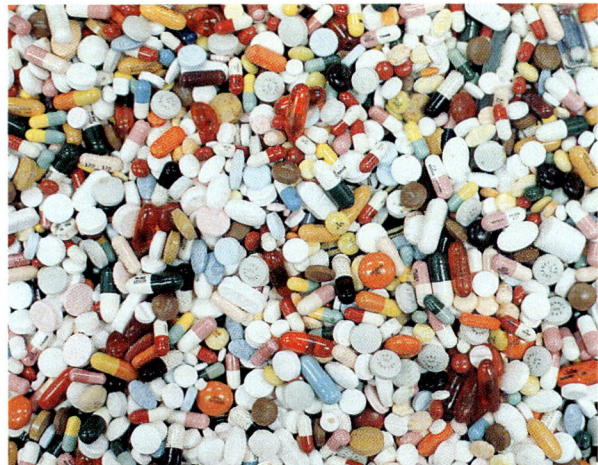

becoming involved with drugs, yet we observe a continual stream of sports figures and celebrities whose careers have been jeopardized, and who in some cases have lost their lives, because of their problems with drugs.

These facts, as contradictory as some of them are, represent the present-day drug scene in the United States. It is not just a "young person's problem" but one that encompasses every segment of our society. The availability of drugs and the potential for drug abuse present a challenge for people of all ages, from the young to the elderly. The personal and social problems associated with drugs extend in one way or another to both men and women and to people of all ethnic groups and socioeconomic levels. No group should believe themselves exempt.

Despite our concerns about the dangers, however, we should recognize another important side to the topic of drugs today. You may know someone whose depression nearly led to suicide but who is now living a normal life after taking antidepressant drugs. You may know someone else who has been helped by a drug that controls anxiety. Millions of individuals in the United States and around the world who suffer from the torment of mental illness have benefited from drug treatment. With new therapeutic drugs continually being developed, you can be certain that in the near future even more effec-

tive drugs will be available to treat psychiatric disorders. There is tremendous excitement among those involved in drug research now, and a good deal of hope.

The purpose of this book is to answer your questions and address your concerns about drugs and behavior, to sort out the facts from the myths. A glance at the contents will show you the wide range of drugs that will be covered. As you will discover, our society has had as many problems contending with legal drugs as it has had dealing with those that are illegal.

There are two basic ways in which we can look at the subject of drugs and behavior. First of all, we can speak of specific drugs that alter our feelings, our thoughts, our perceptions of the world, and our behavior. We call these types of drugs **psychoactive drugs,** because they influence the functioning of the brain and hence our behavior. The most dramatic examples are **illicit** (illegal) **drugs,** such as heroin, cocaine, marijuana, and LSD (lysergic acid diethylamide). Other psychoactive substances are **licit** (legal) **drugs,** such as alcohol, nicotine, and caffeine.

Second, we can speak of factors that lead to *drug-taking behavior.* The use of drugs does not occur in a vacuum but rather can be, at least in part, a consequence of our feelings and perceptions about ourselves in relationship to parents, friends, and the community

psychoactive drugs
Drugs that affect feelings, thoughts, perceptions, or behavior

illicit drugs
Drugs whose manufacture, sale, or possession is illegal.

licit drugs
Drugs whose manufacture, sale, or possession is legal.

we live in. The important question of drug-taking behavior will be discussed throughout this book.

It should not be surprising that psychoactive drugs and drug-taking behavior can often interact with each other, creating a cycle, or behavioral "loop," that is difficult to break. In an extreme example, the intake of heroin or cocaine sets off changes within the brain as well as outward behavioral changes that greatly increase the probability of future drug use. We call this situation a **cycle of dependence.** Smoking is another example of a cycle of dependence; the intake of nicotine in the cigarettes causes internal changes that result in a craving for more at some future time. It should be emphasized, however, that, although dependence is not necessarily a characteristic of psychoactive drugs in general, some psychoactive drugs produce strong dependence reactions. The issues of drug dependence will be considered in Chapter 2.

A matter of definition

t first glance, it should be relatively easy to define what we mean by the word **drug.** Unfortunately, there are significant problems in arriving at a clear definition. The standard approach is to characterize a drug as a *chemical substance that, when taken into the body, alters the functioning of the body in some way.*[2] In doing so, we are accounting for examples such as medications used for the treatment of physical disorders and mental illnesses, as well as for alcohol, nicotine, and the typical street drugs. Unfortunately, this broad definition

cycle of dependence
A process by which the taking of a drug sets up physiological or environmental changes that encourage future drug taking.

drugs
Chemical substances that, when taken into the body, alter the functioning of the body in some way, excluding those nutrients considered to be related to normal functioning.

could also refer to ordinary food and water. Since it does not make much sense for nutrients to be considered drugs, it is helpful to have a modified definition that adds the phrase, *excluding those nutrients considered to be related to normal functioning.*

Bear in mind, however, that we may still be on slippery ground. We can now effectively eliminate the cheese in your next pizza from consideration as a drug, but what about some exotic ingredient in the sauce? Sugar is safely excluded, even though it has significant energizing and therefore behavioral effects on us, but what about the cayenne pepper that burns your tongue? Is it fair to make this distinction?

We can learn two important lessons from this seemingly easy task of defining a drug. First of all, there is probably no perfect definition that would distinguish drugs from non-drugs without leaving a number of cases that fall in some kind of gray area. The best we can do is to set up a definition, as we have, that handles most of the substances we are likely to encounter.

The second lesson is more subtle. We often make the distinction between drugs and non-drugs not in terms of their physical characteristics but rather in terms of whether the substance in question has been *intended to be used* primarily as a way of inducing a bodily or psychological change.[3] If the pizza maker intended to put that spice in the pizza to make it taste better, the spice would not be considered a drug. It would simply be another ingredient in the recipe. If the pizza maker intended the spice to intoxicate you or quicken your heart rate, then it would be considered a drug. Chapter 12 will note that the issue of intent is precisely at the core of determining whether nicotine, a natural component of tobacco, should be considered as a drug by the U.S. Food and Drug Administration (FDA).

Ultimately, the problem is that we are trying to create a definition that fits our intuitive sense of what constitutes a drug. We may find it difficult to define pornography, but (as has been said) we know it when we see it. So it may be with drugs. Whether we realize it or not, when we discuss the topic of drugs we are operating within a context of social and cultural values, a group of shared feelings about what kind of behavior (that is, what kind of drug-taking behavior) is right and what kind is wrong.

The judgments we make about drug-taking behavior even influence the terminology we use when referring to that behavior. When we use the common terms "drug misuse" and "drug abuse," for example, we are implying that something wrong is happening, that a drug is producing some harm to the physical health or psychological well-being of the drug user or to society in general. But what criteria do we use to decide whether misuse or abuse is going on? We cannot use the distinction between legality and illegality, since whether a psychoactive drug is legal may depend not only upon the specific properties of the drug but upon historical and cultural circumstances as well. Tobacco, for example, has deep-rooted associations in American history, going back to the days of Christopher Columbus and the early settlers at Jamestown, Virginia; and although it may be objectionable to many individuals and harmful to a smoker's health and the health of others around them, it is legally available. Alcohol is another substance that is legal, within the bounds of the law, even though it can be harmful to individuals who drink and potentially harmful to others who may be affected by the drinker's behavior. The difficulty of using a criterion based upon legality is further complicated by cultural differences around the world. In Muslim countries, such as Iran and Saudi Arabia, alcohol is illegal; in Nepal and parts of India, marijuana is legal.[4]

Instrumental and recreational use of drugs

As you might expect, the relationship between drugs and behavior can be defined not only in the sense of a drug's legality but also in terms of the motivation of the user. Depending upon the intent of the individual, drug use can be considered either instrumental or recreational.[5] By **instrumental use,** we mean that a person has a specific behavioral goal in mind when taking a drug: the user may want to stay awake longer, fall asleep more quickly, or recover from an illness. The instrumental use of drugs can involve prescription and nonprescription (over-the-counter) drugs that are licitly obtained and taken for a particular medical purpose. Examples include an antidepressant prescribed for depression, a cold remedy for a cold, an anticonvulsant drug to control epileptic seizures, or insulin to maintain the health of a person with diabetes. The instrumental use of drugs can also involve drugs that are illicitly obtained, such as an amphetamine that has been procured through illegal means to help a person stay awake and alert after hours without sleep.

In contrast, by **recreational use** we mean the use of a drug for no other reason than achieving some desirable pleasurable feeling or psychological state. Alcohol and tobacco fit into the category of licit drugs for recreational use; street drugs generally fall into the category of illicit recreational drug use.

Misuse and abuse of drugs

How do misuse and abuse fit into this scheme? **Drug misuse** is typically applied to cases in which a prescription or nonprescription drug is used in an inappropriate way.

---

instrumental use
Referring to the motivation of a drug user who takes the drug for a specific purpose other than getting "high."

recreational use
Referring to the motivation of the drug user who takes the drug only in order to get "high" or achieve some pleasurable effect.

drug misuse
Drug-taking behavior in which a prescription or nonprescription drug is used in an inappropriate way.

Many instances of drug misuse involve instrumental goals. For example, drug doses may be increased beyond the level of the prescription in the mistaken idea that if a little is good, more will work better. Or doses may be decreased from the level of the prescription to make the drug supply last longer. Drugs may be continued past the time during which they were originally needed; or a prescription drug might be shared by family members or lent to a friend even though the medical conditions may differ among them.

Drug misuse can be dangerous and potentially lethal, particularly when alcohol is combined with drugs that depress the nervous system. Drugs that have this particular feature include antihistamines, antianxiety drugs, and sleeping medications. Even if alcohol is not involved, however, drug combinations can still represent serious health risks, particularly for the elderly, who often take a large number of separate medications. They are especially vulnerable to the hazards of drug misuse.

In contrast, **drug abuse** is typically applied to cases in which a licit or illicit drug is used in ways that produce some form of physical, mental, or social impairment. The primary motivation for individuals involved in drug abuse is recreational. We should remember that drugs with abuse potential include not only the common street drugs but also legally available psychoactive substances such as caffeine and nicotine (stimulants) and alcohol (a depressant), as well as a number of prescription drugs used for medical purposes. In this book, when there is no intent to make a value judgment as to the motivation or consequences of a particular type of drug-taking behavior, we will refer to that behavior simply as drug use.

Given the major role that drugs and drug-taking behavior are playing in society today, it is important for us to look at the ways in which drugs and drug-taking behavior have been viewed in the past. Have things changed, or have they remained the same? Have drugs always been around? How did people feel about drugs and drug-taking behavior one hundred years ago, fifty years ago, or twenty-five years ago? These are the questions to which we now turn.

Drugs in early times

t is not difficult to imagine the circumstances under which a psychoactive drug might have been accidentally discovered. For a hunting-and-gathering society thousands of years ago, perhaps hundreds of thousands of years ago, the process of discovery was as natural as eating, and the motivation as basic as simple curiosity. In cool climates, next to a cave may have grown a profusion of blue morning glories or brightly colored mushrooms, plants that produce hallucinations similar to those of LSD. In desert regions, yellow-orange fruits grew on certain cacti, the source of the hallucinogenic drug peyote. Elsewhere, poppy plants, the source of opium, covered acres of open fields. A pink blossom called *Rauwolfia,* the source of a powerful psychiatric drug, grew in the high mountains of Asia. Coca leaves, from which cocaine is made, grew on shrubs along the mountain valleys throughout Central and South America; while the hardy cannabis plant, the source of marijuana, grew practically everywhere.[6] Somewhere along the line, people made the connection between the chewing of willow bark (the source of modern-day aspirin) and the relief of a headache, or the eating of the senna plant (a natural laxative) and the relief of constipation.

Of course, some plants made people sick, and many were sufficiently poisonous to cause death. Probably, however, the plants that had the strangest impact on humans were the ones that produced hallucinations. Having a sudden vision of something totally alien to everyday living must have been overwhelming, like a visit to another world. Individuals with prior knowledge about such

drug abuse
Drug-taking behavior resulting in some form of physical, mental, or social impairment.

plants, as well as about plants with therapeutic powers, would eventually acquire great power over others in the community. This knowledge was the beginning of **shamanism,** a practice among primitive societies in which an individual called a **shaman** acted as a healer through a combination of trances and plant-based medicines, usually in the context of a local religion. Shamans, as will be described later, still function today in South America and Africa, alongside practitioners of modern medicine.

With the development of centralized religions in Egyptian and Babylonian societies, shamanism gradually declined. The principal reasons were essentially political. For a society based on strict and rigidly controlled religious principles, a man or woman who had a trance-like vision, whether induced by a hallucinogenic drug or by some kind of self-hypnosis, could never be considered trustworthy. Who knew what vision might contradict some aspect of official religious doctrine? The guardians of religion, the priests, found it safer to concentrate on elaborate rituals rather than visions. Besides, shamans were independent practitioners, relying on their own personal skills. The duties of an ancient priesthood, by contrast, could be mastered only after extensive training within the priesthood itself. In this way, the priests could stay in control.[7]

Nevertheless, despite the new shift in emphasis from do-your-own-thing hallucinations to prescribed rituals and rules, knowledge of drugs was still a source of great power, since drugs still had the ability to heal, to make a difference between life or death. Probably the most dramatic testament to the development of priestly healing at this time in history is a sixty-five-foot-long scroll known as the **Ebers Papyrus,** named after the British Egyptologist who acquired it in 1872. This mammoth document, dating from 1500 B.C., contains more than eight hundred prescriptions for practically every ailment imaginable, including simple wasp stings and crocodile bites, baldness, constipation, headaches, enlarged prostate glands, sweaty

feet, arthritis, inflammations of all types, heart disease, and cancer. More than a hundred of the preparations contained castor oil as a natural laxative; some contained "the berry of the poppy," which is now recognized as referring to opium. Other ingredients were quite bizarre: lizard's blood, the teeth of swine, the oil of worms, the hoof of an ass, putrid meat with fly specks, and crocodile dung (excrement of all types being highly favored for its ability to frighten off the evil spirits of disease).[8]

How successful were these strange remedies? It is impossible to know, since no records were kept on what happened to the patients. While some of the ingredients, such as opium and castor oil, had truly medicinal value, it may be that much of the improvement from these concoctions was psychological rather than physiological. In other words, improvements in the patient's condition resulted from the *belief* on the patient's part that he or she would be helped, a phenomenon known as the **placebo effect.** Psychological factors have played a critical role throughout the history of drugs. Chapter 3 will examine in more detail the importance of the placebo effect as an explanation of some drug effects.

Along with substances that had genuine healing properties, other psychoactive drugs

shaman (SHAH-men)
A healer whose diagnosis or treatment of patients is based at least in part on trances. These trances are frequently induced by hallucinogenic drugs.

shamanism
The philosophy and practice of healing in which the diagnosis or treatment is based on trance-like states, either on the part of the healer (shaman) or the patient.

Ebers papyrus
An Egyptian document, dating approximately 1500 B.C., containing more than 800 prescriptions for common ailments and diseases.

placebo (pla-CEE-bo) effect
Any change in a person's condition after taking a drug based solely on that person's beliefs about the drug rather than on any physical effects of the drug.

were recognized for their recreational rather than their instrumental possibilities. In the early Middle Ages, Viking warriors ate the mushroom *Amanita muscaria,* known as fly agaric, and experienced increased energy, which resulted in wild behavior in battle. They were called Berserkers because of the bear skins they wore, and reckless, violent behavior has come to be called beserk. Later, witches operating on the periphery of Christian society created "witch's brews." They were said to induce hallucinations and a sensation of flying by consuming mixtures made of various plants called mandrake, henbane, and belladonna. The toads that they included in their recipes did not hurt either, since we know now that the sweat glands of toads contain bufotenine, a powerful hallucinogenic drug.[9]

Drugs in the nineteenth century

Near the end of the nineteenth century, the medical profession could look back on a number of significant accomplishments with regard to drugs. Generally speaking, the transition had been made from working with natural substances, as healers had done for centuries, to working with purified substances that had been chemically isolated from those natural substances. Morphine was identified as the active ingredient in opium, a drug that had been in use for at least three thousand years and had become the physician's most reliable prescription to control the pain of disease and injury. The invention of the syringe made it possible to deliver the morphine directly and speedily into the bloodstream. Cocaine, having been extracted from coca leaves, was used as a stimulant and antidepressant. Sedative powers to calm the

mind or induce sleep had been discovered in bromides and chloral hydrate.[10]

The nineteenth century also saw the development of drugs that were used for specific purposes or specific diseases. Anesthetic drugs had been discovered that made surgery painless for the first time in history. A few diseases could actually be prevented through the administration of vaccines, such as the vaccine against smallpox that had been introduced by Edward Jenner in 1796 and the vaccine against rabies introduced by Louis Pasteur in 1885. With the discovery of new pharmaceutical products, the modern era in the history of the healing arts was beginning.[11]

The social picture of drug-taking behavior during this time, however, was more complicated. By the 1890s, prominent leaders in the medical profession had begun to call attention to social problems resulting from the widespread and uncontrolled access to psychoactive drugs. Remedies called **patent medicines,** sold through advertisements, peddlers, or general stores, contained opium, alcohol, and cocaine and were promoted as answers to every common medical or nonmedical complaint. Opium itself was cheap, easily available, and completely legal. Most people, from newborn infants to the elderly, in the United States and England "took opium" during their lives. The way in which they took it, however, was a critical social factor. The respectable way was to drink it, usually in a liquid form called *laudanum.* By contrast, the smoking of opium, as introduced by Chinese immigrants imported for manual labor in the American West, was considered degrading and immoral. Laws prohibiting opium smoking began to be enacted in 1875. Considering the contrast with the tolerant attitude toward opium drinking, the strong emotional opposition to opium smoking can be viewed as more anti-Chinese than antiopium.[12]

Like opium, cocaine was also a drug in widespread use in Europe and North America and was taken quite casually in the form of beverages. The original formula for Coca-Cola, as the name suggests, contained cocaine until

patent medicine
A drug or combination of drugs sold through peddlers, shops, or mail-order advertisements.

1903, as did Dr. Agnew's Catarrh Powder, a popular remedy for chest colds. In the mid-1880s, Parke, Davis, and Company was selling cocaine and its botanical source, coca, in more than a dozen forms, including coca-leaf cigarettes and cigars, cocaine inhalant, a coca cordial, and an injectable cocaine solution.[13] A Viennese doctor named Sigmund Freud, who was later to gain a greater reputation for his psychoanalytic theories than for his ideas concerning psychoactive drugs, called cocaine a "magical drug," and, in an influential paper published in 1884, he recommended cocaine as a safe and effective treatment for morphine addiction. When a friend and colleague became heavily addicted to cocaine, Freud quickly reversed his position, regretting for the rest of his life that he had been initially so enthusiastic in recommending its use.[14]

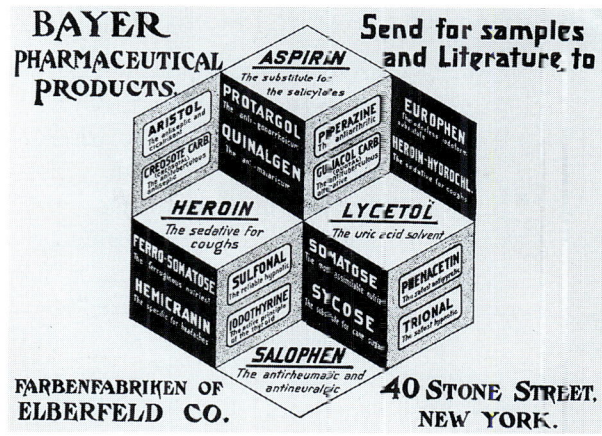

Around 1900, heroin was advertised as a completely safe remedy for common ailments, along with aspirin. No one knows the number of individuals who became dependent upon heroin as a result.

Drugs and behavior in the twentieth century

By 1900, the promise of medical advances in the area of drugs was beginning to be matched by concern about the dependence that some of these drugs could produce. For a short while after its introduction in 1898, heroin (a drug derived from morphine) was completely legal and considered safe. In fact, it was even recommended by many physicians as a treatment for morphine addiction. Its powerful addictive properties, however, were soon evident. One response to this concern was a growing social support for the regulation of access to heroin. By 1914, heroin and other opium-based substances could not be obtained without a medical prescription, and under such restrictive circumstances physicians gave up issuing medical prescriptions for it. Additional restrictive legislation for other psychoactive drugs, including marijuana, would follow in later years, a topic discussed further in Chapter 2.

At the beginning of the twentieth century, neither the general public nor the government considered alcohol as a drug. Nonetheless, the temperance movement dedicated to the prohibition of alcohol consumption, led by the Women's Christian Temperance Union and the Anti-Saloon League, was a formidable political force. In 1920 the Eighteenth Amendment to the U.S. Constitution took effect, ushering in the era of Prohibition, which lasted for thirteen years.

Although succeeding in substantially reducing the rates of alcohol consumption in most states as well as the number of deaths attributed to alcohol-related diseases, the Prohibition Era also succeeded in establishing a nationwide alcohol distribution network dominated by sophisticated criminal organizations.[15] Violent gang wars arose in major cities as one group battled another for control of the liquor trade. By the early 1930s, whatever desirable health-related effects Prohibition may have brought were perceived to be overshadowed by the undesirable social changes that had come along with it. Since its end in 1933, the social problems associated with the era of Prohibition have often been cited as an argument against the continuing restriction of psychoactive drugs in general.

Drugs and behavior from 1945 to 1960

In the years following World War II, a medical revolution was underway. For the first time, physicians were able to control bacteria-carried infectious diseases through the administration of antibiotic drugs. Although penicillin had been discovered in a particular species of mold by Alexander Fleming in 1928, techniques for extracting large amounts from the mold were not perfected until the 1940s. Also during that time, Selman Waksman found that a species of fungus had powerful antibacterial effects, later to be the source of the drug streptomycin.[16] This era marked the birth of present-day chemotherapy.

In the field of psychiatry, advances in therapeutic drugs did not occur until the early 1950s, when quite accidentally a group of psychoactive drugs were discovered that relieved schizophrenic symptoms without producing heavy sedation. The first of these, still commonly used today, was **chlorpromazine** (brand name: Thorazine). Originally used as a drug to facilitate presurgical anesthesia, by 1954 chlorpromazine was identified as a drug that could reduce the hallucinations, agitation, and disordered thinking common to schizophrenia. Soon after, a torrent of new drugs were introduced not only for schizophrenia but for the whole range of mental illnesses. It was a revolution in psychiatric care, equivalent to the impact of antibiotics in medical care a decade earlier.

In the recreational drug scene in the post-World War II United States, a few features stand out. Smoking was considered romantic and sexy, as one could observe by going to the movies and seeing the hero and heroine lighting up their cigarettes or even sharing the same one. It was the era of the two-martini lunch, when social drinking was at its height of popularity and acceptance. Cocktail parties

James Dean was one of many Hollywood actors and actresses in the 1950s whose smoking was part of their glamorous screen image.

dominated the social scene. There was little or no public awareness that alcohol or nicotine consumption were drug-taking behaviors.

However, the general perception of certain drugs such as heroin, marijuana, and cocaine was simple and negative: They were considered bad, illegal, and no one you knew had anything to do with them. Illicit drugs were seen as the province of criminals, the urban poor, and nonwhites.[17] The point is that a whole class of drugs were, during this period of time, outside the mainstream of American life. Furthermore, an atmosphere of fear and suspicion surrounded the idea of people who took such drugs. For the vast majority of Americans at this time, drugs were not considered an issue in their lives.

Drugs and behavior from 1960 to the present

During the 1960s, basic premises of American life—the beliefs that working hard

chlorpromazine
(chlor-PRO-mah-zeen)
An antipsychotic (antischizophrenia) drug. Brand name is Thorazine (THOR-a-zeen).

and living a good life would bring happiness and that society was stable and calm—were being undermined by disturbing events. We watched President John F. Kennedy assassinated in 1963 and Reverend Martin Luther King, Jr. and Senator Robert Kennedy gunned down in 1968. We worried about the continuing cold war and nuclear annihilation. College students found it difficult to believe in the dream of prosperity that their parents had held. The reality of the Vietnam War represented to many of them all that had gone wrong with the previous generation. They were searching for new answers to old problems, and their search led to experimentation with drugs that their parents had been taught to fear. The principal symbol of this era of defiance against the established order, or indeed against anyone over thirty years old, was marijuana. No longer was marijuana something foreign to middle America.

Marijuana, as well as other drugs such as hallucinogenic LSD, "uppers," and "downers," became associated with sons and daughters in our own families and in our own neighborhoods. Along with the turbulence of this period came also a disturbing increase in heroin abuse across the country. The issues surrounding drug abuse, once a problem associated with minority populations and the poor, were now too close to our personal lives for us to ignore.

One of the governmental responses to these events, particularly the increase in heroin addiction, was to finance basic research related to the effects of drugs on the brain. The timing could not have been better. During the early 1970s, a new branch of science, called **neuroscience,** was being established. Its intent was to bring researchers from formerly separate scientific fields together in a new collaborative effort to understand the relationship between brain functioning and human behavior. In the area of drug research, pharmacologists (those specialized in the study of drugs) were joined by biochemists, psychologists, and psychiatrists, among others. One of the important discover-

The famous Woodstock Festival concert drew an estimated 500,000 people to a farm in upstate New York in the summer of 1969. According to historian David Musto, " . . . it was said that the [use of marijuana] at the gigantic Woodstock gathering kept peace—as opposed to what might have happened if alcohol had been the drug of choice."

ies that emerged from this era was the identification of receptors in the brain that are tailored specifically for drugs taken into the body. The findings of neuroscience research will be discussed in Chapter 3 and the chapters that follow.

With the decade of the 1980s came significant changes in the mood of the country in the form of a social and political reaction to earlier decades. If the media symbol had formerly been the "hippie," now it was the "yuppie," a young, upwardly mobile professional. The political climate grew more conservative, in all age groups.[18] In the area of drugs, the concern about heroin addiction was being overshadowed by a new fixation: cocaine. At first, cocaine took on the aura of glamor and (since it was so expensive) became a symbol of material success. The media spotlight shone on a steady stream

neuroscience
A collaborative effort among scientists to understand the human brain and its relationship to behavior.

of celebrities in entertainment and sports who used cocaine. Not long after, however, the harsh realities of cocaine dependence were recognized. The very same celebrities who had accepted cocaine into their lives were now experiencing the consequences; many were in rehabilitation programs, and some had died from cocaine overdoses.

To make matters worse, in 1985, a new form of cocaine called **crack,** smokable and cheap, succeeded in extending the problems of cocaine dependence to urban ghettos, to members of society who could never have afforded cocaine itself. Crack dependence quickly became a national nightmare.

Drugs and behavior today

The attitude toward drug-taking behavior at the close of the twentieth century is quite different from the attitude that prevailed even as recently as twenty years ago. There is a far greater awareness that a wide range of psychoactive drugs, whether they are licit or illicit, all qualify as substances with varying levels of potential for abuse. The "war on drugs," declared in 1971 and now in its third decade in the United States, is no longer a war on a particular drug, such as heroin in the 1970s or cocaine in the 1980s. We have to be concerned with the emergence of designer drugs, substances that present abuse problems but do not fit the technical categories of commonly abused drugs. We have to be concerned with the widespread personal and social problems created by the abuse of alcohol, as well as the misuse of prescription drugs. We have to be concerned with the abuse of steroids, inhalants, and nicotine. The war being waged today is against a wide range of substance misuse and abuse that touches all segments of American society. And yet, in the area of psychiatric treatment, new therapeutic drugs are being designed to be more effective than ever in reducing the suffering of mental illness.

QUICK CONCEPT CHECK   1.1

Understanding the history of drugs and behavior

heck your understanding of the changes in drug-taking behavior over history by matching the statement (on the left) with the appropriate historical period (on the right).

1. Opium and castor oil are first documented as therapeutic drugs.

2. Marijuana use symbolizes a generation's defiance against establishment values.

3. Waksman discovers antibacterial effects of streptomycin.

4. Opium use extends to all levels of Western society.

5. Cocaine use is at its peak as a symbol of glamor and material success.

6. Heroin is first introduced as a treatment for morphine addiction.

7. Antischizophrenic drugs begin widespread use in mental hospitals.

8. Vaccines against smallpox and rabies are introduced.

A. approximately 1500 B.C.

B. late 1700s to late 1880s

C. late 1800s

D. late 1940s

E. mid-1950s

F. late 1960s to early 1970s

G. early 1980s

ANSWERS: 1.A. 2.F. 3.D. 4.B. 5.G. 6.C. 7.E. 8.B.

Patterns of drug use among American youth

n arriving at some statistical idea about drug use today, we first have to ask the question; How could we ever succeed in obtaining such information? Assuming that we could not conduct large-scale random drug testing, the only alternative we have is simply to ask people about their drug-taking behavior through self-reports. We encourage honesty and arrange the data-collection procedure so as to make the respondents feel that their answers are confidential, but the truth is that any questionnaire is inherently imperfect because there is no perfect way to check the validity of what people say about themselves. Nevertheless, questionnaires are all we have, and the statistics on drug use are based upon such survey measures.

One of the best-known surveys, tapping into the drug-taking patterns of young people, has been conducted every year since 1975 by the University of Michigan. In 1993, more than 50,000 American students in the eighth, tenth, and twelfth grades participated in the survey, as well as more than 8,000 college students and young adults between the ages of nineteen and thirty-two.[19] The advantage of repeating the survey with a new sample year after year is the ability it gives us to look at trends in drug-taking behavior over time and compare the use of one drug relative to another. We can assume that the degree of overreporting and underreporting stays relatively constant over the years and does not affect the interpretation of the general trends. A major disadvantage of this survey, however, is the fact that high school dropouts have not been included. Therefore, results may not totally represent drug use for these age groups.

Survey questions concerning drug use are phrased in four basic ways:

1. Whether an individual has ever used a certain drug in his or her lifetime

2. Whether an individual has used a certain drug over the previous year

3. Whether an individual has used a certain drug within the previous thirty days

4. Whether an individual has used a certain drug on a *daily* basis during the previous thirty days.

You can see that these questions separate three important degrees of involvement with a given drug. The first question focuses on the extent of experimentation, including individuals who perhaps may have taken a drug only once in their lives and who have stayed away from it ever since. The second and third questions focus on the extent of current but moderate drug use, while the fourth question focuses on the extent of heavy drug use. What do the numbers tell us? Consider first the data regarding high school seniors.

Drug use among high school seniors

On the one hand, the current picture with high school seniors looks better than it has in the past. In 1993, for example, 31 percent of high school seniors reported use of any illicit drug over the previous year, a substantial reduction from the 53 percent reporting such use in 1980 (Table 1.1). If we look specifically at marijuana use over the previous year, the senior sample was 26 percent, a reduction by nearly one-half from a peak level reported in 1980 (Table 1.2). Cocaine use over the previous year for seniors had declined to 3 percent, less than a third of those reporting such behavior in 1985.

On the other hand, the absolute numbers in 1993 were still substantial. They indicate that nearly one in every three high school seniors had used some form of illicit drug over the last twelve months, about one in four had smoked marijuana, and about one in thirty

TABLE 1.1					
Percentages of high school seniors reporting some level of illicit drug use, 1975–1993					
	1975	1980	1985	1990	1993
In one's lifetime	55	65	61	48	43
Over previous year	45	53	46	33	31
Over last 30 days	31	37	30	17	18

SOURCE: Adapted from Johnston, Lloyd D., O'Malley, Patrick M., and Bachman, Jerald G. (1994). *National survey results on drug use from the Monitoring the Future study, 1975–1993*. Vol. 1. Rockville MD: National Institute on Drug Abuse. Table 1.

TABLE 1.2

Percentage of high school seniors reporting some level of marijuana or hashish use (1975–1993).

	1975	1980	1985	1990	1993
In one's lifetime	47	60	54	41	35
Over previous year	40	49	41	27	26
Over last 30 days	27	34	26	14	16
Daily in last 30 days	6	9	5	2	2

SOURCE: Adapted from Johnston, Lloyd D., O'Malley, Patrick M., and Bachman, Jerald G. (1994). *National survey results on drug use from the Monitoring the Future study, 1975–1993.* Vol. 1. Rockville MD: National Institute on Drug Abuse, Table 1.

TABLE 1.3

Percentage of U.S. high school seniors who ever used a particular drug (University of Michigan survey, 1993)

	White	African American	Latino
Marijuana	36.0	24.0	37.0
Inhalants	20.0	6.0	16.0
Hallucinogens	12.0	1.0	10.0
Cocaine	6.0	2.0	11.0
Crack	2.0	1.0	5.0
Heroin	1.2	0.5	1.4
Alcohol	89.0	81.0	88.0
Cigarettes	66.0	44.0	63.0

SOURCE: Adapted from Johnston, Lloyd D., O'Malley, Patrick M., and Bachman, Jerald G. (1994). *National survey results on drug use from the Monitoring the Future study, 1975–1993.* Vol. 1. Rockville MD: National Institute on Drug Abuse, Table 10.

had used cocaine. As will be shown shortly, the prevalence rates for drug use of many types have begun to rise, not only among high school seniors but among younger students in the eighth and tenth grades as well.

Drugs among youth in a diverse society

When we look at racial and ethnic differences in drug use among adolescents, certain patterns emerge from the University of Michigan survey. Drug use among African Americans in the eighth grade is consistently lower than among white students, and these differences remain approximately the same throughout high school. By the senior year, levels of daily cigarette smoking and binge drinking among African Americans are substantially below those of white students of comparable age. A comparison of white, African American, and Latino seniors shows on the one hand that white students generally have the highest prevalence rates, taking all seven categories together, in using marijuana, nonprescription inhalants, stimulants, hallucinogens, barbiturates, alcohol, and cigarettes. On the other hand, Latino seniors show the highest prevalence rates in using some of the most dangerous drugs: cocaine, crack, and heroin (Table 1.3).[20]

Gender differences among high school seniors have remained roughly the same since 1975. In 1993 male seniors were more than twice as likely to be smoking marijuana or drinking alcohol on a daily basis as female seniors. Rates of cigarette smoking, however, were more comparable, with a slight edge toward higher levels in males.[21]

Drug use among college students and young adults

The University of Michigan study also allows a look at drug use among young people beyond high school. For college students, the trends and basic numbers regarding use of illicit drugs are very similar to that of high school seniors. The annual prevalence rates for use of illicit drugs in general, for marijuana use, and for cocaine use are all substantially lower than levels reported in the 1980s. Young adults one to ten years past high school, however, show much higher levels of cocaine use than college students over a period of one year (4.7 percent), even though this figure has also fallen dramatically when compared to the mid-1980s. The active use of cocaine and illicit drugs in general rises substantially after high school in those individuals who do not go on to college.

Patterns of alcohol use in high school and beyond

As you might imagine, the percentages related to use of alcohol are much higher than those related to use of cocaine or marijuana. In 1993 about one-half of high school seniors (51 percent) drank an alcoholic beverage during the previous month, with about 28 percent reporting at least one instance of binge drinking, defined as five or more drinks in a row over the previous two weeks. These figures were down from a decade earlier, when 72 percent reported in 1980 that they had consumed alcohol over the previous month and 41 percent reported binge drinking. A partial explanation for the decline lies in the reduced accessibility to alcohol for this age group, with all U.S. states now having adopted a twenty-one-year-or-older requirement. Despite the decline, however, the present level of alcohol consumption among high school seniors is a matter of great concern. Alcohol consumption on a regular basis is widespread for individuals in this age group, despite the fact that it is officially illegal for any of them to purchase alcoholic beverages.

In contrast to the seniors, drinking habits of college students have shown much less change over the past years. In 1993, 72 percent of college students surveyed drank at least once in the previous month, and 40 percent reported instances of binge drinking. Evidently, the "know when to say when" message as promoted by the major beer companies has not gotten through.[22]

Patterns of nicotine use in high school and beyond

Roughly 19 percent of high school seniors in 1993 had established a regular habit of nicotine intake by smoking at least one cigarette every day. In fact, nicotine is the most frequently used drug on a daily basis by high school students. Nevertheless, the rate of daily smoking has declined steadily from 1977 (when approximately 29 percent of high school seniors smoked cigarettes) to 1984, after which it has remained relatively steady. About 11 percent of all high school seniors in 1993 reported smoking at least a half a pack of cigarettes a day, a strikingly high level for this age group considering the legal obstacles in many states to buying cigarettes.

Trends in drug use since 1991

Until 1991, prevalence rates among high school and college students for drug use in several categories had showed a steady decline. The University of Michigan surveys in 1992 and 1993, however, show us that the percentage of high school seniors reporting marijuana use increased from 1991 by about a fifth, while the percentage of tenth grade users increased by about a quarter, and the percentage of eighth grade users increased by about one-half. Prevalence rates in 1993 for LSD, inhalants, and stimulants also rose among all grade levels. These trends will be examined in later chapters.

Patterns of drug awareness among young people

Another troubling trend in recent University of Michigan surveys is the beginning of a reversal from the steadily increasing awareness among high school students, college students, and young adults since 1977 that psychoactive drugs present genuine health risks. Since 1991, the percentage of students thinking that marijuana use presented great risk has declined. Lloyd Johnston, speaking on behalf of the Michigan survey in 1993, has remarked:

The changes in use would worry me less if the underlying attitudes and beliefs were not also continuing to shift in a direction favorable to drug use. Unfortunately, the perceived dangers of nearly all of the illicit drugs declined in 1993 at all grade levels.[23]

A look at drug use among younger students

Beginning in 1991, we have also had survey information about drug use among students in the eighth grade (Table 1.4). Forty-five percent of eighth grade students in 1993 reported having tried cigarettes, 67 percent having tried alcohol, 19 percent having tried inhalants such as glues and aerosols, 3 percent having tried cocaine, and 2 percent having tried crack. These percentages are particularly disturbing. They reflect a very early age of entry into the world of psychoactive drugs. Some general estimates of drug use in the overall population in the United States are given in Table 1.5.[24]

Reasons for adolescents taking drugs

hy do students and other young people take drugs? What factors influence the drug-taking behavior that we see in all these statistics? One study asked high school seniors to report their personal reasons for taking drugs.[25] Most frequently occurring responses among the classes of 1983 and 1984 included "to have a good time with my friends" (65 percent), "to experiment or see what it's like" (54 percent), "to feel good or get high" (49 percent), and "to relax or relieve tension" (41 percent). These responses were similar to reasons given by the class of 1976 in earlier surveys.

Is there any way of predicting those individuals who may be more inclined to take drugs? Certain factors that may appear to be strong indicators for drug-taking behavior in general (socioeconomic status, for example) turn out to have an association that is far from simple and may depend on the particular drug under discussion.[26] The most successful set of indicators consist of psychosocial characteristics that reflect a tendency toward nonconformity within society. Young people who take drugs are more inclined to attend school irregularly, have poor relationships

---

T A B L E   1 . 4

Percentage of eighth graders reporting some use of drugs (1993)

Drug use	Percentage of users
Cigarettes in previous 30 days	16.7
Cigarettes every day	8.3
Marijuana in past year	6.2
Cocaine in past year	1.7
Inhalants in past year	11.0
Alcohol, being drunk in past year	17.5

SOURCE: Adapted from Johnston, Lloyd D., O'Malley, Patrick M., and Bachman, Jerald G. (1994). *National survey results on drug use from the Monitoring the Future study, 1975–1993.* Vol. 1. Rockville MD: National Institute on Drug Abuse, Table 1.

T A B L E   1 . 5

Drug use in the United States in 1992

	PERCENTAGE BY AGE RANGE FOR USE EVER/USE IN PAST YEAR					
	12–17	18–25	26–34	35 and above	Total sample	Estimated number of users ever/past year
Any illicit drug	16.0/12.0	52.0/26.0	61.0/18.0	28.0/5.0	36.0/11.0	74,378,000/22,862,000
Marijuana	11.0/8.0	48.0/23.0	59.0/14.0	25.0/3.0	33.0/9.0	67,525,000/17,400,000
Cocaine	2.0/1.0	16.0/6.0	25.0/5.0	7.0/1.0	11.0/2.0	22,603,000/4,973,000
Hallucinogens	3.0/2.0	13.0/5.0	16.0/1.0	5.0/0.2	8.0/1.0	16,437,000/2,440,000
Heroin	0.2/0.1	1.3/0.5	1.6/0.2	0.7/0.1	1.0/0.2	1,840,000/323,000
Alcohol	40.0/33.0	86.0/78.0	92.0/79.0	87.0/63.0	83.0/65.0	170,685,000/133,018,000
Nicotine	34.0/18.0	68.0/41.0	75.0/39.0	77.0/29.0	71.0/31.0	146,012,000/64,262,000

SOURCE: Adapted from Substance Abuse and Mental Health Services Administration (1993). *National Household Survey of Drug Abuse: Population estimates 1992.* Rockville MD: Substance Abuse and Mental Health Services Administration, Office of Applied Studies, Tables 2A, 3A, 4A, 7A, 13A, 14A, and 17.

with their parents, or get into trouble in general. Sociologists refer to such individuals as members of a deviant subculture. The greater the number of risk factors toward becoming part of such a subculture, the higher the probability that an individual will display some level of drug-taking behavior. Some of the risk factors that have been found to be important are the following: an early history of alcohol intoxication beginning at age twelve or earlier, the number of adults you know who have a drug problem, the degree to which your friends would approve of your getting high on drugs, absence from school for reasons other than illness, and generally low educational aspirations.[27]

As the number of risk factors increases, so does the likelihood of abusing specific drugs. If one had to single out the most influential risk factor, it would be peer influence, as measured by the reported number of friends who use drugs.[28] The importance of peer influence evidently is found across cultural groups; white, African American, and Latino youngsters react in very similar ways.[29] By contrast, economic hardship and parental abuse do not appear to correlate with the inclination to use drugs (Focus 1.1).[30]

Peer influence is a major factor in predicting the extent of drug-taking behavior during adolescence.

Looking to the future and learning from the past

hat does the future hold with respect to psychoactive drugs? Predictions are always tricky to make, but in regard to drug-taking behavior there are historical patterns that can serve as guides.

Old drugs, new drugs

One certainty is that specific drugs will continue to come into and out of favor. New drugs will come on the scene, and others may reappear like ghosts from the past, sometimes in new forms and involving new faces in the drug underground. Since 1992, for example, with cocaine declining in popularity in the United States, heroin has been once more on the upswing. Heroin is distributed in potent blends that can be snorted like cocaine or smoked like crack. On the one hand, these new forms circumvent the traditional need for hypodermic syringes and the associated dangers of being infected with the AIDS (acquired immunodeficiency syndrome) virus. On the other hand, new populations of people formerly turned off to heroin because of their fear of needles are being introduced to it for the first time. As mentioned earlier, there are signs that LSD, once the darling of a previous psychedelic generation, has staged a comeback as well.[31]

Along with the reappearance of heroin and LSD, there is a new drug phenomenon just emerging: a group of new psychoactive substances being promoted as ways to enhance memory, clarity of thinking, and general cognitive ability, presumably without the dependence problems of amphetamines and cocaine. Originating in California and now spreading across the country, these so-called smart drugs include Piracetam (a drug currently available in Mexico and unapproved by the U.S.), Hydergine (a

Substance abuse and the college student: An assessment tool

n a recent study conducted at Rutgers University, a cutoff score of five or more "yes" responses to the following 25 questions in the Rutgers Collegiate Substance Abuse Screening Test (RCSAST) was found to distinguish problem users from nonproblem users in a college student population. However, more research must be done to determine if a score of five represents the best cutoff. It is important to remember that the RCSAST is not for use by itself in determining the presence of problem substance abuse or a substance use disorder. Rather, the RCSAST is designed to be used as one part of a larger assessment battery aimed at identifying which young adults experience problems due to substance use and specifically what types of problems a particular individual is experiencing.

1. Have you gotten into financial trouble as a result of drinking or other drug use?

2. Is alcohol or other drug use making your college life unhappy?

3. Do you use alcohol or other drugs because you are shy with other people?

4. Has drinking alcohol or using other drugs ever caused conflicts with close friends of the opposite sex?

5. Has drinking alcohol or using other drugs ever caused conflicts with close friends of the same sex?

6. Has drinking alcohol or using other drugs ever damaged other friendships?

7. Has drinking alcohol or using other drugs ever been behind your losing a job (or the direct reason for it)?

8. Do you lose time from school due to drinking and/or other drug use?

9. Has drinking alcohol or using other drugs ever interfered with your preparations for exams?

10. Has your efficiency decreased since drinking and/or using other drugs?

11. Do you drink alcohol or use other drugs to escape from worries or troubles?

12. Is your drinking and/or using other drugs jeopardizing your academic performance?

13. Do you drink or use other drugs to build up your self-confidence?

14. Has your ambition decreased since drinking and/or drug using?

15. Does drinking or using other drugs cause you to have difficulty sleeping?

16. Have you ever felt remorse after drinking and/or using other drugs?

17. Do you drink or use drugs alone?

18. Do you crave a drink or other drug at a definite time daily?

19. Do you want a drink or other drug the next morning?

20. Have you ever had a complete or partial loss of memory as a result of drinking or using other drugs?

21. Is drinking or using other drugs affecting your reputation?

22. Does your drinking and/or using other drugs make you careless of your family's welfare?

23. Do you seek out drinking/drugging companions and drinking/drugging environments?

24. Has your physician ever treated you for drinking and/or other drug use?

25. Have you ever been to a hospital or institution on account of drinking or other drug use?

SOURCE: Bennett, Melanie E., McCrady, Barbara S., Frankenstein, William, Laitman, Lisa A., Van Horn, Deborah H. A., and Keller, Daniel S. (1992). The Rutgers Collegiate Substance Abuse Screening Test: Identifying young adult substance abusers. Presentation at the meeting of the American Psychological Association, August, Washington DC. Reprinted with permission of the authors of the RCSAST.

medication used in the treatment of senility in elderly patients), antiepileptic medication, and amino acid compounds in nutrient drinks.[32]

Proponents see these drugs as increasing blood flow to the brain and brain metabolism in general. Researchers who know about these drugs, however, are less enthusiastic. They maintain, for example, that even if a drug were to be established as a way of relieving the cognitive deficits of senility, we cannot assume it would benefit healthy brains; any perceived benefits may simply be placebo effects. Besides, the risks in taking such poorly understood substances, much less the risks in taking many different kinds in combination, are presently unknown. It is not difficult to see the dangerous game of smart drugs as an updated revival of the psychedelic era of the late 1960s and early 1970s.

Why drugs?

If the history of drugs teaches us anything, it is that there will always be an attraction to the drug experience. This certainty arises directly from the character of psychoactive drugs themselves, namely their ability to cause an alteration in consciousness. For a time, they can make us feel euphoric, light-headed, relaxed, or powerful, and there is little doubt that all this feels good. There may be other nonpharmacological ways of arriving at this state of mind, but drugs are easy and they are quick. They also seem to increase awareness of the environment and give the impression of a feeling that we are seeing or hearing things in a more intense way. No matter whether we are young or old, rich or poor, drugs can allow us to retreat from an uncomfortable environment, to feel no pain.

There is one further certainty: In every generation there will be young people who are alienated from their families and the community of adults around them, who seek some form of temporary release from an unhappy existence. There will be a younger generation seeking some form of rebellion against traditional values. There will be adolescents testing the limits of their parents' love and tolerance. There will be young people who are willing to try anything new, including drugs. Their curiosity, to find out "what it's like," brings us full circle to the earliest times in human life when we nibbled on the plants in the field just to find out how they tasted. In the modern era, drug experimentation is not a new phenomenon; it can involve an alcoholic drink, an inhaled solvent, a cigarette, or illicit drugs. Whether this experimentation leads to a more intense level of drug use or drug abuse is

another question. Drug-taking behavior as a personal and societal concern will be discussed in the next chapter.

The source of future drugs

The acceleration in the development of new drugs, whether they are psychoactive or not, is in large part a result of an explosion in biomedical technology over the last twenty years or so. We now have the ability to manipulate molecules and come up with new synthetic chemicals that nature never heard of before. It has even become possible to inject patients with genetic material itself, cut-and-pasted strands of DNA, to treat such inherited diseases as hemophilia, cystic fibrosis, dwarfism, and immune deficiencies, as well as cancer and heart disease, through a new

Don Hilde— A present-day shaman

Don Hilde lives in the small town of Pucallpa in the Peruvian rain forest, five hundred miles from the capital city Lima. As an adolescent when experiencing a series of personal visions, he realized his mission in life was to heal others. Like other shamanistic healers in this region, Don Hilde comes out of a folk tradition in which illness is often believed to be a result either of a capricious whim on the part of offended spirits of nature or else of the evil powers of another person who wishes to cause pain or suffering. The task of the shaman is to help the patient deal with such evil influences.

A common feature of their healing practice is the use of a powerful hallucinogenic plant called ayahuasca. For some healers, ayahuasca serves as a diagnostic tool during the course of a therapeutic session. Patients are given an ayahuasca drink to induce visions that help the healer to understand which force or individual is responsible for the illness. It is believed that only then can the evil be deflected, neutralized by the healer, and returned to the perpetrator. Don Hilde, however, chooses to take ayahuasca himself, relying upon his own hallucinogenic visions rather than those of his patients as he passes his hand over the patient's head and "reads the evil energies."

His diagnoses may come from a trance, but his therapies are based upon the careful preparations of herbs and plant-based medicines. Don Hilde and others like him treat their patients largely on the basis of plants available locally. Some of these have common ingredients (arrowroot, avocado, coriander, cumin, garlic, or ginger, prepared as therapeutic teas), while many others come from roots and tree resins that have not been scientifically identified. Don Hilde grows a number of his herbal medicines in his own garden; others he obtains from Indian communities outside the town.

Don Hilde's success as a shamanistic healer in his community stems from several factors. First of all, it is quite possible that the herbal preparations have genuine therapeutic effects on the physical symptoms of the patients. The fact that some of Don Hilde's drugs also have an antianxiety effect, however, indicates that some patients, particularly those suffering from rheumatic or abdominal pain, may be feeling better because they are more relaxed. In Don Hilde's case, there is an interesting connection to Western medical care. He will frequently refer his cases to the local medical facility in Pucallpa if surgery is required or if he thinks his particular drugs are not helping his patients; patients being treated by modern Western physicians will frequently come to Don Hilde for supplementary treatment. He maintains a cordial relationship with medical doctors in Pucallpa. In this region, as in many underdeveloped areas of the world, shamanistic and Western approaches toward healing exist, quite amiably, side by side.

SOURCE: De Rios, Marlene D. (1989). A modern-day shamanistic healer in the Peruvian Amazon: Pharmacopoeia and trance. *Journal of Psychoactive Drugs, 21*, 91–99.

approach called gene therapy.[33] It is ironic that another significant thrust in drug research is directed toward organic compounds that already exist in nature but have yet to be discovered and whose function has not yet been identified. As one scientist has put it, "Plants and animals have infinite patience. They've had a lot more time to manufacture molecules than we have."[34]

The search for natural products that might yield future therapeutic drugs, whether they are used to treat physical or mental disorders, has led scientists to some of the least accessible and most undeveloped regions of the world. One example is the tropical rain forests, where millions of plant species exist, probably more than half the total number of species in the entire earth, with thousands not yet identified. Some of these plants could hold the key to the discovery of the next miracle drug for cancer, AIDS, schizophrenia, or some other disorder. As a result, an international effort has been mounted to collect as many specimens from these areas as possible,

and as quickly as possible, given the fact that approximately 55,000 square miles of rain forests are currently lost each year (about the size of the state of Florida).[35]

Unfortunately, the techniques we have for isolating specific compounds that may have some therapeutic significance cannot keep up with the many thousands of samples being collected for analysis.[36] To offset this difficulty, an interesting strategy has been adopted. Since 1990, a small pharmaceutical company, appropriately named Shaman Pharmaceuticals, has been carrying out initial screenings of specimens with the help of local medicine men and women whose expertise with local plant species has been passed on from generation to generation. With the help of these shamans, a new drug has recently been identified as active against the influenza and herpes viruses; it is likely that more discoveries will be forthcoming.[37] In a curious turn of events, history's first pharmacologists, the shamans of the world, have joined forces with modern pharmaceutical companies in this newest quest for the drugs of the future.

Summary

A MATTER OF DEFINITION

- Psychoactive drugs are those drugs that affect our feelings, perceptions, and behavior. Depending upon the intent of the individual, drug use can be considered either instrumental or recreational.

- Drug abuse refers to cases in which a licit or illicit drug is used in ways that produce some form of impairment. Drug misuse refers to cases in which a prescription or nonprescription drug is used in an inappropriate way.

DRUGS IN EARLY TIMES

- Probably the earliest experiences with psychoactive drugs came from tasting naturally growing plants. Individuals with knowledge about such plants were able to attain great power within their culture.

- Ancient Egyptians and Babylonians in particular had extensive knowledge of both psychoactive and nonpsychoactive drugs. Some of these drugs had genuine beneficial effects.

DRUGS IN THE NINETEENTH CENTURY

- Medical advances in the 1800s had succeeded in the isolation of active ingredients within many psychoactive substances. For example, morphine was identified as the major active ingredient in opium.

- Psychoactive drugs were in widespread use, principally in the form of patent medicines. Only by the end of the century were the risks of drug dependence beginning to be recognized.

DRUGS AND BEHAVIOR IN THE TWENTIETH CENTURY

- Increased concern about the social effects of drug dependence led to restrictive legislation regarding the use of morphine, heroin, cocaine, and marijuana.

- Social pressure from the temperance movement resulted in the national prohibition of alcohol consumption in the U.S. from 1920 to 1933.

- After 1945, important strides were made in the development of antibiotics and psychiatric drugs.

- By the 1940s and 1950s, illicit drugs such as heroin, cocaine, and marijuana were outside the mainstream of American life.

- In the 1960s and 1970s, the use of marijuana and hallucinogenic drugs spread across the nation, along with an increase in problems related to heroin.

- A decline in heroin abuse in the 1980s was matched with an increase in cocaine abuse and the emergence of crack as a cheap, smokable form of cocaine.

- It is now recognized that a wide range of psychoactive drugs, licit or illicit, qualify as potential sources of misuse and abuse.

PATTERNS OF DRUG USE AMONG AMERICAN YOUTH

- Surveys of illicit drug use among high school seniors in 1993 have shown that one in three seniors used an illicit drug over the last twelve months, one in four smoked marijuana, and one in thirty used cocaine.

- Nicotine use, as indicated by smoking at least one cigarette per day, has remained at approximately the same level since 1984.

- Since 1991, marijuana use among high school seniors has risen significantly, as has the use of other illicit drugs.

- Drug use in general and the use of individual psychoactive drugs vary greatly according to racial and ethnic variables.

REASONS FOR ADOLESCENTS TAKING DRUGS

- Risk factors for drug-taking behavior in adolescence include a tendency toward nonconformity within society and peer influence.

LOOKING TO THE FUTURE AND LEARNING FROM THE PAST

- Predictions regarding future drugs and drug-taking behaviors are largely founded on patterns from the past. New drugs will undoubtedly come on the scene; old drugs that were out of favor will regain popularity until their popularity declines again.

- It is unlikely that young people will stop experimenting with drugs, as they experiment with a great many other things.

- It is likely that many new beneficial drugs for the treatment of mental illness and physical disease will come from plant specimens gathered in remote areas of the world.

Key Terms

chlorpromazine, p. 10
cycle of dependence, p. 4
drugs, p. 4
drug abuse, p. 6
drug misuse, p. 5

Ebers Papyrus, p. 7
illicit drugs, p. 3
instrumental use, p. 5
licit drugs, p.3
neuroscience, p. 11

Endnotes

1. Ifill, Gwen (1992, March 30). Clinton admits experiment with marijuana in 1960's. *New York Times,* p. A15.
2. Payne, Wayne A., Hahn, Dale B., and Pinger, Robert R. (1991). *Drugs: Issues for today.* St. Louis: Mosby, p. 2.
3. Jacobs, Michael R., and Fehr, Kevin O'B. (1987). *Drugs and drug abuse: A reference text.* Toronto: Addiction Research Foundation, pp. 3–5.
4. Goode, Erich (1989). *Drugs in American society (3rd ed.).* New York: McGraw-Hill, p. 79.
5. Ibid., pp. 79–84.
6. Caldwell, A. E. (1970). *Origins of psychopharmacology: From CPZ to LSD.* Springfield IL: C. C. Thomas, p. 3.
7. Inglis, Brian (1975). *The forbidden game: A social history of drugs.* New York: Scribners, pp. 11–36.
8. Bryan, Cyril P. (1930). *Ancient Egyptian medicine: The Papyrus Ebers.* Chicago: Ares Publishers.
9. Grilly, David (1989). *Drugs and human behavior.* Boston: Allyn and Bacon, pp. 2–3.
10. Sneader, Walter (1985). *Drug discovery: The evolution of modern medicines.* New York: Wiley, pp. 15–47.
11. Ibid.
12. Levinthal, Charles F. (1988). *Messengers of paradise: Opiates and the brain.* New York: Anchor Press, Doubleday, pp. 3–25.
13. Bugliosi, Vincent (1991). *Drugs in America: The case for victory.* New York: Knightsbridge Publishers, p. 215.
14. Freud, Sigmund (1884). Ueber Coca (On Coca). *Centralblatt feur die gesammte Therapie.* Translated by S. Pollak (1884). *St. Louis Medical and Surgical Journal, 47.*
15. Aaron, Paul, and Musto, David (1981). Temperance and prohibition in America: A historical overview. In Mark H. Moore and Dean R.
Gerstein (Eds.), *Alcohol and public policy.* Washington DC: National Academy Press, pp. 127–181.
16. Sneader, *Drug discovery,* p. 296.
17. Helmer, John (1975). *Drugs and minority oppression.* New York: Seabury Press.
18. Walsh, Kenneth T. (1986, January 13). Campus conservatives on the offensive. *U.S. News and World Report,* pp. 20–21
19. Johnston, Lloyd D., O'Malley, Patrick M., and Bachman, Jerald G. (1994). *National survey results on drug abuse from the Monitoring the Future study, 1975–1993.* Vols. 1 and 2. Rockville MD: National Institute on Drug Abuse.
20. Ibid. Vol. 1, Table 10.
21. Ibid.
22. Ibid., Vol. 1, Table 1.
23. Johnston, Lloyd D. (1994, January 27). News release from the University of Michigan, Ann Arbor MI, p. 3.
24. Johnston, O'Malley, and Bachman. *National survey results.* Vol. 1, Tables 1 and 10. Substance Abuse and Mental Health Services Administration (1993). National household survey on drug abuse: Population estimates 1992. Rockville MD: Office of Applied Studies, Substance Abuse and Mental Health Services Administration.
25. Johnston, Lloyd, and O'Malley, Patrick M. (1986). Why do the nation's students use drugs and alcohol? Self-reported reasons from nine national surveys. *The Journal of Drug Issues, 16,* 29–66.
26. Goode. *Drugs,* pp. 96–98.
27. Newcomb, Michael D., Maddahian, Ebrahim, Skager, Rodney, and Bentler, P. M. (1987). Substance abuse and psychosocial risk factors among teenagers: Associations with sex, age, ethnicity, and type of school. *American Journal of Drug and Alcohol Abuse, 13,* 413–433.

28. Kandel, Denise B. (1980). Drug and drinking behavior among youth. *Annual Review of Sociology, 6,* 235–285.

29. Perez, R., Padilla, A. M., Ramirez, A., and Rodriguez, M. (1980). Correlates and changes over time in drug and alcohol use within a barrio population. *American Journal of Community Psychology, 8,* 621–636.   Watts, W. David, and Wright, Loyd S. (1990). The drug use-violent delinquency link among adolescent Mexican-Americans. In Mario De la Rosa, Elizabeth Y. Lambert, and Bernard Gropper (Eds.), *Drugs and violence: Causes, correlates, and consequences* (NIDA Research Monograph 103). Rockville MD: National Institute on Drug Abuse.

30. Fawzy, F. L., Coombs, R. H., Simon, J. M., and Bowman-Terrell, M. (1987). Family composition, socioeconomic status, and adolescent substance use. *Addictive behaviors, 12,* 79–83.

31. Sabbag, Robert (1994, May 5). The cartels would like a second chance. *Rolling Stone,* pp. 35–37, 43.   Treaster, Joseph B. (1992, April 15). U. S. links trail of heroin to a 'Soviet connection.' *New York Times,* p. B3.

32. Bishop, Katherine (1992, June 10). 'Smart drugs': Elixir or snake oil? *New York Times,* pp. C1, C8.   Dean, Ward, and Morgenthaler, John (1990). *Smart drugs and nutrients: How to improve your memory and increase your intelligence using the latest discoveries in neuroscience.* Santa Cruz CA: B and J Publications.   Lambert, Victor (1993, April). Using smart drugs and drinks may not be smart. *FDA Consumer,* pp. 24–26.

33. Angier, Natalie (1992, April 14). With direct injections, gene therapy takes a step into a new age. *New York Times,* p. C3.

34. Daly, Douglas (1992, March/April). The tree of life. *Audubon Magazine,* pp. 76–85.

35. Wilson, Edward O. (1992, March). Rain forest canopy: The high frontier. *National Geographic Magazine,* pp. 78–107.

36. Pollack, Andrew (1992, March 5). Drug industry going back to Nature. *New York Times,* pp. D1, D9.

37. Stevens, William K. (1992, January 28). Shamans and scientists seek cures in plants. *New York Times,* pp. C1, C9.

Should we legalize drugs?

he following discussion of viewpoints represents the opinions of people on both sides of the controversial issue of the legalization of drugs. Read them with an open mind. Discuss them in your class, with your family, and with your friends. Don't think you have to come up with the final answer, nor should you necessarily agree with the argument you heard last. Many of the ideas in this discussion come from sources listed at the end, where more extensive coverage can be found.

POINT

Legalization would get the problem under some degree of control. The "war on drugs" does nothing but increase the price of illicit drugs to what the market will bear, and it subsidizes the drug dealers and drug barons around the world. If we legalize drugs, we can take the profit out of the drug business because legalization would bring the price down dramatically. We could regulate drug sales, as we do now with nicotine and alcohol, by setting up centers that would be licensed to sell cocaine and heroin, as well as sterile syringes, while any drug sales to minors would remain a criminal offense. Regulations would also ensure that drugs maintained standards of purity; the health risks of drug contamination would be avoided.

COUNTERPOINT

Legalization is fundamentally immoral. How can we allow people to run to the nearest store and destroy their lives? Don't we as a society have a responsibility for the health and welfare of people in general? If the drugs (pure or impure) were available, the only effect would be to increase the number of drug abusers. When Britain allowed physicians to prescribe heroin to "registered" addicts, the number of heroin addicts rose fivefold (or more according to some informal estimates), and there were now cases of medical abuse as well as drug abuse. A few unscrupulous doctors were prescribing heroin in enormous amounts, and a new drug culture was created.

POINT

How moral is the situation now? We have whole communities living at the mercy of drug dealers Any increase in drug users would be more than compensated for by the gains of freedom from such people. Even if the sale of crack were kept illegal, conceding that this drug is highly dangerous to society, we would have an 80 percent reduction in the black market for drugs, a substantial gain for the welfare of society. We can't guarantee that our inner cities would no longer be places of hopelessness and despair, but at least we would not have the systemic violence associated with the drug world. Besides, with all the money saved from programs set up to prevent people from getting hold of illicit drugs, we could increase the funding for drug treatment programs for all the drug abusers who want them and for research into ways of understanding the nature of drug dependence.

COUNTERPOINT

No doubt, many drug abusers seek out treatment and want to break their drug dependence. Perhaps there may be some individuals who seek treatment under legalization because there would no longer be a social stigma associated with drug abuse, but many drug abusers have little or no long-term commitment toward drug treatment. In the present situation, the illegality of their behavior allows us to compel them to seek and stay in treatment, as well as monitor their abstinence by periodic drug testing. How could we do this when the drug was legal?

Besides, how would we approach the education of young people if drugs were legal? We could not tell them that cocaine would give them cancer or emphysema, as we warn them of the dangers of nicotine, only that it would prevent them from being a productive member of society and would have long-term effects on their brains. If the adults around them were allowed to take cocaine, what would be the message to the young? Simply wait until you're twenty-one?

POINT

We already have educational programs about alcohol abuse; the message for heroin and cocaine abuse would be similar. The loss of productivity due to any increased availability of drugs would not be as significant as the present loss of productivity we have with alcohol and cigarettes. With the tax revenues obtained from selling drugs legally, we could have money for more extensive antidrug advertising. We could send a comprehensive message to our youth that there are alternatives to their lives that do not include psychoactive substances. In the meantime, we would be removing the "forbidden fruit" factor in drug-taking behavior. Drugs wouldn't be a big deal.

COUNTERPOINT

Arguing that people take drugs because they are forbidden or hard to get ignores the basic psychological allure of drugs. If

(continued)

you lowered the price of a very expensive sports car, would you have fewer people wanting to buy one? Of course not. People would want a fast car because they like fast cars, just as people will still want to get high on drugs. Legalizing present drugs would only encourage the development of more dangerous drugs in the future. Look at what happened with crack. Cocaine was bad enough but crack appeared on the scene, making the situation far worse.

POINT

It can be argued that crack was marketed because standard cocaine powder was too expensive for people in the inner cities. If cocaine had been legally available, crack might not ever have been created because the market would not have been there. Even with crack remaining illegal under a legalization plan, there is at least the possibility that the appeal of crack would decline. The trend has been lately that illegal drugs are getting stronger, while legal drugs (alcoholic beverages and cigarettes) are getting weaker as people become more health-conscious. Legalization might make presently illicit drugs weaker in strength, as public opinion turns against them. The main problem we face is that spending 60 percent of a multibillion-dollar drug-law-enforcement program on the "supply" side of the question, and only 40 percent on reducing the demand for drugs is not working. If one source of drugs is controlled, another source takes its place. The link between drugs and crime is a direct result of the illegality of drugs. It's not the drug addicts that are destroying the country; it's the drug dealers. Right now, the criminals are in charge. We have to change that. Only legalization would take away their profits, and refocus our law-enforcement efforts on other crimes that continue to undermine our society.

COUNTERPOINT

The frustration is understandable, but let's not jump into something merely because we're frustrated. We can allocate more funds for treatment without making drugs legal. We can increase funds for scientific research without making drugs legal. We need a more balanced program, not an entirely new one. Polls do not indicate general support for drug legalization. Between 60 percent and 80 percent of the U.S. public supports continued prohibition of drugs. Most citizens appear to recognize that legalization would make a bad situation worse, not better.

SOURCES: Dennis, Richard J. (1990, November). The economics of legalizing drugs. *The Atlantic*, pp. 126–132. Hamill, Pete. (1988, August 15). Facing up to drugs: Is legalization the solution? *New York*, pp. 20–27. Inciardi, James. (1991). *The drug legalization debate*. Newbury Park CA: Sage Publications. Jarvik, Murray E. (1990). The drug dilemma: Manipulating the demand. *Science, 250*, 387–392. Miller, Richard L. (1991). *The case for legalizing drugs*. New York: Praeger. Trebach, Arnold S., and Inciardi, James A. (1993). *Legalize it: Debating American drug policy*. Washington DC: American University Press. Wilson, James Q. (1990, February). Against the legalization of drugs. *Commentary*, 21–28.

2

Drug-Taking Behavior: The Personal and Social Dangers

sk someone whether drugs present a major problem in the United States today, and you will get a loud, clear, affirmative answer. This is probably the only aspect of drug-taking behavior on which people are unanimous. Yet, just because people agree there is a problem does not necessarily mean that we are on the way to resolving it. A better question might focus upon a more specific issue. What are the specific problems that drugs present to us as individuals and to society?

It is more than an academic question. If we are to expend our energies as well as our public funds on ways to reduce "the drug problem," it is important to know or at least reach some consensus as to where the problems are and which problems are most deserving of our efforts. Here is where people disagree and controversy exists. This chapter will concern itself with the various aspects of drugs that are known to present significant problems for individuals and for society in general. It will then explore the response U.S. society has made to these problems, in the form of public policy.

At the outset we should recognize that the real culprits are not the drugs per se but rather certain forms of drug-taking behavior. If a drug, for example, were totally without any redeeming value (let us say, it was extremely poisonous), most people would simply avoid it. It would have no street value, and no one would seriously object to, or even see the need for, measures that restricted access to it. It would be a totally "bad" drug, but no one would care. When we characterize cocaine and heroin, for example, as "bad drugs" we are essentially saying that society has balanced the perceived risks of heroin or cocaine *use* against any potential benefits. Heroin as well as other opiates such as opium and morphine, for example, are excellent painkillers and have been used medically in many countries of the world; cocaine is an excellent local anesthetic and has been used in a large number of medical procedures in the United States. Society has decided, however, that these positive applications are far outweighed by the negative consequences, on both a personal and a social level.

The importance of focusing on drug-taking behavior rather than simply on drugs can be highlighted by a bizarre but true story from the mid-1970s. At that time, a number of male patients were being treated for alcoholism in a Veteran's Administration hospital in California. In one ward, a patient was observed moving his bed into the men's room. Shortly afterward, several of his fellow patients, one by one, did the same.

What was behind this curious behavior? Evidently, these men, deprived of alcohol after years of alcohol abuse, had discovered that drinking enormous amounts of water, more than seven gallons a day, produced a "high" by altering the acid-to-base balance of their blood. They had found a medically dangerous but psychologically effective way of getting drunk. The fact that they were also urinating approximately the same amount of water each day accounted for their decision to move into the men's room.[2] The point of the story is that, in this case, water had become a psychoactive substance without technically being a drug (recall the definition from Chapter 1). Once again, the focus should be placed on the particular behavior and its consequences rather than on the substance itself.

Our examination of the personal and social problems associated with drug-taking behavior will focus on three broad categories: the toxicity of the drug being used, the potential for behavioral dependence on the drug, and finally the connection drug-taking behavior can have with violence and crime.

Toxicity

 hen we say that a drug is toxic, we are referring to the fact that it may be dangerous, poisonous, or in some way an interference with a person's normal functioning. Technically, any substance, no matter how benign, has the potential for **toxicity** if the **dose,** the amount in which the substance is taken, is high enough. The question of a drug's safety, or its relative safety when compared to other drugs, centers on the possibility that it may be toxic at relatively low doses. We certainly do not want people to harm themselves accidentally when taking the drug in the course of their daily lives.

To understand the principle of toxicity further, we can examine the S-shaped graph called a **dose-response curve** in Fig. 2.1a, which we will assume is a result of data collected from laboratory tests of a hypothetical sleep-inducing drug. It shows that increases in the dose level of the drug are producing the desired sleep-inducing effect in an increasingly large percentage of a test population of mice. At 10 milligrams (mg), 50 percent of the population has fallen asleep; at 50 mg, 100 percent has done so. There is always

toxicity (tox-IHS-ih-tee)
The physical or psychological harm that a drug might present to the user.

dose
The quantity of drug that is taken into the body, typically measured in terms of milligrams (mg) or micrograms (µg).

dose-response curve
An S-shaped graph showing the increasing probability of a certain drug effect as the dose level rises.

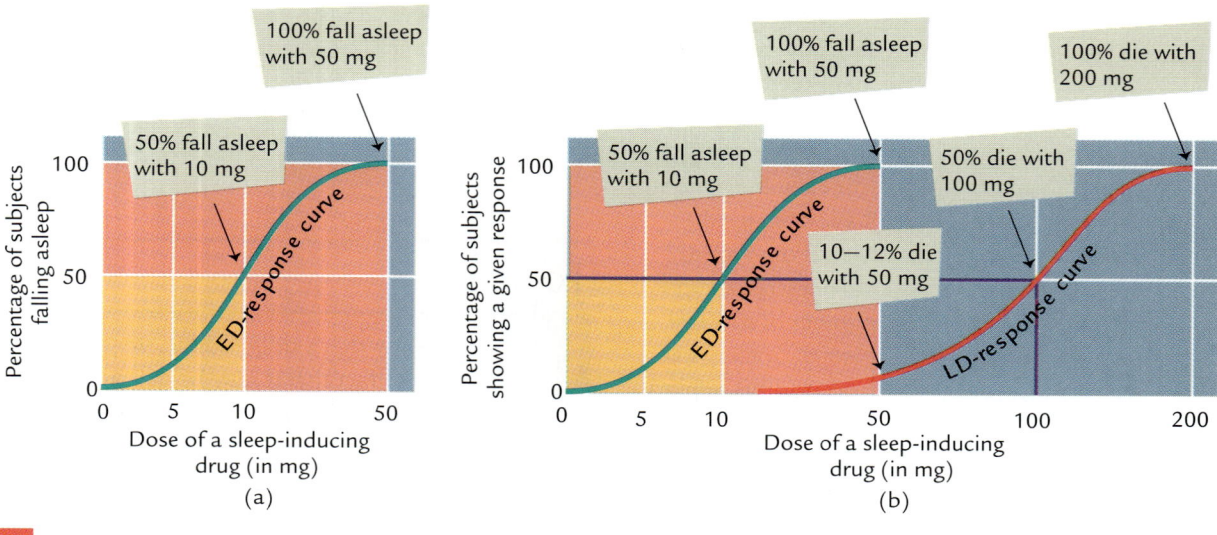

FIGURE 2.1

(a) An effective dose-response curve, and (b) an effective dose-response curve (left) and a lethal dose-response curve along side an effective dose-response curve (right).

some variability in individual reactions to any drug; some mice may be internally resistant to the drug's effect while others may be more susceptible. Any one animal may fall asleep with an extremely low dose or a dose of 50 mg, so we have to think of the **effective dose** (ED) of a drug on a test population in terms of probabilities, from 0 percent to 100 percent.

For example, the ED50 of a drug refers to the effective dose for 50 percent of the population; ED99 refers to the effective dose for 99 percent of the population. In this case, the ED numbers are referring to the drug's effect of producing sleep. The same drug may be producing other effects (muscular relaxation, for instance) at lower doses; these drug

effective dose
The minimal dose of a particular drug necessary to produce the intended drug effect in a given percentage of the population.

lethal dose
The minimal dose of a particular drug capable of producing death in a given percentage of the population.

effects would have their own individual dose-response curves. It is a good idea to remember that we are looking at the properties of a drug *effect* here, not the properties of the drug itself.

Now we can look at Fig. 2.1b, where the effective dose-response curve is represented along with another S-shaped dose-response curve, also gathered from laboratory testing, in which the "response" is death. It makes sense that the second curve should be shifted to the right since the **lethal dose** (LD) generally involves greater amounts of a drug than the amounts necessary to produce an effect. Emphasis should be placed on the word "generally" because the lethal dose-response curve overlaps with the effective dose-response curve in this example. While a 100 mg dose has to be taken in order to kill 50 percent of the test population, it can be seen that a dose of as little as 50 mg (or less) is lethal for at least a few of them. The LD50 of a drug refers to the lethal dose for 50 percent of the population; LD1 refers to a relatively lower dose that is lethal for 1 percent of the population.

It is useful to combine the effective and lethal doses of a drug in a ratio to arrive at some idea of that drug's toxicity. The ratio of LD50/ED50 is called the **therapeutic index.** If the LD50 for a drug is 450 mg and the ED50 is 50 mg, then the therapeutic index is 9. In other words, you would have to take nine times the dose that would be effective for half of the population in order to incur a 50 percent chance of dying. It can be argued, however, that a 50 percent probability of death represents an unacceptably high risk even for a drug that has genuine benefits. To be more conservative in the direction of safety, the ratio of LD1/ED99 is calculated. Here we are calculating the ratio between the dose that produces death in 1 percent of the population and the dose that would be effective in 99 percent. This second ratio, called the **margin of safety,** should be as high as possible. The higher the ratio, the safer, or less toxic, the drug. It can be seen that the margin of safety for the hypothetical drug examined in Fig. 2.1a and 2.1b would present serious toxicity problems.

The therapeutic index or the margin of safety is very helpful when considering the toxicity of drugs that are manufactured by recognized pharmaceutical companies and regulated by the FDA, keeping in mind those circumstances in which a person might intentionally or unintentionally take a higher-than-recommended dose of the drug. But what about the toxicity risks in consuming illicit drugs? The reality of street drugs is that the buyer has no way of knowing what has been bought until the drug has been used, and then it is frequently too late. Few if any illicit drug sellers make a pretense of being ethical businessmen their only object is to make money and avoid prosecution by the law. Frequently, the drugs they sell are diluted with either inert or highly dangerous ingredients. Adulterated heroin, for example, may contain a high proportion of milk sugar as a harmless filler and a dash of quinine to simulate the bitter taste of real heroin, when

the actual amount of heroin that is being sold is far less than the "standard" street dosage. At the other extreme, the content of heroin may be unexpectedly high and may lead to a lethal overdose, or else it may contain animal tranquilizers, arsenic, strychnine, insecticides, or other highly toxic substances.[3] Cocaine, LSD, marijuana, and all the other illicit drugs that are available to the drug abuser, as well as look-alike drugs that are unauthorized copies of popular prescription medications, present hidden and unpredictable risks of toxicity. Even if drugs are procured from a friend or someone you know, these risks remain. Neither of you might know the exact ingredients.

Given the uncertainty that exists about the contents of many abused drugs, what measure can we use to evaluate their effects on individuals in society? There is a natural tendency to look first to the news headlines; well-known public individuals who have died as a direct consequence of drug misuse or abuse easily come to mind (Focus 2.1). Such examples, however, can be misleading. Celebrities are not necessarily representative of the drug-using population in general, and the drugs prevalent among celebrities, because of their expense, may not represent the drugs most frequently encountered by the rest of society. In order to have some idea of the toxic effects of psychoactive drugs in a broader context, we have to turn to the institutions that contend with drug toxicity on a daily basis: the emergency rooms of hospitals around the country.

therapeutic index
A measure of a drug's relative safety for use, computed by the ratio of the lethal dose for 50 percent of the population over the effective dose for 50 percent of the population.

margin of safety
The ratio of a lethal dose for 1 percent of the population to the effective dose for 99 percent of the population.

The DAWN reports

ince 1980, the U.S. government has gathered data concerning drug-related medical emergencies in major metropolitan hospitals, through a program called the **Drug Abuse Warning Network (DAWN).** Two basic pieces of information are reported. The first concerns the number of cases in which a patient comes to an emergency room (ER) and mentions that the emergency was related to a particular drug or combination of drugs. These statistics are referred to literally as ER mentions and can refer to a range of emergency-room situations from a relatively minor attack of panic to a nearly successful suicide attempt. The second piece of information concerns the number of cases in which the patient actually dies and the coroner or medical examiner (ME) reports the death to be drug related. These latter cases are referred to as ME mentions.

The DAWN report for 1992 is shown in Table 2.1, but before we look closely at the numbers, it is important to understand some basic problems we face in trying to interpret the data. The first is that the ER counts are based only on the drugs that are actually mentioned by the patient at the time of the emergency; what the patient says may or may not accurately reflect what is actually inside the patient's body. In the midst of a medical crisis, it is natural that a patient may be either extremely confused and disoriented, in considerable pain, or consciously concealing the reason for coming to the hospital. Consequently, statistical errors can be expected. In one study, laboratory tests, showing the presence of drugs in the patient's body, were compared with the DAWN ER-mention reports. The test results and the DAWN reports were identical in only 20 percent of the cases examined. Ten

Drug Abuse Warning Network (DAWN)
A federal program in which metropolitan hospitals report the incidence of drug-related lethal and nonlethal emergencies.

Understanding dose-response curves

heck your understanding of dose-response curves and the toxicity of drugs by answering the following question.

The following three sets of dose-response curves show the effective and lethal responses to three drugs A, B, and C.

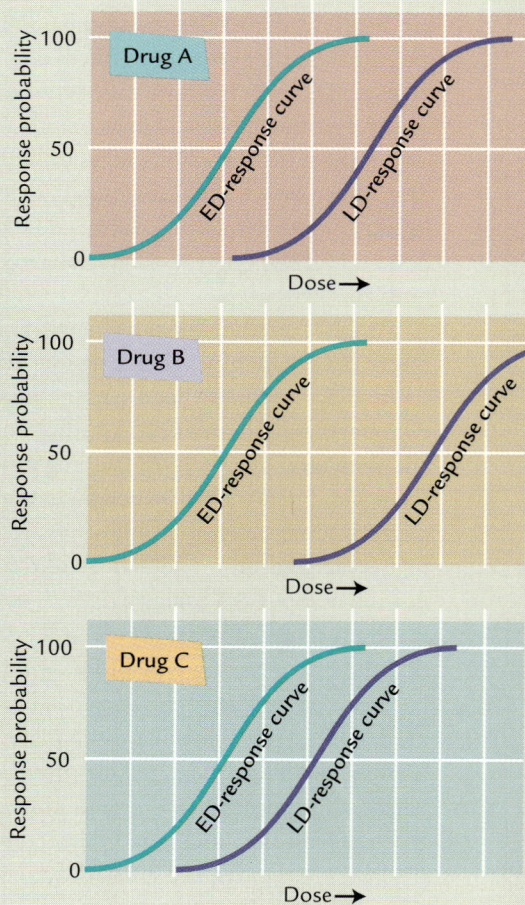

Which drug of the three would be considered the least toxic, and which would be considered the most toxic?

ANSWER: The second set of curves (B) refers to the least toxic drug. The third set of curves (C) refers to the most toxic drug.

percent showed totally different drugs to be involved; in 70 percent the laboratory tests showed a greater number of drugs to be in the patient's body than the drug the patient had mentioned.[4] The DAWN reporting forms allow for the reporting of multiple drugs, up to four in the case of ER mentions and up to six in the case of ME mentions, and therefore give us some idea of medical problems associated with drug combinations, but it turns out that much of this information is incomplete.

The second problem is that we are getting information in the DAWN statistics only from a group of urban hospitals. While approximately one third of the U.S. population is served by these hospitals, we are not examining a random sample of the nation as a whole. Therefore, the absolute numbers may underestimate or overestimate the actual extent of medical emergencies associated with a particular drug.

A third problem centers around the absence of ER or ME mentions concerning alcohol alone. There is a good reason for this omission. If emergencies related to alcohol alone were reported, the numbers would far exceed those related to any other drug, particularly

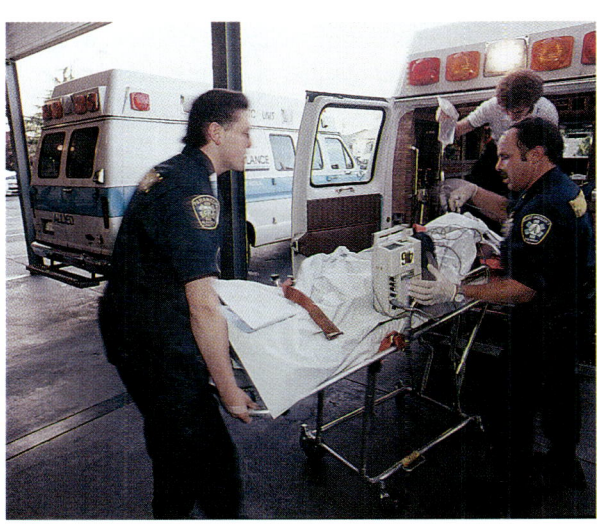

Emergency medical crews frequently have to deal with drug-related cases.

Top twelve emergency room (ER) and medical examiner (ME) mentions in 1992

ER MENTIONS			ME MENTIONS		
Drug	Number of mentions	Percentage of total episodes	Drug	Number of mentions	Percentage of total episodes
1. alcohol-in-combination	141,773	32.7	1. cocaine	3,465	46.0
2. cocaine	119,843	27.7	2. alcohol-in-combination	2,944	39.1
3. heroin/morphine	48,003	11.7	3. heroin/morphine	2,912	38.6
4. acetaminophen (Tylenol)	31,355	7.2	4. codeine	880	11.7
5. marijuana/hashish	23,997	5.5	5. diazepam (Valium)	640	8.5
6. aspirin	18,834	4.3	6. methadone	431	5.7
7. alprazolam (Xanax)	16,498	3.8	7. amitriptyline (Elavil)	414	5.5
8. ibuprofen (Motrin)	16,400	3.8	8. D-propoxyphene (Darvon)	398	5.3
9. diazepam (Valium)	13,947	3.2	9. marijuana/hashish	359	4.8
10. amitriptyline (Elavil)	10,132	2.3	10. nortriptyline (Pamelor)	335	4.5

Note: Percentages will add up to more than 100 since more than one drug is often mentioned in each case. Some representative brand names are included in parentheses.

SOURCES: Adapted from Substance Abuse and Mental Health Services Administration (1994a). Annual Emergency Room Data 1992. Data from the Drug Abuse Warning Network (DAWN), Series I, No. 12A. Rockville MD: Substance Abuse and Mental Health Services Administration, Office of Applied Studies, p. 32.   Substance Abuse and Mental Health Services Administration (1994b). Annual Medical Examiner Data 1992. Data from the Drug Abuse Warning Network (DAWN), Series I, No. 12B. Rockville MD: Substance Abuse and Mental Health Services Administration, Office of Applied Studies, p. 16.

when we consider the high percentage of car accidents and deaths resulting from drunk drivers. Instead of a few thousand mentions, we would be reporting many tens of thousands (see Chapter 10), more than all the other categories combined. What is reported, instead, is the number of emergencies that result from cases in which alcohol is mentioned in conjunction with some other drug. These are referred to as alcohol-in-combination mentions. The high incidence of alcohol-in-combination cases, 33 percent of all ER mentions and 46 percent of all ME mentions, is an indication of the substantial percentage of emergencies arising not from one drug alone but rather from drug mixing, or **polydrug use.** In 1992, 52 percent of ER mentions and 75 percent of ME mentions referred to combinations of two or more drugs.[5]

Clearly, as Table 2.1 shows, cocaine and narcotics such as heroin or morphine account for a large portion of lethal drug-related emer-

gencies, 46 percent and 39 percent, respectively. These statistics are quite dramatic, considering that there are relatively few cocaine and narcotics users in the total population in the first place. In other words, a large percentage of drug-related deaths, as defined by the DAWN reports, is associated with a relatively small segment of society. In contrast, a relatively larger number of people who smoke marijuana are involved in fewer nonlethal emergencies (largely owing to panic attacks that bring them to the hospital). In 1992 the DAWN statistics showed that only 1 case out of the 359 reported ME mentions regarding marijuana was attributed directly to marijuana alone. All the others were the result of a combination of marijuana and some other drug or some other factor present at the time.[6] A reasonable conclusion is that marijuana is considerably less toxic than cocaine or a narcotic drug.

DAWN statistics can also give us a rough idea of different patterns of drug-taking behavior among demographic groups, insofar as that behavior bears upon medical emergencies. While men and women appear in approx-

polydrug use
Drug-taking behavior involving two or more drugs simultaneously.

TABLE 2.2

Circumstances behind emergency room (ER) and medical examiner (ME) mentions in 1992 according to racial and ethnic background

PERCENTAGE OF ALL ER MENTIONS

Motive	White	African American	Latino	Other*
Recreational Use	7.6	7.0	12.9	7.1
Drug dependence	18.4	54.8	37.5	10.3
Suicide	52.7	18.9	28.2	59.6
Other reasons or unknown	21.3	19.3	21.4	23.0
Total	100.0	100.0	100.0	100.0

PERCENTAGE OF ALL ME MENTIONS

Manner of death	White	African American	Latino	Other*
Accidental/unexpected	48.6	62.2	74.5	46.0
Suicide	31.9	9.9	12.4	38.0
Other reasons or unknown	19.5	27.9	13.0	16.0
Total	100.0	100.0	100.0	100.0

Note: Includes Native Americans and Asian/Pacific Islanders

SOURCES: Adapted from Substance Abuse and Mental Health Services Administration (1994a). Annual Emergency Room Data 1992. Data from the Drug Abuse Warning Network (DAWN), Series I, No. 12A. Rockville MD: Substance Abuse and Mental Health Services Administration, Office of Applied Studies, p. 20.   Substance Abuse and Mental Health Services Administration (1994b). Annual Medical Examiner Data 1992. Data from the Drug Abuse Warning Network (DAWN), Series I, No. 12B. Rockville MD: Substance Abuse and Mental Health Services Administration, Office of Applied Studies, p. 13.

example, there has been a drop in both non-lethal and lethal emergencies, particularly with regard to the use of methaqualone (Quaalude) and barbiturates. But there has also been a steady increase in heroin-related emergencies, due to the fact that the purity of available heroin is currently far higher than ever before. There has also been a dramatic increase in the number of cocaine-related emergencies, a result of the greater numbers of individuals using cocaine and changes in the way the drug is consumed. Smoking or injecting cocaine, more common practices since the mid-1980s, is more potentially lethal than snorting it.

The DAWN reports tell us something about the **acute toxicity** of a particular drug, referring to the negative consequences that arise suddenly from a specific administration of the drug, but they do not tell us anything about the negative consequences of using a particular drug over a long period of time, the drug's **chronic toxicity.** The long-term health risks of cigarette smoking or a dependence on any of a range of psychoactive drugs, including alcohol, are examples of chronic toxicity. What are the chronic problems of drug-taking behavior? What is the best way to look at drug dependence in general? These are some of the questions to be examined in the next section.

imately equal numbers among the ER mentions, men outnumber women by roughly two to one in the ME mentions. In other words, the lethal drug-related emergencies are more likely to involve male drug users. Men more frequently mention the use of narcotic drugs, cocaine, amphetamines, hallucinogens, or marijuana when admitted to emergency rooms, while women more frequently mention tranquilizers (antianxiety drugs), over-the-counter pain relievers, antidepressants, and codeine. Table 2.2 shows the distribution of ER and ME mentions among white, African American, and Latino groups in terms of the motivation behind drug-taking behavior.[7]

Since DAWN reports have been issued for more than a decade, we can get some idea of the changes that have taken place in the frequency of medical emergencies related to specific drugs in recent years. In some cases, for

Drug tolerance

egend has it that in the first century B.C., King Mithradates VI of Pontus, a region near the Black Sea, grew despondent following a series of defeats by the Romans and decided to commit suicide by poison. The problem was that no amount of poison was sufficient,

acute toxicity
The physical or psychological harm a drug might present to the user immediately after the time the drug is ingested into the body.

chronic toxicity
The physical or psychological harm a drug might cause over a long period of time.

and the task had to be completed by the sword. It turned out that Mithradates, having lived in fear of being poisoned by others, had taken gradually increasing amounts of poison over the course of his life. By the time he wanted to end his life by his own hand, he could tolerate such large doses that poisoning no longer presented any lethal possibility. It is the first recorded example of drug tolerance. In fact, the phenomenon originally was called mithradatism, and several celebrated poisoners of history, including the notorious Lucretia Borgia, were later to use the same technique.[8]

The concept of **tolerance** refers to the capacity of a drug dose to have a gradually diminished effect on the user as the drug is taken repeatedly. Another way of viewing tolerance is to say that over repeated administrations a drug dose needs to be increased in order to maintain an equivalent effect. A common illustration is the effect of caffeine in coffee. When you are first introduced to caffeine, the stimulant effect is usually quite pronounced; you might feel noticeably "wired" after a five-ounce cup of coffee, containing approximately 100 mg of caffeine. After several days or perhaps a few weeks of coffee drinking, the effect is greatly diminished; you may be on the second or third cup by that time, consuming 200 to 300 mg of caffeine, in order to duplicate the earlier reaction. Some individuals who drink coffee regularly have developed such high levels of tolerance to caffeine that they are able to sleep comfortably even after several cups of coffee, while individuals with more infrequent schedules of caffeine end up awake through the night after a single cup.

The danger that the tolerance effect presents is the possibility of death by drug overdose, frequently the source of lethal

tolerance
The capacity of a drug to produce a gradually diminished physical or psychological effect upon repeated administrations of the drug while maintaining the same dose level.

Understanding statistics in the DAWN reports

heck your understanding of the DAWN report statistics by answering the following questions.

Suppose the following three drugs (A, B, or C) were mentioned by the medical examiner (ME) in major metropolitan hospitals as being the cause of death for 13,500 individuals in a given year. There were no instances of drug combinations.

The distribution of ME mentions are as follows:

Drug A	2,500
Drug B	10,000
Drug C	1,000

1. Let's assume that Drug A is used by four times as many people as Drug B and that Drug C is used by forty times as many people as Drug B. How would you judge the relative danger of the three drugs?

2. Now let's assume that Drug B is used by four times as many people as Drug A and that Drug B is used by ten times as many people as Drug C. How would you judge the relative danger of the three drugs?

ANSWERS: Relative danger can be viewed in terms of the relative proportion of adverse occurrences within the population using a particular drug. 1. Drug B is the most dangerous, followed by Drug A, then by Drug C. 2. Drugs A, B, and C are equivalent in their toxicities.

emergencies (ME mentions) listed in the DAWN reports. Individuals involved in drug abuse are often taking drug doses that are precariously close to the lethal dose-response curve amounts, described earlier. In addition, it is important to point out that these dose increases may be sustainable by the drug abuser but quite lethal to an individual being introduced to the drug for the first time.

Tolerance effects, in general, illustrate the need for us to look at the *interaction* between the actual amount of the drug taken and other factors involved in the drug-taking behavior. For example, as already noted, the number of previous times the drug has been used is crucial; repetition is what tolerance is all about. Another important factor is the setting within which the drug-taking behavior occurs. There is strong evidence that tolerance is maximized when the drug-taking behavior occurs consistently in the same surroundings or under the same set of circumstances.[9] We speak of this form of tolerance as *behavioral tolerance.* Other forms of tolerance are tied to the purely physiological effects of a drug; they will be discussed in Chapter 3.

In order to have a clear idea of behavioral tolerance, we first have to understand the processes of Pavlovian conditioning, upon which behavioral tolerance is based. Suppose you consistently heard a bell ring every time you had a headache. Previously, bells had never had any negative effect on you. The association between the ringing bell and the pain of the headache, however, would have become strong enough that the mere ringing of a bell would now give you a headache, perhaps less painful than the ones you had originally but a headache nonetheless; this effect is Pavlovian conditioning at work. A pioneering study by the psychologist Shepard Siegel showed a similar phenomenon occurring with drug-taking behavior. In his experiment, one group of rats was injected with doses of mor-

phine in a particular room over a series of days and later tested for tolerance to that dose in the same room. Predictably, they displayed a lessened analgesic effect as a sign of morphine tolerance. A second group was tested in a room other than the one in which the injections had been given. No tolerance developed at all. They reacted as if they had never been given morphine before, even though they had received the same number of repeated injections as the first group.

Siegel explained the results by assuming that environmental cues in the room had elicited physiological effects opposite to the effect of the drug, in this case a heightened sensitivity to pain, or hyperalgesia. This compensatory effect produced by the environment would partially counteract the analgesic effect of the drug, and the combination of the two effects would end up as a diminished response. Rats in the first group would be less affected by the morphine over time because there had been a consistent relationship between the environment in which the injections occurred and the injections themselves.[10]

This behavioral account of drug tolerance, also known as *conditioned tolerance,* explains why a heroin addict may easily suffer the consequences of an overdose when the drug has been taken in a different environment from the one more frequently encountered or in a manner different from his or her ordinary routine.[11] The range of tolerated doses of heroin can be enormous: amounts in the 200 to 500 mg range may be lethal for a first-time heroin user while amounts as high as 1800 mg may not even be sufficient to make a long-term heroin user sick.[12] You can imagine how dangerous it would be then if the conditioned compensatory responses a heroin addict had built up were suddenly gone.

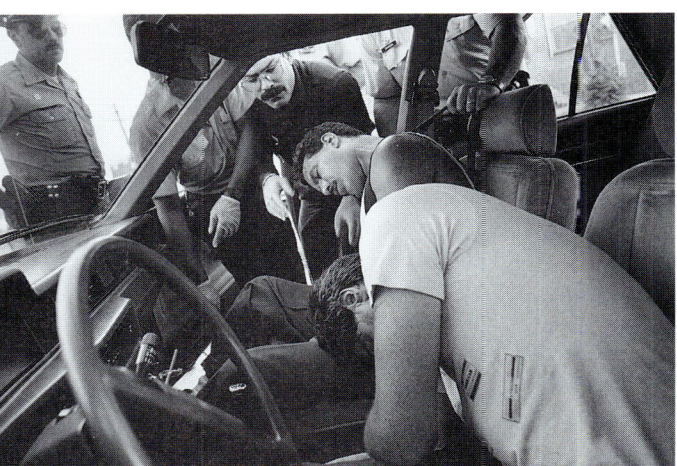

Having overdosed on pure heroin, the driver in the car has already died and the passenger would die soon afterward. The police found a needle injected through the driver's pants leg. The two men had just cashed their paychecks and bought the drugs.

Physical and psychological dependence

hen we refer to the idea of dependence in drug abuse, we are dealing with the fact that a person has a strong compulsion to continue taking a particular drug. Two possible models or explanations for why drug dependence occurs can be considered. The first is referred to as physical dependence, and the second is referred to as psychological dependence. The two models are not mutually exclusive; the abuse of some drugs can be a result of both physical and psychological dependence while others can be a result of psychological dependence alone.

Physical dependence

The concept of **physical dependence** originates from observations of heroin addicts, as well as of those who abuse other opiate drugs, who developed strong physical symptoms following heroin withdrawal: a runny nose, chills and fever, inability to sleep, and hypersensitivity to pain. For barbiturate addicts in a comparable situation, symptoms include anxiety, inability to sleep, and sometimes lethal convulsions.[13] For chronic alcoholics, abstention can produce tremors, nausea, weakness, and tachycardia (a fast heart rate). If severe, symptoms may include delirium, seizures, and hallucinations.[14]

While the actual symptoms vary according to the drug being withdrawn, the fact that we observe physical symptoms at all suggests very strongly that some kind of physical need, perhaps as far down as the cellular level, has developed over the course of drug abuse. It is as if the drug, previously a foreign chemical,

> **physical dependence**
> A model of drug dependence based on the idea that the drug abuser continues the drug-taking behavior in order to avoid the consequences of physical withdrawal symptoms.

has become a normal part of the nervous system, and its removal and absence become abnormal. From this point of view, it is predictable that the withdrawal symptoms would involve symptoms that are opposite to effects the drug originally had on the body. For example, heroin can be extremely constipating, but eventually the body compensates for heroin's intestinal effects. Abrupt abstinence from heroin releases the processes that have been counteracting the constipation and the result of withdrawal is diarrhea. You may have noticed a strong resemblance between the action-counteraction phenomena of withdrawal and the processes Siegel has hypothesized as the basis for behavioral tolerance.

Psychological dependence

The most important implication of the model of physical dependence, as distinct from psychological dependence, is that individuals involved in drug abuse continue the drug-taking behavior, at least in part, *in order to avoid the feared consequences of withdrawal.* This idea can form the basis for a general model of drug dependence only if physical withdrawal symptoms appear consistently for every drug considered as a drug of abuse. It turns out, however, that a number of abused drugs (cocaine, hallucinogens, and marijuana, for example) do not produce physical withdrawal symptoms, and the effects of heroin withdrawal are more variable than we would expect if physical dependence alone were at work. It is possible that drug abusers continue to take the drug not because they want to avoid the symptoms of withdrawal but because they crave the pleasurable effects of the drug itself. They may even feel that they need the drug in order to function at all. This is the way one heroin addict has expressed it:

I'm just trying to get high as much as possible. I would have to spend $25 a day on heroin to avoid withdrawal, but I actually use about $59 worth. If I could get more money, I would spend it all on drugs. All I want is to get loaded. I just really like shooting dope. I don't have any use for sex; I'd rather shoot dope. I like to shoot dope better than anything else in the world. I have to steal something every day to get my dope.[15]

Many heroin addicts (between 56 percent to 77 percent in one major study) who complete the withdrawal process after abstaining from the drug, become readdicted.[15] If physical dependence were the whole story, these phenomena would not exist. The withdrawal symptoms would have been gone by that time, and any physical need that may have been evident before would no longer be present.

When we speak of **psychological dependence,** we are offering an explanation of drug abuse based not upon the attempt of abusers to avoid unpleasant withdrawal symptoms but upon their desire to obtain pleasurable effects from the drug. Unfortunately, we are faced here with a major conceptual problem:

The explanation by itself is circular and tells us basically nothing. If I were to say, for example, that I was taking cocaine because I was psychologically dependent on it, then I could as easily say I was psychologically dependent upon cocaine because I was abusing it. Without some *independent* justification, the only explanation for the concept of psychological dependence would be the behavior that the concept was supposed to explain!

Fortunately, there is independent evidence for the concept of psychological dependence, founded chiefly upon studies showing that animals are as capable of self-administering drugs of abuse as humans are. Using techniques developed in the late 1950s, researchers have been able to insert a **catheter** into the vein of a freely moving laboratory animal and arrange the equipment so that the animal can self-administer a drug intravenously whenever it presses a lever (Fig. 2.2). It had been well known that animals would engage in specific behaviors in order to secure rewards such as food, water, or even electrical stimulation of certain regions of the brain. These objectives were defined as positive reinforcers because animals would learn to work in order to secure them. The question at the time was whether animals would self-administer drugs in a similar way. Could drugs be positive reinforcers as well?

The experiments showed clearly that animals would self-administer drugs such as cocaine and other stimulants, despite the fact that these drugs would not ordinarily produce physical symptoms during withdrawal. In one study, rats would press the lever as many as 6,400 times for one administration of cocaine; others were nearly as eager for administrations

psychological dependence
A model of drug dependence based on the idea that the drug abuser is motivated by a craving for the pleasurable effects of the drug.

catheter (CATH-eh-ter)
A device to deliver intravenous injections of a drug in a free-moving human or animal.

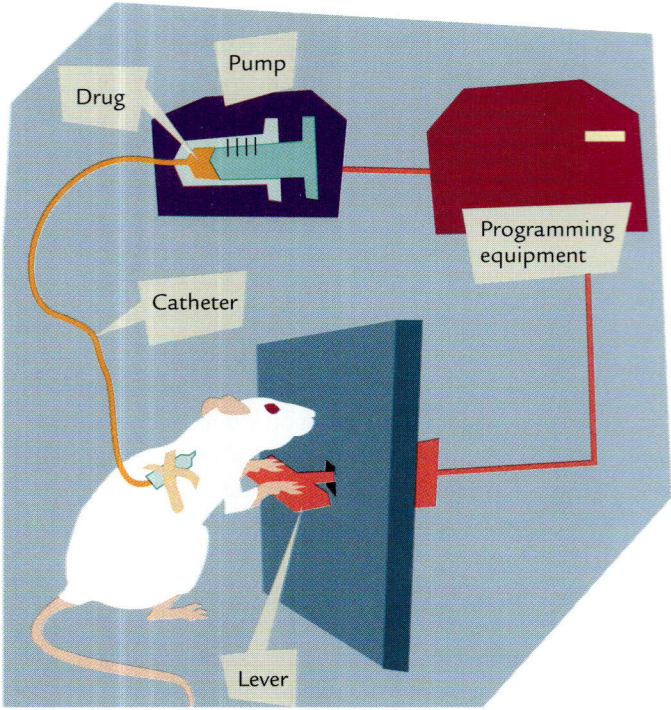

A simplified rendition of how drugs are self-administered in rats. Pressure on a lever causes the pump to inject a drug through a catheter implanted into the rat's vein.

the powerful effects of abused drugs. When presented with a choice of pressing levers for food or for cocaine, cocaine wins hands down even to the point of an animal starving to death.[19] When comparing the effects of heroin with cocaine, the differences are dramatic:

> Those rats that self-administer heroin developed a stable pattern of use, maintained their pretest weight, continued good grooming behavior, and tended to be in good health. Their mortality rate was 36 percent after thirty days. Those self-administering cocaine . . . exhibited an extremely erratic pattern of use, with "binges" of heavy use alternating with brief periods of abstinence. They lost 47 percent of their body weight, ceased grooming behavior, and maintained extremely poor physical health. After thirty days, 90 percent were dead.[20]

Chapter 3 will examine the possibility that the abuse potentials of heroin and morphine as well as cocaine and amphetamines are all linked together on a physiological level. In other words, these drugs may be working in the brain by virtue of a common neural mechanism.[21]

of amphetamines.[17] Interestingly, a number of other drugs were aversive, judging from the reluctance of animals to work for them. Hallucinogens such as LSD, antipsychotic drugs, and antidepressant drugs were examples of drugs that animals clearly did not like.[18]

By connecting the concept of psychological dependence to general principles of reinforcement, it has been possible for us to appreciate

substance dependence
A diagnostic term used in clinical psychology and psychiatry that identifies an individual with significant signs of a dependent relationship upon a psychoactive drug.

substance abuse
A diagnostic term used in clinical psychology and psychiatry that identifies an individual who continues to take a psychoactive drug despite the fact that the drug-taking behavior creates specific problems for that individual.

Psychiatric definitions

ost health professionals use guidelines published by the American Psychiatric Association as a kind of official standard for defining problems associated with drug-taking behavior. In 1994 the fourth edition of the association's Diagnostic and Statistical Manual (DSM-IV) identified two specific behavioral conditions: **substance dependence** and **substance abuse** (Table 2.3).

Two features of these guidelines are worth noting. First, they consist of a series of behavioral criteria for the diagnosis of dependence or abuse. There is no discussion of why these problems have arisen or what circumstances produced them, only their behavioral features. The position of the American Psychiatric Association is that a judgment of whether a person has a problem of dependence or abuse

T A B L E   2 . 3

Criteria for substance dependence and substance abuse according to the DSM-IV

Substance dependence

At least three out of the following must apply within a 12-month period:

1. Tolerance. The person has to take increasingly large doses of the drug to get the desired effect. Or else the person experiences a diminished effect from the same amount of the drug.
2. Withdrawal. When the drug is stopped, there are psychological or physiological withdrawal symptoms. Or else the substance is taken to relieve or avoid these symptoms.
3. Unintentional overuse. The person repeatedly takes more of the drug or takes it over a longer period of time than he or she intended.
4. Persistent desire or efforts to control drug use. The person tries to quit and repeatedly relapses into further drug use.
5. Preoccupation with the drug. The person spends a great deal of time in activities necessary to obtain the substance, use it, or recover from its effects.
6. The reduction or abandonment of important social, occupational, or recreational activities in order to engage in drug use. A person quits a job, neglects a child, or gives up other important activities.
7. Continued drug use despite major drug-related problems. A person repeatedly arrested for drug possession still maintains the drug habit, or a person with serious lung disease continues to smoke cigarettes, for example.

Symptoms of the disturbance must have persisted for more than a month or occurred repeatedly over a longer period of time.

Substance abuse

At least one on the following must apply within a 12-month period:

1. Recurrent substance use resulting in a failure to fulfill major role obligations at work, school, or home. Examples include repeated absences from work, suspensions or expulsions from school, or neglect of children or one's household.
2. Recurrent drug use in situations in which use is physically hazardous.
3. Recurrent substance-related legal problems, such as an arrest for disorderly conduct or drug-related behavior. Symptoms of the disturbance must have persisted for more than a month or occurred over a longer period of time.
4. Continued drug use despite the knowledge of persistent social, occupational, psychological, or physical problems that would be caused or made more difficult by the use of the drug.

Important: The person must have never met the criteria for substance dependence for this particular drug.

SOURCE: Adapted from the *Diagnostic and Statistical Manual* (4th ed.). (1994). Washington DC: American Psychiatric Association, pp. 180–183.

should depend upon the behavior of that person, not the chemical that is being consumed. Second, the broader term "substance" has been substituted for the word "drug" in the guidelines, primarily because there is often confusion in the public mind in deciding what is defined as a drug and what is not, particularly in the instance of alcohol or nicotine use.[22]

Special problems in drug abuse

The discussion so far has dealt with drug-abuse problems, specifically the problems of acute and chronic toxicity, that affect only the drug user. Unfortunately, other people are frequently involved as well. Consider now two special circumstances related to drug abuse that require discussions of their own: the problems of drug abuse in pregnancy and in association with AIDS.

Drug abuse in pregnancy

Prior to the 1960s, doctors and scientists regarded the placenta joining the bloodstream of a pregnant woman with that of the developing fetus as a natural barrier protecting the fetus from toxic substances in the mother. We now know this "placental barrier" is largely a myth. During gestation, almost all drugs cross the placenta and affect the unborn child. In general, women who smoke cigarettes or consume alcohol or illicit drugs during pregnancy increase their risks for obstetrical complications and for premature labor and delivery. They are also more likely to suffer loss of the fetus through spontaneous abortions (miscarriages) and stillbirths than are women who abstain from drugs. The greater the extent of drug-taking behavior, the more likely there will be adverse consequences.

The timing of drug use during a pregnancy has a great deal to do with the specific risks to the fetus. Drug use during the early weeks of pregnancy, from the fourth to the eighth week following conception, is more likely to increase the risks of spontaneous abortions and physical malformations in the newborn than drug use later in the pregnancy. Drug use after the eighth month of pregnancy is frequently associated with growth retardation, prematurity and low birth weight, and neurological damage to the infant.[23] These warnings are generalizations, however, cutting across many categories of psychoactive substances. Focus 2.2 examines the specific risks associated with specific categories of drugs.

Drug abuse and AIDS

One of the hazards associated with intravenous (i.v.) drug use is the spread of disease when needles are shared. In the past, the contamination has primarily involved infectious hepatitis, a serious liver disease. Since the late 1970s, however, attention has turned to the potential spread of the human immunodeficiency virus (HIV) responsible for acquired immunodeficiency syndrome (AIDS). Since HIV-infected individuals may not show discernible AIDS symptoms for a considerable period of time (the median interval being ten years), there is unfortunately ample opportunity for contaminating others, either through sexual contact or some direct exchange of bodily fluids. Almost 60 percent of intravenous drug users in New York have tested HIV-positive, and the prevalence among similar populations in cities as disparate as Edinburgh and Bangkok is only slightly less.[24] Approximately 69 percent of AIDS cases in the United States attributed to heterosexual transmission involve sexual contact with a user of intravenous drugs. Viewed in a different way, about one third of *all* AIDS cases in

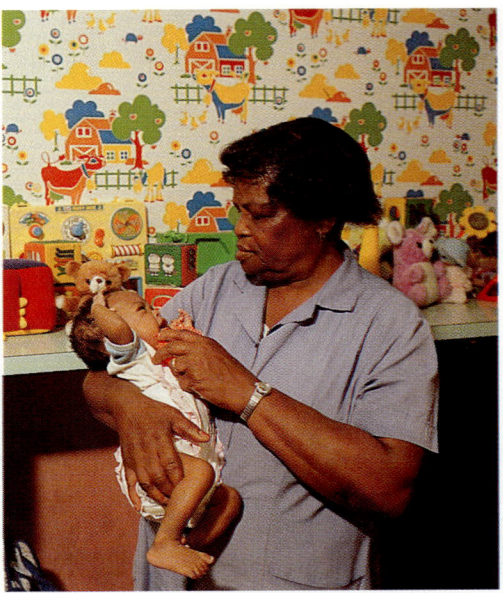

Babies born to women who have abused drugs during their pregnancy require special health care during their early months of development.

the United States have resulted from the use of a needle infected with HIV rather than from sexual transmission.[25]

In an effort to reduce the risk of HIV infection among the intravenous drug user, needle-exchange programs, where addicts have the opportunity to trade in their used needles for sterile ones, have been operating successfully in several countries, including England, Canada, Australia, Sweden, and the Netherlands. In the United States, however, the idea of providing sterile needles to heroin users has met with considerable political and social resistance. Nonetheless, such programs do exist in more than two dozen U.S. communities, either officially sanctioned or operating underground. In a 1993 experimental needle-exchange program in New York City, more than five thousand drug users participated; during the six-month trial period, no increase in drug use was reported.[26]

In addition to the implementation of needle-exchange programs, it is also important to educate drug users on the specific dangers of

Effects of psychoactive drugs on pregnant women and newborns

While psychoactive drugs have an adverse effect on fetal development and pregnancy in general, a number of such drugs carry very specific risks. Here is a review of these effects.

ALCOHOL

- Fetal effects: Impairment in the supply of fetal oxygen and stimulation of excess prostaglandins possibly causing fetal malformations.

- Pregnancy effects: Risk of miscarriage during the second trimester of pregnancy if the mother consumed only one or two drinks a day.

- Newborn effects: Signs of alcohol withdrawal upon birth if the mother drank heavily. Fetal alcohol syndrome involving retardation of postnatal growth and nervous system, abnormal craniofacial features, numerous organ abnormalities.

TOBACCO

- Fetal effects: Reduced oxygen supply compounded by carbon monoxide that interferes with the blood's ability to carry oxygen throughout the body.

- Pregnancy effects: Increased frequency of spontaneous abortions and fetal death.

- Newborn effects: Increased risk of physical defects, lower birth weight. Also a higher risk that infants born to mothers who smoke will die before their first birthday.

MARIJUANA

- Fetal effects: Increased carbon monoxide levels in mother's blood, particularly in the last trimester, resulting in reduced oxygen in fetal blood.

- Pregnancy effects: Inconsistent findings, although there is a tendency for more males to be conceived than females if either parent is a heavy marijuana smoker.

- Newborn effects: Some evidence for abnormal sleep and arousal patterns if mothers have used marijuana.

COCAINE OR CRACK

- Fetal effects: Constriction of blood vessels, which reduces normal fetal blood flow and causes urogenital malformations.

- Pregnancy effects: High rates of spontaneous abortion and early separation of the placenta from the uterine wall, resulting in increased numbers of stillbirths. Increased risks of early onset of labor and preterm delivery.

- Newborn effects: Increased risk of intrauterine growth retardation: lower birth weight and smaller length and head circumference. Tendency to be jittery and easily startled. Fewer discernible withdrawal symptoms than in newborns exposed to heroin or other narcotics in utero. Increased incidence of sudden infant death syndrome (SIDS).

HEROIN OR MORPHINE

- Fetal effects: Reduced oxygen supply to the fetus, as well as reduced pancreatic, liver, and intestinal functioning.

- Pregnancy effects: In 10 to 15 percent of pregnant women using heroin, development of toxemia, a poisoning of the blood between the mother and the fetus.

- Newborn effects: Retardation of intrauterine growth. Likelihood of lung problems, brain hemorrhages, and respiratory distress. Risk for perinatally transmitted HIV infection and the development of AIDS. Dramatic withdrawal symptoms usually beginning forty-eight to seventy-two hours after delivery.

PRESCRIPTION DRUGS

- Accutane (isoretinoin): Major birth defects associated with this antiacne medication and Vitamin A derivative.

- Tetracycline antibiotics: Possibility of permanent discoloration of a child's teeth.

- Salicylates (aspirin products): Possibility of bleeding in the mother or fetus and of delay in delivery if taken close to term or prior to delivery.

- Dilantin (phenytoin): Increased risk of heart malformations, cleft lip, and mental retardation associated with this and other anticonvulsants.

- Hormones in birth control pills: Increased risk of congenital abnormalities, including heart and limb defects.

- Antianxiety drugs: Possible depression of respiration in newborn when taken during labor. Fourfold increase in cleft plates and malformations of the heart and limbs when taken during early pregnancy.

- Barbiturates: Birth defects resembling fetal alcohol syndrome associated with long-acting barbiturates such as phenobarbital. Withdrawal symptoms in the newborn four to seven days after delivery.

SOURCE: Cook, Paddy S., Peterson, Robert C., and Moore, Dorothy T. (1990). *Alcohol, tobacco, and other drugs may harm the unborn.* Rockville MD: Office of Substance Abuse Prevention.

HIV infection. In one educational intervention program in Cleveland in 1990, the percentage of those who reported sharing needles decreased from 67 to 24, with the reductions remaining stable after several months.[27]

Drugs, violence, and crime

mportant questions often end up being the most complicated ones to answer. Consider the question of whether drugs cause violence and crime. We can look at the daily barrage of news about acts of social violence linked to the world of illicit drugs and the impact of those acts on our society: innocent children killed in the crossfire of rival drug gangs, thousands of crimes against individuals and property to pay for the addict's drug habit, terrorization of whole communities by drug dealers. Illicit drugs and crime are bound up together in a web of greed and callous disregard for human life. The association is clearly there. Figure 2.3 shows the results of a continuing survey conducted by the U.S. Department of Justice in which individuals arrested for a serious offense (most commonly burglary, assault, and grand larceny) are tested for various drugs in their bloodstream. During the fourth quarter of 1992, 64 percent of men arrested in Philadelphia, for example, were found to test positive for cocaine. Approximately 79 percent of them tested positive for some illicit drug at the time of arrest. At the same time, the range was substantial; Chicago arrestees showed a similar pattern of positive responses to drug testing as Philadelphia, but among arrestees in Omaha and San Jose, California, the percentage was considerably lower.[28]

In general, a wide range of violent acts and deaths have been connected to some form of alcohol or illicit drug use (Fig. 2.4).[29] But do drugs *cause* violent behavior and crime? Do certain drugs have a greater causal relationship than others? We have to break down the larger question about the effect of drugs on crime and violence into specific issues and try to understand them one by one.

Pharmacological violence

First of all, we should address the issue of whether a drug causes violent or criminal behavior while the drug is actually present in the individual's system. Although the statistics show that a large proportion of people have some illicit drug in their system at the time of arrest, it is difficult to say whether the offense was committed as a result of the influence of that drug. This possibility, often referred to as **pharmacological violence,** appears to depend upon the drug involved. On the one hand, the physiological nature of some illicit drugs makes the probability of pharmacological violence quite unlikely. Marijuana, for example, makes the user more lethargic than active, in effect quite mellow in circumstances in which there may be some interpersonal conflict. Heroin produces a passive state of mind that reduces the inclination toward violent behavior. In fact, as rates of heroin abuse rise, the incidence of crimes against individuals (as opposed to crimes against property) decline.[30]

On the other hand, psychoactive stimulants such as amphetamines and cocaine or the hallucinogenic PCP (known as angel dust) produce an on-edge manner and a social paranoia that can lead to violent behavior, although there is no current evidence that these drugs specifically stimulate violent behavior. We need to be careful in the interpretation of studies reporting violent behavior in unselected populations. For example, in a study conducted at an Atlanta medical center, more than half of all patients being treated for acute cocaine intoxication were reported to be aggressive, agitated, and paranoid just prior to and at the time of hospital admission. It is impossible to determine

pharmacological violence
Violent acts committed while under the influence of a particular psychoactive drug, with the implication that the drug caused the violence to occur.

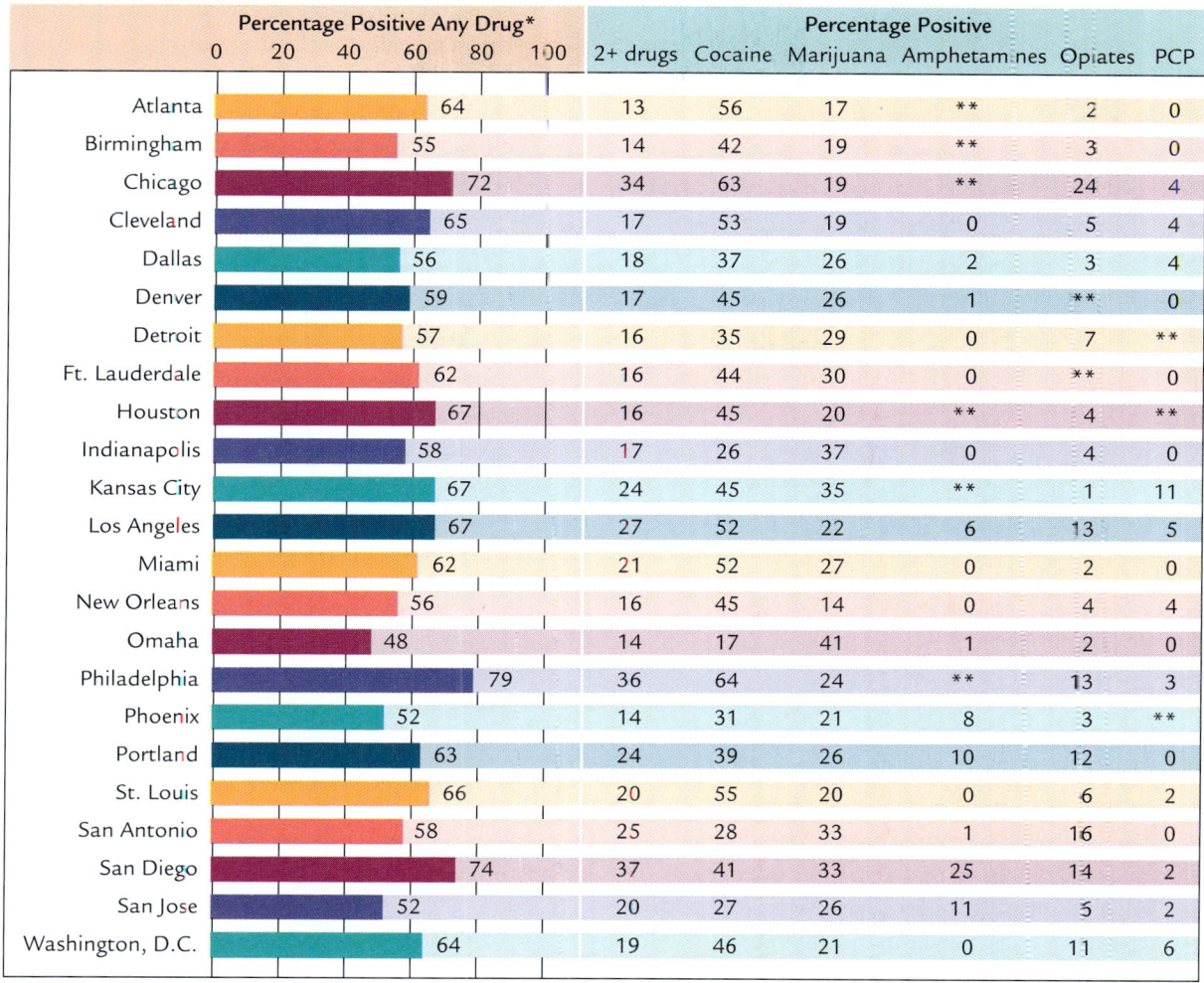

	Percentage Positive Any Drug*		Percentage Positive					
	0 20 40 60 80 100	2+ drugs	Cocaine	Marijuana	Amphetamines	Opiates	PCP
Atlanta	64	13	56	17	**	2	0
Birmingham	55	14	42	19	**	3	0
Chicago	72	34	63	19	**	24	4
Cleveland	65	17	53	19	0	5	4
Dallas	56	18	37	26	2	3	4
Denver	59	17	45	26	1	**	0
Detroit	57	16	35	29	0	7	**
Ft. Lauderdale	62	16	44	30	0	**	0
Houston	67	16	45	20	**	4	**
Indianapolis	58	17	26	37	0	4	0
Kansas City	67	24	45	35	**	1	11
Los Angeles	67	27	52	22	6	13	5
Miami	62	21	52	27	0	2	0
New Orleans	56	16	45	14	0	4	4
Omaha	48	14	17	41	1	2	0
Philadelphia	79	36	64	24	**	13	3
Phoenix	52	14	31	21	8	3	**
Portland	63	24	39	26	10	12	0
St. Louis	66	20	55	20	0	6	2
San Antonio	58	25	28	33	1	16	0
San Diego	74	37	41	33	25	14	2
San Jose	52	20	27	26	11	5	2
Washington, D.C.	64	19	46	21	0	11	6

FIGURE 2.3

Prevalence of drug use among male adult arrestees in major U.S. cities in October–December 1992. Figures for marijuana are overestimates with regard to cocaine, since cocaine is eliminated from the body within days while marijuana can be detected weeks after its last use.
SOURCE: *National Institute of Justice (1993). DUF: Drug use forecasting, 4th quarter 1992. Washington D.C. Department of Justice, p. 2.*

whether these patients were mentally unstable to begin with, prior to their taking cocaine. People who have long-standing psychological problems may be overrepresented in any population of cocaine abusers.[31]

Crack cocaine has the dubious reputation of making the crack smoker irritable, suspicious, and inclined to lash out at another person at the slightest provocation.[32] Whether or not these effects are due to being under the influence of the drug, however, is unclear. Tendencies toward violence are observed during times of *crack withdrawal* as well as crack

intoxication. A seventeen-year-old daily crack user has expressed it this way:

It doesn't seem to matter whether you're on or off crack . . . you're crazy both times If you're high, you think someone's goin' ta do something to you, or try an' take your stuff. If you're comin' down or are waiting to make a buy or just get off, you seem to get upset easy. . . . A lot of people been cut just because somebody looked at them funny or said somethin' stupid.[33]

Of all the psychoactive drugs we could consider, the one with the most definitive and

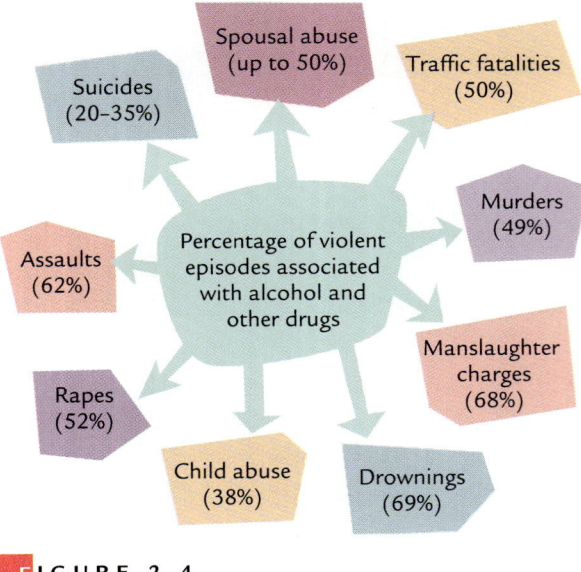

Spousal abuse
(up to 50%)

Suicides
(20–35%)

Traffic fatalities
(50%)

Murders
(49%)

Assaults
(62%)

Percentage of violent
episodes associated
with alcohol and
other drugs

Manslaughter
charges
(68%)

Rapes
(52%)

Child abuse
(38%)

Drownings
(69%)

F I G U R E 2 . 4

*The strong association between alcohol and other drug use
and episodes of violence and death*

widely reported links to violent behavior is
alcohol. On a domestic level, males involved
in spouse abuse commonly report having
been drinking or having been drunk during
many of the times that abuse has occurred.
Alcohol intoxication has been associated with
child-abuse in a subgroup of child-abuse
offenders but does not appear to be a characteristic feature. Violent crime outside the
home, however, is strongly related to alcohol
intoxication. The more violent the crime, the
greater the probability that the perpetrator of
the crime was drunk while committing it.
Studies show at least a majority of all homi-
cides and almost a majority of all sexually
aggressive acts (rapes and attempted rapes)
are committed while the offender is drunk.[34]

Does the chronic use of drugs cause individuals to engage in criminal behavior in general? There is little evidence that drugs *cause*
an increase in one's general inclination toward
antisocial behavior. In other words, it is not

economically compulsive violence
Violent acts that are committed by a
drug abuser in order to secure money to
buy drugs.

true that drugs alone are capable of changing
the personality of the user, turning him or her
from being some kind of upstanding pillar of
the community into a social menace. As discussed in the last chapter, social risk factors
can be identified that lead toward deviant
behavior, as defined by the societal norms,
and that deviant behavior includes both drug
abuse and criminal behavior. One aspect of
that deviant behavior cannot be considered
the cause of the other. Frequently, individuals
with the greatest chance of abusing drugs
have socioeconomic backgrounds that also
produce the greatest chance of criminal
behavior: a low level of education, a broken
family, little or no social supervision, and low
social status.[35] As one researcher has put it,

*Teenagers who begin illegal drug use are also
likely to have committed other criminal acts before-
hand, whether or not they have been caught. It is
likely that this relationship may be sufficient to
explain the higher crime rate of marijuana users. It
is not so much that marijuana use causes crime
(except, of course, the crime of using the drug), but
that those who use marijuana are also the type of
people more likely to commit criminal acts.[36]*

Economically compulsive violence

To what extent are criminal acts being
committed for the expressed purpose of
obtaining the money to support a drug habit?
We can speak of the possibility of **economically compulsive violence,** if the violent act
stems from the costliness of the drug-taking
behavior.

A 1985 study of heroin abusers in New
York City showed a high frequency of robberies, burglaries, and larcenies, as well as of
shoplifting and prostitution. Very few of these
crimes, however, earned them more then $100
at a time, and the average annual income from
crime was less than $12,000. Nearly half of
this income was in the form of drugs obtained
as payment for distributing drugs to others.[37]

A 1990 survey of a sample of 361 adolescent crack users in the Miami area showed

that 59 percent participated in 6,669 robberies over a twelve-month period, averaging 31 robberies per individual, or roughly one every twelve days. Yet, while the majority of these robberies were carried out in order to buy drugs, we cannot assume that they all involved the classic picture of break-ins and holdups. Approximately 25 percent of the sample had robbed drugs from drug dealers or other users, while 40 percent had been themselves victims of a drug robbery.[38] Nonetheless, a large proportion of the crimes committed in order to obtain drug money involved violent acts directed toward individuals within the community. Particular targets included storekeepers, children, and the elderly.

In recent years, U.S. government studies have indicated that the primary means for gaining money to buy drugs has been drug selling rather than robbery. Not all drug sellers, however, use the drugs they sell. A 1993 survey of three hundred gang members in San Francisco has shown that it depends upon the particular drug. The majority of marijuana, powdered cocaine, or heroin sellers use the drugs they sell, while the majority of crack sellers do not use crack themselves. The use of crack by sellers is considered "bad for business."[39]

When robbery is the means for financing drug abuse, the extent of this crime has been shown to be closely related to the market conditions at the time. When heroin prices are high, for example, the level of property crime goes up; when heroin prices are low, the crime level goes down as well. In other words, heroin abusers steal more in order to maintain a stable consumption of heroin if the drug becomes more expensive to obtain. Therefore, deliberate elevation of drug prices when accomplished by reducing the supply not only fails to reduce the incidence of abuse but also tends to increase the incidence of criminal behavior among drug abusers.[40] Economically compulsive violence, therefore, appears to be a major component of the link between drugs and crime in U.S. society

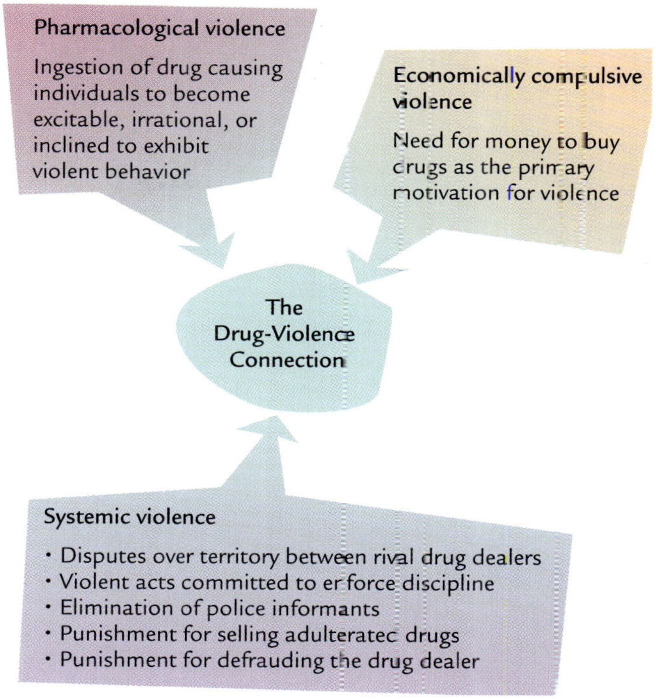

Pharmacological violence
Ingestion of drug causing individuals to become excitable, irrational, or inclined to exhibit violent behavior

Economically compulsive violence
Need for money to buy drugs as the primary motivation for violence

The Drug-Violence Connection

Systemic violence
- Disputes over territory between rival drug dealers
- Violent acts committed to enforce discipline
- Elimination of police informants
- Punishment for selling adulterated drugs
- Punishment for defrauding the drug dealer

FIGURE 2.5

The three aspects of drugs and violence

Systemic violence

A third important source of social violence and criminal behavior is inherent within the drug world itself. Researchers use the term **systemic violence** to refer to the violence that arises from characteristic features of drug dealing (Fig. 2.5). Systemic violence can result from such situations as territorial disputes, the consequences of selling inferior grades of the illicit drug, or fraudulent handling of funds from drug sales (referred to as "messing up the money"). The prominence of systemic violence in crack cocaine abuse since the mid-1980s is particularly striking. Studies show that as the involvement of a youth in crack distribution increases, the more likely that

systemic violence
Violence that arises from the traditionally aggressive patterns of behavior within a network of illicit drug trafficking and distribution.

person is to become a criminal offender. The probability also increases that major felonies will be committed.[41]

The question of which factor causes the other cannot be easily answered. It is quite possible that a combination of modeling behavior and self-selection is occurring here. Inherently violent individuals may be useful in maintaining tight discipline in groups that focus upon drug taking and drug selling; they may be useful as combatants in territorial disputes in general. As a result, the participation of highly violent individuals in the selling and distribution of crack adds an extremely dangerous dimension to the violence and social upheaval already associated with illicit drugs.[42] In addition, the most violent individuals may be the most respected role models for young people. Sociologists have observed that in many communities, adolescents feel the need to prove that they can be brutal in order to avoid being harassed by their peers. The pressure to be an accepted member of such a community may be more responsible for a drug abuser's committing frequent violent acts than the effects of the drugs themselves, or even the need for money to buy drugs.[43]

In addressing the connections between drug-taking behavior and crime, it is important to include patterns of criminal behavior that are associated with more affluent populations. The spread of dependency on illicit drugs to higher socioeconomic levels of society, since the 1970s, has led to an increase in white-collar crimes of fraud and embezzlement that are motivated by the need for drug money. In such cases, we are speaking of economically compulsive acts. While generally nonviolent in nature, these criminal acts involve substantially greater amounts of lost revenue than the burglaries and robberies common to poorer neighborhoods.

laissez-faire (LAY-say FAIR) (Fr.)
The philosophy of exerting as little control and regulation as possible.

Regulating drugs and enforcing drug laws

ow should we as a society respond to the social problems of drug-taking behavior? We are faced with an overwhelming flood of illicit drugs entering the United States from around the world, only a small fraction of which is ever identified, much less confiscated, despite the well-publicized drug seizures.[44] We can express our moral outrage that the situation has become so bad, that drug abuse is costing society such an enormous amount of money and wasting so many lives (Fig. 2.6). Social despair is so well entrenched in some portions of society that solutions seem to be nonexistent. The official responses U.S. society has made through its history, in terms of regulatory controls over drugs, can be understood more clearly in terms of its attitudes toward drug-taking behavior and drug users than in terms of the drugs themselves.

Attempts to regulate drugs 1900–1970

Up until about 1900 in the United States, the public attitude toward addictive behavior was one of **laissez-faire,** roughly translated as "allow [people] to do as they please," which meant there was little regulation or control. It was a well-ingrained philosophy, going back to our early days as a nation, that government should stay out of the lives of its citizens. Nonmedical use of opiates was not considered respectable and in some circles was seen as immoral, but it was no more disreputable than heavy drinking.

Employees were not fired for addiction. Wives did not divorce their addicted husbands, or husbands their addicted wives. Children were not taken from their homes and lodged in foster homes or institutions because one or both parents were addicted. Addicts continued to participate fully in the life of the community. Addicted children and young people continued to go to school, Sunday school, and college.[45]

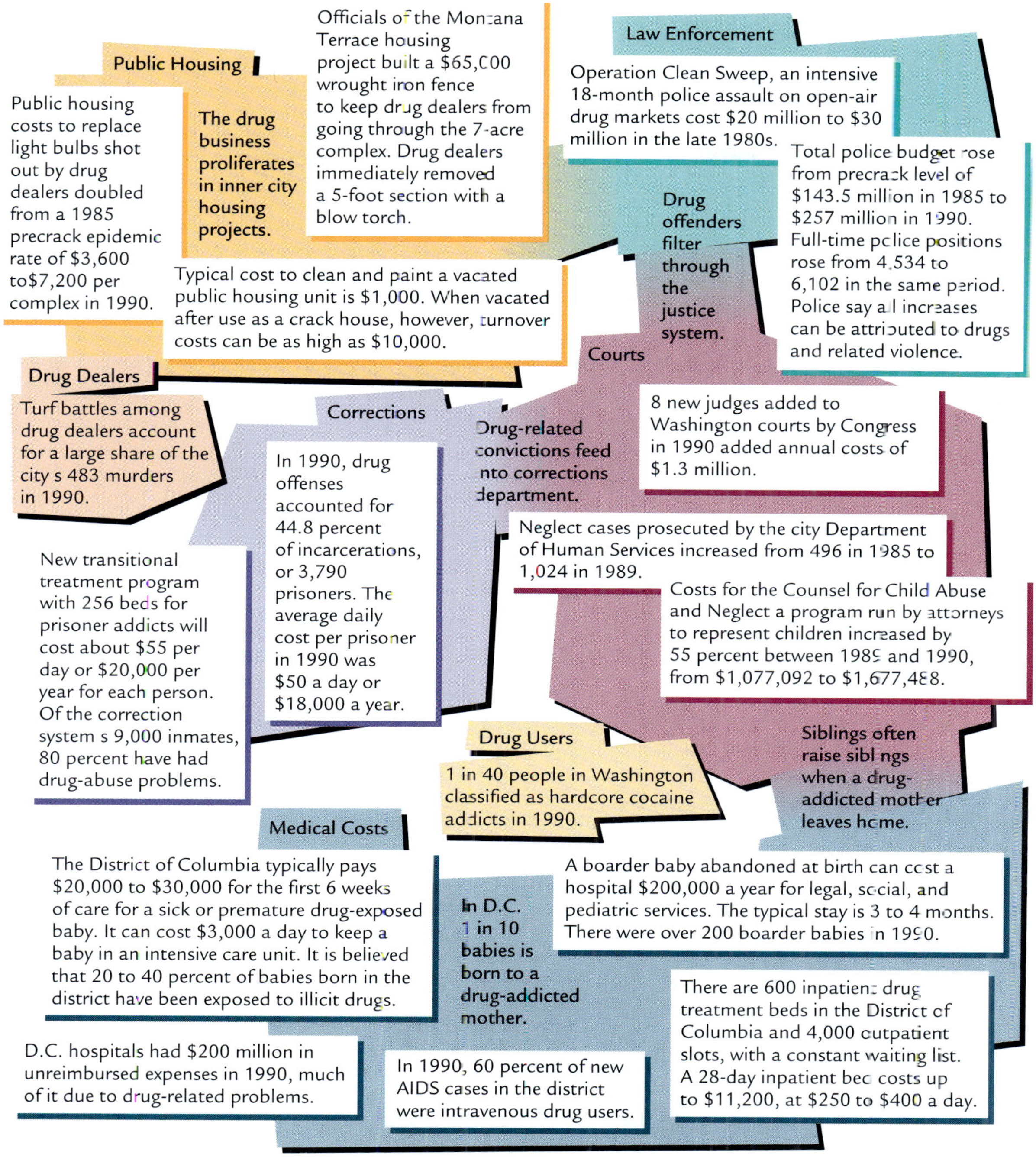

Public Housing

Public housing costs to replace light bulbs shot out by drug dealers doubled from a 1985 precrack epidemic rate of $3,600 to $7,200 per complex in 1990.

The drug business proliferates in inner city housing projects.

Officials of the Montana Terrace housing project built a $65,000 wrought iron fence to keep drug dealers from going through the 7-acre complex. Drug dealers immediately removed a 5-foot section with a blow torch.

Typical cost to clean and paint a vacated public housing unit is $1,000. When vacated after use as a crack house, however, turnover costs can be as high as $10,000.

Law Enforcement

Operation Clean Sweep, an intensive 18-month police assault on open-air drug markets cost $20 million to $30 million in the late 1980s.

Total police budget rose from precrack level of $143.5 million in 1985 to $257 million in 1990. Full-time police positions rose from 4,534 to 6,102 in the same period. Police say all increases can be attributed to drugs and related violence.

Drug offenders filter through the justice system.

Courts

8 new judges added to Washington courts by Congress in 1990 added annual costs of $1.3 million.

Drug Dealers

Turf battles among drug dealers account for a large share of the city's 483 murders in 1990.

Corrections

Drug-related convictions feed into corrections department.

In 1990, drug offenses accounted for 44.8 percent of incarcerations, or 3,790 prisoners. The average daily cost per prisoner in 1990 was $50 a day or $18,000 a year.

New transitional treatment program with 256 beds for prisoner addicts will cost about $55 per day or $20,000 per year for each person. Of the correction system's 9,000 inmates, 80 percent have had drug-abuse problems.

Neglect cases prosecuted by the city Department of Human Services increased from 496 in 1985 to 1,024 in 1989.

Costs for the Counsel for Child Abuse and Neglect a program run by attorneys to represent children increased by 55 percent between 1989 and 1990, from $1,077,092 to $1,677,488.

Drug Users

1 in 40 people in Washington classified as hardcore cocaine addicts in 1990.

Siblings often raise siblings when a drug-addicted mother leaves home.

Medical Costs

The District of Columbia typically pays $20,000 to $30,000 for the first 6 weeks of care for a sick or premature drug-exposed baby. It can cost $3,000 a day to keep a baby in an intensive care unit. It is believed that 20 to 40 percent of babies born in the district have been exposed to illicit drugs.

In D.C. 1 in 10 babies is born to a drug-addicted mother.

A boarder baby abandoned at birth can cost a hospital $200,000 a year for legal, social, and pediatric services. The typical stay is 3 to 4 months. There were over 200 boarder babies in 1990.

There are 600 inpatient drug treatment beds in the District of Columbia and 4,000 outpatient slots, with a constant waiting list. A 28-day inpatient bed costs up to $11,200, at $250 to $400 a day.

D.C. hospitals had $200 million in unreimbursed expenses in 1990, much of it due to drug-related problems.

In 1990, 60 percent of new AIDS cases in the district were intravenous drug users.

FIGURE 2.6

Tracing the direct and indirect costs of drug abuse in Washington DC, in 1990
SOURCE: *By Gus Stuart and John Van Pelt. Reprinted by permission from* The Christian Science Monitor.
© 1990 The Christian Science Publishing Society. All rights reserved.

Prior to the twentieth century, there were movements to ban alcoholic consumption but none to ban the wholesale use of opium, morphine, heroin, or cocaine. The only exception was the strong opposition to the smoking of opium, an attitude directed principally toward Chinese immigrants in the Western states, as noted in Chapter 7.

By the turn of the century, however, a wave of reform sentiment began to sweep the country. In 1905 the popular magazine *Collier's* criticized the fradulant claims and improper labeling of patent medicines that contained large amounts of alcohol, opiates, and cocaine. Large-scale abuses in the meat-packing industry, publicized in 1906 in Upton Sinclair's novel *The Jungle,* turned the stomach of the American public and quickly pressured President Theodore Roosevelt and Congress to take action. The result was the enactment of the Pure Food and Drug Act. The 1906 law required that food and drug manufacturers list the amounts of alcohol or "habit-forming" drugs, specified as any opiate or cocaine, on the label of the product, but the sale or use of any of these substances was left unrestricted. The law was the first of a series of legislative controls over food, drinks, drugs, and eventually cosmetics. As Chapter 15 will describe, this legislation eventually evolved into the present-day Food and Drug Administration.

The second major piece of legislation of the early part of the century was the Harrison Act of 1914. This new law concerned itself with opiate drugs (defined as narcotics) and cocaine. Cocaine was not defined as a narcotic under the law, but it became lumped together with opiates and often was referred to as a narcotic as well. Although the application of the term to cocaine was incorrect (narcotic literally means "stupor-inducing" and cocaine is anything but that), the association has unfortunately stuck. Later, several restricted drugs, including marijuana and the hallucinogenic peyote, were also officially classified as narcotics without regard to their pharmacological characteristics. Today, many people still think of any illegal drug as a narcotic, and for many years the bureau at the Treasury Department charged with drug-enforcement responsibilities was called the Bureau of Narcotics and their agents known on the street as "narks."

The Harrison Act did not make opiates and cocaine illegal, but physicians, dentists, and veterinarians could prescribe these drugs "in the course of their professional practice only." What this last phrase meant was left to a good deal of interpretation. The Treasury Department viewed the maintenance of individuals on these drugs, particularly opiates, as beyond medical intentions, and the courts upheld the interpretation. Between 1915 and 1938, thousands of physicians in the United States were found to be in violation of the law. In what would become a continuing theme in the history of drug-enforcement legislation, the Harrison Act failed to reduce drug-taking behavior. Eventually, American physicians gave up writing prescriptions for their addicted patients, and the emphasis in the field of drug abuse moved from a medical concern to a criminal one.

By 1933, as the Prohibition Era ended, the attention of drug-enforcement policymakers, led by Harry Anslinger, the newly installed director of the Federal Bureau of Narcotics, turned from the control of alcohol consumption to the identification of marijuana as a major public menace. Congressional committees heard testimony from police claiming that marijuana, now called the "killer weed," aroused sexual excitement and led to violent crimes. The movie *Reefer Madness,* now a cult classic on many university campuses, depicted the moral slide of innocent young people introduced to marijuana. The result was the Marijuana Tax Act of 1937, after which, growers, sellers, and buyers of marijuana were subject to tax. State laws made possession of marijuana illegal.

The 1960s saw a number of amendments to the enforcement laws then in effect, as new drugs of abuse came onto the scene. The Bureau of Narcotics became the Bureau of Narcotics and Dangerous Drugs, and Anslinger, whose tenure as director rivaled that of FBI Director J. Edgar Hoover in longevity and power, retired in 1962.

PORTRAIT

Harry J. Anslinger—America's first drug czar

By the time Harry J. Anslinger became the first commissioner of the Federal Bureau of Narcotics (FBN) in 1930, the nation's drug-law-enforcement policy had been established. Despite the obvious failure of the national Prohibition movement, the consensus was that vigilant monitoring and harsh penalties could still help solve the social problems of heroin and cocaine abuse, even if they had not done so for alcohol. Anslinger had been a rising young star in the Prohibition Unit at the Treasury Department during the twenties, convinced that drug addiction was absolutely immoral and that its cure was a matter of preventing the addict from getting hold of the drug.

The end of Prohibition, however, had placed pressure on Congress to reduce the Treasury's enforcement budget, and the Great Depression put strains on federal expenditures in general. Anslinger and the FBN faced hard times. The savior, ironically enough, was marijuana. Beginning in the early 1930s, rumors of "degenerate Spanish-speaking residents" in the Southwest going on criminal rampages while smoking marijuana were being spread in newspapers and popular magazines. Anslinger seized upon these unsubstantiated reports, calling marijuana the "assassin of youth" (the title of an article in *American Magazine* that he co-wrote in 1937). In his view, a new menace at our shores deserved new legislation,

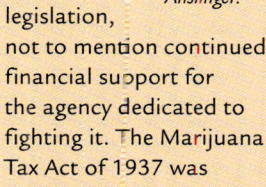

U.S. Commissioner of Narcotics Harry J. Anslinger.

not to mention continued financial support for the agency dedicated to fighting it. The Marijuana Tax Act of 1937 was Anslinger's creation.

Anslinger's thirty-two-year tenure at the FBN and his stature as the defender of the purity of American youth, or at least the purity of their circulatory systems, could not have been possible without strong support from several important conservative U.S. congressmen and senators. During the late 1940s and into the 1950s, Anslinger began to emphasize the link between drug addiction in the United States with the threat of international Communism from abroad. The target was Communist China, which Anslinger repeatedly claimed was the primary source of domestic heroin in the United States, even though the evidence clearly pointed to politically friendlier nations of Southeast Asia as the real culprits. Only after Anslinger's resignation in 1962, following considerable pressure from President John Kennedy, would the focus of attention be turned to the problem of heroin trafficking in Burma, Laos, and Thailand.

Given the anti-Communist stance of the FBN, it is not surprising that one of Anslinger's staunchest supporters during the late 1940s and early 1950s was Senator Joseph R. McCarthy, whose congressional subcommittee was then engaged in a ruthless crusade against "known Communists" inside the government. What was not known at the time, however, was that Anslinger during this period was secretly allowing McCarthy, a morphine addict as well as an alcoholic, to buy unrestricted supplies of morphine without FBN interference.

When McCarthy died in 1957 of "acute hepatitis, cause unknown," Anslinger wrote in a memoir, "I thanked God for relieving me of my burden."

Despite the criticism regarding Anslinger's continued obsession with the evils of marijuana, he is on the one hand credited with being the first to expose the influence of organized crime in the illicit drug market. This was at a time when J. Edgar Hoover, director of the FBI, was still denying the existence of organized crime in the United States. On the other hand, Anslinger's strong opposition to the treatment of drug addicts on an outpatient basis instead of admitting them to hospitals as medical patients, formed a major obstacle toward the development of community-based drug-abuse programs. After the Anslinger era had ended in 1962, there was finally a shift in U.S. drug policy toward a consideration of why an individual might be taking drugs in the first place.

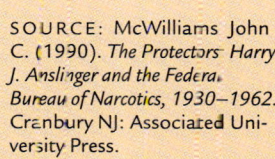

SOURCE: McWilliams, John C. (1990). *The Protectors: Harry J. Anslinger and the Federal Bureau of Narcotics, 1930–1962*. Cranbury NJ: Associated University Press.

Rethinking the approach toward drug regulation

The Comprehensive Drug Abuse Prevention and Control Act of 1970 was an attempt to organize the control of drugs under five classifications called schedules, based upon their potential for abuse (Table 2.4). These categories have defined the degrees of "authorized availability" of drugs ever since. Schedules I and II refer to drugs presenting the highest level of abuse potential, and Schedule V refers to drugs presenting the least. As drugs are considered more dangerous and more easily abused, progressively more stringent restrictions have been placed upon their possession, the number of prescriptions that could be made, or the manner in which the drugs could be dispensed.

The 1970 law moved the administration of drug enforcement from the Treasury Department to the Justice Department, ending the long era of attempts to regulate drug-taking behavior through taxation. As prevention and treatment programs for drug abuse were set up and funds were allocated for educational material, the emphasis started to shift from penalties on the drug user to penalties on drug dealing. In 1988 the Omnibus Drug Act imposed, among its features, penalties for money laundering when associated with drug smuggling and sales. Under this act, a new cabinet-level position, a "Drug Czar," was established to coordinate the many federal agencies and departments that were by now involved in drug regulation and drug-law enforcement.

Enforcement of drug laws on a local and international scale

The enforcement picture today is far more complex than it was fifty years ago, when the consideration was chiefly the "supply" side (the availability of drugs) of the problem, without much consideration of the "demand" side (the dependence of individuals on drugs

---

TABLE 2.4

The five schedules of controlled substances in the Comprehensive Drug Abuse Prevention and Control Act

Schedule I
High potential for abuse, No accepted medical use. Research use only; separate records must be maintained, and the drugs must be stored in secure vaults.

   Examples: heroin, LSD, mescaline, marijuana

Schedule II
High potential for abuse. Some accepted medical use, though use may lead to severe physical or psychological dependence. Prescriptions must be written in ink, or typewritten, and signed by a medical practitioner. Verbal prescriptions must be confirmed in writing within 72 hours and may be given only in a genuine emergency. No prescription renewals are permitted. Separate records must be maintained, and the drugs must be stored in secure vaults.

   Examples: codeine, morphine, cocaine, methadone, amphetamines, methaqualone, short-acting barbiturates

Schedule III
Some potential for abuse. Accepted medical use, though use may lead to low-to-moderate physical dependence or high psychological dependence. Prescriptions may be oral or written. Up to five prescription renewals are permitted within 6 months.

   Examples: long-acting barbituates, narcotic solutions (for example, paregoric or tincture of opium in alcohol) or mixtures (for example, 1.8% codeine)

Schedule IV
Low potential for abuse. Accepted medical use. Prescriptions may be oral or written. Up to five prescription renewals are permitted within 6 months.

   Examples: antianxiety drugs and sedative-hypnotics (for example, Valium and Miltown)

Schedule V
Minimal abuse potential. Widespread medical use. Minimal controls for selling and dispensing.

   Examples: prescription cough medicines not containing codeine, laxatives

SOURCE: *Physicians' desk reference* (48th ed.). (1994). Montvale NJ: Medical Economics Data, p. 2665.

capable of being abused). Society is putting more emphasis on drug-abuse treatment and prevention than ever before. Nonetheless, treatment and prevention programs in the Ronald Reagan and George Bush administrations represented only 30 percent of the federal budget to control drug abuse. During the Bill Clinton administration, the amount allotted to treatment and prevention programs has been increased to approximately 40 percent, but the majority of funds is still budgeted for efforts to reduce the supply of illicit drugs.[46]

An enormous amount of federal funds are expended, approximately $1.2 billion in 1994, specifically to hold back the continuing influx of illicit drugs entering the country. The Drug Enforcement Administration (DEA) has agents in more than forty foreign countries, working with the Departments of Defense and State, Central Intelligence Agency (CIA), U.S. Coast Guard and other branches of the military, and Immigration and Naturalization Service (INS). In 1989, 24,000 U.S. combat forces invaded Panama and brought back the country's dictator, General Manuel Noriega, to face charges of conspiring to smuggle cocaine into the United States; a few months later, the U.S. attorney general brought an indictment against a Burmese warlord, Khun Sa, reputedly the most powerful drug trafficker in the region and the leading heroin supplier to New York City. In 1992 Noriega was sentenced to forty years in jail on eight counts of drug trafficking, money laundering, and racketeering.

What impact, however, an indictment of an individual living securely half a world away or a conviction of a former dictator now in federal custody will have on the drug problem here at home remains open to considerable question. One of the great problems we face in our attempt to control the supply of illicit drugs into this country is that the many Third World countries continue to depend upon the drug trade in order to survive economically.[47]

Where has nearly a century of drug regulation taken us? We are now in the third decade of the U.S. War on Drugs, declared officially by President Richard Nixon in 1971, and the

The large quantities of confiscated illicit drugs are only a small fraction of the actual amount that successfully enters the United States.

price tag for this war as of 1994 has exceeded $100 billion, with more than $13 billion allocated in 1994 alone. More money continues to be requested to carry on the fight, but the struggle continues to be frustrating in the extreme (Fig. 2.7). In 1987 the U.S. Office of Technology Assessment issued a comprehensive report on the efforts to intercept and block the entrance of illicit drugs into the country. It concluded that despite a *doubling* of the money devoted to drug interdiction from 1982 to 1987, the amount of smuggled drugs had continued to increase. In addition, there was no clear-cut correlation between the expenditures for interdiction and the availability of illicit drugs.[48] One federal drug-law-enforcement official has recently commented, "It reminds me of that cartoon. This king is slamming his fist on the table, saying 'If all my horses and all my men can't put Humpty Dumpty together again, then what I need is *more* horses and *more* men!' "[49]

Many experts in the field of drug abuse view the solution not to be in faraway countries, at U.S. borders, or in U.S. prisons, but in the communities of the United States.[50] As one political scientist has put it: "If the 'war' is

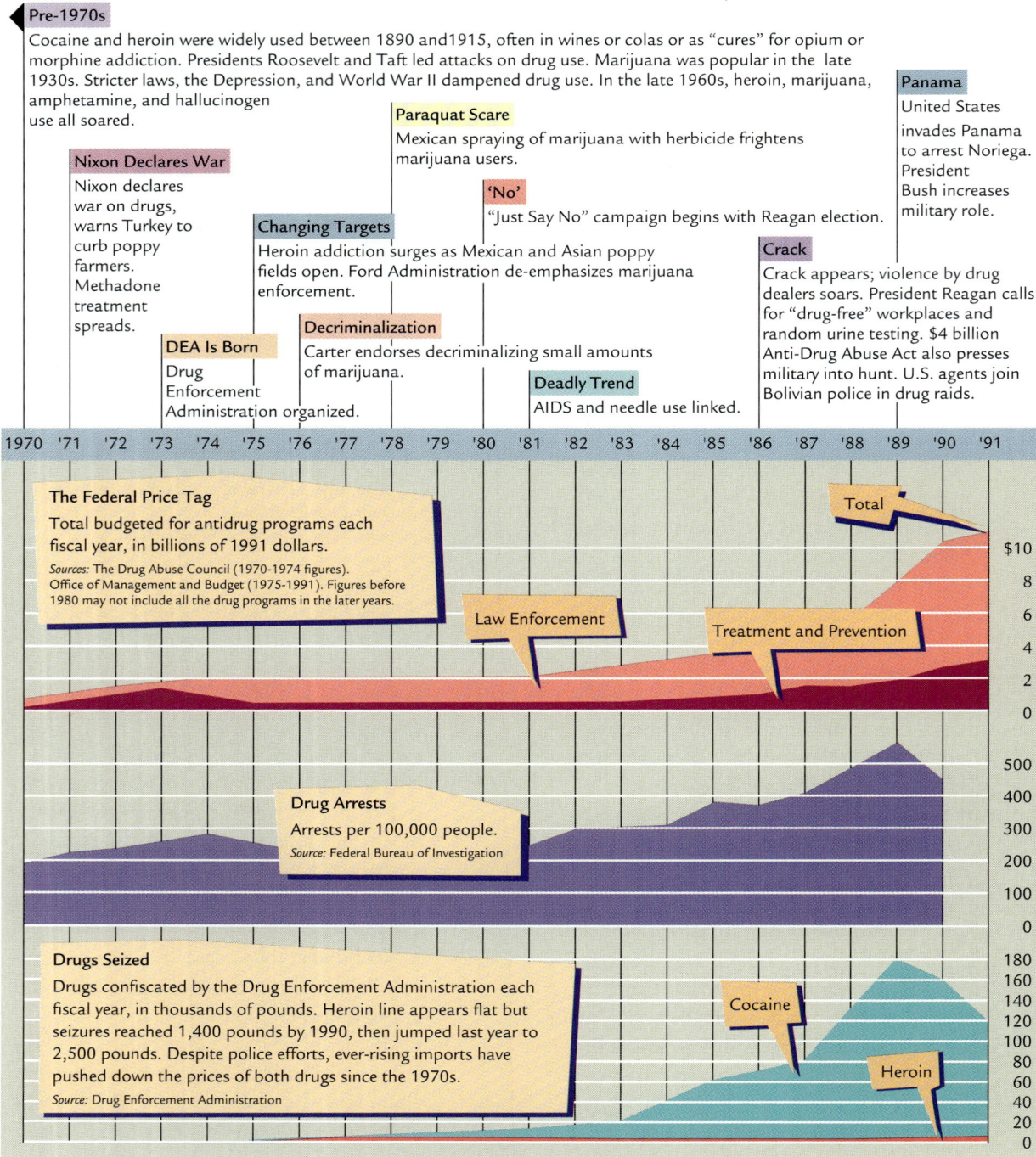

Pre-1970s

Cocaine and heroin were widely used between 1890 and 1915, often in wines or colas or as "cures" for opium or morphine addiction. Presidents Roosevelt and Taft led attacks on drug use. Marijuana was popular in the late 1930s. Stricter laws, the Depression, and World War II dampened drug use. In the late 1960s, heroin, marijuana, amphetamine, and hallucinogen use all soared.

Nixon Declares War

Nixon declares war on drugs, warns Turkey to curb poppy farmers. Methadone treatment spreads.

Changing Targets

Heroin addiction surges as Mexican and Asian poppy fields open. Ford Administration de-emphasizes marijuana enforcement.

DEA Is Born

Drug Enforcement Administration organized.

Decriminalization

Carter endorses decriminalizing small amounts of marijuana.

Paraquat Scare

Mexican spraying of marijuana with herbicide frightens marijuana users.

'No'

"Just Say No" campaign begins with Reagan election.

Deadly Trend

AIDS and needle use linked.

Panama

United States invades Panama to arrest Noriega. President Bush increases military role.

Crack

Crack appears; violence by drug dealers soars. President Reagan calls for "drug-free" workplaces and random urine testing. $4 billion Anti-Drug Abuse Act also presses military into hunt. U.S. agents join Bolivian police in drug raids.

1970 '71 '72 '73 '74 '75 '76 '77 '78 '79 '80 '81 '82 '83 '84 '85 '86 '87 '88 '89 '90 '91

The Federal Price Tag

Total budgeted for antidrug programs each fiscal year, in billions of 1991 dollars.

Sources: The Drug Abuse Council (1970-1974 figures). Office of Management and Budget (1975-1991). Figures before 1980 may not include all the drug programs in the later years.

Total

Law Enforcement

Treatment and Prevention

$10
8
6
4
2
0

Drug Arrests

Arrests per 100,000 people.

Source: Federal Bureau of Investigation

500
400
300
200
100
0

Drugs Seized

Drugs confiscated by the Drug Enforcement Administration each fiscal year, in thousands of pounds. Heroin line appears flat but seizures reached 1,400 pounds by 1990, then jumped last year to 2,500 pounds. Despite police efforts, ever-rising imports have pushed down the prices of both drugs since the 1970s.

Source: Drug Enforcement Administration

Cocaine

Heroin

180
160
140
120
100
80
60
40
20
0

FIGURE 2.7

A summary of the U.S. war on drugs from 1970 to 1991

SOURCE: *Copyright © 1992 by the New York Times Company. Reprinted by permission.*

to be won, it will be won in the hearts and minds of people who might be inclined to consume drugs."[51]

The public policy issues surrounding the "demand side" of the drug abuse equation will be considered in greater detail in Chapter 17.

Summary

TOXICITY

- A drug's harmful effects are referred to as its toxicity. Toxicity can be measured in terms of a drug's therapeutic index or its margin of safety, each of which can be computed from its effective and lethal dose-response curves.

THE DAWN REPORTS

- Drug Abuse Warning Network (DAWN) statistics, which reflect drug-related lethal and nonlethal emergencies in major metropolitan hospitals in the United States, offer another measure of drug toxicity. In general, DAWN statistics show that cocaine and narcotic drugs are both highly toxic and that many emergencies involve drugs being taken in combination with alcohol.

DRUG TOLERANCE

- A tolerance effect refers to the capacity of a drug to have a gradually diminished effect over repeated administrations; in effect, a greater dose has to be taken to maintain the original effect of the drug. Tolerance effects can be quite dangerous, since experienced drug users often end up taking potentially lethal dose levels.

PHYSICAL AND PSYCHOLOGICAL DEPENDENCE

- Drugs can be viewed in terms of a physical dependence model, in which the compulsive drug-taking behavior is tied to an avoidance of withdrawal symptoms, or a psychological dependence model, in which the drug-taking behavior is tied to a genuine craving for the drug and highly reinforcing effects of the drug on the user's body and mind.

PSYCHIATRIC DEFINITIONS

- The American Psychiatric Association currently recognizes two major conditions associated with drug-taking behavior: substance abuse and substance dependence. The broader term "substance" is used instead of "drug," because there is often confusion in the public mind in deciding what is defined as a drug and what is not.

SPECIAL PROBLEMS IN DRUG ABUSE

- Increasing attention has been directed toward the harmful effects that drug abuse has on pregnant women, in terms of problems with the pregnancy itself and with the neural development of the fetus.

- There is also concern with the increased risk of HIV infection (and the spread of AIDS) among intravenous drug users when needles are shared.

DRUGS, VIOLENCE, AND CRIME

- While there is an overall association between the taking of illicit drugs and crime, a careful analysis indicates that the drug with the closest connection to social violence is alcohol, and that heroin and marijuana cause the user to be less inclined toward violence rather than more so.

- It is clear that drug abuse forces many drug users to commit criminal acts (generally property theft) to support the drug habit. It is also clear that there is a high level of social violence and criminal behavior inherent in the trafficking and distribution of illicit drugs.

REGULATING DRUGS AND ENFORCING DRUG LAWS

- Since the beginning of the twentieth century, U.S. society's philosophy toward drug-taking behavior has been that we should restrict it by reducing the availability of illicit drugs and making it as difficult as possible for the potential drug user to engage in drug-taking behavior.

- The Harrison Act of 1914 was the first of several legislative efforts to impose criminal penalties on the use of narcotics and cocaine and later marijuana, hallucinogens, and several other types of drugs.

- The Comprehensive Drug Act of 1970 organized the federal control of drugs under five classifications called schedules.

- Today's drug-law-enforcement program in the United States places considerable emphasis upon the interdiction of drugs entering the country, with less emphasis upon treatment and prevention of drug abuse.

Key Terms

acute toxicity, p. 35
catheter, p. 39
chronic toxicity, p. 35
dose, p. 29
dose-response curve, p. 29
Drug Abuse Warning Network (DAWN), p. 32
economically compulsive violence, p. 46
effective dose, p. 30
laissez faire, p. 48
lethal dose, p. 30
margin of safety, p. 31

pharmacological violence, p. 44
physical dependence, p. 38
polydrug use, p. 34
psychological dependence, p. 39
substance abuse, p. 40
substance dependence, p. 40
systemic violence, p. 47
therapeutic index, p. 31
tolerance, p. 36
toxicity, p. 29

Endnotes

1. Aquinas, Thomas (c. 1265). *Summa theologica.* Cited in Peter Kreeft. (1990). *A summa of the Summa.* San Francisco: Ignatius Press, p. 415.
2. Cummings, Nicholas A. (1979). Turning bread into stone: Our modern antimiracle. *American Psychologist, 34,* 1119–1129.
3. Treaster, Joseph B., and Holloway, Lynette (1994, September 4). Potent new blend of heroin ends 8 very different lives. *New York Times,* pp. 1, 37.
4. Ungerleider, J. Thomas, Lundberg, George D., Sunshine, Irving, and Walberg, Clifford B. (1980). The Drug Abuse Warning Network (DAWN) Program. *Archives of General Psychiatry, 37,* 106–109.
5. Substance Abuse and Mental Health Services Administration (1994a). Annual Emergency Room Data 1992. Data from the Drug Abuse Warning Network (DAWN), Series I, No. 12A. Rockville MD: Substance Abuse and Mental Health Services Administration, Office of Applied Studies.
Substance Abuse and Mental Health Services Administration (1994b). Annual Medical Examiner Data 1992. Data from the Drug Abuse Warning Network (DAWN), Series I, No. 12B. Rockville MD: Substance Abuse and Mental Health Services Administration, Office of Applied Studies.
6. Substance Abuse. Annual Medical Examiner Data, p. 24.

7. Substance Abuse. Annual Emergency Room Data, p. 20.
Substance Abuse. Annual Medical Examiner Data, p. 13.

8. Lankester, E. Ray (1889). Mithradatism. *Nature, 40,* 149.

9. Siegel, Shepard (1990). Drug anticipation and the treatment of dependence. In Barbara A. Ray (Ed.), *Learning factors in substance abuse* (NIDA Research Monograph 84). Rockville MD: National Institute on Drug Abuse, pp. 1–24.

10. Siegel, Shepard (1975). Evidence from rats that morphine tolerance is a learned response. *Journal of Comparative and Physiological Psychology, 89,* 489–506.

11. Siegel, Shepard, Hinson, Riley E., Krank, Marvin D., and McCully, Jane. (1982). Heroin "overdose" death: Contribution of drug-associated environmental cues. *Science, 216,* 436–437.

12. Brecher, Edward M., and the editors of Consumer Reports. (1972). *Licit and illicit drugs.* Mount Vernon NY: Consumers Union.

13. Jaffe, Jerome H. (1985). Drug addiction and drug abuse. In Alfred G. Gilman, Louis S. Goodman, Theordore W. Rall, and Ferid Murad (Eds.), *The pharmacological basis of therapeutics.* New York: Macmillan, pp. 532–581.

14. Blum, Kenneth. (1991). *Alcohol and the addictive brain*. New York, Free Press, p. 17.

15. Pinel, John P. J. (1990). *Biopsychology.* Boston: Allyn and Bacon, p. 483.

16. Simpson, D. Dwayne, and Marsh, Kerry L. (1986). In Frank M. Tims and Carl G. Leukefeld (Eds.), *Relapse and recovery in drug abuse* (NIDA Research Monograph 72). Rockville MD: National Institute on Drug Abuse, pp. 86–103. Simpson, D. Dwayne, and Sells, Saul B. (1982). Effectiveness of treatment for drug abuse: An overview of the DARP research program. *Advances in Alcohol and Substance Abuse, 2,* 7–29.

17. Pickens, Roy, and Thompson, Travis (1968). Cocaine-reinforced behavior in rats: Effects of reinforcement magnitude and fixed-ratio size. *Journal of Pharmacology and Experimental Therapeutics, 161,* 122–129. Yamagita, T. (1975). Some methodological problems in assessing dependence-producing properties of drugs in animals. *Pharmacological Reviews 27,* 503–510.

18. Hoffmeister, F. H., and Wuttke, W. (1975). Psychotropic drugs as negative reinforcers. *Pharmacological Reviews, 27,* 419–428. Yokel, R. A. (1987). Intravenous self-administration: Response rates, the effect of pharmacological challenges and drug preferences. In Michael A. Bozarth (Ed.), *Methods of assessing the reinforcing properties of abused drugs.* New York: Springer-Verlag, pp. 1–34.

19. Johanson, Chris E. (1984). Assessment of the abuse potential of cocaine in animals. In John Grabowski (Ed.), *Cocaine: Pharmacology, effects, and treatment of abuse.* Rockville MD: National Institute on Drug Abuse, pp. 54–71.

20. Quotation from Goode, Erich. (1989). *Drugs in American Society* (3rd ed.). New York: McGraw-Hill, p.49. Data from Bozarth, Michael A., and Wise, Roy A. (1985) Toxicity associated with long-term intravenous heroin and cocaine self-administration in the rat. *Journal of the American Medical Association, 254,* 81–83.

21. Stewart, Jane, De Wit, Harriet, and Eikelboom, Roelof (1984). Role of unconditioned and conditioned drug effects in the self-administration of opiates and stimulants. *Psychological Review, 91,* 251–268.

22. American Psychiatric Association (1994) *Diagnostic and statistical manual.* (4th ed.). Washington DC: American Psychiatric Association, pp. 180–183.

23. Cook, Paddy S., Petersen, Robert C., and Moore, Dorothy T. (1990). *Alcohol, tobacco, and other drugs may harm the unborn* (DHHS Publication No. [ADM] 90–1711). Washington DC: Office of Substance Abuse Prevention.

24. Stimson, Gerry V. (1991, May). The prevention of HIV infection in injecting drug users: Recent advances and remaining obstacles.

Newsletter of the International Working Group on AIDS and Drug Use, 5, 14–19.

25. Schuster, Charles, and Pickens, Roy (1988). AIDS and intravenous drug abuse. *Problems of Drug Dependence, 1988* (NIDA Research Monograph 90). Rockville MD: National Institute on Drug Abuse, pp. 1–11. The Drug Policy Foundation (1992). *The Bush drug war record.* Washington DC: The Drug Policy Foundation, p. 20.

26. Navarro, Mireya (1993, February 18). New York needle exchanges called surprisingly effective. *New York Times,* pp. A1, B4.

27. Stephens, Richard C., Feucht, Thomas E., and Roman, Shadi W. (1991). Effects of an intervention program on AIDS-related drug and needle behavior among intravenous drug users. *American Journal of Public Health, 81,* 568–571.

28. National Institute of Justice (1993). DUF: Drug use forecasting, Fourth quarter 1992. Washington DC: Department of Justice, p. 2.

29. National Clearinghouse for Alcohol and Drug Information (1989). *Prevention Plus II: Tools for creating and sustaining drug-free communities.* Rockville MD: Office of Substance Abuse, p. 3.

30. De La Rosa, Mario, Lambert, Elizabeth Y., and Gropper, Bernard (1990). Introduction: Exploring the substance abuse-violence connection. In *Drugs and violence: Causes, correlates, and consequences* (NIDA Research Monograph 103). Rockville MD: National Institute on Drug Abuse, pp. 1–7.

31. Roth, Jeffrey A. (1994, February). *Psychoactive substances and violence:* Research brief. Washington DC: National Institute of Justice.

32. Gold, Mark S. (1991). *The good news about drugs and alcohol: Curing, treating and preventing substance abuse in the new age of biopsychiatry.* New York: Villard books.

33. Inciardi, James A. (1990). The crack-violence connection within a population of hard-core adolescent offenders. In Mario De La Rosa, Elizabeth Y. Lambert, and Bernard Gropper (Eds.), *Drugs and violence: Causes, correlates, and*

consequences (NIDA Research Monograph 103). Rockville MD: National Institute on Drug Abuse, pp. 92–111.

34. Roth. *Psychoactive substances.*

35. Harris, Jonathan (1991). *Drugged America.* New York: Four Winds Press, p. 112.

36. White, Jason M. (1991). *Drug Dependence.* Englewood Cliffs NJ: Prentice Hall, p. 200.

37. A study of heroin abusers, their drug use patterns, and crime (1985, March). *Street Pharmacologist, 8* (3), 1–2.

38. Inciardi. The crack-violence connection.

39. Roth. *Psychoactive substances.* Waldorf, Dan (1993). Don't be your own best customer: Drug use of San Francisco gang drug sellers. *Crime, Law, and Social Change, 19,* 1–15.

40. Silverman, Lester P., and Spruill, Nancy L. (1977). Urban crime and the price of heroin. *Journal of Urban Economics, 4,* 80–103.

41. Inciardi. The crack-violence connection.

42. Fagan, Jeffry, and Chin, Ko-lin (1990). Violence as regulation and social control in the distribution of crack. In Mario De La Rosa, Elizabeth Y. Lambert, and Bernard Gropper (Eds.), *Drugs and violence: Causes, correlates, and consequences* (NIDA Research Monograph 103). Rockville MD: National Institute on Drug Abuse, pp. 8–43.

43. Berger. Gilda (1989). *Violence and drugs.* New York: Franklin Watts, p. 16. Harris. *Drugged America,* p. 117.

44. Bugliosi, Vincent T. (1991). *Drugs in America: A citizen's call to action.* New York: Knightsbridge Publishing, p. 25.

45. Brecher. *Licit and illicit drugs,* pp. 6–7.

46. Page, Susan (1994, February 10). Clinton shifts drug funds to treatment. *Newsday,* pp. 3, 24.

47. McCoy, Alfred W. (1991). *The politics of heroin.* Brooklyn NY: Lawrence Hill Books.

48. U.S. Congress, Office of Technology Assessment. *The border war on drugs.* Washington DC: Government Printing Office, p. 3.

49. Herbert Kleber, quoted in Joseph B. Treaster. (1992, June 14). Twenty years of war on drugs, and no victory yet. *New York Times,* p. E7.

50. Trebach, Arnold S., and Zeese, Kevin B. (Eds.) (1991). *New frontiers in drug policy.* Washington DC: The Drug Policy Foundation.

51. F. LaMond Tullis, quoted in Joseph B. Treaster (1992, June 14). Twenty years of war on drugs. *New York Times,* p. E7.

3

How Drugs Work in the Body and on the Mind

You may have seen, some years ago on television, the classic public-service announcement with the image of an egg cooking in a frying pan. Its message was immediate and compelling: Stay away from drugs because they fry your brain. Doctors were speaking metaphorically, of course. They were saying, in effect, that there exist certain classes of drugs that have a devastating impact on the human brain. At the same time, it is important to realize that there are other drugs that have enormous beneficial effects (Chapters 15 and 16).

Whether drugs in general have a positive or negative effect on us depends upon how they interact with physiological processes in the body. As noted in Chapter 1, psychoactive drugs in particular affect our behavior and experience through their effects on the functioning of the brain. Therefore, our knowledge about drugs and their effects on our lives ultimately rests upon our understanding of the ways drugs work on a physiological level. This chapter will describe the basic functions of the nervous system and the ways in which drugs alter these functions. A good place to start is the question of how drugs get into the body in the first place.

"Men ought to know that from the brain and from the brain only, arise our pleasures, joys, laughter, and jests, as well as our sorrows, pains, griefs, and tears. Through it, . . . we think, see, hear, and distinguish the ugly from the beautiful, the bad from the good, the pleasant from the unpleasant. . . . In these ways, I hold that the brain is the most powerful organ of the human body."

Hippocrates, 460–377 B.C.[1]

How drugs enter the body

There are four principal routes through which drugs can be delivered into the body: oral administration, injection, inhalation, and absorption through the skin or membranes. In each of these possibilities, the destination is the bloodstream. In the case of psychoactive drugs, a drug effect depends not only on reaching the bloodstream but on reaching the brain as well.

Oral administration

Ingesting a drug by mouth, digesting it, and absorbing it into the bloodstream through the gastrointestinal tract is the oldest and easiest way of taking a drug. On the one hand, oral administration and reliance upon the digestive process for delivering a drug into the bloodstream provides a degree of safety. Many naturally growing poisons taste so vile that we normally spit them out before swallowing; others will cause us to be nauseous and the drug will be expelled through vomiting. In the case of other hazardous substances that are not spontaneously rejected, we can benefit from the relatively long absorption time for orally administered drugs. Most of the absorption process is accomplished between five and thirty minutes after ingestion, and absorption is not usually complete for as long as six to eight hours.[2] Therefore, there is at least a little time after accidental overdoses or suicide attempts to induce vomiting or pump the stomach.

On the other hand, the gastrointestinal tract contains a number of natural barriers that may prevent certain drugs that we *want* absorbed into the bloodstream from doing so. We first have to consider the degree of alkalinity or acidity in a drug, defined as its pH value. The interior of the stomach is highly acidic and the fate of a particular drug depends upon how it reacts with that environment. Weakly acidic drugs such as aspirin are absorbed better in the stomach than highly alkaline drugs such as morphine, heroin, or cocaine. Insulin is destroyed by stomach acid so it cannot be administered orally, while a neutral substance like alcohol is readily absorbed at all points in the gastrointestinal tract.

If it survives the stomach, the drug needs to proceed from the small intestine into the bloodstream. The membrane separating the intestinal wall from blood capillaries is made up of two layers of fat molecules, making it necessary for substances to be *lipid-soluble* or soluble in fats, in order to pass through. Even after successful absorption into blood capillaries, however, substances must still pass through the liver for another "screening" before being released into the general circulation. There are enzymes in the liver that destroy a drug by metabolizing (breaking down) its molecular structure, prior to its excretion from the body. There is a further barrier separating the circulatory system from brain tissue, which will be discussed in a later section.

As a result of all these natural barriers, orally administered drugs must be ingested at deliberately elevated dose levels, in order to allow for the fact that some proportion of the drug will not make it through to the bloodstream. We can try to compensate for the loss of the drug during digestion, but even then we may be only making a good guess. The state of the gastrointestinal tract changes constantly over time, making it more or less likely that a drug will reach the circulatory system. The presence or absence of undigested food or

Orally consumed drugs are absorbed into the brain relatively slowly, though a liquid beverage containing alcohol has the advantage of being easily absorbed.

whether the undigested food interacts with the chemical nature of the drug are examples of factors that make it difficult to make exact predictions about the strength of the drug when it finally enters the bloodstream.

Injection

A solution to the problems of oral administration is to bypass the digestive process entirely and deliver the drug more directly into the bloodstream. One option is to inject the drug through a hypodermic syringe and needle.

The fastest means of injection is an **intravenous** (i.v.) injection, since the drug is delivered into a vein without any intermediary tissue. An intravenous injection of heroin in the forearm, for example, arrives at the brain in less than fifteen seconds.[3] The effects of abused drugs delivered in this way, often called *mainlining*, are not only rapid but extremely intense. In a medical setting, intravenous injections provide an extreme amount of control over dosage and the opportunity to administer multiple drugs at the same time. The principal disadvantage, however, is that the effects of intravenous drugs are irreversible. In the event of a mistake or unexpected reaction, there is no turning back unless some other drug is available that can counteract the first one. In addition, repeated injections through a particular vein may cause the vein to collapse or develop a blood clot.

With **intramuscular** (i.m.) injections, the drug is delivered into a large muscle (usually in the upper arm, thigh, or buttock) and is absorbed into the bloodstream through the capillaries serving the muscle. Intramuscular injections have slower absorption times than intravenous injections, but they can be administered more rapidly in emergency situations. Our exposure to intramuscular injections comes early in our lives when we receive the standard schedule of inoculations against diseases such as measles, diphtheria, and typhoid fever. Tetanus and flu shots are also administered in this way.

A third injection technique is the **subcutaneous** (s.c. or sub-Q) delivery, in which a needle is inserted into the tissue just underneath the skin. On the one hand, since the skin has a less abundant blood supply relative to a muscle, a subcutaneous injection has the slowest absorption time of all the injection techniques. It is best suited for situations in which it is desirable to have a precise control over the dosage and a steady absorption into the bloodstream. On the other hand, the skin may be easily irritated by this procedure. As a result, only relatively small amounts of a drug can be injected under the skin, compared to the quantity that can be injected into a muscle or vein. When involved in drug abuse, subcutaneous injections are often referred to as *skin-popping.*

All injections require a needle to pierce the skin, so there is an inherent risk of bacterial or viral infection if the needle is not sterile. The practice of injecting heroin or cocaine with shared needles, for example, promotes the spread of infectious hepatitis and AIDS (Chapter 2). If administered orally, drugs do not have to be any more sterile than the foods we eat or the water we drink.

Inhalation

Next to ingesting a drug, the simplest way of receiving its effects is to inhale it in some form of gaseous or vaporous state. The alveoli within the lungs can be imagined as a huge surface area with blood vessels lying immediately behind it. Our bodies are so dependent upon the oxygen in the air we breathe that we have evolved an extremely efficient system for getting oxygen to its destinations. As a consequence of this highly developed system, the psychoactive effect of an inhaled

> **intravenous (i.v.)**
> Into a vein.
>
> **intramuscular (i.m.)**
> Into a muscle.
>
> **subcutaneous (s.c. or sub-Q)**
> Underneath the skin.

drug is even faster than a drug delivered through intravenous injection. Traveling from the lungs to the brain takes only five to eight seconds.[4]

One way of delivering a drug through inhalation is to burn it and breathe in the smoke-borne particles in the air. Drugs administered through smoking include nicotine from cigarettes, opium, tetrahydrocannabinol (THC) from marijuana, free-base cocaine, crack cocaine, and crystallized forms of methamphetamine. Drugs such as paint thinners, gasoline, and glues can also be inhaled because they evaporate easily and the vapors travel freely through the air. In medical settings, general anesthetics are administered through inhalation, since the concentration of the drug can be precisely controlled.

The principal disadvantage of inhaling smoked drugs, as you probably expect, arises from the long-term hazards of breathing particles in the air that contain not only the active drug but also tars and other substances produced by the burning process. Emphysema, asthma, and lung cancer can result from smoking in general (see Chapter 12). There is also the possibility in any form of drug inhalation that the linings leading from the throat to the lungs can be severely irritated over time.

Absorption through the skin or membranes

Drug users over the ages have been quite creative in finding other routes through which drugs can be administered. One way is to sniff or snort a drug in dust or powder form into the nose. Once inside the nose, it adheres to thin mucous membranes and dissolves

intranasal
Applied to the mucous membranes of the nose.

sublingual
Applied under the tongue.

transdermal patch
A device attached to the skin that slowly delivers the drug through skin absorption.

Drugs consumed by inhalation are absorbed extremely quickly, aided by a very efficient delivery system from lungs to brain.

through the membranes into the bloodstream. This technique, referred to as an **intranasal** administration, is commonly used in taking snuff tobacco or cocaine. Snuff tobacco, chewing tobacco, and cocaine-containing coca leaves can also be chewed without swallowing over a period of time or simply placed in the cheek so that they are slowly absorbed through the membranes of the mouth. Nitroglycerin tablets for heart-disease patients are typically administered **sublingually,** with the drug placed underneath the tongue and absorbed into the bloodstream.

At the opposite end of the body, medicines can be placed as a suppository into the rectum, where the suppository gradually melts and the medicine is absorbed through thin rectal membranes. This method is less reliable than an oral administration, but it may be necessary if the individual is vomiting or unconscious. The newest technique involves a **transdermal patch** through which a drug can slowly diffuse through the skin without breaking the skin surface. Transdermal patches have been used for long-term administration of nitroglycerin, estrogen, and motion-sickness medication, and more recently nicotine.[5]

Focus 3.1 summarizes the various ways drugs can be administered into the body.

Factors determining the physiological impact of drugs

The type of delivery route into the bloodstream, as has been discussed, places specific constraints upon the effect a drug might produce. Some drug effects are optimized, for example, by an oral administration, while others require more direct access to the bloodstream. There are other factors that must be considered. If a drug is administered repeatedly, the timing of the administrations plays an important role in determining the final result. If two drugs are administered together, we must also consider how these drugs interact with each other. Finally, it is possible that two identical drugs taken by two individuals may have different effects by virtue of the characteristics of the drug taker at the time of administration. These three factors will now be considered.

Timing

All drugs, no matter how they are delivered, share some common features when we consider their effects over time. There is initially an interval (the **latency period**) during which the concentration of the drug is increasing in the blood but is not yet high enough for a drug effect to be detected. How long this latency period will last is related generally to the absorption time of the drug. As the concentration of the drug continues to rise, the effect will become stronger. A stage will be eventually reached when the effect attains a maximum strength, even though the concentration in the blood continues to rise. This point is unfortunately the point when the drug might produce undesirable side effects. One solution to this problem is to administer the drug in a time-release form. In this approach, a large dose is given initially in order to enable the drug effect to be felt; then smaller doses are programmed to be released at specific intervals afterward to postpone, up to twelve hours or so, the decline in the drug's concentration in the blood. The intention is to keep the concentration of the drug in the blood within a "therapeutic window" high enough for a drug to be effective while low enough to avoid any toxic effects. When drugs are administered repeatedly, there is the risk of the second dose boosting the concentration of the drug in the blood too high before the effect of the first dose has a chance to decline (Fig. 3.1).

Drug interactions

Two basic types of interactions may occur when two drugs are mixed together. In the first type, two drugs in combination may produce an effect that is greater than the effect of either drug administered alone. In some cases, the combination effect is purely *additive*. For example, if the effect of one drug alone is

latency period
An interval of time during which the blood levels of a drug are not yet sufficient for a drug effect to be observed.

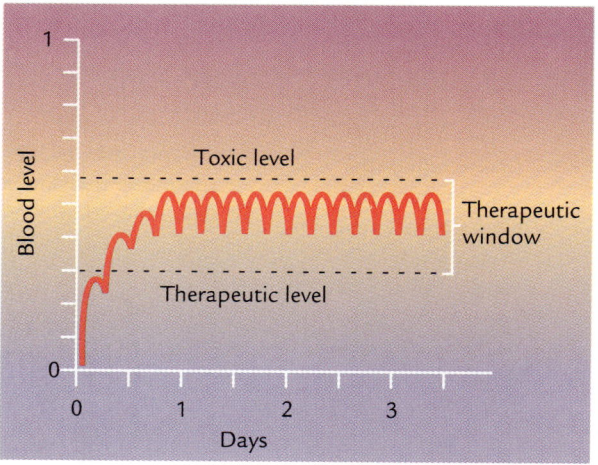

FIGURE 3.1

The therapeutic window. Time-release drugs administer the drug in small amounts over time in order to stay between the therapeutic level and the toxic level.

equivalent to a 4 and the effect of another drug is a 6, then the combined additive effect is equivalent to a value of 10. In other cases, however, the combination effect is *hyperadditive*, with the combined effect exceeding the sum of the individual drugs administered alone, as in the two drugs in the first example combining to a value of 13 or more. Any hyperadditive effect produced by a combination of two or more drugs is referred to as **synergism.** In some synergistic combinations, one drug may even double or triple the effect of another. It is also possible that one drug might have no effect at all by itself unless it is taken simultaneously with another. This special form of synergism is called **potentiation;** it is as though a drug with no effect at all by itself when combined with a drug having an effect of 6 produces a result equivalent to a 10.

In the second type of interaction, two drugs can be *antagonistic* if the effect of one drug is diminished to some degree when administered with another, a situation comparable to a drug with the effect of 6 and a drug with the effect of 4 ending up as an effect of 3. Later chapters will discuss drugs that are perfectly antagonistic to each other, in that the second exactly cancels out the effect of the first. Table 3.1 shows some examples of various drug interactions..

Individual differences

Some variations in drug effects may have nothing to do with the drug itself. Instead, it may be the particular characteristics of the person taking the drug that make the difference. One characteristic is an individual's weight. In general, a heavier person will require a greater amount of a drug than a lighter person to receive an equivalent drug effect, all other things being equal. It is for this reason that drug dosages are expressed as a ratio of drug amount to body weight, in metric terms as milligrams-per-kilogram (mg/kg).

Another characteristic is gender. Even if a man and a woman are exactly the same weight, differences in drug effects can still result on the basis of gender differences in body composition and sex hormones. Women have, on average, a higher proportion of fat, due to a greater fat-to-muscle ratio, and a lower proportion of water than men. When we look at the effects of alcohol consumption in terms of gender, we find that the lower water content (a factor that tends to dilute the alcohol in the body) in women makes them feel more intoxicated than men, even though the same amount of alcohol is consumed. Relative to men, women also have reduced levels of enzymes that metabolize alcohol in the liver, resulting in higher alcohol levels in the blood and a higher level of intoxication.[6] We suspect that the lower level of alcohol metabolism may be related to an increased level of estrogen and progesterone in women. Whether gender differences exist with regard to drugs other than alcohol is presently unknown.

TABLE 3.1

Examples of possible drug interactions

Hyperadditive effects
Alcohol with barbiturate-related sleep medications, cardiovascular medications, insulin, anti-inflammatory medications, antihistamines, painkillers, tranquilizers

Trimethoprim with sulfamethoxazole (two antibiotic medications)

Additive effects
Two types of barbiturates in combination

Antagonistic effects
Morphine/heroin with naloxone or naltrexone

---

synergism (SIN-er-gih-zum)
The property of a drug interaction in which the combination effect of two drugs exceeds the effect of either drug administered alone.

potentiation
The property of a drug interaction in which one drug combined with another drug produces an effect when one of the drugs alone would have had no effect.

heart rate, facial flushing, and nausea.[7] As a result, many Asians find drinking to be quite unpleasant. Ethnic variability can be seen in terms of other drug effects as well. It has also been found that Caucasians metabolize antipsychotic and antianxiety medications faster than Asians and, as a result, end up with relatively lower concentrations of drugs in the blood. One consequence of this difference is in the area of psychiatric treatment. Asian schizophrenic patients require significantly lower doses of antipsychotic medication in order for their symptoms to improve, and they experience medication side effects at much lower doses than do Caucasian patients. Since other possible factors such as diet, life-style, and environment do not account for these differences, we can speculate that these differences have a genetic basis.[8]

Introducing the nervous system

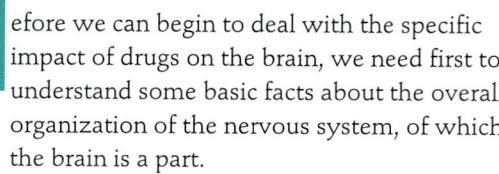

Before we can begin to deal with the specific impact of drugs on the brain, we need first to understand some basic facts about the overall organization of the nervous system, of which the brain is a part.

In simplest terms, the nervous system is designed to do two basic things: to take in information from the environment around us and to control our bodily responses so that we can live effectively in that environment. But, of course, we do a lot more than that. We interpret the information coming in, try to make sense of it, remember some of it for a later time, and more than occasionally generate some information on our own in a process called thinking.

We can understand these different functions in terms of divisions within the nervous system. In general, the nervous system is divided into the **central nervous system** (CNS), consisting of the brain and the

Still another individual characteristic that influences the ways certain drugs affect the body is ethnic background. About 50 percent of all people of Asian descent, for example, show low levels of one of the enzymes that normally metabolize alcohol in the liver shortly before it is excreted. With this particular deficiency, alcohol by-products tend to build up in the blood, producing a faster

central nervous system (CNS)
The portion of the nervous system that consists of the spinal cord and the brain.

spinal cord, and the **peripheral nervous system,** consisting of all the nerves and nerve fibers that connect the CNS to the environment and to our muscles and glands (Fig. 3.2).

Peripheral nervous system

The peripheral nervous system is essentially the system that brings information in and later, after processing in the CNS, executes our behavioral response. On the input side, it includes the visual pathway, the auditory pathway, and other channels of sensory information about the world around us. On the output side, motor pathways in the peripheral nervous system that control our reactions to that world produce two basic acts. The first type, called a *somatic* response, is a voluntary reaction, executed by skeletal muscles that are attached to bone. When you lift your arm, for example, you have

executed a series of motor commands that ultimately results in contractions of flexor and extensor muscles. In this case, the movement is deliberate, conscious, and controlled. A second type of reaction, called a *autonomic* response, is usually involuntary and executed by smooth muscles that form the walls of arteries, veins, capillaries, and internal organs as well as cardiac muscles that form the walls of the heart. When you blush, for example, the capillaries are dilating, or enlarging, underneath the surface of your skin, an effect that produces a reddening color and a feeling of warmth. As most of us know from personal experience, blushing often comes on when we do not necessarily want it to, and it is difficult to make it go away. And yet, it is a reaction to a situation that has been processed through our sensory pathways and interpreted within the brain; in this case, some emotional content has triggered this autonomic response.

We should not think of autonomic responses, however, as merely an annoyance. Indeed, we need them to survive. If we were to take the time to execute deliberate commands to breathe regularly, to have our hearts beat at an appropriate rate, or to carry out the thousands of changes that our internal organs make, we certainly would not last very long. The autonomic control that we have evolved is a product of the interplay of two subsystems, each delivered to smooth and cardiac muscles and to glands through its own set of nerve fibers. These subsystems are referred to as the **sympathetic** and

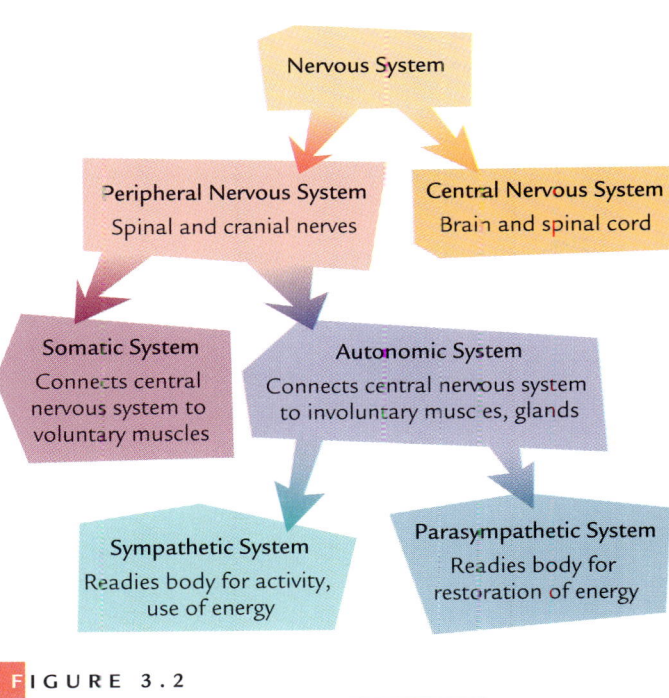

peripheral nervous system
The portion of the nervous system consisting of nerves and nerve fibers that carry information to the central nervous system and outward to muscles and glands.

sympathetic branch of the autonomic nervous system
The portion of the autonomic nervous system controlling bodily changes that deal with stressful or emergency situations.

F IGURE 3.2

Organizational chart of the nervous system
SOURCE: *Robert A. Baron,* Psychology *2/E. Copyright © 1992 by Allyn and Bacon. Adapted by permission.*

Specific bodily changes during emergency situations are produced through stimulation of the sympathetic branch of the autonomic nervous system.

parasympathetic branches of the auto-nomic nervous system.

Sympathetic and parasympathetic responses

Autonomic responses are divided into two general categories (Fig. 3.3). The first is oriented toward dealing with some kind of emergency or stress. If we are in a situation that is perceived as a threat to our internal well-being or to our survival, the sympathetic system is in charge. During times of *sympathetic activation,* the heart rate goes up, blood pressure goes up, the bronchi in the lungs dilate to accommodate a greater amount of oxygen, the pupil dilates to allow more light into the eye, and other bodily systems alter their level of functioning, so we are in a better position to fight, to flee, or simply to feel frightened. Not all systems, however, increase their activity during sympathetic activation.

parasympathetic branch of the autonomic nervous system
The portion of the autonomic nervous system controlling the bodily changes that lead to increased nurturance, rest, and maintenance.

The gastrointestinal tract is inhibited; we obviously do not want to be digesting our lunch when we are battling for our lives.

The second category of response is totally opposite to the first. We cannot be "on alert" all our lives; we need some time to regroup our forces, to orient ourselves toward a state of calm and rest necessary for nurturance and internal maintenance. Heart rate and blood pressure now go down, bronchi and pupils constrict, and the gastrointestinal tract is now excited rather than inhibited. These and other changes constitute *parasympathetic activation* and are an important counterpoint to the activation of the sympathetic system.

We can swing back and forth between sympathetic and parasympathetic activation as the need arises and the situation presents itself, and in many instances the momentary state of the autonomic nervous system is somewhere in the middle of the two extremes. Some psychoactive drugs, however, produce autonomic changes, in addition to their direct effects on the brain. They may produce a swing toward sympathetic activation or a swing toward parasympathetic activation. Later in the chapter the biochemical basis for these autonomic reactions and some of the drugs that affect them will be discussed.

The central nervous system

The central nervous system, located along the central axis of the body, consists of the spinal cord and the brain. It is here that interpretations of our sensory input occur and the intricate processing of information is accomplished. Some of our sensory nerves, such as those originating at locations from the neck down, enter the CNS at the level of the spinal cord; others, such as those nerves coming from our eyes and ears, enter at the level of the brain. Complex information entering at the spinal cord is carried by neural pathways upward into the brain for further processing; the processing of simpler information may not involve the brain at all, resulting in merely reflexive responses.

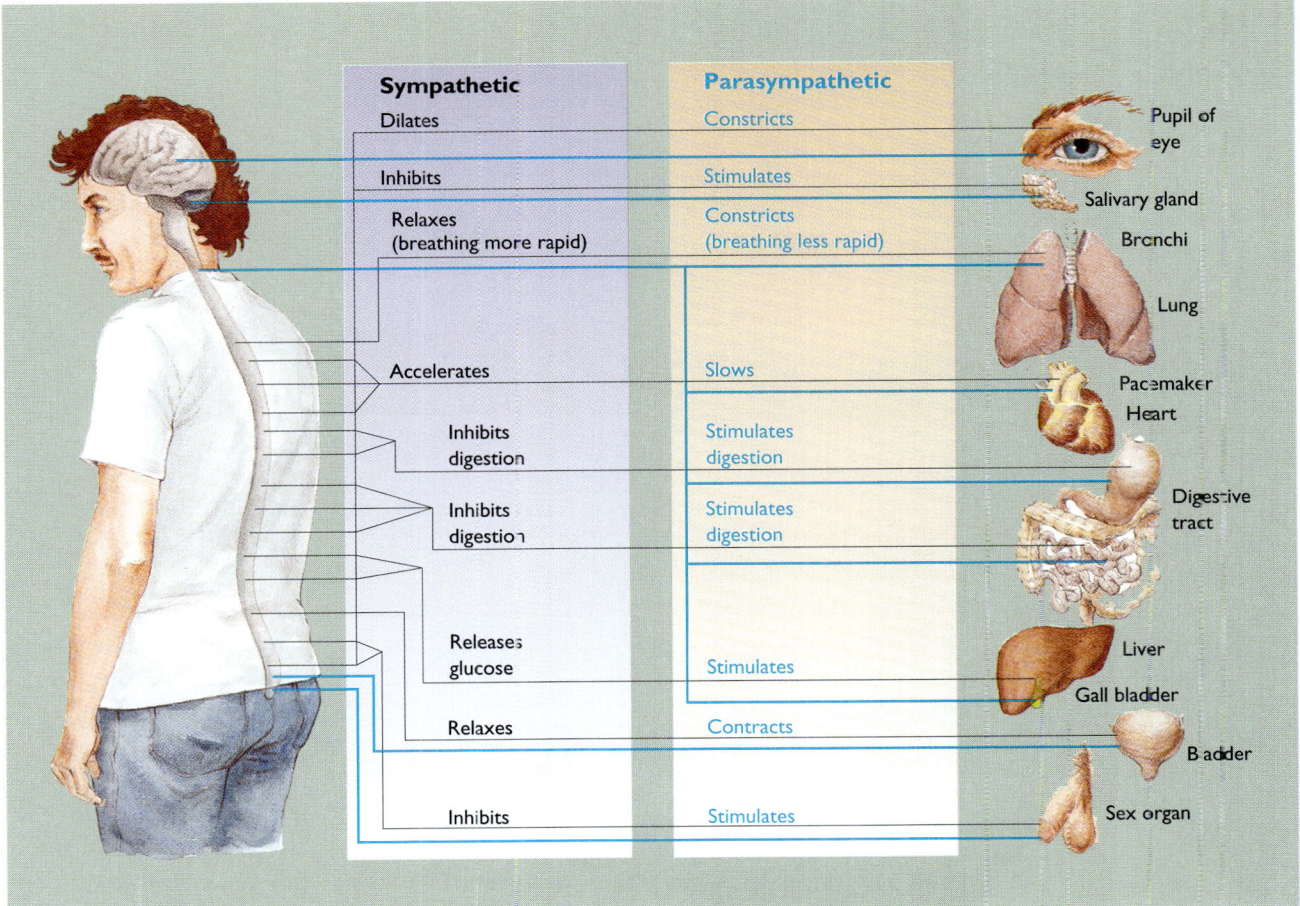

Sympathetic	Parasympathetic	
Dilates	Constricts	Pupil of eye
Inhibits	Stimulates	Salivary gland
Relaxes (breathing more rapid)	Constricts (breathing less rapid)	Bronchi
		Lung
Accelerates	Slows	Pacemaker Heart
Inhibits digestion	Stimulates digestion	Digestive tract
Inhibits digestion	Stimulates digestion	
Releases glucose	Stimulates	Liver
		Gall bladder
Relaxes	Contracts	Bladder
Inhibits	Stimulates	Sex organ

FIGURE 3.3

Functions of the sympathetic and parasympathetic branches of the autonomic nervous system
SOURCE: *Robert A. Baron, Psychology 2/E. Copyright © 1992 by Allyn and Bacon. Reprinted by permission.*

Consider how your body might react, in terms of the systems discussed so far. Imagine, as you read this page, that someone is sneaking up behind you and grabbing your shoulder. A sudden start and jerking of your body is a result of information that has little to do with the brain; the reaction is accomplished at a spinal level. You may then decide to look around and see who it is, in which case you are now dealing with visual and possibly some auditory information, and the brain will be interpreting the input either as a practical joke or a real threat. In the latter case, the sympathetic nervous system will begin after a few seconds to be activated, orienting your body toward dealing with this situation through changes in your smooth and cardiac muscles.

The most important part of the CNS, at least for advanced species such as ourselves, is the brain. It is nearly impossible to overestimate its role in our everyday lives. Every gesture we make, every feeling, every experience we have of our surroundings, every insight or memory, is a result of a complex, beautifully modulated pattern of activity among approximately 100 billion specialized cells called **neurons.** We owe our entire cognitive universe, all of what we are or think we are, to the functioning of these cells. It is here that

neuron
The specialized cell in the nervous system designed to receive and transmit information.

psychoactive drugs are doing their work, for good or for bad.

Understanding the brain

Proceeding upward from the spinal cord, starting at the point where the CNS enlarges into the brain, neuroanatomists have classified brain tissue into three major sections: the *hindbrain,* the *midbrain,* and finally the *forebrain* (Fig. 3.4). The older and more primitive systems of the brain tend to be underneath the newer and more sophisticated ones, so as we travel upward from hindbrain to midbrain to forebrain on our quick tour of the brain we are dealing with structures that have evolved ever more recently and have greater involvement in complex behaviors. You can think of this arrangement in brain anatomy as similar to an archaeological dig, where the strata of previous civilizations extend downward to greater and greater antiquity. Understanding the brain in terms of the orderliness of its development over the span of evolutionary history helps to make sense of its complexity.

The hindbrain

At the top of the spinal cord, neural tissue suddenly widens and enlarges into the hindbrain. The *medulla* lies at the point of the hindbrain where this enlargement has just begun. It is essentially the coordinator of the basic life-support systems in our body. Blood pressure is controlled here, as are the rhythms of breathing, heart rate, digestion, and even vomiting. Death would be seconds away, were it not for the normal functioning of the medulla. Unfortunately, it is highly sensitive to opiates, alcohol, barbiturates, and other depressants. When levels of any of these drugs are excessive in overdose cases, the respiratory controls in the medulla are inhibited and death can result from asphyxiation. Even if a person survives, the lack of oxygen in the blood while he or she is not breathing can result in severe brain damage. On a more positive note, the vomiting center in the medulla is sensitive to the presence of poisons in the blood and is able to initiate vomiting to get rid of unwanted and potentially harmful substances.

Another hindbrain structure, situated just above the medulla, is the *pons.* We can view the pons in terms of our ability to maintain the necessary level of alertness to survive. Within the pons are structures that deter-

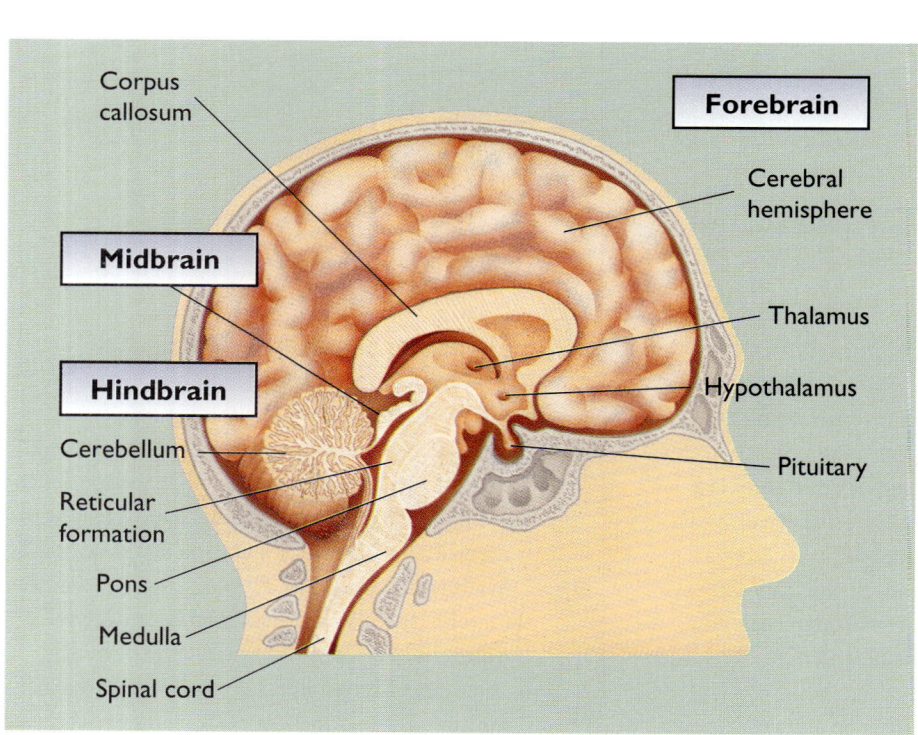

F I G U R E 3 . 4

Basic structures of the human brain
SOURCE: *Robert A. Baron,* Psychology 2/E. *Copyright © 1992 by Allyn and Bacon. Reprinted by permission.*

Corpus callosum
Midbrain
Hindbrain
Cerebellum
Reticular formation
Pons
Medulla
Spinal cord
Forebrain
Cerebral hemisphere
Thalamus
Hypothalamus
Pituitary

mine when we sleep and when we wake up, as well as the main portion of a structure called the *reticular formation* that energizes the rest of the brain to be alert to incoming information. Drugs that affect the patterns of our sleep influence the sleep centers in the pons.

Behind the medulla and the pons in the hindbrain is the *cerebellum,* an important structure for the maintenance of balance and for the execution of smooth movements of the body. The dizziness and lack of coordination we experience after consuming alcohol is related in large part to alcohol's depressive effect on the cerebellum.

The midbrain

The midbrain, located just above the hindbrain, is a center for the control of important sensory and motor reflexes. For example, if an object were to pass quickly across our visual field, our eyes would reflexively shift in that object's direction, with the movement being so fast that we would have been hardly aware of it. A major portion of our processing of pain information is handled by the midbrain as well.

Without a specific region of the midbrain called the *substantia nigra,* we would not be able to control the movements of our bodies effectively. Parkinson's disease, a disorder characterized by muscular tremors and other motor difficulties, is a result of a degeneration of the substantia nigra. Unfortunately, symptoms that resemble Parkinson's disease are frequently observed in patients taking antipsychotic medication, an issue that will be explored further in Chapter 16.

The forebrain

In the uppermost section of the brain, there are two important areas to consider. The first area, lying immediately above the midbrain, includes the *hypothalamus* and the *limbic system.* It is through these structures that we are able to carry out the appropriate motivational and emotional acts that ensure our survival as a species. Feeding behavior, drinking behavior, and sexual behavior are controlled by the hypothalamus. Given the critical nature of these behaviors, it might not be surprising that experimental lesions in the hypothalamus produce gross behavioral abnormalities. Depending upon the location of the lesion, for example, an animal might suddenly eat enormous amounts of food and become obese or eat nothing at all until it starves to death. The hypothalamus is also critical for the activation of sympathetic autonomic changes in the body.

The limbic system surrounds the hypothalamus and plays a central role in organizing emotional behavior during times of stress. Experimental lesions in points within the limbic system can turn a tame animal into a rageful monster or a wild animal into a docile one. Near the side of the hypothalamus runs a limbic pathway called the *medial forebrain bundle,* which has a very special property. If this pathway is electrically stimulated, the animal reacts in such a way that the stimulation can be viewed as a reward. Animals will learn to press levers as frequently as 700 times per hour for such stimulation, so powerful is the effect. As you might suspect, theories about the basis for psychological dependence have focused on the medial forebrain bundle. Some of these ideas will be explored later in the chapter. It also turns out that drugs that deal with symptoms of anxiety, depression, and schizophrenia affect regions within the limbic system

The second forebrain area of concern, and the most important from the standpoint of understanding human behavior, is a two-sided, wrinkled sheet of neural tissue, with a thickness approximately equivalent to the height of a capital letter on this page and overhanging almost all of the brain: the hemispheres of the **cerebral cortex.** Its appearance resembles that of a giant walnut, an association by the way that prompted early

cerebral cortex
The portion of the forebrain devoted to sophisticated processing of information.

physicians in the Middle Ages to prescribe walnuts as medicine for diseases of the brain.[9]

When we arrive at the cerebral cortex (or cortex, for short), we have arrived at the pinnacle of the brain both functionally and spatially. In the occipital lobes located in the back of the cortex is a system for processing visual information; on the sides, in the temporal lobes, is a system for processing auditory information; on top, in the parietal lobes, is a system for processing somatosensory, or touch, information. Also on top and toward the front of the cortex, in the frontal lobes, is a system for organizing complex, watchmaker-like movements of the fingers. Each of these cortical systems has taken over responsibilities formerly held by brain regions located beneath the cortex. The older systems still exist in our brains, but the newer ones are in charge.

Beyond the sensory and motor areas of the cortex, a large percentage of cortical tissue is taken up with the task of associating one piece of information with another. In the human brain, more than 80 percent of the cortex, called the association cortex, concerns itself with the integration of ideas. Of all the areas within the association cortex, the most recently evolved is a region closest to the front of the brain called the prefrontal cortex. Our higher-order, intellectual abilities as well as personality characteristics emerge from activity in this region.

Understanding the biochemistry of psychoactive drugs

aining some perspective about brain anatomy lays the foundation for us to understand *where* certain psychoactive drugs are active, but it does not help to understand *how* they work. In order to answer this second question, we need to know something about neurons themselves, the specialized cells designed to communicate information within the nervous system.

Introducing neurons

Here is a scary thought. There are an estimated 100 billion neurons in the brain, and the number of possible interconnections that exist among them all has been estimated to be greater than the total number of atomic particles in the known universe.[10] It is then an understatement that the brain is the most complex organ of the body. How can we possibly begin to understand the brain amidst such complexity? Or rather, are our own brains good enough to understand how our brains work? It seems impossible.

Fortunately, the task is not as insurmountable as it appears. The neuron itself, as the basic unit of the nervous system, can be understood in relatively simple terms. Imagine the neuron at any moment in time as a tiny device that is either on or off, like a light switch. There is no intermediate state. In this respect, the nervous system is digital like a computer, since a computer consists simply of electrical circuits that are permitted only two states, open or closed. In terms of the neuron, the "on" state is accomplished by the generation of an electrical change in its membrane, referred to as an action potential, or a nerve impulse. Just as the neuron is the basic unit that forms the structure of the nervous system, the action potential is the basic unit that forms the language of the nervous system.

The role of the neuron is to receive information and to transmit information, carrying out this mission through its three principal components: the *cell body,* the *dendrites,* and the *axon* (Fig. 3.5). The cell body comprises the bulk of the neuron and contains the nucleus and other elements that relate it to other types of cells in the body, such as muscle cells, skin cells, and blood cells. What makes the neuron unique is its appendages, extending out from

the cell body, some rather short and one quite long. The short ones are called dendrites and represent the part of the neuron that receives information from the outside. The long appendage, called the axon, is the part that transmits information outward. The axon is essentially the carrier of the messages of the neuron. When an action potential is generated, that action potential travels down the length of the axon at speeds up to 120 meters per –second (roughly 270 miles per hour) until it reaches the axon's end point. If we followed the axon along its length, starting from the cell body (and sometimes that distance may be as long as a meter in length), we would see that toward its end the axon diverges like the branches of a tree. At the terminal point of each of these branches is a small button-like structure called a *synaptic knob.*

After the anatomy of the neuron has been explored, the important question can be addressed: How does one neuron communicate information to another? To answer this, we turn to the gap between neurons known as the **synapse.**

Synaptic communication

The basic scenario is as follows: Located inside each synaptic knob are *synaptic vesicles* which produce and store millions of chemical molecules called **neurotransmitters.** Without neurotransmitters, the action potential, upon arrival at the terminal points of the axon, would sputter out like a wet fuse, and the neuron would have no function at all. Instead, the action potential causes the release of neurotransmitter molecules out of the vesicle, into the synaptic cleft, and eventually into

Cell body
Dendrites
Myelin sheath
Axon terminals

F I G U R E 3 . 5

Basic structure of a neuron
SOURCE: *Robert A. Baron,* Psychology 2/E. *Copyright © 1992 by Allyn and Bacon. Reprinted by permission.*

synapse (SIN-apse)
The juncture between neurons. It consists of a synaptic knob, the synaptic cleft, and receptor sites on a receiving neuron.

neurotransmitter
A chemical substance that a neuron uses to communicate information at the synapse.

special receptor sites in the membrane on the other side of the synapse. These receptors have internal shapes that are designed to match the external shape of the neurotransmitter, which allows for the neurotransmitter and receptor to fit together closely. When the neurotransmitter has successfully made it into the receptor site, a change occurs in the membrane of the receiving neuron. Neuron A has now communicated with neuron B.

But what exactly is the message? It takes one of two forms, either a message to excite or a message to inhibit. The receiving neuron, like all neurons in the nervous system, is continually creating its own action potentials. In other words, it is continually "firing." This activity leaves two alternatives for change: either an increase in the rate of firing (excitation) or a decrease (inhibition). Excitation, therefore, is not a matter of creating an action potential out of silence but rather of making a neuron emit a greater number of action potentials per second's time, just as inhibition is a matter of making a neuron emit a lesser number of action potentials per second's time. As will be discussed, the message that is communicated depends upon the specific neurotransmitter that is present at the synapse.

This description concerns one synaptic knob at one synapse, but we have to realize that a typical neuron may have a thousand synaptic knobs near its membrane surface; some neurons have more than that. Adding to this complexity is the fact that the receiving neuron itself may have a thousand or more synaptic knobs of its own that can communicate with other neurons. It is easy to see how the idea of many billions of neurons in the nervous system, impressive as it may be, cannot begin to convey the functional complexity of the nervous system as a whole.

reuptake
The process by which a neurotransmitter returns from the receptor site back to the synaptic knob.

This description of synaptic communication also does not indicate that it is happening hundreds of times every second. In fact, in order to allow neurons to fire in very quick succession, the neurotransmittter molecules cannot remain in the receptor sites for more than a millisecond or two. Once the neurotransmitter binds itself to the receptor, it is expelled and returns back to the vesicles in the synaptic knob.

The process of "returning back," called **reuptake,** is essentially a way of getting the neurotransmitter back to the knob where it can be released again (as shown in Fig. 3.6). Successful reuptake, however, is not a certainty. In the vicinity of the synapse are enzymes that are capable of breaking down the neurotransmitter molecule. These enzymes control the amounts of neurotransmitter in the region of the synapse so as to prevent too many molecules from "clogging up" the receptor sites and interfering with the normal process of one neuron communicating with another. As a result of the enzymes, some of the neurotransmitter molecules do not make it back safely to the vesicles. Under normal circumstances the vesicles then synthesize more to make up for any deficiency.

While the principle of synaptic communication rests upon the possibility of conveying either excitation or inhibition, it turns out that there are dozens of neurotransmitters. Why do we need more than simply two? One way of looking at it might be to assume that there exist two classes of neurotransmitters: "encouragers," which are excitatory, and "discouragers," which are inhibitory. In an analogy to human communication, different arguments could exist to provide encouragement or discouragement, each effective in its own way, depending upon the particular circumstance. So it may be in the brain. More than fifty neurotransmitters have been studied, but this chapter will focus principally on the six most prominent ones in relation to psychoactive drugs.

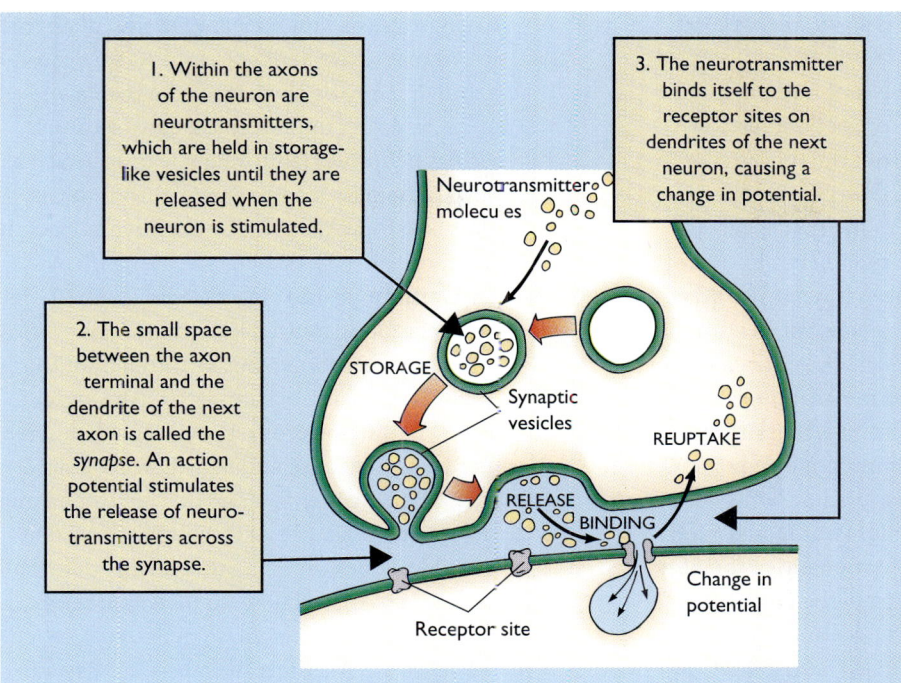

1. Within the axons of the neuron are neurotransmitters, which are held in storage-like vesicles until they are released when the neuron is stimulated.

2. The small space between the axon terminal and the dendrite of the next axon is called the *synapse.* An action potential stimulates the release of neuro-transmitters across the synapse.

3. The neurotransmitter binds itself to the receptor sites on dendrites of the next neuron, causing a change in potential.

Neurotransmitter molecules

STORAGE

Synaptic vesicles

REUPTAKE

RELEASE

BINDING

Change in potential

Receptor site

FIGURE 3.6

Sequence of events in synaptic communication
SOURCE: *Robert A. Baron, Psychology 2/E. Copyright © 1992 by Allyn and Bacon. Reprinted by permission.*

The major neurotransmitters in brief: The big six

Acetylcholine was the first molecule to be firmly established as a neurotransmitter. There are two types of receptor sites that are sensitive to acetylcholine. The first type, muscarinic receptors, so named because they are responsive to the drug muscarine, are located in the parasympathetic autonomic nervous system. If a drug is antimuscarinic, that means that it interferes with the role of acetylcholine in stimulating parasympathetic reactions of the body. Examples are atropine and scopolamine. Atropine, when applied to the eyes, for example, causes the pupils to dilate by inhibiting the parasympathetic tendency for the pupils to constrict. This is useful in eye examinations where the retina needs to be inspected for possible problems. The second type, nicotinic receptors, so named because they are responsive to nicotine, are found near the end points of motor neurons, where skeletal muscles are innervated, as well as through-

out the cerebral cortex. Some antinicotinic drugs, such as the poison curare, affect these motor neurons so dramatically that the body can become paralyzed within seconds. Deficiencies in acetylcholine, in nicotinic receptors, or in both, have been tied to Alzheimer's disease, a degenerative condition resulting in memory loss and mental confusion.

Norepinephrine, the second major neuro-transmitter, is concentrated in the hypothalamus and limbic system but also found throughout the brain. In the peripheral nervous system, it is the principal neurotransmitter for sympathetic autonomic activation, but its role here is independent of its effects in the

acetylcholine (a-SEE-til-KOH-leen)
A neurotransmitter active in the parasympathetic autonomic nervous system, cerebral cortex, and peripheral somatic nerves.

norepinephrine (NOR-ep-ih-NEH-frin)
A neurotransmitter active in the sympathetic autonomic nervous system and in many regions of the brain.

brain. Norepinephrine helps to regulate our mood states; Chapter 16 will discuss how drugs that boost the levels of norepinephrine also help relieve symptoms of depression.

The role of **dopamine,** the third major neurotransmitter, lies in two important aspects of our behavior. The first aspect is motor control: the ability to start a movement when we want to, to stop it when we want to, and to execute the movement in a smooth, precisely determined manner. A deficiency in motor control, as mentioned earlier, is dramatically seen in symptoms of Parkinson's disease, a disorder arising from a degeneration of dopaminergic (dopamine-using) neurons in the substantia nigra of the midbrain. The second aspect is emotionality. Problems in dopaminergic neurons in the cortex and limbic system are strongly suspected to be at the root of schizophrenia. The role of dopamine in schizophrenia and efforts to develop drugs that relieve schizophrenic symptoms will be discussed in Chapter 16.

Serotonin, the fourth neurotransmitter, is concentrated in the pons and medulla, in the limbic system, and in the cortex. At the level of the hindbrain, serotonin plays an important role in regulating patterns of sleep. At the level of the limbic system, it shares with norepinephrine responsibility for establishing appropriate levels of mood, avoiding wild swings upward that result in mania or downward that result in depression. As you can predict, many drugs that relieve mania and depression act upon serotonergic (serotonin-using) neurons. Hallucinogenic drugs, such as LSD, stimulate serotonergic neurons in the cortex, a topic that will be explored further in Chapter 8.

Gamma aminobutyric acid (GABA), the fifth neurotransmitter, is an important inhibitory neurotransmitter throughout the brain. Tranquilizers stimulate GABAergic (GABA-using) neurons, providing a reduction in feelings of stress and fear, as will be discussed in Chapter 5. Since this neurotransmitter is a major source of inhibitory control, it should not be surprising that GABA deficiencies are associated with an increased tendency to suffer epileptic seizures.

The sixth major neurotransmitter is actually a grouping of neurotransmitters collectively known as **endorphins.** They are natural painkillers produced by the brain and bear a remarkable resemblance to morphine. Chapter 7 will discuss how the discovery of endorphins has helped us understand more clearly not only the nature of pain but also the nature of opiate addiction.

Focus 3.2 shows the ways that various psychoactive drugs work in the brain, in terms of how they alter the activity of a specific neurotransmitter. Some drugs, such as amphetamines for example, work at the synapse in multiple ways.

dopamine (DOPE-ah-meen)
A neurotransmitter in the brain whose activity is related to emotionality and motor control.

serotonin (SER-ah-TOH-nin)
A neurotransmitter in the brain whose activity is related to emotionality and sleep patterns.

gamma amino-butyric acid (GABA) (GAM-ma a-MEEN-o byoo-TEER-ik ASS-id)
An inhibitory neurotransmitter in the brain. Antianxiety drugs tend to facilitate the activity level of GABA in the brain.

endorphins (en-DOR-fins)
A class of chemical substances, produced in the brain and elsewhere in the body, that mimic the effects of morphine and other opiate drugs.

Physiological aspects of drug-taking behavior

There are three important concepts related to drug-taking behavior that arise from the physiology of the nervous system. The first is the blood-brain barrier; the second is the physiological basis for drug tolerance; and the third is the current theory that psychological dependence may be related to activity in a specific area of the brain.

Drug effects and synaptic communication in the nervous system

Drug	Result	Mechanism
amphetamines	CNS stimulation	Mimicking of norepinephrine at the receptor site; inducement of norepinephrine release at the synaptic knob without the presence of an action potential
antianxiety drugs in general	Reduction in anxiety and stress	Stimulation of GABA receptors in the brain
antidepressant drugs, MAO-inhibitor type	Reduction in depressive symptoms	Inhibition of enzymes that metabolize norepinephrine and serotonin
antidepressant drugs, tricyclic type	Reduction in depressive symptoms	Slowing down of reuptake of norepinephrine and serotonin at their receptor sites
antipsychotic drugs, typical type	Reduction in schizophrenic symptoms	Dopamine blocked from entering receptor sites in the brain
atropine	Stimulation of the sympathetic autonomic system	Inhibition of acetylcholine at muscarinic receptor sites

Drug	Result	Mechanism
botulinus toxin	Paralysis of skeletal muscles (known as botulism)	Acetylcholine prevented from being released at the synaptic knobs of somatic motor neurons
caffeine	CNS stimulation	Adenosine (an inhibitory neurotransmitter) blocked from entering its receptor sites
cocaine	CNS stimulation and local anesthesia	Blocking the reuptake of norepinephrine and dopamine at their receptor sites
curare	Paralysis of skeletal muscles	Acetylcholine blocked from entering receptor sites in muscle cells
LSD	Visual hallucinations and disordered thinking	Stimulation of receptor sites sensitive to serotonin
morphine, heroin, and codeine	Pain relief and euphoria	Stimulation of endorphins at receptors in the spinal cord and brain
strychnine sulphate	Generalized convulsions; possible death by asphyxiation	Glycine (an inhibitory neurotransmitter) blocked from entering receptor sites in the spinal cord
tetanus toxin	Generalized convulsions; possible death by asphyxiation	Glycine and GABA prevented from being released at the synaptic knobs

The blood-brain barrier

Mentioned earlier in the chapter was a barrier that restricts the passage of drugs and other molecules from the bloodstream to the brain. This exclusionary system is called the **blood-brain barrier.** Since it is important to maintain a level of stability in the brain, it is quite fortunate that this "gatekeeper" keeps the environment of the brain free from the biochemical ups and downs that are a fact of life in the bloodstream. The key factor in determining whether or not a drug passes through the blood-brain barrier is the degree to which that drug is fat-soluble.

Despite the obstacles, many types of drugs easily pass into the brain: nicotine, alcohol, cocaine, barbiturates, and caffeine, to name a few. Among the opiates, heroin, which is

blood-brain barrier
A system whereby substances in the bloodstream are excluded from entering the nervous system.

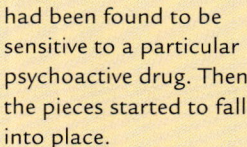

PORTRAIT

Solomon H. Snyder— On the cutting edge of discovery

Progress in science comes about sometimes in small steps and sometimes in great leaps. If you look at the real breakthroughs in any specific field, you will find the work of people who simply have had a new way of thinking about a problem and the courage to take some risks with new ideas.

Consider the career of Solomon H. Snyder, distinguished pharmacologist and director of neuroscience research at Johns Hopkins University in Baltimore. Early in the 1970s, at the very beginning of the neuroscience revolution (see Chapter 1), Snyder turned to the study of morphine. At that time, scientists knew that morphine had to act upon neurons in the brain, but no one understood how this happened. They knew that morphine was highly

addictive, but no one knew why.

Snyder saw the advantage of looking at the receptors on the surface of neurons as the key elements in linking morphine to the functions of the brain. By 1973, together with a graduate student in his laboratory, Candace Pert, he succeeded in identifying the opiate receptor. It was the first time a specific receptor

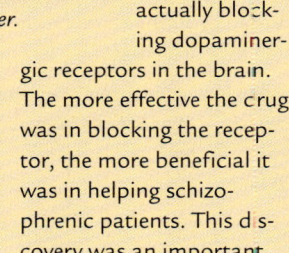

Solomon H. Snyder.

had been found to be sensitive to a particular psychoactive drug. Then the pieces started to fall into place.

If these receptors existed, could they be sensitive to something we produce ourselves, a morphine-like

substance that helps us to kill pain and gives us a natural euphoria similar to what we get from opiate drugs? That substance was soon identified by Snyder and scientists in other laboratories as a family of chemicals called endorphins.

Success with the opiate receptor led Snyder to study the possibility that other receptors could be identified that were sensitive to brain neurotransmitters. By 1978, Snyder and his students found the receptors for dopamine and argued that it was the dopaminergic receptor that held the key for understanding schizophrenia. They showed that antipsychotic drugs effective in reducing schizophrenic symptoms were actually blocking dopaminergic receptors in the brain. The more effective the drug was in blocking the receptor, the more beneficial it was in helping schizophrenic patients. This discovery was an important step toward our present understanding that schizo-

phrenia is related to higher-than-normal levels of dopamine in the brain.

Snyder's laboratory team has since identified receptors for serotonin, GABA, and even caffeine. More recently, his studies have shown that carbon monoxide, normally a highly toxic molecule, acts in very small quantities as an important neurotransmitter in the brain, responsible for setting down memories.

Largely through Snyder's efforts, the investigation of receptors has become the fundamental basis for understanding the brain itself. In the ability to conceive novel experiments, according to his colleagues, Snyder has no equal. In the words of one of his students, Snyder has "ideas rolling out of his head like silver dollars from a Las Vegas slot machine."

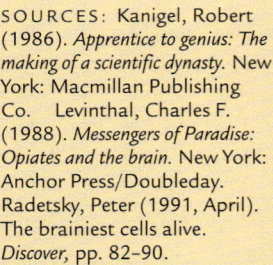

SOURCES: Kanigel, Robert (1986). *Apprentice to genius: The making of a scientific dynasty.* New York: Macmillan Publishing Co. Levinthal, Charles F. (1988). *Messengers of Paradise: Opiates and the brain.* New York: Anchor Press/Doubleday. Radetsky, Peter (1991, April). The brainiest cells alive. *Discover,* pp. 82–90.

---

highly fat-soluble, crosses the blood-brain barrier faster and more completely than morphine. Penicillin, by contrast, hardly enters the brain at all.[11]

The presence of a blood-brain barrier is an issue not only for the study of psychoactive drugs but for certain medical treatments as

well. For example, one of the effective treatments for Parkinson's disease is the administration of the drug L-Dopa, a shortened name for levodopa. The reason for using this drug stems from the root cause of Parkinson's disease: a dopamine deficiency in the substantia nigra. Taking dopamine itself is of no help, since its lack of fat-solubility excludes it from ever getting into the brain. Fortunately, L-Dopa, a metabolic precursor to dopamine, is fat-soluble. Therefore, L-Dopa can enter the brain and then metabolize into dopamine. As a result, dopamine levels in the brain rise, and the symptoms of Parkinson's disease are relieved.[12]

It has recently been possible to create a fat-soluble molecule in the laboratory rather than find one in nature. Pharmacologists have succeeded in combining protein-based drugs that are presently excluded by the blood-brain barrier with a fatty acid, making the drug able to slip through into the brain. It may be possible in the future to design special molecules that not only ferry protein drugs across the barrier but also regulate the release of the drugs once they are in the brain.[13]

There is recent evidence that the blood-brain barrier is changeable, depending upon situational factors. During sympathetic arousal, increased levels of stress hormones in the bloodstream make it less likely for substances to pass from the blood to the brain.[14] On the one hand it is possible that times of stress may be periods when it would be particularly hazardous for the brain to be exposed to various substances in the blood. These circumstances would be comparable to raising the bridge over a moat and isolating the castle at the first sign of an assault On the other hand, trauma to the brain through a concussion or cerebral infection can damage a crucial component of the blood-brain barrier and decrease its effectiveness.[15] In this case, then, the brain would be more vulnerable to substances in the blood.

Biochemical processes underlying drug tolerance

The last chapter covered the phenomenon of drug tolerance as a behavioral effect, accomplished through Pavlovian conditioning. Tolerance can also be a result of two types of physiological processes, one in the liver and the other in the neuron itself. In the first type, called *metabolic (dispositional) tolerance,* a drug may facilitate over repeated administrations the processes that produce the drug's chemical breakdown in the liver. Alcohol, as an example, increases over time the rate of its own elimination. When the liver metabolizes the drug faster than it had initially, a smaller amount is left available for absorption into the blood. In the case of alcohol, the habitual drinker feels less of an alcoholic effect and compensates by increasing the amount consumed. In the second type, called *cellular (pharmacodynamic) tolerance,* changes occur in the synapses of neurons themselves. Receptors that have been stimulated by the drug over time may become less sensitive, and the effect on the receiving neuron at a synapse may be diminished. Repeated blocking of receptor sites by a drug over time may cause a compensatory reaction through an increase in the number of receptor sites or an increased amount of neurotransmitter released from the synaptic knob.[16]

A physiological basis for psychological dependence

Amphetamines, cocaine, and opiate drugs may be very different from a pharmacological standpoint, but they are remarkably similar in the way people and animals react to them. There is a tremendous "rush" as these drugs enter the bloodstream and the brain, and an intense craving for repeating the experience. The parallels are numerous enough to entertain the idea that there might exist a common physiological process in the brain that links them all together. It may not be a coincidence that there is a system of neurons, the medial forebrain bundle, near the hypothalamus and limbic system, that animals will work hard to stimulate electrically. We cannot say how they are feeling at the time but their behavior indicates that they want to "turn on" this region of their brains. Could there be a connection to the craving and intense "rush" of heroin, cocaine, or amphetamine?

A key element in the rewarding effect of these psychoactive drugs seems to be dopamine, and the region of dopaminergic neurons involved is an area near to the medial forebrain bundle called the *mesotelencephalic dopamine pathway, (MTDP).* The cell bodies of neurons in this pathway lie in the midbrain, and their axons pass through the medial forebrain bundle, then fan out to regions of the limbic system, through a critical structure at the base of the forebrain called the *nucleus accumbens,* and finally onward to the frontal lobes of the cortex.[17] Injections of amphetamines, heroin, and cocaine, in laboratory animals, excite the nucleus accumbens and the MTDP in general, while any lesion in the nucleus accumbens or blockage of dopamine receptors in the MTDP eliminates the desire to inject these drugs.[18] Each of these drugs either directly or indirectly increases the activity of dopaminergic neurons. Bringing all this evidence together, a persuasive argument can be made that there is a common dopamine-related system in the brain that underlies the effect of pleasurable drugs. Continued research into the nature of this system cannot fail to help us in grappling with the problems of drug abuse.

Psychological factors in drug-taking behavior

This chapter has covered current understanding about the physiological effects of psychoactive drugs, down to the level of a single neuron in the brain. It has also pointed out that certain physiological factors such as weight and gender must be taken into account in order to predict particular drug effects. Yet,

> **placebo (pla-CEE-bo)**
> Latin term translated as "I will please."
> Any inert substance that produces a
> psychological or physiological reaction.

even if we controlled these factors completely, we would still frequently find a drug effect in an individual person to be different from time to time, place to place, and situation to situation. Predictions about how a person might react would be far from perfectly accurate.

One of the most uncontrollable factors in drug-taking behavior is the set of expectations a person may have about what the drug will do. If you believe that a beer will make you drunk or feel sexy, the chances are increased that it will do so; if you believe that a marijuana cigarette will make you high, the chances are increased that it will do so. You can consider the impact of negative expectations in the same way; when the feelings are strong that a drug will have no effect on you, the chances are lessened that you will react to it. In the most extreme case, you might experience a drug effect even when the substance you ingested was completely inert, that is, pharmacologically ineffective. Such inert substances are called **placebos** (Latin for "I will please"), and the reaction to them is referred to as the placebo effect.

The concept of a placebo goes back to the earliest days of pharmacology. The bizarre ingredients prescribed in the Ebers Papyrus (see Chapter 1) were effective to the extent that people *believed* that they were effective, not from any known factor in these ingredients. No doubt, the placebo effect was strong enough for medical symptoms to diminish. During the Middle Ages, in one of the more extreme cases of the placebo effect, Pope Boniface VIII reportedly was cured of kidney pains when his personal physician hung a gold seal bearing the image of a lion around the pope's thigh.[19]

It would be a mistake to think of the placebo effect as involving totally imaginary symptoms or totally imaginary reactions. Physical symptoms, involving specific bodily changes, can occur on the basis of placebo effects alone. How likely is it that a person will react to a placebo? The probability will

vary from drug to drug, but in the case of morphine, the data are very clear. In 1959 a review of studies in which morphine or a placebo was administered in clinical studies of pain concluded that a placebo-induced reduction in pain occurred 35 percent of the time. Considering that morphine itself had a positive result in only 75 percent of the cases, the placebo effect is a very strong one.[20] Unfortunately, it is not clear how we can predict whether a person will react strongly or weakly to a placebo. We do know, however, that the enthusiasm or lack of enthusiasm of the prescribing physician can play a major role. In one study that varied the attitude of the physician toward a particular drug, negative attitudes toward the drug resulted in the least benefits, while positive attitudes resulted in the most.[21]

It is not at all clear how the placebo effect is accomplished. In the case of pain relief, there is evidence that we have the natural ability to increase the levels of endorphins in

the bloodstream and the brain from one moment to the next, but the nature of our abilities to alter other important substances in our bodies is virtually unknown.[22] Yet, the very fact that the placebo effect occurs at all indicates that we have a great deal of psychological control over the physiological processes in our bodies, in ways that are seldom, if ever, on a conscious level.

Given the power of the placebo effect in drug-taking behavior, it is necessary to be very careful when carrying out drug research. For a drug to be deemed truly effective, it must be proved to be better not only in comparison to a no-treatment condition (which could conceivably be due to a placebo effect) but also in comparison to an identical-looking drug that lacks the active ingredients of the drug being evaluated. For example, if the drug under study is in the shape of a round red pill, another round red pill without the active ingredients of the drug (called the active placebo) must also be administered for comparison. The procedures of these studies also have to be carefully executed. Neither the individual administering the drug or placebo nor the individual receiving the drug or placebo should know which substance is which. Such precautions, referred to as **double-blind** procedures, represent the minimal standards for separating the pharmacological effects of a drug from the effects that arise from one's expectations and beliefs.

double-blind
A procedure in drug research in which neither the individual administering nor the individual receiving a chemical substance knows whether the substance is the drug being evaluated or an active placebo.

Summary

HOW DRUGS ENTER THE BODY

- There are four basic ways of administering drugs into the body: oral administration, injection, inhalation, and absorption through the skin or membranes. Each of these has advantages and disadvantages, and each presents constraints on which kinds of drugs will be effectively delivered into the bloodstream.

FACTORS DETERMINING THE PHYSIOLOGICAL IMPACT OF DRUGS

- The physiological effect of a drug can vary as a factor of the time elapsed since its administration, the possible combination of its administration with other drugs, and finally the personal characteristics of the individual consuming the drug.

- Some characteristics that can play a definite role in the effect of a drug include the individual's weight, gender, and ethnic background.

INTRODUCING THE NERVOUS SYSTEM

- Understanding the organization of the nervous system helps us to understand where psychoactive drugs are working in our bodies.

- The nervous system consists of the peripheral nervous system and the central nervous system, with the latter divided into the brain and spinal cord. Within the peripheral nervous system are autonomic nerves that control our cardiac and smooth muscles to respond either to stress (sympathetic activation) or to demands for nurturance and renewal (parasympathetic activation).

UNDERSTANDING THE BRAIN

- Within the brain are three major divisions: the hindbrain, midbrain, and forebrain. The forebrain is the most recently evolved region of the brain and controls the most complex behaviors and processes the most complex information.

- Many drugs affect all levels of the brain, in one way or another.

UNDERSTANDING THE BIOCHEMISTRY OF PSYCHOACTIVE DRUGS

- Understanding the functioning of neurons and their interaction through synaptic communication helps us to understand how psychoactive drugs work in our bodies.

- In general, drugs work at the neuronal level by altering the way in which neurotransmitters are released and bind to receptor sites.

- While the mechanisms behind the effects might vary, psychoactive drugs cause neurotransmitters to be either more or less active at the synapse.

PHYSIOLOGICAL ASPECTS OF DRUG-TAKING BEHAVIOR

- Three important issues need to be understood in looking at the physiological effect of drugs: The extent to which drugs pass from the bloodstream to the brain, the extent to which tolerance effects occur, and the extent to which a drug activates the mesotelencephalic dopamine pathway in the midbrain and forebrain.

PSYCHOLOGICAL FACTORS IN DRUG-TAKING BEHAVIOR

- While the physiological actions of psychoactive drugs are becoming increasingly well understood, there still remains great variability in the effect of these drugs, due to psychological factors.

- The most prominent psychological factor is the influence of personal expectations on the part of the individual consuming the drug. The impact of expectations on one's reaction to a drug, a phenomenon called the placebo effect, is an important consideration in drug research.

Key Terms

acetylcholine, p. 77
blood-brain barrier, p. 79
central nervous system (CNS), p. 68
cerebral cortex, p. 73
dopamine, p. 78
double-blind, p. 83
endorphins, p. 78
gamma aminobutyric acid (GABA), p. 78
intramuscular, p. 63
intranasal, p. 64

intravenous, p. 63
latency period, p. 66
neuron, p. 71
neurotransmitter, p. 75
norepinephrine, p. 77
parasympathetic branch of the autonomic nervous system, p. 70
peripheral nervous system, p. 69
placebo, p. 82
potentiation, p. 67

reuptake, p. 76
serotonin, p. 78
subcutaneous, p. 63
sublingual, p. 64
sympathetic branch of the autonomic nervous system, p. 69
synapse, p. 75
synergism, p. 67
transdermal patch, p. 64

Endnotes

1. Jones, W. H. S. (1923). *Hippocrates* (Vol. 2). London: Heinemann. Quotation on p 179.
2. Palfai, Tibor, and Jankiewicz, Henry (1991). *Drugs and human behavior.* Dubuque IA: W. C. Brown, p. 27.
3. Grilly, David M. (1989). *Drugs and human behavior.* Boston: Allyn and Bacon, p. 83.
4. Ray, Oakley, and Ksir, Charles (1990). *Drugs, society, and human behavior.* St. Louis: Times Mirror/Mosby, p. 102.
5. Langer, Robert (1990). New methods of drug delivery. *Science, 249,* 1527–1533.
6. Frezza, Mario, DiPadova, Carlo, Pozzato, Gabrielle, Terpin, Maddalena, Baraona, Enrique, and Lieber, Charles S. (1990) High blood alcohol levels in women: The role of decreased gastric alcohol dehydrogenase activity and first-pass metabolism. *New England Journal of Medicine, 322,* 95–99.
7. Nakawatase, Tomoko V., Yamamoto, Joe, and Sasao, Toshiaki (1993). The association between fast-flushing response and alcohol use among Japanese Americans. *Journal of Studies on Alcohol, 54,* 48–53.
8. Goodman, Deborah (1992, January-February). NIMH grantee finds drug responses differ among ethnic groups. *ADAMHA News,* pp. 5,15.
9. Levinthal, Charles F. (1990). *Introduction to physiological psychology* (3rd ed.). Englewood Cliffs NJ: Prentice Hall, p. 63.
10. Thompson, Richard F. (1985). *The brain: An introduction to neuroscience.* San Francisco: Freeman.
11. Julien, Robert M. (1995). *A primer of drug action* (7th ed.). New York: Freeman, p. 20.
12. Levinthal, *Introduction to physiological psychology,* p. 155.
13. Sneaking drugs past the brain's barrier. (1992, September 26). *Science News,* p. 207.
14. Long, J. B., and Holaday, J. W. (1985). Blood-brain barrier: Endogenous modulation by adrenal-cortical function. *Science, 227,* 1580–1583.
15. Goldstein, Gary W., and Betz, A. Lorris (1986). The blood-brain barrier. *Scientific American, 255* (3), 74–83.   Oldendorf, William (1987). The blood-brain barrier. In George Adelman (Ed.), *Encyclopedia of Neuroscience.* Boston: Birkhauser, pp. 139–141.
16. Martin, William R. (1987). Tolerance and physical dependence. In George Adelman (Ed.), *Encyclopedia of Neuroscience.* Boston: Birkhauser, pp. 1223–1225.
17. Groves, Philip M., and Rebec, George V. (1988). *Introduction to Biological Psychology* (3rd

ed.). Dubuque IA: W. C. Brown, p. 406.
Koob, George F., and Bloom, Floyd E. (1988). Cellular and molecular mechanisms of drug dependence. *Science, 242,* 715–723.

18. Goeders, N. E., and Smith, J. E. (1983). Cortical dopaminergic involvement in cocaine reinforcement. *Science, 221,* 773–775. Wise, Roy A., and Rompre, Pierre-Paul. (1989). Brain dopamine and reward. *Annual Review of Psychology, 40,* 191–225.

19. Kornetsky, Conan (1976). *Pharmacology: Drugs affecting behavior.* New York, Wiley, p. 23.

20. Beecher, H. K. (1959). *Measurement of subjective responses: Quantitative effects of drugs.* New York: Oxford University Press.

21. Schindel, L. E. (1962). Placebo in theory and practice. *Antibiotica et Chemotherapia, Advances, 10,* 398–430. Cited in Kornetsky, *Pharmacology* p. 36.

22. Levine, J. D., Gordon, N. C., and Fields, Howard L. (1979). The role of endorphins in placebo analgesia. In J. J. Bonica, John C. Liebeskind, and D. Albe-Fessard (Eds.), *Advances in pain research and therapy.* Vol. 3. New York: Raven Press, pp. 547–557.

4

The Major Stimulants: Cocaine and Amphetamines

THIS CHAPTER WILL INTRODUCE YOU
TO THE FOLLOWING SUBJECTS:

- The history of cocaine

- How cocaine works
  in the brain

- Patterns of cocaine abuse

- Treatment programs for
  cocaine abuse

- The history of amphetamines

- How amphetamines work
  in the brain

- Patterns of
  amphetamine abuse

- Treatment programs for
  amphetamine abuse

S. F. is a brilliant, young physician attending a case conference at a metropolitan medical center where he is a resident. He has been on call for thirty-six hours and cannot concentrate on the presentation. S. F. is lonely, depressed, and overworked. All he can think about is his fiancée, who is several hundred miles away. He knows that her father will not permit her to marry until he is able to support her, and with his loans and meager salary, that could take years. He excuses himself from the conference, takes a needle syringe from the nurses' station, and locks himself in a bathroom stall. He fills the syringe with cocaine and plunges the needle into his arm. Within seconds, the young doctor feels a rush of euphoria. His tears dry up; he regains his composure and quickly rejoins the conference.

The date is 1884, the place is Vienna, and the doctor is Sigmund Freud.

he time, place, and identity of S. F. in this fictionalized clinical vignette, based upon the facts of Freud's life, may have surprised you, but unfortunately the overall picture of cocaine abuse is all too familiar.[1] The year could have been 1984 instead of 1884, and the individual involved could have been anyone twenty-eight years old, as Freud was at the time, or some other age. Freud was extremely lucky; he never became dependent upon cocaine, though a close friend did and millions of people have since Freud's time. The story of cocaine is both ancient and modern. While its origins stretch back more than four thousand years, cocaine abuse continues to represent a major portion of the present-day drug crisis. For this reason, it is important to understand its history, the properties of the drug itself, and the ways in which it has the ability to destroy a person's life.

This chapter will focus not only on cocaine but also on another group of stimulant drugs, referred to as amphetamines. While cocaine and amphetamines are distinct in terms of their pharmacology (their characteristics as biochemical substances), there are enough similarities in their behavioral and physiological effects and patterns of abuse to warrant their being discussed together. In general, cocaine and amphetamines represent the two major classes of psychoactive stimulants, drugs that energize the body and create feelings of euphoria. Other less powerful stimulants, such as nicotine, caffeine, and clinical antidepressants, will be discussed in later chapters.

The history of cocaine

ocaine is derived from small leaves of the coca shrub (Erythroxylon coca), grown in the high-altitude rain forests and fields that run along the slopes of the Peruvian and Bolivian Andes in South America. We know that the chewing of coca leaves, which contain about 2 percent cocaine, played a central role in the Inca civilization that flourished from the thirteenth century to its conquest by the Spaniards in 1532, as well as in other cultures that predated it. One immediate benefit of coca chewing was the increased strength and stamina that it gave those who worked in this harsh mountainous environment. It is not surprising that coca leaves were prized as a euphoriant as well. Inca shamans went into a trance from the burning of coca leaves and supposedly saw future events in the smoke. It had long been the custom to bury coca leaves next to the dead to help them deal with the afterlife, judging from the contents of graves dating from 500 B.C., and coca was part of the sacrifices to the gods.[2]

Coca was even used to measure time and distance; a journey would be commonly described in terms of the mouthfuls of coca leaves that a person would chew in making the trip.[3] Legends abounded concerning the origins of the coca plant. In one story, coca was a gift from the god Inti to the Incas, allowing them to endure life in the Andes without suffering from hunger or thirst. Another story had the first coca plant growing from the buried corpse of a beautiful woman who had been executed for adultery.[4]

To this day, coca chewing is part of the culture of this region. It is estimated that about 2 million Peruvian men who live in the Andean highlands, representing 90 percent of the male population in that area, chew coca leaves.[5] These people, called acullicadores, mix their own blend of coca, chalk, lime, and ash to achieve the desired effects, whether it is to fight fatigue or socialize with friends.[6]

Despite this continued drug taking, there are few instances of toxicity or abuse. The reason lies in the very low doses of cocaine that chewed coca leaves provide; in this form, absorption from the digestive system is slow and relatively little cocaine is distributed to the brain. A much more serious problem for these people, however, has been the introduction of an addictive mixture of coca paste containing a much higher percentage of cocaine combined with tobacco, called a bazuco, which is then smoked as a cigarette. Making matters worse, dangerously high levels of kerosene, gasoline, and ether are involved in the coca-refining process and end up in the cigarettes themselves.[7]

Cocaine in nineteenth-century life

Coca leaves were brought back to Europe from the Spanish colonies soon after the conquest of the Incas, but their potency was nearly gone after the long sea voyage. Perhaps, it was said at the time, the effects of coca were merely exaggerations after all Coca leaves were ignored for nearly three hundred years. By the late 1850s, however, the active ingredient of the coca plant had been chemically isolated. In 1859 Alfred Niemann, a German chemist, observed in 1859 its anesthetic effect on his tongue and its bitter taste, and named it "cocaine." Interest in the drug was renewed, and by the 1860s the patent medicine industry in the United States and Europe lost no time in taking advantage of cocaine's appeal.

Commercial uses of cocaine

By far the most successful commercial product of this type was a mixture of coca and wine invented in 1863 by a Corsican

cocaine
An extremely potent and dependence-producing stimulant drug, derived from the coca leaf.

chemist and businessman, Angelo Mariani. "Vin Mariani" became an instant sensation. A long list of endorsements by celebrities accumulated over the next few decades from satisfied customers such as U.S. President William McKinley, Thomas Edison, the surgeon general of the U.S. Army, General Ulysses S. Grant, Sarah Bernhardt, Jules Verne, the Prince of Wales, the czar of Russia, and both Pope Pius X and Leo XII. In a letter to Mariani, Frederic Bartholdi, the sculptor of the Statue of Liberty, wrote that if he had been drinking Vin Mariani while designing the statue it would have been more than three times taller.[8] We can only assume that this comment was intended to be complimentary.

In the United States, an Atlanta pharmacist, James Pemberton, promoted an imitation form of Vin Mariani that he called French Wine Cola. Shortly after, in 1885, he took out the alcohol, added soda water, and reformulated the basic mixture to combine coca with the syrup of the African kola nut containing about 2 percent caffeine: Coca-Cola was born. Early advertisements for Coca-Cola emphasized the drink as a brain tonic that made you feel more productive and as a remedy for assorted nervous ailments such as sick headaches and melancholia (a word used at the time to mean depression).[9] The medicinal slant to the early promotion of Coca-Cola is probably the reason why soda fountains began to appear in drugstores.[10]

A number of competing brands with similar formulations sprang up with names such as Care-Cola, Dope Cola, Kola Ade, and Wiseola, and the Parke-Davis Company began to sell several products containing cocaine.[11] Eventually, public pressure brought about official restrictions on the patent medicine industry, which, by the beginning of the twentieth century, was marketing more than fifty thousand unregulated products.[12] The Pure Food and Drug Act of 1906 specified that all active ingredients would have to be listed on patent medicine labels. In Canada, the Proprietary and Patent Medicine Act of 1908

In the late nineteenth century, the Coca-Cola Co. advertised their beverage in medicinal terms. A company letterhead of this period spoke of Coca-Cola as containing "the tonic properties of the wonderful coca plant."

banned cocaine from patent medicines entirely, but in the United States no further restrictions on cocaine sales or use were imposed until the Harrison Act of 1914 (see Chapter 2). The Coca-Cola Company, aware of the growing tide of sentiment against cocaine, had changed the formula in 1903 from regular coca leaves to decocainized coca leaves, which retained the coca flavoring that remains to this day (Focus 4.1). The "pause that refreshed" America would now be due only to the sugar and caffeine in the drink.

The use of cocaine was also becoming a major factor in the practice of medicine. In the United States, William Halstead, one of the most distinguished surgeons of the time and one of the founders of Johns Hopkins

What happened to the coca in Coca-Cola?

Every day, in a drab factory building in a New Jersey suburb of Maywood, a select team of employees of the Stepan Company carries out a chemical procedure that has been one of the primary responsibilities of the company since 1903. They remove cocaine from high-grade coca leaves. The remainder, technically called a "decocainized flavor essence" is then sent to the Coca-Cola Company as part of the secret recipe for Coca-Cola.

Each year, the Stepan Company is legally sanctioned by the U.S. government (and carefully monitored by the DEA) to receive shipments of about 175,000 kilograms of coca leaves from South American coca farms, separate the cocaine chemically, and produce about 1,750 kilograms of high-quality cocaine. Its annual output is equivalent to approximately 20 million hits of crack, worth about $200 million if it were to make it to the illicit drug market. Fortunately, the Stepan Company has an impeccable security record.

In case you are wondering what happens to the cocaine after it is removed from the coca leaves, it turns out that Stepan finds a legitimate market in the world of medicine. Tincture of cocaine is regularly used as a local anesthetic to numb the skin prior to minor surgical procedures such as stitching up a wound. Surgeons frequently use cocaine as a topical ointment when working on the nose or throat. As a result, the Stepan Company essentially has it both ways. It is the exclusive U.S. supplier of cocaine for use in medical settings as well as decocainized coca for your next can of Coke. As a recent article in the *Wall Street Journal* has put it, "The two markets end up sending Stepan's products into virtually every bloodstream in America."

SOURCE: Miller, Michael W. (1994, October 17). Quality stuff: Firm is peddling cocaine, and deals are legit. *The Wall Street Journal*, pp. A1, A14.

Medical School, studied the effect of cocaine on anesthetizing nerves and whole limbs. In the process, he acquired a cocaine habit of his own, which was replaced several years later by a dependence on morphine. It was in Europe, however, that the psychological implications of cocaine were most extensively explored, ironically by the triumphs and tragedies of Sigmund Freud.

Freud and cocaine

In 1884 Freud was a struggling young neurologist, given to bouts of depression and self-doubt but nonetheless determined to make his mark in the medical world. He had read a report by a German army physician that supplies of pure cocaine could help soldiers endure fatigue and feel better in general. Freud secured some cocaine for himself and found the experience exhilarating; his depression lifted, and he felt a new sense of boundless energy. His friend and colleague Dr. Ernst von Fleischl-Marxow, addicted to morphine and enduring a painful illness, borrowed some cocaine from Freud and found favorable results as well. Freud immediately saw the prospects of fame and fortune. In a letter to his fiancée, Martha, he wrote: "If it goes well I will write an essay on it and I expect it will win its place in therapeutics by the side of morphium [morphine] and superior to it."[3]

Before long, Freud was distributing cocaine to his friends and his sisters and even sent a supply to Martha. In the words of Freud's biographer Ernest Jones, "From the vantage point of our present knowledge, he was rapidly becoming a public menace."[14] We can gain some perspective on the effect cocaine was having on Freud's life at this time through an excerpt from a subsequent letter to Martha:

Woe to you, my Princess, when I come. I will kiss you quite red and feed you till you are plump. And if you are forward you shall see who is the stronger, a gentle little girl who doesn't eat enough or a big wild man who has cocaine in his body [underlined in the original]. *In my last severe depression I took coca again and a small dose lifted me to the heights in a wonderful fashion. I am just now busy collecting the literature for a song of praise to this magical substance.*[15]

Within four months, his "song of praise" essay, *Über Coca* (Concerning coca), was written and published.

Unfortunately, however, the sweetness of Freud's romance with cocaine turned sour. While Freud himself never became dependent on the cocaine, his friend Fleischl did. Within a year, Fleischl had increased his cocaine dose to twenty times the amount Freud had taken and had developed a severe cocaine-induced psychosis in which he experienced hallucinations that snakes were crawling over his skin (a phenomenon now referred to as **formication**). Fleischl suffered six years of painful agony and anguish until his death.

The story of Freud's infatuation with cocaine and his later disillusionment with it can be seen as a miniature version of the modern history of cocaine itself.[16] Between 1880 and 1910, the public reaction to cocaine had gone from wild enthuasiasm to widespread disapproval. As this chapter will later describe, a similar cycle of attitudes swept the country and the world between 1970 and 1985.

Acute effects of cocaine

hile the effects of cocaine on the user vary in degree with the route of administration, the purity of the dose, and the user's expectations about the experience, certain features remain the same. The most characteristic reaction is a powerful burst of energy. If the cocaine is injected intravenously, the effect is virtually instantaneous and extremely intense (often

---

formication
Hallucinatory behavior, produced by chronic cocaine or amphetamine abuse, in which the individual feels insects or snakes crawling either over or under the skin.

referred to as a "rush"), peaking in three to five minutes and wearing off in thirty to forty minutes. If snorted through the nose, the effect begins in about three minutes, peaking after fifteen to twenty minutes, and wearing off in sixty to ninety minutes.

There is also a general sense of well-being, although in some instances cocaine may precipitate a panic attack.[17] When cocaine levels return to normal, the mood changes dramatically. The user becomes irritable, despondent,

The depiction of actor Al Pacino as a cocaine kingpin. Scarface *was an example of Hollywood's glamorization of cocaine during the early 1980s.*

and depressed (Fig. 4.1). These aftereffects are uncomfortable enough to produce a powerful craving for another dose.

The depression induced in the aftermath of a cocaine high can lead to suicide. In 1985, during one of the peak years of cocaine abuse in the United States, as many as one out of five suicide victims in New York City showed evidence of cocaine in their blood at autopsy. The prevalence of cocaine use was greatest among victims who were in their twenties and thirties, and for African Americans and Latinos. Those who relied upon guns to end their lives were twice as likely to have also taken cocaine.[18] In a 1989 survey of teenage callers to the 800–COCAINE hotline, one out of seven reported a previous suicide attempt.[19] On the basis of these studies, cocaine use has become a significant risk factor for suicide attempts.

Cocaine's effect on sexual arousal is often cited as the basis for calling it "the aphrodisiac of the 1980s." On the one hand, interviews of cocaine users frequently include reports of spontaneous and prolonged erections in males and multiple orgasms in females during initial doses of the drug. On the other hand, cocaine's reputation for increasing sexual performance (recall Freud's reference in his letter to Martha) may bias users toward a strong

expectation that there will be a sexually stimulating reaction, when in reality the effect is a much weaker one. As one cocaine abuser expressed it, "Everybody says that it's an aphrodisiac. Again, I think some people say it because it's supposed to be. I think that it's just peer group identification. . . . I never felt that way. I was more content to sit there and enjoy it."[20] The fact is that prolonged cocaine use results in decreased sexual performance and a loss of sexual desire, as the drug essentially takes the place of sex.

Cocaine produces a sudden elevation in the sympathetic branch of the autonomic nervous system. Heart rate and respiration are increased, while appetite is diminished. Blood vessels constrict, pupils in the eyes dilate, and blood pressure rises. The cocaine user may start to sweat and appear suddenly pale. The powerful sympathetic changes can lead to a cerebral hemorrhage or congestive heart failure. Cardiac arrhythmia results from cocaine's binding to heart tissue itself.[21]

The extreme effects of cocaine on bodily organs, particularly the heart, stem from its ability not only to excite the sympathetic system but to inhibit the parasympathetic system as well (Focus 4.2). Given the high level of sympathetic arousal, it is not surprising that

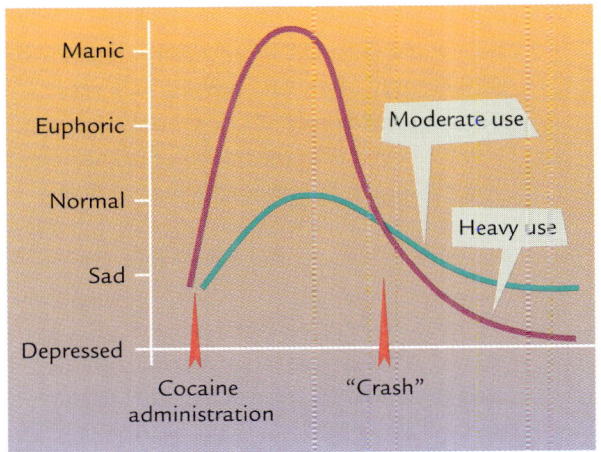

FIGURE 4.1

Ups and downs of a typical dose of cocaine

Ways cocaine can kill you

1. Abnormal heart rhythms can lead to ventricular tachycardia (extremely rapid heart rate) or ventricular fibrillation (very weak contractions of the heart).

2. A rapid increase in blood pressure can produce a cerebral hemorrhage.

3. Increased body temperature can reach very dangerous levels, from 108 to 110 degrees Fahrenheit.

4. Epileptic seizures can be triggered. Through the "kindling" effect, extensive cocaine use can sensitize the brain to increasingly lower doses of the drug.

5. Respiratory effects can lead to labored breathing, gasping, or respiratory arrest.

6. In rare individuals, a deficiency in pseudo-cholinesterase, an enzyme normally present that breaks down cocaine, can produce an accumulation to toxic levels even when the dose is very low.

7. Sugar levels in the blood can rise, endangering the lives of diabetics.

SOURCE: Weiss, Roger D., and Mirin, Steven M. (1987). *Cocaine.* Washington DC: American Psychiatric Press, pp. 27–28.

Chronic effects of cocaine

Repeated and continued use of cocaine produces undesirable mood changes that can only be alleviated when the person is under the acute effects of the drug. Chronic cocaine abusers are often irritable, depressed, and paranoid. As was true in Fleischl's experience with cocaine, long-term abuse can produce the disturbing hallucinatory experience of formication. The sensation of "cocaine bugs" crawling on or under the skin can become so severe that abusers may scratch the skin into open sores or even pierce themselves with a knife to cut out the imaginary creatures. These hallucinations, together with feelings of anxiety and paranoia, make up a serious mental disorder referred to as **cocaine psychosis.**

When snorted, cocaine causes bronchial muscles to relax and nasal blood vessels to constrict; the opposite effects occur when the drug wears off. As the bronchial muscles contract and nasal blood vessels relax, chronic abusers endure continuously stuffy or runny noses and bleeding of nasal membranes. In advanced cases of this problem, the septum of the nose can develop lesions or become perforated with small holes, both of which present serious problems for breathing.

behavioral skills will be adversely affected. In a 1993 study of drivers showing reckless behavior on the road, those who were found to have been under the influence of cocaine were wildly overconfident in their abilities, taking turns too fast or weaving through traffic. One highway patrol officer called this behavior "diagonal driving. They were just as involved in changing lanes as in going forward." Yet they passed the standard sobriety tests designed to detect alcohol intoxication.[22]

cocaine psychosis
A set of symptoms, including hallucinations, paranoia, and disordered thinking, produced from chronic use of cocaine.

Medical uses of cocaine

When applied topically on the skin, cocaine has the ability to block the transmission of nerve impulses, deadening all sensations from the area. This local anesthetic effect of cocaine remains its only legitimate medical application. In procedures in which tubes are passed through the nose or throat, cocaine is applied on the membranes to ease the discomfort. There are, however, potential problems in the use of cocaine even for these specific circumstances. One danger is that cocaine may be inadvertently absorbed into the bloodstream. There is also the possibility for abuse. Finally, the local anesthetic effects are brief, since cocaine is rapidly metabolized. Synthetic drugs such as lidocaine (brand name: Xylocaine) have the advantage of acting as local anesthetics over a longer period of time, and since they do not have the euphoriant effects of cocaine, the abuse potential is reduced. Consequently, lidocaine and other similar drugs, by injection into the gums, are widely used as local anesthetics during dental procedures.

How cocaine works in the brain

ocaine greatly enhances the activity of dopamine, and to a lesser extent, norepinephrine in the brain. In the case of both neurotransmitters, the actual effect is to block the reuptake process at the synapse, so the neurotransmitters stimulate the postsynaptic receptors longer and to a greater degree.[23] Unlike the amphetamines (discussed later in this chapter), the structure of cocaine does not appear to resemble the structure of either norepinephrine or dopamine, so why cocaine should block their reuptake so effectively is not at all clear. What has been determined, however, is that the euphoria experienced through cocaine is directly related to the effect of dopamine in those regions of the brain that control pleasure and reinforcement in general: the nucleus accumbens and the mesotelencephalic dopamine pathway (MTDP, see Chapter 3).

One feature of cocaine is quite unlike that of other psychoactive drugs. While many cocaine abusers develop a pattern of drug tolerance (Chapter 2), requiring increased doses to duplicate the initial cocaine effect, others sometimes experience the opposite: a hypersensitization to the drug. In other words, long-term cocaine abusers may become *more* sensitive to the drug over repeated administrations. This phenomenon, referred to as the **kindling effect,** makes cocaine particularly dangerous, since cocaine has the potential for

setting off brain seizures (see Focus 4.2). Repeated exposure to cocaine can lower the threshold for seizures, through a sensitization of neurons in the limbic system over time. As a result of the kindling effect, deaths from cocaine overdose may occur from relatively low dose levels.[24]

Present-day cocaine abuse

he difficult problems of cocaine abuse in the United States and around the world arose during the early 1970s and continue to the present day, though the incidence of abuse is considerably down from a peak level reached around 1986. In ways that resembled the brief period of enthusiasm for cocaine in 1884, attitudes during the early period of this "second epidemic" were incredibly naive. Fueled by media reports of use among the rich and famous, touted as the "champagne of drugs," cocaine became synonymous with the glamorous life.

The medical profession at this time was equally nonchalant about cocaine. The widely respected *Comprehensive textbook of psychiatry* (1980) stated the following: "If it is used no more than two or three times a week, cocaine creates no serious problem. . . . At present chronic cocaine use does not usually present a medical problem."[25]

These attitudes began to change as the 1980s unfolded. The death of actor-comedian John Belushi, followed by the drug-related deaths of other entertainers and sport figures (see Focus 2.1) produced a slow but steady reversal of opinion about the safety and desirability of cocaine. The greatest influence, however, was the arrival of crack cocaine on the drug scene in 1985, which will be examined in the next sections.

kindling effect
A phenomenon in the brain that produces a heightened sensitivity to repeated administrations of a drug. This heightened sensitivity is the opposite to the phenomenon of tolerance.

Cocaine in this form, however, is not water-soluble and therefore cannot be injected into the bloodstream. An additional step of treatment with oxidizing agents and acids is required to produce a water-soluble drug. The result is a white crystalline powder called **cocaine hydrochloride,** about 99 percent pure cocaine and classified chemically as a salt.

When in the form of cocaine hydrochloride, the drug can be injected intravenously or snorted. The amount injected at one time is about 16 mg. Intravenous cocaine can also be combined with heroin in a highly dangerous mixture called a speedball.

If cocaine is snorted, the user generally has the option of two methods. In one method, a tiny spoonful of cocaine is carried to one nostril while the other nostril is shut, and the drug is taken with a rapid inhalation. In the other method, cocaine is spread out on a highly pol-

In order to understand the ways in which cocaine is abused, we should look at the various steps that the raw coca goes through to become reasonably pure cocaine (Fig. 4.2). During the initial extraction process, coca leaves are soaked in various chemical solvents so that cocaine can be drawn out of the plant material itself. Leaves are then crushed, and alcohol is percolated through them to remove extraneous matter. After sequential washings and a treatment with kerosene, the yield is cocaine that is approximately 60 percent pure. This is the coca paste, which, as mentioned earlier, is combined with tobacco and smoked in many South American countries.

cocaine hydrochloride
The form of cocaine that is injectable into the bloodstream.

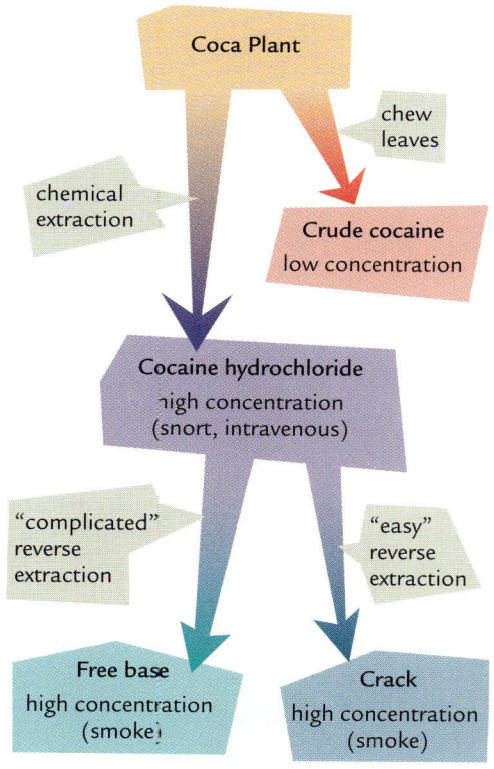

FIGURE 4.2

Steps in producing various forms of cocaine from raw coca

ished surface (often a mirror) and arranged with a razor blade in several lines each containing from 20 to 30 mg. The cocaine is then inhaled into one nostril, by means of a straw or rolled piece of paper. During the early 1980s, a $100 bill was a fashionable option, emphasizing the level of income necessary to be taking cocaine in the first place.[26]

Options beyond the intake of cocaine hydrochloride widened with the development of **free-base cocaine** during the 1970s and **crack cocaine** (or simply **crack**) during the mid-1980s. In free-base cocaine, the hydrochloride is removed from the salt form of cocaine, thus liberating it as a free base. The aim is to obtain a smokable form of cocaine, which by entering the brain more quickly, produces a more intense effect. The technique for producing free-base cocaine, however, is extremely hazardous, since it is necessary to treat cocaine powder with highly flammable agents such as ether. If the free base still contains some ether residue, the lighting of the drug will cause it to explode into flames.

Crack cocaine is the result of a cheaper and safer chemical method, but the result is essentially the same: a smokable form of cocaine. Treatment with baking soda yields small rocks, which can then be smoked in a small

TABLE 4.1	
Street names for cocaine	
Type of cocaine	Street name
Cocaine	blow, C, coke, big C, lady, nose candy, snowbirds, snow, stardust, toot, white girl, happydust, cola, flake, pearl, Peruvian lady, freeze, geeze, doing the line
Free-base cocaine	freebase, base
Crack cocaine	crack, rock, kibbles and bits
Crack cocaine combined with PCP (see Chapter 8)	beam me up Scottie, space cadet, tragic magic
Cocaine combined with heroin	speedball
Cocaine combined with heroin and LSD	Frisco special, Frisco speedball

SOURCE: Bureau of Justice Statistics Clearinghouse (1992). *Drugs, behavior and crime.* Washington DC: Department of Justice pp. 24–25.

pipe.[27] When they are smoked, there is a small cracking noise during the burning, hence the origin of the name "crack."

How dangerous is crack? There is no question that the effect of cocaine when smoked exceeds the effect of cocaine when snorted; for some users, it even exceeds the effect of cocaine when injected. Inhaling high-potency cocaine (the purity of cocaine in crack averages about 75 percent) into the lungs, and almost immediately into the brain, sets the stage for uncontrollable psychological dependence. And at a price of $5 to $10 per dose cocaine is no longer beyond one's financial means (Table 4.1). The answer is that crack is very dangerous indeed. Beyond its effect on the user, however, is the effect on the society where crack is prevalent. As discussed in Chapter 2, the enormous monetary profits from the selling of crack have created dramatic increases in inner-city crime and violence.

The emergence of crack cocaine has brought desolation and misery to many communities in the United States and around the world.

free-base cocaine
A smokable form of cocaine.

crack cocaine or **crack**
A smokable form of cocaine.

Patterns of cocaine abuse

n 1992 the National Household Survey on Drug Abuse estimated that approximately 23 million Americans had used cocaine at some time in their lives, 5 million had used it during the past year, and 1.3 million had used it during the past month. Of these totals, approximately 2.8 million Americans had used crack at some time in their lives, 800,000 had used it during the past year, and 300,000 had used it during the past month (Focus 4.3). Equivalent estimates from other countries are less precise, but it is safe to assume that abuse of cocaine and crack cocaine has spread throughout Europe and on other continents as well.[28]

While the incidence of cocaine abuse in the United States was lower in the 1990s than it had been during the 1980s, medical emergencies associated with cocaine use, as measured through the DAWN statistics, have increased dramatically. In 1992 there were approximately 120,000 cocaine-emergencies reported by metropolitan hospitals, a 50 percent jump from 1990. Evidently, the emergency wards are bearing the greatest burden in the acute care of cocaine abuse.[29] What choices are there for the long-term treatment of individuals with a cocaine dependence?

Treatment programs for cocaine abuse

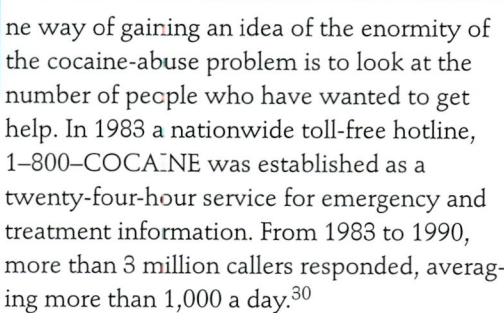

ne way of gaining an idea of the enormity of the cocaine-abuse problem is to look at the number of people who have wanted to get help. In 1983 a nationwide toll-free hotline, 1–800–COCAINE was established as a twenty-four-hour service for emergency and treatment information. From 1983 to 1990, more than 3 million callers responded, averaging more than 1,000 a day.[30]

We can also see, through the statistics gathered from the hotline over the years, the changing face of cocaine abuse. In 1983 the typical cocaine abuser was college educated (50 percent), employed (83 percent), earning more than $25,000 a year (52 percent), and taking cocaine powder intranasally (61 percent). By 1988, however, the typical cocaine abuser had not gone to college (83 percent) and was earning less than $25,000 a year (80 percent). From 1983 to 1988, the percentage of individuals reporting an abuse of a free-base form of cocaine had more than doubled to 56 percent. In 1986 alone, one year after the introduction of crack, one half of all calls to the hotline referred to problems of crack abuse. These demographic changes require new challenges in treatment; new programs must be sensitive not only to the ethnic diversity of present-day cocaine abusers but also to the diversity in the pattern of cocaine abuse. As noted in an earlier chapter, the relative decline in media coverage in the mid-1990s regarding cocaine and crack should not be misleading; abused cocaine and crack continues to be pervasive in many, if not all, urban centers in the United States.[31]

Treating cocaine abuse presents difficulties that are peculiar to the power of cocaine itself. This is the way one treatment expert has put it:

Coming off cocaine is one of the most anguished, depressing experiences. I've watched people talk about coming off freebase and one of the things I noticed was the nonverbal maneuvers they use to describe it. It looks like they're describing a heart attack. They have fists clenched to the chest. You can see that it hurts. They can recreate that hurt for you because it's a devastating event. They'll do almost anything to keep from crashing on cocaine. And on top of that they'll do just about anything to keep their supply coming. Postcocaine anguish is a strong inducement to use again—to keep the pain away.[32]

The varieties of treatment for cocaine abuse all have certain features in common. The initial phase is detoxification and total abstinence, where the cocaine abuser undergoes total withdrawal with the least possibility of physical injury and minimal psychological discomfort. During the first twenty-four to forty-eight hours, the chances are high that there will be profound depression, along with severe headaches, irritability, and disturbances in sleep.[33]

In severe cases, where a pattern of compulsive use cannot be easily broken, the cocaine abuser needs to be admitted for inpatient treatment in a hospital facility. The most intensive interventions, medical supervision, and psychological counseling can be made in this kind of environment. The early stages of withdrawal are clearly the most difficult, and the recovering abuser can benefit from around-the-clock attention that only a hospital staff can give. The alternative approach is an outpatient program, where the individual remains at home but travels regularly to a facility for treatment. An outpatient program is clearly a less expensive route to take, but it may work only for those who recognize the destructive impact of cocaine dependence on their lives and enter treatment with a sincere desire to do whatever is needed to stop.[34] For cocaine abusers who have failed in previous attempts in outpatient treatment or for those who are in denial of their cocaine dependence, an inpatient approach may be the only answer (Focus 4.4). For some, it is important to stay

FOCUS 4.4

Seven rules for cocaine abusers who want to quit

1. **The time to stop using cocaine is now.** If you say, "I'll quit tomorrow," then you are saying, "I have no intention of quitting."

2. **Stop all at once, not gradually.** Each time you use cocaine, you are fueling the desire for more and postponing the process of recovery.

3. **Stop using all other drugs of abuse, including alcohol and marijuana.** Cocaine abusers often think that the problem is with cocaine alone. Use of alcohol and marijuana can be the initial step to a relapse back to cocaine.

4. **Change your life-style.** If you encounter conditions that are associated with cocaine, your craving will increase. This problem is particularly difficult in the early stages of cocaine withdrawal.

5. **Whenever possible, avoid situations, people, and places that cause drug urges.** Yesterday's abstinences cannot guarantee the same result today. It's a matter of "one day at a time." Trying to test yourself by approaching drug situations and monitoring your reaction is a big mistake, according to drug-treatment experts.

6. **Find other rewards** Learn to enjoy life without cocaine. Learn how to reconnect with a drug-free world. You may have even forgotten how to talk about anything except cocaine.

7. **Take good care of your body. Eat right and exercise.** Normal eating habits are wrecked while you are abusing cocaine. Chances are good that your physical condition has deteriorated, and you may be suffering from significant vitamin deficiencies. A healthy diet and a program of regular exercise are two major factors in your long-term recovery prospects.

SOURCE: Weiss, Roger D., and Mirin, Steven, M. (1987). *Cocaine*. Washington DC: American Psychiatric Press, pp. 136–139.

away from an environment where cocaine and other drugs are associated and peer pressure to resume drug-taking behavior is intense. This factor is particularly crucial among adolescents:

Peer acceptance is of utmost importance to adolescents. In order to interrupt the addiction cycle, youth are cautioned to avoid drug-using friends. Since many addicted adolescents are alienated from the mainstream and what few friends they have are users, this challenge can appear overwhelming. Recovering adolescents often comment that they can't find friends who don't at least drink.[35]

A third alternative is a combined approach in which a shortened inpatient program, seven to fourteen days in length, is followed by an intensive outpatient program that continues for several months.

Whether on an inpatient or outpatient basis, there are several approaches for treatment. For cocaine abusers specifically, there is the self-help support group Cocaine Anonymous, modeled after the famous Alcoholics Anonymous program (Chapter 11). In these group sessions, recovering cocaine abusers feel less isolated, learn from the life experiences of other members, and attain a sense of accomplishment from remaining drug free. In many cases, an intensive relearning process has to go on, since cocaine abusers often cannot remember a life without cocaine. Formal psychotherapy sessions can also be provided, on an individual, group, or family basis. Finally, new advances in the understanding of the physiological basis for cocaine dependence have led to the development of therapeutic drugs that can be taken during treatment and recovery to reduce the intense craving (Table 4.2).

Success rates in an outpatient program depend on a host of factors: the severity of the cocaine abuse, the strength of the motivation to give it up, and the extent to which the program matches up with the abuser's personal needs. In one study of 127 abusers who took part in an outpatient treatment program, 65 percent completed the program after six to twelve months and more than 75 percent were still drug free after a one-to-two-year follow-up.[36] Nonetheless, relapse is always a significant concern among recovering cocaine abusers. A specialist in cocaine abuse rehabili-

TABLE 4.2

Therapeutic drugs for cocaine-abuse treatment

Generic name	Brand name	Function
bromocriptine	Parlodel	Reduces craving during cocaine withdrawal
desipramine	Norpramin	Reduces depression during cocaine abstinence
amantadine	Symmetrel	Reduces craving during cocaine withdrawal
lithium		Prevents the euphoric effects of cocaine, should a relapse occur

SOURCE: Adapted from Spitz, Henry I., and Rosencan, Jeffrey S. (1987). Overview of cocaine abuse treatment. In *Cocaine abuse: New directions in treatment and research.* New York: Brunnel/Mazel, pp. 97–118.

tation tells this story: "A woman was doing very well in treatment. Then one day she was changing her baby's diaper. She used baby powder and the sight of the white powder induced a tremendous craving for cocaine."[37]

Amphetamines

ne of humanity's fondest dreams is to have the power of unlimited endurance, to be able to banish fatigue from our lives, to be capable of endless energy as if we had discovered some internal perpetual-motion machine. We all have wanted, at one time in our lives, to be a super-hero. Cocaine, as we know, gives us that illusion. The remainder of this chapter will examine another powerful drug source for these feelings: amphetamines. As will be explained, the attractions and problems of abuse of cocaine and amphetamines are very similar, but amphetamines are less prominent in the current drug scene. About three decades ago, just the opposite was true; amphetamines were the object of concern, and cocaine was yet to make the headlines. Had this book been written at that time, the proportion of attention given to these two psychostimulant drugs would have been reversed.

Otis Nixon—Trials and tribulations

I n the continuing story of athletes who struggle against drug abuse, we have seen the casualties of college basketball player Len Bias and professional football player Dan Rodgers. These were star performers whose deaths from cocaine overdose in 1986 galvanized the nation to take a serious look at the power of this drug to take the lives of healthy, talented young men. There are other victims who have escaped death but whose athletic careers have been demolished: Stanley Wilson, Cincinnati Bengals running back, for example, whose suspension from football after testing positive for cocaine took place on the eve of Super Bowl XXIII in 1989.

And then there are the small but steady victories, cases in which you feel yourself rooting for an athlete in his or her battle against cocaine just as you would cheer a home run or an interception play. In the life of Otis Nixon, major league baseball player, we are watching an emotional roller-coaster of a baseball career in which there have been defeats and triumphs, and we can't be sure how the ride will end.

It was in 1979, while a freshman at Louisburg College in North Carolina, that Nixon first tried cocaine. He didn't know anything about it, much less how to use it. In an all too familiar pattern of events, however, innocence evolved into a pattern of cocaine abuse. In 1987 his problems with cocaine caused him to be released from the Cleveland Indians, and he entered his first drug-rehabilitation program. It was a four-week program, the kind of casual approach to drug dependence that represents, in the words of sports professionals, "the standard cosmetic treat-

ment that so often fails." Nixon has said, "I came out and wasn't worried. It was major denial."

In July 1991, in Atlanta, Nixon tested positive for cocaine. He convinced the baseball commissioner that he was clean and the test had to have been flawed, but in September he failed again. This time, there was a sixty-day suspension. Nixon's hopes for a free-agent contract in the $5 million range were ended.

Otis Nixon

At this point in the story, the picture brightens. "It was the best thing that could possibly have happened to me because I got my life straightened out," Nixon has said, as he remembers his decision to extend his stay in rehabilitation by an additional two months. He made a film called *Strikeout* to teach kids about drug addiction. He fought to get back into the Atlanta lineup in 1992 and establish himself as part of a winning ball club.

Like the thousands of other recovering drug abusers, Nixon recognizes the fragile nature of cocaine-abuse rehabilita-

tion. His contract now includes monetary incentives if his tests stay negative, but as we know from many case histories money often fails to be enough incentive to keep athletes clean of drugs. Nixon understands the environmental cues associated with drug abuse. He knows where he cannot go: "the old friends, old stomping grounds." He still attends rehabilitation meetings and keeps in touch with others who are in the same struggle.

As of 1994, Nixon has tested negative in more than two hundred random drug tests. He still takes it one day at a time.

SOURCES: Jacobson, Steve (1992, October 13). Nixon's life would make a great movie. *Newsday*, pp. 120 (Pt. 1), 119 (Pt. 2). Gergen, Joe (1992, October 26). Just happy to be there. *Newsday*, p. 107. "Nixon: Gooden needs a lot of strength" (1994, June 29). *Newsday*, p. A72. Vecsey, George (1991, September 18). Another way to lose a pennant. *New York Times*, p. E5. Vecsey, George (1992, October 25). This year, Otis Nixon has control. *New York Times*, p. L8.

The history of amphetamines

The origin of modern amphetamines dates back almost five thousand years to a Chinese medicinal herb called *ma huang (Ephedra vulgaris)* that was used to clear bronchial pas-

sageways during bouts of asthma and other respiratory problems. According to Chinese legend, this herb was first identified by the Emperor Shen Nung, who also is credited with the discovery of tea and marijuana. In 1887 German chemists isolated the active ingredient of *ma huang,* naming it ephedrine. It was soon obvious that ephedrine stimulated the sympathetic nervous system in general. In 1927 Gordon Alles, a research chemist from Los Angeles, developed a synthetic form of ephedrine and named the new drug **amphetamine.** The pharmaceutical company Smith, Kline and French Laboratories marketed the Alles formula under the brand name Benzedrine in 1932 as a nonprescription inhalant for asthma sufferers.

By the beginning of World War II, amphetamine had gained the reputation of being a CNS stimulant as well as a bronchial dilator. Now available as a prescription tablet, amphetamine was found to be useful as a treatment for narcolepsy (a sleep disorder in which a person spontaneously and unpredictably falls asleep numerous times during the day), as an antidepressant, and as an appetite suppressant for dieting. Wartime conditions, however, provided an additional application for amphetamine: to keep soldiers "pepped up" during long hours of battle. During the war, both U.S. and German troops were being given amphetamine to keep them awake and alert. Japanese kamakazi pilots were on amphetamine during their suicide missions. The advantages over cocaine, the other stimulant drug available at the time, were twofold: amphetamine was easily absorbed into the nervous system from the gastrointestinal tract so it could be taken orally, and its effects were much longer lasting, generally about seven hours.

After the war, amphetamine use was adapted for peacetime purposes. Amphetamine, often referred to as bennies, was a way for college students to stay awake to study for exams, and long-distance truck drivers used it to stay awake for days on the road. Truckers would take a "St. Louis" if they had to go from New York to Missouri and back or a "Pacific turnabout" if they needed to travel completely across country and back, without stopping to sleep.[38]

In the meantime, the word got around that amphetamine produced euphoria as well. As you can imagine, this news created a flourishing black market, as amphetamine began to be seen in recreational terms. People found ways of opening up the nonprescription amphetamine inhalers, withdrawing the contents, and getting high by drinking it or injecting it intravenously. Since each inhaler contained 250 mg of amphetamine, there was enough for several powerful doses. During the early 1960s, injectable amphetamines could be bought with forged prescriptions or even by telephoning a pharmacy and posing as a physician. By 1965, amendments to federal drug laws tightened the supply of prescription amphetamines, requiring manufacturers, wholesalers, and pharmacies to keep careful records of amphetamine transactions, but amphetamines soon became available from illegal laboratories.[39]

Amphetamine abuse in the United States reached a peak about 1967, declining slowly over the 1970s as other drugs of abuse, notably cocaine, grew in popularity. By 1970, 10 percent of the U.S. population over fourteen years of age had used amphetamine, and more than 8 percent of all drug prescriptions were for amphetamine in some form.[40]

The different forms of amphetamine

In order to understand the pharmacology of amphetamine, it is necessary to know something about the molecular structures of drugs in general. As you can see at the top of Fig. 4.3, amphetamine can be represented in terms of carbon (C), hydrogen (H), and nitrogen (N) atoms, in a prescribed arrangement. What you are seeing, however, is only one version of amphetamine, the "right-handed" form, since amphetamine contains a "left-handed" version as well (imagine a mirror image of Fig. 4.3). The more potent version is

amphetamine (am-FEH-ta-meen)
A family of ephedrine-based
stimulant drugs.

the right-handed form, called dextroamphet-amine or **d-amphetamine** (brand name: Dexedrine). It is stronger than the left-handed form, called levoamphetamine or l-amphetamine, which is not commonly available. A modified form of d-amphetamine, accomplished by substituting CH_3 (called a methyl group) instead of H at one end, is called **methamphetamine** (brand name: Methedrine). This slight change in the formula allows for a quicker passage across the blood-brain barrier. It is methamphetamine, often called meth or speed, that has been the primary form of amphetamine abuse.

How amphetamines work in the brain

We can get a good idea of how amphetamines work in the brain by looking carefully at the molecular structures of dopamine and norepinephrine alongside d-amphetamine and methamphetamine in Fig. 4.3. Notice how similar they all are, with only slight differences among them. Because of the close resemblance to dopamine and norepinephrine, it is not hard to imagine amphetamines increasing the activity level of these two neurotransmitters. Specifically, amphetamines cause increased amounts of dopamine and norepinephrine to be released from the synaptic knobs and also slow down their reuptake from receptor sites. As described in Chapter 3, dopamine figures prominently in regions of the brain associated with positive reinforcement. The euphoric effects of amphetamines, and the craving for them during abstinence, are very likely direct results of the increase in neural activity in these regions.

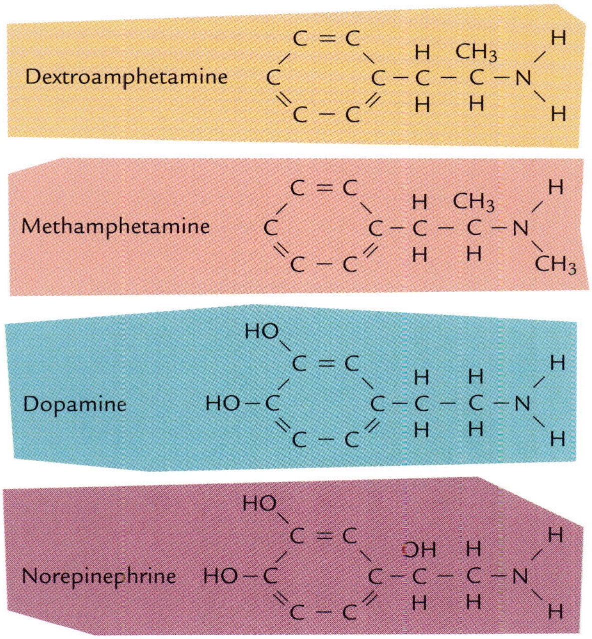

FIGURE 4.3

The molecular structure of dextroamphetamine, methamphetamine, dopamine, and norepinephrine

Acute and chronic effects of amphetamines

he acute effects of amphetamines closely resemble those of cocaine. There is a general increase in sympathetic autonomic activity, increased energy, and a feeling of euphoria. The chronic effects of amphetamine abuse, particularly in the case of methamphetamine, however, are far less pleasant. Heavy users, often referred to as speed freaks, may experience formication hallucinations similar to those endured by cocaine abusers. Behavioral fixations may develop, in which actions are repeated over and over again; an entire night might be spent, for example, counting the cornflakes in a cereal box.[41] Here is an

d-amphetamine
Shortened name for dextroamphetamine, a potent form of amphetamine, marketed under the brand name Dexedrine.

methamphetamine
An often abused type of amphetamine, once marketed under the brand name Methedrine. Amphetamine abusers refer to it as speed.

anecdote of how extreme the behaviors of chronic amphetamine use can get:

One speed freak . . . had spent two years engaged in covering an entire wall with heads of George Washington, carefully cut out from cancelled postage stamps; supposedly, he had pasted 60,000 of these figures on the wall.[42]

The most serious consequence of chronic amphetamine abuse is the appearance of paranoia, wildly bizarre delusions, hallucinations, tendencies toward violence, and mood swings. Collectively, these symptoms are referred to as **amphetamine psychosis,** a product of high-dose amphetamine abuse, persisting even for weeks after the drug has been withdrawn.[43] Since the behavioral features of amphetamine psychosis so closely resemble those of paranoid schizophrenia, it has been speculated that the two conditions have the same underlying basis in the brain: an over-stimulation of dopamine-involving neurons in those regions that control emotional reactivity.

The danger of amphetamine psychosis is bad enough in the case of an ordinary individual, but what would we be dealing with if a public figure were involved? According to many historical accounts, Adolf Hitler's disintegrating personality toward the end of World War II was strongly influenced by heavy use of methamphetamine. This is how one historian has put it:

No one who has read about his behavior during the time or about the pronouncements at the situation conferences on 23, 25, and 27 April 1945, then still being recorded, can fail to recognize what it was that made him conjure up in all good faith such patently hare-brained schemes. The rapid alternation of depression and euphoria, exhaustion and artificially induced buoyancy clearly reflect Hitler's dependence on the stimulants prescribed by [his physician] Morell.[44]

amphetamine psychosis
A set of symptoms, including hallucinations, paranoia, and disordered thinking, resulting from high doses of amphetamines.

Patterns of amphetamine abuse and treatment

Considering the powerful reinforcing effects of amphetamines, it is not surprising that cases of amphetamine abuse began to surface soon after the drug became widely available. The first wave of abuse took place in Japan, shortly after World War II. In order to reduce stockpiles of methamphetamine accumulated during the war, the drug was sold without prescription. By 1954, 2 million out of a Japanese population of about 88 million, were amphetamine abusers, primarily teenagers and young adults. Similar epidemics arose in other countries as well. In the case of Japan, a concerted effort to tighten controls and educate the public managed to cause the abuse to subside by the early 1960s, only to have it renew itself in the 1970s.[45]

In the United States, the emergence of widespread methampetamine abuse was intermingled with the marijuana and LSD scene during San Francisco's "Summer of Love and Peace" in 1967. Almost from the beginning, however, these speed freaks, whose behaviors were anything but loving or peaceful, became the outcasts of that society:

A subculture of drug users who used speed almost exclusively—popping it or shooting it— developed, and began to evince all the symptoms we now associate with classic amphetamine abuse. These wild-eyed, manic burnout cases would blither on endlessly, rip off anything not welded in place, then go into fits of erratic and violent behavior. . . . They were shunned by other sorts of drug users, and ended up congregating with the only segment of the population who could stomach their company—other speed freaks.[46]

In the meantime, prescription amphetamines, widely administered during the 1960s for weight control and as a way to combat drowsiness, resulted in large numbers of abusers from practically every segment of society. Even though d-amphetamine was classified as a Schedule II drug in 1970 and the number of d-amphetamine prescriptions decreased by 90 percent from 1971 and 1986 (methamphetamine had become a Schedule I drug in 1970 and therefore was no longer legally available), the pills were still cut there, and people found ways to continue an abusive pattern of behavior.

What is the present picture of amphetamine abuse? With the shift to cocaine as the major psychostimulant of abuse in the 1980s, amphetamine problems failed to make major headlines. In the 1990's, however, there is increasing concern about a comeback in amphetamine abuse, particularly in the form of methamphetamine (Table 4.3).[47] Since the late 1980s, the number of illegal speed laboratories has increased dramatically, particularly in western U.S. states. From 1988 to 1992, about 25 to 30 percent of males and females arrested in San Diego, for example, were found with amphetamine metabolites in their bloodstream. Recently, the distribution of methamphetamine in general has shifted to well-organized Mexican drug syndicates, and increasing levels of methamphetamine abuse have been reported not only on the West Coast but in central and midwestern states as well.[48]

Kitty Dukakis and Gov. Michael Dukakis, Democratic Presidential candidate in 1988, at a campaign rally. Her 26-year amphetamine dependence, followed by alcohol dependence and depression, came to light in 1989.

One of the aspects of methamphetamine abuse that has been a particular cause for concern is the emergence of a smokable form of a high-potency crystallized form of methamphetamine called **ICE**. In many ways, the physical appearance of this new drug and many of its effects on the user are similar to those of crack cocaine. It looks like pieces of rock candy and contains from 98 percent to 100 percent pure methamphetamine. Since smoking ICE gives a powerful and virtually instantaneous euphoria and it lasts from four to twenty-four hours (a period far longer than crack), the potential for psychological dependence is substantial. As in the ingestion of any form of methamphetamine, there is the possibility of amphetamine psychosis; in the case of ICE, it can occur from even a single large-dose administration. Outbreaks of ICE abuse began in Hawaii in 1988, with its popularity being concentrated among Japanese, Korean, and Filipino communities. There was concern that ICE abuse might expand to the mainland United States, but as of the mid-1990s that has not happened.[49]

TABLE 4.3	
Street names for amphetamines	
Type of amphetamines	Street name
amphetamines in general	bennies, uppers, ups, A, pep pills, white crowns, whites
dextroamphetamine	dexies, cadillacs, black beauties
methamphetamine	meth, speed, crank, little whites, white crosstops
smokable methamphetamine	crystal, crystal meth, ICE
methamphetamine mixed with heroin	speedball
methcathinone (an analog form of amphetamine)	cat

ICE
A smokable form of methamphetamine.

The course of amphetamine withdrawal for people who have developed an amphetamine dependence is very similar to the course of events described earlier for cocaine. First there is the "crash" when the abuser feels intense depression, agitation, and anxiety within one to four hours after the drug-taking behavior has stopped. Withdrawal from amphetamines, during total abstinence from the drug, takes between six and eighteen weeks, during which the intense craving for amphetamine slowly subsides. As in cocaine-abuse treatment, there are inpatient and outpatient programs, depending on the circumstances and motivation of the abuser. Self-help groups such as Cocaine Anonymous are useful as well, since the symptoms of amphetamine withdrawal and cocaine withdrawal are closely related.[50]

Medical uses for amphetamines and similar stimulant drugs

hile amphetamines in general continue to present potential problems of abuse, there are approved medical applications for amphetamine-like stimulant drugs in specific circumstances. The two most widely prescribed drugs in this regard are methylphenidate (brand name: Ritalin) and pemoline (brand name: Cylert) for elementary-school-age children diagnosed as hyperactive and unable to maintain sufficient attention levels in school, technically referred to as **attention-deficit hyperactivity disorder** (ADHD). These children, more than three times as many boys as girls, are of normal to above average intelligence but are underperforming academically.

> **attention-deficit hyperactivity disorder (ADHD)**
> A childhood disorder characterized by increased motor activity and reduced attention span.

About 70 percent of the approximately 750,000 children who take stimulants for ADHD each year successfully respond to the treatment. Typically, the prescribed drug is taken only during the school year and in conjunction with behavior-modification training and counseling with the family and teachers. The major side effect of this treatment, however, is a suppression of height and weight gains during these formative years, reducing growth to about 80 to 90 percent of normal levels. Fortunately, growth spurts during the summer, when the child is no longer taking the drug, usually compensate for this problem.

Why a stimulant drug would successfully *reduce* childhood hyperactivity, rather than

Common amphetamine-like drugs in present use

For appetite suppression in weight control		For relief of nasal congestion	
Generic name	Brand name	Generic name	Brand name
diethylpropion	Tenuate	ephedrine	Broncholate, Primatene
fenfluramine	Pondimin	metaraminol	Aramine
mazindol	Sanorex	naphazoline	Privine
phendimetrazine	Bondril, Plegine, Preludin, Prelu-2	oxymetazoline	Afrin, Dristan
phenylpropanolamine	Acutrim, Dexatrim	phenylephrine	Neo-Synephrine
		phenylpropanolamine	Contac, Dimetapp, Triaminic, many others
		pseudoephedrine	Sudafed, Comtrex, many others

SOURCE: *Physician's desk reference* (48th ed.). (1994). Montvale NJ: Medical Economics Data.   *Physician's desk reference for nonprescription drugs* (13th ed.). (1992). Montvale NJ: Medical Economics Data.

increase it, has been a great mystery among professionals in this field, and several theories have been advanced in an attempt to explain this apparent paradox. Children with ADHD may have an underlying depression, in which case a stimulant would be useful in alleviating the symptoms. If there is a less-than-normal level of cortical activity that would normally inhibit movement, then a stimulant might bring the cortical activity back to a normal level and the child would have a greater degree of self-control. It is also possible that ADHD children are overly tired as a result of a CNS arousal level that is too low. By this reasoning, a stimulant would set the arousal level higher, making them more alert and attentive. Anyone who has watched a child who is up well past his or her bedtime will recognize the hyperactivity that seems to contradict the fact that the child is exhausted.[51] The fact is that ADHD in general is still poorly understood, and no one is entirely certain how the stimulant treatment works.

Other medical applications include d-amphetamine treatment for narcolepsy and obesity. Once again, however, the potential for abuse has steered physicians away from amphetamines themselves and toward less potent amphetamine-like stimulants (Table 4.4).

There is also a wide range of amphetamine-like drugs available to the public, many of them on a nonprescription basis, to be used as nasal decongestants. In most cases, their effectiveness stems from their primary action on the peripheral nervous system rather than on the CNS. Even so, there is the potential for continuing to take these drugs over a long period of time, since stopping their use may result in unpleasant rebound effects such as nasal stuffiness. This reaction, by the way, is similar to the stuffy nose that is experienced in the chronic administration of cocaine.[52]

Summary

THE HISTORY OF COCAINE

- Cocaine, as one of the two major psychoactive stimulants, is derived from coca leaves grown in the mountainous regions of South America. Coca chewing is still prevalent among certain groups of South American indians.

- During the last half of the nineteenth century, several patent medicines and beverages were sold that contained cocaine, including the original formulation for Coca-Cola.

- Sigmund Freud was an early enthusiast of cocaine as an important medicinal drug, promoting cocaine as a cure for morphine dependence and depression. Soon afterward, Freud realized the strong dependence that cocaine could bring about.

ACUTE EFFECTS OF COCAINE

- Cocaine produces a powerful burst of energy and sense of well-being. In general, cocaine causes an elevation in the sympathetic autonomic nervous system.

CHRONIC EFFECTS OF COCAINE

- Long-term cocaine use can produce hallucinations and deep depression, as well as physical deterioration of the nasal membranes if cocaine is administered intranasally.

MEDICAL USES OF COCAINE

- The only accepted medical application for cocaine is its use as a local anesthetic.

HOW COCAINE WORKS IN THE BRAIN

- Within the CNS, cocaine blocks the reuptake of receptors sensitive to dopamine and norepinephrine. As a result, the activity level of these two neurotransmitters in the brain is enhanced.

PRESENT-DAY COCAINE ABUSE

- Despite a permissive attitude toward cocaine use during the 1970s and early 1980s, attitudes toward cocaine use since the second half of the 1980s have changed dramatically.

- The emergence in 1986 of relatively inexpensive, smokable crack cocaine has expanded the cocaine-abuse problem to new segments of the U.S. population and made cocaine abuse one of the major social issues of our time.

TREATMENT PROGRAMS FOR COCAINE ABUSE

- Cocaine abusers can receive treatment through inpatient programs, outpatient programs, or a combination of the two. Relapse is a continual concern for recovering cocaine abusers.

AMPHETAMINES

- Amphetamines, the second of the two major psychoactive stimulants, have their origin in a Chinese medicinal herb, used for thousands of years as a bronchial dilator; its active ingredient, ephedrine, was isolated in 1887.

- The drug amphetamine (brand name: Benzedrine) was developed in 1927 as a synthetic form of ephedrine. By the 1930s, various forms of amphetamines, specifically d-amphetamine and methamphetamine, became available around the world.

ACUTE AND CHRONIC EFFECTS OF AMPHETAMINES

- Amphetamine is effective as a general arousing agent, as an antidepressant, and as an appetite suppressant, in addition to its ability to keep people awake for long periods of time.

- While the acute effects of amphetamines resemble those of cocaine, amphetamines have the particular feature of producing (when taken in large doses) symptoms of paranoia, delusions, hallucinations, and violent behaviors, referred to as amphetamine psychosis. The bizarre behaviors of the "speed freak," the name given to a chronic abuser of methamphetamine, illustrate the dangers of amphetamine abuse.

PATTERNS OF AMPHETAMINE ABUSE AND TREATMENT

- With the emphasis on cocaine abuse during the 1980s, amphetamine abuse has been less prominent in the public mind. Recently, however, there has been a resurgence of amphetamine-abuse cases involving a new smokable form of methamphetamine called ICE.

- Treatment for amphetamine abuse generally follows along the same lines as treatment for cocaine abuse.

MEDICAL USES FOR AMPHETAMINES AND SIMILAR STIMULANT DRUGS

- Amphetamines themselves are rarely prescribed, given their potential for abuse, but other less potent, amphetamine-like drugs

have been developed for approved medical purposes.

- Two drugs, methylphenidate (brand name Ritalin) and pemoline (brand name: Cylert), are prescribed for children diagnosed with attention-deficit hyperactivity disorder.

- Other medical applications for amphetamine-like drugs include their use as a treatment for narcolepsy, as an appetite suppressant for weight control, and as a means for temporary relief of nasal congestion.

Key Terms

amphetamine psychosis, p. 104
amphetamine, p. 102
attention-deficit hyperactivity disorder, ADHD, p. 106
cocaine, p. 89
cocaine hydrochloride, p. 96
cocaine psychosis, p. 94

crack cocaine or crack, p. 97
d-amphethamine, p. 103
formication, p. 92
free-base cocaine, p. 97
ICE, p. 105
kindling effect, p. 95
methamphetamine, p 103

Endnotes

1. Rosencan, Jeffrey S., and Spitz, Henry I. (1987). Cocaine reconceptualized: Historical overview. In Henry I. Spitz and Jeffrey S. Rosencan (Eds.), *Cocaine abuse: New directions in treatment and research*. New York: Brunner/Mazel, p. 5.
2. Inglis, Brian (1975). *The forbidden game: A social history of drugs*. New York: Scribner's, pp. 49–50.
3. Flynn, John C. (1991). *Cocaine: An in-depth look at the facts, science, history, and future of the world's most addictive drug*. New York: Birch Lane/Carol Publishing, p. 20.
4. Weiss, Roger D., and Mirin, Steven M. (1987). *Cocaine*. Washington DC: American Psychiatric Press, p. 4.
5. Jaffe, Jerome (1985). Drug addiction and drug abuse. In Louis S. Goodman and Alfred Gilman (Eds.), *The pharmacological basis of therapeutics* (7th ed.). New York: Macmillan, p. 552.
6. Nahas, Gabriel G. (1989). *Cocaine: The great white plague*. Middlebury VT: Paul S. Eriksson, pp. 154–162.
7. Kusinitz, Marc (1988). *Drug use around the world*. New York: Chelsea House Publishers, pp. 91–95.
8. Nuckols, Cardwell C. (1989). *Cocaine: From dependency to recovery* (2nd ed.). Blue Ridge Summit PA: Tab Books, p. x.
9. Weiss and Mirin. Cocaine, p. 6   Brecher, Edward M., and the editors of Consumer Reports (1972). *Licit and illicit drugs*. Boston Little, Brown, p. 270.
10. McKim, William A. (1991). *Drugs and behavior* (2nd ed.). Englewood Cliffs NJ: Prentice Hall p. 203.
11. Erickson, Patricia G., Adlaf, Edward M., Murray, Glenn F., and Smart, Reginald G. (1987). *The steel drug: Cocaine in perspective*. Lexington MA: D. C. Heath, p. 9.

12. Musto, David (1973). *The American disease: Origins of narcotic control.* New Haven CT: Yale University Press.

13. Jones, Ernest (1953). *The life and work of Sigmund Freud.* Vol. 1. New York: Basic Books, p. 81.

14. Ibid., p. 81.

15. Ibid., p. 84.

16. Brecher. *Licit and illicit drugs,* pp. 272–280.

17. Aronson, T. A., and Craig, T. J. (1986). Cocaine precipitation of panic disorder. *American Journal of Psychiatry, 143,* 643–645.

18. Marsuk, Peter M., Tardiff, Kenneth, Leon, Andrew C., Stajic, Marina, Morgan, Edward B., and Mann, J. John (1992). Prevalence of cocaine use among residents of New York City who commited suicide during a one-year period. *American Journal of Psychiatry, 149,* 371–375.

19. Office of Substance Abuse Prevention (1989). *What you can do about drug use in America* (DHHS publication No. ADM 88–1572). Rockville MD: National Clearinghouse for Alcohol and Drug Information.

20. Philips, J. L., and Wynne, R. D. (1974). *A cocaine bibliography—nonannotated.* Rockville MD: National Institute on Drug Abuse, 1974. Cited in Ernest L. Abel. (1985). *Psychoactive drugs and sex.* New York: Plenum Press, p. 100.

21. Volkow, Nora D., Fowler, Joanna S., Wolf, Alfred P., et al. (1990). Effects of chronic cocaine abuse on postsynaptic dopamine receptors. *American Journal of Psychiatry, 147,* 719–724.

22. Experiment in Memphis suggests many drive after using drugs (1994, August 28). *New York Times,* p. 30.

23. Clouet, D., Asqhar, K., and Brown, R. (Eds.) (1988). *Mechanisms of cocaine abuse and toxicity* (NIDA Research Monograph 88). Rockville MD: National Institute on Drug Abuse. Wise, Roy A. (1984). Neural mechanisms of the reinforcing action of cocaine. In J. Grabowski (Ed.), *Cocaine: Pharmacology, effects, and treatment of abuse* (NIDA Research Monograph 50). Rockville MD: National Institute on Drug Abuse, pp. 15–33. Koob, George T., Vaccarino, Franco J., Amalric, Marianne, and Swerdlow, Neal R. (1987). In Seymour Fisher, Allen Raskin, and E. H. Uhlenhuth (Eds.), *Cocaine: Clinical and biobehavioral aspects.* New York: Oxford University Press, pp. 80–108.

24. Weiss and Mirin. *Cocaine,* pp. 48–49. Post, Robert M., Weiss, Susan R. B., Pert, Agu, and Uhde, Thomas W. (1987). Chronic cocaine administration: Sensitization and kindling effects. In Seymour Fisher, Allen Raskin, and E. H. Uhlenhuth (Eds.), *Cocaine: Clinical and biobehavioral aspects.* New York, Oxford University Press, pp. 109–173.

25. Kaplan, Harold I., Freedman, Arnold M., and Sadock, Benjamin J. (1980). *Comprehensive textbook of psychiatry.* Vol. 3. Baltimore MD: Williams and Wilkins, p. 1621.

26. Flynn, *Cocaine,* pp. 38–46.

27. Ibid., p. 44.

28. Substance Abuse and Mental Health Services Administration (1993). *National Household Survey on Drug Abuse: Population Estimates 1992.* Rockville MD: Substance Abuse and Mental Health Services Administration, Office of Applied Studies, Tables 4A and 5A. Kusinitz. *Drug use.*

29. Drug emergencies up. (1992, October 25). *Newsday,* p. 18. Substance Abuse and Mental Health Services Administration (1994). Annual Emergency Room data 1992. Data from the Drug Abuse Warning Network (DAWN). Series I, Number 12-A. Rockville MD: Substance Abuse and Mental Health Services Administration, Office of Applied Studies, p. 32.

30. Gold, Mark S. (1990). *800–COCAINE.* New York: Bantam books.

31. Nuckols, Cardwell C. (1989). *Cocaine: From dependency to recovery* (2nd ed.). Blue Ridge Summit PA: Tab Books, pp. 144–146. Lee, Felicia R. (1994, September 10). A drug dealer's rapid rise and ugly fall. *New York Times,* pp. 1, 22.

32. Nuckols. *Cocaine,* p. 42.

33. Ibid., pp. 71–72.

34. Weiss and Mirin. *Cocaine,* p. 125.

35. Fox, C. Lynn, and Forbing, Shirley E. (1992). *Creating drug-free schools and communities: A*

comprehensive approach. New York: Harper-Collins, p. 165.

36. Washton, Arnold M., Gold, Mark S., and Pottash, A. C. (1986). Treatment outcome in cocaine abusers. In L. S. Harris (Ed.), *Problems of drug dependence, 1985* (NIDA Research Monograph 67). Rockville MD: National Institute on Drug Abuse, pp. 381–384.

37. Barnes, Deborah M. (1988). Breaking the cycle of addiction. *Science, 241,* p. 1029.

38. McKim. *Drugs and behavior,* p. 205.

39. Brecher. *Licit and illicit drugs,* pp. 282–283.

40. Peluso, Emanuel, and Peluso, Lucy S. (1988). *Women and drugs.* Minneapolis: CompCare Publishing.   Greaves, George B. (1980). Psychosocial aspects of amphetamine and related substance abuse. In John Caldwell (Ed.), *Amphetamines and related stimulants: Chemical, biological, clinical, and sociological aspects.* Boca Raton FL: CRC Press, pp. 175–192.

41. Goode, Erich (1989). *Drugs in American society* (3rd ed.). New York, McGraw-Hill, p. 192.

42. Ibid., p. 192.

43. Ibid., p. 192.

44. Maser, Werner (1971). *Adolf Hitler: Legend, myth, and reality.* New York: Harper and Row, pp. 228–229.

45. Austin, G. A. (1978). *Perspectives on the history of psychoactive substance abuse* (NIDA Research Issues 24). Rockville MD: National Institute on Drug Abuse, p. 42.

46. Young, Stanley (1989, July). Zing! Speed: The choice of a new generation. *Spin magazine,* pp. 83, 124–125. Reproduced in Erich Goode (Ed.) (1992), *Drugs, society, and behav-ior 92/93.* Guilford CT: Dushkin Publishing, p. 116.

47. Lovett, Anthony R. (1994, May 5). Wired in California. *Rolling Stone,* pp. 39–40.

48. Drug agents see shift in trafficking in speed (1994, September 4). *New York Times,* p. 24. National Institute of Justice (1993). Drug Use Forecasting 1992 Annual Report: Drugs and crime in America's Cities. Washington DC: Department of Justice, p. 32.

49. "Ice" poses a new threat to public health. (1990, August). *The fact is . . . ,* Rockville MD: National Clearinghouse for Alcohol and Drug Information, Office of Substance Abuse Prevention, p. 1.   Lauderback, David, and Waldorf, Dan (1993). Whatever happened to ICE: The latest drug scare. *Journal of Drug Issues, 23,* 597–613.   National Institute of Justice (1993). *The rise of crack and ICE: Experiences in three locales.* Washington DC: Department of Justice.

50. Gawin, Frank H., and Ellinwood, Everett H. (1988). Cocaine and other stimulants: Action, abuse, and treatment. *New England Journal of Medicine, 318,* 1173–1182.

51. Abikoff, Howard, and Gittleman, Rachel (1985). Children treated with stimulants. *Archives of General Psychiatry, 42,* 953–961. Jacobvitz, D., Sroufe, A., Stewart, M., and Leffert, N. (1990). Treatment of attentional and hyperactivity problems in children with sympathomimetic drugs: A comprehensive review. *Journal of the American Academy of Child and Adolescent Psychiatry, 29,* 677–688.

52. Julien, Robert M. (1995). *A primer of drug action* (7th ed.). New York: Freeman, p. 151.

5

Sedative-Hypnotics and Antianxiety Drugs

Jennie never expected to be addicted to a prescription drug. After all, weren't the really dangerous drugs the ones you got from a pusher? It started with stress and anxiety, an engagement that didn't work out, trouble with the boss at work. The doctor gave her the prescription to fall asleep on those nights that seemed endless, to calm her down and get her through the day. And the drug worked, all too well. She was frightened of the thought of stopping. After several months, when she was embarrassed to ask for the fifth refill, she found another doctor who didn't ask any questions. So it went, from doctor to doctor, pharmacist to pharmacist, until she started to realize she was in trouble.

Just as cocaine, amphetamines, and other stimulants bring us up, depressants bring us down. Just as there is a desire to be stronger, faster, and more attuned to the world, there is also the desire to move apart from that world, reduce the stressors and anxieties of our lives, and fall asleep more easily. Historically, the prime psychoactive depressant drug has been alcohol. As will be discussed in Chapter 10, practically every culture in the world has discovered in one way or another the effects of alcohol on the body and the mind. This chapter, however, will focus on a group of drugs called **sedative-hypnotics,** so named since they calm us down and produce sleep (from the Greek word *hypnos,* meaning "to sleep"). There are several types of depressants that promote sedation and sleep, ranging from drugs that were introduced in the nineteenth century to drugs that are only recently available.

This chapter will also look at drugs that provide specific relief from stress and anxiety without sedating us. These drugs have often been referred to as *tranquilizers* by virtue of their ability to make us feel peaceful or tranquil, but we will call them by their more current name, **antianxiety drugs.**

Unfortunately, sedative-hypnotics and antianxiety drugs have been subject not only to legitimate medical use but to misuse and abuse as well. Although they are available as prescribed medications, many of them can be obtained from illicit sources as street drugs and are consumed for recreational purposes. The psychological problems and physical dangers associated with the misuse and abuse of these depressants, as will be noted, are of particular concern.

Barbiturates

In 1864 the German chemist Adolf von Baeyer (better known for the development of Bayer's aspirin) combined a waste product in urine called urea and an apple extract called malonic acid to form a new chemical compound called barbituric acid. There are two often told stories about how this compound got its name. One story has it that Von Baeyer went to a local tavern to celebrate his discovery and encountered a number of artillery officers celebrating the feast day of St. Barbara, the patron saint of people who handle explosives. Inspired by their celebration, the name "barbituric acid" came to mind. The other story attributes the name to a favorite barmaid at the same tavern whose name was Barbara.[1]

Whichever story is true (if either is), Von Baeyer's discovery of barbituric acid set the stage for the development of a large class of drugs called **barbiturates.** Barbituric acid itself, however, has no behavioral effects. It is only when additional molecular groups combine with the acid to form derivatives of Von Baeyer's compound that depressant effects are observed. In 1903 the first true barbiturate, diethylbarbituric acid, was created and marketed under the name Veronal. Over the next thirty years, several major barbiturate drugs were introduced: **phenobarbital** (brand name: Luminal), **amobarbital** (brand name: Amytal), **pentobarbital** (brand name: Nembutal), and **secobarbital** (brand name: Seconal).

Categories of barbiturates

Dozens of different barbiturates have been marketed over the years, all sharing a number of common features. They are relatively tasteless and odorless, and at sufficient dosages they reliably induce sleep, although the quality of sleep is a matter that will be discussed later. Since they slow down the activity of the central nervous system, barbiturates are also useful in the treatment of epilepsy.

The principal difference among them lies in how long the depressant effects will last; a classification of barbiturates is based upon this factor. Barbiturates are categorized as long-acting (six or more hours), intermediate-acting (four to six hours), or short-acting (less than four hours). Bear in mind, however, that these groups are only relative to one another. Injectable forms of barbiturates will be shorter-acting than orally administered forms of the same drug, since it takes longer for the drug to be absorbed when taken by mouth and longer for it to be eliminated from the body. Naturally, a higher dose of any drug will last longer than a lower dose because it will take longer for all of the drug to be eliminated from the body (Table 5.1).

The barbiturates used in surgical anesthesia, such as thiopental (brand name: Pentothal), take effect extremely rapidly (within seconds) and last only a few minutes. For this reason, they are referred to as ultra-short-acting barbiturates. Since these features are undesirable for a person seeking a recreational drug, these forms of barbiturates are not commonly abused.

sedative-hypnotics
A category of depressant drugs that provide a sense of calm and sleep.

antianxiety drugs
Drugs that make the user feel more peaceful or tranquil, also called tranquilizers.

barbiturate (bar-BIT-chur-rit)
A drug within a family of depressants derived from barbituric acid and used as a sedative-hypnotic and antiepileptic medication.

phenobarbital (FEEN-oh-BAR-bih-tall)
A long-acting barbiturate drug. Brand name is Luminal.

amobarbital (AY-moh-BAR-bih-tall)
An intermediate-acting barbiturate drug. Brand name is Amytal.

pentobarbital (PEN-toh-BAR-bih-tall)
A short-acting barbiturate drug. Brand name is Nembutal.

secobarbital (SEC-oh-BAR-bih-tall)
A short-acting barbiturate drug. Brand name is Seconal.

TABLE 5.1

Major barbiturates in present use

Generic name*	Brand name	Duration of action	Relative potential for abuse
phenobarbital	Luminal	Long	Low
butabarbital	Butisol	Intermediate	Moderate
amobarbital	Amytal	Intermediate	High
secobarbital and amobarbital	Tuinal	Short, intermediate	High
talbutal	Lotusate	Short	Moderate
pentobarbital	Nembutal	Short	High
secobarbital	Seconal	Short	High

Note: Short-acting barbiturates begin to take effect in about 15 minutes, intermediate-acting barbiturates in 30 minutes, and long-acting barbiturates in one hour.

*In Great Britain, generic names for barbiturates end in -one (as in phenobarbitone) instead of -al.

SOURCE: Henningfield, Jack E., and Ator, Nancy A. (1986). *Barbiturates: Sleeping potion or intoxicant?* New York: Chelsea House, p. 24.

Effects of barbiturates

You can visualize the effects of barbiturates on the body and the mind as points along a scale ranging from mild relaxation on one end to coma and death on the other (Fig. 5.1). In this sense, barbiturate effects are the same as the effects of depressants in gen-

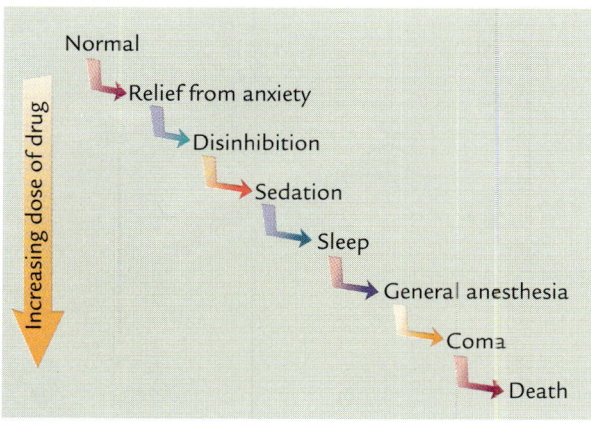

FIGURE 5.1

The downward continuum of arousal levels, as induced by depressants
SOURCE: *A Primer of Drug Action by Julien.*
Copyright © 1992 by W. H. Freeman and Company.
Reprinted with permission.

eral. The particular point that is achieved depends upon the dose level that is taken.

At very low doses, the primary result of oral administrations of a barbiturate is relaxation and, paradoxically, a sense of euphoria. These effects are chiefly due to a "disinhibition" of the cerebral cortex, in which normal inhibitory influences from the cortex are reduced. You might recognize these symptoms as similar to the inebriating or intoxicating effects that result from low-level doses of alcohol (Focus 5.1).

As the dose level increases, lower regions of the brain become affected, specifically the reticular formation (Chapter 3). At therapeutic doses (one 100 mg capsule of secobarbital, for example), barbiturates make you feel sedated and drowsy. For this reason, patients are typically warned that barbiturates may impair the performance of driving a car or operating machinery. At higher doses, a hypnotic (sleep-inducing) effect will be achieved.

Historically, the primary use of barbiturates has been in the treatment of insomnia, and they were widely recommended for this purpose from 1903, when they were first introduced, until the development of the benzodiazepines in the 1960s. One of the reasons why barbiturates fell from favor was that the sleep induced by these drugs turned out to be far from normal. Barbiturates tend to suppress rapid-eye movement (REM) sleep, a phase of everyone's sleep that comprises about 20 percent of the total sleep time each night. REM sleep is associated with dreaming and general relaxation of the body. If barbiturates are consumed over many evenings and then stopped, the CNS will attempt to "catch up" for the lost REM sleep by producing longer REM periods on subsequent nights This **REM-sleep rebound** effect will produce vivid and upsetting nightmares. There will also be a barbiturate hangover the next

REM-sleep rebound
A phenomenon associated with the withdrawal of barbiturate drugs in which the quantity of rapid-eye movement (REM) sleep increases, resulting in disturbed sleep and nightmares.

Is there any truth about "truth serum"?

he idea that sedative-hypnotic drugs such as amobarbital sodium (Sodium Amytal) or thiopental (Pentothal) may function as "truth serums" is not at all new. It has been known for centuries that depressants can produce remarkable candor and freedom from inhibition. The oldest example is simple alcohol, whose effect on loosening the tongue has led to the Latin phrase *in vino veritas* ("in wine, there is truth").

Whether or not we are guaranteed truthfulness under any of these circumstances, however, is another matter entirely. Courts have ruled that expert opinion in criminal cases based *solely* upon drug-assisted testimony cannot be admitted as evidence. Controlled laboratory studies have shown that individuals under the influence of Sodium Amytal or Pentothal, when pressed by questioners, are as likely to give convincing renditions of fabrications (outright lies) or fantasies as they are to tell the truth.

So, perhaps, Sodium Amytal or Pentothal might be better described as "tell anything serum."

SOURCES: Leavitt, Fred (1982). *Drugs and behavior* (2nd ed.). New York: Wiley, p. 236. Michaelis, James I. (1966). Quaere, whether 'in vino veritas': An analysis of the truth serum cases. *Issues in Criminology, 2* (2), pp. 245–267.

centers in the medulla. The mixture of barbiturates with alcohol produces a synergistic effect (see Chapter 2), in which the combined result is greater the sum of the effects of each drug alone (Focus 5.2).

Half of the lethal dose of secobarbital combined with ¼ the lethal dose of alcohol can kill in a synergistic double whammy. In another typical case of accidental overdose, a person takes a sleeping pill and awakens drugged and confused a few minutes later, annoyed at being aroused. The person then forgetfully takes another pill, or several, from the nightstand, and goes to sleep forever. This is called "drug automatism," a good reason not to keep medications within reach of the bed.[3]

During the period between 1973 and 1976, barbiturates were implicated in more than half of all drug-related deaths labeled as suicide by medical examiners. In fact, the suicide potential of barbiturates is the primary reason for their decline as a prescription drug.[4]

Barbiturates and alcohol have frequently been combined in attempts to commit suicide.

day, during which the user feels groggy and out of sorts. In other words, barbiturates may induce sleep, but a refreshing sleep it definitely is not.[2]

The most serious acute risks of barbiturate use involve the possibility of a lethal overdose either from taking too high a dose level of the drug alone or from taking the drug in combination with alcohol, as when a barbiturate might be taken after an evening of drinking. In these instances, sleep can all too easily slip into coma and death, since an excessive dose produces an inhibition of the respiratory

Chronic effects of barbiturates

When barbiturates are used as sleep medications, there are a number of ways a cycle of behavior can arise, leading to dependence. Even after brief use of barbiturates, anxiety might be temporarily increased during the day and there might be an even greater degree of insomnia than before. In addition, since a barbiturate-induced sleep typically leaves a person feeling groggy the next morning, it is tempting to take a stimulant drug during the day in order to feel completely alert. When it comes time for sleep, a person still feels the stimulant effects and is inclined to continue taking a barbiturate in order to achieve any sleep at all. To make matters worse, the brain builds up a pharmacological tolerance to barbiturates quite quickly, requiring increasingly higher doses for an equivalent effect.

Withdrawal symptoms, observed when barbiturates are discontinued, indicate a strong physical dependence of the body on the drug. A person may experience a combination of tremors (the "shakes"), nausea and vomiting, intense perspiring, general confusion, convulsions, hallucinations, high fever, and increased heart rate. Not surprisingly, considering the parallels mentioned so far with alcohol, the barbiturate withdrawal syndrome closely resembles that of withdrawal after chronic alcohol abuse (Chapter 11).

Professionals in the treatment of drug dependence often view the effects of barbiturate withdrawal as the most distressing as well as the most dangerous type of drug withdrawal. From a medical perspective, the withdrawal process is potentially life-threatening unless it is carried out in gradual fashion in a hospital setting. Without medical supervision, abrupt withdrawal from barbiturates carries approximately a 5 percent chance of death.[5]

Current medical uses of barbiturates

Considering the problems of barbiturate use in the treatment of insomnia, it should not be surprising that a 1988 review in the *Harvard*

Medical School Health Letter concluded that the clinical use of barbiturates for this problem was essentially "obsolete."[5] Nonetheless, barbiturates continue to play an important role in the treatment of epileptic seizures. Phenobarbital, one of the long-acting varieties of barbiturates, is often used to prevent convulsions. Dose levels need to be monitored carefully, however, since the concentration must be high enough to control the development of seizures (despite the tendency for tolerance effects to occur over time) without being so high as to produce drowsiness.

Patterns of barbiturate abuse

There are clear indications that taking barbiturate drugs is positively reinforcing. Laboratory animals will eagerly press a lever to deliver intravenous injections of barbiturates, particularly for the short-acting types, at rates that are equal to pressing levers for cocaine.[7] When given the choice between pentobarbital and a nonbarbiturate depressant and given no knowledge as to the identity of the drugs, human drug abusers reliably select an oral dose of pentobarbital.[8]

Barbiturate abuse reached its peak in the 1950s and 1960s, later to be overshadowed by abuses of heroin, hallucinogens, nonbarbiturate depressants, amphetamine, and, more recently, abuses of cocaine and crack (Table 5.2). The principal reason was that barbiturates became less widely available as prescription drugs. Stricter controls were placed on obtaining excessive amounts of barbiturates from pharmacies, while physicians, concerned with the potential of barbiturates as ways of committing suicide, became more reluctant to prescribe them on a routine basis.

Despite their decline as major drugs of abuse, however, barbiturates are still being abused. The University of Michigan survey of 1993 high school seniors found that 6 percent of them had made some recreational use of barbiturates during their lifetime, down from 17 percent in 1975, and 3 percent had taken them within the past year, down from 11 percent in 1975.[9]

Nonbarbiturate sedative-hypnotics

s the hazards of barbiturate use became increasingly evident in the 1950s, the search was on for sedative-hypnotic drugs that were not derivatives of barbituric acid and, it was hoped, had fewer undesirable side effects. One such drug, **chloral hydrate,** had been first

chloral hydrate
A depressant drug once used for the treatment of insomnia. It is highly reactive with alcohol and can severely irritate the stomach.

T A B L E   5 . 2

Street names for various barbiturates

Type of barbituate	Street name
pentobarbital (Nembutal)	abbotts, blockbusters, nebbies, nembies, nemmies, yellow bullets, yellow dolls, yellow jackets, yellows
amobarbital (Amytal)	blue angels, bluebirds, blue bullets, blue devils, blue dolls, blue heavens, blues
secobarbital (Seconal)	F-40s, Mexican reds, R.D.s, redbirds, red bullets, red devils, red dolls, reds, seccies, seggies, pinks
secobarbital and amobarbital (Tuinal)	Christmas trees, double trouble, gorilla pills, rainbows, tootsies, trees, tuies
barbiturates in general	downers, down, goofballs, G.B.s, goofers, idiot pills, King Kong pills, peanuts, pink ladies, sleepers, softballs, stumblers

Note: Like any other street drug, illicit barbiturate capsules often contain an unknown array of other substances, including strychnine, arsenic, laxatives, or milk sugars. Any yellow capsule may be "marketed" as Nembutal, any blue capsule as Amytal, or any red capsule as Seconal.

SOURCE: Henningfield, Jack E., and Ator, Nancy A. (1986). *Barbiturates: Sleeping potion or intoxicant?* New York: Chelsea House, p. 82.

---

synthesized as early as 1832. As a depressant for the treatment of insomnia, it has the advantage of not producing the REM sleep rebound effect or bringing on the typical barbiturate hangover. A major disadvantage, however, is that it can severely irritate the stomach. Like other depressants, it is also highly reactive when combined with alcohol. In the nineteenth century, a few drops of chloral hydrate in a glass of whiskey became the infamous Mickey Finn, a concoction that left many an unsuspecting sailor unconscious and eventually "shanghaied" onto a boat for China.

Two other nonbarbiturate sedative-hypnotics, glutethimide (brand name: Doriden) and methylprylon (brand name: Noludar), were briefly popular in the 1950s, but both drugs were eventually found to have undesirable side effects and are now considered to be even less safe than barbiturates.

The development of **methaqualone** (brand names: Quaalude, Sopor), first introduced in the United States in 1965, was a further attempt toward achieving the perfect sleeping pill. In 1972 methaqualone had become the sixth best-selling drug for the treatment of insomnia. It was also during this time that reports from elsewhere in the world had been received of links between the drug and suicide, as well as of widespread abuse. During the early 1970s, recreational use of methaqualone (popularly known as ludes or sopors) was rapidly spreading across the country, aided by the unfounded reputation that it had aphrodisiac properties. The problem was compounded by the extensive number of prescriptions written by physicians who mistakenly saw the drug as a desirable alternative to barbiturates. On the street, quantities of methaqualone were obtained from medical prescriptions or stolen from pharmacies. Methaqualone-associated deaths started to be prominent "mentions" in the DAWN reports of the period (see Chapter 2). In 1984 its legal status changed to that of a Schedule I drug, the most restricted classification, which indicates a high potential for abuse and no medical benefits.[10] While no longer manufactured by any pharmaceutical company, methaqualone is still available as an illicit drug. It is either manufactured in domestic underground laboratories or smuggled into the country from underground laboratories abroad.

The development of antianxiety drugs

f historians consider the 1950s as "the age of anxiety," then it is appropriate that this period would also be marked by the development of drugs specifically intended to combat that anxiety. These drugs were originally called minor tranquilizers, in order to distinguish them from other drugs, called major tranquilizers, developed at about the same time to relieve symptoms of schizophrenia. This terminology is no longer used today, since we now know that the difference between the two drug categories is more than simply a difference of degree. Anxious people or even people who are not bothered by anxiety will not be helped by drugs designed to treat schizophrenia. As a result, the current philosophy is to refer to drugs in terms of a specific action and purpose. The minor tranquilizers are now called antianxiety drugs. The major tranquilizers are now called antipsychotic drugs and will be reviewed in Chapter 16.

The first antianxiety drug to be developed was **meprobamate** (brand name: Miltown), named in 1955 for a New Jersey town near the headquarters of the pharmaceutical company that first introduced it. Spurred on by its manufacturer's recommendation to physicians that "the choice of Miltown . . . means the comfortable assurance that it will relieve nervousness and tension without impairing your patient's mental efficiency, motor control, normal behavior or autonomic balance," Miltown became an immediate hit among prescription drugs, making its name a household word and essentially a synonym for tranquilizers in general.[11]

Even though meprobamate was the first psychoactive drug in history to be marketed as an antianxiety medication, most pharmacologists have identified the effects of this drug more in terms of sedation than of relief from anxiety.[12] Nonetheless, meprobamate is different from the other depressant drugs discussed so far in this chapter. The primary difference is in the way it works in the nervous system. Instead of inhibiting the reticular formation and the respiratory centers in the medulla as barbiturates do, meprobamate reduces the activity of acetylcholine at

methaqualone (MEH-tha-QUAY-lone)
A nonbarbiturate depressant drug once used as a sedative. Brand name is Quaalude.

meprobamate (MEH-pro-BAYM-ayt)
A nonbarbiturate antianxiety drug and sedative. Brand name is Miltown.

the nicotinic synapses where the motor nerves innervate the body's skeletal muscles (Chapter 3). As a result, there are weaker muscle contractions and general relaxation.

On the positive side, the toxic dose of meprobamate is relatively high, making the possibility of suicide more remote than with alcohol, barbiturates, and other depressants. In addition, there are genuine signs, judging from the reduction in autonomic responses to stressors, that people under this medication are actually less anxious. On the negative side, motor reflexes are diminished, making driving more hazardous. People often complain of drowsiness, even at dose levels that should only be calming them down. Meprobamate can also produce both physical and psychological dependence, at slightly more than twice the normal recommended daily dose.[13] This is not a very wide margin for possible abuse, and as a result meprobamate is classified as a Schedule IV drug, requiring limits on the number of prescription refills. Meprobamate is still occasionally prescribed for anxiety and insomnia, but since 1960 it has been far eclipsed by a different class of antianxiety drugs called benzodiazepines.

Benzodiazepines

The introduction of a new group of drugs, called **benzodiazepines,** was a dramatic departure from all earlier attempts to treat anxiety. On the one hand, for the first time, there now were drugs that had a *selective* effect on anxiety itself, instead of producing some generalized reduction in the body's overall level of functioning. It was their tranquilizing effects, rather than their sedative effects, that made benzodiazepines so appealing to mental health professionals. On the other hand, it is important to distinguish between the well-publicized virtues of benzodiazepines when they were first introduced in the 1960s and the data that accumulated during the 1970s as millions of people experienced these new drugs. While very useful in the treatment of anxiety and other stress-related problems, benzodiazepines are no longer recognized as the miracle drugs they were promoted to be when they were first marketed.

Before taking up the specific facts about benzodiazepine drugs, it is important to understand how their discovery has given us some insight into the nature of anxiety itself. As the pharmacologist Robert Julien has defined it;

Anxiety can be described as apprehension, tension, or uneasiness that stems from the anticipation of danger, which may be internal or external. It may be a response to stress that is associated with external stimuli, or it may be devoid of any apparent precipitating stimulus.[14]

As Fig. 5.2 shows, feelings of anxiety can be considered along a continuum of emotions that range in magnitude or intensity from a complete lack of concern, to moderate apprehension, justified or unjustified anxiety, finally to outright panic. You can see that some of these emotional states have a gen-

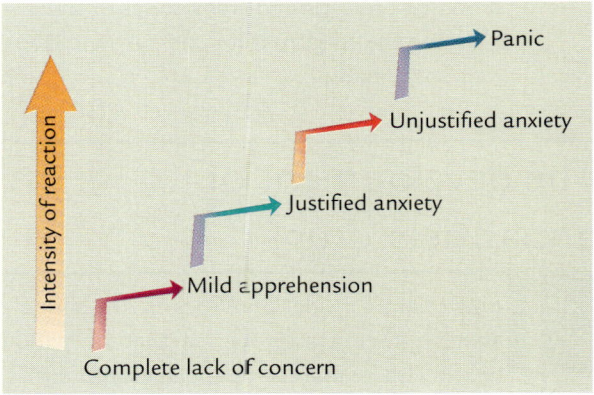

FIGURE 5.2

Levels of anxiety and stress
SOURCE: A Primer of Drug Action *by Julien. Copyright © 1992 by W. H. Freeman and Company.*

> **benzodiazepines (BEN-zoh-dye-AZ-eh-pins)**
> A family of antianxiety drugs. Examples are diazepam (Valium), chlordiazepoxide (Librium), and triazolam (Halcion).

uine adaptive purpose; we would be less able to survive in a hostile and potentially dangerous world if we were not on our guard and capable of anticipating or responding to possible hazards surrounding us. Our highly developed sympathetic autonomic nervous system (see Chapter 3) is designed to mobilize the resources of our bodies to deal with threats and challenges.

When anxiety interferes with our daily lives or when it causes us great personal distress, however, then an adaptive emotion has become maladaptive. We refer to these conditions as **anxiety disorders.** It has been estimated that approximately 16 percent of the U.S. population (more than 40 million people) has suffered from an anxiety disorder sometime in their lifetime.[15]

Given the importance of some level of anxiety in our survival as a species, it should not be surprising that specific mechanisms in the brain have developed that concern themselves specifically with this emotion. In that sense, we can view antianxiety drugs in terms of their ability to help in the treatment of conditions in which a normal physiological process has gotten essentially out of hand.[16] The neural basis for anxiety will be examined later in this chapter.

Public speaking is often regarded as one of the most anxiety-producing situations in an individual's life.

TABLE 5.3

The leading benzodiazepines on the market

Trade name	Generic name	Half-life (in hours)*
Long-acting benzodiazepines		
Valium	diazepam	20–100
Librium	chlordiazepoxide	8–100
Dalmane	flurazepam	70–160
Centrax	prazepam	50–100
Tranxene	chlorazepate	50–100
Intermediate-acting benzodiazepines		
Ativan	lorazepam	10–24
Klonopin	clonazepam	18–50
Restoril	temazepam	8–35
Short-acting benzodiazepines		
Versed	midazolam	2–5
Serax	oxazepam	5–15
Halcion	triazolam	2–5
Xanax	alprazolam	11–18

*A half-life is the interval of time for a drug to be half of its original strength.

SOURCE: Adapted from Julien, Robert M. (1995). *A primer of drug action* (7th ed.). New York: Freeman, p. 80.

Medical uses of benzodiazepines

The first marketed benzodiazepine, **chlordiazepoxide** (brand name: Librium), was introduced in 1960, followed by **diazepam** (brand name: Valium) in 1963. Table 5.3 lists twelve of the major benzodiazepine drugs currently on the market. While they are all chemically related, their potencies and time courses vary considerably. Valium, for example, is five to ten times stronger than Librium

anxiety disorder
A psychological condition dominated by excessive worry, sympathetic autonomic activity, and maladaptive behavior.

chlordiazepoxide (CHLOR-dye-az-eh-POX-eyed)
A major benzodiazepine drug for the treatment of anxiety. Brand name is Librium.

diazepam (dye-AZ-eh-pam)
A major benzodiazepine drug in the treatment of anxiety. Brand name is Valium.

and takes effect about one hour sooner. The relatively quicker response from Valium is a principal factor in making it more popular than Librium.

The variations in benzodiazepine effects have led to different recommendations for their medical use. Oral administrations of the relatively long-acting benzodiazepines, in general, are recommended for relief from anxiety, with the effects beginning thirty minutes to four hours after ingestion. Besides Librium and Valium, other examples of this type include flurazepam (brand name: Dalmane) and prazepam (brand name: Centrax). When a very quick effect is desired, an injectable form of diazepam is used either to reduce the symptoms of agitation that follow alcohol withdrawal (delirium tremens, or the D.T.s), as an anticonvulsant for epileptic patients, or as a preanesthetic drug to relax the patient just prior to surgery. In contrast, shorter-acting oral benzodiazepines are recommended for sleeping problems because their effects begin more quickly and wear off well before morning. Examples of this type include triazolam (brand name: Halcion), alprazolam (brand name: Xanax), and temazepam (brand name: Restoril).

How effective are benzodiazepines for the treatment of anxiety? In order to answer this question, it is very important to conduct a double-blind study (see Chapter 3) and compare a representative benzodiazepine such as Valium to a placebo control that looks like Valium but produces no physiological effects. In studies of this type, Valium is observed to be helpful for about 70 to 80 percent of people with an anxiety disorder. Approximately 25 to 30 percent of them, however, are helped by the placebo alone, so it is also evident that psychological factors play some role in the final outcome.[17] Interestingly, benzodiazepines work best when the physician prescribing the medication is perceived as being warm, has a positive attitude toward use of antianxiety drugs, and believes that the patient would improve (Table 5.4).[18] The positive impact of such factors upon the outcome of treatment

TABLE 5.4
Factors that predict successful treatment with benzodiazepines
Physician attributes
Warmth
Liking the patient
Feeling comfortable with the patient
Believing the patient has good prospects for improvement
Patient attributes
High verbal intelligence
Compliance with the physician
Realistic treatment goals
Low verbal hostility
High level of education
High occupational status
Marital stability
Orientation and expectations prior to treatment
Realization that problems are emotional rather than physical
Expectation that drugs will be part of the treatment

SOURCE: Adapted from Rickels, Karl (1981). Benzodiazepines: Clinical use patterns. In Stephen I. Szara and Jacqueline P. Ludford (Eds.), *Benzodiazepines: A review of research results 1980* (NIDA Research Monograph 33). Rockville MD: National Institute on Drug Abuse, p. 46.

underscores the importance of the physician-patient relationship, along with the genuine antianxiety effects of the drug itself.

Acute effects of benzodiazepines

In general, benzodiazepines are absorbed relatively slowly into the bloodstream, so their relaxant effects last longer and are more gradual than those of barbiturates. The primary reason for these differences lies in the fact that benzodiazepines are absorbed from the small intestine rather than the stomach, as is the case with barbiturates. The relatively greater water-solubility, and by implication the relatively lower fat-solubility, of benzodiazepines also is a factor.

The major advantage that benzodiazepines have over barbiturates is their higher level of safety. Respiratory centers in the medulla are not affected by benzodiazepines, so it is rare that a person will die of respiratory failure from an accidental or intentional overdose.

Even after taking fifty or sixty times the therapeutic dose, the person will still not stop breathing. It is almost always possible to arouse a person from the stupor that such a drug quantity would produce. In contrast, doses of barbiturates or nonbarbiturate sedatives that are ten to twenty times the therapeutic dose are lethal.[19]

Yet, we should understand that this higher level of safety assumes that *combinations are not being made with alcohol or other depressant drugs taken at the same time.* If we looked at the DAWN statistics for 1992, we would see a major difference between the consequences of an overdose of benzodiazepines alone and an overdose of benzodiazepines in combination. For example, of the total 1992 emergency room (ER) mentions involving Valium, the patient reported in only 21 percent of these cases having ingested the drug alone. In all other cases, there was at least one other drug involved. When we look at the record of medical examiner (ME) mentions that resulted in death, the combination-drug effect is also apparent. Valium is reported to have been involved in 9 percent of the cases (the fifth highest-mentioned drug), but less than 2 percent of these ME mentions involved Valium alone.[20] The bottom line is that taking Valium or another benzodiazepine drug by itself is relatively safe, but taking it in combination with other drugs (particularly alcohol) is quite dangerous.

Nonetheless, despite the very low risk of successful suicide from Valium and other benzodiazepines, there are a number of medical risks for special populations. For elderly patients, for example, the rate of elimination of these drugs is slowed down significantly, resulting in the risk of a dangerously high buildup of benzodiazepines after several doses. In the case of a long-acting benzodiazepine such as Valium or Librium, the half-life (the time it takes for the drug level in the body to be reduced by one half) is for them as long as ten days. An elderly patient with this rate of elimination would not be totally drug free until sixty days or so have passed. The continued accumulation of benzodiazepines produces a type of drug-induced dementia in which the patient suffers from confusion and loss of memory. There have been reports of birth defects, when women have taken benzodiazepines during the first trimester of their pregnancy but it is unclear whether the mothers were taking other drugs during this period.[21]

Chronic effects of benzodiazepines

The benzodiazepines were originally viewed as having few if any problems relating to a tolerance effect or an acquired dependence. We now know that the anxiety-relieving aspects of benzodiazepines show little or no tolerance effects when the drugs are taken at prescribed dosages, but there is a tolerance to the sedative effects. In other words, if the drugs are taken for the purpose of relieving anxiety, there is no problem with tolerance, but if they are taken for insomnia, more of the drug may be required in later administrations to induce sleep.[22]

We also now know that physiological symptoms appear when benzodiazepines are withdrawn. In the case of Valium and other long-acting benzodiazepines, the slow rate of elimination delays the appearance of withdrawal symptoms until between the third and sixth day following drug withdrawal. The first signs include an anxiety level that may be worse than the level for which the drug was originally prescribed. Later, there are symptoms of insomnia, restlessness, and agitation. In general, however, withdrawal symptoms are less severe than those observed after barbiturate withdrawal. occur only after long-term use, and are gone in one to four weeks (Focus 5.3).[23]

Patterns of benzodiazepine misuse and abuse

Benzodiazepines do not present the same potential for abuse that cocaine, alcohol, or the barbiturates do, for two primary reasons. First, benzodiazepines are only weak rein-

Nine guidelines for avoiding the misuse of benzodiazepine drugs

1. Do not think of benzodiazepines as cures. These drugs are optimally used to give temporary relief until the cause of the anxiety can be removed.

2. Do not think of benzodiazepines as the main treatment. Think of them instead as a supporting treatment. Get appropriate medical, psychological, or pastoral help.

3. Do not take benzodiazepines without first having a psychiatric examination to make sure that your anxiety is not due to a depression, bipolar disorder (where mania alternates with depression), or some other treatable mental illness.

4. Do not use benzodiazepines if you are a heavy drinker or suffer from alcoholism.

5. Do not use benzodiazepines for insomnia for more than four nights in a row.

6. Do not use benzodiazepines continuously for more than two months without a "drug holiday" (a discontinuation of the drug) lasting several weeks.

7. Do not increase the dose of a benzodiazepine without consulting a physician. Do not refill your prescription without revisiting your physician.

8. Do not keep more than fourteen daily doses of benzodiazepines on hand at any one time.

9. Do not drive under the influence of benzodiazepines, and whatever you do, do not drive under the influence of benzodiazepines and alcohol.

SOURCES: Lickey, Marvin E., and Gordon, Barbara (1983). *Drugs for mental illness: A revolution in psychiatry.* New York: Freeman, pp. 263–264. Lickey, Marvin E., and Gordon, Barbara (1991). *Medicine and mental illness: The use of drugs in psychiatry.* New York: Freeman, pp. 325–326.

forcers of behavior. When trained to press a lever for an injection of Valium, for example, laboratory animals will self-administer the drug but at far less robust levels than they would show for self-administering pentobarbital or methaqualone. Studies with normal college-student volunteers show that, when given the choice between a placebo and Valium and the true identity of neither choice is known, the placebo is actually preferred. For these individuals, presumably nondrug abusers and relatively anxiety free, the results show no indication of a positive Valium reaction.[24] Second, the slow onset of a benzodiazepine effect prevents the sudden "rush" feeling that is characteristic of many abused drugs such as cocaine or heroin.

The foregoing is *not* to say, however, that benzodiazepines fail to be abused. It is simply that their abuse exists in the context of abusing other drugs as well, often referred to as multiple substance abuse or polydrug abuse. Alcoholics, for example, will sometimes take benzodiazepines at work, in order to relax and avoid having the smell of alcohol on their breath. Heroin abusers may take benzodiazepines to augment their euphoria and reduce their anxiety when the opiate levels in their blood begin to fall. Cocaine abusers may take the drugs to soften the crashing feeling that is experienced as the cocaine starts to wear off.[25]

Therefore, the principal social problems surrounding the taking of benzodiazepine drugs, since their introduction in the 1960s, have arisen more from their *misuse* than from their abuse (Chapter 1). The greatest concern during the 1960s and 1970s was the enormous quantity of benzodiazepine prescriptions that were being written. In 1972 Valium ranked first (and Librium third) among the most frequently prescribed drugs of any type. In 1975 alone, more than 100 million such prescriptions were processed around the world, with 85 million in the United States. In Western Europe and North America, it was estimated that 10 to 20 percent of adults were taking benzodiazepines on a fairly regular basis.[26]

More recently, the number has declined substantially, but benzodiazepines currently remain among the "top thirty" prescription medications. A major problem has been that such prescriptions were and continue to be written not by psychiatrists but by general practitioners and family doctors who respond to their patient's need for a medical answer to stress and anxiety. It is important to understand that antianxiety drugs may reduce a patient's stress and anxiety but do not really help resolve any of the social, family, and personal problems that produce that stress and anxiety (Focus 5.4). Specialists in the problems of drug misuse have phrased it this way:

> Taking a sleeping pill may help you sleep on the nights you take one, but pills do not make one's relationship with one's spouse any better, or improve one's job situation, or change any of the stressors that may be causing the insomnia in the first place. In fact, a hidden danger occurs when the use of drugs masks these symptoms and allows the person to function under less than optimal environmental conditions.[27]

Cross tolerance and cross dependence

If you were taking a barbiturate for an extended length of time and you developed a tolerance for its effect, you might have also

---

FOCUS 5.4

The controversy over Halcion

When triazolam (brand name: Halcion) was introduced in 1983, it was hailed as an effective benzodiazepine with a brief onset time that made it ideal for the treatment of insomnia. Halcion soon became the most widely prescribed sleeping pill. Sold in more than ninety countries, in 1991 Halcion had annual worldwide sales of $250 million. Approximately 7 million prescriptions for Halcion were written in the United States alone.

Disturbing reports gained wide attention, however, that pointed to significant adverse side effects. In 1989 a multimil-lion-dollar civil suit was brought against the Upjohn Pharmaceutical Company (which manufactures Halcion) by a woman who claimed that she had been involuntarily intoxicated while taking Halcion as a prescription drug for insomnia and killed her mother as a result. In 1991 the suit was settled out of court just prior to the beginning of the trial, with an undisclosed amount paid by the company.

While obviously an extreme case, the situation that precipitated the lawsuit was not an isolated one. The FDA, through a system of "post-marketing surveillance," has collected reports on Halcion (as it does on all prescription drugs), submitted by physicians whenever unusual or adverse reactions are observed. Specific reactions have included anxiety, memory loss, hostility, and paranoia. The number of adverse-reaction reports for Halcion from 1983 to 1986 was eight to thirty times the combined number of reports received with regard to two other benzodiazepine medications, Dalmane and Restoril. This comparison is particularly striking, since it covered a period of time when the latter two drugs were more widely available than Halcion. In light of the accumulated facts about Halcion, it was a matter of public concern in 1991 that President George Bush and Secretary of State James Baker were both taking Halcion for insomnia while on trips abroad.

Gradually, the warning information on Halcion medication has been made more specific. A revised package insert in 1987 reduced the recommended starting dose by 50 percent and acknowledged that "bizarre or abnormal behavior, agitation, and hallucinations" might possibly be responses to higher dosages. Two years later, the label was changed to state that amnesia "may occur at a higher rate with Halcion than with other benzodiazepine hypnotics." Nonetheless, in 1992, the FDA ruled that Halcion was safe and effective, though the label warnings should be strengthened beyond the ones presently in force. It also recommended a large-scale study to investigate its safety and whether the dosage levels should be reduced even more.

SOURCES: Sweet dreams or nightmare? (1991, August 19). *Newsweek*, pp. 44–51. Kolata, Gina (1992, May 19). FDA panel recommends keeping sleeping pill on market. *New York Times*, p. C3.

developed a tolerance for another depressant drug even though you have not ever in your life taken the second drug. In other words, a tolerance effect for one drug automatically induced a tolerance for another. We can see this phenomenon, called **cross tolerance,** when we look at the physiological and psychological effects of alcohol, barbiturates, and benzodiazepines. As a result of cross tolerance, an alcoholic will have already developed a tolerance for a barbiturate, or a barbiturate abuser will need a greater amount of an anesthetic when in surgery.

We see the interconnectedness of depressant drugs in another way. If we can relieve the withdrawal symptoms of one drug by administering another drug, then the two drugs show **cross dependence.** In other words, if cross dependence exists between two drugs, one drug can substitute for whatever physiological effects have been produced by a second drug that has been discontinued. The family of depressant drugs show this phenomenon. Unfortunately, cross dependence provides a means for continuing an abused drug in the guise of a new one:

When drug abuse becomes obvious and embarrassing or when the preferred drug becomes unavailable, the user can switch to a cross-dependent drug to avoid the withdrawal illness. A woman who wants to conceal her drinking from the family might substitute some diazepam for her morning eye opener.[28]

The effects of cross tolerance and cross dependence would not be possible if there were not a common mechanism in the brain that produced the behavioral and physiological effects. It turns out that in the case of benzodiazepines, a special receptor has been discovered that not only explains benzodiazepine effects but also explains the relationship between benzodiazepines and depressant drugs in general.

How benzodiazepines work in the brain

The key factor in the action of benzodiazepines is the neurotransmitter gamma aminobutyric acid (GABA), which normally exerts an inhibitory effect on the nervous system (Chapter 3). When benzodiazepines are in the vicinity of GABA receptors, the actions of GABA are increased. The antianxiety drugs attach themselves to their own receptors on the membrane of neurons and in doing so heighten the effect of GABA. The facilitation of GABA produces a greater inhibition and a decreased activity level in the neurons involved.[29]

The receptor that is involved here is a large protein molecule that has at least three binding locations, arranged like docking sites for three different kinds of boats. As displayed in Fig. 5.3, there exists a binding site for sedative-hypnotics (including the barbiturates

cross tolerance
A phenomenon in which the tolerance that results from the chronic use of one drug induces a tolerance effect with regard to a second drug that has not been experienced.

cross dependence
A phenomenon in which one drug can be used to reduce the withdrawal symptoms following the discontinuance of another drug.

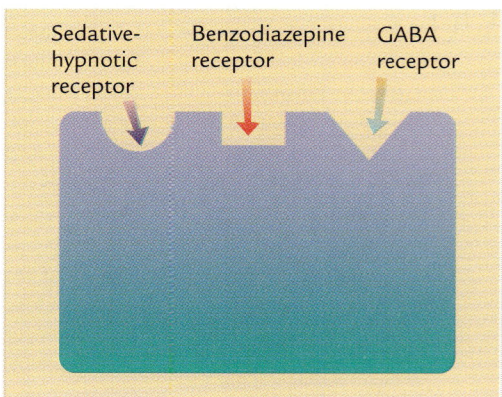

F I G U R E   5 . 3

The benzodiazepine receptor

Barbara Gordon—
A case history of
Valium withdrawal

Jill Clayburgh as Barbara Gordon in the 1982 film, I'm dancing as fast as I can.

Barbara Gordon's 1979 autobiographical account of her experience with Valium, *I'm dancing as fast as I can,* has come to represent the dark side of an era when Valium was at its peak. In the mid-1970s, 100 million prescriptions were being written for Valium each year, at dosages that were often far higher than we now know are considered safe. While Gordon's experiences are not typical, her dramatic retelling of her symptoms during an abrupt withdrawal from Valium nonetheless created a sensation. Her book and the 1982 film based on the book helped to alert the public to the potential of Valium dependence.

As a successful career woman and award-winning television producer with a satisfying personal and social life, Barbara Gordon could be considered to have had it all. But underneath the appearance of apparent success, there was significant anxiety in her life, temporarily masked by the effects of Valium. She described her experience as follows:

I had started taking Valium for a back problem, beginning with four milligrams a day. Now I was up to thirty and couldn't get out of the house without taking them. I was taking them before an anxiety attack, trying to ward it off, or to minimize the terror. And that didn't always work either.

Gordon decided to stop taking the drug and try to get on with her life. Her psychiatrist, however, gave little support in this regard, as revealed in this conversation:

"I've enough pills for a while, Dr. Allen," I said. "Besides, I've come to a decision this morning. I'm not going to take Valium again—ever." . . . I waited for his response to this new-found independence of mine.

"I've told you many times, Miss Gordon," he said with a hint of impatience, "they are nonaddictive and do a great deal to help you. Perhaps you'd like a little Stelazine [an antipsychotic medication]?" . . .

"No, no more pills, Dr. Allen, no more pills. I'm going off Valium. What do you think of that?" And again, I waited for his response, for him to tell me how strong I was, that I was doing the right thing.

"All right, Miss Gordon, then don't take one, not one. Do it absolutely cold. As a matter of fact, don't even have a sip of wine and I'm sure you'll do fine. Call me if you need anything or if you change your mind. But remember, don't take even one."

The withdrawal from Valium was anything but uneventful. Once again, in her words:

By early afternoon, I began to feel a creeping sense of terror. It felt like little jolts of electricity, as if charged pins and needles were shooting through my body. My breathing became rapid and I began to perspire. . . . My scalp started to burn as if I had hot coals under my hair. Then I began to experience funny little twitches, spasms, a jerk of a leg, a flying arm, tiny tremors that soon turned into convulsions. I held on to the bed, trying to relax. It was impossible.

When her relationships began to come apart and her anxiety grew, Gordon required hospitalization for several months.

It is important to understand that some of her withdrawal symptoms may have been manifestations of the underlying anxiety disorder that had been masked over the years by Valium. Fortunately, despite the "bumpy ride," Gordon eventually recovered. Her decision to publish her experiences was in part motivated by her realization that others would benefit from knowing the long-term consequences of antianxiety drugs. As she concludes:

They aren't just medicines. They are drugs that can be anesthetics of the emotions. And their sudden withdrawal can precipitate psychosis and, in some cases, death. Because of my strong feelings about medical mismanagement, because of the prevalence of drug abuse—and the soft-core prescription-pad variety is drug abuse all the same—I felt I had to tell my story.

SOURCE: Quotes from pages 50–51, 52, 311 from *I'm dancing as fast as I can* by Barbara Gordon. Copyright © 1979 by Barbara Gordon. Reprinted by permission of HarperCollins Publishers, Inc.

and possibly alcohol), a binding site for benzodiazepines, and finally a binding site for GABA. When GABA attaches to its binding site, there is greater inhibition if the benzodiazepine sites are also occupied at the time by a benzodiazepine drug than if they are not occupied.[30] A successful binding of chemicals at each of the separate sites will facilitate the binding at the others. It is not difficult, therefore, to imagine how cross tolerance and cross dependence among depressant drugs might occur.

Where are these receptors? They are understood to be localized primarily in the limbic system and the cerebral cortex. It is believed that receptors in the limbic system underlie the antianxiety action of benzodiazepines (since the limbic system is involved with emotionality), while receptors in the cortex underlie their sedative actions.

Buspirone: The antianxiety drug for the 1990s?

ince 1986 a new type of antianxiety drug has been available called **buspirone** (brand name: BuSpar), with a number of remarkable features. It has been found to be equivalent to Valium in its ability to relieve anxiety. Yet, unlike the benzodiazepines in general, buspirone shows no cross tolerance or cross dependence with alcohol or other depressants and no withdrawal symptoms when discontinued after chronic use. When compared to benzodiazepines, side effects are observed less frequently and are less troublesome to the patient; 9 percent report dizziness and 7 per-

buspirone (BYOO-spir-rone)
A nonbenzodiazepine antianxiety drug, first introduced in 1986, for the treatment of anxiety. Brand name is BuSpar.

Understanding cross tolerance and cross dependence

heck your understanding of cross tolerance and cross dependence by answering the following questions.

Suppose you have two receptors in the brain, as shown below.

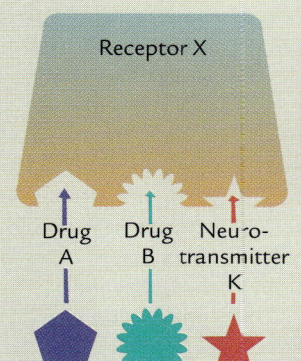

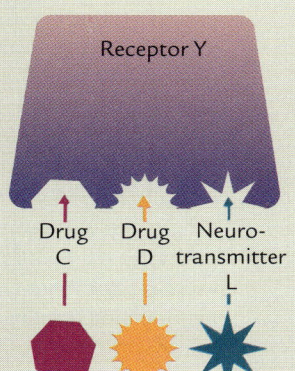

Notice that Receptor X has three binding sites, one for drug A, one for drug B, and one for neurotransmitter K. Receptor Y also has three binding sites, one for drug C, one for drug D, and one for neurotransmitter L.

Based upon this information, answer yes or no whether the following pairs of drugs show cross tolerance and cross dependence with each other.

1. drug A and drug B	❑ yes	❑ no
2. drug A and drug C	❑ yes	❑ no
3. drug B and drug C	❑ yes	❑ no
4. drug C and drug D	❑ yes	❑ no
5. drug B and drug D	❑ yes	❑ no
6. drug A and drug D	❑ yes	❑ no

ANSWERS: 1. Yes 2. No 3. No 4. Yes 5. No 6. No

cent report headaches. Animals will not self-administer buspirone in laboratory studies, and human volunteers indicate an absence of euphoria.

Buspirone also fails to show the impairments in motor skills that are characteristic of benzodiazepines. In other words, the relief of anxiety is attainable without the accompanying feelings and behavioral consequences of sedation. Perhaps anxiety and sedation do not have to be necessarily intertwined after all. Unlike benzodiazepines, buspirone does not affect GABA receptors in the brain but rather acts upon a special subclass of serotonin receptors instead. It remains unclear how the influence of buspirone on serotonin produces the antianxiety effects.

Despite its virtues, however, buspirone has a distinct disadvantage: a very long delay before anxiety relief is felt. Several weeks may need to pass before the drug becomes effective. This feature makes buspirone clearly inappropriate for relieving acute anxiety on an emergency basis, and many patients suffering from chronic anxiety may simply be

QUICK CONCEPT CHECK 5.2

Understanding the abuse potential in drugs

Each of the following statements refers to the description of a particular attribute of a new drug. Based upon material in this chapter, judge whether each description, when taken by itself, either increases or decreases the abuse potential of the drug.

1. Drug fails to produce euphoria at any dose levels.

2. Drug acts very quickly.

3. Drug is cross tolerant to barbiturates and alcohol.

4. Drug is not available to the public.

5. There are tolerance effects when taking th s drug.

6. The drug can be used without the need for medical supervision of dose or dosage schedule.

ANSWERS: 1. decreases 2. increases 3. increases 4. decreases 5. increases 6. increases

---

TABLE 5.5

The advantages of buspirone over other means to reduce anxiety

Factor for possible abuse	Alcohol	Barbituates	Benzodiazepines	Buspirone
Euphoria	++	+++	+	0
Rapid action	+++	++	+	0
Unsupervised use	++++	++	++	0
Social encouragement	++++	++	+	0
Tolerance	++	++	+	0
Physical dependence	++++	+++	++	0
Cross-tolerance	+++	+++	+++	0
Cross-dependence	+++	+++	+++	0
Total	25	20	14	0

Note: Each plus sign indicates a degree of abuse potential. The greater the total number of plus signs, the greater the overall abuse potential for each drug. A zero indicates that the drug has no value with regard to a particular factor.

SOURCE: Modified from Lickey, Marvin E., and Gordon, Barbara (1991). *Medicine and mental illness.* New York: Freeman, p. 324.

too impatient to wait for the drug to take hold. Yet, on a positive side, the long delay in the action of buspirone makes it highly undesirable as a drug of abuse. We should not expect to see news headlines in the future warning us of an epidemic of buspirone abuse (Table 5.5)

Whether or not buspirone fulfills its promise as the ultimate antianxiety drug without the dangers of sedation is a question yet to be fully answered. For the long-term treatment of anxiety, buspirone appears to be a positive development. As has been recently noted, however, "It is too soon . . . to launch a buspirone bandwagon Buspirone is a very new drug, and unforeseen problems may come to light as time goes on."[31]

Summary

BARBITURATES

- The primary sedative-hypnotics, drugs that produce sedation and sleep, from 1903 to approximately 1960 have belonged to the family of barbiturate drugs.

- Barbiturates are typically classified by virtue of how long their depressant effects are felt, from long-acting (example: phenobarbital) to intermediate-acting (examples: secobarbital and amobarbital) to short-acting (example: pentobarbital).

- A major disadvantage of barbiturates is the potential of a lethal overdose, particularly when combined with other depressants such as alcohol. In addition, barbiturate withdrawal symptoms are very severe and require careful medical attention.

NONBARBITURATE SEDATIVE-HYPNOTICS

- Methaqualone (Quaalude) was introduced in the 1960s as an alternate to barbiturates for sedation and sleep. Unfortunately, this drug produced undesirable side effects and became subject to widespread abuse. It is no longer available as a licit drug.

THE DEVELOPMENT OF ANTIANXIETY DRUGS

- Beginning in the 1950s, a major effort in the pharmaceutical industry was made to develop a drug that would relieve anxiety (tranquilize) rather than merely depress the CNS.

- Meprobamate (Miltown) was introduced in 1955 for this purpose, though it is now understood that the effects of this drug result more from its sedative properties than its ability to relieve anxiety.

BENZODIAZEPINES

- The introduction of benzodiazepines, specifically diazepam (Valium) and chlordiazepoxide (Librium), in the early 1960s, was a significant breakthrough in the development of antianxiety drugs. These drugs selectively affected specific receptors in the brain instead of acting as general depressants of the nervous system.

- In general, benzodiazepines are safer drugs than barbiturates, when taken alone. When taken in combination with alcohol, however, dangerous synergistic effects are observed.

- Social problems concerning the taking of benzodiazepine drugs during the 1970s centered around the widespread misuse of the drug. Prescriptions were written too frequently and for excessive dosages.

- Benzodiazepines produce their effects by binding onto receptors in the limbic system and cerebral cortex in the brain that are sensitive to the inhibitory neurotransmitter gamma amino-butyric acid (GABA).

BUSPIRONE: THE ANTIANXIETY DRUG FOR THE 1990S?

- The search for the perfect sedative-hypnotic or the perfect antianxiety drug continues. The latest candidate for the latter role is buspirone (BuSpar), introduced in 1986.

- Buspirone offers a number of advantages over barbiturates and benzodiazepines. A disadvantage of buspirone, however, is the very long delay before its effects are felt, which makes it useful for long-term anxiety relief but not for emergency purposes.

Key Terms

Endnotes

1. Palfai, Tibor, and Jankiewicz, Henry *Drugs and human behavior.* Dubuque IA: W. C. Brown, p. 203.

2. Jacobs, Michael R., and Fehr, Kevin O'B. (1987). *Drugs and drug abuse: A reference text* (2nd ed.). Toronto: Addiction Research Foundation, pp. 183–194.

3. Palfai and Jankiewicz. *Drugs and human behavior,* p. 213.

4. Jacobs and Fehr. *Drugs and drug abuse,* p. 189.

5. Kauffman, Janice F., Shaffer, Howard, and Burglass, Milton E. (1985). The biological basics: Drugs and their effects. In Thomas E. Bratter and Gary G. Forrest (Eds.), *Alcoholism and substance abuse: Strategies for clinical intervention.* New York: Free Press, pp. 107–136.

6. Sleeping pills and antianxiety drugs (1988). *The Harvard Medical School Mental Health Letter, 5* (6), 1–4.

7. Griffiths, Roland R., Lukas, Scott E., Bradford, L. D., Brady, Joseph V., and Snell, Jack D. (1981). Self-injection of barbiturates and benzodiazepines in baboons. *Psychopharmacology, 75,* 101–109.

8. Griffiths, Roland R., Bigelow, George, and Liebson, Ira (1979). Human drug self-administration: Double-blind comparison of pentobarbital, diazepam, chlorpromazine, and placebo. *Journal of Pharmacology and Experimental Therapeutics, 210,* 301–310.

9. Johnston, Lloyd, O'Malley, Patrick M., and Bachman, Jerald (1994). *National survey results on drug use from the Monitoring the Future study, 1975–1993.* Vol. 1. Rockville MD: National Institute on Drug Abuse, Table 1.

10. Carroll, Marilyn, and Gallo, Gary (1985). *Quaaludes: The quest for oblivion.* New York: Chelsea House.

11. Text of advertisement of Miltown by Wallace Laboratories, New Brunswick, New Jersey. In Palfai and Jankiewicz. *Drugs and human behavior,* p. 222.

12. Julien, Robert M. (1995). *A primer of drug action* (7th ed.). New York: Freeman, p. 64.

13. Berger, Philip A., and Tinklenberg, Jared R. (1977). Treatment of abusers of alcohol and other addictive drugs. In Jack D. Barchas, Philip A. Berger, Roland D. Caranello, and Glen R. Elliott (Eds.), *Psychopharmacology: From theory to practice.* New York: Oxford University Press, pp. 355–385.

14. Julien. *A primer of drug action,* p. 94.

15. Robins, Lee N., Helzer, John E., Weissman, Myrna M., Orvaschel, Helen, Gruenberg, Ernest, Burke, Jack D., Jr., and Regier, Darrel A. (1984). Lifetime prevalence of specific psychiatric disorders in three sites. *Archives of General Psychiatry, 41,* 949–958.

16. Julien. *A primer of drug action,* pp. 74–75.

17. Leavitt, Fred (1982). *Drugs and behavior* (2nd ed.). New York: Wiley.

18. Rickels, Karl (1981). Benzodiazepines: Clinical use patterns. In Stephen I. Szara and Jacqueline P. Ludford (Eds.), *Benzodiazepines: A review of research results 1980* (NIDA Research Monograph 33). Rockville MD: National Institute on Drug Abuse, pp. 43–60.

19. Lickey, Marvin E., and Gordon, Barbara (1991). *Medicine and mental illness.* New York: Freeman, p. 280.

20. Substance Abuse and Mental Health Services Administration (1994). Annual emergency room data 1992. Data from the drug abuse warning network (DAWN). Series I, Number 12-A. Rockville MD: Substance Abuse and Mental Health Services Administration, Office of Applied Studies, pp. 30, 49. Substance Abuse and Mental Health Services Administration (1994). Annual medical examiner data 1992. Data from the drug abuse warning network (DAWN). Series I, Number 12-B. Rockville MD: Substance Abuse and Mental Health Services Administration, Office of Applied Studies, pp. 16, 31.

21. Julien. *A primer of drug action,* pp. 81–86.

22. Rickels, Karl, Case, W. George, Downing, Robert W., and Winokur, Andrew (1983). Long-term diazepam therapy and clinical outcome. *Journal of the American Medical Association, 250,* 767–771.

23. Julien. *A primer of drug action,* p. 85–86.

24. Griffiths, Roland R., and Ator, Nancy A. Benzodiazepine self-administration in animals and humans: A comprehensive literature review. In Stephen I. Szara and Jacqueline P. Ludford (Eds.), *Benzodiazepines: A review of research results, 1980* (NIDA Research Monograph 33). Rockville MD: National Institute on Drug Abuse, pp. 22–36.

25. Julien. *A primer of drug action,* pp. 86-87.

26. Lickey and Gordon. *Medicine and mental illness,* p. 278.

27. Maistro, Stephen A., Galizio, Mark, and Connors, Gerard J. (1991). *Drug use and misuse.* Fort Worth TX Holt, Rinehart, and Winston, p. 239.

28. Lickey and Gordon. *Medicine and mental illness,* p. 323.

29. Mohler, H., and Okada, T. (1977). Benzodiazepine receptors in rat brain: Demonstration in the central nervous system. *Science, 198,* 849–851. Squires, Richard F., and Braestrup, Claus (1977). Benzodiazepine receptors in rat brain. *Nature, 266,* 732–734.

30. Lickey and Gordon. *Medicine and mental illness,* p. 291.

31. Ibid., pp. 293–325, quotation on p. 325. Julien. *A primer of drug action,* pp. 81–86.

6

Glues, Solvents, and Other Inhalants

ometimes, psychoactive drugs do not originate in a pharmacy or a liquor store or even on the street. They can be found under the sink, in kitchen or bathroom cabinets, in the basement, or in the garage. Ordinary household products frequently have the potential for giving euphoriant effects if they are sniffed or inhaled. When you consider that these substances are available to anyone in a family, including its youngest members, the consequences of their abuse become particularly troubling. This chapter will concern itself with glues, solvents, and other inhalant products, as dangerous recreational drugs.

Inhalants through history

he mind-altering effects of substances inhaled into the lungs has been known since the beginnings of recorded history. Burnt spices and aromatic gums were used in acts of worship in most parts of the ancient world; perfumes were inhaled during Egyptian worship as well as in Babylonian rituals. Inhalation effects also figured prominently in the famous rites of the oracle at Delphi in ancient Greece, where trances induced by the inhaling of vapors led to mysterious utterances that were interpreted as predictions of future events.[2] Whether any of these phenomena were due to genuine psychoactive effects rather than to placebo effects is difficult to tell, since it is not known what substances were involved. It was not until the latter part of the eighteenth century that reports about the inhalation of specific drugs began to appear. The two most prominent examples were cases involving nitrous oxide and ether.

"I remember," Julio says, taking quick, nervous puffs from his cigarette, "when I was a little kid, maybe eight or nine, and I used to take the garbage out for my mother, I'd always see tubes from airplane glue under the stairwell in our apartment house and in the alley out back. At first, glue just meant building models to me. But I'd see people sniffing it, under the stairwell. I was curious, and one day I tried it. It made me feel like I was in a trance. It wasn't really exciting, but I did it again and again until we moved, and in the new neighborhood people weren't into glue and I didn't see the empty tubes to remind me anymore."[1]

These anesthetic drugs were first used as surgical analgesics in the 1840s, but they had been synthesized decades earlier. From the very start, the word had spread that there were recreational possibilities.

Nitrous oxide

The British chemist Sir Humphrey Davy synthesized the gas **nitrous oxide** in 1798 at the precocious age of nineteen. He immediately observed the pleasant effects of this "laughing gas" and proceeded to give nitrous-oxide parties for his literary and artistic friends. By the early 1800s, recreational use of nitrous oxide became widespread both in England and the United States as a nonalcoholic avenue to drunkenness. In the 1840s, public demonstrations were being organized in cities and towns, as a traveling show, by entrepreneurs eager to market the drug commercially.

It was at such an exhibition in Hartford, Connecticut, that a young dentist, Horace Wells, got the idea for using nitrous oxide as an anesthetic. One of the intoxicated participants in the demonstration had stumbled and fallen, resulting in a severe wound in the leg. Seeing that the man showed no pain despite his injury, Wells was sufficiently impressed to try out the anesthetic possibilities himself. The next day, he underwent a tooth extraction while under the influence of nitrous oxide. He felt no pain during the procedure, and nitrous oxide has been a part of dental practice ever since, though recently its role as a routine anesthesia has become a matter of controversy (see Point/Counterpoint later in this chapter).[3]

During the 1960s, nitrous-oxide inhalation reappeared as a recreational drug. Tanks of compressed nitrous oxide were diverted for illicit use, and health professionals, like their counterparts one hundred years earlier, were reportedly sponsoring nitrous oxide parties. Small cartridges of nitrous oxide called **whippets,** generally used by restaurants to make whipped cream, became available through college campus "head shops" and mail-order

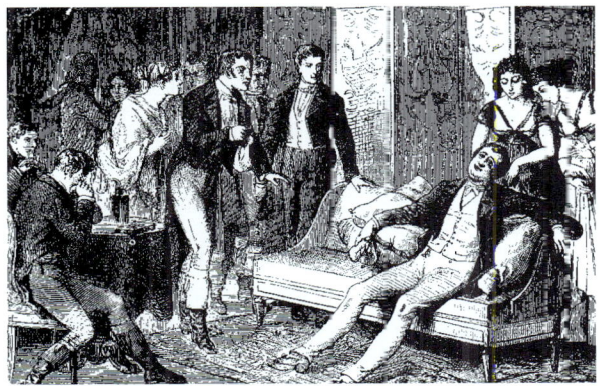

Inhalation of nitrous oxide provided an extra ingredient in an evening of entertainment in the early nineteenth century.

catalogs. The customary pattern of nitrous-oxide abuse was to fill up a balloon from these cylinders and inhale the gas from the balloon. The result was a mild euphoric high that lasted for a few minutes and a sense of well-being that remained for several hours. Sometimes, there would be a loss of consciousness for a few seconds and an experience of "flying." Once consciousness returned, there was the possibility of sensory distortions, nausea, or vomiting. Ordinary cans of commercial whipped cream, in which nitrous oxide is the propellant gas, currently provide easy access to this inhalant.

While nitrous oxide itself is a nontoxic gas, its inhalation presents serious risks. As with any euphoriant drug, the recreational use of nitrous oxide can be extremely dangerous when a person is driving under its influence. In addition, if nitrous oxide is inhaled through an anesthetic mask and the mask is worn over the mouth and nose without the combination of oxygen, the consequences can be lethal Unless there is a minimum of 21 percent oxy-

nitrous oxide (NEYE-trus OX-eyed)
An analgesic gas commonly used in modern dentistry. It is also referred to as laughing gas.

whippets
Small canisters containing pressurized nitrous oxide.

gen in the mixture, reproducing the 21 percent oxygen content in the air we breathe, the lack of oxygen (called **hypoxia**) will produce suffocation or irreversible brain damage.[4]

Ether

As was true of nitrous oxide, **ether** came into use well before its anesthetic effects were appreciated by the medical profession. It was introduced by Friedrich Hoffmann at the beginning of the 1700s, under the name Anodyne, as a liquid "nerve tonic" for intestinal cramps, toothaches, and other pains. Whether it was swallowed or inhaled (since it evaporated very quickly), ether also produced effects that resembled intoxication from alcohol. In fact, during the mid-1800s, when the combination of a heavy tax on alcohol and an antialcohol temperance campaign in England and Ireland forced people to consider alternatives to alcoholic beverages, ether drinking as well as ether inhalation became quite popular. It was also used for the same purpose later in the United States during the Prohibition years and in Germany during World War II when alcohol was rationed. Ether's flammability, however, made its recreational use highly dangerous.[5]

Glue, solvent, and aerosol inhalation

The abuse of nitrous oxide and ether may have a relatively long history, but the more familiar reports of inhalation abuse involving glue and solvent chemicals have only appeared since the late 1950s. Table 6.1 gives a listing of some of the common products that have been subject to abuse, including glues, paint thin-

ners, lighter fluid, and stain removers. In addition, there are aerosol products that are also inhalable: hair sprays, deodorants, vegetable lubricants for frying pans, and spray paints. Unfortunately, new products are continually being introduced for genuinely practical uses, without a great enough awareness of what may be the consequences, should someone inhale their ingredients on a recreational basis (Table 6.2).

The abuse potential of inhalants

Commercial glues, solvents, and aerosol sprays are prime candidates for drug abuse for a number of reasons. First of all, since they are inhaled into the lungs, they give a feeling of intoxication that is more rapid than the effects of orally administered alcohol. "It's a quicker drunk," in the words of one solvent abuser.[6] The feeling is often described as a "floating euphoria," similar to the effect of

T A B L E 6 . 1
Common household products with abuse potential as inhalants
Gasoline
Hobby glues and cements
Paint thinners
Lacquers and enamels
Varnishes and varnish removers
Cigarette or charcoal lighter fluid
Fingernail polishes and polish remover
Stain removers, degreasers, and other dry-cleaning products
Upholstery protection spray products (e.g., Scotchgard*)
Windshield deicers
Disinfectants
Fire extinguishing volatile chemicals
Typewriter correction fluid
Permanent felt marker ink
Aerosol hair sprays
Vegetable frying pan lubricants
Spray deodorants
Spray paints
Whipped cream propellants
Freon

Note: The above is a partial list. New products are continually being introduced.

*Scotchgard is a registered product of the 3M Corporation.

TABLE 6.2

Household products with abuse potential and their ingredients

Household product	Possible ingredients
Glues, plastic cements, and rubber cements	Acetates, acetone, benzene, chloroform, hexane, toluene
Cleaning solutions	Trichloroethylene, petroleum products, carbon tetrachloride
Nail polish removers	Acetone
Lighter fluids	Butane, propane
Paints and paint thinners	Acetone, butylacetate, methanol, toluene
Other petroleum products	Acetone, benzene, ether, gasoline, hexane, petroleum, tetraethyl lead, toluene
Typewriter correction fluid	Trichloroethylene
Hair sprays	Butane, propane

SOURCES: Sharp, Charles W., and Rosenberg, Neil L. (1992). Volatile substances. In Joyce H. Lowinson, Pedro Ruiz, and Robert B. Millman (Eds.), *Substance abuse: A comprehensive textbook (2nd ed.).* Baltimore: Williams & Wilkins, pp. 303–327.

alcohol but with a shorter course of intoxication. The high is over in an hour or so, and the hangover is considered less unpleasant than that following alcohol consumption. Second, the typical packaging of inhalant products makes it easy to carry them around and conceal them from others. Even if they are discovered, many products are so common that it is not difficult to invent an excuse for having them on hand.

Finally, most inhalants are easily available in hardware stores, pharmacies, and supermarkets, where they can be bought cheaply or else stolen. Among some inhalant abusers, shoplifting these products from open shelves is not only routine but an expected way of acquiring these drugs. Inhalants are even more widely available than alcohol in poor households; liquor may be in short supply but gasoline, paints, or aerosol products are usually around the house or garage.[7] All these factors contribute to the considerable potential for abuse.

Acute effects of glues, solvents, and aerosols

The fumes from commercial inhalant products fall into the general category of depressant drugs, in that the central nervous system is inhibited after they are inhaled. Brain waves, measured objectively through the electroencephalograph (EEG), slow down. Subjectively, the individual feels intoxicated within minutes after inhalation. The most immediate effects include giddiness, euphoria, dizziness, and slurred speech, lasting for fifteen to forty-five minutes. This state is followed by one to two hours of drowsiness and sometimes a loss of consciousness. Along with these effects, there can be experiences of double vision, ringing in the ears, and hallucinations.[8]

The dangers of inhalant abuse

We should realize that inhalant abuse often involves concentrations of glue and solvent products that are usually fifty to a hundred times greater than the maximum allowable concentration in industry. While industrial workers are generally protected from the toxic effects of these chemicals by governmental standards, the health of the inhalant abuser is obviously at risk (Focus 6.1).

The dangers of inhalant abuse lie not only in the toxic effects of the inhaled compound on body organs but in the behavioral effects of the intoxication itself. Inhalant-produced feelings of euphoria also include feelings of recklessness and omnipotence. There have been instances of young inhalant abusers leaping off roof tops in an effort to fly, running into traffic, lying on railroad tracks, or incurring severe lacerations when pushing their hand through a glass window that has been perceived as open. The hallucinations that are sometimes experienced carry their own personal risks. Walls may appear to be closing in or the sky may appear to be falling. Ordinary objects may be perceived to be changing their shape, size, or color. Any one of these experiences can easily lead to impulsive and potentially destructive behavior.[9]

acetone (ASS-eh-tohn)
A chemical found in nail polish removers and other products.

benzene
A carcinogenic (cancer-producing) compound found in many solvent products, representing a serious health risk when these products are inhaled.

hexane
A dangerous compound present in many glues and adhesive products. Inhalation of these products has been associated with muscular weakness and atrophy.

toluene (TOL-yoo-ene)
A compound in glues, cements, and other adhesive products. Inhalation of these products results in behavioral and neurological impairments.

There are also hazards in the ways in which inhalants are administered. While solvents are sometimes inhaled from a handkerchief or from the container in which they were originally acquired ("huffing"), glues and similar vaporous compounds are often squeezed into a plastic bag and inhaled while the bag is held tightly over the nose and mouth ("bagging"). Potentially, a loss of consciousness can result in hypoxia and asphyxiation. Choking can occur if there is vomiting while the inhaler is unconscious. In an early investigation in the 1960s of nine documented deaths attributed to glue inhalation, at least six were due specifically to a lack of oxygen.[10] Another danger lies in the inhalation of freon, a refrigerant gas so cold that the larynx and throat can be frozen upon contact.

The toxic effects of inhalant drugs themselves depend upon the specific compound, but the picture is complicated by the fact that most products subject to inhalant abuse contain a variety of compounds and in some cases the list of ingredients on the product label is incomplete. Therefore, often we do not know if the medical symptoms resulted from a particular chemical or an interaction with others. Nonetheless, there are specific chemicals that have known health risks. The most serious concern involves sudden-death cases, due to cardiac dysrhythmia, that have been reported following the inhalation of propane and butane, commonly used as a propellant for many commercial products (Table 6.3). Of twenty reported cases of inhalant abuse-related deaths in the United States in 1990, ten were caused specifically by butane or propane.[11] Other inhalant ingredients that present specific hazards are **acetone, benzene, hexane, toluene,** and gasoline.

1. Acetone: Acetone inhalation causes significant damage to the mucous membranes of the respiratory tract.

2. Benzene: Prolonged exposure to benzene has been associated with carcinogenic (cancer-related) disorders, specifically leukemia, as well as anemia. Benzene is generally used as a

T A B L E   6 . 3

Sudden death of males in the Midwestern United States: Five months in 1991

Date	Age	Location	Circumstances
July	16	Kokomo IN	Inhaling butane lighter fuel while driving, held his head out of car window, gasping for air, then crashed; no traumatic cause for death shown in autopsy
August	16	West Michigan	Died after inhaling butane lighter fuel
October	16	Dayton OH	Died after inhaling butane lighter fuel
October	15	Noblesville IN	Died after inhaling aerosolized shoe polish
November	14	Madisonville KY	Died after inhaling aerosolized solvent
November	29	Portsmouth OH	Died after inhaling aerosolized paint
December	17	West Michigan	Died after inhaling butane lighter fuel

SOURCE: Adapted from Siegel, Earl, and Wason, Suman (1992). Sudden sniffing death following inhalation of butane and propane: Changing trends. In Charles N. Sharp, Fred Beauvis, and Richard Spence (Eds.), *Inhalant abuse: A volatile research agenda* (NIDA Research Monograph 129). Rockville MD: National Institute on Drug Abuse, pp. 193–201.

solvent in waxes, resins, lacquers, paints, and paint removers.

3. Hexane: The inhalation of hexane, primarily in glues and other adhesive products, has been associated with peripheral nerve damage leading to muscular weakness and muscle atrophy. There is a latency period of a few weeks before the symptoms appear.

4. Toluene: Toluene inhalation through glue sniffing has been associated with a reduction in short-term memory, anemia, and a loss of hearing, as well as dysfunctions of the cerebellum that result in difficulties in movement and coordination. Toluene has also been implicated as a principal factor in cases of lethal inhalation of spray paints and lacquers,

though it is difficult to exclude the contribution of other solvents in these products

5. Gasoline: Concentrated vapors from gasoline can be lethal when inhaled. Medical symptoms from gasoline inhalation are also frequently attributed to gasoline additives that are mixed in the fuel. The additive **triorthocresyl phosphate (TCP)** in particular, has been associated with spastic muscle disorders and liver problems. Lead content in gasoline is generally linked to long-term CNS degeneration, but fortunately leaded gasoline is no longer commonly available in the United States. On the other hand, present-day gasoline mixtures contain large amounts of toluene, acetone, and hexane to help achieve the "anti-knock" quality that lead had previously provided.[12]

Patterns of inhalant abuse

mong all the psychoactive drugs, inhalants are associated most closely with the young and often the very young. For those who engage in inhalant abuse, these compounds frequently represent the first experience with a psychoactive drug, preceding even alcohol or tobacco. Most of these drug abusers are between eleven and thirteen years old. The University of Michigan survey of 1993 found that almost one out of five eighth-grade students (19 percent) had used inhalants at some previous time. More than 5 percent reported that they had used inhalants within the past month, and 11 percent within the past year. These prevalence rates were significantly higher than equivalent figures for 1992

Inhalants were the only class of drugs for which the incidence of usage in the eighth grade significantly exceeded the incidence in

triorthocresyl phosphate (TCP)
(tri-OR-thoh-CREH-sil FOS-fate)
A gasoline additive. Inhalation of TCP-containing gasoline has been linked to spastic muscle disorders and liver problems.

the tenth or twelfth grades. In contrast, only about 1 percent of college students and young adults not in college reported inhalant use in the past month.[13]

In other cultures and under different circumstances, however, inhalant abuse affects even younger children and a wider proportion of that age group. Interviews of Native American children age six to twelve living in a southwestern U.S. village in 1973 revealed a lifetime prevalence rate for gasoline inhalation of 63 percent, with half of these children reporting that they had used these inhalants on more than one occasion. In Mexico City, among street children as young as eight or nine who live without families in abandoned buildings, rates of inhalant abuse are extremely high, with 22 percent reporting some form of solvent inhalation on a daily basis.[14]

Inhalant abuse, on an experimental basis, is not restricted to social or geographic boundaries. Chronic inhalant abuse, however, is overrepresented among the poor and those youths suffering emotional challenges in their lives and seeking some form of escape. Studies of young inhalant abusers show high rates of delinquency, poor school performance, and emotional difficulties. They often come from disorganized, multiproblem homes in which the parents are actually or effectively absent or else engage themselves in abuse of alcohol or some other substance.[15] The diversity of

ethnic subgroups showing high prevalence rates for inhalant abuse include such disparate groups as Latino children in a rural community in the Southwest, Native American children on U.S. reservations, and white children in an economically disadvantaged neighborhood in Philadelphia.

Whatever the ethnic identity of the chronic inhalant abuser, however, a critical factor is peer influence. Most studies indicate that glue, solvent, or aerosol inhalation is generally experienced in small groups, often at the urging of friends or relatives. Young inhalant abusers tend to be more alienated than others at this age, and the feelings of alienation can be an important factor in leading a youth to others who are also alienated, thus creating a cluster of peers who engage in this form of drug-taking behavior. One survey among Native American youth, for example, found that when friends strongly encouraged inhalant use or would not try to stop it, 84 percent of the sample reported having tried inhalants and 41 percent reported having used them recently. In contrast, when friends discouraged inhalant use or would be perceived as applying strong sanctions against it, only 19 percent reported having tried inhalants and only 3 percent had used them recently.[16]

Questions about chronic inhalant abuse

The long-term effects of inhalant abuse are not well documented, owing to the fact that inhalant abuse frequently does not extend over more than a year or two in a person's life and may occur only sporadically. There have been reports of cases showing a tolerance to the euphoriant effects of glues and gasoline. While it is difficult to determine the dosages that are involved with these tolerance effects,

A group of abandoned Brazilian children inhale glue from bags in Rio de Janeiro.

Scott Pecor— The Scotchgard high

n a secluded beach in south Florida, a group of friends would meet on a weekend and pass around the $5 spray can of Scotchgard, a substance that is sprayed on sofas to prevent stains from spills. A saturated washcloth held against the mouth for a few seconds was all it would take to get a few minutes of tingling and intoxication. There would be no worry about beer cans or liquor bottles that their parents might discover, no need for a fake ID to buy it, no telltale signs to give them away.

"That's all that you really needed to get high," Courtney Knief, a fifteen-year-old girl from Fort Pierce, later recalled. She doesn't, however, sniff Scotchgard anymore.

"It killed my boyfriend and my best friend. I had no idea somebody could die from it. I wish I would have had the sense to open my eyes and say hey this is stupid."

Courtney's boyfriend was sixteen-year-old Scott Pecor of nearby Port St. Lucie, who had died of heart failure from a large dose of inhaled Scotchgard. His older brother had found him unconscious in his backyard and had found the near-empty can on the family's couch. Scott and Courtney had been "huffing" Scotchgard for about three months; they had gotten high three days before he died.

Scott was a soccer player and honors student in his high school, with aspirations to be an archi-

tect. He wasn't an angry or rebellious kid, his parents say. Without any signs of overt drunken behavior or obvious aftereffects, Scott's inhalant abuse went totally unnoticed by them. "I didn't know he was doing it alone," Courtney says. "I guess he was hooked."

Family and friends comfort each other at Scott Pecor's funeral in 1991.

From 1989 to 1991, the local medical examiner had recorded three teenage deaths in three nearby counties. One boy died after inhaling butane lighter refills, another from inhaling paint thinner. Scott was the first casualty from Scotchgard itself, though the manufacturer, the 3M Company of Minneapolis, reported that from 1989 to 1991 more than twenty people died from inhaling

the fabric protector. On a nationwide scale, the National Institute on Drug Abuse estimates that there are about 440,000 inhalant abusers between the ages of twelve and seventeen and 344,000 between eighteen and twenty-five.

Unfortunately, the dangers of inhalants are not fully appreciated. In a 1990 school district survey in a Florida county immediately south of where Scott lived, 10 percent of seventh graders indicated that inhalants were not perceived as harmful and between 8 and 10 percent of them reported having used them. Scotchgard and Freon were current favorites.

SOURCE: Hiaasen, Rob (1991, March 29). The newest deadly high. *Palm Beach Post*, p. 1D.

it appears that individuals exposed only to low concentrations for brief periods of time or high levels occasionally do not show tolerance to the inhalants.

Psychological dependence occurs frequently. Inhalant abusers have been reported as feeling restless, irritable, and anxious, when prevented from inhaling glues, solvents, or aerosols. Since physiological withdrawal symptoms are observed only rarely, we can

conclude that physical dependence does not play a major role in cases of inhalant abuse.[17]

A gateway for future drug abuse?

The young age at which inhalant abuse occurs leads to the question of whether there is a causal link between inhalant abuse and later abuse of other drugs. While some youths will subsequently replace inhalants with alcohol, marijuana, and other recreational drugs, the experience of inhalants cannot be considered to lead, per se, to other drug experimentation or long-term abuse. This is how one author has put it:

The socially and emotionally healthy juvenile casually experimenting with solvent sniffing does not bear any greater potential for heroin addiction than had he not sniffed solvents. Conversely, the disturbed youth from a broken home, who is frequently exposed to pushers, probably bears the same high risk of ultimate narcotic abuse whether or not he sniffs glue. Regardless of surrounding circumstances, however, any significant resort to intoxicating substances in childhood should be carefully noted as a potential warning of a growing emotional disturbance or as a predictor of a future drug-dependent personality.[18]

A similar "gateway argument" with respect to marijuana will be presented in Chapter 9.

Responses of society to inhalant abuse

niffing gasoline or paint is a grubby, dirty, cheap way to get high. Inhalant users are, therefore, likely to be the social rejects, the emotionally disturbed, the disadvantaged minorities, the maladjusted, as well as angry and alienated. There is nothing attractive, exciting, or appealing about inhalant use or inhalant users and, in our attempts to deal with drug use, inhalants may be ignored.[19]

Certainly, the concern about inhalant abuse takes a backseat to more widely publicized concerns about cocaine and heroin abuse. Despite the relatively low priority given to inhalant abuse, however, steps have been taken over the years to reduce some of its hazards. One major approach has been to restrict the availability and sales of glues to young people, a strategy, as you might predict, that has met with mixed success. Some U.S. cities have restricted sales of plastic cement unless it is purchased with a model kit, but such legislation is largely ineffective when model kits are relatively inexpensive. As with the official restriction of alcohol and tobacco to minors, young people can find a way around these laws.

More direct action has been taken since 1969 by the Testor Corporation, a leading manufacturer of plastic cement for models, by incorporating **oil of mustard** into the formula. This additive produces severe nasal irritation similar to the effect of horseradish, while not affecting its use as a glue or the effect on the user who does not inhale it directly.

Other brands of glues and adhesives, however, may not contain this additive and as a result could still be available for abuse, and additives in general may not be desirable for certain products that are used for cosmetic purposes. In addition, concentrations of benzene in many household products sold in the United States have been reduced or eliminated, though it is difficult to determine the exact composition of them by merely inspecting the label. Standards for products manufactured and sold in foreign countries may be significantly less stringent.[20]

Beyond the difficulty in identifying the toxicity of specific solvent compounds, there is the overriding general problem of the enormous variety and easy availability of solvent-containing products. As one researcher has expressed it, "If sales of gold paint or paint thinner are curtailed, people may choose to use typewriter correction fluid, or shoe polish or nail polish remover, or hundreds of other items that have legitimate uses in everyday life."[21]

Ultimately, some sort of educational strategy must be coordinated that is targeted at children in the elementary grades in school and their parents at home. Different countries have differing educational approaches, ranging from nonalarmist, low-key programs to those based on the assumption of absolute

oil of mustard
An additive in Testor brand hobby-kit glues that produces nasal irritation when inhaled, thus reducing the potential for inhalant abuse.

A chronology of nitrite inhalation abuse

Date	Example of inhalation	Date	Example of inhalation
1859	Flushing of skin with amyl nitrite first described	1976	$50 million sales reported in nitrites in one U.S. city
1867	First therapeutic use of amyl nitrite for angina pain	1977	Nitrite inhalation predominant among homosexual men
1880s	Butyl nitrite studied but not used clinically		
1960	Amyl nitrite prescription requirement eliminated by FDA	1979	More than 5 million people estimated to have used nitrites more than once per week
1963	First reports of recreational use of nitrites		19 cases of Kaposi's sarcoma found in retrospect
1960s	Widespread recreational use of nitrites among young adults	1980	56 cases of Kaposi's sarcoma reported
		1981	Increased suspicions of a link between nitrite use and Kaposi's sarcoma
1969	Amyl nitrite prescription requirement reinstated		
1970	Street brands of butyl nitrite beginning to be widely available	1985	Concerns about AIDS and HIV infection beginning to receive widespread media attention
1974	Popper craze beginning	1990s	Nitrite inhalation abuse greatly reduced among nonhomosexual populations

SOURCE: Updated from Newell, Guy R., Spitz, Margaret R., and Wilson, Michael B. (1988). Nitrite inhalants: Historical perspective. In Harry W. Haverkos and John A. Dougherty (Eds.), *Health hazards of nitrite inhalants* (NIDA Research Monograph 83). Rockville MD: National Institute of Drug Abuse, p. 6.

abstinence, and it is not clear which strategy is most effective in controlling inhalant abuse. In the meantime, attention has been drawn to abusive inhalation of two specific products, amyl and butyl nitrite, affecting a different population from the one traditionally associated with glue, solvent, or aerosol inhalants. Like nitrous oxide and ether, these nitrites have been around for some time, but their abuse has been relatively recent.

Amyl nitrite and butyl nitrite inhalation

Amyl and butyl nitrites were first identified in the nineteenth century. When inhaled, they produce an intense vasodilation, a relaxation of smooth muscle, a fall in blood pressure, and a reflex increase in heart rate. Since 1867, **amyl nitrite** has been used medically, on a prescription basis, in the treatment of angina pain in heart patients and as an antidote in cyanide poisoning. **Butyl nitrite** produces similar therapeutic effects but has never been used clinically.

News of the recreational potential of nitrite inhalation began to spread in the 1960s and reached a peak in the 1970s, particularly within the homosexual community, as it was recognized that the vasodilation of cerebral blood vessels produced a euphoric high, anal sphincter muscles were relaxed, and vasodilation of genital blood vessels enhanced sexual pleasure (Table 6.4). By 1979, more than 5 million people in the United States were using amyl or butyl nitrites more than once a week. The con-

amyl nitrite (AY-mil NEYE-trite)
An inhalant drug that relaxes smooth muscle and produces euphoria. Clinically useful in treating angina pain in cardiac patients, it is also subject to abuse.

butyl nitrite (BYOO-til NEYE-trite)
An inhalant drug, similar in its effects to amyl nitrite. It is commonly abused since it induces feelings of euphoria.

cern, however, that nitrites might be linked to the development of **Kaposi's sarcoma,** a rare form of cancer affecting the immune system, frequently observed in AIDS patients, has led to a significant decline in its popularity, although it continues to be abused.[22]

Patterns of nitrite inhalation abuse

Amyl nitrite is often referred to as poppers or snappers, since it is commonly available in a mesh-covered glass ampule and there is a popping sound as the ampule is broken and the vapors of the nitrite are released into the air. It is quick-acting, with vasodilatory effects appearing within thirty seconds. Light-headedness, a flushing sensation, blurred vision, and euphoria last for about five minutes, followed by headache and nausea. Butyl nitrite follows a similar time course in its effects and is available in pornography shops and mail-order catalogs. Many of the various "trade names" for butyl nitrite (Table 6.5) suggest its supposed sexual benefits and the fact that its vapors emit a strong odor resembling that of sweaty socks.

While frequently identified with homosexual activity, cases of nitrite inhalation have also been found among heterosexual adolescents, for whom the primary attraction is a feeling of general euphoria. The University of Michigan survey began looking at prevalence rates for nitrite inhalation in 1979. In that year, approximately 11 percent of high school seniors reported having tried nitrite inhalants at least once in their lifetime. By 1993, the rate had dropped substantially to approximately 1 percent.[23]

Health risks in nitrite-inhalation abuse

Nitrites increase intraocular pressure and as a result are associated with the development of glaucoma. Blood-cell abnormalities are also observed. The primary concern, how-

Kaposi's sarcoma
A form of cancer affecting the immune system and associated with AIDS.

QUICK CONCEPT CHECK 6.1

Understanding the history of inhalants

Check your understanding of the history of inhalant drugs by answering whether a particular substance was used (a) first recreationally, then as an application in medicine or (b) first as an application in medicine, then recre- ationally, or (c) used recreationally and no application in medicine has been found.

1. amyl nitrite
2. hexane
3. nitrous oxide

ANSWERS: 1. b 2. c 3. a

ever, is the potential carcinogenic effects of nitrites. Studies of individuals with Kaposi's sarcoma have showed a high incidence of nitrite inhalation. Although it is now known that AIDS is produced by an infection of the human immunodeficiency virus (HIV), the growing consensus is that nitrite inhalation is a cofactor in the suppression of the immune system that is characteristic of AIDS and increases the risk of Kaposi's sarcoma.[24]

TABLE 6.5
"Brand names" for butyl nitrite

Aroma of Men	Hardware	Mama Poppers
Ban Apple Gas	Heart On	Oz
Bang	Highball	Quick Silver
Bullet	Jac Aroma	Rush
Climax	Lightning Bolt	Satan's Scent
Crypt Tonight	Liquid Increase	Thrust
Discorama	Locker Room	Toilet Water

SOURCE: Maickel, Roger P. (1988). The fate and toxicity of butyl nitrites. In Harry W. Haverkos and John A. Dougherty (Eds.), *Health hazards of nitrite inhalants* (NIDA Research Monograph 83). Rockville MD: National Institute on Drug Abuse, p. 16.

Summary

GLUE, SOLVENT, AND AEROSOL INHALATION

- Present-day inhalant abuse involves a wide range of commercial products: gasoline, glues and other adhesives, household cleaning compounds, aerosol sprays, and solvents of all kinds.

- These products are usually cheap, easily available, and easily concealable, and their intoxicating effects when inhaled are rapid. All of these factors make inhalants prime candidates for abuse.

- The principal dangers of inhalant abuse lie in the behavioral consequences of intoxication and in the possibility of asphyxiation when inhalants are administered by an airproof bag held over the nose and mouth.

- Specific toxic substances contained in inhalant products include acetone, benzene, hexane, toluene, and gasoline.

PATTERNS OF INHALANT ABUSE

- Inhalant abuse respects no social or geographic boundaries, though prevalence rates are particularly high among poor and disadvantaged populations.

- Research studies indicate the presence of psychological dependence rather than physical dependence in inhalant abuse behavior.

- Tolerance effects are seen for chronic inhalant abusers when the inhalant concentration is high and exposure is frequent.

RESPONSES OF SOCIETY TO INHALANT ABUSE

- Concern about the dangers of inhalant abuse has led to restriction of the sale of model-kit glues to minors and a modification of the formulas for model-kit glue in order to lessen the popularity of deliberate inhalation.

- There are so many products presently on the open market that contain volatile chemicals that a universal restriction of abusable inhalants is practically impossible.

AMYL NITRITE AND BUTYL NITRITE INHALATION

- Two types of inhalants, amyl nitrite and butyl nitrite, appeared on the scene in the 1960s, reaching a peak in the late 1970s. While they are chiefly identified with homosexual individuals, populations of heterosexual adolescents and young adults have also engaged in this form of inhalant abuse.

- These nitrites are recognized now as a cofactor in the development of Kaposi's sarcoma, a form of cancer associated with AIDS.

Key Terms

Endnotes

1. Quotation from Silverstein, Alvin, Silverstein, Virginia, and Silverstein, Robert (1991). *The addictions handbook.* Hillside NJ: Enslow Publishers, p. 51.

2. Preble, Edward, and Laury, Gabriel V. (1967). Plastic cement: The ten cent hallucinogen. *International Journal of the Addictions, 2,* 271–281.

3. Nagle, David R. (1968). Anesthetic addiction and drunkenness. *International Journal of the Addictions, 3,* p. 33.

4. Julien, Robert M. (1995). *A primer of drug action* (7th ed.). New York: Freeman, pp. 65–71. Layzer, Robert B. (1985). Nitrous oxide abuse. In Edmond I. Eger (Ed.), *Nitrous oxide/N$_2$O.* New York: Elsevier, pp. 249–257. Morgan, Roberta (1988). *The emotional pharmacy.* Los Angeles: Body Press, pp. 212–213.

5. Nagle. Anesthetic addiction and drunkenness, pp. 26–30.

6. Cohen, Sidney (1977). Inhalant abuse: An overview of the problem. In Charles W. Sharp and Mary Lee Brehm (Eds.), *Review of inhalants: Euphoria to dysfunction* (NIDA Research Monograph 15). Rockville MD: National Institute on Drug Abuse, p. 7.

7. Ibid., pp. 6–8.

8. Schuckit, Marc A. (1989). *Drug and alcohol abuse: A clinical guide to diagnosis and treatment* (3rd ed.). New York: Plenum Medical Book Co., pp. 185–186.

9. Hofmann, Frederick G. (1983). *A handbook on drug and alcohol abuse: The biomedical aspects* (2nd ed.). New York: Oxford University Press, pp. 136–137.

10. Brecher, Edward M., and the editors of Consumer Reports (1972). *Licit and illicit drugs.* Boston: Little, Brown, p. 331.

11. Siegel, Earl, and Wason, Suman (1992). Sudden sniffing deaths following inhalation of butane and propane: Changing trends. In Charles W. Sharp, Fred Beauvais, and Richard Spence (Eds.), *Inhalant abuse: A volatile research agenda* (NIDA Research Monograph 129). Rockville MD: National Institute on Drug Abuse, pp. 193–201.

12. Bruckner, James V., and Peterson, Richard G. (1977). Toxicology of aliphatic and aromatic hydrocarbons. In Charles W. Sharp and Mary L. Brehm (Eds.), *Review of inhalants: Euphoria to dysfunction* (NIDA Research Monograph 15). Rockville MD: National Institute on Drug Abuse, pp. 124–163. Comstock, Eric G., and Comstock, Betsy S. (1977). Medical evaluation of inhalant abusers. In Charles W. Sharp and Mary L. Brehm (Eds.), *Review of inhalants: Euphoria to dysfunction* (NIDA Research Monograph 15). Rockville MD: National Institute on Drug Abuse, pp. 54–80. Garriott, James C. (1992). Death among inhalant abusers. In Charles W. Sharp, Fred Beauvais, and Richard Spence (Eds.), *Inhalant abuse: A volatile research agenda* (NIDA Research Monograph 129). Rockville MD: National Institute on Drug Abuse, pp. 171–193. Jacobs, Michael R., and Fehr, Kevin O'B. (1987). *Drugs and drug abuse: A reference text* (2nd ed.). Toronto: Addiction Research Foundation, pp. 322–323.

13. Johnston, Lloyd D., O'Malley, Patrick M., and Bachman, Jerald G. (1994). *National survey results on drug use from the Monitoring the Future study, 1975–1993.* Vol. 1. Rockville MD: National Institute on Drug Abuse, Table 1.

14. Kaufman, A. (1973). Gasoline sniffing among children in a Pueblo Indian village. *Pediatrics, 51,* 1060–1064. Leal, Hermán, Mejía, Laura, Gómez, Lucila, and Salina de Valle, Olga (1978). Naturalistic study on the phenomenon of inhalant use in a group of children in Mexico City. In Charles W. Sharp and L. T. Carroll (Eds.), *Voluntary inhalation of industrial solvents.* Rockville MD: National Institute on Drug Abuse, pp. 95–108. Beauvais, Fred, and Oetting E. R. (1988). Inhalant abuse by young children. In Raquel A. Crider and Beatrice A. Rouse (Eds.), *Epidemiology of inhalant abuse: An update* (NIDA Research Monograph 85). Rockville MD: National Institute on Drug Abuse, pp. 30–33.

15. Hofmann. *Handbook on drug and alcohol abuse,* p. 134.

16. Oetting, E. R., Edwards, Ruth W., and Beauvais, Fred (1988). Social and psychological factors underlying inhalant abuse. In Raquel A. Crider and Beatrice A. Rouse (Eds.), *Epidemiology of inhalant abuse: An update* (NIDA Research Monograph 85). Rockville MD: National Institute on Drug Abuse, pp. 172–203.

17. Hofmann. *Handbook on drug and alcohol abuse,* pp. 138–139. Korman, Maurice (1977). Clinical evaluation of psychological factors. In Charles W. Sharp and Mary Lee Brehm (Eds.), *Review of inhalants: Euphoria to dysfunction* (NIDA Research Monograph 15). Rockville MD: National Institute on Drug Abuse, pp. 30–53.

18. Hofmann. *Handbook on drug and alcohol abuse,* p. 134.

19. Oetting, Edwards, and Beauvais. Social and psychological factors, p. 197.

20. Sharp, Charles W. (1977). Approaches to the problem. In Charles W. Sharp and Mary Lee Brehm (Eds.), *Review of inhalants: Euphoria to dysfunction* (NIDA Research Monograph 15). Rockville MD: National Institute on Drug Abuse, pp. 226–242.

21. Kerner, Karen (1988). Current topics in inhalant abuse. In Raquel A. Crider and Beatrice A. Rouse (Eds.), *Epidemiology of inhalant abuse: An update* (NIDA Research Monograph 85). Rockville MD: National Institute on Drug Abuse, p. 20.

22. Newell, Guy R., Spitz, Margaret R., and Wilson, Michael B. (1988). Nitrite inhalants: Historical perspective. In Harry W. Haverkos and John A. Dougherty (Eds), *Health hazards of nitrite inhalants* (NIDA Research Monograph 83). Rockville MD: National Institute on Drug Abuse, pp. 1–14.

23. Johnston, O'Malley, and Bachman. *National survey results on drug use,* Table 1.

24. Haverkos, Harry W. (1988). Epidemiological studies—Kaposi's sarcoma vs. opportunistic infections among homosexual men with AIDS. In Harry W. Haverkos and John A. Dougherty (Eds.), *Health hazards of nitrite inhalants* (NIDA Research Monograph 83). Rockville MD: National Institute on Drug Abuse, pp. 96–105.

POINT/COUNTERPOINT

Should dentists continue to use nitrous oxide?

he following discussion represents the opinions of people on both sides of the controversial issue of nitrous oxide. Read them with an open mind. Discuss them in your class, with your family, and with your friends. Don't think you have to come up with the final answer, nor should you necessarily agree with the argument you heard last. Many of the ideas in this feature come from sources listed at the end, where more extensive discussions can be found.

POINT

If we were to imagine nitrous oxide being brought to the FDA for consideration as a new anesthetic drug, the chances for its approval would be far from assured. Look at some of the problems. First of all, you have to make sure the proportion of oxygen mixed with it exceeds 21 percent; otherwise you get hypoxia. Survey studies show that the offspring of pregnant women chronically exposed to trace levels of nitrous oxide may develop birth abnormalities. There is an increased probability of spontaneous abortions not only in exposed women but also in the wives of exposed men, with the increased risk being directly related to the extent of the exposure to the gas. The incidence of kidney and liver disease is higher for dentists and their chairside assistants who use nitrous oxide in their practice. Animal studies show that nitrous oxide increases blood pressure and other sympathetic factors in the body, as well as leading to a reduction of white blood cell counts in bone marrow after prolonged exposure.

COUNTERPOINT

Results from animal studies can be frightening to read,

(continued)

unless you also read the fine print. Some animal studies show no signs of toxicity at all, and those that do usually impose nitrous oxide for far longer periods of time than would be characteristic of a dental practice. Epidemiological studies that are carried out by questionnaires are not adequate to get an idea of cause and effect. The response rate to the surveys may have been biased by how the responders viewed the safety of nitrous oxide. Those that were exposed to nitrous oxide could very well have been sensitized to report all sorts of abnormalities. As a result, nitrous oxide would be unfairly blamed.

POINT
It's true that survey data do not represent the final answer, but they raise a red flag as to the potential dangers. Besides, the effects aren't always physiological; some mental patients can have significant relapses under nitrous oxide while other people find the loss of control very disturbing. Doesn't it make more sense to suspend nitrous

oxide use until we know more about it?

COUNTERPOINT
Suspend it after more than 150 years of use? We have to realize that nitrous oxide has been used for mild anesthesia for a longer period of time and administered to more patients over the years than any other inhaled anesthetic. The untoward effects are rare. Besides, the weaknesses of nitrous oxide are known with great precision, thanks to the research literature in the last thirty years. Can we say the same thing about some of the candidates you might suggest as a replacement? We know better what we are dealing with in the case of nitrous oxide than in the case of any other anesthetic drug that's around.

POINT
You are still missing the essential message. People can be at significant risk from exposure to nitrous oxide, and the risks extend to dental professionals as well as patients.

COUNTERPOINT
This is nothing new. If you are careful in screening patients

for psychoses, fear of loss of control, pregnancy, pulmonary difficulties, liver or kidney disease, and any previous problem with anesthesia, you are greatly lessening the risks. If the equipment prevents leakage of the gas into the air, dental professionals will be protected. We have to consider the benefits as well as the potential costs.

POINT
Then what about the potential for inhalant abuse? The popular perception that nitrous oxide is innocuous (after all, some dentists call it merely sweet air), we are inadvertently reinforcing an avenue for drug abuse. While not quite in vogue to the extent that it was n the 1960s and 1970s, nitrous oxide is still available for recreational use. The whippet cartridges can be obtained from a variety of sources, and if nitrous oxide is perceived as safe then people will seek them out. Meanwhile the tanks in dental offices provide an easy tranquilizing break for dentists,

their assistants, and nurses.

COUNTERPOINT
If nitrous oxide remains as accessible as the nearest can of whipped cream, we do not have to worry about the tanks in dental offices or mail-order catalogs. The point is that we are singling out the dentists and blaming them for a larger problem of substance abuse in America.

SOURCES: Brodsky, Jay B. (1985). Toxicity of nitrous oxide. In Edmond I. Eger (Ed.), *Nitrous oxide/N_2O*. New York: Elsevier, pp. 259–280. Eger, Edmond I. (1985). Should we not use nitrous oxide? In Edmond I. Eger (Ed.), *Nitrous oxide/N_2O*. New York: Elsevier, pp. 339–344. Hornbein, Thomas F. (1985). Epilogue. In Eger, *Nitrous oxide/N_2O*, pp. 355–358. Saidman, Lawrence, J., and Hamilton, William K. (1985). We should continue to use nitrous oxide. In Eger, *Nitrous oxide/N_2O*, pp. 345–354. Smith, Richard A., and Beirne, Owen R. (1985). The use of nitrous oxide by dentists. In Eger, *Nitrous oxide/N_2O*, pp. 281–304.

7

The Major Narcotics: Opium, Morphine, and Heroin

I took it; and in an hour—oh heavens! What a revulsion! What an upheaving, from its lowest depths, of the inner spirit! What an apocalypse of the world within me!. . . Here was a panacea . . . for all human woes; here was the secret of happiness about which philosophers had disputed for so many ages, at once discovered.

Thomas DeQuincey
Confessions of an English opium eater, 1821

All dope can do for you is kill you—and kill you the long slow hard way. And it can kill people you love right along with you. And that's the truth, the whole truth, and nothing but.

Billie Holiday
Lady sings the blues, 1956

here is no escaping the ambivalence we feel about opium and the opiates that are derived from it. Here is a family of drugs that has the power to banish pain from our lives and at the same time the power to enslave our minds.

This chapter will concern itself with the medical uses and recreational abuses of opiate-derived and opiate-related drugs. Together, these drugs are referred to as **narcotics** (from the Greek word for "stupor"), in that they produce a dreamlike effect on the user and at higher doses induce a state of sleep. The most important characteristic of narcotic drugs, however, is that they have powerful analgesic properties; they greatly reduce feelings of pain.

As noted in Chapter 2, the term "narcotic" was at one time used inappropriately to mean *any* illicit psychoactive drug or at least any drug that causes some degree of dependence, including such unlikely examples as cocaine and amphetamine. Even today, the term is at the very least misleading, because other drugs having no relationship to opium are far more effective in inducing sleep (Chapter 5). Nonetheless, we are stuck with this inexact terminology; it is not likely to disappear anytime soon.

Narcotic drugs, in general, may be divided into three main categories. The first includes **opium** and three natural components that can be extracted from it: morphine, codeine, and thebaine (Fig. 7.1). The second category includes opium derivatives that are created by making slight changes in the chemical composition of morphine. The best example of this type of opiate derivative is heroin. Morphine, codeine, thebaine, and heroin are commonly

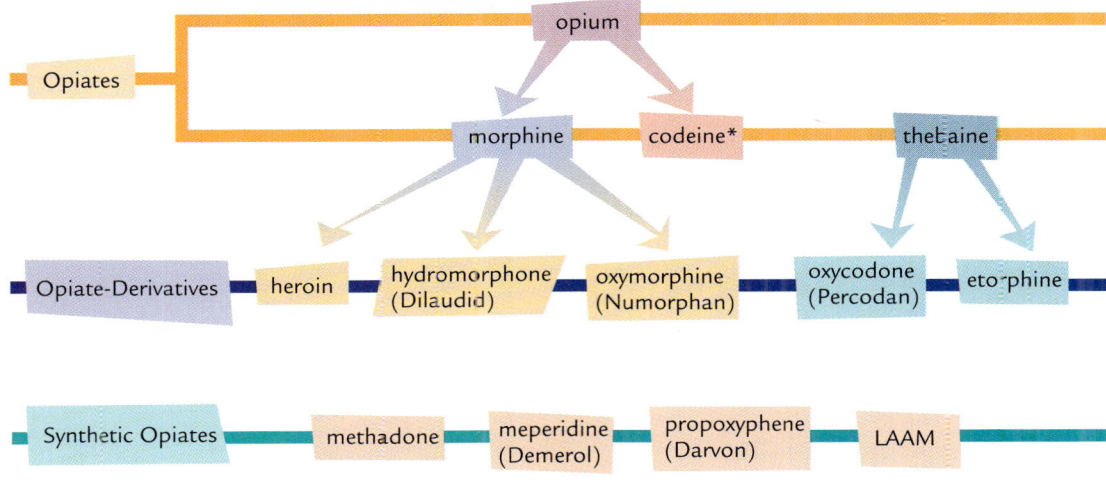

Opiates		opium			
		morphine	codeine*		thebaine
Opiate-Derivatives	heroin	hydromorphone (Dilaudid)	oxymorphone (Numorphan)	oxycodone (Percodan)	etorphine
Synthetic Opiates	methadone	meperidine (Demerol)	propoxyphene (Darvon)	LAAM	

FIGURE 7.1

Major opiates, opiate-derivatives, and synthetic opiates
Morphine is the present-day source for codeine.
(Note: Brand names are shown in parentheses.)

referred to simply as **opiates.** The third category includes synthetic drugs that are not chemically related to morphine or any of its derivatives but nonetheless produce opiate-like effects that are behaviorally indistinguishable from the effects of opiates themselves. Drugs of this type are commonly referred to as **synthetic opiates** or *synthetic opiate-like drugs.* This last category is a result of a continuing effort to discover a drug that achieves the same degree of analgesia as the opiates but without the potential for abuse. Unfortunately, such drugs have yet to be found.

Opium in history

ike cocaine, the origins of heroin and other opiates go back to the fields of faraway places. This particular story begins with the harvesting of raw opium in remote villages of Myanmar (formerly Burma), Laos, Thailand, Vietnam, Mexico, and a dozen other countries where the weather is hot and dry and labor is cheap. The source is the opium poppy, known by its botanical name as *Papaver somniferum* (literally "the poppy that brings

sleep"), an annual plant growing three to four feet high. Its large flowers are typically about four or five inches in diameter and can be white, pink, red, or purple. This variety is the only type of poppy that produces opium; common garden plants such as the red Oriental poppy or the yellow California poppy look similar but do not have any psychoactive ingredients.

The present-day method of opium harvesting has not essentially changed for more

narcotics
A general term technically referring to opiate related or opiate-derived drugs. It is often mistakenly used to include several other illicit drug categories as well.

opium
An analgesic and euphoriant drug acquired from the dried juice of the opium poppy.

opiate
Any ingredient of opium or a chemical derivative of these ingredients. Opiates generally refer to opium, morphine, codeine, thebaine, and heroin.

synthetic opiates
synthetic drugs unrelated to morphine that produce opiate-like effects.

than three thousand years. In the seven to ten days each year when the petals of the opium poppy have fallen but the seed capsule of the plant underneath the petals is not yet completely ripe, laborers make small, shallow incisions in the capsules, allowing a milky white juice to ooze out. The next day, this substance will have oxidized and hardened by contact with the air. At this point, now reddish brown and having a consistency of heavy syrup, it is collected, plant by plant, onto large poppy leaves. Later, it will darken further and form small gumlike balls that look like tar, taste bitter, and smell like new-mown hay.[1]

Opium was first described in specific detail in the early third century B.C., but we can be fairly sure that it was used for at least a thousand years before that. A ceramic opium pipe has been excavated in Cyprus, dating from the Late Bronze Age, about 1200 B.C. Cypriot vases from that era depict incised poppy capsules. From evidence contained in the Ebers Papyrus writings (Chapter 1), Egyptians knew of the medicinal value of opium as well.[2]

Raw opium is harvested in an Afghan poppy field.

In the second century A.D., Claudius Galen, the famous Greek physician and surgeon to Roman gladiators, recommended opium for practically everything. He wrote that it

. . . resists poison and venomous bites, cures chronic headache, vertigo, deafness, apoplexy, dimness of sight, loss of voice, asthma, coughs of all kinds, spitting of blood, tightness of breath, colic, . . . jaundice, hardness of the spleen, . . . urinary complaints, fever, . . . leprosies, the troubles to which women are subject, melancholy, and all pestilences.[3]

Western Europe was introduced to opium in the eleventh and twelfth centuries from returning crusaders who had learned of it from the Arabs. At first, opium was only used by sorcerers as an ingredient in their potions. Later, during the first stirrings of modern medicine in Europe, opium began to be used as a therapeutic drug. In 1520 a physician named Paracelsus, promoting himself as the foremost medical authority of his day, introduced a medicinal drink combining opium, wine, and an assortment of spices. He called the mixture *laudanum* (derived from the Latin phrase meaning "something to be praised"), and before long the formula of Paracelsus was being called the stone of immortality. Even though Paracelsus himself denounced many of the doctrines of earlier physicians in history, he continued the time-honored tradition of recommending opium for practically every known disease.

In 1680 the English physician Thomas Sydenham, considered the father of clinical medicine, introduced a highly popular version of opium drink similar to that of Paracelsus, called Sydenham's Laudanum. For the next two hundred years or so, the acceptable form of taking opium among Europeans and later Americans would be in the form of a drink, either Sydenham's recipe or a host of other variations. Sydenham's enthusiasm for the drug was no less than that of many of his predecessors: "Among the remedies which it has pleased Almighty God to give man to relieve his sufferings, none is so universal and so efficacious as opium."[4]

Opium in China

The association of opium with China and Chinese culture seems to be so well established that we tend to assume that opium was a major part of Chinese life for thousands of years. It is true that sometime in the eighteenth century, China invented a novel form of opium use, opium smoking, which became synonymous in the Western mind with China itself. Nevertheless, for at least eight hundred years after the Arabs introduced opium to China, the Chinese used opium only in a very limited way. They took it almost exclusively on a medicinal basis, consuming it in its raw state as a painkiller and treatment for diarrhea.

The picture changed dramatically in the eighteenth century for the basic reason that the British people had fallen in love with Chinese tea. British merchants wanted to buy tea and send it home, but what could they sell to China in exchange? The problem was that there were few, if any, commodities that China really wanted from the outside. In their eyes, the rest of the world were simply "barbarians" with an inferior culture, offering little or nothing the Chinese people needed.

The answer was opium. In 1773 British forces had conquered Bengal Province in India and suddenly had a monopoly on raw opium. It was now easy to introduce opium to China as a major item of trade. Opium was successfully smuggled into China through local British and Portuguese merchants, allowing the British government and its official trade representative, the East India Company, to carry off the public image of not being directly involved in the opium trade. Opium, flooding into the country from its southern port of Canton, found a ready market, and opium dependence soon became a major Chinese problem. Despite repeated edicts by the Chinese emperor to reduce the use of opium within China or cut the supply line from India, the monster flourished.[5]

By 1839, the tension had reached a peak. In a historic act of defiance against the European powers, including Britain, an imperial commissioner appointed by the emperor to deal with the opium problem once and for all confiscated a huge quantity of opium and burned it publicly in Canton. Events escalated shortly after until open fighting broke out. The Opium War had begun.

By 1842, British artillery and warships had overwhelmed a nation unprepared to deal with European firepower. In a humiliating treaty, China was forced to sign over to Britain the island of Hong Kong and its harbor, grant to British merchants exclusive trading rights in major Chinese ports, and pay a large amount of money to reimburse British losses during the war. Despite these agreements, fighting broke out again between 1858 and 1860, with the British soldiers and sailors being joined by the French and Americans. Finally, in a treaty signed in 1860, China was required to legalize opium within its borders. The Opium War had succeeded in opening up the gates of China, much against its will, to the rest of the world.[6]

Opium in Britain

To the average Briton in the mid-1800s, the Opium War in China was totally a trade issue, with little or no direct impact upon his daily life. In fact, opium itself was everywhere. The important difference between China and Britain with respect to opium, as noted in Chapter 1, was not in the extent of its consumption but in the way it was consumed. The acceptable form of opium use in Victorian England was opium drinking in the form of laudanum, while the Oriental practice of opium smoking was identified by the British with vice and degradation and associated with the very lowest fringes of society. The contrast was strikingly ironic. Opium dens, with all the evil connotations that the phrase has carried with it into modern times, were places where opium was *smoked;* the respectable parlors of middle-class British families were the places where opium was *drunk.*

In a sense, opium was the aspirin of its day. Supplies were unlimited and cheaper than gin or beer; medical opinion was at most divided on the question of any potential harm; there was no negative public opinion and seldom any trouble with the police. An opium addict, as long as there were no signs of opium smoking, was considered no worse than a drunkard. Nearly all infants and young children in Britain during this period were given opium, often from the day they were born. Dozens of laudanum-based patent medicines, with appealing names such as Godfrey's Cordial, A Pennysworth of Peace, and Mrs. Winslow's Soothing Syrup were used for teething pain, colic, or merely as a way to keep the children quiet. The administration of opium to babies was particularly attractive in the new, industrial-age life-style of female workers, who had to leave their infants in the care of elderly women or young children when they went off to work in the factories.[7]

Out of this atmosphere of acceptance sprang a new cultural phenomenon: the opium-addict writer. Just as LSD was to be promoted in the 1960s as an avenue toward a greatly expanded level of creativity and imagination (Chapter 8), a similar belief was spreading during this period with respect to opium. The leader of the movement was Thomas DeQuincey, and his book *Confessions of an English Opium Eater,* published in 1821, became the movement's bible. It is impossible to say how many people started to use opium recreationally as a direct result of reading DeQuincey's *Confessions,* but there is no doubt that the book made the practice fashionable.

Opium in the United States

In many ways, opium consumption in the United States paralleled its widespread use in Britain. In one survey of thirty-five Boston drugstores in 1838, 78 percent of the prescriptions that had been refilled three or more times contained opium. Opium poppies were cultivated in Vermont and New Hampshire, in Florida and Louisiana, and later in California and Arizona. It was not until 1942 that the growing of opium poppies was made illegal in the United States.

Women outnumbered men in opium use during the nineteenth century by as much as three to one. The principal reason for this gender difference lay in the attitudes toward women at the time. Men could engage in the recreational use of alcohol in the time-honored macho tradition, but such use among women was not considered respectable. Only opium, in the form of laudanum and similar products, was open to American women. As one researcher has expressed it, the consequence was that "husbands drank alcohol in the saloon; wives took opium at home."[8]

Throughout the 1800s, opium coexisted alongside alcohol, nicotine (in tobacco products), and cocaine as dominant recreational drugs. As late as 1897, the Sears, Roebuck catalog was advertising laudanum for sale for about six cents an ounce, while other opium products were addressed specifically to the alcoholic. For example, Sears' "White Star Secret Liquor Cure" was advertised as designed to be added to the gentleman's after-dinner coffee so that he would be less inclined to join his friends at the local bar. In effect, he would probably nearly fall asleep at the table, since the "cure" was opium. If the customer were to become dependent on opium, perhaps as a result of the "opium cure," he could fortunately order "A Cure for the Opium

A nineteenth-century advertising card for a popular opium remedy was directed toward young mothers and their children.

Habit" on another page of the same catalog. Chances were good that the ingredients in this one included alcohol.[9] Opium habits were often replaced by cocaine habits (see Chapter 4) and vice versa.

Given the openness of opium use in the nineteenth-century United States, we can only surmise that the fanatical reaction against opium smoking was based on anti-Chinese prejudice. It is clear that intense hostility existed toward the thousands of Chinese men and boys brought to the West in the 1850s and 1860s to build the railroads. Since most of the Chinese workers were recruited from the Canton area, where opium traffic was particularly intense, the practice of opium smoking was well known to them and it served as a safety valve for an obviously oppressed society of men. In 1875 San Francisco outlawed opium smoking for fear, to quote a newspaper of the time, that "many women and young girls, as well as young men of respectable family, were being induced to visit the dens, where they were ruined morally and otherwise."[10] No mention was ever made of any moral ruin coming out of drinking opium at home.

A federal law forbidding opium smoking soon followed, while the regulation of opium use by any other means failed to receive legislative attention at that time. By the beginning of the twentieth century, however, the social control of opium dens became overshadowed by the emergence of opium-related drugs that were seen as more threatening than smoked opium.[11]

Morphine and the advent of heroin

n 1803 a German drug clerk named Friedrich Wilhelm Adam Sertürner first isolated a yellowish white substance in raw opium that turned out to be its primary active ingredient. He called it morphium, later changed to **morphine,** in honor of Morpheus, the Greek god of dreams. For the first time more than three fourths of the total weight of opium (containing inactive resins, oils, and sugars) could be separated out and discarded. Morphine represented roughly 10 percent of the total weight of opium, but it was found to be roughly ten times stronger than raw opium. All the twenty-five or so opiate products that were eventually isolated from opium were found to be weaker than morphine and formed a far smaller proportion of opium. Besides morphine, other major opiate products were **codeine** (0.5 percent of raw opium) and **thebaine** (0.2 percent of raw opium), both of which were found to have a considerably weaker opiate effect.

In the scientific community, Sertürner's discovery was recognized as a major achievement of its time. It was not until 1856, however, with the invention of the hypodermic syringe, that morphine became a widely accepted medical drug. With the syringe it could be injected into the bloodstream rather than administered orally, bypassing the gastrointestinal tract, and the effects could be felt much faster. The new potential of a morphine injection coincided with the traumas of the Civil War in the United States (1861–1865) and later the Franco-Prussian War in Europe (1870–1871). Information about the syringe came too late for morphine injections to be widespread during the American conflict, but millions of opium pills and oral doses of morphine were distributed to soldiers injured in battle. It is not surprising that large numbers of soldiers became dependent on opiates and maintained the condition in the years that followed by morphine injections. After the

morphine
The major active ingredient in opium.

codeine (COH-deen)
One of the three active ingredients in opium, used primarily to treat coughing.

Thebaine (THEE-bayn)
One of three active ingredients in opium.

Civil War, opiate dependence in general was so widespread among returning veterans that the condition was often called the soldier's disease.[12]

Against the backdrop of increasing worry about opiate dependence, a new painkilling morphine derivative called **heroin** was introduced into the market in 1898 by the Bayer Company in Germany, the same company that had been successful in developing aspirin (acetylsalicylic acid) as an analgesic drug (Chapter 15). About three times stronger than morphine, and strangely enough believed initially to be free of morphine's dependence-producing properties, heroin (from the German *heroisch,* meaning "powerful") was hailed as an entirely safe cough suppressant preferable to codeine. It is incredible that from 1898 to 1905, no fewer than forty medical studies concerning injections of heroin failed to pick up on its potential for dependence! The abuse potential of heroin, which we now know exceeds that of morphine, was not fully recognized until as late as 1910.[13]

Why is heroin more potent than morphine? The answer lies in the fact that heroin consists of two acetyl groups joined to a basic morphine molecule. These attachments make heroin more fat-soluble and hence more rapidly absorbed into the brain. Once inside the brain, however, the two acetyl groups break off, making the effects of heroin chemically identical to that of morphine. One way of seeing the relationship between the two drugs is to imagine morphine as the contents inside a plain cardboard box and the heroin as the gift wrapping. The contents remain the same, but the wrapping increases the chances the box will eventually be opened.

heroin
A chemical derivative of morphine. It is approximately three times as potent as morphine and a major drug of abuse.

Heroin and opiate dependence in the twentieth century

The end of the nineteenth century marked a turning point in the history of opium and its derivatives. Opiate dependence would never again be treated casually. By 1900, there were, by one conservative estimate, 250,000 opiate-dependent people in the United States, and the actual number could have been three times that. If we rely upon the upper estimate, then we would be speaking of one out of every hundred Americans, young or old, living at the time. Compare these figures with the estimate of 300,000 opiate (chiefly heroin) abusers in the United States in the 1990s, with the population at large being at least four times greater than in 1900, and you can appreciate how extensive opiate abuse was during the turn of the century.

The size of the opiate-abusing population alone at this time would probably have been sufficient grounds for social reformers to seek some way of controlling these drugs, but there was also the growing fear that, despite the popularity of opiates among all levels of society, the problem of opiate abuse was becoming closely associated with criminal elements or the underworld. There was a gnawing anxiety that opiates were causing a significant disruption in American society.

Opiate use after 1914

The Harrison Act of 1914 (see Chapter 2) radically changed the face of opiate use and abuse in the United States. It ushered in an era in which the addict was

. . . no longer seen as a victim of drugs, an unfortunate with no place to turn and deserving of society's sympathy and help. He became instead a base, vile, degenerate who was weak and self-indulgent, who contaminated all he came in contact with and

who deserved nothing short of condemnation and society's moral outrage and legal sanction.[14]

The situation, however, did not change overnight. Most important, the 1914 legislation did not actually ban opiate use. It simply required that doctors register with the Internal Revenue Service the opiate drugs (as well as cocaine and other coca products) that were being prescribed to their patients and pay a small fee for the right to prescribe such drugs. The real impact of the new law came later, in the early 1920s, as a result of several landmark decisions sent down from the U.S. Supreme Court. In effect, the decisions interpreted the Harrison Act more broadly. Under the Court's interpretation of the Harrison Act, no physician was permitted to prescribe opiate drugs for "nonmedical" use. In other words, it was now illegal for addicted individuals to obtain drugs merely to maintain their habit, even from a physician.

Without a legal source for their drugs, opiate abusers were forced to turn to illegal means or else abandon opiates altogther, and the drug dealer suddenly provided the only place where opiate drugs could be obtained. In 1924 a new law outlawed the importation of opium into the United States, if the opium was to be made into heroin. Since there was ordinarily no way of telling what the destination of imported opium might be, the presumption was always that its purpose was illegal. As a result, legitimate opium sources were cut off, and the importation of any opiate-related drug was now in the hands of the smuggler.

Heroin became the perfect black market drug. It was easier and more profitable to refine it from raw opium overseas and ship it into the country in small bags of odorless heroin powder than it was to transport raw opium with its characteristic odor. In addition, because it had to be obtained illegally, heroin's price tag skyrocketed to thirty to fifty times what it had cost when it was available from legitimate sources.[15]

With the emergence of restrictive legislation, the demographic picture also changed dramatically. No longer were the typical takers of narcotic drugs characterized as female, predominantly white, middle-age, and middle-class, as likely to be living on a Nebraskan farm as in a house in Chicago. In their place were young, predominantly white, urban adult males, whose opiate drug of choice was intravenous heroin and whose drug supply was controlled by organized crime.[16]

Heroin addiction in the 1960s and 1970s

Three major social developments in the 1960s brought the heroin story back into the consciousness of the United States. The first began in late 1961 when a crackdown on heroin smuggling resulted in a significant shortage of heroin on the street. The price of heroin suddenly increased, and heroin dosages became more adulterated than ever before. Predictably, the high costs of maintaining heroin dependence encouraged new levels of criminal behavior, particularly in urban ghettos. Heroin abuse soon forced a cultural stranglehold on many African American and Latino communities in the major cities.

A second development, beginning in the 1960s, affected the white majority more directly. Fanned by extensive media attention, a youthful counterculture of hippies, flower children, and the sexually liberated swept the country.

It was a time of unconventional fashions and anti-establishment attitudes. In unprecedented numbers, middle- and upper-class people experimented with illegal drugs to get high. They smoked marijuana; tried the new synthetic properties of amphetamines and barbiturates; rediscovered the almost forgotten product of the coca plant, cocaine; and, for the first time, people from the mainstream of American life began to experiment with derivatives of the opium poppy. Thus, heroin addiction made its insidious way back to the forefront of national concern.[17]

Finally, disturbing news about heroin addiction began to appear that focused not only on Americans at home but also on American armed forces personnel stationed in Southeast Asia in connection with the Vietnam War. Faced with a combination of despair and boredom, a lack of definable military mission or objective, opposition at home to the conflict itself, and the unusual stresses of fighting a guerrilla war, many of these soldiers turned to psychoactive drugs as a way of coping. Reports beginning in the late 1960s indicated an increasingly widespread recreational abuse of heroin, along with alcohol, marijuana, and other drugs, among U.S. soldiers. One returning Vietnam veteran related the atmosphere of polydrug abuse at the time:

> The last few months over there were unbelievable. My first tour there in '67, a few of our guys smoked grass, you know. Now the guys walk right in the hootch with a jar of heroin or cocaine. Almost pure stuff. Getting smack [heroin] is like getting a bottle of beer. Everybody sells it. Half my company is on the stuff.[18]

With respect to heroin, the problem was exacerbated by the fact that Vietnamese heroin was 90 to 98 percent pure, compared to 2 to 10 percent pure in the United States at the time, and incredibly cheap to buy. A 250-mg dose of heroin, for example, could be purchased for $10, while the standard intravenous dose on the streets of a major U.S. city would amount to only 10 mg. A comparable 250 mg of highly diluted U.S. heroin would have cost about $500. With the purity of heroin supplies so high, most U.S. soldiers smoked or sniffed it to get an effect; some drank it mixed with alcohol, even though most of the drug was lost through the absorption in the gastrointestinal tract.[19]

Beyond the concern about the soldiers overseas, there was also the worry that tens of thousands of Vietnam veterans would be returning home hopelessly addicted to heroin. It has been estimated, from survey

Military involvement in Vietnam brought U.S. soldiers in contact with unusually potent doses of heroin and other psychoactive drugs.

data, that about 11 percent of Army returnees in 1971 were regular users of heroin and about 22 percent had tried it at least once. Urine tests (appropriately named Operation Golden Flow), conducted near the end of a soldier's tour of duty, revealed a percentage about one half of that level, but there were strong indications that servicemen had voluntarily given up heroin prior to their being shipped home.

Fortunately, the worst fears were not borne out. A comprehensive investigation in 1974 showed that only 1 to 2 percent of Vietnam veterans were regular heroin abusers, one year following their return from overseas, approximately the same percentage as those entering the military from the general population.[20] Why were we so lucky? Evidently, the use of heroin was situationally specific to involvement in Vietnam. Does that mean that it is possible to abuse heroin without becoming dependent upon it? This question will be addressed later in the chapter.

Heroin and synthetic opiates in the 1980s and 1990s

Since the late 1980s, the supply routes for heroin smuggled into the United States have originated in the "Golden triangle" region of Laos, Myanmar (formerly Burma), and Thailand; in parts of Afghanistan, Pakistan, and Iran; and in Mexico. Prior to 1973, the major source of heroin had been Turkey, where the opium was grown, and the center of heroin manufacture and heroin distribution had been Marseilles in southern France (the infamous French Connection, as popularized in the 1970 movie of the same name). A ban on the cultivation of opium poppies in Turkey and enforcement of laws against smuggling operations in France, however, greatly reduced heroin trafficking from that region, but it unfortunately encouraged other parts of the world to fill the vacuum that was created. Soon after, a new form of heroin from Mexico, brownish in color instead of white, began entering the United States. In addition, remote regions in Southeast Asia, controlled by chieftains largely independent of formal governmental control, became the dominant source of U.S. heroin. One consequence was the increase in the purity of imported heroin from around 5 percent to more than 18 percent.

More recently, a number of other countries have joined the list of international heroin suppliers. While Myanmar remains the largest opium-producing nation in the world in the 1990s (accounting for 60 to 70 percent of the U.S. heroin supply in 1995), opium cultivation and heroin trafficking has been growing in the central Asian states of Kazakhstan, Kyrgystan, Tajikistan, Turkmenistan and Uzbekistan, all of which are regions of the former Soviet Union. In 1994 a major State Department report identified Nigeria as being centrally involved in the trafficking of heroin into the United States as well as Europe.[21]

While the growth of crack-cocaine abuse in the 1980s pushed the issue of heroin abuse temporarily out of the major headlines, heroin abuse itself continued in new forms and variations. One significant development was the appearance around 1985 of a relatively pure and inexpensive form of Mexican heroin called **black tar** (Focus 7.1). At about the same time, new synthetic forms of heroin were appearing on the street, created in illegal drug laboratories within the United States. One such synthetic drug was derived from **fentanyl,** a prescription narcotic drug. Chemical modifications of fentanyl, anywhere from ten to a thousand times stronger than heroin, were sold under the common name "China White." The risks of overdose death increased dramatically. From a technical point of view, however, this and other similar "designer drugs" were not illegal, through a loophole in the drug laws; because they were not chemically identical to heroin, no specific law applied to them. In 1986, however, through the Controlled Substance Analogue Act, this unfortunate loophole was closed. The laws now state that any drug with a chemical structure or pharmacological effect similar to that of a controlled substance is as illegal as the genuine article. Nonetheless, such look-alike opiates are still available as drugs of abuse.

In the 1990s, with the decline in the popularity of cocaine abuse, there has been a resurgence in heroin abuse (see Chapter 1) and the appearance of heroin purities in the neighborhood of at least 60 percent, at least ten times more powerful than the typical street heroin of the 1970s. In 1994 a brand of heroin sold in New York City with a purity of 90 percent took heroin abusers by surprise, resulting in several overdose deaths within a period of five days.

With the availability of nearly pure heroin, heroin no longer needs to be injected. Instead, it can be snorted or smoked. The new heroin

> **black tar**
> A potent form of heroin, generally brownish in color, originating in Mexico.
>
> **fentanyl (FEN-teh-nil)**
> A chemical derivative from thebaine, used as a prescription pain-killer. The street name for fentanyl and related compounds is China White.

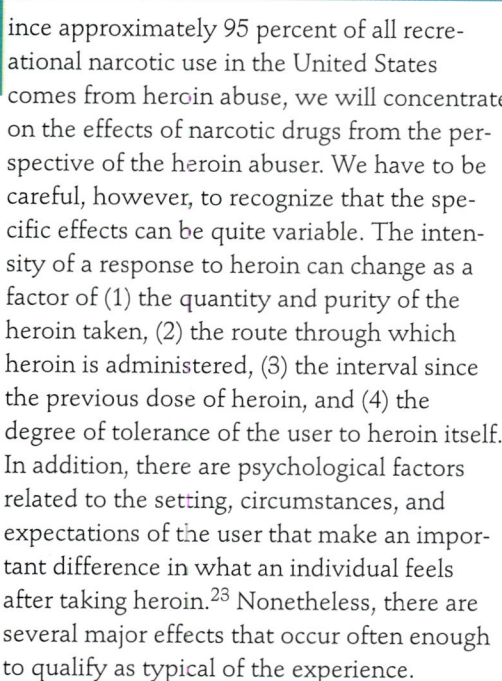

FOCUS 7.1

Black tar heroin in the United States

n the late 1980s, a new form of heroin, quite unlike heroin powder, hit the streets of U.S. cities: black tar. As the name suggests, black tar is a sticky substance, dark brown or black in color, produced by a relatively crude process that leaves many plant by-products still in the drug. In the western United States, black tar has been sold uncut, in purities that range from 2 percent to an astounding 93 percent. Most frequently, the purity of black tar is in the 40 to 60 percent range, considerably higher than that of ordinary powdered heroin. Despite its purity, however, black tar is sold very cheaply, often for about one tenth the price of other forms of heroin.

Black tar is typically administered by injection. Since it is usually gummy, it is relatively easy to smoke by heating it on a piece of aluminum foil and inhaling the vapor through a straw, a method called "chasing the dragon's tail."

Black tar heroin traffic is controlled almost totally by Mexicans and Mexican Americans living legally or illegally within the United States. The increased availability of black tar, originating in Latino communities in the Southwest, is a major drug-related concern across the country.

SOURCE: *Black tar heroin in the United States.* (1986) (Special Report). Washington DC: U.S. Department of Justice, Drug Enforcement Administration.

abusers are frequently mixing the heroin with crack cocaine or heating the heroin and inhaling the vapors that are created. While these methods avoid potentially HIV-contaminated needles, they do not prevent the dependence that heroin can produce or the risk of overdose. Unfortunately, heroin snorting or smoking has also opened the door to a new population of potential heroin abusers who have previously stayed away from the drug on the basis of their aversion to hypodermic needles.[22]

Effects on the mind and the body

ince approximately 95 percent of all recreational narcotic use in the United States comes from heroin abuse, we will concentrate on the effects of narcotic drugs from the perspective of the heroin abuser. We have to be careful, however, to recognize that the specific effects can be quite variable. The intensity of a response to heroin can change as a factor of (1) the quantity and purity of the heroin taken, (2) the route through which heroin is administered, (3) the interval since the previous dose of heroin, and (4) the degree of tolerance of the user to heroin itself. In addition, there are psychological factors related to the setting, circumstances, and expectations of the user that make an important difference in what an individual feels after taking heroin.[23] Nonetheless, there are several major effects that occur often enough to qualify as typical of the experience.

If heroin is injected intravenously, there is an almost immediate tingling sensation and sudden feeling of warmth in the lower abdomen, resembling a sexual orgasm, for the first minute or two. There is a feeling of intense euphoria, variously described as a "rush" or a "flash," followed later by a state of tranquil drowsiness that heroin abusers often call being "on the nod." During this period, lasting from three to four hours, any interest in sex is greatly diminished. In the case of male heroin abusers, the decline in sexual desire is due, at least in part, to the fact that narcotics reduce the levels of testosterone, the major male sex hormone.[24]

An individual's first-time experience with heroin, however, may be considerably less pleasant. Opiates in general cause nausea and vomiting, as the reflex centers in the medulla are suddenly stimulated. Some first-time abusers find the vomiting so aversive that they never try the drug again; others consider the discomfort largely irrelevant because the euphoria is so powerful.

There are a number of additional physiological changes in the body. A sudden release of histamine in the bloodstream produces an often intense itching over the entire body and a reddening of the eyes. Heroin will also cause pupillary constriction, resulting in the characteristic "pinpoint pupils" that are used as an important diagnostic sign for narcotic abuse in general. As with sedative-hypnotic drugs (see Chapter 5), heroin also reduces the sensitivity of respiratory centers in the medulla to levels of carbon dioxide, resulting in a depression in breathing. At high doses, respiratory depression is a major risk factor that can result in death. Blood pressure is also depressed from heroin intake. Finally, a distressing, though nonlethal, effect of heroin is the slowing down of the gastrointestinal tract, causing a labored defecation and long-term constipation.[25]

Medical uses of narcotic drugs

e have focused upon the acute effects of narcotic drugs in the context of heroin abuse, but it is also important to look at the beneficial effects that narcotic drugs can have in a medical setting (Table 7.1).

Beneficial effects

Excluding heroin, which is a Schedule I drug in the United States and therefore unavailable for medical use, narcotic drugs have been administered with three primary therapeutic goals in mind: the relief of pain, the treatment of acute diarrhea, and the suppression of coughing. These applications are not at all new; they have been employed throughout the long history of opiate drugs.

The first and foremost medical use of narcotic drugs today is for the treatment of pain. For a patient suffering severe pain following surgical procedures or from burns or incurable cancer, morphine is the drug of choice. The actual impact on pain, however, is not a simple one. Patients report that morphine has indeed reduced their suffering caused by pain

T A B L E 7 . 1		
Major narcotic drugs in medical use		
Generic name	Brand name*	Recommended dose for adults
morphine	Duramorph	2–10 mg (i.v.)
	Roxanol	10–30 mg (oral)
codeine		30–60 mg (oral, i.m., or s.c.)
hydromorphone	Dilaudid	1–2 mg (i.m. or s.c.)
oxymorphone	Numorphan	1–1.5 mg (i.m. or s.c.)
oxycodone	Percodan	4.5 mg (oral) with aspirin
	Percocet	5 mg (oral) with acetaminophen
hydrocodone	Hycodan	5 mg (oral)
	Hydrocet	5 mg (oral) with acetaminophen
methadone	Dolorphine	2.5–10 mg (oral, i.v., or s.c.)
meperidine	Demerol	50–150 mg (oral, i.m., or s.c.)
propoxyphene	Darvon	65 mg (oral)
	Darvon-N	65 mg (oral) with acetaminophen
pentazocine	Talwin	30 mg (i.v., i.m., or s.c.)
fentanyl	Sublimaze	.05–.10 mg (i.v.)
	Duragesic	.05–.10 mg (time release by transdermal patch)

*Only a portion of the brands are listed here. Some narcotic drugs are available only under their generic names or under either their generic or brand names.

SOURCE: *Physicians' desk reference* (48th ed.). (1994). Montvale NJ: Medical Economics Data.

but not their perception of pain itself. They say that the pain can now be ignored because it does not bother them anymore, but if their attention is drawn to the pain they will acknowledge that it is still there. Strangely enough, they are aware of the pain, but the pain no longer distresses them.

The second application capitalizes on the effect of opiates in slowing down peristaltic contractions in the intestines that occur as part of the digestive process. As noted earlier, one problem associated with the chronic abuse of heroin, as well as of other opiates, is constipation. However, for individuals with dysentery, a bacterial infection of the lower intestinal tract causing pain and severe diarrhea, this negative side effect can prove a positive benefit. In fact, the control of diarrhea by morphine is literally life-saving, since acute dehydration (loss of water) from diarrhea can frequently be fatal. An added benefit is that it takes much less morphine to affect gastrointestinal activity than to produce analgesia, so dose levels can be smaller. A traditional treatment is the administration of a camphorated form of opium called **paregoric.**

The third application focuses on the effect of narcotic drugs to suppress the cough reflex center in the medulla. In cases in which an **antitussive** (cough-suppressing) drug is necessary, codeine is frequently prescribed, either by itself or combined with other medications such as aspirin or acetaminophen (brand names: Tylenol among others). As an alternative treatment for coughing, there is a nonaddictive, nonopiate drug, **dextromethorphan,** that is available in over-the-counter syrups and lozenges as well as in combination with antihistamines (see Chapter 15). The "DM" designation in many of these cough-control preparations refers to the presence of dextromethorphan hydrobromide.

Possible complications

Since opiates have so many simultaneous effects on the body, it is natural that there should be some concerns attached to their medical use, even though the overall effect is beneficial. For example, respiration will be depressed for four to five hours even following a therapeutic dose of morphine, so caution is advised when the patient suffers from asthma, emphysema, or pulmonary heart disease. Nausea and vomiting can also be a prob-

---

QUICK CONCEPT CHECK 7.1

Understanding the history of drugs

heck your understanding of the historical background for opiates and other psychoactive drugs discussed in earlier chapters by answering the following multipart question. Imagine yourself to be living as a male adult in the year 1900. Write yes or no whether or not the following psychoactive drugs would be available to you.

1. heroin   ❑ yes   ❑ no
2. cocaine   ❑ yes   ❑ no
3. sodium phenobarbital   ❑ yes   ❑ no
4. crack cocaine   ❑ yes   ❑ no
5. d-amphetamine   ❑ yes   ❑ no
6. morphine   ❑ yes   ❑ no
7. nicotine   ❑ yes   ❑ no
8. alcohol   ❑ yes   ❑ no
9. benzodiazepines of
   any type   ❑ yes   ❑ no
10. ether or nitrous oxide   ❑ yes   ❑ no

If you were a woman in 1900, would your answers be different? Be specific as to the drugs listed above.

ANSWERS: 1. yes 2. yes 3. no 4. no 5. no 6. yes 7. yes 8. yes 9. no 10. yes
   With regard to women, answers to items 7 and 8 would be no. It would not have been generally acceptable for women to have used alcohol or nicotine.

---

paregoric (PAIR-a-GORE-ik)
A form of opium used medically for the control of gastrointestinal difficulties.

antitussive
Having an effect that controls coughing.

dextromethorphan
(DEX-troh-meh-THOR-fan)
A popular nonnarcotic ingredient used in OTC cough remedies.

---

lem for patients receiving morphine, especially if they walk around immediately afterward. As a result, patients are advised to remain still, either sitting or lying down, for a short period following their medication. In addition, opiate medications decrease the secretion of hydrochloric acid in the stomach and reduce the pushing of food through the intestines, a condition that can lead to intestinal spasms. Finally, while opiates will have a sleep-inducing effect in high doses, it is not recommended that they be used as a general sedative-hypnotic treatment, unless sleep is being prevented by pain or coughing.[26]

How opiates work in the brain

Earlier chapters looked at the neurochemical basis for a number of psychoactive drugs in terms of their influence upon various neurotransmitters in the brain. For example, the stimulant effects of cocaine and amphetamine were related to changes in norepinephrine and dopamine (Chapter 4), while the antianxiety effects of benzodiazepines were related to changes in GABA (Chapter 5). In the case of opiate drugs, however, as a result of major discoveries in the 1970s, it is clear that we are dealing with a more direct effect: the activation of receptors in the brain that are specifically sensitive to morphine.

During the 1960s, suspicions grew that a morphine-sensitive receptor, or a family of them, exist in the brain. One major clue came from the discovery that small chemical alterations in the morphine molecule would result in a group of new drugs with strange and intriguing properties. Not only would these drugs produce little or no *agonistic* effects, that is they would not act like morphine, but instead they would act as *opiate antagonists*, that is they would reverse or block the effects of morphine (Fig. 7.2).

The most complete opiate antagonist to be identified, **naloxone** (brand name: Narcan), turned out to have enormous therapeutic benefits in the emergency treatment of narcotic-overdose situations. In such cases, intramuscular or intravenous injections of naloxone reverse the depressed breathing and blood pressure in a matter of a minute or so, an effect so fast that emergency-room special-

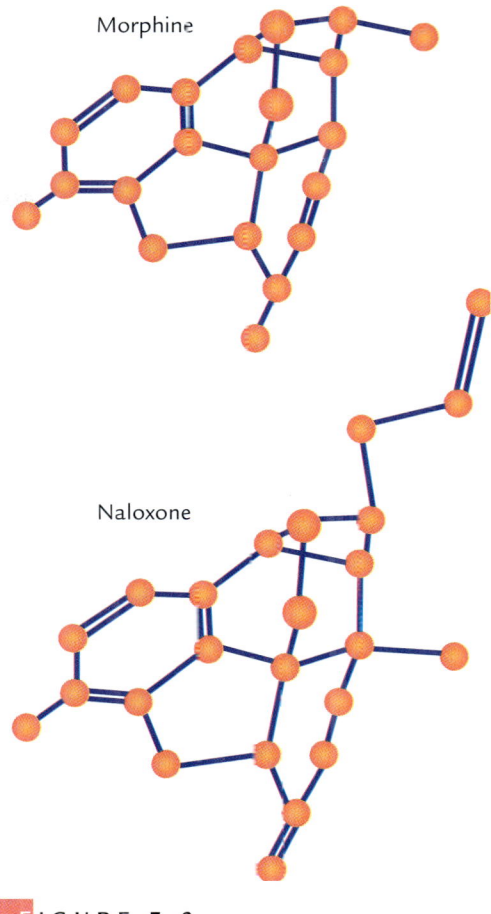

F I G U R E   7 . 2

Only minor differences exist between a morphine molecule and a naloxone molecule

ists view the reaction as "miraculous." The effect lasts for one to four hours. Higher doses of naloxone bring on symptoms that are very similar to those observed following an abrupt withdrawal of narcotic drugs. Interestingly, in normal undrugged people, naloxone produces only negligible changes, either on a physiological or a psychological level. Only if morphine or other narcotic drugs are already in the body does naloxone have an effect.[27]

Beyond its practical application, the discovery of naloxone had theoretical implications as

naloxone (nah-LOX-ohn)
A pure antagonist for morphine and other opiate drugs. Brand name is Narcan.

well. The argument went as follows: If such small molecular changes could so dramatically transform an agonist into an antagonist, then some receptor in the brain must exist in such a way that it can be easily excited or inhibited. The concept of a special morphine-sensitive receptor fits these requirements.

The actual receptors themselves were discovered in 1973, precisely where you would have expected them to be, in the spinal cord and brain, where pain signals are known to be processed, and in the limbic system of the brain, where emotional behaviors are coordinated. In other words, it was clear that the analgesic and euphoric properties of morphine were due to the stimulation of these receptors.

Why would these receptors exist in the first place? No one seriously considers the possibility that receptors in the brain have been patiently waiting millions of years in evolutionary history for the day that the juice of the opium poppy could finally slip inside them! The only logical answer is that we must be producing our own morphine-like chemicals that activate these receptors.

As a result of a series of important discoveries from 1975 to the early 1980s, three groups of natural morphine-like molecules have been identified: enkephalins, beta-endorphin, and dynorphins. Together, they are known as **endogenous opioid peptides,** inasmuch as they are (1) all peptide molecules (amino acids strung together like a necklace), (2) opiate-like in function, and (3) produced within the central nervous system. Unfortunately, this is such an unwieldy name that more frequently they are simply referred to as *endorphins*. Since their discovery, endorphins have been studied with regard to a wide range of human behaviors. Focus 7.2 lists some of the findings of these studies.

endogenous opioid peptides (en-DODGE-eh-nus OH-pee-oid PEP-teyeds) also known as **endorphins** A class of chemicals produced inside the body that mimic the effects of opiate drugs.

What can we then conclude about the effect of opiates on the brain? The answer, as we now understand it, is that the brain has the ability to produce its own "opiate-like" substances, called endorphins, and contains a special set of receptor sites to receive them. By an amazing quirk of fate, the opium poppy yields a similarly shaped chemical that fits into these receptor sites, thus producing equivalent psychological and physiological effects. Naloxone acts as an opiate antagonist because its structural features enable it to fit into these receptor sites, replacing the drug molecules that have gotten in. This is why naloxone can "undo" the acute effects of an opiate drug like heroin.

Patterns of heroin abuse

The dominant route of administration in heroin abuse is intravenous injection, usually referred to as either mainlining or shooting. Heroin can also be administered by a variety of other routes. Heroin smoking is popular in Middle Eastern countries and in Asia, but until very recently (because of the AIDS epidemic) it has seldom been observed in the United States. Newcomers to heroin may begin their abuse either by snorting the drug through the nose or injecting it subcutaneously (skin-popping). Experienced heroin abusers may snort heroin in order to avoid using a needle or choose the subcutaneous route when they can no longer find veins in good enough condition to handle an intravenous injection. An oral administration for heroin or any other narcotic (except for methadone) is virtually worthless because absorption is extremely poor. American soldiers in Vietnam who were abusing heroin often took the drug orally, but they were consuming dose levels that far exceeded the levels found on American streets at that time.

Tolerance and withdrawal symptoms

A prime feature of chronic heroin abuse is the tolerance that develops, but the tolerance

What do endorphins tell us about ourselves?

Here is a sampling of research findings that have dealt with endorphins:

1. Under stressful circumstances, people can become temporarily analgesic (insensible to pain) without any external drugs. There are well-documented cases of soldiers who have been oblivious to their injuries during the heat of battle, athletes who are unaware of their pain until the game is over, and individuals in primitive societies who endure painful religious rituals or initiation rites without complaint. Increased levels of endorphins, released in these situations, are considered to provide this analgesia.

2. Electrical stimulation of a midbrain region in experimental animals results in a profound analgesia. This effect is reversible, at least in part, by naloxone. As a consequence, it is believed that the analgesia results from an increased level of endorphins.

3. The analgesia that is accomplished by acupuncture, the Chinese technique of inserting needles into the skin at precisely defined points in the body, is completely reversible by naloxone. Therefore, it is reasonable to conclude that acupuncture produces increased levels of endorphins.

4. Endorphin levels measured in the placental bloodstream of pregnant women near to the time of childbirth are greatly elevated from levels normally present in nonpregnant women, reaching a peak during labor itself. It is believed that as a result, women during labor are enduring less pain than they would have if endorphin levels were unchanged. In other words, endorphins are protecting them against an even greater amount of discomfort at this important time.

5. Some studies have shown increased levels of endorphins among compulsive runners and other athletes. This increase could explain the euphoria, and in some instances analgesia, felt during strenuous physical exercise. Nonetheless, there are also increased levels of adrenalin at the same time, which cannot be ruled out as contributing to this effect.

6. Emaciated anorexic women have been found to have higher endorphin levels than control patients without anorexic symptoms. When body weights return to normal, the endorphin levels decline. Anorexic women often report feeling high and often engage compulsively in physical exercise. These feelings and this behavior might be tied in with endorphin disturbances in the body.

7. Laboratory rats like chocolate, seemingly as much as humans do. In tasks in which they are trained to work for chocolate rewards, injections of naloxone will make them less anxious to perform the tasks. It is possible that at least a portion of the pleasure of eating chocolate may be linked to the release of endorphins.

SOURCES: Levinthal, Charles F. (1988). *Messengers of paradise: Opiates and the brain.* New York: Anchor Press/Doubleday. Dum, J., and Herz, A. (1984). Endorphinergic modulation of neural reward systems indicated by behavioral changes. *Pharmacology, Biochemistry, and Behavior 21,* 259–266.

effects themselves are not "across the board" with regard to all of the responses commonly associated with heroin. Gastrointestinal effects of constipation and spasms do not show much tolerance at all; while distinctive pupillary responses (the pinpoint feature of the eyes) will eventually subside over chronic use. The greatest signs of tolerance are seen in the degree of analgesia, euphoria, and respiratory depression. The intense thrill of the intravenous injection will be noticeably lessened. The overall decline in heroin reactions, however, is dose-dependent. If the dose level is high, then tolerance effects will be more dramatic than if the dose level is low.

The first sign of heroin withdrawal, a marked craving for another fix, generally begins about four to six hours after the previous dose and gradually intensifies to a peak over the next thirty-six to seventy-two hours, with other symptoms beginning from a few hours later (see Table 7.2). The abuser is essentially over the withdrawal period in five to ten days, though mild physiological disturbances, chiefly elevations in blood pressure and heart rate, are observed as long as six

TABLE 7.2

Symptoms of administering heroin and of withdrawing heroin

Administering	Withdrawing
Lowered body temperature	Elevated body temperature
Decreased blood pressure	Increased blood pressure
Skin flushed and warm	Piloerection (gooseflesh)
Pupillary constriction	Tearing, runny nose
Constipation	Diarrhea
Respiratory depression	Yawning, panting, sneezing
Decreased sex drive	Spontaneous ejaculations and orgasms
Muscular relaxation	Restlessness, involuntary twitching and kicking movements*
Nodding, stupor	Insomnia
Analgesia	Pain and irritability
Euphoria and calm	Depression and anxiety

*Probably the source of the expression, "kicking the habit."

SOURCE: Adapted from Grilly, David M. (1989). *Drugs and human behavior*. Boston: Allyn and Bacon, p. 207.

months later. Generally, these long-term effects are associated with a gradual withdrawal from heroin rather than an abrupt one.

The overall severity of heroin-withdrawal symptoms is a function of the dosage levels of heroin that have been sustained. When dosage levels were in the "single digits" (under 10 percent), the withdrawal symptoms were comparable to a moderate to intense case of the flu. In more severe cases, the withdrawal process can result in a significant loss of weight and body fluids. With recent increases in the purities of street heroin in the 1990s, the symptoms of withdrawal are greater. Only rarely, however, is the process of heroin withdrawal life threatening, unlike the withdrawal from barbiturate drugs (see Chapter 5).

It should not be surprising that withdrawal symptoms are essentially the mirror image of symptoms observed when a person is under the influence of heroin. If we are dealing with a group of endorphin-sensitive receptors that are, in the case of the heroin abuser, being stimulated by the opiates coming in from the outside, then it is reasonable to assume that over time, the production of endorphins would decline. Why produce stuff on your own when you are getting it from an external source? By that argument, withdrawal from heroin would then be a matter of cutting off those receptors from that external source, resulting in a reaction opposite to the one that would have occurred, had the receptors been satisfied in the first place. Over a period of time, coinciding with the withdrawal period for a heroin abuser, we would expect that the normal production of endorphins would reestablish itself and there would be little or no need for the external supply of heroin.

The receptor explanation for heroin dependence sounds reasonable and does account for the presence of withdrawal symptoms, but unfortunately it has to be an oversimplification for heroin abuse in general. We would expect that once the endorphin-sensitive receptors regained their natural supply of endorphins, heroin abuse would end, but we know that it does not.

In the case of heroin abusers, their tendency to continue taking heroin is propelled by a number of factors. There is, first of all, the combination of fear and distress associated with the prospect of experiencing withdrawal symptoms, along with a genuine craving for the effects themselves, as a result of the physical and psychological dependence that heroin brings. In addition, long-term heroin abuse frequently produces such a powerful conditioned-learning effect that the social setting in which the drug-taking behavior has occurred takes on reinforcing properties of its own. Even the act of inserting a needle can become pleasurable. Some heroin abusers (called needle freaks) will continue to insert needles into their skin and experience heroin-like effects even when there is no heroin in the syringe. In effect, the heroin abuser is responding to a placebo. Any long-term treatment for heroin abuse, as will be discussed in a later section, must address itself to a range of physical, psychological, and social factors in order to be successful.

However rocky the road from heroin abuse to rehabilitation might be, the first step is to stop. Fortunately, in most cases, the withdrawal process can be made less distressing if the drug is reduced gradually under medical supervision than if the heroin abuser is abruptly withdrawn from heroin "cold turkey" (a name probably inspired by the gooseflesh appearance of an abuser's skin during withdrawal). In a medical setting, a synthetic opiate, either **propoxyphene** (brand name: Darvon) or **methadone,** is frequently administered to lessen the distress of withdrawal, and doses of this transitional drug are decreased over a period of two weeks or so.[28]

The withdrawal process can also be lessened by the administration of **clonidine** (brand name: Catapres), a drug traditionally prescribed for the control of high blood pressure. Clonidine is helpful because it inhibits norepinephrine in a small region of the pons called the **locus coeruleus,** where there exists a high concentration of neurons that are sensitive to both norepinephrine and endorphins.

Through animal studies, researchers know that when the locus coeruleus is stimulated, the behavioral result includes symptoms of fear and anxiety that are virtually identical to symptoms produced by withdrawal from narcotic drugs. Since opiates inhibit norepinephrine-sensitive neurons, the locus coeruleus remains relatively quiet while the individual is taking heroin. When heroin is withdrawn, however, the norepinephrine-sensitive neurons rebound to a hyperactive state. Clonidine inhibits these hyperactive neurons and, as a result, reduces the intensity of withdrawal symptoms.[29]

The lethality of heroin abuse

Considering the statistics of deaths resulting from heroin abuse (see Chapter 2), you might be surprised to learn that heroin itself is considered a relatively nontoxic drug. As one expert has put it:

Unlike alcohol, the amphetamines, and the barbiturates, which are toxic to the body over the long run with relatively heavy use, the narcotics are relatively safe. The organs are not damaged, destroyed, or even threatened by even a lifetime of narcotic addiction. There are no major malformations of the body, no tissue damage, no physical deterioration directly traceable to the use of any narcotic, including heroin.[30]

If chronic heroin intake is nontoxic, why are there deaths? The answer lies in the potentially lethal acute effects. First of all, heroin has a relatively small ratio of LD (lethal dose) to ED (effective dose). Increase a dose that produces a high in a heroin abuser by ten or fifteen times and you will be in the dosage range that is potentially fatal. As a result, death by overdose is an ever present risk. If we now take into account the virtually unknown potency of street heroin in any given fix, we can begin to appreciate the hazards involved. While the "bag" sold to a heroin abuser may look like the same amount each time, the actual heroin content may be anywhere between none at all and 90 percent. Therefore, it is easy to underestimate the amount of heroin being taken in. In addition, there is the risk of possible adverse effects from any toxic substance that has been "cut" with the heroin. Adding to the complexity, deaths from heroin overdose are frequently consequences of synergistic combinations of heroin with other

propoxyphene (pro-POX-ee-feen)
A synthetic opiate useful in treating heroin abuse. Brand name is Darvon.

methadone
A synthetic opiate useful in treating heroin abuse.

clonidine (CLAHN-eh-deyen)
A drug, ordinarily used for treating high blood pressure that reduces the distress of narcotic withdrawal. Brand name is Catapres.

locus coeruleus (LOH-cus ser-ROOL-ee-us)
A region of the pons in the brain, having a high concentration of receptors sensitive to norepinephrine and endorphins.

abused drugs such as stimulants like cocaine or depressants like alcohol, Valium, or barbiturates. Seldom do heroin abusers restrict their drug-taking behavior simply to heroin. A listing of street names for heroin and heroin combinations is given in Table 7.3.

As noted in Chapter 3, it is also possible that some heroin abusers develop unstable levels of tolerance that are tied to the environmental setting in which the heroin is administered. A heroin dose, experienced in an environment that has not been previously associated with drug taking, may have a significantly greater effect on the abuser than the same dose taken in more familiar surroundings. As a result of all these factors, the specific effect on the abuser is largely unpredictable.

While the overriding danger of excessive amounts of heroin is the potentially lethal effects of respiratory depression, abusers can die from other physiological reactions. In some instances, death can come so quickly that the victims are found with a needle still in their veins, possibly due to a massive release of histamine or an allergic reaction to some filler in the heroin to which the abuser was hypersensitive. Intravenous injections of heroin increase the risks of hepatitis or HIV infections, while unsterile water used in the mixing of heroin for these injections can be contaminated with bacteria.

An extra risk began to appear during the mid-1980s. In some forms of synthetic heroin illicitly produced in clandestine laboratories in the United States, an impurity called MPTP was isolated that destroys dopamine-sensitive neurons in the substantia nigra of the midbrain. As a result, young people exposed to this type of heroin have acquired full-blown symptoms of Parkinson's disease (see Chapter 3) that are virtually identical in character to the symptoms observed in elderly patients suffering from a progressive loss of dopamine-sensitive neurons in their brains.

Heroin abuse and society

hile society over the last thirty years has had to deal with the reality of drug abuse in many forms, many people still see heroin abuse as the ultimate drug addiction and the heroin abuser as the ultimate "dope addict." It is true that many heroin abusers fit this image: people driven to stay high on a four- to eight-hour schedule, committing a continuing series of predatory crimes. Yet the actual picture of the present-day heroin abuser is more complex. A major study has shown that while robbery, burglary, and shoplifting accounted for 44 percent of an abuser's income and nearly two thirds of that abuser's criminal

TABLE 7.3

Street names for narcotic drugs

Type of narcotic	Street name
morphine	Big M, Miss Emma, white stuff, M, dope, hocus, unkie, stuff, morpho
white heroin	Junk, smack, horse, scag, H, stuff, hard stuff, cope, boy, boot, blow, jolt, spike, s am
brown heroin (from Mexico)	Black tar, tootsie roll, chapapote (Spanish for "tar"), mexican mud, peanut butter, poison, gummy balls, black jack
heroin combined with amphetamines	Bombitas
heroin combined with cocaine	Dynamite, speedball, whizbang, goofball
heroin combined with marijuana	Atom bomb, A-bomb
heroin combined with cocaine and marijuana	Frisco Special, Frisco speedball
heroin combined with cocaine and morphine	Cotton brothers
codeine combined with Doriden (a nonbarbituate sedative-hypnotic)	Loads, four coors, hits
Talwin combined with pyribenzamine (an antihistamine)	T's and blues

SOURCES: Adapted from Carroll, Charles R. (1993). *Drugs in modern society* (3rd ed.). Dubuque, IA: Brown and Benchmark, pp. 188, 201–202. U.S. Department of Justice, Drug Enforcement Administration. (1986). *Special Report: Black tar heroin in the United States*, p. 4. U.S. Department of Justice, Bureau of Justice Statistics Clearinghouse. (1992). *Drugs, crime, and the justice system*, pp. 24–25.

income, a substantial amount of income came from either victimless crimes (such as pimping or prostitution) or noncriminal activity. Often a heroin abuser would work in some capacity in the underground drug industry and be paid in heroin instead of dollars.[31]

A related question with regard to our image of the heroin abuser is whether or not controlled heroin abuse is possible. Is heroin abuse a situation that is, by definition, out of control? For thousands of heroin abusers, the answer is yes. Yet for other individuals, heroin is not a compulsion. It has been estimated that for every regular heroin abuser in the United States, there are three or four occasional abusers who do not appear to be physically dependent on the drug. The practice of controlled or paced heroin intake is referred to as **chipping**, and the occasional heroin abuser is known as a *chipper*.

An important study conducted by Norman E. Zinberg in 1984 analyzed a group of people who had been using heroin on a controlled basis for more than four years.[32] Over the course of one year, 23 percent reported taking heroin less than once a month, 36 percent reported taking it one to three times a month, and 41 percent reported taking it twice a week. Four years of exposure to heroin would seem to have been sufficient time to develop a compulsive dependence, but that did not happen. The observation that most compulsive heroin-dependent individuals never had any period of controlled use implies that controlled heroin abuse is not merely a early transitional stage that would eventually turn into uncontrolled heroin dependence. The chipper and the classic heroin abuser seem to belong to two separate populations. What factors differentiate them?

Zinberg's study showed that relative to the compulsive heroin abusers, occasional abusers tend to avoid heroin use in the presence of known addicts, rarely use heroin on a binge basis, and most often know the heroin dealer personally. Their motivations are different as well. Occasional abusers tend to use heroin for relaxation and recreation rather than to escape from difficulties in their lives or to reduce depression.

While from a behavioral standpoint the chipper appears to be avoiding the environmental influences (the social setting) that reinforce drug dependence, there may be a physiological distinction as well. Suppose for a moment that one group of people had more endorphin-sensitive receptors in their brains than another group, or else had some defi-

chipping
The taking of heroin on an occasional basis.

ciency in the ability to produce endorphins for those receptors. It is possible that the first group would not have the capacity for these receptors to be properly filled, resulting in a natural tendency to seek out external agents to do the job. This group would be inclined toward greater psychological and physical dependence than a group with a more normal internal endorphin system.

While this account is highly speculative, it may explain differences between occasional and compulsive heroin abuse. It may, in part, help to explain why the vast majority of Vietnam veterans who had been exposed to heroin overseas discontinued its abuse upon their return to their homes and why patients exposed to morphine for the relief of postsurgical pain seldom if ever develop dependence. Naturally, we cannot ignore the role of sociocultural differences in the development of chronic heroin abuse. Nonetheless, it is entirely possible that differences within the chemical makeup of the brain are a contributing factor.[33]

Treatment and long-term recovery programs

For the heroin abuser seeking out medical treatment for heroin dependence, the most immediate problem is getting the drug out of the abuser's system, a process called **detoxification** ("detox"), with a minimum of discomfort and distress. As mentioned earlier, clonidine has been particularly important in speeding up withdrawal and reducing the severity of physiological symptoms. Naloxone has also been used in combination with clonidine to complete the withdrawal process.

detoxification
The process of drug withdrawal in which the body is allowed to rid itself of the chemical effects of the drug in the bloodstream.

methadone maintenance
A treatment program for heroin abusers in which heroin is replaced by the long-term intake of methadone.

After detoxification, however, the long-term problem of drug dependence remains. The craving for heroin is still there, and the abuser most often has little choice but to return to a drug-oriented environment where the temptations to satisfy the craving still exist. Since the mid-1960s, one strategy has been to have a detoxified heroin abuser participate in a program in which oral administrations of the synthetic opiate methadone are essentially substituted for the injected heroin. This treatment approach, called **methadone maintenance,** was initiated in New York City through the joint efforts of Vincent Dole, a specialist in metabolic disorders, and Marie Nyswander, a psychiatrist whose interest has focused on narcotic dependence. Their idea was that if a legally and carefully controlled narcotic drug was available to heroin abusers on a regular basis, the craving for heroin would be eliminated, their drug-taking life-style would no longer be needed, and they could now turn to more appropriate social behaviors such as steady employment and a more stable family life.

For the Dole-Nyswander treatment program, now commonplace throughout the United States, methadone has definite advantages. First of all, since it is a legal, inexpensive narcotic drug (when dispensed through authorized drug-treatment centers), criminal activity involved in the purchase of heroin on the street can be avoided. Methadone is slower acting and more slowly metabolized, so withdrawal symptoms are less severe than with heroin. In addition, unlike heroin, methadone effects last approximately twenty-four hours and can be easily absorbed through an oral administration. Since it is a narcotic drug, methadone binds to the endorphin-sensitive receptors in the brain and prevents feelings of craving, yet its slow action avoids the rush of a heroin high.

Typically, clients in the program come to the treatment center daily for an oral dose of methadone, dispensed in orange juice, and the dose is gradually increased to a maintenance level over a period of four to six weeks.

A recent study indicates that the chances of an abuser turning away from illicit drug use are increased if the higher doses of methadone are made conditional upon a "clean" (drug-free) urinanalysis.[34] Successful maintenance has also improved by the introduction of a new form of methadone, **LAAM** (levo-alpha-acetylmethadol). The advantage of LAAM is a longer duration so that treatment clients need to receive the drug only three times a week instead of every day. Another drug showing promise for use in maintenance programs is the synthetic opiate **buprenorphine** (brand name: Buprenex). Though it must be taken daily, buprenorphine does not induce physical signs of dependence and effectively suppresses the craving for heroin among abusers.[35]

The general philosophy behind maintenance programs is that heroin abuse is a metabolic disorder requiring a maintenance drug for the body, just as a diabetic patient needs a maintenance supply of insulin. Whether this assumption is true has yet to be determined. As a social experiment, methadone-maintenance programs have met with a mixture of success and failure. On the one hand, evaluations of this program have found that 71 percent of former heroin abusers who have stayed in methadone maintenance for a year or more have stopped intravenous drug taking, thus lessening the risk of AIDS. In a major study, drug-associated problems declined from about 80 percent to between 17 and 28 percent, criminal behavior was reduced from over 20 percent to less than 10 percent, and there was a slight increase in permanent employment.[36] While never attracting more than 20 percent of the heroin-dependent community, methadone maintenance does attract those who perceive themselves as having a negligible chance of becoming abstinent on their own. It is reasonable to assume that we are looking at the potential rehabilitation of a hard-core subpopulation within heroin abusers.[37]

On the other hand, there have been several problems. The first has to do with the moral question of opiate maintenance itself. Some critics have seen these treatments as a cop-out that perpetuates rather than discourages the sense of low self-esteem among heroin abusers, a system that serves the needs of society over the needs of the individual.[38] While maintenance programs do help many heroin abusers, particularly those who stay in the program over an extended period of time, there are strong indications that the programs do not help the overall vulnerability toward drug abuse in general. Alcohol abuse among methadone-maintenance clients, for example, ranges from 10 percent to 40 percent, suggesting that alcohol may be substituting for narcotics during the course of treatment, and one study found that as many as 43 percent of those who had successfully given up heroin had become dependent on alcohol.[39] Furthermore, there is a problem with the diversion of methadone away from the clinics to the street for illicit use. As a result of the growth in methadone-maintenance clinics, the availability of street methadone has increased dramatically, adding to the already long list of abusable drugs.[40]

The shortcomings of the methadone-maintenance approach and variations of it have pointed to the inadequacy of solving the problem of heroin abuse on an exclusively physiological level.

In order to help deal with the tremendous social stresses that reinforce a continuation of heroin abuse, programs called **therapeutic communities** (Synanon and Odyssey House are examples) have developed, in which the

LAAM
The synthetic narcotic drug levo-alpha-acetylmethadol used in the treatment of heroin abuse.

buprenorphine (BYOO-preh-NOR-feen)
A synthetic opiate useful in heroin abuse treatment. Brand name is Buprenex.

therapeutic communities
Living environment for individuals in treatment for heroin and other drug abuse, where they learn social and psychological skills needed to lead a drug-free life.

Mother Hale and her thousand babies

It began in 1969, when Clara Hale of Harlem took into her home her first drug-addicted baby. Hale's daughter had seen a woman sitting on a wooden crate, nodding off from heroin, with a two-month-old baby slipping out of her arms, and she told the woman to go to her mother's house. Hale was sixty-four at the time, looking forward to retirement as a foster mother, but she could see that the baby had acquired the effects of the heroin from the mother and she quickly accepted the baby's care. She had no medical or nursing education or experience with drug rehabilitation, but word soon began to spread of her special brand of caring and love. "It wasn't their fault they were born addicted," she would say. Over the next three months, twenty-two cribs filled her house.

When Hale's babies eventually overwhelmed the facilities of her home, she moved to a five-story brownstone that became known as Hale House. Many of her little patients arrived still trembling from the withdrawal of heroin and alcohol. When crack cocaine joined heroin as the prominent drugs of abuse, Hale accepted crack babies as well, helping them recover from fetal toxins with hugging and rocking. At least one baby, often the neediest one, would sleep in her room at night, next to her bed.

The policy of Hale House was to reunite the children with their families when the parents recovered from drug abuse. They were able to do so with about 90 percent of the children, and a large number of them remained extremely close to Hale over the years. Hale House's multimillion-dollar budget, once government funded, needed to be supported by private fund raising in 1989. Despite the financial constraints, however, Hale House now provides not only housing for about seventeen babies but also education programs for mothers coming out of detoxification and apprenticeship training programs for young people. Recently, babies infected with HIV through their mothers have presented special challenges for Hale House, but they have not been turned away.

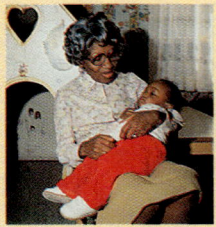

Clara Hale and one of her many babies.

Mother Hale, as she has been known, died in 1992 at the age of eighty-seven. She had received presidential tribute as "an American hero," the woman who founded a haven for nearly a thousand babies over the years. "I'm not an American hero," she said recently before her death, "I'm simply a person who loves children."

SOURCES: Lambert, Bruce (1992, December 20). Clara Hale, 87, who aided addicts' babies, dies. *New York Times*, p. 50. Rist, Curtis (1992, December 19). "Mother" Hale dies. *Newsday*, p. 6.

---

abuser establishes temporary residence in a drug-free group setting and receives intensive counseling, often from former heroin abusers or former abusers of other drugs, who have successfully given up drugs. Other approaches have been developed that combine detoxification, treatment with a long-term form of naloxone called **naltrexone** (brand name: Trexan), psychotherapy, and vocational rehabilitation, under one comprehensive plan of action. These programs, called **multimodality programs,** are designed to focus simultaneously on the multitude of needs facing the heroin abuser, with the goal being a successful reintegration into society. As a continuing effort to help the recovering heroin abuser, there are also twelve-step group support programs such as Narcotics Anonymous, modeled after similar programs for those recovering from alcohol or cocaine dependence.

naltrexone (nal-TREX-ohn)
A long-lasting form of naloxone. Brand name prior to 1994 was Trexan; brand name has changed to ReVia.

multimodality programs
Treatment programs in which a combination of detoxification, psychotherapy, and group support is implemented.

Summary

OPIUM IN HISTORY

- Opium has a very long history; its medicinal and recreational use stretch back approximately 5,000 years.

- During the nineteenth century, opium even figured into global politics, as the instigating factor for the Opium War fought between China and Britain. At the time, opium use was widespread in Britain and the United States at all levels of society.

MORPHINE AND THE ADVENT OF HEROIN

- The discovery of morphine in 1803 as the principal active ingredient in opium revolutionized medical treatment of pain and chronic diseases.

- At the end of the nineteenth century, heroin was introduced by the Bayer Company in Germany. Initially, it was believed that heroin lacked the dependence-producing properties of morphine.

HEROIN AND OPIATE DEPENDENCE IN THE TWENTIETH CENTURY

- The abuse potential of morphine and especially heroin was not fully realized until the beginning of the twentieth century. Social and political developments in the United States after the passage of the Harrison Act in 1914 drove heroin underground, with a growing association with criminal life.

- While heroin abuse became associated with African American and other minority communities in urban ghettos after World War II, the drug revolution and the military involvement in Vietnam during the 1960s and 1970s brought the issues of heroin abuse to a wider population.

EFFECTS ON THE MIND AND THE BODY

- The effects of narcotic drugs such as heroin include euphoria, analgesia, gastrointestinal slowing, and respiratory depression.

- Respiratory depression is the major risk factor for heroin intake.

MEDICAL USES OF NARCOTIC DRUGS

- In medical settings, narcotic drugs have been extremely helpful in the treatment of pain, in the treatment of dysentery, and in the suppression of coughing.

- Side effects of narcotic medication include respiratory depression, nausea, intestinal spasms, and sedation. There is also concern that narcotic drugs may be misused and diverted to nonmedical purposes.

HOW OPIATES WORK IN THE BRAIN

- Since the 1970s, we know that the effects of morphine and similar drugs are due to the activation of morphine-sensitive receptors in the brain.

- Three families of chemical substances produced by the brain bind to these receptors. These chemicals are collectively known as endorphins.

PATTERNS OF HEROIN ABUSE

- Chronic heroin abuse is subject to tolerance effects over time. Withdrawal effects include intense craving for heroin and physical symptoms such as diarrhea and dehydration.

- One of the major problems surrounding heroin abuse is the unpredictability in the content of a heroin dose.

TREATMENT AND LONG-TERM RECOVERY PROGRAMS

- Treatment for heroin abuse includes short-term detoxification and long-term interventions addressing the continuing craving for the drug and physical dependence factors in the body.

- Methadone-maintenance programs focus on the physiological needs, while therapeutic communities and support groups focus on a long-term reintegration into society.

Key Terms

antitussive, p. 162
black tar, p. 159
buprenorphine, p. 171
chipping, p. 169
clonodine, p. 167
codeine, p. 155
detoxification, p. 170
dextromethorphan, p. 162
endogenous opioid
    peptides, p. 164
fentanyl, p. 159

heroin, p. 156
LAAM, p. 171
locus coeruleus, p. 167
methadone, p. 167
methadone
    maintenance, p. 170
morphine, p. 155
multimodality
    programs, p. 172
naloxone, p. 163
naltrexone, p. 172

narcotics, p. 151
opiate, p. 151
opium, p. 151
paregoric, p. 162
propoxyphene, p. 167
synthetic opiates, p. 151
thebaine, p. 155
therapeutic
    communities, p. 171

Endnotes

1. Levinthal, Charles F. (1988). *Messengers of paradise: Opiates and the brain.* New York: Anchor/Doubleday, p. 4.
2. Merlin, M. D. (1984). *On the trail of the ancient opium poppy.* Cranbury NJ: Associated University Press.
3. Scott, James M. (1969). *The white poppy: A history of opium.* New York: Funk and Wagnalls, p. 111.
4. Snyder, Solomon H. (1977). Opiate receptors and internal opiates. *Scientific American, 236* (3), p. 44. Levinthal. *Messengers of paradise,* pp. 3–25.
5. Beeching, Jack (1975). *The Chinese opium wars.* New York: Harcourt Brace Jovanovich, p. 23.
6. Owen, David E. (1934). *British opium policy in China and India.* New Haven CT: Yale University Press. Waley, Arthur (1958). *The opium war through Chinese eyes.* London: Allen and Unwin.
7. Fay, Peter W. (1975). *The opium war 1840–1842.* Chapel Hill: University of North Carolina Press, p. 11.
8. Brecher, Edward M., and the editors of Consumer Reports (1972). *Licit and illicit drugs.* Boston: Little, Brown, p. 17.
9. Kaplan, Eugene H., and Wieder, Herbert. (1974). *Drugs don't take people; People take drugs.* Secaucus NJ: Lyle Stuart.
10. Brecher. *Licit and illicit drugs,* pp. 42–43.
11. Levinthal. *Messengers of paradise,* pp. 16–17.
12. Courtright, David T. (1982). *Dark paradise: Opiate addiction in America before 1940.* Cambridge MA: Harvard University Press, p. 47.
13. Terry, Charles E., and Pellens, Mildred. (1928/1970). *The opium problem.* Montclair NJ: Patterson Smith.
14. Smith, Roger (1966). Status politics and the image of the addict. *Issues in Criminology, 2* (2), pp. 172–173.
15. Zackon, Fred (1986). *Heroin: The street narcotic.* New York: Chelsea House Publishers, p. 44.
16. McCoy, Alfred W., with Read, Cathleen B., and Adams, Leonard P. (1972). *The politics of heroin in southeast Asia.* New York: Harper and Row, pp. 5–6.
17. Zackon. *Heroin,* p. 45.
18. Bentel, David J., Crim, D., and Smith, David E. (1972). Drug abuse in combat: The crisis of drugs and addiction among American troops in Vietnam. In David E. Smith and George R. Gay (Eds.), *It's so good, don't even try it once: Heroin in perspective.* Englewood Cliffs NJ: Prentice Hall, p. 58.
19. McCoy. *The politics of heroin,* pp. 220–221.
20. Robins, Lee N , David, Darlene H., and Goodwin, Donald W. (1974). Drug use by U.S. Army enlisted men in Vietnam: A follow-up on their return home. *American Journal of Epidemiology, 99* (4), 235–249.

21. Greenhouse, Steven (1995, February 12). Heroin from Burmese surges as U.S. debates strategy. *New York Times,* p. 3. Sciolino, Elaine (1994, April 5). State Department report labels Nigeria major trafficker of drugs to U.S. *New York Times,* pp. A1, A11.

22. Holloway, Lynette (1994, August 31). 13 heroin deaths spark wide police investigation. *New York Times,* p. A1, B2. Sabbag, Robert (1994, May 5). The cartels would like a second chance. *Rolling Stone,* pp. 35–37.

23. Hofmann, Frederick G. (1983). *A handbook on drug and alcohol abuse: The biomedical aspects.* New York: Oxford University Press, 1983, p. 74.

24. Abel, Ernest L. (1985). *Psychoactive drugs and sex.* New York: Plenum Press, pp. 175–204.

25. Hofmann. *Handbook on drug and alcohol abuse,* pp. 74–78.

26. Jaffe, Jerome H., and Martin, William M. (1985). Opioid analgesics and antagonists. In Alfred G. Gilman, Louis S. Goodman, Theodore W. Rall, and Ferid Murad (Eds.), *The pharmacological basis of therapeutics* (7th ed.). New York: Macmillan, pp. 491–531.

27. Ibid., pp. 525–527.

28. Hofmann. *Handbook on drug and alcohol abuse,* pp. 79–80. Schuckit, Marc A. (1989). *Drug and alcohol abuse: A clinical guide to diagnosis and treatment* (3rd ed.). New York: Plenum Press, pp. 132–135.

29. Riordan, Charles E., and Kleber, Herbert D. (1980). Rapid opiate detoxification with clonidine and naloxone. *Lancet, 1,* 1079–1080.

30. Goode, Erich (1989). *Drugs in American society* (3rd ed.). New York: McGraw-Hill, pp. 245–246.

31. Johnson, Bruce D.; Goldstein, Paul J.; Preble, Edward; Schmeidler, James; Lipton, Douglas S.; Spunt, Barry; and Miller, Thomas (1985). *Taking care of business: The economics of crime by heroin abusers.* Lexington MA: Lexington Books.

32. Zinberg, Norman E. (1984). *Drug, set, and setting: The basis for controlled intoxicant use.* New Haven CT: Yale University Press, pp. 46–81.

33. Melzack, Ronald (1990). The tragedy of needless pain. *Scientific American, 262* (2), 27–33.

34. Stitzer, Maxine L.; Bickel, Warren K.; Bigelow, George E.; and Liebson, Ira A. (1986). Effect of methadone dose contingencies on urinalysis test results of poly-drug-abusing methadone-maintenance patients. *Drug and Alcohol Dependence, 18,* 341–348.

35. Mendelson, Jack H., and Mello, Nancy K (1992). Human laboratory studies of buprenorphine. In Jack D. Blaine (Ed.), *Buprenorphine: An alternative treatment for opioid dependence* (NIDA Research Monograph 121). Rockville MD: National Institute on Drug Abuse, pp. 58–60.

36. Ball, John C.; Lange, W. Robert; Myers, C. Patrick; and Friedman, Samuel R. (1988). Reducing the risk of AIDS through methadone maintenance treatment. *Journal of Health and Social Behavior, 29,* 214–226. Hubbard, Robert L.; Allison, Margaret; Bray, Robert M.; Craddock, S Gail; Rachal, J. Valley; and Ginzburg, Harold M. (1983). An overview of client characteristics, treatment services, and during-treatment outcomes for outpatient methadone clinics in the treatment outcomes prospective study (TOPS). In James R. Cooper, Fred Altman, Barry S. Brown, and Dorynne Czechowicz (Eds.), *Research on the treatment of narcotic addiction,* pp. 714–751.

37. Hargreaves, William A. (1983). Methadone dose and duration for maintenance. In James R. Cooper, Fred Altman, Barry S. Brown, and Dorynne Czechowicz (Eds.), *Research on the treatment of narcotic addiction,* pp. 19–79.

38. Myerson, D. J. (1969). Methadone treatment of addicts. *New England Journal of Medicine, 281,* 380.

39. Kosten, Thomas R., Rounsaville, Bruce J., and Kleber, Herbert D. (1986). A 2.5 year follow-up of treatment retention and reentry among opioid addicts. *Journal of Substance Abuse Treatment, 3,* 181–189. Maddux, James F., and Desmond, David P. (1986). Relapse and recovery in substance abuse careers. In Frank M. Tims and Carl G. Leukefeld (Eds.), *Relapse and recovery in drug abuse* (NIDA Research Monograph 72). Rockville MD: National Institute on Drug Abuse, pp. 49–71.

40. Faupel, Charles E. (1991). *Shooting dope: Career patterns of hard-core heroin users.* Gainesville: University of Florida Press, pp. 170–173

LSD and Other Hallucinogens

n an April afternoon in 1943, Albert Hofmann,
a research chemist at Sandoz Pharmaceuticals in Basel, Switzerland, went home early
from work, unaware that his fingertips had
made contact with an extremely minute
trace of a new chemical he had been testing
that day. The chemical was **lysergic acid
diethylamide (LSD)**, and as the opening
quotation indicates, Hofmann unknowingly
experienced history's first "acid trip." Three
days later, having pieced together the origin
of his strange experience, he decided to try a
more deliberate experiment. He chose a dose
of 0.25 mg, a concentration that could not,
so he thought, possibly be effective. His plan
was to start with this dose and gradually
increase it to see what would happen

The dose Hofmann had considered inadequate was actually about five times greater
than the typical dose for LSD. As he later
recalled his experiences,

*My condition began to assume threatening
forms. Everything in my field of vision wavered
and was distorted as if seen in a curved mirror. I
also had the sensation of being unable to move
from the spot.*[1]

A little while later, his experiences turned for
the worse:

*The dizziness and sensation of fainting became
so strong at times that I could no longer hold myself
erect, and had to lie down on a sofa. My surroundings had now transformed themselves in more terri-
fying ways. Everything in the room spun around,
and the familiar objects and pieces of furniture
assumed grotesque, threatening forms. . . . I was
seized by the dreadful fear of going insane. I was
taken to another place, another time.*[2]

His experience then became pleasant:

Kaleidoscopic, fantastic images surged in on me, alternating, variegated, opening and then closing themselves in circles and spirals. . . . It was particularly remarkable how every acoustic perception, such as the sound of a door handle or a passing automobile, became transformed into optical perceptions. Every sound generated a vividly changing image, with its own consistent form and color.[3]

Hofmann's vivid remembrances are presented here at length because they succinctly convey some of the major facets of a hallucinogenic drug experience: the distortions of visual images and body sense, the frightening reaction that often occurs when ordinary reality is so dramatically changed, and the strange intermingling of visual and auditory sensations. These effects will be considered later as this chapter explores the strange world of hallucinogenic drugs.

Like many of the drugs that have been examined in the preceding chapters, hallucinogenic drugs such as LSD and several others have a story that belongs both in the twentieth century and in the distant past. Hofmann worked in the modern facilities of an international pharmaceutical company, but the basic material on his laboratory bench was derived from a fungus that has been around since before the human species emerged. There have always existed natural products with the potential to strengthen and stimulate those who taste them (Chapter 4), to sedate and relax them (Chapter 5), or to reduce pain and intoxicate (Chapter 7). It has been estimated that as many as six thousand plant species around the world have some psychoactive properties.[4] This chapter will focus on a collection of special chemicals called *hallucinogenic drugs* or simply **hallucinogens,** often pharmacologically dissimilar to one another but with the common ability to distort perceptions and alter one's sense of reality.

A matter of definition

efinitions are frequently reflections of the definer's attitude toward the thing that is being defined, and the terminology used to describe hallucinogens is no exception. For those viewing these drugs with a "positive spin," particularly for those who took LSD in the 1960s, they have been described as *psychedelic,* meaning "mind-expanding" or "making the mind manifest." In contrast, for others viewing these drugs with more alarm than acceptance, the popular descriptive adjectives have been *psychotomimetic,* meaning "having the appearance of a psychosis," *psychodysleptic,* meaning "mind-disrupting," or even worse, *psycholytic,* meaning "mind-dissolving." Therefore, you can see that the description one chooses to use carries with it a strong attitude, pro or con, toward the drug's effects.

As a result of all this emotional baggage, the description of these drugs as hallucinogenic, meaning "hallucination-producing" is probably the most evenhanded way of defining their effects; that is the way they will be referred to in this chapter. There still are some problems, however, that need to be considered. Technically, a hallucination is the reported perception of something that does not physically exist. For example, a schizophrenic might hear voices that no one else hears, and therefore we must conclude (at least the nonschizophrenic world must conclude) that such voices are not real. In the case of hallucinogens, the effect is more complicated because we are dealing with a perceived alteration in the existing physical

lysergic acid diethylamide (LSD) (leye-SER-jik ASS-id di-ETH-il-la-meyed)
A synthetic, serotonin-related hallucinogenic drug.

hallucinogens (ha-LOO-sin-oh-jens)
A class of drugs producing distortions in perception and one's body image at moderate doses.

environment. Drug experts have used the term *illusionogenic,* as a more accurate way of expressing the experiences of those who take these drugs.

We should also be aware of another qualification when we use the term "hallucinogen." There are many drugs that produce distinctive effects when taken at low to moderate dose levels but that produce hallucinations when the dose levels are extremely high. Examples of this phenomenon appeared in Chapter 4 with cocaine and amphetamines and in Chapter 6 with inhalants. Here the category of hallucinogens will be limited only to those drugs that produce marked changes in perceived reality at relatively low dosages.

Classifying hallucinogens

ost hallucinogens can be classified in terms of the particular neurotransmitter in the brain that bears a close resemblance to the molecular features of the drug. As shown in Table 8.1, there are three principal categories: (1) hallucinogens that are chemically similar to serotonin (LSD psilocybin, morning glory seeds, DMT, bufotenine, and harmine), (2) those that are chemically similar to norepinephrine (mescaline, DOM, MDMA, and MDA), and (3) those that are chemically similar to acetylcholine (atropine, hyoscyamine, scopolamine, and ibotenic acid). The implication is that any drug that resembles a

TABLE 8.1

Major categories of hallucinogens

Category	Source
Hallucinogens related to serotonin	
lysergic acid diethylamide (LSD)	A synthetic derivative of lysergic acid, which is in turn a component of ergot
psilocybin	Various species of North American mushrooms
lysergic acid amide or morning glory seeds	Morning glory seeds
dimethyltryptamine (DMT)	The bark resin of several varieties of trees and some nuts native to Central and South America
bufotenine	The beans of several species of Central and South American trees as well as the skin of a species of toad
harmine	The bark of a South American vine
Hallucinogens related to norepinephrine	
mescaline	The peyote cactus in Mexico and the U.S. Southwest
2,5,-dimethoxy-4-methylamphetamine (DOM or more commonly STP)	A synthetic mescaline-like drug
MDA and MDMA (Ecstasy)	Two synthetic amphetamine-like drugs
Hallucinogens related to acetylcholine	
atropine	*Atropa belladonna* plant, known as deadly nightshade, and the datura plant
scopolamine (hyoscine)	Roots of the mandrake plant, henbane herb, and the datura plant
hyoscyamine	Roots of the mandrake plant, henbane herb, and the datura plant
ibotenic acid	*Amanita muscaria* mushrooms
Miscellaneous hallucinogens	
phencyclidine (PCP)	A synthetic preparation, developed in 1963
ketamine	A PCP-like drug

SOURCE: Schultes, Richard E., and Hofmann, Albert (1979). *Plants of the gods: Origins of hallucinogenic use.* New York: McGraw-Hill.

neurotransmitter has the potential either to stimulate the receptors sensitive to that neurotransmitter or to inhibit them. In addition, there is a fourth category of a few hallucinogens (PCP and ketamine are examples) that are chemically unlike any known neurotransmitter; these drugs will be called miscellaneous hallucinogens. As Figure 8.1 indicates, most of these drugs have natural origins.

Lysergic acid diethylamide (LSD)

The most famous hallucinogen is LSD, which does not exist in nature but is synthetically derived from **ergot,** a fungus present in moldy rye and other grains. One of the compounds in ergot, lysergic acid, is highly toxic, resulting in a condition called **ergotism.** Historians have surmised that widespread epidemics of ergotism (called St. Anthony's fire) occurred periodically in Europe during the Middle Ages, when extreme famine forced people to bake bread from infected grain. In one particularly deadly episode in 944 A.D., an outbreak of ergotism claimed as many as forty thousand fatalities.[5]

The features of this calamity were twofold. One form of ergotism produced a reduction in blood flow toward the extremities, leading to gangrene, burning pain, and the eventual loss of limbs. The other form produced a tingling sensation on the skin, convulsions, disordered thinking, and hallucinations.

While the scientific link between this strange affliction and lysergic acid has been known since the 1700s, outbreaks of ergotism have occurred in recent times. A major one took place in a small French community in 1951. Hundreds of townspeople went totally mad on a single night:

Many of the most highly regarded citizens leaped from windows or jumped into the Rhone, screaming that their heads were made of copper, their bodies wrapped in snakes, their limbs swollen to gigantic size or shrunken to tiny appendages. . . . Animals went berserk. Dogs ripped bark from trees until their teeth fell out.[6]

Albert Hofmann's professional interest in lysergic acid centered on its ability to reduce bleeding and increase contractions in smooth muscle, particularly the uterus. He was trying to find a nontoxic chemical version that would be useful in treating problems associated with childbirth. The LSD molecule was number twenty-five in a series of variations that Hofmann studied in 1938, and his creation was officially named LSD-25 for that reason. He thought at the time that it had possibilities for medical use but went on to other pursuits, returning to it five years later in 1943, the year of his famous LSD experience.

The beginning of the psychedelic era

Sandoz Pharmaceuticals applied for FDA approval of LSD in 1953, and as was a common practice at the time, the company sent out samples of LSD to laboratories around the world for scientific study. The idea was that LSD could possibly be helpful in the treatment of schizophrenia by allowing psychiatrists to gain insight into subconscious processes, apparently unlocked by this drug. One of the researchers intrigued by the potential psychotherapeutic applications of LSD was the psychiatrist Humphrey Osmond of the University of Saskatchewan in Canada, who coined the word "psychedelic" to describe its effects and whose interest also extended to other hallucinogens such as mescaline.

In 1953 Osmond introduced the British writer Aldous Huxley to mescaline, and Hux-

ergot (ER-got)
A fungus infecting rye and other grains.

ergotism
A physical and/or psychological disorder acquired by ingesting ergot-infected grains. One form of ergotism involves gangrene and eventual loss of limbs; the other form is associated with hallucinations, convulsions, and disordered thinking.

F IGURE 8.1

Botanical sources for four hallucinogenic drugs: (a) Amanita muscaria
(ibotenic acid), (b) Atropa belladonna (atropine), (c) Claviceps tulasne
(ergot), (d) Datura stramonium (atropine, scopolamine, and hyoscyamine).

ley later reported his experiences, under Osmond's supervision, in his essay *The Doors of Experience*. Prior to 1960 LSD was being administered to humans under fairly limited circumstances, chiefly as part of research studies in psychiatric hospitals and psychotherapy sessions on the West Coast. As would be later revealed in court testimony in the 1970s, there were also clandestine experiments conducted by governmental agencies such as the CIA that were interested in LSD for possible application in espionage work. Word of its extraordinary effects, however, gradually spread to regions outside laboratories or hospitals. One of those who picked up on these events was a young clinical psychologist and lecturer at Harvard University named Timothy Leary.

Leary's first hallucinogenic experience (in fact his first psychoactive drug experience of any kind) was in Mexico in 1960, when he ate some mushrooms containing the hallucinogen psilocybin. This is his recollection of the effect on him: "During the next five hours, I was whirled through an experience which could be described in many extravagant metaphors but which was above all and without question the deepest religious experience of my life."[7]

Back at Harvard, his revelations sparked the interest of a colleague, Richard Alpert. The two men were soon holding psilocybin sessions with university students and whoever else was interested on and off campus At first there was some semblance of scientific control in these studies. For example, a physician was on hand, and objective observers of behavior reported the reactions of the subjects. Later, these procedures were altered. Physicians were no longer invited to the sessions and Leary himself began taking the drug at the same time. His argument was that he could communicate better with the subject during the drug experience, but his participation seriously undermined the objective nature of the studies.

In 1961, Leary, Alpert and other associates turned to LSD as the focus of their investigations, in their homes and other locations off the Harvard campus. Though these experiments were technically separate from the university itself, public-relations concerns on the part of the academic community were mounting. Leary further aggravated the situation through his writings. In a 1962 article published in the *Bulletin of the Atomic Scientists,* he suggested that the Soviets could conceivably dump LSD into the water supply and, in order to prepare for such an attack, Americans should dump LSD into their own water supply so that citizens would then know what to expect. The U.S. government was not amused.

In 1963, after a Harvard investigation, Leary and Alpert were dismissed from their academic positions, making it the first time in the twentieth century that a Harvard faculty member had been fired. As you can imagine, such events brought enormous media exposure. Leary was now "Mr. LSD," and suddenly the public was acquainted with a class of drugs that had been previously unknown to them. [8]

For the rest of the 1960s, LSD became not only a drug but also one of the symbols for the cultural revolt of a generation of youth against the perceived inadequacies of the established, older generation. Leary himself told his followers that they were "the wisest and holiest generation that the human race has ever seen" and advised them to "turn on, tune in, and drop out."[9] Lester Grinspoon and James Bakalar have described the era in this way:

There were psychedelic churches, ashrams, rock festivals, light shows, posters, comic books and newspapers, psychedelic jargon and slang. Every middle-sized city had its enclaves, and there was a drug culture touring circuit. . . . Everyone had his own idea of what was meant by turning on, tuning in, and dropping out—his own set and setting— and the drug culture provided almost as many variations in doctrine, attitude, and way of life, from rational and sedate to lewd and violent, as the rest of society.[10]

A psychedelic bus in the 1960s.

To paraphrase the words of songwriter and singer Bob Dylan, "the times were a-changin'," but not always for the better. LSD became a battleground unto itself. In congressional hearings on LSD among the nation's youth, scientists, health officials, and law-enforcement experts testified to a growing panic over the drug. Newspaper stories emphasized the dangers with headlines such as "A monster in our midst—a drug called LSD" and "Thrill drug warps mind, kills." Sandoz quietly let its LSD patent lapse in 1966 and did everything it could to distance itself from the controversy. Hofmann himself called LSD his "problem child."

In 1966, LSD was made illegal, later becoming a Schedule I drug, with its penalties for possession originally set as a misdemeanor and later upgraded to a felony. By the 1970s, LSD had become entrenched as a street drug, and the taking of LSD had become a component of the already dangerous world of illicit drugs. The story of LSD will be updated in a later section, but first it is important to understand the range of effects LSD typically produces.

Acute effects of LSD

LSD is considered one of the most, if not *the* most, powerful psychoactive drugs

Timothy Leary— Whatever happened to him?

For the average college student of the 1990s, the question regarding Timothy Leary might not be "Whatever happened to him?" but rather "Who was this guy anyway?" So for those of you who ask the latter question, here is a capsule rendition of Leary's impact on the drug scene in the 1960s, along with an update.

Until 1960 Leary's career was conventional. As a clinical psychologist, he had written a widely acclaimed textbook and devised a respected personality test (called the Leary) that has since been used by many organizations to screen prospective employees. His experience with psilocybin in Mexico in 1960 turned his life around, and the more extensive his exposure to hallucinogenic drugs became, the more he took on the self-appointed role of Pied Piper for what was referred to then as the acid generation. There were many characters in the confusing drama of the 1960s, but Leary managed to stay at the forefront of media attention.

By the middle of the 1970s, Leary had been sentenced to twenty years for marijuana possession (the longest sentence ever imposed for such an offense), had gone to federal prison, escaped, evaded the authorities in Algeria and Switzerland for a few years, been recaptured, and finally released. LSD advocacy was no longer on his agenda by this time, and in fact LSD had lost its mystique years earlier. Leary hit the college lecture circuit, talking about space migration and life extension and calling himself a "stand-up philosopher."

Since the late 1980s, however, Leary has discovered computers. In his latest reincarnation, he has formed a Beverly Hills software company called Futique (by merging the words *future* and *antique*), has marketed a number of successful video games, and sees interactive computer programming and virtual reality in particular as the consciousness expansion of the 1990s, the newest route to cerebral stimulation. As Leary puts it, "People need some way to activate, boot up, and change the discs in their minds. LSD may not be as necessary now." In his seventies, Leary admits that "I've been exploring for the first time in my life the amazing wonderland known as senility. There's a little clutter in the organization of the files."

Not enough clutter, evidently, to prevent Leary from being a social activist on occasion. In 1994 he was detained by the police in an Austin, Texas, airport for smoking—a cigarette,

Timothy Leary in the 1990s.

this time. Leary said that he wanted to draw attention to people being "demonized" by no-smoking restrictions on their lives. "We were told by an official that smoking in the airport would get us a citation. So we did look for a policeman to check this out."

SOURCES: Brozan, Nadine (1994, May 12). Chronicle: Timothy Leary lights up. *New York Times*, p. D26. Lee, Martin A., and Shlain, Bruce (1985). *Acid dreams: The complete social history of LSD*. New York: Grove Weidenfeld. Sheff, David (1987, November 5–December 10). Interview with Timothy Leary. *Rolling Stone*, pp. 226–228. Stone, Judith (1991, June). Light elements: Turn on, tune in, boot up. *Discover*, pp. 32–35. Timothy Leary: Getting high on high tech (1986, December 22). *Newsweek*, p. 48.

known. Its potency is so great that effective dose levels have to be expressed in terms of micrograms, one millionths of a gram, often called mikes. The typical street dose ranges from 50 to 150 micrograms, though sellers often claim that their product contains more. The effective dose can be as small as 10 micrograms, with only one hundredth of a percent being absorbed into the brain. Compare these figures to the fact that a single pain-relief tablet contains 300,000 micrograms of aspirin, and you can appreciate the enormous potency of LSD.[11]

Taken orally, LSD is rapidly absorbed into the bloodstream and the brain, with effects beginning within forty-five to sixty minutes. Once its concentration has peaked (in about ninety minutes), the half-life, or the time it takes for 50 percent of the drug to diminish in the bloodstream, is approximately three hours. Within five to twelve hours, LSD effects are over.[12]

Surprisingly, given its extreme potency, the toxicity of LSD is relatively low. Generalizing from studies of animals given varying doses of LSD, we can estimate that a lethal dose of LSD for humans would have to be roughly three hundred to six hundred times the effective dose, a fairly comfortable margin of safety. In 1992 the DAWN statistics listing the frequency of admissions to hospital emergency rooms showed that only about 1 percent were related to ingestion of LSD, and to this day there has never been a single definitive case in which a death has been attributed to an LSD overdose.[13]

Street forms of LSD may contain color additives or adulterants with specific flavors, but the drug itself is odorless, tasteless, and colorless. LSD is sold on the street in single-dose "hits." It is typically swallowed in the form of powder pellets (microdots) or gelatin chips (windowpanes) or else licked off small squares of absorbent paper that have been soaked in liquid LSD (blotters). In the past, blotters soaked with LSD have been decorated with pictures of mystical symbols and signs, rocket ships, or representations of Mickey Mouse, Snoopy, Goofy, or other cartoon characters.

LSD initially produces an excitation of the sympathetic autonomic activity: increases in heart rate and blood pressure, dilated pupils, and a slightly raised body temperature. There is an accompanying feeling of restlessness, euphoria, and a sensation that inner tension has been released. There may be laughing or crying, depending upon the expectations and setting.[14] Between thirty minutes and two hours later, a "psychedelic trip" begins, characterized by several of these distinctive features. The best way to describe these effects are in the words of individuals who have experienced them.[15]

synesthesia
A subjective sensation (as of vision) other than the one (as of sound) being stimulated.

1. Images seen with the eyes closed:

   Closing my eyes, I saw millions of color droplets, like rain, like a shower of stars, all different colors.

2. An intermingling of senses called **synesthesia,** which often involves sounds appearing as hallucinatory visions:

   "I clapped my hands and saw sound waves passing before my eyes."

3. Perception of a multilevel reality:

   I was sitting on a chair and I could see the molecules. I could see right through things to the molecules.

4. Strange and exaggerated appearances of common objects or experiences:

   A towel falling off the edge of my tub looked like a giant lizard crawling down.

   When my girlfriend was peeling an orange for me, it was like she was ripping a small animal apart.

During the third and final phase, approximately three to five hours after first taking LSD, the following features begin to appear.

1. Great swings in emotions or panic:

   It started off beautifully. I looked into a garden . . . and suddenly, it got terrible . . . and I started to cry. . . . And then, my attention wandered, and something else was happening, beautiful music was turned on. . . . Then suddenly I felt happy.

2. A feeling of timelessness:

   Has an hour gone by since I last looked at the clock? Maybe it was a lifetime. Maybe it was no time at all.

3. A feeling of ego disintegration, or a separation of one's mind from one's body:

   Boundaries between self and nonself evaporate, giving rise to a serene sense of being at one with the universe. I recall muttering to myself again and again, "All is one, all is one."

Whether these strong reactions result in a "good trip" or a "bad trip" depends heavily upon the set, or expectations, for the drug, the setting, or environment, in which the LSD is experienced, and the overall psychological health of the individual.

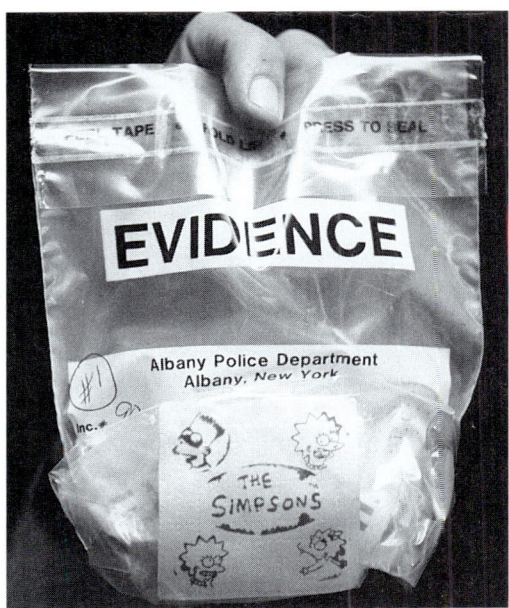

A recently confiscated bag of LSD blotters bearing the likeness of TV cartoon family "The Simpsons."

Effects of LSD in the brain

Since LSD closely resembles the molecular structure of serotonin, it is not surprising that there should be effects on receptors in the brain that are sensitive to serotonin. As a result of research in the 1980s, it turns out that the critical factor behind LSD's hallucinogenic effects lies in its ability to stimulate a special subtype of serotonin-sensitive receptors, commonly called S_2 receptors. In fact, all hallucinogens, even those drugs whose structures do not resemble serotonin, are linked together by the common ability to excite S_2 receptor sites. Drugs that specifically block S_2 receptors, leaving all other subtypes unchanged, will block the behavioral effects of hallucinogens. In addition, the ability of a particular drug to produce hallucinogenic effects is directly proportional to its ability to bind to S_2 receptors. [16]

Patterns of LSD use

The enormous publicity surrounding Timothy Leary and his followers in the 1960s made LSD a household word. In one estimate, as many as fifty popular articles about LSD were published in major U.S. newspapers and magazines between March 1966 and February 1967 alone. By 1970, however, the media had lost interest, and hardly anything was appearing about LSD (see Portrait). Even so, while media attention was diminishing, the incidence of LSD abuse was steadily rising. In four Gallup Poll surveys conducted between 1967 and 1971, the percentage of college students reported to have taken LSD at least once in their lives rose dramatically from 1 to 18 percent. [17]

From the middle 1970s to the early 1990s, the numbers showed a steady decline. By 1986, the University of Michigan survey indicated that the lifetime incidence of LSD taking among high school seniors was 7 percent, down from 11 percent in 1975. In 1993, however, the incidence had risen sharply to 10 percent. Along with the increased rate of overall exposure to LSD, there has also been an increase in the percentage of seniors thinking that LSD is not dangerous The trends with regard to LSD use will need to be carefully monitored in the years ahead. Fortunately, the upsurge in LSD use has not been reflected in an increase in hospital emergency cases (according to the DAWN reports). The likely reason is that the dosage of street LSD is lower than the dosages common to the 1960s and 1970s. [18]

Facts and fictions about LSD

Given the current upsurge in LSD abuse (if not in publicity about it), it is all the more important to look at the facts about LSD and also the myths. Six basic questions that are often asked about this drug are examined here.

Will LSD produce a dependence?

There are three major reasons why LSD is not likely to result in a drug dependence, despite the fact that the experience at times is quite pleasant.[19] First, LSD and other hallucinogens cause the body to build up a tolerance to their effects faster than any other drug category. As a result, one cannot remain on an LSD-induced high day after day, for an extended period of time. Second, LSD is not the drug for someone seeking an easy way to get high. As one drug expert has put it:

The LSD experience requires a monumental effort. To go through eight hours of an LSD high—sensory bombardment, psychic turmoil, emotional insecurity, alternations of despair and bliss, one exploding insight upon the heels of another, images hurtling through the mind as fast as the spinning fruit of a slot machine—is draining and exhausting in the extreme.[20]

Third, the LSD experience seems to control the abuser rather than the other way around. It is virtually impossible to "come down" from LSD at will. Besides, the unpredictability of the LSD experience is an unpopular feature for those who would want a specific drug effect every time the drug is taken.

Will LSD produce a panic or a psychosis?

One of the most notorious features of LSD is the possibility of a bad trip. Examples have been given of how a sweet, dreamlike state can rapidly turn into a nightmare. Perhaps the greatest risks are taken when a person is slipped a dose of LSD and begins to experience its effect without knowing that he or she has taken a drug. Panic reactions do occur, however, even when a person is fully aware of the fact that he or she has taken LSD. While the probability of having a bad trip is difficult to estimate, there are very few regular LSD abusers who have not experienced a bad trip or had a disturbing experience as part of an LSD trip. The best advice for treating adverse effects is the companionship and reassurance of others throughout the period when LSD is active. Focus 8.1 includes some specific procedures for LSD panic episodes.

Despite the possibility of an LSD panic, there is no strong evidence that the panic will

---

F O C U S **8.1**

DRUG ABUSE ALERT

Emergency guidelines for a bad trip on LSD

1. Stay calm with the individual. Do not move around quickly, shout, cry, or become hysterical. Any sense of panic on your part will make an LSD panic worse. Speak in a relaxed, controlled manner.

2. Reassure the individual that the situation is temporary and that you will not leave until he or she returns to a normal state. Encourage the individual to breathe deeply and calmly. Advise him or her to view the trip as though watching a movie or TV program.

3. Reduce any loud noises or bright lights but do not let the individual go into the dark. Darkness tends to encourage hallucinations in a person under LSD.

4. Allow the individual to move around without undue restrictions. He or she can sit, stand, walk, or lie down if this helps the situation. You can divert attention from the panic by encouraging the individual to beat time to music or by dancing.

5. If your assistance does not produce a reduction in the panic, seek out medical attention immediately. Under medical supervision, LSD panics can be treated with benzodiazepines such as chlordiazepoxide (Librium) or diazepam (Valium), or if the symptoms are severe by antipsychotic medication such as haloperidol (Haldol).

SOURCES: Carroll, Charles R. (1993). *Drugs in modern society* (3rd ed.). Dubuque IA: W. C. Brown, p. 311. Palfai, Tibor, and Jankiewicz, Henry (1991). *Drugs and human behavior.* Dubuque IA: W. C. Brown, p. 445. Trulson, Michael E. (1985). *LSD: Visions or nightmares.* New York: Chelsea House, p. 101.

---

lead to a more permanent psychiatric breakdown. Long-term psychiatric problems are relatively uncommon, with one study conducted in 1960 showing that there was no greater probability of a person's attempting suicide or developing a psychosis after taking LSD than when undergoing ordinary forms of psychotherapy.[21] The incidents that do occur typically involve people who were unaware that they were taking LSD, showed unstable personality characteristics prior to taking LSD, or were experiencing LSD under hostile or threatening circumstances.

The possible link between the character of LSD effects and symptoms of schizophrenia has also been examined closely. It is true that on a superficial level, the two behaviors show some similarities, but there are important differences. LSD hallucinations are primarily visual, best seen in the dark, and, as mentioned earlier, more accurately characterized as illusions or pseudohallucinations; schizophrenic hallucinations are primarily auditory, seen with open eyes, and qualify as true hallucinations. Individuals taking LSD are highly susceptible to suggestion and will usually try to communicate the experience to others; the schizophrenic individual is typically resistant to suggestion and withdrawn from his or her surroundings. Therefore, it is not true that LSD is mimicking the experience of a schizophrenic psychosis (see Chapter 16).

Will LSD increase creativity?

The unusual visual effects of an LSD experience may lead you to expect that your creativity is enhanced, but the evidence indicates otherwise. Professional artists and musicians creating new works of art or songs while under the influence of LSD typically think that their creations are better than anything they have yet produced, but when the LSD has worn off, they are far less impressed. Controlled studies generally show that individuals under LSD *feel* that they are creative, but objective ratings do not show a significant difference from levels prior to the LSD.[22]

Will LSD damage chromosomes?

In March 1967 a study was published in the prestigious scientific journal *Science* describing a marked increase in chromosomal abnormalities in human white blood cells that had been treated with LSD in vitro

(that is, the cells were outside the body at the time).[23] Shortly after, three other studies were reported in which chromosomal abnormalities in the white blood cells of LSD abusers were higher than those of people who did not use drugs, while three additional studies reported no chromosomal effect at all.

By the end of that year, a second study was published by the people whose report had started the controversy in the first place. They wrote that eighteen LSD abusers had two to four times the number of chromosomal abnormalities in their white blood cells, when compared with fourteen control subjects. Interestingly, the subjects in this study were not exactly model citizens. Everyone of them had taken either one or more of amphetamines, barbiturates, cocaine, hallucinogens, opiates, or antipsychotic medication. How the authors got away with describing their study as "chromosomal damage induced by LSD-25" is anyone's guess.

The picture was confused, to say the least. Not only were many of these studies unreplicable, but many were methodologically flawed as well. Most important, when studies actually looked at the chromosomes of reproductive cells themselves for signs of breakage from exposure to LSD, the results were either ambiguous or entirely negative. By 1971, after nearly a hundred studies had been carried out, the conclusion was that LSD did not cause chromosomal damage in human beings at normal doses, and that there was no evidence of a high rate of birth defects in the children of LSD users.[24] Yet, in the highly politicized climate of the late 1960s, the media tended to emphasize the negative findings without any scrutiny into their validity or relevance. The public image of LSD causing genetic damage still persists, despite the lack of scientific evidence. This is not to say, however, that there is no basis of exercising some degree of caution. Women should avoid LSD, as well as other psychoactive drugs, during pregnancy, especially in the first three months.[25]

Will LSD have a residual effect?

One of the most disturbing aspects of taking LSD is the possibility of reexperiencing the effects of the drug long after the drug has worn off, sometimes as long as a year later. The likelihood that such occurrences, called *flashbacks,* might occur is not precisely known. Some studies estimate its rate of incidence as only 5 percent, while others estimate it as high as 33 percent.[26] Flashback effects can sometimes be frightening and other times be quite pleasant; they can occur among LSD novices or "once-only" drug takers as well as among experienced LSD abusers. While they appear without warning, there is a higher probability that they will occur when the individual is beginning to go to sleep or has just entered a dark environment.[27]

The reason why LSD flashbacks might occur, since they are not common to any other psychoactive drug, is not well understood. It is possible that LSD has a peculiar ability to produce some biochemical changes that remain dormant for a period of time and then suddenly reappear or that some remnant of the drug has the ability to remain over extended periods of time. It is also possible that individuals who ingest LSD are highly suggestible to social reminders about the original exposure to LSD.

Will LSD increase criminal or violent behavior?

As noted in Chapter 2, it is very difficult to establish a clear cause-and-effect relationship between a drug and criminal or violent behavior. Once again, in the highly charged era of the 1960s, stories related to this question were publicized and conclusions were drawn without any careful examination of the actual facts. For example, in 1964 a case was reported of a woman undergoing LSD

> **psilocybin (SIL-oh-SEYE-bin)**
> A serotonin-related hallucinogenic drug originating from a species of mushrooms.

therapy treatment who murdered her lover, three days after the last LSD session.[28] The details of the case, often overlooked by subsequent media reports, reveal that the woman had been physically abused by the man, he had caused her to have an abortion, and the woman already had a serious mental disorder before going into treatment. The fact that the homicide took place well after the LSD had left her body indicates that the murder was not an instance of pharmacological violence. Other cases in which violent behavior appeared to be associated with an LSD experience turned out in fact to be associated with the use of other hallucinogenic drugs.

It is possible, however, that an individual can "freak out" on LSD. As noted in Chapter 6, the effects of a euphoriant drug such as an inhalant or LSD can lead to a feeling of invulnerability. This feeling, in turn, can lead to dangerous and possibly life-threatening behavior. While we cannot reliably estimate the likelihood of these effects or pinpoint the circumstances under which they might occur, we should recognize that psychological reactions to LSD are inherently unpredictable, and caution is advised.

Psilocybin and other hallucinogens related to serotonin

The source of the drug **psilocybin** is a family of mushrooms native to southern Mexico and Central America. Spanish chroniclers in the sixteenth century wrote of "sacred mushrooms" revered by the Aztecs as *teonanacatl* (roughly translated as "God's flesh") and capable of providing extraordinary visions when eaten. Their psychoactive properties had been known for a long time, judging from stone-carved representations of these mushrooms discovered in El Salvador and dating back to as early as 500 B.C.

Psilocybin in the twentieth century

Native use of these mushrooms continued to the present day but disappeared from historical accounts until the late 1930s, when several varieties were identified. In 1955 a group of Western observers documented the hallucinogenic effects of the *Psilocybe mexicana* in a native Indian group living in a remote mountainous region of southern Mexico. Three years later, samples worked their way to Switzerland, where Albert Hofmann, already known for his work on LSD, identified the active ingredient and named it psilocybin. As was his habit, Hofmann sampled some of the mushrooms himself and wrote later of his reactions:

Thirty minutes after my taking the mushrooms, the exterior world began to undergo a Mexican character. . . . I saw only Mexican motifs and colors. When the doctor supervising the experiment bent over me to check my blood pressure, he was transformed into an Aztec priest.[29]

We can never know whether the Aztec character of these hallucinogenic effects was a result of suggestion or that Aztec designs may have been inspired by the effects of psilocybin.

Effects of psilocybin

Once it is ingested, psilocybin loses a portion of its molecule, making it more fat-soluble and more easily absorbed into the brain. This new version, called **psilocin,** is the actual agent that works on the brain. Since LSD and psilocin are chemically similar to serotonin, the biochemical effects are also similar. In fact, the resemblance is so close that there is cross tolerance between the two.[30]

Far less potent than LSD, psilocybin is effective at dose levels measured in the more traditional units of milligrams rather than micrograms. At doses of 4 to 5 mg, psilocybin causes a pleasant, relaxing feeling; at doses of 15 mg and more, hallucinations, time distor-

tions, and changes in body perception appear. A psilocybin trip generally lasts from two to five hours, considerably shorter than an LSD trip.

Individuals who have experienced both kinds of hallucinogens report that, relative to LSD, psilocybin produces effects that are more strongly visual, less emotionally intense, and more euphoric, with fewer panic reactions and less chance of paranoia. As with LSD, psilocybin (often called "shrooms") has been increasingly available among young people as a drug of abuse.

Lysergic acid amide (LAA)

In addition to their reverence for psilocybin mushrooms, the Aztecs also ingested locally grown morning glory seeds, calling them *ololuiqui,* and used their hallucinogenic effects in religious rites and healing. Like many Native American practices, the recreational use of morning glory seeds has survived in remote areas of southern Mexico. In 1961 Albert Hofmann (once again) identified the active ingredient in these seeds as **lysergic acid amide (LAA)**, after having sampled its hallucinogenic properties. As the chemical name suggests, this drug is a close relative to LSD.

The LAA experience judging from Hofmann's report, is similar to that of LSD, though LAA is only one tenth to one thirtieth as potent and the hallucinations tend to be dominated by auditory rather than visual images. Commercial varieties of morning glory seeds are available to the public, but suppliers have taken the precaution of coating

---

psilocin
A brain chemical related to serotonin, resulting from the ingestion of psilocybin.

lysergic acid amide
(leye-SER-jik ASS-id A-meyed)
A hallucinogenic drug found in morning glory seeds, producing effects similar to those of LSD. It is abbreviated LAA.

them with an additive that causes nausea and vomiting to minimize their abuse.[31]

Dimethyltryptamine (DMT)

The drug **dimethyltryptamine (DMT)** is obtained chiefly from the resin of the bark of trees and nuts native to the West Indies as well as to Central and South America, where it is generally inhaled as a snuff. An oral administration does not produce psychoactive effects. The similarity of this drug's effects to those of LSD and its very short duration gave DMT the reputation during the psychedelic years of the 1960s of being "the business-man's LSD." Presumably, someone could take a DMT trip during lunch and be back in time for work in the afternoon.

An inhaled 30 mg dose of DMT produces physiological changes within ten seconds, with hallucinogenic effects peaking around ten to fifteen minutes later. Paranoia, anxiety, and panic can also result at this time, but most symptoms are over in about an hour.[32]

Bufotenine

Another serotonin-related hallucinogen, **bufotenine,** is found, strangely enough, in both animal and plant species. One primary source is a family of beans native to Central and South America; the other is the skin of a toad. As noted in Chapter 1, toads figured

dimethyltryptamine (DMT) (dye-METH-il-TRIP-ta-meen)
A short-acting hallucinogenic drug.

bufotenine (byoo-FOT-eh-neen)
A serotonin-related hallucinogenic drug, generally inhaled as a snuff. It is obtained either from a bean plant or the skin of a particular species of toad.

cyanosis (seye-ah-NOH-sis)
A tendency for the skin to turn bluish purple. It can be a side effect of the hallucinogenic drug, bufotenine.

harmine (HAR-meen)
A serotonin-related hallucinogenic drug frequently used by South American shamans in healing rituals.

prominently in the potions of European witches, and it is likely that the psychoactive effects of these concoctions were at least partially due to the presence of bufotenine. Reports of individuals experiencing the effects of bufotenine after ingesting the venom squeezed from live toads (called toad licking) or smoking the venom after it has dried (called toad smoking) have surfaced from time to time since the 1970s. While this strange practice is well documented, it has attracted relatively few supporters as a hallucinogenic experience.[33]

Like DMT, bufotenine is generally inhaled as a hallucinogenic snuff, since an oral administration is ineffective. Indians in southern Venezuela mix bufotenine with the lime of ground seashells prior to inhaling it to speed up its absorption, in a similar way to that of Indians in Peru and neighboring countries ingesting coca leaves. Very strong sympathetic autonomic reactions, greater than the autonomic reactions to LSD, make bufotenine relatively unpopular as a street hallucinogen. One particularly distressing toxic reaction to bufotenine is **cyanosis,** the tendency for the skin to turn bluish purple. Perhaps it was better suited for a witch's brew.

Harmine

Among native tribes in the western Amazon region of South America, the bark of the *Banisteriopsis* vine yields the powerful drug **harmine.** A drink containing harmine, called *ayahuasca,* is frequently used by local shamans for healing rites (see Portrait in Chapter 1). It is chemically similar to serotonin, like LSD and the other hallucinogens examined so far. Its behavioral effects, however, are somewhat different. Unlike LSD, harmine makes the individual withdraw into a trance, and the hallucinatory images (often visions of animals and supernatural beings) are experienced within the context of a dreamlike state. Reports among shamans refer to a sense of suspension in space or flying, falling into one's body, or experiencing one's own death.[34]

Hallucinogens related to norepinephrine

everal types of hallucinogens have a chemical composition similar to norepinephrine. As you may recall from Chapter 4, amphetamines are also chemically similar to norepinephrine. Consequently, norepinephrine-related hallucinogens are closely related to amphetamine drugs, though they do not generally produce amphetamine-like stimulant effects.

Mescaline

The hallucinogen **mescaline** is derived from the **peyote** plant, a spineless cactus with a small greenish crown that grows above ground and a long carrotlike root. This cactus is found over a wide area, from the southwestern United States to northern regions of South America, and many native tribes have discovered its psychoactive properties. Given the large distances between these tribes, it is remarkable that they prepare and ingest mescaline in a highly similar manner. The crowns of the cactus are cut off, sliced in small disks called buttons, dried in the sun, and then consumed. An effective dose of mescaline from peyote is 200 mg, equivalent to about five buttons, though some Indians increase the dose to four times that level. Peak response to the drug takes place thirty minutes to two hours after consumption. As Focus 8.2 describes, mescaline is still used today as part of religious worship among many Native Americans in the United States and Canada.

The psychological and physiological effects of mescaline are highly similar to those of LSD, though some have reported that mescaline hallucinations are more sensual, with fewer changes in mood and the sense of self. In contrast, double-blind studies comparing the reactions to LSD and mescaline show that subjects cannot distinguish between the two when dose levels are equivalent. While the reactions may be the same, the mescaline trip comes at a greater price, as far as physiological reactions are concerned. Peyote buttons taste extremely bitter and can cause vomiting, headaches, and unless the stomach is empty, distressing levels of nausea.[35]

Today mescaline can be synthesized as well as obtained from the peyote cactus. The mescaline molecule resembles the chemical structure of norepinephrine but stimulates the same S_2 receptors as LSD and other hallucinogens that resemble serotonin. As a result, mescaline use shows cross-tolerance with these other drugs.[36]

DOM and MDMA

A group of synthetic hallucinogens have been developed that share mescaline's resemblance to amphetamine but do not produce the strong stimulant effects of amphetamine. There are several dozen of them, since the amphetamine molecule is relatively easy to manipulate chemically. Two prominent examples will be discussed here.

The first of these synthetic drugs, **DOM**, appeared in the 1960s and 1970s, when it was frequently combined with LSD and carried the street name of STP. The nickname supposedly was a reference to the well-known engine oil additive, while others took it to mean a "super terrific psychedelic." It is roughly eighty times more potent than mescaline, though still far weaker than LSD. At low doses of about 3 to 5 mg, DOM

mescaline (MES-kul-leen)
A norepinephrine-related hallucinogenic drug. Its source is the peyote cactus.

peyote (pah-YO-tay)
A species of cactus and the source for the hallucinogenic drug mescaline.

DOM
A synthetic norepinephrine-related hallucinogenic drug, derived from amphetamine. DOM or a combination of DOM and LSD is often referred to by the street name STP.

Present-day peyotism and the Native American Church

Among Native Americans within the United States, the ritual use of peyote buttons, called peyotism, can be traced to the eighteenth century when the Mescalero Apaches (from whom the word *mescaline* was derived) adopted the custom from Mexican Indians who had been using peyote for more than three thousand years. By the late 1800s, peyotism had become widely popular among tribes from Wisconsin and Minnesota to the West Coast. It was not, however, until the early twentieth century that peyote use became incorpo-

rated into an official religious organization, the Native American Church of North America, chartered in 1918.

The beliefs of the Native American Church membership, estimated to include anywhere from 50,000 to 250,000 Native Americans in the United States and Canada, combine traditional tribal customs and practices with Christian morality. To them, life is a choice between two roads that meet at a junction. The Profane Road is paved and wide, surrounded by worldly passions and temptations. The Peyote Road is a narrow and

windy path, surrounded by natural, unspoiled beauty; it is also a path of sobriety (since alcohol poisons the goodness of the body), hard work, caring for one's family, and brotherly love. Only the Peyote Road leads to salvation. In their weekly ceremonies, lasting from Saturday night until Sunday afternoon, church members swallow small peyote buttons as a sacrament, similar to the ritual of taking communion, or drink peyote tea. It is considered sacriligious to take peyote outside the ceremonies in the church.

While peyote remains classified as a Schedule I drug and therefore banned, federal law and the laws of twenty-three U.S. states have exempted the sacramental use of peyote from criminal penalties. The American Indian Religious Freedom Act of 1978 affirmed the sentiment of the U.S. Congress that peyote was sacred to

Native American Church members and that peyote use should be constitutionally protected. Nonetheless, in 1990, the Supreme Court ruled that a state has the constitutional right to ban all peyote use regardless of the circumstances, if it chooses to do so. This decision leaves open the possibility of prosecution in states that do not specifically exempt the use of peyote as a sacrament. So far, no criminal charges have been brought up.

SOURCES: Indian religion must say no (1990, October 6). *The Economist*, pp. 25–26. Morgan, George (1983). Recollections of the peyote road. In Lester Grinspoon and James B. Bakalar (Eds.), *Psychelic reflections*. New York: Human Sciences Press, pp. 91–99. Oregon peyote law leaves 1983 defendant unvindicated (1991, July 9). *New York Times*, p. A14.   Schultes, Richard E., and Hofmann, Albert (1979). *Plants of the gods: Origins of hallucinogenic use*. New York: McGraw-Hill, pp. 132–143.

---

produces euphoria; with higher doses of 10 mg or more, severe hallucinations result, often lasting from sixteen to twenty-five hours. While like LSD in many respects, DOM has the reputation of producing a far higher incidence of panic attacks, acute psychoses, and other symptoms of a very bad trip. Cases have been reported of STP being added as an adulterant to marijuana.[37]

MDMA
A synthetic norepinephrine-related hallucinogenic drug. Once considered useful (under the name Ecstasy) for psychotherapeutic purposes, this drug is now known to produce permanent brain damage.

Another amphetamine-related hallucinogen, abbreviated **MDMA,** achieved a brief notoriety and controversy in the 1980s. On the street, MDMA had been subject to abuse as a new designer drug referred to as "ecstasy." It also became known that a number of psychiatrists, believing that MDMA had a special ability to enhance empathy, were using the drug as part of their therapy. At the same time, animal studies, using amounts barely two to three times the effective dose levels in humans, showed that MDMA produced permanent brain damage, specifically in those regions sensitive to serotonin.[38]

After a number of decisions and reversals, the Drug Enforcement Administration in

1989 put MDMA permanently on the Schedule I list of controlled substances. It has not, however, prevented MDMA from becoming in the 1990s a popular street drug. Widely available under names such as Ecstasy, XTC, X, Essence, Clarity, and Adam, MDMA on the one hand has the reputation of having the stimulant qualities of amphetamine and the hallucinogenic qualities of mescaline. Recently, reports of MDMA use at "rave parties" in dance clubs have received considerable media attention. On the other hand, the toxicity of MDMA exceeds the toxicity of most other hallucinogenic drugs. Even moderate doses of MDMA have produced extremely high body temperatures, cardiovascular difficulties, jaundice, and convulsions.[39]

Hallucinogens related to acetylcholine

f the acetylcholine-related hallucinogens, some enhance the neurotransmitter and some inhibit it. Some examples include *Amanita muscaria* mushrooms, atropine, scopolamine, and hyoscyamine.

Amanita muscaria

The **Amanita muscaria** mushroom, also called the *fly agaric* mushroom because of its ability to lure and sedate flies and other insects, grows in the upper latitudes of the Northern Hemisphere, usually among the roots of birch trees. The mushroom has a bright red cap speckled with white dots; the dancing mushrooms in Walt Disney's film *Fantasia* were inspired by the appearance (if not the hallucinogenic effects) of this fungus.

Amanita mushrooms are one of the world's oldest intoxicants. Most historians agree that this mushroom was the basis for the mysterious and divine substance called soma that is celebrated in the *Rig-Veda*, one of Hinduism's oldest holy books, dating from 1000 B.C. It is strongly suspected that amanita mushrooms were used in Greek mystery cults and were probably the basis for the legendary nectar of the Gods.[40]

The effects of amanita mushrooms can be lethal if dose levels are not watched very carefully. They produce muscular twitching and spasms, vivid hallucinations, dizziness, and heightened aggressive behavior. It was briefly mentioned in Chapter 1 that Viking warriors were reputed to have ingested amanita mushrooms prior to sailing off to battle. The drug-induced strength and savagery of these "berserk" invaders were so widely known that a medieval prayer was written especially for their attacks: "From the intolerable fury of the Norseman, O Lord, deliver us."[41]

Until the 1960s it was believed that the active ingredient in *Amanita muscaria* was, as the name suggests, muscarine, and that this was the drug that excited receptors sensitive to acetylcholine in the parasympathetic autonomic nervous system. Our present knowledge, however, is that the principal psychoactive agent in these mushrooms that accomplishes this effect is a chemical called *ibotenic acid.*

A hallucinogenic drug related to ibotenic acid, called **ibogaine,** is found in the iboga root in the western coastal region of central Africa. While higher doses of ibogaine are potentially lethal, powdered forms of the iboga root in small amounts have been used in ceremonies of the Bwiti cult among several tribal groups in Gabon and the Congo, in an effort to communicate with the spirit world and seek advice from the ancestors. Among these people, iboga root is slowly chewed and the intoxication from ibotenic acid, often lasting for as long as thirty hours, is believed to allow an individual to travel down a road

Amanita muscaria
(a-ma-NEE-ta mus-CAR-ee-ah)
A species of mushroom containing the hallucinogenic drug ibotenic acid.

ibogaine (EE-bo-gayn)
A hallucinogenic drug originating from the West African iboga root.

through a visionary landscape to the dwellings of the spirits of the dead. It is interesting that the imagery of a "trip" pervades so many experiences with hallucinogenic drugs, in both primitive and modern settings.

The hexing drugs and witchcraft

A number of natural plants contain chemicals that share a common feature: the ability to block the parasympathetic effects of acetylcholine in the body. The drugs with this ability, called *anticholinergic drugs,* produce specific physiological effects. The production of mucus in the nose and throat, as well as saliva in the mouth, is reduced. Body temperature is elevated, sometimes to very high fever levels. Heart rate and blood pressure go up, and the pupils dilate considerably. Psychologically, there is a feeling of delirium, confusion, and generally a loss of memory for events occurring during the drugged state.[42] The amnesic property is one of the principal reasons these drugs hold little or no street appeal.

The principal anticholinergic drugs are **atropine, scopolamine** (also called

---

atropine (A-tro-peen)
An anticholinergic hallucinogenic drug derived from the *Atropa belladonna* plant.

scopolamine (scoh-POL-ah-meen)
An anticholinergic hallucinogenic drug. Also called hyoscine.

**hyoscyamine
(HEYE-oh-SEYE-eh-meen)**
An anticholinergic hallucinogenic drug found in mandrake and henbane plants.

Atropa belladonna
(a-TROH-pah BEL-ah-DON-ah)
A plant species, also called deadly nightshade, whose berries can be highly toxic. It is the principal source of atropine.

mandrake
A potato-like plant containing anticholinergic hallucinogenic drugs.

henbane
An herb containing anticholinergic hallucinogenic drugs.

---

hyoscine), and **hyoscyamine.** They are found in various combinations and relative amounts in a large number of psychoactive plants. Four of the most famous ones are examined here.

1. Atropine is principally derived from the ***Atropa belladonna*** plant, also called deadly nightshade. Its lethal reputation is quite justified, since it is estimated that ingesting only a dozen or so berries is sufficient for death to occur. Many recipes for poisons through history have been based upon this plant. At lower, more benign dose levels, plant extracts can be applied to the eyes, causing the pupils to dilate. Egyptian and Roman women used this technique to enhance their beauty or at least improve their appearance. The term *belladonna* ("beautiful lady") originates from this application. The psychological effects of atropine are generally associated with the anticholinergic effects of heart-rate acceleration and general arousal.

2. The **mandrake** plant is an oddly shaped potatolike plant with a long forked root that has traditionally been imagined to resemble a human body. In ancient times, mandrake was considered to have aphrodisiac properties. According to medieval folklore, mandrake plants supposedly shrieked when they were uprooted, understandably driving people mad.

    Mandrake contains a combination of atropine, scopolamine, and hyoscyamine. Since low doses act as a depressant, mandrake has been used as a sedative-hypnotic drug to relieve anxiety and induce sleep. At higher doses, it produces bizarre hallucinations and muscular paralysis.

3. **Henbane** is a strong-smelling herb, native to widespread areas of the Northern Hemisphere, with purple-veined, yellowish flowers and hairy leaves. Its English name, meaning "harmful to hens," originates from the observation that henbane seeds were toxic to chickens and other birds. The lethal possibilities for henbane potions have been described

by writers since the days of the Roman Empire. Hamlet's father in Shakespeare's play was supposedly murdered in this way. Lower doses of henbane, however, have been used in a more benign way, as an anesthetic and painkiller. We now know that the predominant drugs in henbane are scopolamine and hyoscyamine.

4. Various species of the *datura* plant, containing a combination of atropine, scopolamine, and hyoscyamine, grow wild in locations throughout the world. In the United States, one particular species, **Datura stramonium,** is called jimsonweed, a contraction from "Jamestown weed" (a name given to it by early American colonists). Consumption of the seeds or berries of jimsonweed produces hypnotic and hallucinogenic effects, together with disorientation, confusion, and amnesia. At high doses, jimsonweed is quite toxic. In recent years, there have been occasional reports of hospitalizations and occasional deaths among teenagers who have eaten jimsonweed seeds as an inexpensive way to get high.[43]

During medieval times, mixtures of deadly nightshade, mandrake, and henbane were major factors in the psychoactive effects of witches' potions, producing a disastrous combination of physiological and psychological effects. Satanic celebrations of the "Black mass" centered on the ingestion of such brews. The atropine, in particular, produced a substantial elevation in arousal, probably leading to the feeling that the person was flying or else was capable of it, while the hallucinogenic effects enabled the person to imagine that one was communing with the Devil.[44] Witches were reputed to have prepared these mixtures as ointments and rubbed them on their bodies and on broomsticks, which they straddled. The chemicals would have been easily absorbed through the skin and the membranes of the vagina. The Halloween image of a witch flying around on a broomstick has been with us ever since.

QUICK CONCEPT CHECK 8.1

Understanding variations in hallucinogens

heck your understanding of the psychological differences among major hallucinogens by matching the hallucinatory experience (in the left column) with the hallucinogenic drug most apt to produce such effects (in the right column).

Psychological experience	Hallucinogen
1. "The images I saw were Mexican designs as if they were created by an Aztec artist."	A. PCP
2. "As I heard the bells, I also saw the vibrations move through the air."	B. DMT
	C. LSD
3. "You tell me that a wave of aggressiveness swept over me. But, to tell you the truth, I don't remember a thing."	D. *Atropa belladonna*
	E. ibogaine
4. "The hallucinations were gone sixty minutes after they had started."	F. psilocybin
5. "As I ate the red-topped mushrooms, I felt my muscles twitch. I could see vivid hallucinations."	G. mescaline
6. "I felt as if I were flying through the air."	H. *Amanita muscaria*

ANSWERS: 1. psilocybin 2. LSD, principally 3. PCP 4. DMT 5. *Amanita muscaria* 6. *Atropa belladonna*

Datura stramonium
(duh-TOOR-ah strah-MOH-nee-um)
A species of the datura family of plants with hallucinogenic properties. In the United States, the plant is called jimsonweed.

Phencyclidine (PCP)

Perhaps the most notorious of all the hallucinogens is **phencyclidine (PCP),** often referred to as *angel dust.* The appearance of this drug from the miscellaneous group as an illicit drug in the late 1960s brought special problems to the already dangerous drug scene.

History and use of PCP

Technically PCP is a synthetic depressant, and it was originally introduced in 1963 as a depressant drug by the Parke-Davis pharmaceutical company, under the brand name of Sernyl. It was marketed as a promising new surgical anesthetic that had the advantage of not depressing respiration or blood pressure or causing heart-beat irregularities like other anesthetics. In addition, PCP had a higher therapeutic ratio than many other anesthetics available at that time. By 1965, however, it was withdrawn from human applications after reports that nearly half of all patients receiving PCP showed signs of delirium, disorientation, hallucinations, intense anxiety, or agitation. For a time, PCP was used for animal anesthesia, but this application ended by the late 1970s.

PCP can be taken orally, intravenously, or by inhalation, but commonly it is smoked either alone or in combination with other drugs. Whatever its mode of administration, the results are extremely dangerous, with an unpredictability that far exceeds that of LSD or other hallucinogens. The symptoms may include manic excitement, depression, severe anxiety, sudden mood changes, disordered

> **phencyclidine (PCP)**
> **(fen-SEYE-kluh-deen)**
> A dissociative anesthetic hallucinogen that produces disorientation, agitation, aggressive behavior, analgesia, and amnesia. It carries various street names, including angel dust.
>
> **ketamine (KET-ah-meen)**
> A dissociative anesthetic hallucinogen related to phencyclidine (PCP).

and confused thought, paranoid thoughts, and unpredictable aggression. Because PCP has analgesic properties as well, individuals taking the drug often feel invulnerable to threats against them and may be willing and able to withstand considerable pain. Hallucinations also occur, but they are quite different from the hallucinations under the influence of LSD. There are no colorful images, no intermingling of sight and sound, no mystical sense of being "one with the world." Instead, a prominent feature of PCP-induced hallucinations is the change in one's body image. As one PCP abuser has expressed it,

> The most frequent hallucination is that parts of your body are extremely large or extremely small. You can imagine yourself small enough to walk through a key hole, or you can be lying there and all of a sudden you just hallucinate that your arm is twice the length of your body.[45]

Individuals under the influence of PCP may also stagger, speak in a slurred way, and feel depersonalized or detached from people around them. A prominent feature is a prolonged stare, often called doll's eyes.

The effects of PCP last from as little as a few hours to as long as two weeks, and they are followed by partial or total amnesia and dissociation from the entire experience. Considering these bizarre reactions, it is not surprising that PCP deaths occur more frequently from the behavioral consequences of the PCP experience than from its physiological effects. Suicides, accidental or intentional mutilations, drownings (sometimes in very small amounts of water), falls, and threatening behavior leading to the individual's being shot are only some of the possible consequences.[46]

Ketamine, a drug chemically similar to PCP, has also been subject to abuse. Like PCP, ketamine has a mixture of stimulant and depressive properties, though its depressive effect is more extreme and does not last as long as that of PCP. Ketamine was used as an emergency surgical anesthetic on the battlefield in Vietnam as well as in standard hospital-based operations in which gaseous anesthetics could not be employed. It is no longer used in any medical context due to its adverse side effects.[47]

The weird combination of stimulant, depressant, and hallucinogenic effects makes PCP and ketamine difficult to classify. Some textbooks treat the discussion of PCP and ketamine in a chapter on hallucinogens, as is done here, while others include it in a chapter on stimulants because some features of PCP and ketamine intoxication resemble the effect of cocaine, though their medical use has always been as depressants. A growing consensus of opinion has it that PCP and ketamine should be described as dissociative anesthetic hallucinogens since they produce a feeling of being dissociated or "cut off" from oneself and the environment.[48]

Patterns of PCP abuse

It is strange that a drug with so many adverse effects would be subject to deliberate abuse, but such is the case with PCP. Reports of PCP abuse began surfacing in 1967 among the hippie community in San Francisco, where it became known as the PeaCe Pill. Word quickly spread that PCP did not live up to its name. Inexperienced PCP abusers were suffering the same bizarre effects as had the clinical patients earlier in the decade. By 1969, PCP had been written off as a garbage drug, and it dropped out of sight as a drug of abuse.

In the early 1970s, PCP returned under new street names and in new forms (Table 8.2). No longer a pill to be taken orally, PCP was now in powdered or liquid form. Powdered PCP could be added to parsley, mint, oregano, tobacco, or marijuana, rolled as a cigarette, and smoked.[49] Liquid PCP could be used to soak leaf mixtures of all types, including manufactured cigarettes, which could then be dried and smoked. Many new users have turned to PCP as a way to boost the effects of marijuana. Making matters worse, as many as 120 different designer-drug variations of PCP have been developed in illicit laboratories around the country and the world. The dangers of PCP abuse, therefore, are complicated by the difficulty in knowing whether or not a street drug has been adulterated with PCP and what version of PCP may be present.

Understanding PCP

Check your understanding of the effects of PCP by listing three major features of PCP intoxication that are significantly different from the effects of other hallucinogens.

ANSWER: Correct responses can include any of the following: analgesia, amnesia, prolonged stare, absence of synesthesia, absence of mysticism, unpredictable aggression, extreme disorientation

TABLE 8.2

Street names for phencyclidine (PCP) and PCP-like drugs	
PCP	jet fuel
angel dust	sherms (derived from the reaction that it hits you like a Sherman tank)
monkey dust	
peep	super-kools
supergrass	cyclones
killer weed	zombie dust
ozone	ketamine
embalming fluid	special K
rocket fuel	

Note: In the illicit drug market, PCP and ketamine are frequently misrepresented and sold as mescaline, LSD, marijuana, amphetamine, or cocaine.

SOURCES: Carroll, Charles R. (1993). *Drugs in modern society* (3rd ed.). Dubuque IA: Brown and Benchmark, p. 317. Milburn, H. Thomas (1991). Diagnosis and management of phencyclidine intoxication. *American Family Physician, 43,* 1293.

The 1992 DAWN statistics give us some idea of the demographic features of the PCP abuser who ends up receiving emergency treatment: predominantly male (73 percent), between eighteen and thirty-four years old (68 percent), and a large proportion dependent on PCP (32 percent).[50] African Americans are 38 percent of these cases, whites are 34 percent, and Latinos 22 percent. Amazingly, some regular PCP abusers have managed to avoid medical-care facilities, even as they mix PCP with alcohol or marijuana, combinations that only add to the unpredictability of the final result.[51]

Summary

A MATTER OF DEFINITION

- Hallucinogens are, by definition, drugs that produce distortions of perception and one's sense of reality. These drugs have also been called psychedelic ("mind-expanding") drugs. In some cases, users of hallucinogens feel that they have been transported to a new reality.

- Other classes of drugs may produce hallucinations at high dose levels, but hallucinogens produce these effects at low or moderate dose levels.

CLASSIFYING HALLUCINOGENS

- Hallucinogens can be classified in four basic groups. The first three relate to the chemical similarity between the particular drug and one of three major neurotransmitters: serotonin, norepinephrine, or acetylcholine.

- The fourth, miscellaneous group includes synthetic hallucinogens, such as phencyclidine (PCP), which bear little resemblance to any known neurotransmitter.

LYSERGIC ACID DIETHYLAMIDE (LSD)

- Lysergic acid diethylamide (LSD), the best known hallucinogenic drug, belongs to the serotonin group. It is synthetically derived from ergot, a toxic rye fungus that has been documented to be responsible for thousands of deaths over the centuries.

- Albert Hofmann synthesized LSD in 1943, and Timothy Leary led the psychedelic movement in the 1960s that popularized LSD use.

- While the experience is often unpredictable, certain features are commonly observed: colorful hallucinations, synesthesia in which sounds often appear as visions, a distortion of perceptual reality, emotional swings, a feeling of timelessness, and a separation of one's mind from one's body.

- It is now known that LSD affects a subtype of brain receptors sensitive to serotonin, referred to as S_2 receptors.

- Since the early 1990s, there has been a resurgence in LSD abuse, particularly among young individuals.

FACTS AND FICTIONS ABOUT LSD

- LSD does not produce psychological or physical dependence and has only a slight chance of inducing a panic or psychotic state (providing that there is a supportive setting for the taking of LSD).

- LSD does not elevate one's level of creativity, does not damage chromosomes (though there remains the chance for birth defects if LSD is ingested when pregnant), and a relationship between LSD abuse and violent behavior has not been established. Flashback experiences, however, are potential hazards.

PSILOCYBIN AND OTHER HALLUCINOGENS RELATED TO SEROTONIN

- Hallucinogens related to serotonin are psilocybin, lysergic acid amide (LAA), dimethyltryptamine (DMT), bufotenine, and harmine.

HALLUCINOGENS RELATED TO NOREPINEPHRINE

- Mescaline is chemically related to norepinephrine, even though S_2 receptors are responsible for its hallucinogenic effects.

- Two synthetic hallucinogens, DOM and MDMA, are variations of the amphetamine molecule.

HALLUCINOGENS RELATED TO ACETYLCHOLINE

- A number of anticholinergic hallucinogens, so named because they diminish the effects of acetylcholine in the parasympathetic nervous system, have been involved in sorcery and witchcraft since the Middle Ages.

- These hexing drugs contain a combination of atropine, scopolamine, and/or hyoscyamine.

Sources for such drugs include the deadly nightshade plant, mandrake roots, henbane seeds, and the datura plant family.

PHENCYCLIDINE (PCP)

- A dangerous form of hallucinogen abuse involves phencyclidine (PCP). Originally a psychedelic street drug in the 1960s, PCP quickly developed the reputation for producing a number of adverse reactions.

- PCP reappeared in the early 1970s, in smokable forms either alone or in combination with marijuana. Extremely aggressive tendencies, as well as behaviors resembling acute schizophrenia, have been associated with PCP intoxication.

Key Terms

Endnotes

1. Hofmann, Albert (1980). *LSD: My problem child.* New York: McGraw-Hill, p. 17.
2. Ibid., pp. 17–18.
3. Ibid., p. 19.
4. Brophy, James J. (1985). Psychiatric disorders. In Marcus A. Krupp, Milton J. Chatton, and David Werdegar (Eds.), *Current medical diagnosis and treatment.* Los Altos CA: Lange Medical Publication, p. 674.
5. Mann, John (1992). *Murder, magic, and medicine.* New York: Oxford University Press, pp. 41–51.

6. Fuller, John G. (1968). *The day of St. Anthony's Fire.* New York: Macmillan, preface.

7. Leary, Timothy (1973). The religious experience: Its production and interpretation. In Gunther Weil, Ralph Metzner, and Timothy Leary (Eds.), *The psychedelic reader.* Secaucus NJ: Citadel Press, p. 191.

8. Lee, Martin A., and Shlain, Bruce (1985). *Acid dreams: The complete social history of LSD.* New York: Grove Weidenfeld, pp. 71–118.

9. Leary, Timothy (1968). *High Priest.* New York: New American Library, p. 46.

10. Grinspoon, Lester, and Bakalar, James B. (1979). *Psychedelic drugs reconsidered.* New York: Basic Books, p. 68.

11. Brown, F. Christine (1972). *Hallucinogenic drugs.* Springfield IL: C. C. Thomas, pp. 46–49. Goode, Erich (1989). *Drugs and American society* (3rd ed.). New York: McGraw-Hill, p. 164.

12. Schuckit, Marc A. (1989). *Drug and alcohol abuse: A clinical guide to diagnosis and treatment* (3rd ed.). New York: Plenum, pp. 159–160.

13. Jacobs, Michael R., and Fehr, Kevin O'B. (1987). *Drugs and drug abuse: A reference text* (2nd ed.). Toronto: Addiction Research Foundation, p. 345. Substance Abuse and Mental Health Services Administration (1994). *Annual Emergency Room Data 1992. Data from the Drug Abuse Warning Network (DAWN).* Rockville MD: Substance Abuse and Mental Health Services Administration, Office of Applied Studies, p. 32.

14. Brophy. *Psychiatric disorders.* Jacobs and Fehr. *Drugs and drug abuse,* pp. 337–347.

15. Goode. *Drugs and American society,* pp. 166–171. Snyder, Solomon H. (1986). *Drugs and the brain.* New York: Freeman, pp. 180–181.

16. Jacobs, Barry J. (1987). How hallucinogenic drugs work. *American Scientist, 75,* 386–392. Snyder. *Drugs and the brain,* pp. 195–205.

17. Goode. *Drugs and American society,* pp. 178–179.

18. Johnston, Lloyd D., O'Malley, Patrick M., and Bachman, Jerald G. (1994). *National survey results on drug use from the Monitoring the Future study, 1975–1993.* Vol. 1. Rockville MD: National Institute on Drug Abuse, Tables 1 and 20. Johnston, Lloyd D., O'Malley, Patrick M., and Bachman, Jerald G. (1993). Summary of the 1992 survey *Drug use among American high school seniors, college students, and young adults.* Ann Arbor: University of Michigan, Institute for Social Research, p. 3.

19. Goode. *Drugs and American society,* pp. 180–181.

20. Ibid., p. 180.

21. Cohen, Sidney (1960). Lysergic acid diethylamide: Side effects and complications. *Journal of Nervous and Mental Diseases, 130,* 30–40. Levine, Jerome, and Ludwig, Arnold M. (1964). The LSD controversy. *Comprehensive Psychiatry, 5*(5), 314–321.

22. Wells, Brian (1974). *Psychedelic drugs: Psychological, medical, and social issues.* New York: Jason Aronson, pp. 170–188.

23. Cohen, M. M., and Marmillo, M. J. (1967). Chromosomal damage in human leukocytes induced by lysergic acid diethylamide. *Science, 155,* 1417–1419.

24. Dishotsky, Norman I., Loughman, William D., Mogar, Robert E., and Lipscomb, Wendell R. (1971). LSD and genetic damage. *Science, 172,* 431–440. Grinspoon and Bakalar. *Psychedelic drugs reconsidered,* pp. 188–191.

25. Brown. *Hallucinogenic drugs,* pp. 61–64. Wells. *Psychedelic drugs,* pp. 104–109.

26. Frosh, William A. (1969). Patterns of response to self-administration of LSD. In Roger E. Meyer (Ed.), *Adverse reactions to hallucinogenic drugs* (Publication No. 1810). Washington DC: Public Health Service. Schlaadt, Richard G., and Shannon, Peter T. (1994). *Drugs: Use, misuse, and abuse.* Englewood Cliffs NJ: Prentice Hall, p. 273.

27. Abraham, Henry D. (1983). Visual phenomenology of the LSD flashback. *Archives of General Psychiatry, 40,* 884–889.

28. Knudsen, Knud (1964). Homicide after treatment with lysergic acid diethylamide. *Acta Psychiatrica Scandinavica, 40* (Supplement 180), 389–395.

29. Hofmann. *LSD,* p. 112.

30. Brown. *Hallucinogenic drugs,* pp. 81–88.

31. Hofmann. *LSD,* pp. 119–127.   Schultes, Richard E., and Hofmann, Albert (1979). *Plants of the gods: Origins of hallucinogenic use.* New York: McGraw-Hill, pp. 158–163.

32. Jacobs and Fehr. *Drugs and drug abuse,* pp. 499–500.

33. Richards, Bill (1994, March 7). Toad-smoking gains on toad-licking among drug users *Wall Street Journal,* pp. A1, A8.

34. Grinspoon and Bakalar. *Psychedelic drugs reconsidered,* pp. 14–15.

35. Ibid., pp. 20–21.   Hollister, Leo E., and Sjoberg, Bernard M. (1964). Clinical syndromes and biochemical alterations following mescaline, lysergic acid diethylamide, psilocybin, and a combination of the three psychotomimetic drugs. *Comprehensive Psychiatry, 5,* 170–178.

36. Jacobs. *How hallucinogenic drugs work,* pp. 386–392.

37. Brecher, Edward, and the editors of Consumer Reports (1972). *Licit and illicit drugs.* Boston: Little, Brown, pp. 376–377.

38. Schmidt, C. J. (1987). Psychedelic amphetamine, methylendioxymethamphetamine. *Journal of Pharmacology and Experimental Therapeutics, 240,* 1–7.   Henry, J. A., Jeffreys, K. J., and Dawling, S. (1992). Toxicity and deaths from 3,4-methylenedioxymethamphetamine ("ecstasy"). *Lancet, 340,* 384–387.

39. Milkman, Harvey, and Sunderwirth, Stanley (1987). *Craving for ecstasy: The consciousness and chemistry of escape.* Lexington MA: D. C. Heath.   Randall, Teri (1992). Ecstasy-fueled "rave" parties become dances of death for English youths. *Journal of the American Medical Association, 268,* 1505–1506.   Randall, Teri (1992). "Rave" scene, ecstasy use, leap Atlantic. *Journal of the American Medical Association, 268,* 1506.

40. Wasson, R. Gordon (1968). *Soma: Divine mushroom of immortality.* New York: Harcourt, Brace and World.

41. Cohen, Sidney (1964). *The beyond within: The LSD story.* New York: Atheneum, p. 17.

42. Levinthal, Charles F. (1990). *Introduction to physiological psychology,* (3rd ed.). Englewood Cliffs NJ: Prentice Hall, pp. 157–158.

43. Freedman, Mitchell (1994, October 15). One teen's tale of jimsonweed. *Newsday,* p. A14. Schultes and Hofmann. *Plants of the gods,* pp. 106–111.

44. Ibid., pp. 86–91.

45. James, Jennifer, and Andresen, Elena (1979). Sea-Tac and PCP. In Harvey V. Feldman, Michael H. Agar, and George M. Beschner (Eds.), *Angel dust: An ethnographic study of PCP users.* Lexington MA: Lexington Books, p. 133.

46. Grinspoon and Bakalar. *Psychedelic drugs reconsidered,* pp. 32–33.   Petersen, Robert C., and Stillman, Richard C. (1978). Phencyclidine: An overview. In Robert C. Petersen and Richard C. Stillman (Eds.), *Phencyclidine (PCP) abuse: An appraisal* (NIDA Research Monograph 21). Rockville MD: National Institute on Drug Abuse, pp. 1–17.

47. Jacobs and Fehr. *Drugs and drug abuse,* pp. 89–106.   *Physicians' desk reference* (1994). Montvale NJ: Medical Economics Data.

48. Julien, Robert M. (1995). *A primer of drug action* (7th ed.). New York: Freeman, pp. 321–326.

49. Linder, Ronald L., Lerner, Steven E., and Burns, R. Stanley (1981). *PCP: The devil's dust.* Belmont CA: Wadsworth, pp. 2–19.

50. Substance Abuse and Mental Health Services Administration. *Annual Emergency Room Data 1992,* pp. 41–43.

51. Ciancutti, Caroline J. (1980). PCP in perspective. *Street Pharmacologist, 3* (1), 3–4.

9

Marijuana

It needs little care to thrive. . . . it is ubiquitous. It flourishes under nearly every possible climatic condition. It sprouts from the earth not meekly . . . but defiantly, arrogantly, confident that whatever the conditions it has the stamina to survive.

Ernest L. Abel
Marijuana: The first twelve thousand years
(1980)

t might be fair to characterize *Cannabis sativa,* the source of marijuana, as a weed with an attitude. Whether it is hot or cold, wet or dry, cannabis will grow abundantly from seeds that are unbelievably hardy and prolific. A handful of cannabis seeds, tossed on the ground and pressed in with one's foot, will usually anchor and become plants. Its roots devour whatever nutrients there are in the soil, like a vampire sucking the life blood from the earth.[1] It is not surprising that, as a result, marijuana has managed to grow in some unorthodox places. It can be found in median strips of interstate highways or in ditches alongside country roads. The top prize for most unusual location, assuming the story is accurate, has to go to a variety known as Manhattan Silver. Reportedly, it originated from cannabis seeds flushed down a New York sewer during a sudden police raid in the 1960s. Once the seeds hit the sewer, they produced a plant that, in the absence of light, grew silverish white leaves instead of green, hence its name.[2]

Considering its botanical source, it is fitting that the psychological and physiological effects of marijuana should show something of an independent nature as well. It is not easy to place marijuana within a classification of psychoactive drugs. When we consider a category for marijuana, we are faced with an odd assortment of unconnected properties. Marijuana produces some excitatory effects, but it is not generally regarded as a stimulant. It produces some sedative effects, but it carries no danger of slipping into a coma or dying. It produces mild analgesic effects, but it is not related pharmacologically to opiates or opiate-like drugs. It

A Mexican harvester gathers up his crop of Cannabis sativa, *later to be processed into marijuana or hashish.*

produces hallucinations at high doses, but there is no cross tolerance with LSD or any other drug formally categorized as a hallucinogen. Marijuana is clearly a hybrid drug, in a league of its own.

At the same time, few other drugs have been so politicized in recent history as marijuana. It is frequently praised by one side or condemned by the other, on the basis of emotional issues rather than an objective view of research data. The pro-marijuana faction tends to dismiss reports of potential dangers and emphasize the benefits, while the antimarijuana faction tends to do the opposite. Marijuana has often been regarded, over the last thirty years or so, not only as simply a drug with psychoactive properties but also as a symbol of an individual's attitude toward the establishment. This makes

> **Cannabis sativa**
> **(CAN-uh-bus sah-TEE-vah)**
> A plant species, commonly called hemp, from which marijuana and hashish are obtained.

it even more critical that we look at the effects of marijuana as dispassionately as possible.

A matter of terminology

Marijuana (marihuana) is frequently referred to as a synonym for cannabis, but technically the two terms are separate. Cannabis is the botanical term for the hemp plant ***Cannabis sativa***. With a potential height of about eighteen feet, cannabis has sturdy stalks, four-cornered in cross-section, that have been commercially valuable for thousands of years in the manufacture of rope, twine, shoes, sailcloth, and containers of all kinds. Pots made of hemp fiber discovered at archaeological sites in China date the origins of cannabis cultivation as far back as the Stone Age. It is arguably the oldest cultivated plant not used for food.[3]

Spaniards brought cannabis to the New World in 1545, and English settlers brought it to Jamestown, Virginia, in 1611, where it became a major commercial crop, along with tobacco. Like other eighteenth-century farmers in the region, George Washington grew cannabis in the fields of his estate at Mount Vernon. Entries in his diary indicate that he maintained a keen interest in cultivating better strains of cannabis, but there is no reason to believe he was interested in anything more than a better-quality rope.

In contrast, marijuana is obtained not from the stalks of the cannabis plant but from its serrated leaves. The key psychoactive factor is contained in a sticky substance, or resin, that accumulates on these leaves. Depending on the growing conditions, cannabis will produce either a greater amount of resin or a greater amount of fiber. In a hot, dry climate, such as North Africa, for example, the fiber content is weak, but so much resin is produced that the plant looks as if it is covered with dew. In a cooler, more humid climate, such as North America, less resin is produced, but the fiber is stronger and more durable.[4]

As many as eighty separate chemical compounds, called **cannabinoids,** can be extracted specifically from cannabis resin. Among these, the chief psychoactive compound and the active ingredient that produces the intoxicating effects is **delta-9-tetrahydrocannabinol (THC)**. The isolation and identification of THC in 1964 was a major step toward understanding the effects on the brain of marijuana and similar preparations obtained from *Cannabis sativa*.

Knowing these facts, we are now in a position to categorize various forms of cannabis products in terms of the origin within the cannabis plant and the relative THC concentration. The first and best-known of these products, **marijuana,** consists of leaves and occasionally flowers of the cannabis plant that are first dried and then shredded. During the 1960s and 1970s, the typical THC concentration of street marijuana imported from Mexico was about 1 to 2 percent; more recently, marijuana has been imported principally from Colombia and other South American countries and contains a THC concentration of about 4 percent. Marijuana, when smoked as a cigarette, is the form of cannabis that is most familiar to North Americans.

A more potent form of marijuana, originating in California and Hawaii, is obtained by cultivating only the unpollinated, or seedless, portion of the cannabis plant. Without pollination, the cannabis plant grows bushier, the resin content is increased, and a greater THC concentration, as high as 6 percent, is achieved. This form is called **sinsemilla,** from the Spanish meaning "without seeds."

Still stronger is a form in which the resin itself is scraped from cannabis flowers, dried, and either smoked by itself or in combination with tobacco. This form, called **hashish,** has a THC concentration of 8 to 14 percent and is commonly available in Europe, Asia, and the Middle East. The most potent forms of cannabis are **hashish oil** and **hashish oil crystals,** produced by boiling hashish in alco-

hol or some other solvent, filtering out the alcohol, and leaving a residue with a THC concentration ranging from 15 to 60 percent.[5]

The history of marijuana and hashish

he first direct reference to a cannabis product as a psychoactive agent dates from 2737 B.C., in the writings of the mythical Chinese emperor Shen Nung. The focus was on its powers as a medication for rheumatism, gout, malaria, and, strangely enough, absent-mindedness.[6] Mention was made of its intoxicating properties, but the medicinal possibilities evidently were considered more important. In India, however, its use was clearly recreational. The most popular form, in ancient

cannabinoids (CAN-a-bih-noyds)
Any of several dozen active substances in marijuana and other cannabis products.

delta-9-tetrahydrocannabinol (THC) (DEL-tah 9-TEH-trah-HEYE-dro-CAN-a-bih-nol)
The active psychoactive ingredient in marijuana and hashish.

marijuana
The most commonly available psychoactive drug originating from the cannabis plant. The THC concentration ranges from approximately 1 to 4 percent. Also called marihuana

sinsemilla
A form of marijuana obtained from the unpollinated or seedless portion of the cannabis plant. It has a higher THC concentration than regular marijuana, as high as 6 percent.

hashish (hah-SHEESH)
A drug containing the resin of cannabis flowers. The THC concentration ranges from approximately 8 to 14 percent.

hashish oil
A drug produced by boiling hashish, leaving a potent psychoactive residue. The THC concentration ranges from approximately 15 to 60 percent.

hashish oil crystals
A solid form of hashish oil.

times as well as in the present day, was a liquid made from cannabis leaves called **bhang,** with a potency usually equal to that of a marijuana cigarette in the United States.

The Muslim world also grew to appreciate the psychoactive potential of cannabis, encouraged by the fact that, in contrast to its stern prohibition of alcohol consumption, the Koran did not specifically ban its use. It was here in a hot, dry climate conducive to maximizing the resin content of cannabis that hashish was born, and its popularity spread quickly during the twelfth century from Persia (Iran) in the east to North Africa in the west.

Hashish in the nineteenth century

In Western Europe knowledge about hashish or any other cannabis product was limited until the beginning of the nineteenth century. Judging from the decree made by Pope Innocent VIII in 1484 condemning witchcraft and the use of hemp in the Black Mass, we can assume that the psychoactive potential of cannabis was known by some portions of the population. Nonetheless, there is no evidence of widespread use.

By about 1800, however, cannabis became more widely known and the subject of a popular craze. One reason was that French soldiers who had served in Napoleon's military campaigns in Egypt brought hashish back with them to their homes in France. Another reason was a wave of Romanticism that swept Europe, including an increased interest in the exotic stories of the East, notably the *Arabian Nights* and the tales of Marco Polo, which latter contained references to hashish. In Paris during the 1840s, a small group of prominent French artists, writers, and intellectuals formed the Club des Hachichins ("Club of the Hashish-Eaters"), where they would gather together, in the words of their leader, "to talk of literature, art, and love" while con-

bhang
A form of marijuana popular in India.

suming large quantities of hashish. The mixture consisted of a concentrated hemp paste, mixed with butter, sweeteners, and flavorings such as vanilla and cinnamon. Members included Victor Hugo, Alexandre Dumas, Charles Baudelaire, and Honoré de Balzac.

Marijuana and hashish in the twentieth century

Chances are that anyone living in the United States at the beginning of the twentieth century would not have heard of marijuana, much less hashish. By 1890, hemp had been replaced by cotton as a major cash crop in southern states, although cannabis plants continued to grow wild along roadsides and in the fields. Some patent medicines during this era contained marijuana, but it was a small percentage compared to the number containing opium or cocaine.[7]

It was not until the 1920s that marijuana began to be a noticeable phenomenon. Some historians have related the appearance of marijuana as a recreational drug to social changes brought on by Prohibition, when it was suddenly difficult to obtain good-quality liquor at affordable prices. Its recreational use was largely restricted to jazz musicians and people in show business. "Reefer songs" became the rage of the jazz world; even the clarinetist and bandleader Benny Goodman had his popular hit, "Sweet Marihuana Brown." Marijuana clubs, called tea pads, sprang up in the major cities; more than five hundred were estimated in Harlem alone, outnumbering the speakeasies where illegal alcohol was being dispensed. These marijuana establishments were largely tolerated by the authorities because marijuana was not illegal and patrons showed no evidence of making a nuisance of themselves or disturbing the community. Marijuana was not considered a social threat.[8]

The antimarijuana crusade

This picture started to change by the end of the 1920s and early 1930s. Even though millions of people had never heard of the plant, much less smoked it, marijuana became widely publicized as a "killer weed." The anti-marijuana campaign was so intense that, in the eyes of the American public, marijuana was a pestilence singlehandedly destroying a generation of American youth.

How did this transformation occur? In order to understand the way in which marijuana smoking went from a localized, negligible phenomenon to a national social issue, we have to look at some important changes in American society that were taking place at that time. First of all, the practice of smoking marijuana and the cultivation of cannabis plants for that purpose had been filtering slowly into the United States since 1900 as a result of the migration of Mexican immigrants. They entered the country through towns along the Mexican border and along the Gulf Coast. In Mexican communities, marijuana was, in the words of one historian, "a casual adjunct to life . . .—a relaxant, a folk remedy for headaches, a mild euphoriant cheaply obtained for two cigarettes for the dollar."[9] It is no exaggeration to say that the immigrant communities were met with hostility and prejudice, and the smoking of an alien and foreign-sounding substance did not help their reception. In effect, it was a social rerun of the Chinese-opium panic of the 1880s (Chapter 7) but with the Mexicans on the receiving end. Rumors about the violent behavioral consequences of marijuana smoking among Mexicans began to spread, largely unchallenged by objective data.

Through the decade of the 1920s, the nation had been obsessed with lawlessness, especially among the foreign born. As a result, the association between an ingrained bias against Mexican Americans and the practice of marijuana smoking became a natural one. In addition, economic upheavals during the Depression made it particularly convenient to vent frustrations upon immigrant communities that were perceived as competing for a dwindling number of American jobs and straining an already weak economy. By 1933, thirty-two states had made marijuana illegal; by 1936, all the rest of the states, even those with negligible immigrant populations, followed suit. The stage was now set for a national policy on marijuana. Leading the crusade was Harry Anslinger, director of the Federal Bureau of Narcotics (FBN), whose career was reviewed in Chapter 2.

Considering the hysteria against marijuana smoking and cannabis use in general, it is not surprising that the Marijuana Tax Act of 1937 had little difficulty in gaining support in Congress. Like the Harrison Act of 1914, the regulation of marijuana was accomplished indirectly. The act did not ban marijuana; it merely required everyone connected with marijuana, from growers to buyers, to pay a tax. It was a deceptively simple procedure that, in effect, made it virtually impossible to comply with the law. In the absence of compliance, a person was in violation of the act and therefore subject to arrest. It was the state's responsibility to make possession of marijuana or any other product of *Cannabis sativa* illegal. Shortly after the tax act of 1937 was enacted, all of the states adopted a uniform law that did just that.

During the rest of the 1940s and 1950s, marijuana research was virtually at a standstill. The theory that marijuana was connected with violence slowly faded away, only to be replaced, with the encouragement of the FBN, with a new position, the gateway theory. According to this idea, marijuana was purported to be dangerous because its abuse would lead to the abuse of heroin, cocaine, or other illicit drugs.

While marijuana research declined, penalties for involvement with it steadily increased. In certain states, the penalties were harsh. Judges frequently had the option of sentencing a marijuana seller or user to life imprisonment. In Georgia, a second offense of selling marijuana to a minor could be punishable by death.

Ironically, in 1969, more than three decades after its passage, the U.S. Supreme Court ruled the 1937 Marijuana Tax Act to be unconstitutional precisely because marijuana possession was illegal. The argument was made that requiring a person to pay a tax (and that was all that the 1937 act concerned) in order to possess an illegal substance amounted to a form of self-incrimination, which would be a specific violation of the Fifth Amendment to the Constitution. It turns out that the case in question here was brought to the high court by Timothy Leary of LSD fame (see Chapter 8), and the court's decision succeeded in overturning a marijuana conviction judged against him.[10]

Challenging old ideas about marijuana

In 1960 arrests and seizures for possession of marijuana were relatively rare and attracted little or no public attention. There was a social consensus that marijuana was a drug that could be comfortably associated with, and isolated to, ethnic and racial minorities. It was relatively easy for most Americans to avoid the drug entirely. In any event, up until 1960, involvement with marijuana was a deviant act, during an era when there was little tolerance for personal deviance.

By the mid-1960s, this consensus began to come apart. Marijuana smoking was suddenly an attraction on the campuses of U.S. colleges and universities, affecting a wide cross-section of the nation. At the same time, the experimental use of drugs, particularly marijuana, by young people set the stage for a wholesale questioning of what it meant to respect authority, on an individual as well as governmental level.

reefer
A name commonly given for a marijuana cigarette.

joint
A marijuana cigarette.

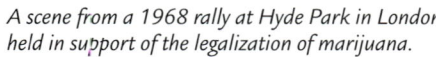

A scene from a 1968 rally at Hyde Park in London held in support of the legalization of marijuana.

Acute effects of marijuana

n the United States, THC is usually ingested by smoking a hand-rolled marijuana cigarette referred to as a **reefer** or, more commonly, a **joint.** Exactly how much THC is administered depends on the specific THC concentration level in the marijuana (often referred to as its quality), how deeply the smoke is inhaled into the lungs, and how long it is held in the lungs before being exhaled. In general, an experienced smoker will ingest more THC than a novice smoker by virtue of being able to inhale more deeply and hold the marijuana smoke in his or her lungs longer, for twenty-five seconds or longer, thus maximizing THC absorption into the bloodstream.

The inhalation of any drug into the lungs produces extremely rapid absorption, as noted in earlier chapters, and marijuana is no exception. In the case of THC, effects are felt within seconds. Peak levels are reached in the blood within thirty minutes and start to decline after about one hour. Behavioral and psychological effects generally last from two to four hours. At this point, low levels of THC stay around for several days, since they are absorbed into fatty tissue, and excretion from fatty tissue is notoriously slow.[11]

One implication arising from a slow metabolic rate is that the residual THC, left over from a previous administration, can intensify the effect of marijuana on a subsequent occasion. In this way, regular marijuana smokers often report a quicker and more easily obtained high, achieved with a smaller-quantity of drug, than more intermittent smokers.[12]

It is important to see the implication of slow marijuana metabolism also with regard to drug testing (see Chapter 14). Urine tests for possible marijuana abuse typically measure levels of THC metabolites (broken down remnants of THC); because of the slow metabolism of marijuana these metabolites are detectable in the urine even when the smoker no longer feels high or shows any behavioral effects. Metabolites can remain in the body several days after smoking a single joint and several weeks later if there has been chronic marijuana smoking. Some tests are so sensitive that a "positive level for marijuana" can result from passive inhalation of marijuana smoke-filled air in a closed environment, even though the THC levels in these cases are substantially below levels that result from active smoking. The bottom line is that marijuana testing procedures are unable to indicate *when* marijuana has been smoked (if it has been smoked at all), only that exposure to marijuana has occurred.[13]

Acute physiological effects

Immediate physiological effects after smoking marijuana are relatively minor. It has been estimated that a human would need to ingest a dose of marijuana that was from twenty thousand to forty thousand times the effective dose before death would occur; in fact, there is no clearly documented case of a human death occurring from marijuana alone.[14] Nonetheless, there is a dose-related increase in heart rate during early stages of marijuana ingestion, up to 160 beats per minute when dose levels are high. Blood pressure either increases, decreases, or remains the same, depending primarily on whether the individual is standing, sitting, or lying down.[15] A dilation of blood vessels on the cornea resulting in bloodshot eyes peaks in about an hour after first smoking a joint. Frequently there is a drying of the mouth and an urge to drink.

Other physiological reactions are inconsistent, and at least part of the inconsistency can be attributed to cultural and interpersonal influences. For example, the observation that marijuana smoking makes you feel extremely hungry and crave especially sweet things to eat (often referred to as having the munchies) generally holds true in studies of North Americans but not for Jamaicans, who consider marijuana an appetite suppressant. Likewise, North Americans often report enhanced sexual responses following marijuana, while in India marijuana is considered a sexual depressant. These reactions, being subjective in nature, can very well be slanted to one direction or the other by the set, or expectations, the marijuana smoker has going into the experience. A good example is the effect on sexual responses. If you believe that marijuana turns you on sexually, the chances are that it will.

While expectations undoubtedly play a prominent role here, we should be aware of the possibility that varying effects may also be due to differences in the THC concentration of the marijuana being smoked. In the case of sexual reactivity, studies of male marijuana smokers have shown that low-dose marijuana tends to enhance sexual desire while high-dose marijuana tends to depress it, even to the point of impotence. It is quite possible that the enhancement is a result of a brief rise in the male sex hormone, testosterone, and the depression a result of a rebound effect that lowers testosterone below normal levels. Typically, the THC concentration in India is higher than that in North America. As a result, we would expect different effects on sexual reactivity. The same argument could be made with respect to the differences in marijuana's effect on appetite.[16]

Acute psychological and behavioral effects

Chapter 7 noted that a first-time heroin abuser frequently finds the experience more aversive than pleasurable. With marijuana, it is likely that a first-time smoker will feel no discernible effects at all. It takes some practice to be able to inhale deeply and keep the smoke in the lungs long enough for a minimal level of THC, particularly in low-quality marijuana, to take effect. Novices often have to be instructed to focus on some aspect of the intoxicated state in order to start to feel intoxicated. The psychological reactions, once they do occur, however, are fairly predictable.

The marijuana high, as the name implies, is a feeling of euphoria, well-being, and peacefulness. Marijuana smokers typically report an increased awareness of their surroundings, as well as a sharpened sense of sight and sound. Frequently they feel that everything is suddenly very funny, and even the most innocent comments or events can set off uproarious laughter. Usually mundane ideas can be filled with profound implications, and the individual may feel that creativity has been increased. As with LSD, however, no objective evidence shows that creativity has been enhanced while under the influence of marijuana. Commonly, time passes more slowly while a person is under the influence of marijuana, and events appear to be elongated in duration. Finally, marijuana smokers frequently report that they feel drowsy, sleepy, and sometimes dreamy. The usual THC concentrations of a marijuana joint are not sufficient to be particularly sleep-inducing, though stronger cannabis preparations with higher THC can have strong sedative-hypnotic effects, particularly when combined with alcohol.[17]

At the same time, marijuana produces significant deficits in behavior. The major deficit is a decline in the ability to carry out tasks that involve attention and memory. Speech will be increasingly fragmented and disjointed; individuals will often forget what they have just said or what others have just said. The problem is that marijuana typically causes such a rush of distracting ideas to come to mind that it is difficult to concentrate on new information coming in. By virtue of a diminished focus of concentration, the performance of both short-term and long-term memory tasks is impaired. All

these difficulties increase in magnitude as a direct function of the level of THC in the marijuana (Focus 9.1).[18]

It should not be surprising that complex motor tasks, just like driving a car, are also more poorly performed while a person is under the influence of marijuana. It is not necessarily a matter of reaction time; studies of marijuana smokers in automobile simulators indicate that they are as quick to respond as control subjects. The problem arises from a difficulty in attending to peripheral information and making an appropriate response while driving.[19] One researcher has put it this way:

Marijuana-intoxicated drivers might be able to stop a car as fast as they normally could, but they may not be as quick to notice things that they should stop for. This is probably because they are attending to internal events rather than what is happening on the road.[20]

In a survey of nearly six thousand teen-age drivers conducted in 1982, results showed that those who had driven six or more times a month after smoking marijuana were approximately two and a half times as likely to have an accident than those who did not. For those individuals who had driven fifteen or more times a month after smoking the marijuana, the increased changes rose to three times as likely.[21]

There is an additional problem that is quite serious. The decline in sensory-motor performance will persist well after the point at which the marijuana smoker no longer feels high. A study involving private airplane pilots, tested in a flight simulator after smoking one joint, showed a significant impairment in average flying performance as long as twenty-four hours later. While their performance was not as greatly impaired as when they were tested one to four hours after smoking the marijuana, it was still below predrug levels. In the case of one of the pilots, the performance would have resulted (assuming a real-life situation) in a plane landing completely off the runway. In summary, we

have to recognize the possibility that some important aspects of behavior can be impaired following marijuana smoking, even when an individual is not aware of it. This effect may be due to the very slow rate with which marijuana is excreted from the body.[22]

Emotional problems as a result of smoking marijuana are rare among Americans who are typically exposed to relatively low THC concentrations, though some distortion of body image, paranoia, and anxiety may occur. It is possible that marijuana smoking among individuals predisposed toward or recovering from a psychosis may trigger off psychotic behavior. Nonetheless, there is little or no support for the idea that low doses of marijuana will trigger such reactions in otherwise normal individuals.

In contrast, a substantially higher incidence of psychiatric problems arising from THC exposure has been reported in India and North Africa. In such cases, however, the THC concentrations being ingested, the frequency with which THC is ingested, and the duration of THC exposure over a lifetime are all far greater than would be encountered in the United States.[23]

Effects of marijuana in the brain

ver since THC was isolated in 1964 as the primary agent for the intoxicating properties of marijuana, the next step has been to find out specifically how THC affects the brain to produce these effects. In 1990 the mechanism was discovered. It turns out that, just as with morphine, special receptors exist in the brain that are stimulated specifically by THC. They are concentrated in areas of the brain that are important for short-term memory and motor control. Unlike morphine-sensitive receptors, however, the THC-sensitive receptors are not found in the lower portions of the brain that control breathing. As a result, no matter how high the THC concentration in the brain, there is no danger of an accidental death by asphyxiation.

Once we have identified a specific receptor for a drug, the question inevitably becomes, Why is it there? As noted in Chapter 7, when the morphine-sensitive receptor was discovered, it made sense to speculate about a natural morphine-like substance that would fit into that receptor. The same speculation sur-

> **anandamide (a-NAN-duh-meyed)**
> A naturally occuring chemical in the brain that fits into THC-sensitive receptor sites, producing many of the same effects as marijuana.

rounded the discovery of the THC-sensitive receptor until 1992. Researchers have now isolated a natural substance, dubbed **anandamide,** that turns on this receptor and appears to produce the same effects as THC in the brain. The question of why the brain would be producing a THC-like substance in the first place remains a subject for future research.[24]

Long term effects of marijuana

s chronic marijuana smoking harmful over a period of time? What is the extent of tolerance and dependence? Are there long-term consequences for organ systems in the body? Will marijuana lessen one's potential as a productive human being in society? Will marijuana abuse lead to the abuse of other drugs? These are questions to be considered next.

Tolerance

It is frequently reported that experienced marijuana smokers tend to become intoxicated more quickly and to a greater extent than nonexperienced smokers, when exposed to marijuana joints with equivalent THC concentrations. For many years, this observation suggested that marijuana upon repeated administrations was producing sensitization, or reverse tolerance (a greater sensitivity), rather than tolerance (a lesser sensitivity). If this were true, then we would have been faced with the troubling conclusion that marijuana operates in a totally opposite way to that of any other psychoactive drug considered so far. Fortunately, when animals are studied or humans are studied in the laboratory, marijuana smoking shows tolerance effects that are consistent and clear-cut.

Why then the difference with the experience of humans outside the laboratory? One factor involves the way in which we measure the quantity of THC consumed. Reaching an effective high from marijuana requires some degree of practice. For example, novice marijuana smokers may not have mastered the breathing technique necessary to allow the minimal level of THC to enter the lungs. They may have to smoke a relatively large number of marijuana joints initially before they achieve a high. Later, when they have acquired the technique, they may need fewer joints to accomplish the same effect. In these circumstances, however, a calculation of the number of joints consumed does not reflect the amount of THC ingested. If you were to control the THC content entering the body, as is done in laboratory studies, you would find the predictable results of tolerance over repeated administrations.

Another factor involves the slow metabolic rate of marijuana. Regular marijuana smokers are likely to have a residual amount of THC still in the system. This buildup of THC would elevate the total quantity of THC consumed with every joint and encourage a quicker high. Once again, we would be left with the impression of sensitization when actually we are observing the enhanced effects of a greater amount of THC in the body. As before, once dosage levels are controlled, the results indicate a consistent pattern of tolerance rather than sensitization. As a rule, tolerance effects following repeated administrations of THC are greater as the dosage level of THC increases.

Dependence

It is possible to observe signs of physical dependence (that is, withdrawal symptoms) following chronic administrations of marijuana, but the level of marijuana smoking has to be quite extreme. In one study, human volunteers were administered large doses of THC every four hours over a ten- to twenty-day period. Within twelve hours after the last administration, subjects reported irritability, restlessness, hot flashes, nausea, and vomiting.[25] In contrast, when another group was required to smoke one marijuana joint daily for twenty-eight days, a condition far closer

to the typical exposure to marijuana, no withdrawal symptoms were observed.[26]

While physical dependence is not much of an issue with marijuana, there may be nonetheless evidence of psychological dependence. Yet, the consensus among experts in the field is that while marijuana is generally reinforcing, there is nowhere near the degree of craving and compulsiveness in the smoking of marijuana that there is for taking alcohol, opiates, stimulants or sedative-hypnotic drugs. It is interesting to note that the popularity of marijuana intoxication among many humans is not at all shared by other members of the animal kingdom. In general, animals will not work in order to self-administer THC (Chapter 2). Humans may find it pleasurable to lose a bit of control and predictability in their lives for a while, but other animals evidently do not.

Cardiovascular effects

THC produces significant increases in heart rate, but there is no conclusive evidence of adverse effects in the cardiovascular functioning in young, healthy people. The reason why the emphasis is on a specific age group is that most of the studies looking at possible long-term cardiovascular effects have involved marijuana smokers under the age of thirty-five, and there is little or no information about older populations. For those people with pre-existing disorders such as heart disease, high blood pressure, or arteriosclerosis (hardening of the arteries), it is known that the acute effects of marijuana on heart rate and blood pressure can worsen their condition.

Respiratory effects and the risk of cancer

The technique of marijuana smoking involves the deep and maintained inhalation into the lungs of unfiltered smoke on a repetitive basis, probably the worst scenario for incurring chronic pulmonary problems. In addition, a marijuana joint (when compared to a tobacco cigarette) typically contains about the same number of tars, 50 percent more hydrocarbons, and an unknown amount of possible contaminants (Table 9.1). Joints are often smoked more completely because the smoker tries to waste as little marijuana as possible. Given all these factors, marijuana smoking presents several risks. One of the immediate consequences affects the process of breathing. When marijuana is inhaled initially, the passageways for air entering and leaving the lungs widen, but after chronic exposure, an opposite reaction occurs. As a result, symptoms of asthma and other breathing difficulties are increased. Overall, while the effects of a single inhalation of marijuana smoke presents greater problems than a single inhalation of tobacco smoke, we need to remember that the patterns of consumption are far from comparable. On a statistical basis, it has been found that the daily smoking of one to three marijuana joints produces approximately the same lung damage and potential cancer risk as the daily smoking of five to fifteen tobacco cigarettes.[27]

TABLE 9.1

A comparison of the components of marijuana and tobacco smoke

Component	Marijuana	Tobacco
Carbon monoxide (mg)	17.6	20.2
Carbon dioxide (mg)	57.3	65.0
Ammonia (micrograms)	228.0	178.0
Acetaldehyde (micrograms)	1200.0	980.0
Acetone (micrograms)*	443.0	578.0
Benzene (micrograms)*	76.0	67.0
Toluene (micrograms)*	112.0	108.0
THC (tetrahydrocannabinol) (micrograms)	820.0	—
Nicotine (micrograms)	—	2850.0
Napthalene (nanograms)	3000.0	1200.0

*See Chapter 6 for information about the health risks of inhaling these chemicals.

SOURCE: Julien, Robert M. (1995). *A primer of drug action* (7th ed.). New York: Freeman, p. 347.

Effects on the immune system

When THC is administered to animals, there is a suppression of the immune system, resulting in a reduction in the body's defense reactions to infection and disease. In humans, the evidence is inconclusive. Some studies indicate that THC has a suppressive effect, while others indicate that no immunological changes occur at all. Because marijuana smoking has not been found to be associated with a higher incidence of any major disease, we can tentatively conclude that marijuana smoking does not have a major impact on the immune system. Yet, long-term epidemiological studies, in which marijuana-exposed and control populations are compared with regard to the frequency of various diseases, have not been conducted on a large-scale basis.[28]

Effects on sexual functioning and reproduction

The reproductive systems of both men and women are adversely affected by marijuana smoking. In men, marijuana reduces the level of testosterone, reduces sperm count in the semen, and increases the percentage of abnormally formed sperm. In women, marijuana results in a reduction in the level of luteinizing hormone (LH), a hormone necessary for the fertilized egg to be implanted in the uterus. As little as one marijuana joint smoked immediately following ovulation is evidently sufficient for this LH suppression to occur. Despite these hormonal changes in both males and females, however, little or no effect on fertility has been observed.[29]

While the research is sparse on the question, there does not appear to be evidence of birth defects in the offspring of women who have smoked marijuana during their pregnancy. Studies indicate, however, a lower birth weight and shorter length among newborns, as well as a reduction in the mother's milk. It may be unfair to associate these effects specifically with marijuana smoking, since other drugs including alcohol and nicotine are often being consumed during the same period. Even so, the best advice remains that marijuana should be avoided during pregnancy.[30]

Neural effects and the amotivation syndrome

Though chronic exposure to marijuana has frequently been suspected of producing some form of brain damage or long-term impairment in neural functioning, there is little or no evidence in support of this idea.[31] It has also been suspected that marijuana may produce more subtle neurological changes that would affect one's personality, motivation to succeed, or outlook on life. In 1968 William McGlothin, a psychologist, and Louis West, a psychiatrist, proposed that chronic marijuana smoking among young people was responsible for a generalized sense of apathy in their lives and an indifference to any long-term plans or conventional goals. These changes were called the **amotivational syndrome.** In their words,

> Regular marijuana use may contribute to the development of more passive, inward-turning personality characteristics. For numerous middle-class students, the subtly progressive change from conforming, achievement-oriented behavior to a state of relaxed and careless drifting has followed their use of significant amounts of marijuana. . . . Such individuals exhibit greater introversion, become totally involved with the present at the expense of future goals, and demonstrate a strong tendency toward regressive, childlike magical thinking.[32]

In effect, McGothlin and West, and probably a large number of other people in the late 1960s, were saying, "These people don't seem to care anymore and marijuana's to blame for it."

The issue of the amotivational syndrome breaks down to two basic questions that can be examined separately. The first question deals with whether such a syndrome exists in the first place, and the second deals with whether chronic abuse of marijuana is a

causal factor. As to the existence of the syndrome, the evidence does suggest that students who smoke marijuana are at a disadvantage academically. Studies of high school students indicate that those who smoke marijuana have lower grades in school, are less likely to continue to college, are more likely to drop out, and miss more classes than those who do not smoke it.[33] In

QUICK CONCEPT CHECK 9.2

Understanding the adverse effects of chronic marijuana abuse

heck your understanding of the possible adverse effects of either acute or chronic exposure to marijuana by checking off true or false next to each of the assertions.

Assertion	True	False
1. The immune system will be impaired.	_____	_____
2. The chances of getting cancer will be unaffected.	_____	_____
3. Driving ability will be significantly impaired.	_____	_____
4. Birth defects will be more frequent.	_____	_____
5. It is likely that academic performance will decline when a person smokes marijuana regularly.	_____	_____
6. Marijuana smoking will cause the smoker to experiment with harder drugs in the future.	_____	_____

ANSWERS: 1. false   2. false   3. true   4. false   5. true   6. false

amotivational syndrome
A state of listlessness and personality change involving a generalized apathy and indifference to long-range plans.

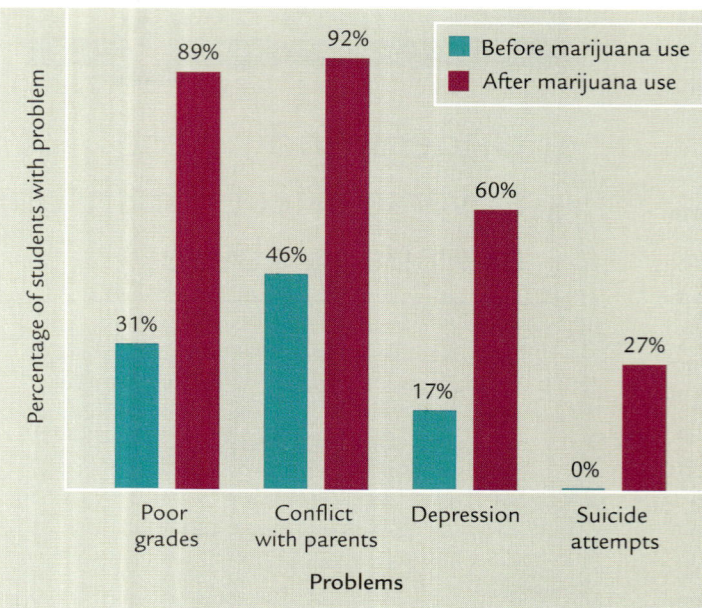

A deceptively simple comparison of adolescent problems before and after marijuana use.

and suicide attempts.[35] The changes are genuine, but we cannot so easily determine a cause-and-effect relationship merely on the basis of such information. We cannot exclude the possibility that marijuana smoking may be, in the words of one expert in the field, "just one behavior in a constellation of related problem behaviors and personality and familial factors" that hamper an adolescent's ability to do well in school and in life.[36] We also cannot exclude the possibility that an involvement with marijuana may closely correlate with involvement in a deviant subculture, a group of friends and associates who feel alienated from traditional values such as school achievement and a promising future. Either of these factors, in combination with the regular ingestion of a sedative drug such as marijuana, can account for the motivational changes that are observed. The point is that we cannot conclude that such changes are purely pharmacological.

a survey of high school students graduating in 1980 and 1981, those who smoked marijuana on a daily basis reported several problems in their lives that are involved in motivation: a loss of energy (43 percent), negative effects on relationships (39 percent), interference with work and the ability to think clearly (37 percent), less interest in other activities (37 percent) and inferior performance in school or on the job (34 percent).[34]

The involvement of marijuana smoking as a causal agent in these problems, however, is doubtful. To understand the difficulties in analyzing data on this question, consider the results of a 1987 study comparing problems before and after the onset of marijuana abuse (Fig. 9.1) and showing substantial increases in the incidence of poor grades, conflict with parents, feelings of depression,

The gateway hypothesis

The final concern regarding chronic effects of marijuana deals with the extent to which marijuana smoking leads to a greater incidence of drug abuse in general, a contention that is often referred to as the **gateway hypothesis.** As in consideration of the issues surrounding the amotivational syndrome earlier, the evidence must be studied very carefully. Statistically, the evidence is overwhelming and uncontroversial. Marijuana smokers are more likely during their lifetimes to consume a wide range of illicit drugs, including heroin, cocaine, and the hallucinogens. The greater the frequency of marijuana smoking and the earlier a person first engages in marijuana smoking, the greater the likelihood of his or her becoming involved in these other drugs in a serious way. These facts are unquestioned.

But is marijuana responsible for this relationship? Erich Goode, sociologist and drug-abuse researcher, distinguishes between two

gateway hypothesis
The idea that the abuse of a specific drug will inherently lead to the abuse of other more harmful drugs.

explanations, which he calls the intrinsic and the sociocultural schools of thought. The intrinsic argument is that there is some inherent property of marijuana exposure itself that leads to physical or psychological dependence on other illicit drugs. According to this viewpoint, pleasurable sensations of marijuana create a biological urge to consume more potent substances, through a combination of drug tolerance and drug dependence. In contrast, the sociocultural argument holds that the relationship exists not because of the pharmacological effects of marijuana but because of the activities, friends, and acquaintances that are associated with marijuana smoking. In other words, the sociocultural explanation asserts that those who smoke marijuana tend to have friends who not only smoke marijuana themselves but also abuse other drugs. These friends are likely to have positive attitudes toward substance abuse in general and provide opportunities for drug experimentation.

Professionals in the drug-abuse field have concluded that there is no support for the intrinsic explanation. It turns out that the relationship between marijuana and later drug abuse is not a unique phenomenon; a similar relationship exists with regard to the exposure to alcohol and cigarettes. A major study of high school students graduating in 1985 has shown that those who had smoked a pack or more of cigarettes each day had a ten times greater likelihood of using cocaine and a six times greater likelihood of smoking marijuana. Alcohol consumption also related positively to marijuana and cocaine abuse. If any gateway drugs exist, they are the legally available substances of alcohol and tobacco, not marijuana. But even in these cases, we are not speaking of a pharmacological property that causes people to engage in further drug experimentation. The consensus is that any early exposure to psychoactive substances in general represents a "deviance-prone pattern of behavior" that will be reflected in a higher incidence of exposure to psychoactive drugs of many types later in life.[37]

Medical uses for marijuana

ven though the medicinal benefits of marijuana have been noted for thousands of years, strong antimarijuana sentiment has made it difficult until the last twenty or so years to conduct an objective appraisal of possible clinical applications. Three principal medical uses have been explored: the treatment of glaucoma, the treatment of asthma, and the treatment of nausea resulting from chemotherapy.[38]

Glaucoma

In 1971 it was found that smoked marijuana significantly reduced intraocular (within the eye) pressure in normal, human subjects. This discovery led to an important potential application for individuals suffering from glaucoma, a disease in which intraocular pressure rises so high as to damage the optic nerve and eventually produce blindness. Since then, experimental studies have examined the effectiveness of marijuana (either smoked or ingested orally) or THC eye drops in reducing glaucoma symptoms. These approaches have been shown to be effective, but the medical consensus is that other nonmarijuana drugs are of equal or greater value.[39]

Asthma

Marijuana produces an initial bronchodilation, followed by a subsequent bronchoconstriction. In the case of asthmatic conditions, in which the primary problem is a bronchoconstriction reducing the flow of air into and out of the lungs, it would appear that marijuana would not be advised at all. In fact, it turns out that orally administered THC results in bronchodilation without the expected contriction later on. Consequently, THC has a positive effect on asthmatic symptoms. As in its application for the treatment of glaucoma, however, other forms of treatment have been shown to be at least equally effective.[40]

Nausea

Chemotherapy in the course of cancer treatment produces an extreme and debilitating nausea, lack of appetite, and loss of body weight, symptoms that are clearly counterproductive in helping an individual contend with an ongoing fight against cancer. AIDS patients suffer from similar symptoms. During these circumstances, standard antiemetic (antivomiting) drugs are frequently ineffective. The beneficial effects of marijuana, specifically THC, as an antiemetic drug is an important application of marijuana as a medical treatment. You may have seen stories in the news highlighting the plight of individuals suffering from AIDS or the side effects of cancer treatment for whom marijuana smoking has provided significant relief. This chapter's Portrait will examine the present-day dilemma of turning to an illegal drug for medical purposes.

Medical and political issues

The use of marijuana per se as a therapeutic agent has distinct disadvantages. First of all, the typical administration through smoking presents, as described earlier, a significant health risk to the lungs. In addition, since marijuana is insoluble in water, suspensions in an injectable form cannot be prepared. Since 1985, however, two legal prescription drugs containing THC or variations of it have been made available in capsule form. **Dronabinol** (brand name: Marisol) is essentially THC in a sesame oil suspension; **nabilone** (brand name: Cesamet) is a synthetic variation of THC. Both drugs have been shown to be clinically effective as antinausea treatments, though the

personal reactions of patients taking these drugs vary considerably.[41]

While these prescription drugs are presently in use, U.S. federal authorities, as administered through FDA guidelines, have until recently been reluctant to reclassify marijuana itself or any other cannabis product from a Schedule I category (defining drugs that are considered to have no medical applications) to a Schedule II category. Only a handful of compassionate-use applications have been approved, and the entire procedure for reviewing new compassionate-use requests was terminated in 1992. Nonetheless, in the event that FDA policy changes in the future, thirty-six states have passed legislation allowing the limited use of marijuana when carried out under a physician's care. In the last few years, prominent figures in law enforcement and government have endorsed a liberalization of the marijuana-as-medicine policy, but no action has as yet been taken.[42]

Patterns of marijuana smoking

From their days in elementary school on, most young Americans have had to come to terms with marijuana as a pervasive element in their lives. Just as nearly all adolescents have had to make the decision to drink or not to drink, smoke cigarettes or not to smoke them, they have also had to decide whether or not to smoke marijuana.

In sheer numbers, marijuana is clearly the dominant illicit drug in U.S. society. From the house-to-house survey conducted by the National Institute on Drug Abuse in 1992, it is estimated that an astounding 67 million Americans, representing roughly one third of the U.S. population over the age of twelve, have smoked marijuana at least once during their lives. If we look specifically at people between the ages of twenty-six and thirty-four, roughly six out of every ten have smoked marijuana at least once. More than 17 million Americans

---

dronabinol (droh-NAB-ih-nol)
A prescription drug containing delta-9-tetrahydrocannabinol (THC). Brand name is Marisol.

nabilone (NAB-ih-lone)
A prescription drug containing a synthetic variation of delta-9-tetrahydrocannabinol (THC). Brand name is Cesamet.

Kenny and Barbra Jenks vs. America's war on drugs

n the late 1980s, Kenny Jenks, a hemophiliac, and his wife, Barbra, both developed AIDS. Neither of them had smoked marijuana in their lives before, but the nausea and weight loss that the disease brought on gave them little choice. Every antinausea medication their physician had prescribed failed to work; Kenny's weight dropped from 155 to 112 pounds in six weeks. For them, smoking two or three joints of marijuana, harvested from two ten-inch cannabis plants in their Panama City Beach, Florida, home, was the only way to keep their weight up and their nausea down. All went well until one day in March 1990,

when twelve policemen bashed a battering ram through their door, seized the plants, and arrested the Jenkses on charges of growing marijuana and possessing more than one ounce of it.

Forbidden to grow their own, Kenny and Barbra then applied for and won approval to be two of approximately a dozen individuals in the United States with permission to smoke marijuana for medical purposes. The marijuana they receive comes from a special farm in Louisiana where the federal government harvests its own crop of cannabis. The Jenkses call their marijuana ditch weed, and it is conceded that the potency leaves much to be desired.

Even so, the Jenkses prefer smoking government-variety marijuana to taking Marisol pills, an FDA-approved antinausea medication containing pure THC. They speculate that there must be other components in the marijuana besides THC that are helping to relieve their symptoms. Besides, Marisol gets them too high; they don't want to be intoxicated, only to make their symptoms go away.

Kenny, Barbra, and a handful of others are the lucky ones to have received approval for their marijuana smoking before the program was canceled in 1992. Others who have been denied approval essentially operate outside the law.

The future for the medical use of marijuana on a nationwide basis is uncertain, although there are signs that attitudes toward this particular application are changing. The medical establishment has already agreed to go on record as supporting the medical use of marijuana. In a 1991

survey of more than a thousand oncologists (specialists in the treatment of cancer) around the country, 44 percent said they had already recommended marijuana smoking to at least one patient to control nausea during chemotherapy even though it was in violation of the law. In addition, a number of individual states now permit the medical use of marijuana.

SOURCES: Baum, Dan (1993, August 5–11). Doctor's orders: The Clinton administration relaxes the ban on marijuana—for medical purposes only, of course. *Ithaca Times*, pp. 6–7, 9. Berger, Joseph (1993, October 11). Mother's homemade marijuana. *New York Times*, pp. B1, B5. Doolin, Richard E., and Kleiman, Mark A. R. (1991). Marijuana as medicine: A survey of oncologists. In Arnold S. Trebach and Kevin B. Zeese (Eds.), *New frontiers in drug policy*. Washington DC: Drug Policy Foundation, pp. 242–245. Grinspoon, Lester, and Bakalar, James B. (1993). *Marihuana, the forbidden medicine*. New Haven CT: Yale University Press.

are estimated as having smoked marijuana at least once during the past year; almost 9 million are estimated as having done so at least once during the past month.[43]

Through the University of Michigan survey we can get an idea of the prevalence rates among younger people. Among high school seniors surveyed in 1993, approximately 26 percent reported having smoked marijuana in the past year, 16 percent reported having done so in the past month, and 2 percent smoked on a daily basis. The data from college students in 1993 were relatively similar; approximately 28 percent reported having smoked marijuana in the past year, 14 percent in the past month, and 2 percent on a daily basis Comparable figures are also reported for young adults eighteen to thirty-two in 1993.

On the one hand, the prevalence of marijuana as an illicit drug among high school seniors today is less than half the prevalence during the late 1970s, with the incidence of daily marijuana smoking down to one fifth of what it was previously.

FOCUS 9.2

Street language for marijuana in the 1990s

n the 1960s, when marijuana smoking first became widely popular, the street language was fairly simple. Marijuana was either grass or pot, and a marijuana cigarette was a joint. Here is a sampling of the street language of the 1990s, though the names are constantly changing.

- marijuana: skunk, boom, doobie

- marijuana and alcohol: Herb and Al

- getting high on marijuana: getting lifted, booted, red, smoked out or choked out, hit the hay, poke, toke up, blast a stick, burn one, fly Mexican Airlines, mow the grass, boot the gong

- $3 bag of marijuana: a tray

- $5 "nickel" bag: a nick (usually just enough for one joint)

- $40 bag: a sandwich bag

- kinds of marijuana: chronic, chocolate tide, indigo, Hawaiian, Tropicana, Acapulco gold, Panama red

- water pipe similar to a bong: a shotgun

- joints: "blunts" (after the Phillies Blunt cigars that marijuana smokers cut open, hollow out, and fill with marijuana; other brands used, White Owls and Dutch Masters)

SOURCES: Bureau of Justice Statistics Clearinghouse (1992). *Drugs, crime, and the justice system*, Washington DC: Department of Justice pp. 24–25. Henneberger, Melinda (1994, February 6). "Pot" surges back, but it's, like, a whole new world. *New York Times*, Sect. 4, p. 18.

Future trends as causes for concern

n addition to the rise in the number of marijuana smokers among young people, there is also a change in the way marijuana use is perceived. Chapter 1 noted that until recently, there has been a steady upward trend over the years in the percentage of students who think that marijuana smoking and drug abuse in general carry significant personal risks. The 1993 survey results show a reversal since 1991. While 72 percent of high school seniors in 1993 considered "regular marijuana smoking" harmful, this figure was down from 77 percent in 1992 and 79 percent in 1991.[45]

We are also currently seeing a growing popular culture that reinforces the behavior of marijuana smoking as a cool thing to do. The transformation since the beginning of the 1990s has been dramatic. In 1990 marijuana smoking was nearly invisible and considered uncool. According to one college student in

The image of Cannabis sativa *in the 1990s.*

On the other hand, since 1991, the survey indicates an increasing trend in the prevalence rates, particularly among young people in the junior high grades.[44] The percentages of eighth graders surveyed in 1993 who have reported smoking marijuana over the previous year or the previous month are 9 and 5 respectively, a significant increase over comparable data collected in 1991 (Focus 9.2). Marijuana smoking is not alone in this regard;

1993, "The image of the pot smoker was very much a hippie thing. Now it's completely different. There's a whole mode of dress, music and style that didn't exist three years ago."[46]

A further concern with regard to present-day marijuana use has to do with an increased potency in the cannabis products available for abuse. A typical marijuana joint in the psychedelic era contained approximately 1 to 2 percent THC; in the 1990s, the average concentration was 4 percent. The higher-potency form, sinsemilla, is more widely available than ever before, as is hashish. It is reasonable to assume that the adverse effects of chronic marijuana smoking, with THC concentrations approaching 15 percent in some strains of sinsemilla, will be more intense than the relatively mild symptoms we have encountered in the past.

A final concern has to do with an issue that applies to any illicit street drug, the possibility for adulteration. As emphasized in earlier chapters, what you buy is not always what you get. Each year brings with it a new cast of ingredients, some of them newly introduced drugs and others merely inventive creations from already available materials, ready to be combined with marijuana either to weaken its effects (and increase the profits of the seller) or to change the overall psychoactive result by some synergistic or other interactive effect.

A DEA officer is confiscating and destroying a domestic crop of Cannabis sativa in Kentucky.

The issue of decriminalization

What then should public policy be toward marijuana smoking in the United States today? To deal with this question, we need first to review how public policy with respect to marijuana regulation has evolved since the 1970s. As described earlier, the dramatic emergence during the 1960s of marijuana as a major psychoactive drug initiated a slow but steady reassessment of myths that had been attached to it for decades. By 1972, the American Medical Association, the American Bar Association, and even the leading conservative commentator and author William F. Buck-ley were proposing a liberalization of laws regarding the possession of marijuana. During the same year, the National Commission on Marijuana and Drug Abuse, authorized by the Comprehensive Drug Abuse Prevention and Control Act of 1970, encouraged state legislators around the country to consider changes in their particular regulatory statutes related to marijuana.[47] Since that time, eleven states, including California, New York, Colorado, Minnesota, and North Carolina, have adopted some form of decriminalization laws with respect to the possession of marijuana in small amounts (usually less than one ounce or so). Essentially, **decriminalization** has meant that possession under these circumstances is considered a civil rather than a criminal offense, punishable by a small fine rather than imprisonment. Alaska in 1990, however, recriminalized marijuana possession, so far the only state to do so. While many other states still have criminal penalties in their statutes, the era of strenuous law enforcement against marijuana smoking in general has essentially ended. As the sociologist Erich Goode has expressed it,

decriminalization
The policy of making the possession of small amounts of a drug subject to a small fine but not criminal prosecution.

For all practical purposes, the possession of marijuana has become decriminalized in the United States. Since present trends are moving toward de facto legal acceptance of small-quantity marijuana possession, it will not make a great deal of difference whether this attitude is recognized by law or not. Consequently, the debate over decriminalization is swiftly becoming obsolete.[48]

You may find it surprising or not surprising (depending on your personal views) that decriminalization has not resulted in an upturn in the incidence of marijuana smoking. Statistics drawn from states that either have or have not decriminalized show little or no difference.[49] In addition, attitude surveys, conducted in California before and after the enactment of decriminalization statutes, have indicated that the acceptance of marijuana among college students has actually declined as a result.[50]

Given the current climate of opinion, the question now remains: Should the practice of marijuana smoking be legalized as well? This issue will be examined in the Point/Counterpoint feature.

Summary

A MATTER OF TERMINOLOGY

- Marijuana is one of several products of the *Cannabis sativa,* or common hemp plant, grown abundantly throughout the world.

- Various cannabis products are distinguished in terms of the content of cannabis resin and, in turn, the concentration of THC, the active psychoactive agent.

THE HISTORY OF MARIJUANA AND HASHISH

- The earliest records of marijuana come from Chinese writings nearly five thousand years ago; hashish has its origins in North Africa and Persia in the ninth or tenth centuries A.D.

- In the United States, marijuana was available in patent medicines during the late 1800s, but its popularity did not become extensive until the 1920s.

- Federal and state regulation of marijuana began in the 1930s; penalties for possessing and selling marijuana escalated during the 1940s and 1950s.

- The emergence of marijuana on American college campuses and among American youth in general during the late 1960s, however, forced a reexamination of public policy regarding this drug, leading to a more lenient approach in the 1970s.

ACUTE EFFECTS OF MARIJUANA

- Since marijuana is almost always consumed through smoking, the acute effects are rapid; since it is absorbed into fatty tissue, its metabolism is slow. It may require days or weeks in the case of extensive exposure to marijuana for THC to leave the body completely.

- Acute physiological effects include cardiac acceleration and a reddening of the eyes. Acute psychological effects, with typical dosages, include euphoria, giddiness, a perception of time elongation, and an increased hunger and sexual desire. There are impairments in attention and memory, which interfere with complex visual-motor skills such as driving an automobile.

- The acute effects of marijuana are now known to be due to the binding of THC at special receptors in the brain.

LONG-TERM EFFECTS OF MARIJUANA

- Chronic marijuana use produces tolerance effects; there is no physical dependence when doses are moderate and only a mild psychological dependence.

- Carcinogenic effects are suspected since marijuana smoke contains many of the same harmful components that tobacco smoke does, and in the case of marijuana smoking inhalation is deeper and more prolonged.

- The hypothesis that there exists an amotivational syndrome attributed to the pharmacological effects of marijuana has been largely discredited, as has the idea that marijuana inherently sets the stage for future drug abuse.

MEDICAL USES FOR MARIJUANA

- While marijuana has been useful in the treatment of glaucoma and asthma, its most effective application to date has been in the treatment of symptoms of chemotherapy-induced nausea.

PATTERNS OF MARIJUANA SMOKING

- While the current incidence of marijuana smoking among adolescents and young adults is lower than the incidence in the late 1970s, there are clear indications of a resurgence.

- Other areas of concern are the greater potency of marijuana that is now available and the continuing potential risk of marijuana adulteration.

- Present public policy toward marijuana smoking has focused upon a decriminalization of possession of small amounts.

Key Terms

amotivational syndrome, p. 215
anandamide, p. 212
bhang, p. 206
cannabinoids, p. 205
Cannabis sativa, p. 204
decriminalization, p. 221
delta-9-tetrahydrocannabinol (THC), p. 205
dronabinol, p. 218
gateway hypothesis, p. 216

hashish oil crystals, p. 205
hashish oil, p. 205
hashish, p. 205
joint, p. 208
marijuana, p. 205
nabilone, p. 218
reefer, p. 208
sinsemilla, p. 205

Endnotes

1. Abel, Ernest L. (1980). *Marihuana, the first twelve thousand years.* New York: Plenum Press, p. ix.
2. Bloomquist, E. R. (1968). *Marijuana.* Beverly Hills CA: Glencoe Press, pp. 4–5.
3. Abel. *Marihuana*, p. 4. Palfai, Tibor, and Jankiewicz, Henry (1991). *Drugs and human behavior.* Dubuque IA: W. C. Brown, p. 452.
4. Abel. *Marihuana*, pp. x–xi.
5. Goode, Erich (1989). *Drugs in American Society* (3rd ed.). New York: McGraw-Hill, p. 37.
6. Abel. *Marihuana*, p. 12.
7. Bonnie, Richard J., and Whitebread, Charles H. (1974). *The marihuana conviction: A history of marihuana prohibition in the United States.* Charlottesville VA: University Press of Virginia, p. 3.
8. Abel. *Marihuana*, pp. 218–222.
9. Bonnie and Whitebread. *The marihuana conviction*, p. 33.
10. Lee, Martin A., and Shlain, Bruce (1985). *Acid dreams: The complete social history of LSD.* New York: Grove Weidenfeld.
11. Julien, Robert M. (1995). *A primer of drug action* (7th ed.). New York: Freeman, pp. 338–340.
12. Julien. *A primer of drug action*, p. 340.
13. *Allen and Hanbury's athletic drug reference* (1992). Research Triangle Park NC: Clean

Data, p. 33.   Wadler, Gary I., and Hainline, Brian (1989). *Drugs and the athlete.* Philadelphia: F. A. Davis, pp. 208–209.

14. Grinspoon, Lester (1971). *Marihuana reconsidered.* Cambridge MA: Harvard University Press, pp. 227–228.

15. Jones, Reese T. (1980). Human effects: An overview. In Robert C. Petersen (Ed.), *Marijuana research findings: 1980* (NIDA Research Monograph 31). Rockville MD: National Institute on Drug Abuse, p. 65.

16. Grilly, David M. (1989). *Drugs and human behavior.* Boston: Allyn and Bacon, p. 245.

17. Hofmann, Frederick G. *A handbook on drug and alcohol abuse* (2nd ed.). New York: Oxford University Press, pp. 204–211.

18. Hooker, William D., and Jones, Reese T. (1987). Increased susceptibility to memory intrusions and the Stroop interference effect during acute marijuana intoxication. *Psychopharmacology, 91,* 20–24.

19. Delong, Fonya L., and Levy, Bernard I. (1974). A model of attention describing the cognitive effects of marijuana. In Loren L. Miller (Ed.), *Marijuana: Effects on human behavior.* New York: Academic Press, pp. 103–117. Gieringer, Dale H. (1988). Marijuana, driving, and accident safety. *Journal of Psychoactive Drugs, 20,* 93–101.

20. McKim, William A. (1991). *Drugs and behavior* (2nd ed.). Englewood Cliffs NJ: Prentice Hall, p. 286.

21. Hingson, R., Heeren, T., Mangione, T., Morelock, S., and Mucatel, M. (1982). Teenage driving after using marijuana or drinking and traffic accident involvement. *Journal of Safety Research, 13,* 33–38.

22. Meer, J. (1986, February). Marijuana in the air: Delayed buzz bomb. *Psychology Today,* pp. 68–69.

23. Hofmann. *A handbook on drug and alcohol abuse,* pp. 214–215.

24. Fackelman, Kathy A. (1992). Marijuana and the brain. *Science News, 143,* 88–89, 94.

25. Jones, Reese T., and Benowitz, Neal (1976). The 30-day trip: Clinical studies of cannabis tolerance and dependence. In Monique C. Braude and Stephen Szara (Eds.), *Pharmacology of marijuana.* Vol. 2. Orlando FL: Academic Press, pp. 627–642.

26. Frank, Ira M., Lessin, Phyllis J., Tyrrell, Eleanore D., Hahn, Pierre M., and Szara, Stephen. (1976). Acute and cumulative effects of marijuana smoking on hospitalized subjects: A 36-day study. In Monique C. Braude and Stephen Szara (Eds.), *Pharmacology of marijuana.* Vol. 2. Orlando FL: Academic Press, pp. 673–680.

27. Julien. *A primer of drug action,* p. 346.   Marijuana update (1989, May). *NIDA capsules.* Rockville MD: National Institute on Drug Abuse, p. 2.

28. Hollister, Leo E. (1988). Marijuana and immunity. *Journal of Psychoactive Drugs, 20,* 3–7. Petersen, Robert C. (1984). Marijuana overview. In Meyer D. Glantz (Ed.), *Correlates and consequences of marijuana use* (Research Issues 34). Rockville MD: National Institute on Drug Abuse, p. 10.

29. Harclerode, Jack (1980). The effect of marijuana on reproduction and development. In Petersen, Robert C. (Ed.), *Marijuana: Research findings 1980* (NIDA Research Monograph 31). Rockville MD: National Institute on Drug Abuse, pp. 137–166.   Jacobs, Michael R., and Fehr, Kevin O'B. (1987). *Drugs and drug abuse: A reference text.* Toronto: Addiction Research Foundation, p. 235.   Marijuana update, p. 2.

30. Harclerode. The effect of marijuana, p. 154.

31. Hollister, Leo E. (1986). Health aspects of cannabis. *Pharmacological Reviews, 38,* 1–20.

32. McGothlin, William H., and West, Louis J. (1968). The marijuana problem: An overview. *American Journal of Psychiatry, 125,* 372.

33. Goode. *Drugs in American society,* pp. 152–155.

34. Fox, C. Lynn, and Forbing, Shirley E. (1992). *Creating drug-free schools and communities: A comprehensive approach.* New York: HarperCollins, p. 60.

35. *Drug Abuse Update* (1987, September). Atlanta: National Families in Action, p. 4.

36. Goode. *Drugs in American society,* p. 154.

37. Johnston, Lloyd D., O'Malley, Patrick M., and Bachman, J. G. (1987). *National trends on drug use and related factors among American high school students and young adults, 1975–1986.*

Rockville MD: National Institute on Drug Abuse, pp. 133–153.   Petersen. Marijuana overview, p. 4.

38. Cohen, Sidney (1980). Therapeutic aspects. In Robert C. Petersen (Ed.), *Marijuana Research findings: 1980* (NIDA Research Monograph 31). Rockville MD: National Institute on Drug Abuse, pp. 199–221.   Julien. *A primer of drug action,* p. 344.

39. Ibid., p. 344.

40. Ibid., p. 344.

41. Plasse, Terry F., Gorter, Robert W., Krasnow, Steven H., Lane, Montague, Shepard, Kirk V., and Wadleigh, Robert G. (1991). Recent clinical experience with dronabinol. International conference on cannabis and cannabinoids, Chania, Greece. *Pharmacology, Biochemistry, and Behavior, 40,* 695–700.

42. Baum, Dan (1993, August 8–11). Doctors orders: The Clinton administration relaxes the ban on marijuana—for medical purposes only. *Ithaca Times,* pp. 6–7, 9.

43. Substance Abuse and Mental Health Services Administration (1993). *National Household Survey on Drug Abuse: Population estimates 1992.* Rockville MD: Substance Abuse and Mental Health Services Administration, Office of Applied Studies, Table 3A.

44. Johnston, Lloyd D., O'Malley, Patrick M., and Bachman, Jerald G. (1994). *National survey results on drug use from the Monitoring the Future study, 1985–1993.* Vol. 1. Rockville MD: National Institute on Drug Abuse, Table 1.

45. Johnston, O'Malley, and Bachman. *National survey results,* Table 19.

46. Leland, John (1993, November 1). Just say maybe. *Newsweek,* pp. 50–54, quotation on p. 52.

47. National Commission on Marihuana and Drug Abuse (1972). *Marihuana: A signal of misunderstanding.* Washington DC: Government Printing Office, pp. 151–167.

48. Goode. *Drugs in American society,* p. 278.

49. Johnston, Lloyd D. (1980, January 16). Marijuana use and the effects of marijuana decriminalization. Unpublished testimony delivered at the hearings on the effects of marijuana held by the Subcommittee on Criminal Justice, Judiciary Committee, U.S. Senate, Washington DC, p. 5.

50. Sommer, Robert (1988). Two decades of marijuana attitudes: The more it changes, the more it is the same. *Journal of Psychoactive Drugs, 20,* 67–70.

Should marijuana be a legally available substance?

he following discussion presents the opinions of people on both sides of the controversial issue of the legalization of marijuana. Read them with an open mind. Discuss them in your class, with your family, and with your friends. Don't think you have to come up with the final answer, nor should you necessarily agree with the argument you heard last. Many of the ideas in this feature come from the sources listed at the end, where more extensive discussions can be found.

POINT

Now that several U.S. states have decriminalized the possession of marijuana in small amounts, it's about time we took the final step: legalizing marijuana entirely. We would be eliminating the black market that presently exists for marijuana and reducing a sizable portion of our law-enforcement costs in the bargain. The state of California alone saved at least $1 billion in arrest costs and court expenses from 1976, when decriminalization statutes first took effect, to 1988. This money can be spent for drug-abuse treatment programs throughout the state; expand the figure to include all the United States and the savings are enormous. Despite decriminalization in some states, approximately 400,000 individuals are arrested on marijuana-related charges nationwide each year.

COUNTERPOINT

The same tired dollar-and-cents argument. But what about the health risks? We would be sanctioning the chronic use of a substance for which, at best, the adverse health consequences are not fully known. It's quite possible that legalization would bring with it a dramatic increase in marijuana smoking, in segments of the population that up to now have stayed away from it. Do you want little children suddenly smoking marijuana?

POINT

First of all, you're correct that we do not know the long-range health problems right now. But you could argue that we cannot wait until we do; the immediate social costs are too important. Besides, we now know the health problems associated with alcohol and tobacco, and we are not making them illegal substances. As to the increased-incidence issue, look at the situation in Oregon in 1973, when it decriminalized possession of small amounts of marijuana. From 1974 to 1977, the number of people, age eighteen or older, who have "ever used" marijuana went up from 19 to 25 percent; "current users" increased from 9 to 10 percent. These small increases were no different from those seen in states that had not changed their marijuana laws. As far as children are concerned, any legalization would be regulated to protect them. A minimum age of eighteen for marijuana smoking would be a prudent and reasonable restriction.

COUNTERPOINT

A minimum-age restriction hasn't kept children from drinking or from smoking tobacco cigarettes; why would it magically work for marijuana? But let's look at another question. Who would make marijuana and who would sell it? Pharmaceutical companies, wine and liquor corporations, cigarette manufacturers? Wouldn't we be creating a whole new industry with a windfall of profits going to companies who get into the marijuana business?

POINT

There already is a marijuana business, but you don't see it because it's underground. One plan might be to issue licenses to sellers who meet certain conditions (such as purity of ingredients and accurate information regarding dosage) and make any sales by others who are unlicensed a criminal offense. As far as this above-ground industry is concerned, we would be assured that they pay their taxes. Can we say that now about the underground?

COUNTERPOINT
Marijuana commercials polluting our airwaves?

POINT
Let's ban all advertising of marijuana products. There's no reason we have to benefit the advertising industry as a result of these changes.

COUNTERPOINT
But isn't there a moral argument? As it has been said, one could argue that marijuana smoking "makes a mockery of virtue." We would be saying that we accept this practice as appropriate in our society. Many people object to that.

POINT
We're talking about an end to prohibition, not an end to temperance. Many people would object to open marijuana smoking, just as many people already object to open tobacco smoking or excessive drinking. We have ways to regulate and restrict these practices already, so people who object do not have to compromise their values or their life-style.

COUNTERPOINT
We have been talking about marijuana smoking up to now. What about hashish, with its far greater THC concentrations? Is there a greater potential for abuse here? Where do we draw the line between acceptable and nonacceptable THC concentrations?

POINT
That could be a problem. To be consistent, a legalization program would have to include hashish as well as any other cannabis product. The health consequences would be more severe, but more than likely individuals consuming high concentrations of THC would be also involved in harder drugs, and the latter involvement would be prosecutable.

COUNTERPOINT
Not only would we be exacerbating the problems we now have on the roads with drunk driving, but we would be saddled with the extra burden of proof because diagnoses for marijuana usage are far more difficult than tests for alcohol in the blood.

POINT
Driving under the influence of any intoxicant would be severely punished. You could argue that tests for driving under the influence of alcohol are not perfect either. In any event, we should force the emphasis toward the penalties for the behavior of dangerous driving rather than the specific pharmacological reason for it. In the meantime, legalization has eliminated the "forbidden fruit" motivation. Marijuana would be no big deal.

COUNTERPOINT
Think about this. If marijuana isn't fun anymore because it's now legal, what would stop children from applying the "forbidden fruit" argument to more dangerous drugs? As one expert has put it, "If pot is so cool and the other drugs are so bad, will we now precipitate a rush to more dangerous drugs by legalizing the less dangerous intermediate?"

POINT
The key would be education.

COUNTERPOINT
I'm not convinced that legalization is the way to go. Let's expand the decriminalization policy first, then see what happens. It may be premature to legalize at the present time. For now, let's encourage an ongoing research program on the long-term health consequences of marijuana smoking and continue monitoring the incidence patterns. We can always decide on legalization at some future time.

SOURCES: Bloomquist, Edward R. (1971). *Marijuana: The second trip.* Beverly Hills CA: Glencoe Press, pp. 285-319. Kaplan, John (1970). *Marijuana: The new prohibition* New York: World Publishing. Alcrich, Michael R., and Mikuriya, Tod (1988). Savings in California marijuana law enforcement costs attributable to the Moscone Act of 1976— A summary. *Journal of Psychoactive Drugs, 20,* 75–81.

10

Alcohol:
Social Beverage,
Social Drug

I was invited to address a convention of high school teachers on the topic of drug abuse. When I arrived at the convention center to give my talk, I was escorted to a special suite, where I was encouraged to join the executive committee in a round of drug taking—the drug was a special high-proof single-malt whiskey. Later, the irony of the situation had its full impact. As I stepped to the podium under the influence of a psychoactive drug (i.e., the whiskey), I looked out through the haze of cigarette smoke at an audience concerned with the unhealthy impact of drugs on their students. The welcoming applause gradually gave way to the melodic tinkling of ice cubes in liquor glasses, and I began. They did not like what I had to say.

John P. J. Pinel
Biopsychology (1993)

inel's observation in this opening quotation sums up the central problem American society has in dealing with alcohol use and abuse the frequent failure to acknowledge that alcohol is indeed a psychoactive drug.[1] You may have heard someone remark, "He drinks a little too much, but at least he's not doing drugs." To many people, an alcoholic beverage is simply a social beverage; in actuality, it is a social drug.

We can see this inherent problem reflected in a number of ways. College courses that concern drug abuse and its effect on society, perhaps the one you are taking right now, are often entitled "Drugs and Alcohol." Would you personally have expected to cover the effects of alcohol in a course simply entitled "Drugs" in your college catalog? If you answer no, then alcohol had better stay in the course title.

Even the U.S. federal government perpetuates the distinction, with separate agencies for alcohol abuse (the National Institute for Alcohol Abuse and Alcoholism, NIAAA) and the abuse of other drugs (the National Institute on Drug Abuse, NIDA). This bureaucratic partitioning has admittedly historic roots, and there may be valid reasons to continue the division from a management or budgetary point of view, but it has inadvertently reinforced an unfortunate and inaccurate notion that alcohol is somehow a substance that stands apart from other drugs of potential abuse. Fortunately, the phrase "alcohol and other drugs" has become increasingly popular as a way of conveying the idea that problems of substance abuse can come from many sources. This chapter will consider alcohol as a drug with a unique history and tradition and its own set of acute risks. The next chapter will turn to the chronic effects of alcohol abuse, specifically the problem of alcoholism.

What makes an alcoholic beverage?

Creating **ethyl alcohol,** through a process known as **fermentation,** is one of the easier things to do. Almost every culture in the world, at one time or another, has stumbled upon the basic procedure. All you need is organic material with a sugar content (honey, grapes, berries, molasses, rye, apples, corn, sugar cane, rice, pumpkins, to name some examples) left undisturbed in a warm container for a time, and Nature does the work. Microscopic yeast cells, floating through the air, will land on the substance and literally consume the sugar in it, so that, for every one sugar molecule consumed, two molecules of

alcohol and two molecules of carbon dioxide will be left behind as waste. The carbon dioxide bubbles out, and what remains is an alcoholic beverage, less sweet than the substance that began it all but with a new, noticeable kick. Basic fermentation results in an alcohol content of approximately 12 percent, best exemplified by standard grape wine.

The process of fermenting starchy grains such as barley to produce beer, called **brewing,** is somewhat more complicated. The barley needs first to be soaked in water until it sprouts, producing an enzyme that is capable of breaking down the starch into sugar. It is then slowly dried, the sprouts are removed, and the remainder (now called **barley malt**) is crushed into a powder. The barley malt is combined with water, corn, and rice to form a mixture called a **mash.** The water activates the enzyme so that the starches convert into sugars. The addition of yeast to the mash starts the fermentation process and produces an alcohol content of approximately 4.5 percent. The dried blossoms of the hop plant, called hops, are then added to the brew for the characteristic pungent flavoring and aroma.

Relying on fermentation alone gives potentially a maximal concentration of alcohol of about 15 percent. The reason for this limit is that an alcohol content above this level starts to kill the yeast and, in doing so, stops the fermentation process. In order to obtain a higher alcoholic content, another process called **distillation** must be carried out. In this process a container of some fermented mixture is heated until it boils. Because alcohol has a lower boiling temperature than water, the vapor produced has a higher alcohol-to-water ratio than the original mixture. This alcohol-laden vapor is then drawn off into a special coiled apparatus (often referred to as a still), cooled until it condenses back to a liquid, and poured drop by drop into a second container. This new liquid, referred to as **distilled spirits** or simply *liquor,* has an alcohol content considerably higher than 15 percent, generally in the neighborhood of 40 to 50 percent. It is possi-

ethyl alcohol
The product of fermentation of natural sugars. It is generally referred to simply as alcohol, though several types of nonethyl alcohols exist.

fermentation
The process of converting natural sugars into ethyl alcohol by the action of yeasts.

brewing
The process of producing beer from barley grain.

barley malt
Barley after it has been soaked in water, sprouts have grown, sprouts have been removed, and the mixture has been dried and crushed to a powder.

mash
Fermented barley malt, following liquification and combination with yeasts.

distillation
A process by which fermented liquid is boiled then cooled, so that the condensed product contains a higher alcoholic concentration than before.

distilled spirits
The liquid product of distillation, also known as liquor.

ble through further distillations to achieve an alcohol content of up to 95 percent. The alcohol content of distilled spirits is not, however, commonly described by percentage but rather by the designation "proof." Any proof is twice the percentage of alcohol: an 80-proof whiskey contains 40 percent alcohol, a 190-proof contains 95 percent alcohol.

The three basic forms of alcoholic beverages are wine, beer, and distilled spirits. Table 10.1 shows the sources of some well-known examples.

Alcohol through history

istorians point out that fermented honey, called *mead,* was probably the original alcoholic beverage, dating from approximately 8000 B.C.[2] Beer, requiring more effort than simple fermentation, came on the scene much later, with the Egyptians establishing the first official brewery about 3700 B.C. At that time, beer was quite different from the watery forms we know today. It was more similar to

T A B L E 1 0 . 1

Prominent alcoholic beverages and their sources

Beverage	Source
Wines	
Red table wine	Fermented red grapes
White table wine	Fermented skinless grapes
Champagne	White wine bottled before yeast is gone, so that remaining carbon dioxide produces a carbonated effect
Sparkling wine	Red wine prepared like champagne or with carbonation added
Dessert wines	Wines whose alcohol content is raised or fortified to 20% by the addition of brandy (see below), for example, sherry, port, Marsala, and Madeira
Wine-like variations	
Hard cider	Fermented apples
Sake	Fermented rice
Beers	
Draft beer	Differences in types of beer due to variations in brewing procedures. Draft and lager beers and ales contain
Lager beer	3–6% alcohol; malt liquor contains up to 8% alcohol
Ale	
Malt liquor	
Distilled spirits	
Brandy	Distilled from grape wine, cherries, peaches, or other fruits
Liqueur or cordial	Brandy or gin, flavored with blackberry, cherry, chocolate, peppermint, licorice, etc. Alcohol content ranges from 20% to 55%
Rum	Distilled from the syrup of sugar, cane, or from molasses
Scotch whiskey	Distilled from fermented corn and barley malt
Rye whiskey	Distilled from rye and barley malt
Blended whiskey	A mixture of two or more types of whiskey
Bourbon whiskey	Distilled primarily from fermented corn
Gin	Distilled from either barley, potato, corn, wheat, or rye, and flavored with juniper berries
Vodka	Approximately 95% pure alcohol diluted by mixing with water
Tequila	Distilled from the fermented juice of the maguey plant
Aquavit or akvavit	Distilled from grains or potatoes, flavored with caraway seeds
Grain neutral spirits	Approximately 95% pure alcohol, used either for medicinal purposes or diluted and mixed in less-concentrated distilled spirits

S O U R C E : Adapted from Becker, Charles E., Roe, Robert L, and Scott, Robert A. (1979). *Alcohol as a drug: A curriculum on pharmacology, neurology, and toxicology.* Huntington NY: Robert Krieger Publishing, pp. 10–12.

a bread than a beverage, and the process of producing it was closer to baking bread than to brewing a liquid.[3]

Evidence of the development of wine comes from references to its sale in the Code of Hammurabi, king of Babylonia, dating about 1700 B.C. By the time of the ancient Greeks, in the eighth century B.C., wine was a central feature of their culture and religion. When Homer described the Mediterranean as a "wine-dark sea," everyone knew what he meant.

The first documented distillation of alcohol was the conversion of wine into brandy during the Middle Ages, at a medical school in Salerno, Italy, and the emphasis at first was on its medicinal applications rather than the level of intoxication that could be achieved with it. The new beverage became known in Latin as **aqua vitae** ("the water of life"). People quickly caught on, however, to its inebriating possibilities, and brandy became the primary distilled liquor in Europe until the middle of the seventeenth century. At that time the Dutch perfected the process of distilling liquor and flavoring it with juniper berries. A new alcoholic beverage was born: gin.

The enormous popularity of gin throughout Europe marked a crucial point in the history of alcohol's effect on European society. Because it was easily produced, as well as cheaper than brandy and faster-acting than wine, great quantities of gin were available to poor classes of people. By the mid-1700s, alcohol abuse was clearly seen as a major societal problem, and concerns about drunkenness had become a public issue. In England, as one observer reported at the time, "One half of the town [London] seems set up to furnish poison to the other half."[4]

Although gin affected life in many parts of Europe, it was in English cities that the gin epidemic became a genuine crisis. By 1750,

Gin Lane in London, as interpreted by William Hogarth (1697–1764). Notice that only the pawnbroker and the coffin maker seem to be benefiting from the gin epidemic.

gin consumption in England had grown to twenty-two times the level in 1685, and the social devastation was obvious. In London, infant mortality had risen during this period, with only one of four baptized babies between 1730 and 1749 surviving to the age of five, despite the fact that mortality rates were falling in the countryside. In one section of the city, as many as one in five houses was a gin shop. Consumption of other distilled spirits, such as rum and whiskey, added to the overall problem, but it was gin that was seen as the prime culprit. The epidemic of gin drinking in England during the first half of the eighteenth century illustrated how destructive the introduction of a potent psychoactive drug into a newly urban society already suffering from social dislocation and instability could be. The consequences were in many ways similar to the introduction of crack cocaine into the ghettos of the United States during the 1980s.[5]

aqua vitae (AH-kwa VEE-tay)
A brandy, the first distilled liquor in recorded history.

Alcohol in U.S. history

Judging from the records of Pilgrims aboard the *Mayflower* in 1620, alcohol played a pivotal role in the earliest days of settling the American colonies. William Bradford, historian of the *Mayflower* voyage and later governor of Plymouth Colony in Massachusetts, wrote that in looking for a place to land, they had decided not to "take time for further search or consideration, our victuals [supplies] being much spent, especially our Beere." Evidently, the Pilgrims arrived not only with a passion for freedom but also with a considerable thirst.[6]

We have to understand, however, that these English settlers, like other travelers at that time, had little choice but to take along alcoholic beverages. Water would have spoiled easily during the sea voyage. Besides, they were not against alcohol per se, merely against the drunken behavior that resulted from its excessive use. The general approval of the moderate use of alcohol was a fact of American life well into the nineteenth century.[7]

It is not surprising, therefore, that the social focus for communities in colonial America was the tavern. Not only did taverns serve as the public dispenser of alcoholic beverages but they also served as the center for local business dealings and town politics as well. Mail was delivered there; travelers could stay the night; elections were held there. As an institution, the tavern was as highly regarded, and as regularly attended, as the local church.[8]

By today's standards, it is difficult to imagine the extent of alcohol consumption during the early stages of American history. In 1830 the average intake was an immoderate five drinks a day, roughly two and one half times the level of consumption today. As far as types of liquor were concerned, rum was the favorite in New England and along the North Atlantic coast, but elsewhere whiskey was king. George Washington himself went into the whiskey business at Mount Vernon in

1798, raising rye for the local distillers; Thomas Jefferson was persuaded to do the same.[9]

Yet given the extent of heavy drinking, reports of public drunkenness in the populated areas of the country were remarkably infrequent. Only in the West, where societal restrictions were more relaxed, was drunkenness commonly observed.

The rise of temperance in the United States

The year 1830 marked the peak in alcohol consumption in the United States. The gradual decline after that point coincided with the growing influence of a **temperance movement** among religious leaders, physicians, and social reformers. Temperance goals originally focused on the moderation, not necessarily the prohibition, of alcohol consumption in society and drew attention to the long-term consequences of chronic alcohol abuse. The distinction between temperate use and total prohibition, however, began to blur over the years. The shift from temperance to prohibition, from 1830 through the beginning of the twentieth century, will be examined in the next chapter.

Patterns of alcohol consumption today

t has been theorized that the earliest systems of agriculture in the history of mankind grew out of the desire to secure a dependable supply of beer.[10] If this is so, then alcohol, commercialization, and economics have been linked together from the very beginning. Today, of course, alcohol is not only a big business but an enormous business. In 1992 Americans spent about $50 billion on beer

> **temperance movement**
> The social movement in the United States, beginning in the nineteenth century, that advocated the renunciation of alcohol consumption.

$12 billion on wine and wine coolers, and $34 billion on liquor, according to industry sources. In terms of international trade, imports of alcoholic beverages outnumbered exports four to one. Approximately, $1.1 billion were spent in 1992 on promoting and advertising alcohol.[11]

Overall patterns of alcohol consumption

How much do Americans drink? The per capita consumption of pure alcohol among Americans in 1990, depending on whether industry or government information is used, was between 2 and two and a half gallons a year, roughly equivalent to approximately one ounce of alcohol a day.[12] How many drinks would equal this amount of pure alcohol? Table 10.2 shows four ways that a single half ounce of pure alcohol could be represented in terms of beer, wine, wine cooler, or liquor. As indicated, one ounce of alcohol is equivalent to a double portion of any of these alcoholic beverages.

A prime consideration, however, in looking at average alcohol consumption figures is the enormous disparity among Americans in terms of how much each person consumes during a given year. *Only 30 percent of Ameri-*

The stainless-steel tanks of the world's largest wine maker, the Ernest and Julio Gallo Winery, are located in Modesto, California.

TABLE 10.2

Alcoholic beverages and their alcohol equivalencies

Beverage	Alcohol equivalency
1 glass of wine	
4 oz. quantity	4 x .12 = .48 oz. alcohol
12% alcohol concentration	(approx. 1/2 oz.)
1 can of regular beer	
12 oz. quantity	12 x .04 = .48 oz. alcohol
4% alcohol concentration	(approx. 1/2 oz.)
1 shot of 80-proof liquor	
1.25 oz. quantity	1.25 x .40 = .50 oz. alcohol
40% alcohol concentration	(exactly 1/2 oz.)
1 bottle of wine cooler	
12 oz. quantity	12 x .04 = .48 oz. alcohol
4% alcohol concentration	(approx. 1/2 oz.)

The bottom line: 1 glass of wine, 1 can of beer, 1 shot of liquor, and 1 bottle of wine cooler have roughly equivalent amounts of alcohol in them.

cans who drink account for 80 percent of the total consumed each year. And one third of that 30 percent, or 10 percent of the drinking population, account for roughly half of the total alcohol consumption.

Trends in alcohol consumption since the late 1970s

Overall, alcohol consumption levels among Americans have been steadily declining each year since the late 1970s, and forecasters predict a continued decline through the rest of the 1990s. Since a large part of this decline has been tied to a growing attention to weight, health, and fitness, the industry has responded with the introduction of lighter wines, with fewer calories and a reduced alcohol content, as well as a popular line of wine coolers (wine mixed with sugar and fruit juice), equal in alcoholic content to regular beer. In addition to brands of lighter beers, introduced with fewer calories and an alcohol content of about 3.2 percent, there has been a growing market for "ice beer," created from a brewing method in which below-freezing temperatures temporarily create crystals and supposedly smooth out the taste.[13] A series of lower-proof liquors are scheduled for test marketing in the years ahead.[14]

The demographics of alcohol consumption

Preferences among types of alcoholic beverages are influenced by a host of factors, including age, gender, education, and income. In general, among individuals who drink alcoholic beverages, women are twice as likely as men not to prefer beer, three times as likely as men to prefer wine, somewhat more likely than men to prefer liquor, and less likely than men to be undecided. The preference for wine and liquor over beer increases as people get older.

Increased years of education are associated with an increased preference for wine over beer and liquor. The same is true with income levels, except for the fact that there is a less clear change in preference for liquor. Individuals earning more than $50,000 prefer wine and beer to liquor, and those earning less than $20,000 prefer beer to liquor and wine.[15]

Binge drinking among college students and other young adults is a common social ritual as well as a continuing social concern.

In general, college students consume a large amount of alcohol, though it appears that the establishment of twenty-one in all states as a mandated legal drinking age has delayed the occurrence of *peak* consumption levels to the junior or senior year. Nonetheless, the prevalence of moderate alcohol consumption in college, assessed by those having a drink in the last thirty days, rises substantially from levels encountered in high school, from 51 to 72 percent. Among young adults, binge drinking, defined as having five or more drinks in a row, rises sharply from age eighteen, peaking at ages twenty-one to twenty-two, and steadily declining over the next ten years. The prevalence of daily drinking, however, rises from levels encountered in high school but remains relatively stable through age thirty-two.

Problems and secondary effects of binge drinking among college students

Percentage of students reporting alcohol-related problems

Problem	Nonbinge drinkers (1 or more drinks in past year)	Infrequent binge drinkers (1 or 2 binges in a 2-week period)	Frequent binge drinkers (3 or more binges in 2-week period)
Had a hangover	30	75	90
Did something I regretted	14	37	63
Forgot where I was or what I did	8	26	54
Argued with friends	8	22	42
Missed class	8	30	61
Engaged in unplanned sexual activity	8	20	41
Did not use protection when having sex	4	10	22
Got into trouble with campus or local police	1	4	11

Percentage of nonbinge drinkers reporting secondary effects, in relation to the binge drinking level of the school

Secondary effects	Low-level schools (fewer than 35% binge drinkers)	Middle-level schools (36–50% binge drinkers)	High-level schools (more than 51% binge drinkers)
Was insulted or humiliated	21	30	34
Had a serious argument or quarrel	13	18	20
Was pushed, hit, or assaulted	7	10	13
Had my property damaged	6	13	15
Had to take care of a drunken student	31	47	54
Experienced an unwanted sexual advance (women only)	15	21	26

SOURCE: Adapted from Wechsler, Henry, Davenport, Andrea, Dowdall, George, Moeykens, Barbara, and Castillo, Sonia (1994). Health and behavioral consequences of binge drinking in college. *Journal of the American Medical Association, 272,* 1672–1677.

Table 10.3 shows the results of a 1993 survey of the drinking habits of more than seventeen thousand college students on 140 U.S. campuses. Overall, 44 percent reported having engaged in binge drinking in a two-week period, 39 percent of the women and 50 percent of the men. The average proportion of binge drinkers on a particular campus ranged from 1 to 70 percent. Not surprisingly, the likelihood of alcohol-related problems increased as a direct function of the level of alcohol consumed. The survey, however, also reported that more than 62 percent of *nondrinkers* were adversely affected by binge drinking patterns on campus. These reactions, called second-hand drinking (since the individuals themselves were not drinking), are analogous to the problems of second-hand smoking which will be examined in Chapter 12.[16]

Looking at the early years of teenage drinking, we find that alcohol use has been extensive by the eighth grade. According to the Michigan survey, 67 percent of eighth graders reported in 1993 that they had consumed alcohol, 26 percent reported having been drunk at some time in their lives, and 8 percent reported having been drunk in the previous month.[17]

The pharmacology of alcohol

lcohol is a very small molecule, in liquid form, that is moderately soluble in fat and highly soluble in water—all characteristics that make it easily absorbed through the gastrointestinal tract once it is ingested, without the need for any digestion. About 20 percent of it is absorbed into the bloodstream directly from the stomach, while the remaining 80 percent is absorbed from the upper portion of the small intestine.

On entering the stomach, alcohol acts initially as an irritant, increasing the flow of hydrochloric acid and pepsin, chemicals that aid digestion. Therefore, in small amounts, alcohol can help digest a meal; in large amounts, however, alcohol will irritate the stomach lining. This is a concern for those already having stomach problems; preexisting ulcers will be worsened by drinking alcohol, and heavy alcohol drinking can produce ulcers. The irritating effect on the stomach also explains why the alcohol proceeds on to the small intestine more quickly if alcohol concentrations are high. The stomach is simply trying to get rid of its irritant. Over time, the chronic consumption of alcohol can produce an inflammation of the stomach (gastritis) or the pancreas (pancreatitis).

Since the small intestine assumes the lion's share of the responsibilities and acts extremely rapidly (more rapidly than the stomach), the rate of total alcohol absorption is based largely on the condition of the stomach when the alcohol arrives and the time required for the stomach to empty its contents into the small intestine. If the stomach is empty, an intoxicating effect (the "buzz") will be felt very quickly. If the stomach is full, absorption will be delayed since the alcohol is retained by the stomach along with the food being digested and the passage of alcohol into the small intestine will slow down.

Besides the condition of the stomach, there are other factors related to the alcohol itself and the behavior of the drinker that influence the rate of alcohol absorption. The principal factor is the concentration of alcohol in the beverage being ingested. An ounce of 80-proof (40 percent) alcohol will be felt more quickly than an ounce of 12 percent wine, and of course the level of alcohol in the blood will be higher as well. Also, if the alcoholic beverage is carbonated, as are champagne and other sparkling wines, the stomach will

empty its contents faster and effects will be felt sooner. Finally, if the alcohol is entering the body at a rapid pace, as when drinks are consumed in quick succession, the level of alcohol in the blood will be higher because the process of getting rid of the alcohol in the liver, cannot keep up with the amount coming in. All other factors being equal, a bigger person will require a larger quantity of alcohol to have equivalent levels accumulating in the blood, simply because there are more body fluids to absorb the alcohol, thus diluting the overall effect.[18]

Distribution and metabolism of alcohol

Its solubility in water helps alcohol to be distributed to all bodily tissues, with those tissues having greater water content receiving a relatively greater proportion of alcohol. The excretion of alcohol is accomplished in two basic ways. About 5 percent will be excreted by the lungs through exhalation, causing the characteristic "alcohol breath" of heavy drinkers. Breatholyzers, designed to test for alcohol concentrations in the body and used frequently by law-enforcement officials to test for drunkenness, work on this principle.[19] The remaining 95 percent of the alcohol will be excreted in the urine, after it has been metabolized into carbon dioxide and water.

The solubility of alcohol in fat easily facilitates its passage across the blood-brain barrier (Chapter 3). As a result, approximately 90 percent of the alcohol in the blood reaches the brain almost immediately. Unfortunately, alcohol also passes the blood-placental barrier with equal ease, so that alcohol intake by women during pregnancy affects the developing fetus. As a result, fetal alcohol levels are essentially identical to those of the mother who is drinking.[20] This important matter will be discussed in the next chapter, when it considers a type of mental and physical retardation called fetal alcohol syndrome.

The body recognizes alcohol as a visitor with no real biological purpose. It contains calories but no vitamins, minerals, or other components that would have any nutritional value. Therefore, the primary reaction is for the body to metabolize it for eventual removal, through a process called **oxidation.** This metabolic process consists of two basic steps. First, an enzyme, **alcohol dehydrogenase,** breaks down alcohol into **acetaldehyde.** This enzyme is present in the stomach, where about 20 percent of alcohol is broken down prior to absorption into the bloodstream, and in the liver, where the remaining 80 percent is metabolized from accumulations in the blood. Second, another enzyme, **acetaldehyde dehydrogenase,** breaks down acetaldehyde in the liver into **acetic acid.** From there, further oxidation results in oxygen, carbon dioxide, and calories of energy.

The entire process is determined by the speed with which alcohol dehydrogenase does its work, and, for a given individual, it works at a constant rate, no matter how much alcohol needs to be metabolized. Imagine a bank where only one teller window stays open, no matter how long the line of customers, and then you will understand the limitations on our capacity to metabolize alcohol.

The specific rate is approximately 100 milligrams of alcohol per kilogram of body weight. To put this in perspective, 8 grams of alcohol will be metabolized in an hour if you weigh 176 pounds (80 kilograms), and 5 grams of alcohol will be metabolized in an hour if you weigh 110 pounds (50 kilograms). There are conditions and circumstances, however, that will alter this basic metabolic rate (Focus 10.1).

In terms of alcoholic beverages, the oxidation rate for adults in general is approximately one third to one half ounce of pure alcohol an hour. If you sipped (not gulped) slightly less than the contents of one twelve-ounce bottle of beer, four-ounce glass of wine, or any equivalent portion of alcohol (see Table 10.2) over an hour's time, the enzymes in the stomach and liver would keep up, and you would not feel intoxicated. Naturally, with larger amounts of alcohol consumed and faster rates of consumption, all bets are off.[21]

It is no secret that alcohol consumption is conducive to the accumulation of body fat, particularly in the form of the notorious beer belly. It turns out that alcohol does not have significant effects on the metabolism of dietary carbohydrates and proteins, so a drinking individual who consumes a healthy diet does not have to worry. Alcohol does, however, reduce the metabolism of fat, so that dietary fat has a greater chance of being stored than expended. The accumulation of fat in the liver is particularly serious because it will interfere eventually with liver functioning. This condition will be examined in the next chapter as one of the major adverse effects of chronic alcohol consumption on the body.[22]

Measuring alcohol in the blood

Alcohol levels in the blood, like levels of any drug, vary considerably not only by virtue of how much is ingested and how long ago but also as a result of differences in body size and relative proportions of body fat. As a consequence, we have to consider a specific ratio

oxidation
A chemical process in alcohol metabolism.

alcohol dehydrogenase (AL-co-haul DEE-heye-DRAW-juh-nays)
An enzyme in the stomach and liver that converts alcohol into acetaldehyde.

acetaldehyde (ASS-ee-TAL-duh-heyed)
A by-product of alcohol metabolism, accomplished through the action of alcohol dehydrogenase.

acetaldehyde dehydrogenase (ASS-ee-TAL-duh-heyed DEE-heye-DRAW-juh-nays)
An enzyme in the liver that converts acetaldehyde to acetic acid in alcohol metabolism.

acetic acid (A-SEE-tik ASS-id)
A by-product of alcohol metabolism, accomplished through the action of acetaldehyde dehydrogenase.

Gender, race, and medication: Factors in alcohol metabolism

Since enzymes play such a critical role in alcohol metabolism, it is important to consider factors that alter the levels of these enzymes. As mentioned in Chapter 3, two of the factors involve gender and ethnicity. In general, women have about 60 percent less alcohol dehydrogenase in the stomach than men, so that their oxidation of alcohol is relatively slower, even when different body weights have been taken into account.

In addition, about 50 percent of all people of Asian descent have a genetically imposed lower level of acetaldehyde dehydrogenase in the liver. As a consequence, acetaldehyde builds up, causing nausea, itching, facial flushing, and cardiac acceleration. The combination of these symptoms, often referred to as fast-flushing, makes alcohol consumption very unpleasant for many Japanese.

It would be reasonable to expect then that those who experienced fast-flushing would drink less alcohol than those who do not. A recent study of Japanese Americans indicates that this is true when you look at a large community sample. For Japanese American college students who have to contend with peer pressure to drink, however, the relationship between the physiological response and the quantity of alcohol consumed is not nearly as strong. For them, environmental factors encourage alcohol consumption, despite their genetically determined predisposition to get sick. In a similar way, the social life of Japanese businessmen has promoted alcohol consumption, though many get sick as a result. A journalist describes the dilemma in present-day Japan in this way:

Perhaps in no other nation is drinking so expensively and tightly woven in business. Drinking after work is not only an extension of the company, it is virtually a requirement. Refuse the boss's offer to go out drinking, and your standing in the firm begins to slide.

Medications can also influence alcohol metabolism by altering levels of alcohol dehydrogenase in the stomach. Aspirin, for example, when taken on a full stomach, reduces enzyme levels by one half, causing more alcohol to accumulate in the blood. Among women, aspirin has a greater inhibiting effect than among men, so it is possible that enzyme levels may be reduced to nearly zero if a woman is taking aspirin prior to drinking alcoholic beverages. Gastric ulcer medications also inhibit alcohol dehydrogenase and thus increase the physiological impact of alcohol. Any combination of these factors appears to produce additive effects.

SOURCES: Frezza, Mario, DiPadova, Carlo, Pozzato, Gabrielle, Terpin, Maddalena, Baraona, Enrique, and Lieber, Charles S. (1990). High blood alcohol levels in women: The role of decreased gastric alcohol dehydrogenase activity and first-pass metabolism. *New England Journal of Medicine, 322,* 95–99. Gibbons, Boyd (1992, February). Alcohol: The legal drug. *National Geographic Magazine, 181,* p. 27. Goodman, Deborah (1992, January–February). NIMH grantee finds drug responses differ among ethnic groups. *ADAMHA News,* pp. 5,15. Nakawatase, Tomoko V., Yamamoto, Joe, and Sasao, Toshiaki (1993). The association between fast-flushing response and alcohol use among Japanese Americans. *Journal of Studies on Alcohol, 54,* 48–53. Roine, Risto, Gentry, Thomas, Hernandez-Muñoz, Rolando, Baraona, Enrique, and Lieber, Charles S (1990). Aspirin increases blood alcohol concentrations in humans after ingestion of ethanol. *Journal of the American Medical Association, 264,* 2406–2408

referred to as the **blood-alcohol concentration (BAC)** when assessing physiological and psychological effects (an alternative term is blood-alcohol level [BAL]). The BAC is the number of milligrams of alcohol in the blood relative to one hundred milliliters of blood, expressed as a percentage. The timing of drinking is crucial because BAC levels rise to a maximum over time and then decline as the alcohol is oxidized. Table 10.4 shows the BAC levels that can be estimated from one's body weight, number of drinks consumed, and hours elapsed since starting the first drink. From these figures, BAC levels can be considered in terms of three broad categories of behavior: caution (.01 to .05 percent), driving impaired (.05 to .10 percent), and legally drunk in most states (.10 percent and higher).[23]

> **blood-alcohol concentration (BAC)**
> The number of milligrams of alcohol in the blood relative to 100 milliliters of blood, expressed as a percentage.

Calculating your blood-alcohol concentration (BAC) level

						Drinks					
Weight (lb.)		1	2	3	4	5	6	7	8	9	10
	100	.029	.058	.088	.117	.146	.175	.204	.233	.262	.290
	120	.024	.048	.073	.097	.121	.145	.170	.194	.219	.243
	140	.021	.042	.063	.083	.104	.125	.146	.166	.187	.208
	160	.019	.037	.055	.073	.091	.109	.128	.146	.164	.182
	180	.017	.033	.049	.065	.081	.097	.113	.130	.146	.162
	200	.015	.029	.044	.058	.073	.087	.102	.117	.131	.146
	220	.014	.027	.040	.053	.067	.080	.093	.106	.119	.133
	240	.012	.024	.037	.048	.061	.073	.085	.097	.109	.122

CAUTION   DRIVING IMPAIRED   LEGALLY DRUNK

Alcohol is "burned up" by your body at .015% per hour, as follows:

No. hours since starting first drink	1	2	3	4	5	6
Percent alcohol burned up	.015	.030	.045	.060	.075	.090

In order to calculate your BAC level correctly, you must consider the number of drinks you have consumed, your body weight, and how much time has passed since the first drink. Note that a BAC level of .10% or higher is the standard for drunk driving in 40 states. A BAC level of .08% or higher is the standard in California, Florida, Kansas, Maine, New Hampshire, New Mexico, North Carolina, Oregon, Utah, and Vermont, as well as all of Canada.

SOURCE: From *A primer of drug action* 3/e by Julien. Copyright © 1981 by W. H. Freeman and Company. Used with permission.

The effect of alcohol on the brain

Alcohol is a CNS depressant drug, though its effects are often misinterpreted as stimulating. The reason for this confusion is that alcohol, at low doses, first releases the cerebral cortex from its inhibitory control over subcortical systems in the brain, a kind of double-negative effect. In other words, alcohol is depressing an area of the brain that normally would be an inhibitor, and the result is the illusion of stimulation. The impairment in judgment and thinking (the classic features of being drunk) stems from a loosening of social inhibitions that allow us to be relatively civil and well behaved. As the BAC level increases, more widespread areas of the brain are affected until an inhibition of the respiratory centers in the medulla becomes a distinct possibility. As with other depressant drugs, acute alcoholic poisoning produces death by asphyxiation.[24] The LD50 BAC level for alcohol, where death is likely to occur, is approximately .50 percent. Remember, however, the nature of the LD50 curve (Chapter 2); deaths can occur at lower concentrations and fail to occur at higher ones.

The effect of alcohol at the neuronal level is less well understood, but the picture is starting to emerge. At present, the leading candidate for a mechanism is the GABA receptor in the brain. Chapter 5 stated that this receptor had three locations within it: one sensitive to the neurotransmitter GABA, one sensitive to benzodiazepines, and one sensitive to sedative-hypnotics. The last location is sensitive also to alcohol, and the research suggests that alcohol acts at this site, making it more difficult for the neuron to be stimulated.[25]

Beyond alcohol's depressive effects on the brain, however, is its ability to set up a pattern of craving for more. In other words, there is the very real possibility of the development of psychological dependence (Chapter 3). Since the late 1980s, there is increasing evidence that a byproduct of alcohol metabolism called **tetrahydroisoquinoline (TIQ)** affects morphine-sensitive receptors in the same way as do heroin and other opiates. By combining with these receptors, TIQ decreases the supply of the natural endorphins produced in the brain. The receptors, therefore, begin to rely on the outside source. This familiar scenario (see Chapter 7) not only accounts for the similar pattern of psychological dependence between opiate and alcohol abuse but also implies that some of the same pharmacological treatments for heroin abusers, such as administrations of the opiate antagonist naltrexone, can also be useful in the treatment of alcoholism.[26] Chapter 11 will consider this possibility.

Acute physiological effects

here are a number of physiological effects that alcohol can produce on an immediate basis. They will be examined here, leaving the physiological effects resulting from chronic alcohol consumption for the next chapter.

Toxic reactions

We need to consider potentially life-threatening situations with alcohol as seriously as we would those with any other depressant drug. In general, the therapeutic index, as measured by the LD50/ED50 ratio (Chapter 2), is approximately 6. Since this figure is not very high, caution is strongly advised; the risks in being the "big winner" in a drinking contest should be weighed very carefully. On the one hand, in order to achieve a lethal BAC level of .50 percent, a 165-pound man needs to have consumed approximately twenty-three drinks over a four-hour period.[27] On the other hand, consuming ten drinks in one hour, a drinking schedule that achieves a BAC level of .35 percent, puts a person in extremely dangerous territory. We have to remember that LD50 is the *average* level for a lethal effect; there is no

way to predict where a particular person might be located on the normal curve!

Fortunately, two mechanisms are designed to protect us to a certain degree. First, alcohol acts as a gastric irritant so that frequently the drinker will feel nauseous and vomit. Second, the drinker may simply pass out, and the risk potential from further drinking becomes irrelevant. Nonetheless, there are residual dangers in becoming unconscious; vomiting while in this state can prevent breathing and death can occur from asphyxiation (Focus 10.2).

Heat loss and the Saint Bernard myth

Alcohol is a peripheral dilator, leading to a warmth and redness of the skin as the blood vessels near the surface enlarge. This effect is most likely the basis for the myth that alcohol can keep you warm in freezing weather. In actuality, however, alcohol will produce a greater heat loss than would be the case without it. In studies conducted of exercising men and women following consumption of alcohol, exaggerated heat loss was significantly greater in men than in women.[28] So if you are marooned in the snow and you see an approaching Saint Bernard with a cask of brandy strapped to its neck, politely refuse the offer. It will not help and could very well do you harm.

Diuretic effects

As concentration levels rise in the blood, alcohol begins to inhibit the **antidiuretic hormone (ADH)**, a hormone that normally would act to reabsorb water in the kidneys

tetrahydroisoquinoline (TIQ)
(TEH-trah-HEYE-droh-EYE-soh-QWEYE-nuh-leen)
A by-product of alcohol metabolism that binds with receptors normally sensitive to endorphins.

antidiuretic hormone (ADH)
A hormone that acts to reabsorb water in the kidneys prior to excretion from the body.

Emergency signs and procedures in acute alcohol intoxication

EMERGENCY SIGNS

- stupor or unconsciousness

- cool or damp skin

- weak, rapid pulse (more than 100 beats per minute)

- shallow and irregular breathing rate, averaging around one every three or four seconds

- pale or bluish skin

Note: Among African Americans, color changes will be apparent in the fingernail beds, mucous membranes inside the mouth, or underneath the eyelids.

EMERGENCY PROCEDURES

- Seek medical help immediately.

- Drinker should lie on his or her side, with the head slightly lower than the rest of the body. This will prevent blockage of the airway and possible asphyxiation if the drinker starts to vomit.

- If drinker is put to bed, maintain some system of monitoring until consciousness is regained.

Note: There is no evidence that home remedies for "sobering up," including cold showers, strong coffee, forced activity, or induction of vomiting have any effect in reducing the level of intoxication. The only factor is the passage of time, rest and perhaps an analgesic if there is a headache.

SOURCES: Payne, Wayne A., and Hahn, Dale B. (1992). *Understanding your health* (3rd ed.). St Louis: Times Mirror Mosby, pp. 237–238. Victor, Maurice (1976). Treatment of alcohol intoxication and the withdrawal syndrome: A critical analysis of the use of drugs and other forms of therapy. In Peter G. Bourne (Ed.), *Acute drug abuse emergencies: A treatment manual.* New York: Academic Press, pp. 197–228.

prior to excretion in the urine. As a result, urine is more diluted and, because large amounts of liquid are typically being consumed at the time, more copious. Once blood alcohol concentrations have peaked, however,

antidiuresis
A condition resulting from excessive reabsorbtion of water in the kidneys.

the reverse occurs. Water is now retained in a condition called **antidiuresis,** resulting in swollen fingers, hands, and feet. This effect is more pronounced if salty foods (peanuts or pretzels, for example) have been eaten along with the alcohol.

The inhibition of ADH during the drinking of alcoholic beverages can be a serious concern, particularly following vigorous exercise when the body is already suffering from a loss of water and fluid levels are low. Therefore, the advice for the marathoner, whose body may lose more than a gallon of water over the course of a warm three-hour run, is not to celebrate the end of the race with a beer but with nonintoxicating liquids such as Gatorade or similar mineral-rich drinks.[29]

Cardiovascular effects

On the one hand, alcohol acts to increase both heart rate and blood pressure, as well as to constrict arteries. As a result, alcohol consumption is not advised for individuals with heart disease or hypertension. On the other hand, moderate wine consumption, about 2.5 ounces a day, has been shown to be actually beneficial in reducing the risk of cardiovascular disease. The mechanism appears to be an increase in high-density lipoprotein and a decrease in low-density lipoprotein in the blood. In general, when the ratio of the first type to the second rises, the incidence of heart disease declines.[30]

Effects on sleep

While it may be tempting to induce sleep with a relaxing "nightcap," we should recognize that the resulting sleep patterns are adversely affected. Alcohol reduces the amount of REM sleep (Chapter 5). Depending on the dose, REM sleep can be either partially or completely suppressed during the night. When alcohol is withdrawn, REM sleep rebounds and represents a higher percentage of total sleep time than before alcohol consumption began. As a result, individuals sleep poorly and experience nightmares.

Interactions with other drugs

A very serious concern is the complex interaction of alcohol with many drugs. As noted in Chapter 2, the DAWN reports of emergency room admissions and deaths show an extremely high incidence of medical crises arising from the combination of alcohol not only with prescribed medications but also with virtually all of the illicit drugs on the street. Depressant drugs (from barbiturates to benzodiazepines), opiates and opiate-like drugs, marijuana, and many prescription medicines interact with alcohol so that the resulting combination produces effects that are either the sum of the parts or greater than the

sum of the parts. In other cases, the ingestion of medications with alcohol significantly lessens the medication's benefits. Anticoagulants, anticonvulsants, and monoamine oxidase inhibitors (used as an antidepressant medication) fit into this second category. Table 10.5 shows a partial listing of major therapeutic drugs that interact with alcohol. The total list is so lengthy that it is fair to say that, whenever any medication is taken, questions should be asked regarding possible interactions with alcohol.

Hangovers

About four to twelve hours after heavy consumption of alcohol, usually the next day, unpleasant symptoms of headache, nausea, fatigue, and thirst may occur, collectively

TABLE 10.5

A partial listing of possible drug-alcohol interactions

Generic drug (brand name or type)	Condition being treated	Effect of interaction
chloral hydrate (Noctec)	Insomnia	Excessive sedation that can be fatal; irregular heartbeat; flushing
glutethimide (Doriden)	Insomnia	Excessive sedation; reduced driving and machine-operating skills
antihypertensives (Apresoline, Diuril)	High blood pressure	Exaggeration of blood pressure-lowering effect; dizziness upon rising
diuretics (Aldactone)	High blood pressure	Exaggeration of blood pressure-lowering effect; dizziness upon rising
antibiotics (penicillin)	Bacterial infections	Reduced therapeutic effectiveness
nitroglycerin (Nitro-bid)	Angina pain	Severe decrease in blood pressure; intense flushing; headache; dizziness upon rising
warfarin (Coumadin)	Blood clot	Increased anti-blood clotting effect, easy bruising
insulin	Diabetes	Excessive low blood sugar; nausea; flushing
disulfiram ((Antabuse)	Alcoholic drinking	Intense flushing; sever headache; vomiting; heart palpitations; could be fatal
methotrexate	Various cancers	Increased risk of liver disorders
phenytoin (Dilantin)	Epileptic seizures	Reduced drug effectiveness in preventing seizures; drowsiness
prednisone (Deltasone)	Inflammatory conditions (arthritis, bursitis)	Stomach irritation
Various antihistamines	Nasal congestion	Excessive sedation that could be fatal

SOURCES: Office of Substance Abuse Prevention (1988). *The fact is . . . It's dangerous to drink alcohol while taking certain medications.* Rockville MD: National Institute on Drug Abuse. Parker, Christy (1985). *Simple facts about combinations with other drugs.* Phoenix AZ: Do It Now Foundation.

known as the hangover. At least one such experience has been reported by 40 percent of all men and 27 percent of all women over the age of eighteen.[31] Why these symptoms occur is not at all clear. The probable explanations at present focus on individual aspects of a hangover, though it is likely that a combination of factors contribute to the total phenomenon.

One factor, beyond the simple fact of drinking too much, is the type of alcohol that has been consumed. Among distilled spirits, for example, vodka has a lower probability of inducing hangovers than whiskey. A possible reason is the relatively lower amount of **congeners.** These are substances in alcoholic beverages, including trace amounts of nonethyl alcohol, oils, and other organic matter, that are by-products of the fermentation and distillation processes and give the drinks their distinctive smell, taste, and color. While there is no harm caused by congeners in such minute concentrations, they are still toxic substances, and some adverse effects may show up as a component of the hangover.

Other possible factors include traces of nonoxidized acetaldehyde in the blood, residual irritation in the stomach, and a low blood sugar level rebounding from the high levels induced by the previous ingestion of alcohol. The feeling of swollenness from the antidiuresis, discussed earlier, may contribute to the headache pain, while the thirst may be due to the dehydration that occurred the night before.

Numerous "remedies" for the hangover have been prescribed over the centuries, but it appears that the best treatment consists of rest, an analgesic medication for the headache (Chapter 15), and the passage of time. Since the hangover can be considered basically as symptoms of withdrawal from alcohol, some people have taken to the remedy of consuming more alcohol, a strategy known as "the hair of the dog that bit you." This approach can relieve the symptoms, but it inevitably merely delays the consequences.

Acute behavioral effects

The consumption of alcoholic beverages is so pervasive in American society that it seems almost unnecessary to comment on how it feels to be intoxicated by alcohol. The behavioral effects of consuming alcohol in more than very moderate quantities range from the relatively harmless effects of exhilaration and excitement, talkativeness, slurred speech, and irritability to behaviors that have the potential for causing great harm: uncoordinated movement, drowsiness, sensorimotor difficulties, and stupor.[32] Some of the prominent behavioral problems associated with acute alcohol intoxication will be examined in this section.

Blackouts

A **blackout** is an inability to remember events that occurred during the period of intoxication, even though the individual was conscious at the time. For example, a drinker having too much to drink at a party drives home, parks the car on a nearby street, and goes to bed. The next morning, he or she has no memory of having driven home and cannot locate the car. Owing to the possibility of blackouts, drinkers can be easily misled into thinking that because they can understand some information given to them during drinking they will remember it later. The risk of blackouts is greatest when alcohol is consumed very quickly, forcing the BAC to rise rapidly.[33]

congeners (KON-jen-ers)
Nonethyl alcohols, oils, and other organic substances found in trace amounts in some distilled spirits.

blackout
Amnesia for events occurring during the period of alcoholic intoxication, even though consciousness had been maintained at that time.

Driving skills

There is no question that alcohol consumption significantly impairs the ability to drive or deal with automobile traffic, particularly among young people. In 1990 among the 44,529 traffic fatalities that occurred, 40 percent of them involved an intoxicated driver or pedestrian showing a BAC level of .10 percent or higher and 50 percent of them showing a BAC level of .05 percent. In that year, about 355,000 individuals suffered injuries in crashes where police officers reported that alcohol was present, an average of one person every ninety seconds. Among fatally injured teenage drivers, more than 60 percent had been drinking prior to the crash.

It is important to recognize that we do not have to reach the state of legal intoxication, defined as a BAC level of .10 percent in most states, to feel the impairment in driving. It has been estimated that the chance of an automobile accident doubles when the driver's BAC level reaches .06 percent. At a BAC level of .10 percent, the chance is six times greater; at a BAC level of .15 percent, it is twenty-five times greater. So it is quite possible for the probability of an accident to increase even though the driver is not officially "driving while intoxicated" (DWI). At present, several states have considered reducing the BAC level limit, following the model already set by most European countries.[34]

All these statistics could be viewed as correlational and not necessarily proof of a causal relationship between alcohol and automobile accidents, were it not for the data from laboratory-based experiments showing a clear deterioration of sensorimotor skills following the ingestion of alcohol. First of all, reaction times are significantly increased following even small amounts of alcohol, as is the ability to concentrate on a particular task. More important, however, there is a major decline in the ability to be aware of peripheral events and stimuli. A major researcher in this area expresses the deficit in this way:

The overwhelming majority of accidents involving alcohol are not accidents in which tracking is the prime error. Contrary to what most people think, it isn't that people are weaving down the road, which is a sign of very high blood alcohol levels, it's that they have failed to see something. They go through a red light, they fail to see a pedestrian or a motorcyclist, they fail to see that the road is curving. Their perceptual and attentive mechanisms are affected very early, after just one drink. These are the things that are the prime causes of accidents.[35]

Unfortunately, it is the weaving behavior or other extreme example of driving impairment that most often signals the police to stop a car for a possible DWI violation; other impairments frequently go unnoticed.

There is evidence that increasing the minimum age for alcoholic consumption from eighteen to twenty-one, now mandated throughout the United States, has made an impact on the chances of accident fatalities among young people. On average, fatal nighttime accidents involving eighteen- and nineteen-year-old drivers decreased 13 percent between 1975 and 1984 in twenty-six states that raised the minimum drinking age during

Every community has at least a few stories of tragedy that are results of drunk driving.

Candace Lightner— Founder of MADD

n 1980 Candace Lightner's thirteen-year-old daughter, Cari, was killed by a hit-and-run intoxicated driver in California. The driver had been out of jail on bail for only two days, a consequence of another hit-and-run drunk driving crash, and he had three previous drunk driving arrests and two previous convictions. He was allowed to plea bargain to vehicular manslaughter. Although the sentence was to serve two years in prison, the judge allowed him to serve time in a work camp and later a halfway house.

It was appalling to Lightner that drunk drivers, similar to the one who had killed her daughter, were receiving such lenient treatment, with many of them never going to jail for a single day. Lightner quit her job and started an organization that has become a household name: Mothers Against Drunk Driving (MADD).

Since then, MADD has campaigned for stricter laws against drunk driving, and most of the present DWI legislation around the country is a result of its intense efforts. In addition, MADD acts as a voice for victims of drunk-driving injuries and the families of those who have been killed. From a single act of courage, despite enormous grief, Lightner has spawned an organization that boasts more than 3 million members in the United States, with groups in virtually every state and more than four hundred local chapters. While Lightner is no longer associated with MADD in an official capacity, a number of activities that she initiated continue. For example, MADD sponsors an annual candlelight vigil for thousands of people who, like Cari Lightner, have been killed on the streets by drivers who have had too much to drink.

Candace Lightner, founder of MADD.

More recently, MADD has set for itself the goal of "20 by 2000," referring to a commitment of a 20 percent reduction by the year 2000 in the number of all traffic fatalities associated with alcohol drinking. In 1992 the percentage was 45; MADD wants it to be 40. These are some of their proposals for change:

1. More effective enforcement of the minimum-drinking-age law

2. A ".00 percent BAC" criterion for drivers under twenty-one, making it illegal to drive with *any* measurable level of blood alcohol in any state. In 1994, the criterion ranging from .00 to .02 percent was in effect in seventeen states and the District of Columbia.

3. Driver's license suspensions for underage persons convicted of purchasing or possession of alcoholic beverages.

4. Alcohol-free zones for youth gatherings

5. Criminal sanctions against adults who provide or allow alcoholic beverages at events for underage participants

6. A new minimum BAC level of .08 percent for adult drivers in all fifty states. In 1994, ten states had this provision.

7. Mandatory alcohol and drug testing for all drivers in all traffic crashes resulting in fatalities or serious bodily injury

8. Sobriety checkpoints to detect and apprehend alcohol-impaired drivers and as a visible deterrent to drinking and driving

SOURCE: Information courtesy of Mothers Against Drunk Driving, Dallas, Texas. Interview with Candace Lightner.

that interval. A decrease of 16 percent in nighttime accidents in Michigan following the change in the drinking law was maintained six years later.[36]

There is also optimism that educational programs in the schools, emphasizing the advantage of "designated drivers," as well as public education and lobbying groups such as Mothers Against Drunk Driving (MADD) and Students Against Drunk Driving (SADD) are having positive effects (see Portrait). Some progress is being made. In 1982, 30 percent of all drivers involved in a fatal automobile crash were found to be drunk; in 1992 the percentage had declined to about 22. Even so, much work remains to be done.[37]

Alcohol, violence and aggression

It is difficult to avoid sweeping generalizations when confronted with statistics about alcohol and violent behavior both in the United States and other countries. In a major study conducted in a community in northwestern Ontario, Canada, reported in 1991, more than 50 percent of the most recent occasions of physical violence were found to be preceded by alcohol use on the part of the assailant and/or the victims themselves.[38] Other studies show from 50 to 60 percent of all murders being committed when the killer had been drinking. About 40 percent of all acts of male sexual aggression against adult women and from 60 to 70 percent of male-instigated domestic violence occur when the offender has been drunk; more than 60 percent of all acts of child molestation involved drunkenness.[39]

Researchers have advanced several theories to account for the linkage between alcohol intoxication and violent behavior. The traditional *disinhibition theory* holds that alcohol on a pharmacological level impairs normal cortical mechanisms responsible for inhibiting the expression of innate or suppressed aggressive inclinations. Another viewpoint, referred to as the *cognitive-expectation theory,* holds that learned beliefs or expectations about alcohol's effects can facilitate aggressive behaviors. This second theory implies that violence is induced by virtue of the act of drinking and one's personal view of how a person is "supposed to respond" rather than by the pharmacological effects of alcohol itself.

Expectations about the consequences of drug-taking behavior or of any behavior at all, as noted in Chapter 3, are studied experimentally through the placebo research design. In the case of the cognitive-expectation theory, it is necessary to use a variation of this design, called the **balanced placebo design.** Subjects are randomly divided into four groups. Two groups are given an alcoholic drink, with one group being told that they are ingesting alcohol and the other that they are ingesting a nonalcohol substitute that tastes and smells like alcohol. Two other groups are given the nonalcohol substitute, with one group being told that they are ingesting this substitute and the other that they are ingesting alcohol.

Studies using the balanced placebo design have shown clearly that beliefs (mind-sets) concerning the effects of drinking are more influential in determining a subject's behavior than the more direct physiological effects of the alcohol. In other words, what they are told they are consuming is more important than what they consume. Unfortunately, for a true test of the cognitive-expectation theory, a balanced placebo design cannot be used with BAC levels above .035 percent because subjects are no longer fooled by the deception with larger quantities, and most alcohol-associated acts of violence occur with BAC levels at least six times higher.[40]

Sex and sexual desire

If they were asked, most people would say that alcohol has an enhancing or aphrodisiac effect on sexual desire and performance. The actual effect of alcohol, however, is more complex than these commonly held beliefs. In fact, it is because of these beliefs that people are frequently more susceptible to the expectations of what alcohol should do for them than they are to the physiological effects of alcohol.

To examine the complex relationship between alcohol and sex, we need to turn again to studies using the balanced placebo design. The general results from such studies

> **balanced placebo design**
> An experimental design that can separate the psychological effects (due to subjective expectations) and physiological effects (due to the pharmacology of the drug).

are quite different for men and women. Among men, those who expected to be receiving low levels of alcohol had greater penile responses, reported greater subjective arousal, and spent more time watching erotic pictures, *regardless of whether or not they did indeed receive alcohol.* When alcohol concentrations rise to levels that reflect genuine intoxication, however, the pharmacological actions outweigh the expectations, and the overall effect is definitely inhibitory. Men who are drunk have less sexual desire and a decreased capacity to perform sexually.

In contrast, expectations among women play a lesser role. They are more inclined to react to the pharmacological properties of alcohol itself, but the direction of their response depends upon whether we are talking about subjective or physiological measures. For women receiving increasing alcohol concentrations, measures of subjective arousal increase but measures of vaginal arousal decrease. Ironically, the pattern of their responses mirrors Shakespeare's quotation in *Macbeth* that alcohol "provokes the desire, but it takes away from the performance," a comment originally intended to reflect the male point of view.[41]

Strategies for responsible drinking

he various negative consequences alcohol can have on physiological responses and behavior have been considered. Yet it is necessary to remember that there are very large numbers of people who drink alcoholic beverages and avoid the adverse effects that have been detailed here. An overwhelming proportion of the population, for example, drink on occasion and have never engaged in any violent or aggressive acts. The question of responsible drinking is an important one; it may not be easy for us to accomplish but fortunately there exist guidelines that make it easier.[42] Focus 10.3 includes a listing of some strategies that reduce the problems associated with alcoholic intake. At the same time, however, we should also remember that, regardless of how it is consumed, alcohol remains a drug with a high level of potential for dependence. It is not difficult to get hooked. As it has been said, people may plan to get drunk, but no one plans to be an alcoholic. The problems surrounding chronic alcohol abuse and alcoholism will be examined in the next chapter.

Guidelines for responsible drinking

1. Know how much you are drinking. Measure your drinks. Beer is often pre-measured (unless you are drinking draft beer from a keg), but wine and liquor drinks frequently are not. Learn what a 4-ounce quantity of wine or a 1 ¼ or 1 ½ ounce shot of liquor looks like, and use these measures to guide your drinking.

2. Choose beer or wine over liquor. Beer especially will make you feel fuller more quickly, with a smaller intake of alcohol. But be careful. A 12-ounce beer is equivalent in alcohol content to a 4-ounce glass of wine or a 1-shot drink of liquor.

3. Drink slowly. One drink an hour stays relatively even with your body's metabolism of the alcohol you consume. Sipping your drinks is a good strategy for slowing down your consumption.

4. Don't cluster your drinking. If you are going to have seven drinks during a week, don't drink them all on the weekend.

5. Eat something substantial while you are drinking. Protein is an excellent accompaniment to alcohol. Avoid salty foods because they will make you thirstier and more inclined to have another drink.

6. Drink only when you are already relaxed. Chronic alcohol abuse occurs more easily when alcohol is viewed as a way to relax. If you have a problem, seek some nondrug alternative.

7. When you drink, savor the experience. If you focus on the quality of what you drink rather than the quantity you are drinking, you will avoid drinking too much.

8. Never drink alone. Drinking cannot be dealt with as a phenomenon of social isolation. Having people around you provides the means to have someone looking out for you.

9. Never drive a car after having had a drink. Driving impairment begins from very low quantities of alcohol.

10. Be a good host or hostess. If you are giving a party where alcohol is served, do not make drinking the focus of activity. Do not refill your guests' glasses. Discourage intoxication and do not condone drunkenness. Provide transportation options for those who drink at your party.

11. Support organizations that encourage responsible drinking. If you are on a college campus, get involved with the local chapter of BACCHUS (Boost Alcohol Consciousness Concerning the Health of University Students). If there is no chapter, start one.

SOURCES: Gross, Leonard (1983). *How much is too much? The effects of social drinking.* New York: Random House, pp. 149–152. *Managing alcohol in your life.* Marsfield MA: Steele Publishing and Consulting.

Summary

WHAT MAKES AN ALCOHOLIC BEVERAGE?

- Drinkable alcohol is obtained from the fermentation of sugar in some natural product such as grapes, apples, honey, or molasses. The result is some form of wine.

- Beer is obtained from barley, after the starch has first been converted into sugar and then fermented along with other grains and hops, and aged.

- To obtain very strong alcoholic beverages, it is necessary to boil the fermented liquid and condense it later by cooling. This process, called distillation, results in alcohol concentrations of up to 95 percent, and the products are known as distilled spirits or liquors.

ALCOHOL THROUGH HISTORY

- The history of alcohol use dates back many thousands of years, since the process of fermentation is very simple and its discovery was probably accidental.

- Distillation techniques were perfected during the Middle Ages, with brandy being the first distilled spirit. In later centuries, gin gained popularity in Europe, as did whiskey in the United States.

PATTERNS OF ALCOHOL CONSUMPTION TODAY

- The demographics of alcohol consumption reveal a large disparity in the population. About a third do not drink at all, and only about 20 percent drink nearly 80 percent of all the alcoholic beverages available.

- Peak alcohol consumption occurs at ages twenty-one to twenty-two.

THE PHARMACOLOGY OF ALCOHOL

- Alcohol is a very small molecule, easily soluble in both water and fat. Its absorption into the bloodstream is extremely rapid. The metabolism of alcohol is handled by two special enzymes in the stomach and liver.

- The rate of alcohol metabolism is constant, so that alcohol can only leave the body at a specific pace, despite the quantity taken in.

- The effective level of alcohol in the body is measured by the blood-alcohol concentration (BAC) level, which must adjust for differences in body weight and the time since ingesting the last alcoholic beverage.

THE EFFECT OF ALCOHOL ON THE BRAIN

- While alcohol affects several neurotransmitters in the brain, it is presently agreed that the principal effect is the stimulation of the GABA receptor.

- Generally, the neural effect of alcohol proceeds downward, beginning with an inhibition of the cerebral cortex, then lower brain sites. Inhibition of respiratory systems in the medulla, usually accomplished at BAC levels in the neighborhood of .50 percent, results in asphyxiation and death.

ACUTE PHYSIOLOGICAL EFFECTS

- Alcohol at very high levels produces serious life-threatening consequences and at moderate levels produces a loss of body heat, increased excretion of water, an increase in heart rate and constriction of coronary arteries, disturbed patterns of sleep, and serious interactions with other drugs.

ACUTE BEHAVIORAL EFFECTS

- On a behavioral level, serious adverse effects include blackouts, significant impairment in sensorimotor skills such as driving an automobile, and an increased potential for aggressive acts.

- The relationship between alcohol consumption and sexual desire and performance is a complex one, with differences being observed for men and women.

STRATEGIES FOR RESPONSIBLE DRINKING

- Despite the potential for alcohol consumption to produce adverse effects, most people can drink in a responsible way that avoids these adverse effects. However, the risk of alcohol dependence is always present.

Key Terms

acetaldehyde, p. 238
acetaldehyde dehydrogenase, p. 238
acetic acid, p. 238
alcohol dehydrogenase, p. 238
antidiuresis, p. 242

antidiuretic hormone (ADH), p. 241
aqua vitae, p. 232
balanced placebo design, p. 247
barley malt, p. 230
blackout, p. 244

Endnotes

1. Pinel, John P. J. (1993). *Biopsychology* (2nd ed.). Boston: Allyn and Bacon, p. 424.

2. Roueché, Berton (1963). Alcohol in human culture. In Salvatore P. Lucia (Ed.), *Alcohol and civilization.* New York: McGraw-Hill. pp. 167–182.

3. Rose, Anthony H. (1977). History and scientific basis of alcoholic beverage production. In Anthony H. Rose (Ed.), *Alcoholic beverages.* New York: Academic Press, pp. 1–41. Gibbons, Boyd (1992, February). Alcohol: The legal drug. *National Geographic Magazine,* pp. 2–35.

4. Webb, Sidney, and Webb, Beatrice. (1903). *The history of liquor licensing in England principally between 1700 and 1830.* In U.S. Department of Health, Education, and Welfare, (1978), *Perspectives on the history of psychoactive substance use* (Research Issues 24). Rockville MD: National Institute on Drug Abuse, p. 72.

5. Sournia, Jean-Charles (1990). *A history of alcoholism.* Cambridge MA: Basil Blackwell, pp. 14–50. U.S. Department of Health, Education, and Welfare (1978). *Perspectives on the history of psychoactive substance use,* pp. 67–75.

6. Grimes, William (1993). *Straight up or on the rocks: A cultural history of American drink.* New York: Simon and Schuster, p. 36.

7. Ibid., p. 37.

8. Lender, Mark E., and Martin, James K. (1982). *Drinking in America: A history.* New York: Free Press, pp. 13–14.

9. Grimes. *Straight up,* p. 51.

10. Gibbons. *Alcohol,* p. 7

11. *U.S. Industrial Outlook 1993.* Washington DC: U.S. Department of Commerce, pp. 20–31. *Jobson's liquor handbook 1993.* New York: Jobson Publishing Corp., p. 172. *Jobson's wine handbook 1992.* New York: Jobson Publishing Corp., p. 7.

12. *Jobson's liquor handbook 1993,* p. 231.

13. Berkowitz, Harry (1994, August 1). Beer drinkers say, "Put it on ice." *Newsday,* p. C2.

14. *Jobson's liquor handbook 1993,* p. 12.

15. *Jobson's wine handbook 1992,* p. 126.

16. Wechsler, Henry, Davenport, Andrea, Dowdall, George, Moeykens, Barbara, and Castillo, Sonia (1994) Health and behavioral consequences of binge drinking in college. *Journal of the American Medical Association, 272,* 1672–1677.

17. Johnston, Lloyd D., O'Malley, Patrick M., and Bachman, Jerald G. (1994). *National survey results on drug use from the Monitoring the Future study, 1975–1993* Vol. 1. Rockville MD: National Institute on Drug Abuse, Table 1.

18. U.S. Department of Health and Human Services (1990). *Alcohol and health.* (The Seventh Special Report to the U.S. Congress). Rockville MD: National Institute on Alcohol Abuse and Alcoholism.

19. Dubowski, Kurt M. (1991). *The technology of breath-alcohol analysis.* Rockville MD: National Institute on Alcohol Abuse and Alcoholism.

20. Julien, Robert M. (1995). *A primer of drug action* (7th ed.). New York: Freeman, p. 102.

21. Friedman, Nancy (1985, August-September). Anatomy of a drink. *Campus Voice* pp 61–63. Julien. *A primer of drug action,* pp. 102–104.

22. Suter, Paolo M., Schutz, Yves, and Jequier, Eric (1992). The effect of ethanol on fat storage in healthy subjects. *New England Journal of Medicine, 326,* 983–987

23. Julien, Robert M. (1981). *A primer of drug action* (3rd ed.). San Francisco Freeman, p. 216.

24. Levinthal, Charles F. (1990). *Introduction to physiological psychology* (3rd ed.). Englewood Cliffs NJ: Prentice Hall, pp. 166–169.

25. U.S. Department of Health and Human Services. *Alcohol and health,* pp. 69–80.

26. Blum, Kenneth, and Payne, James E. (1991). *Alcohol and the addictive brain: Hope for alcoholics from biogenetic research.* New York: Free Press. Schuckit, Marc A. (1994, August). Naltrexone and the treatment of alcoholism. *Drug Abuse and Alcoholism Newsletter,* San Diego CA: Vista Hill Foundation.

27. Grilly, David M. (1989). *Drugs and human behavior.* Boston: Allyn and Bacon, pp. 140–141.

28. Luks, Allan, and Barbato, Joseph (1989). *You are what you drink.* New York: Villiard, p. 44.

29. Ibid., pp. 42–43.

30. Julien. *A primer of drug action,* (7th ed.), p. 108.

31. Schuckit, Marc A. (1989). *Drug and alcohol abuse: A clinical guide to diagnosis and treatment* (3rd ed.). New York: Plenum, p. 62.

32. Victor, Maurice (1976). Treatment of alcohol intoxication and the withdrawal syndrome: A critical analysis of the use of drugs and other forms of therapy. In Peter G. Bourne (Ed.), *Acute drug emergencies: A treatment manual.* New York: Academic Press, p. 199.

33. Luks and Barbato. *You are what you drink,* pp. 52–53.

34. Fox, Jean M. (1988)., pp. 19, 44. National Center for Statistics and Analysis (1991). *Drunk driving facts.* Washington DC: U.S. Department of Transportation, p. 1.

35. Gross, Leonard (1983). *How much is too much: The effects of social drinking.* New York: Random House, p. 29. Quotation of Dr. Herbert Moskowitz.

36. U.S. Department of Health and Human Services. *Alcohol and health,* pp. 216–217.

37. Ayres, R. Drummond (1994, May 22). Big gains are seen in battle to stem drunken driving. *New York Times,* pp. 1, 24. *Drug Abuse Update* (1987, September). Decatur GA: *Families in Action* National Drug Information Center, p. 11.

38. Pernanen, Kai (1991). *Alcohol in human violence.* New York: Guilford Press, pp. 192–193.

39. Collins, James J., and Messerschmidt, Pamela M. (1993). Epidemiology of alcohol-related violence. *Alcohol Health and Research World, 17,* 93–100. Goode, Erich (1989). *Drugs in American society* (2nd ed.). New York: McGraw-Hill, p. 118.

40. Pernanen, Kai (1993). Research approaches in the study of alcohol-related violence. *Alcohol Health and Research World, 17,* 101–107. Taylor, Stuart P. (1993). Experimental investigation of alcohol-induced aggression in humans. *Alcohol Health and Research World, 17,* 108–112.

41. Abel, Ernest L. (1985). *Psychoactive drugs and sex.* New York: Plenum Press, pp. 19–54. George, William H., and Norris, Jeanette (1993). Alcohol, disinhibition, sexual arousal, and deviant sexual behavior. *Alcohol Health and Research World, 17,* 133–138.

42. Darby, William, and Heinz, Agnes (1991, January). *The responsible use of alcohol: Defining the parameters of moderation.* New York: American Council on Science and Health, pp. 1–26.

11

Chronic Alcohol Abuse and Alcoholism

THIS CHAPTER WILL INTRODUCE YOU
TO THE FOLLOWING SUBJECTS:

- Problems surrounding the definition of alcoholism

- The history of attempts to regulate chronic alcohol abuse

- Chronic effects of alcohol

- Patterns of chronic alcohol abuse

- Special problems among the elderly

- Social and family dynamics in alcoholism

- Genetic and environmental influences in alcoholism

- Approaches to treatment for alcoholism

- Alcoholism in the workplace

Chronic abuse of alcohol has been called the hidden addiction. There is no need to get out on the street and find a pusher; for many people, it is remarkably easy to conceal their addiction (at least in the beginning) from family and friends. Alcohol consumption is so tightly woven into the fabric of U.S. social life that it can be difficult to catch on that people may be drinking too much too often. All too frequently, chronic abuse of alcohol has been treated as a genteel affair, not with the same degree of concern as that associated with the chronic abuse of other drugs. Yet from a pharmacological point of view, it is the same, and we have to realize that fact. This chapter will deal with the very serious consequences of this condition on millions of people and on society at large.

Alcoholism: Stereotypes, definitions, and criteria

Picture in your mind an alcoholic; you might form an image of someone, usually male, who is down on his heels, perhaps a dirty, skid-row bum with a bottle of very cheap wine in his hands, living from day to day in a state of deteriorating health, with no one caring about him except a social worker or police officer or inevitably the medical examiner. You would be imagining less than 5 percent of all alcoholics; more than 95 percent of them look quite different. The demographics of alcoholism include every possible category. They can be fourteen years old or eighty-four, male or female, professional or blue-collar worker, urbanite, suburbanite, or rural resident in every community large or small.

When you live in an alcoholic family, you sometimes lie in bed and dream. You dream that your parents are going to quit drinking, that you are going to get closer to them. You are going to have a better life. . . . You picture your parents beginning to care for themselves and for you. You imagine it being beautiful. Your home is clean and organized. Instead of abusing you, or being nice to you just to get rid of you, your parents are helping you with your homework.

Teens talk about alcohol and alcoholism (1987)

The typical alcoholic American

Doctor, age 54

Farmer, age 35

Unemployed, age 40

College student, age 19

Counselor, age 38

Retired editor, age 86

Dancer, age 22

Police officer, age 46

Military officer, age 31

Student, age 14

Executive, age 50

Taxi driver, age 61

Homemaker, age 43

Bricklayer, age 29

Computer programmer, age 25

Lawyer, age 52

There's no such thing as typical. We have all kinds.
10 million Americans are alcoholic.
It's our number one drug problem.

Alcoholism affects so many different kinds of people that generalizations about "who is an alcoholic" are impossible.

What aspects of their behavior tie them all together, if we are to call them by one single label? Because of the diversity in alcoholics, no one has successfully come up with one encompassing definition of alcoholism. Instead, we are left with a set of criteria, basically a collection of signs, symptoms, and behaviors that help us in making the diagnosis. A single individual may not fulfill all of these criteria; but if he or she fulfills enough of them, we decide that the standard has been met.

The criteria adopted here focus on four basic life problems that are tied to the consumption of alcohol: (1) problems associated with a preoccupation with drinking, (2) emotional problems, (3) vocational, social, and family problems, and (4) problems associated with physical health.[1] Notice that a statement is not being made about the cause or causes of alcoholism, only about its behavioral, social, and physical consequences. In short, we are recognizing that **alcoholism** is a complex phenomenon that has psychological-behavioral components (criteria 1 and 2), social components (criterion 3), and a physical component (criterion 4).

Problems associated with a preoccupation with drinking

A major characteristic of alcoholics is their preoccupation with the act of drinking and the incorporation of drinking into their everyday lives. An alcoholic may need a drink prior to a social occasion in order to feel "fortified." With increasing frequency, such a person sees alcohol as a way of dealing with stress and anxiety. Drinking itself becomes a routine, no longer a social, affair. The habit of taking a few drinks on a daily basis upon arriving home from work is an example of **symptomatic drinking** in which alcohol is viewed specifically as a way of relieving tension. Also increasing are incidences of unintentional states of severe intoxication and blackouts for events surrounding the time of drinking, a condition quite different from "passing out" from the increased BAC level. One such occurrence may not be a particularly critical sign, but recurrences definitely are.[2]

Traditionally, alcoholism is associated with consumption of a large quantity of alcohol. This sounds pretty obvious and it is true of most alcoholics, but we still have to be careful. There is a wide diversity in the way alcoholics consume their alcohol. Not all of them drink alone or begin every day with a drink. Many of them drink on a daily basis, but others are spree or binge alcoholics who might become grossly intoxicated on occasion and totally abstain from drinking during the rest of the time. It is even possible for an individual engaged in a busy schedule of social or business entertainment to consume a greater quantity of alcohol than a spree alcoholic.[3]

Another characteristic frequently attributed to alcoholics is the loss of control over their drinking. The alcoholic typically craves drinking and frequently engages in compulsive behavior that is related to alcohol. There may be a stockpiling of liquor, taking a drink or two prior to going to a party, or feeling uncomfortable unless alcohol is present. The alcoholic may be sneaking drinks or having drinks that others do not know about, such as surreptitiously having an extra drink or two in the kitchen apart from guests at a party.[4] Particularly when the alcoholic is trying to abstain from or reduce the quantity of alcohol consumed, his or her thoughts become focused on the possibility of drinking or ways to rationalize it. Because of the intense craving that alcoholics experience, alcoholism qualifies as an example of psychological dependence (Chapter 2).[5]

Yet, professionals disagree whether all alcoholics are necessarily out of control with

---

alcoholism
A condition in which the consumption of alcohol has produced major psychological, physical, social, or occupational problems.

symptomatic drinking
A pattern of alcohol consumption aimed at reducing stress and anxiety.

respect to alcohol. As discussed later in the chapter, this controversy has major implications for the approach adopted in treatment for alcohol abuse. If it is true that even a small amount of alcohol will propel a recovering alcoholic back to alcohol abuse, then a primary focus of treatment should be on no drinking at all, better known as absolute **abstinence.** If it is not true, then there is the possibility of controlled drinking without the fear of "falling off the wagon." The famous alcohol treatment organization Alcoholics Anonymous, in particular, functions under the premise that an alcoholic must never drink again, even in minute quantities, in order for recovery to be long lasting.

Emotional problems

Since alcohol is a depressant drug, it should not be surprising that chronic alcohol intake produces depressive reactions. It has been estimated that between one third and one half of all alcoholics experience depressive symptoms sometime in their lives. Only 5 percent of them, however, show depression prior to the onset of the alcoholic condition. Instead, the depression is thought to be alcohol induced, and when the alcoholic abstains from drinking the depressive symptoms subside.[6]

Vocational, social and family problems

No one questions the potential problems that chronic alcohol abuse can bring to the maintenance of one's job or career, to the maintenance of social relationships, and to the maintenance of a stable family life. These three areas frequently intertwine and exacerbate one another: The loss of one's job puts stress on marital and family relationships, just as marital and family difficulties put stress on one's occupational performance.

While numerous clinical studies support the idea of increased domestic instability in the lives of alcoholics, the extent of these problems is difficult to assess. Family violence, for example, is frequently examined through cases seen in treatment or social-service programs. As a result, these agencies may interpret the domestic behavior of a father not known to have a drinking problem differently from that of a father with a history of alcoholism. A man who drinks heavily and abuses his children may be more likely to be "counted" as an alcoholic than a nonabusive father who consumes just as much alcohol. It is much easier to assess the likelihood of domestic violence or decline in job performance due to acute intoxication than it is to evaluate the influence of chronic abuse of alcohol. Even so, the cumulative effects of alcoholism on family dynamics can be devastating.[7]

Physical problems

There is also no question as to the destructive effect that chronic alcohol consumption can have on the body. While many alcoholics do not exhibit physical problems that are typically associated with alcoholism, the risks are greatly increased.[8] Whether or not specific physical problems arise from chronic alcohol abuse, alcohol is establishing a pattern of physical dependence, as demonstrated by the presence of tolerance and physical withdrawal symptoms. These phenomena, as well as potential damage to organs of the body, will be examined later in the chapter in connection with the chronic effects of alcohol.

Hiding the problems: denial and enabling

The major life problems that serve as rough criteria for determining the condition of alcoholism are often not recognized by alcoholics because of their tendency to deny that their drinking is having any influence on their lives or the lives of people around them. When in denial, the alcoholic can be extremely sensitive to any mention of prob-

abstinence
The complete avoidance of some consumable item.

lems associated with drinking. A hangover the next day, for example, is seldom discussed, since it would draw attention to the drinking that has occurred.[9]

Denial can also be manifest among the people around the alcoholic. Members of an alcoholic's family, for example, may try to function as if nothing is happening. Through their excuse making and efforts to undo the frequent physical and psychological damage the alcoholic causes, they inadvertently prevent the alcoholic from seeking treatment or delay that treatment until the alcoholism is more severe. These people are referred to as **enablers,** since they enable the alcoholic to function as an alcoholic as opposed to a sober person. Both processes of denial and enabling present major difficulties not only in the establishment of problem-oriented criteria for diagnosing alcoholism but also in the establishment of necessary interventions. Denial and enabling are clearly relevant processes in the area of alcoholism, but it is not difficult to see how they present problems with regard to *any* form of drug abuse.

Focus 11.1 shows a useful self-survey for determining the signs of potential alcoholism. You may want to try it out on yourself and people that you know.

Alcohol abuse and alcohol dependence: The professional's view

s you can see, the criteria commonly employed in determining the presence of alcoholism are at times quite murky, and often there are as many counterexamples to each of the criteria as there are examples. The American Psychiatric Association, through its Diagnostic and

enablers
Individuals whose behavior consciously or unconsciously encourages a continuation of a pattern of alcohol or other drug abuse.

FOCUS 11.1

A self-administered Short Michigan Alcoholism Screening Test (SMAST)

he Michigan Alcoholism Screening Test (MAST), twenty-four questions to be answered in ten to fifteen minutes, is designed as a structured interview instrument to detect alcoholism. A shorter thirteen-question version (SMAST), shown here, has approximately the same level of reliability and validity. Score one point for each response that matches the one in parentheses. According to the authors of the test, a total score of 0 or 1 indicates a nonalcoholic, 2 a possible alcoholic, and 3 or more an alcoholic.

1. Do you feel you are a normal drinker? (By normal we mean you drink less than or as much as most other people.) (NO)

2. Does your wife, husband, a parent, or other near relative ever worry or complain about your drinking? (YES)

3. Do you ever feel guilty about your drinking? (YES)

4. Do friends or relatives think you are a normal drinker? (NO)

5. Are you able to stop drinking when you want to? (NO)

6. Have you ever attended a meeting of Alcoholics Anonymous? (YES)

7. Has drinking ever created problems between you and your wife, husband, a parent, or other near relative? (YES)

8. Have you ever gotten into trouble at work because of drinking? (YES)

9. Have you ever neglected your obligations, your family, or your work for two or more days in a row because you were drinking? (YES)

10. Have you ever gone to anyone for help about your drinking? (YES)

11. Have you ever been in a hospital because of drinking? (YES)

12. Have you ever been arrested for drunken driving, driving while intoxicated, or driving under the influence of alcoholic beverages? (YES)

13. Have you ever been arrested, even for a few hours, because of other drunken behavior? (YES)

SOURCE: Selzer, Melvin L., Vinokur, Amiram, and van Rooijen, Louis (1975). A self-administered Short Michigan Alcoholism Screening Test (SMAST). *Journal of Studies on Alcohol, 36,* 117–126.

Statistical Manual, fourth edition (DSM-IV), has attempted to put as many common features together as possible and has established two basic syndromes. DSM-IV definitions were used in Chapter 2 when considering the issue of substance abuse vs. substance dependence. It is important to look at these technical definitions, because professionals in the field of alcoholism commonly use the DSM-IV either in their research or in clinical work.[10]

The first syndrome, referred to as **alcohol abuse,** is characterized as either (1) the continued use of alcohol for at least one month despite the knowledge of having a persistent or recurring physical problem or some difficulty in social or occupational functioning or (2) the recurring use of alcohol in situations (such as driving) when alcohol consumption is physically hazardous.

The second syndrome, referred to as **alcohol dependence,** is characterized as alcohol abuse that also involves any three of the following seven situations:

1. consuming alcohol in amounts or over a longer period than the person intends

2. a persistent desire or one or more unsuccessful attempts to cut down or control drinking

3. a great deal of time spent drinking or recovering from the effects of drinking

4. alcohol consumption continuing despite knowledge that drinking either causes or exacerbates recurrent physical or psychological problems

5. important social, occupational, or recreational activities given up or reduced because of alcohol

6. marked tolerance or the need to drink more than before to achieve previous levels of intoxication

7. symptoms of alcohol withdrawal or the consumptions of alcohol in order to relieve or avoid withdrawal symptoms

Obviously, individuals fitting the second definition are considered more greatly impaired than individuals fitting the first. That was true in regard to the more general criteria for substance abuse and substance dependence. Approximately 4% of U.S. adults are alcohol abusers, and 6% are alcohol dependent.[11]

A history of efforts to regulate chronic alcohol abuse

n the late 1700s, prominent physicians, writers, and scientists began to consider the long-term adverse effects of alcohol consumption and tried to formulate some kind of social reform to reduce them. The goal at that time was to reduce the consumption of distilled spirits (liquor) only. It was a temperate attitude toward drinking (hence the phrase "temperance movement") rather than a total prohibition of alcohol.

In the United States, where the temperance movement was to be stronger than anywhere else, its most influential spokesman was Benjamin Rush, a physician, Revolutionary War hero, and signer of the Declaration of Independence. In his 1785 pamphlet *An inquiry into the effects of ardent spirits on the human mind and body,* Rush vividly described the range of mental and physical dangers associated with alcohol abuse.

Strong liquor is more destructive than the sword. The destruction of war is periodic whereas alcohol exerts its influence upon human life at all times and in all seasons. . . . A nation corrupted by alcohol can never be free.[12]

alcohol abuse
A syndrome characterized primarily by the continued use of alcohol despite the drinker's knowledge of having a persistent physical problem or some social or occupational difficulty.

alcohol dependence
A syndrome in which alcohol abuse involves a variety of significant physical, psychological, social, and behavioral problems.

Understanding the psychology of alcoholism

heck your understanding of the psychological aspects of alcoholism by associating the quotations or behavioral descriptions, on the left, with the appropriate term, on the right.

1. Brad tries to call his estranged wife on the telephone. She hangs up on him. Now angry and frustrated, Brad takes a drink.

2. Mary stays sober during the work week, but on the weekend she downs at least two quarts of vodka.

3. "Despite what my family says, I am convinced I am not an alcoholic."

4. "If I'm with her when she's drinking, I can make sure she doesn't overdo her drinking."

5. "I'm going to the theater later. I don't think there will be any liquor there so I had better have a couple of drinks before I go."

a. denial

b. enabling

c. out-of-control drinking

d. spree or binge drinking

e. symptomatic drinking

ANSWERS: 1. e   2. d   3. a   4. b   5. c

Rush did not have a major effect on the drinking habits of American society during his lifetime. As described in Chapter 10, alcohol consumption in the United States at that time was enormous and continued to rise until about 1830. Rush's words, however, served as an inspiration to political and religious groups around the country who saw alcohol abuse in social and moral terms. In their view, drunkenness led to poverty, a disorderly society, and civil disobedience. In short, it was unpatriotic at best and subversive at worst to be drunk from consuming liquor. When we hear the phrase "demon rum," we have to recognize that many Americans during the nineteenth century took the phrase quite literally. Liquor was "demonized" as a direct source of evil in the world. The idea, like any other form of scapegoating, spread like wildfire. In 1831 the American Temperance Society reported that nearly 2 million Americans had renounced strong liquor and more than eight hundred societies had been established. By the 1850s, twelve U.S. states and two Canadian provinces had introduced legislation forbidding the sale of "alcoholic" (distilled) drink.

Whether or not they may have been justified in doing so, temperance groups took credit for a drastic change that was occurring in the levels of alcohol consumption in the United States. From 1830 to 1850, consumption of all types of alcohol plummeted from an annual per capita level of roughly seven gallons to roughly two gallons, close to the consumption levels in the present day (Chapter 10). It is quite possible that this moderation in drinking habits encouraged the temperance movement to consider their ultimate goal, a prohibition of alcohol consumption in any form.

The road to national prohibition

A major development in the temperance movement was the formation of a women's organization in 1873 called the Women's Christian Temperance Union (WCTU). Almost from the beginning, its primary target was a highly visible fixture of late nineteenth-century American life: the saloon. These establishments, ranging from the relatively rough-and-tumble bars in the West to the elegant and opulent gathering places in the East, were now demonized as the source of all the troubles alcohol could bring. It is not difficult to imagine how the saloon could have been seen as a significant threat to American women in general.

Bars appeared to invite family catastrophe. They introduced children to drunkenness and vice and drove husbands to alcoholism; they also caused squandering of wages, wife beating, and child abuse; and, with the patron's inhibitions lowered through drink, the saloon led many men into the arms of prostitutes (and not incidentally, contributed to the alarming spread of syphilis).[13]

No wonder the WCTU hated the saloon, and no saloon in the country was safe from their "pray-in" demonstrations, vocal opposition, and in some cases violent interventions. Their influence eventually extended into every aspect of American culture. The WCTU and other antialcohol forces, such as the newly formed Anti-Saloon League and National Prohibition Party, were soon electing congressional candidates pledged to enact national legislation banning alcohol consumption in the land.

Even though this 1874 engraving shows a temperance crusader in full battle regalia, relatively few temperance activists resorted to physical violence.

The beginning and ending of a "noble experiment"

n December 1917 Congress passed a resolution "prohibiting the manufacture, sale, transportation, or importation of intoxicating liquors," the simple wording that would form the basis for the Eighteenth Amendment to the U.S. Constitution. (Notice that it did not forbid purchase or use of alcohol, and alcohol for "medicinal purposes" was still legal.) The Volstead Act of 1919 set up the enforcement procedures and defined an intoxicating liquor as any beverage containing more than .05 percent alcohol concentration. By the end of the year, the necessary thirty-six states had ratified the amendment, and Prohibition took effect in January 1920.

Despite its lofty aims, Prohibition was doomed to failure. In the countryside, operators of illegal stills (called moonshiners, since they worked largely at night) continued their production, despite the efforts of an occasional half-hearted raid by Treasury agents (known as "revenooers"). The major cities became centers of open defiance. Liquor, having been smuggled into the country, flowed abundantly as saloons turned into speakeasies and operated in violation of the law.

Early years of Prohibition did, however, show positive effects in the area of public health. Alcohol-related deaths, cirrhosis of the liver, mental disorders, and alcohol-related crime declined in 1920 and 1921, but in a few years, the figures began to creep up again and the level of criminal activity associated with illegal drinking was clearly intolerable.[14] By the end of the decade, for the vast majority of Americans, it had become obvious that the experiment was not working. In 1933 President Franklin D. Roosevelt, having run on a platform to repeal the Volstead Act, signed the necessary legislation that became the Twenty-first Amendment; ratification was swift. Alcohol was restored as a legal commodity and its regulation was returned once more to local authorities. Since that time, state prohibition laws have gradually been repealed, with Mississippi in 1966 being the last state to do so.

Present-day regulation by taxation

One immediate benefit of repealing Prohibition was the return of federal revenue from taxes on alcohol. In 1933 alone, such taxes brought in $500 million, which was used to finance social programs during the Depression. The concept of collecting taxes on the basis of alcohol consumption dates back to the very beginning of the United States as a nation. In 1794 the newly formed U.S. Congress passed a law requiring an excise tax on the sale of whiskey. After a short-lived Whiskey Rebellion in which President Washington had to order federal militia to subdue Appalachian farmers who had refused to pay the new tax, the practice of taxing alcohol was accepted and has continued to the present day as a legal way of raising tax money. Indirectly, these taxes, often referred to as sin taxes, have been a mechanism of regulating the consumption of alcohol by increasing its price. Such governmental revenue from the sales of alcohol in 1992 amounted to practically $8 billion. Today, alcoholic beverages are one of the most heavily taxed consumer products. Approximately 42 percent of the retail price of an average bottle of distilled spirits, for example, is earmarked for federal, state, or local taxes.[15]

An interesting question is how the price of alcohol affects the pattern of consumption. As noted in Chapter 10, alcohol consumption rates have declined over the last decade or so, in part as a result of changing attitudes toward personal health and dieting. On the one hand, the alcohol beverage industry is quick to blame the governmental taxes for decreasing their retail sales and often observes that because of reduced sales the net income to the government actually ends up less than prior to the tax increase. On the other hand, those in favor of these taxes argue that the

nation's taxation policy with regard to alcohol and other legal psychoactive drugs (such as nicotine) that have negative consequences on society should not be oriented toward the quantity of revenue in the first place.

One strategy would be to set alcohol taxes high enough to begin to offset the total societal costs resulting from alcohol abuse. This approach would place a type of "user fee" on the consumption of alcohol. Recent studies have estimated that if the average tax on a gallon of pure alcohol were raised from $35 to about $80, not only would consumption rates decline significantly but the tax revenue on the sales that remain would be substantial enough to pay the health-care costs of patients whose medical expenses arise from alcohol-related illnesses. However, there is also the possibility that raising the costs of alcohol might lead to the development of a black market for its purchase and a net decline in tax revenues.[16]

Chronic effects of alcohol

This section will deal with what we know about the consequences of long-term, or chronic, consumption of alcohol over and above the acute effects that were discussed in the last chapter.

Tolerance and withdrawal

As with other CNS depressants (Chapter 5), alcohol consumption over a period of time will result in a tolerance effect. On a metabolic level, alcohol dehydrogenase activity during tolerance is higher in the stomach and liver, allowing the alcohol to leave the body somewhat faster; on a neural level, the brain is less responsive to alcohol's depressive effects.[17] Therefore, if alcohol consumption were to remain steady, the individual would feel less of an effect.

As a result of tolerance and the tendency to compensate for it in terms of drinking a greater quantity, the chronic alcohol abuser is subject to increased physical risks. There is a serious behavioral risk as well, since an alcohol-tolerant drinker may consider driving with a BAC level that exceeds the standard for drunk driving, thinking he or she is not intoxicated and hence not impaired. A person's driving ability, under these circumstances, will be substantially overestimated.

An alcohol-dependent person's abrupt withdrawal from alcohol can result in a range of serious physical symptoms, beginning from six to forty-eight hours after the last drink, but estimates vary as to how many people are typically affected. Among hospitalized patients, only 5 percent appear to show withdrawal symptoms, while other studies of alcoholics using outpatient facilities have estimated the percentage to be as high as 18. Although the exact incidence may be somewhat unclear, there is less disagreement as to what takes place. Physical withdrawal effects are classified in two clusters of symptoms.

The first cluster, called the **alcohol withdrawal syndrome** is the more common of the two. It begins with insomnia, vivid dreaming, and a severe hangover; these discomforts are followed by tremor (the "shakes"), sweating, mild agitation, anxiety (the "jitters"), nausea, and vomiting, as well as increased heart rate and blood pressure. In some patients, there are also brief tonic-clonic (grand mal) seizures, as the nervous system rebounds from the chronic depression induced by alcohol. The alcohol withdrawal syndrome usually reaches a peak from twenty-four to thirty-six hours after the last drink and is over after forty-eight hours.

The second cluster, called **delirium tremens (DTs),** is much more dangerous and is fortunately less common. The symptoms include extreme disorientation and confusion, profuse sweating, fever, and disturbing nightmares. Typically, there are also periods of frightening hallucinations, when the individual might experience seeing snakes or insects on the walls, ceiling, or his or her skin. These effects generally reach a peak three to four days after the last drink. During this time,

there is the possibility of life-threatening events such as heart failure, dehydration, or suicide, so it is critical for the individual to be hospitalized and medical supervision to be available at all times. The current medical practice for treating individuals undergoing withdrawal is to administer benzodiazepines (Chapter 5) to relieve the symptoms. After the withdrawal period has ended, the dose levels of the benzodiazepines are gradually reduced and discontinued.[18]

Liver disease

Chronic consumption of alcohol produces three forms of liver disease. The first of these is a **fatty liver,** resulting from an abnormal concentration of fatty deposits inside liver cells. Normally, the liver metabolizes fats adequately, but when alcohol is in the body the liver metabolizes the alcohol at the expense of fats. As a result, fats accumulate and ultimately interfere with the functioning of the liver. The condition is fortunately reversible, if the drinker abstains. The accumulated fats are gradually metabolized, and the liver returns to normal.

The second condition is **alcoholic hepatitis,** an inflammation of liver tissue causing fever, jaundice (a yellowing of the skin), and

---

alcohol withdrawal syndrome
The more common of two general reactions to the cessation of alcohol consumption in an alcoholic. It is characterized by physiological discomfort, seizures, and sleep disturbances.

delirium tremens (DTs)
The less common of two general reactions to the cessation of drinking in an alcoholic. It is characterized by extreme disorientation and confusion, fever, hallucinations, and other symptoms.

fatty liver
A condition in which fat deposits accumulate in the liver as a result of chronic alcohol abuse.

alcoholic hepatitis
(AL-co-HAUL-ik hep-ah-TEYE-tus)
A disease involving inflammation of the liver as a result of chronic alcohol abuse.

abdominal pain, resulting at least in part from a lower functioning level of the immune system. It is also reversible with abstinence, though some residual scarring may remain.

The third, most serious liver condition is **alcoholic cirrhosis,** characterized by the progressive development of scar tissue that chokes off blood vessels in the liver and destroys liver cells by interfering with the cell's utilization of oxygen. At an early stage, the liver is enlarged from the accumulation of fats, but at later stages the liver is shrunken as liver cells begin to degenerate (Fig. 11.1). Though abstinence helps to prevent further liver degeneration when cirrhosis is diagnosed, the condition is not reversible except by liver transplantation surgery.

Prior to the 1970s, alcoholic cirrhosis was attributed to nutritional deficiencies that are often associated with an alcoholic's diet. We know now that, although nutritional problems play a role, alcohol itself is toxic to the liver. After a pattern of heavy alcohol consumption of many years, it is possible to develop cirrhosis, even when nutrition is adequate. A major cause of liver cell damage is the toxic accumulation of free radicals, molecule fragments that are by-products of acetaldehyde, the enzyme involved in alcohol metabolism.

Cirrhosis is ranked as the ninth leading cause of death in the United States, with most deaths occurring in people forty to sixty-five years old. Daily drinkers are at a higher risk of developing cirrhosis than binge drinkers, though this risk may be due to the relatively larger quantity of alcohol consumed over a long period of time. Generally, patients showing liver damage have been drinking for ten to twenty years. Only 10 to 20 percent, however, of all heavy drinkers develop cirrhosis, in contrast to 90 to 100 percent who show evidence either of fatty liver or hepatitis.

**alcoholic cirrhosis
(AL-co-HAUL-ik seer-OH-sis)**
A disease involving scarring and deterioration of liver cells as a result of chronic alcohol abuse.

There may be a genetic predisposition for cirrhosis that puts a subgroup of alcoholics at increased risk.[19]

Cardiovascular problems

On the one hand, about one in every four alcoholics develops cardiovascular problems due to the chronic consumption of alcohol. The effects include inflammation and enlargement in the heart muscle, poor blood circulation to the heart, reduced heart contractions, fatty accumulations in the heart and arteries, high blood pressure, and cerebrovascular disorders such as stroke. Alcohol is also capable of triggering angina pain from spasms in heart muscle in those individuals who are otherwise susceptible to it.

On the other hand, as mentioned in Chapter 10, large survey studies have shown that a moderate level of alcohol consumption (up to two drinks a day) may actually reduce the incidence of coronary heart disease, in both men and women. We should not take this information to conclude that abstinent individuals should suddenly take up drinking, only that those who already are drinking at this level are not running a significant medical risk and in fact may be protecting themselves from possible cardiac problems.[20]

Cancer

Chronic alcohol abuse is associated with the increased risk of several types of cancers, especially cancers of the esophagus, pharynx, and larynx. Nearly 50 percent of all such cancers are associated with heavy drinking. If alcohol abusers also smoke cigarettes, the increased risk is even more dramatic. An increased risk of liver cancer is also linked to chronic alcoholic abuse, whether or not cirrhosis is also present. However, there is either a weaker association or no association at all with cancers of the breast, stomach, colon, pancreas, or lungs. Alcohol is not technically considered a carcinogen (a direct producer of cancer), so why the risks are increased in cer-

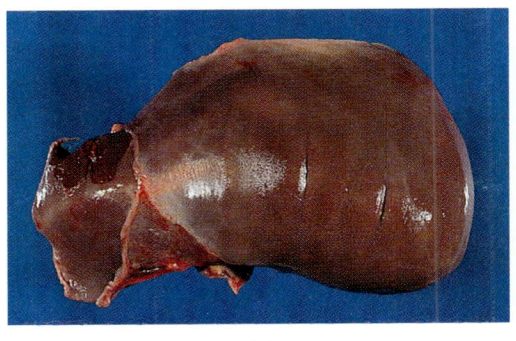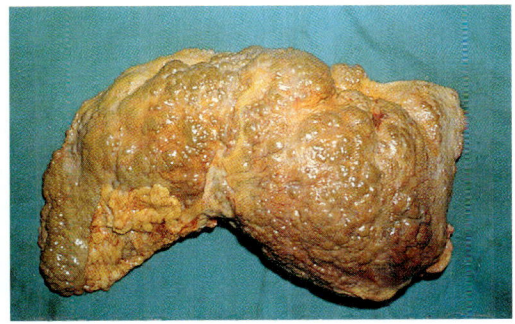

(a)   (b)

F I G U R E   1 1 . 1

A healthy liver (a) and a cirrhotic liver (b)

tain cancer types is presently uncertain. It is possible that the increased risk is a combined result of alcohol enhancing the carcinogenic effects of other chemicals and, as is true with the development of hepatitis, depressing the immune system. With a reduced immune response, the alcoholic risks having a lowered resistance to the development of cancerous tumors.[21]

Wernicke-Korsakoff syndrome

Chronic alcohol consumption produces longer-lasting deficits in the way an individual solves problems, remembers information, and organizes facts about his or her identity and surroundings. These cognitive deficits are commonly referred to together as **alcoholic dementia** and are associated with a structural loss of brain tissue. Specifically, there is an enlargement of brain ventricles (the interior fluid-filled spaces within the brain), a widening of fissures separating sections of cerebral cortex, and a loss of acetylcholine-sensitive receptors in the frontal cortex. The combination of these effects results in a net decrease in brain mass. CT-scans and MRI-scans, two imaging techniques that reveal the structural features of the brain, show that the degree of enlargement of the ventricles correlates with a decline in overall intelligence, verbal learning and retention, and short-term memory, particularly for middle-aged and elderly alcoholics.

It has been estimated that from 50 to 75 percent of all detoxified alcoholics and nearly 20 percent of all individuals admitted to state mental hospitals show signs of alcohol-related dementia. Through abstinence, it is possible to reverse some of the cognitive deficits and even some of the abnormalities in the brain depending on the age of the alcoholic when treatment begins. As you might suspect, younger alcoholics respond better than older ones.[22]

A more severe form of cognitive impairment related to chronic alcohol consumption is a two-stage disease referred to as **Wernicke-Korsakoff syndrome**. In the first stage, called *Wernicke's encephalopathy* or simply *Wernicke's disease,* the patient shows

alcoholic dementia
(AL-co-HAUL-ik dih-MEN-cnee-ah)
A condition in which chronic alcohol abuse produces cognitive deficits such as difficulties in problem solving and memory.

Wernicke-Korsakoff syndrome
(VERN-ih-kee KOR-sa-kof SIN-drohm)
A condition resulting from chronic alcohol consumption, characterized by disorientation, cognitive deficits, amnesia, and motor difficulty.

confusion and disorientation, abnormal eye movements, and difficulties in movement and body coordination. These neurological problems arise from a deficiency in Vitamin B$_1$ **(thiamine),** a necessary nutrient for glucose to be consumed by neurons in the brain. Extreme alcoholics may go days or weeks at a time eating practically nothing and receiving calories exclusively from drinking alcoholic beverages. As a result of thiamine deficiency, large numbers of neurons die in areas of the brain specifically concerned with thinking and movement. About 15 percent of patients with Wernicke's disease, however, respond favorably to large amounts of thiamine supplements in combination with abstinence from alcohol, restoring their previous level of orientation, eye movements, and coordination.

Many Wernicke's disease patients, whether or not they recover from confusion and motor impairments, also display a severe form of chronic amnesia and general apathy called *Korsakoff's psychosis.* Specifically, such patients cannot remember information that has been presented to them and have only a patchy memory for distant events prior to their alcoholic state. They frequently attempt, through a behavior called **confabulation,** to compensate for their gaps in memory by telling elaborate stories of imagined past events, as if trying to fool others that they remember more than they actually do.

Thiamine deficiency is linked to Korsakoff's psychosis as well, since about 20 per-cent completely recover and 60 percent partially recover their memory after being treated with thiamine supplements. Yet, the remaining 20 percent, generally the most severely impaired patients and those with the longest history of alcohol consumption, show little or no improvment and must require chronic institutionalization.[23]

Fetal alcohol syndrome

The disorders just reviewed have generally been associated with consumption of large quantities of alcohol over a long period of time. In the case of the adverse effects of alcohol during pregnancy on unborn children, we are dealing with a unique situation. First of all, we need to recognize the extreme susceptibility of a developing fetus to conditions in the mother's bloodstream. In short, if the mother takes a drink, the fetus takes one too. And to make matters worse, the fetus does not have efficient levels of acetaldehyde to metabolize the alcohol properly, with the result that the alcohol actually stays in the fetus's system longer than in the mother's. In addition, the presence of alcohol is coinciding with a period of time in prenatal development when critical processes are occurring that normally would insure a healthy, alert child.

Although it has long been suspected that alcohol abuse among pregnant women might present serious risks to the fetus, a specific syndrome was not established until 1973, when Kenneth L. Jones and David W. Smith described a cluster of characteristic features in children of alcoholic mothers that has since been defined as **fetal alcohol syndrome (FAS).**[24] Their studies, and research conducted since then, have clearly shown that alcohol is **teratogenic,** that is, it produces specific birth defects in offspring by disrupting fetal development during pregnancy, even when differences in prenatal nutrition have been accounted for.

Present-day diagnoses of FAS are made on the basis of three criteria: (1) prenatal or postnatal growth retardation in which the child's

thiamine
(THEYE-ah-meen or THEYE-ah-min)
Vitamin B$_1$.

confabulation
The tendency to make up elaborate past histories to cover the fact that long-term memory has been impaired.

fetal alcohol syndrome (FAS)
A serious condition involving mental retardation and facial-cranial malformations in the offspring of an alcoholic mother.

teratogenic (TER-ah-tuh-JEN-ik)
Capable of producing specific birth defects.

weight or length is below the 10th percentile, (2) evidence of CNS abnormalities or mental retardation, and (3) a characteristic skull and facial appearance that includes a smaller-than-normal head, small wide-set eyes, drooping eyelids, a flattening of the vertical groove between the mouth and nose, a thin upper lip, and a short upturned nose. If all of these criteria are not met but some of them are, the condition is referred to as possible **fetal alcohol effect (FAE)**.

The incidence of FAS is approximately one to three cases per thousand live births in the general population, but the rates vary greatly within that population. When studies concern only heavy-drinking alcoholic mothers, the prevalence rate rises to approximately twenty-five per thousand. Studies have also shown that African American and Native American women are more vulnerable to both FAS and FAE than women in other ethnic and racial categories, despite similar patterns of drinking behavior and other key factors such as nutrition. These differences suggest that a genetic factor may be contributing to the increase in risk.[25]

We do not know at present how alcohol produces FAS or FAE, except that the greatest risk is in the first trimester of pregnancy, especially the third week of gestation when craniofacial formation and brain growth are prominent developmental milestones. Binge drinking during this time appears to be very damaging to the fetus. For example, if two mothers consumed a similar overall quantity of alcohol during their pregnancies but Mother A consumed one drink on each of seven days in a week and Mother B consumed all seven drinks on two weekend evenings, then Mother B would have run a far greater risk to her child than Mother A. The compressed schedule of consumption would have had a greater adverse impact.[26]

Although not all alcoholic mothers will give birth to babies with FAS or FAE, the research findings are clear: Risks are greatly increased when excessive drinking is taking place, and although an occasional drink may have mini-

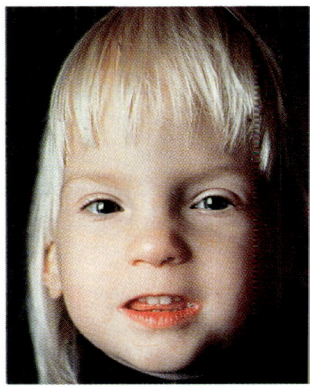

The face of a child with fetal alcohol syndrome.

mal effects, no one has determined a "safe" level of drinking during pregnancy that would make this behavior risk free. The objective of prevention, therefore, is to educate women to the dangers of drinking at any level and to encourage abstinence from alcohol (as well as other psychoactive drugs) during their pregnancy. Since 1989, all containers of alcoholic beverages must contain two warning messages, one of which is that "according to the Surgeon General, women should not drink alcoholic beverages during pregnancy because of the risk of birth defects."

Fortunately, the public is aware of the problem and that the number of women who consume alcohol during pregnancy has declined over the last twenty years. It is also encouraging that it has been possible to affect prenatal exposure to alcohol in a positive way through broad social change. For example in 1978, a change in social policy among members of a Southwestern Plains Native-American tribe, shifting the distribution of mineral-rights income toward social programs on the reservation, resulted in the prevalence rate for FAS decreasing from fourteen per

fetal alcohol effect (FAE)
A cognitive deficiency in the offspring of an alcoholic mother. It is considered less serious than fetal alcohol syndrome.

thousand live births to none at all. A combined prevalence rate of FAS and the rate of FAE decreased from twenty-seven per thousand live births to five. The potential influence of sociocultural factors in altering alcohol consumption patterns needs to be examined closely in all high-risk populations.[27]

The bad news, however, is that the rates of alcohol consumption among several other high-risk populations in the United States, such as pregnant smokers, unmarried women, women under the age of twenty-five, and women with the fewest years of education, have remained unchanged. Twenty percent of pregnant women nationwide continue to consume alcohol, with the percentage rising to 37 among smokers.[28] Until these statistics improve, FAS and FAE will continue to be the third leading cause of mental retardation not only in the United States but in the entire Western world, exceeded only by Down syndrome and spina bifida. Because the development of alcohol-related fetal effects is entirely preventable, the incidence of these conditions becomes all the more tragic (Focus 11.2).

Patterns of chronic alcohol abuse

When we consider the range of direct and indirect costs to society that result from chronic abuse of alcohol, the price we pay is enormous. These costs include the expense of treatment for alcoholism and of medical intervention for alcohol-related diseases, lost productivity from absenteeism and decreases in worker performance, treatment for alcohol-related injuries, and the value of future earnings of individuals who die prematurely because of alcoholism. The total costs are estimated to have exceeded $136 billion in 1990 and $150 billion in 1995, even without taking into consideration the incalculable costs of human suffering that are involved as well. These expenses are proportionally no different from expenses incurred from other

F O C U S   11.2

The T-ACE screening instrument for pregnant women

One of the major difficulties in obtaining information about possible alcoholic behavior is the tendency for the individual to deny that alcohol abuse is going on. It is especially important to find out whether or not pregnant women are engaging in this behavior. Robert J. Sokol and his associates at the Fetal Alcohol Research Center, Wayne State University, in Detroit, Michigan, have developed a very brief screening questionnaire, called the T-ACE, that produces less denial than direct questions about drinking. The T-ACE consists of only four questions:

1. (T—it asks about tolerance) How many drinks does it take to make you feel high?

2. (A—it refers to being annoyed) Have people annoyed you by criticizing your drinking?

3. (C—it refers to cutting down) Have you felt you ought to cut down on your drinking?

4. (E—it refers to an eye opener) Have you ever had a drink first thing in the morning to steady your nerves or get rid of a hangover?

A positive answer to the first question is "two or more" and a positive answer to the other three is yes. A positive answer to the T question counts for two points; a positive answer to the A, C, or E question counts for one point each. The total score can range from 0 to 5, with a score of 2 or more used as the criterion for "risk-drinking" among pregnant women (defined as the consumption of more than one ounce of alcohol a day).

Using this very simple screening questionnaire, Sokol was able to identify approximately 70 percent of the risk-drinkers, a major step in efforts to prevent FAS.

SOURCE: Sokol, Robert J., Martier, Susan S., and Ager, Joel W. (1989). The T-ACE questions: Practical prenatal detection of risk-drinking. *American Journal of Obstetrics and Gynecology, 160,* 863–870.

types of drug abuse, but because of the large numbers of alcoholics and alcohol abusers in the general population, the bottom line figures are far greater.[29]

The demographics of alcoholism

As mentioned earlier, alcoholics can be found in every age, gender, racial, ethnic, and religious group, and in all socioeconomic levels and geographic regions of the country. Nonetheless, large differences in prevalence exist within these categories. For example, men outnumber women in the incidence of alcoholism by about six to one, with men tending to be steadier from day to day in their consumption of alcohol and women tending to abstain from drinking for lengths of time and to binge once they start drinking again.[30] Figure 11.2 shows that, when the severity of alcohol problems is measured by the rate of alcohol-related deaths from disease or injury,

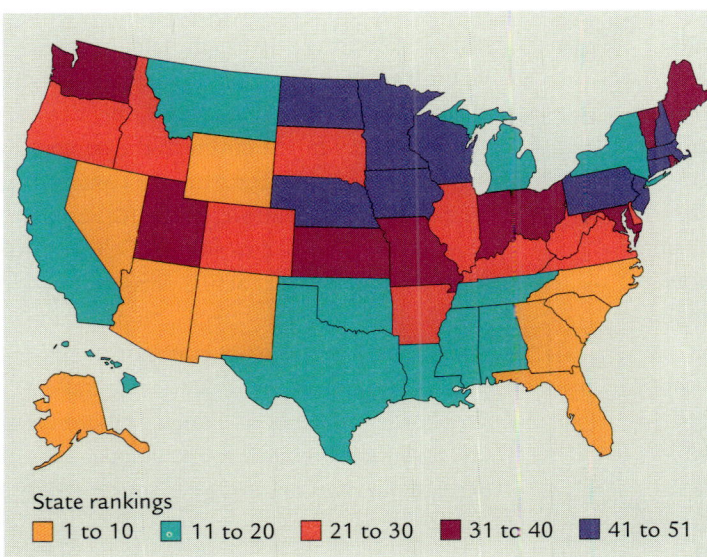

State rankings
■ 1 to 10   ■ 11 to 20   ■ 21 to 30   ■ 31 to 40   ■ 41 to 51

F I G U R E 1 1 . 2

The 50 U.S. states and the District of Columbia ranked from 1 to 51 (one being the highest) in terms of deaths resulting from any alcohol-related disease or injury.
SOURCE: Caces, M. F., et al. (1991). Comparative alcohol-related mortality statistics in the United States by state, 1979–1985. Alcohol Health and Research World, 15, 166.

the highest levels in the United States generally occur in the South, the West, and Alaska.[31] For a discussion of some of the other demographic differences, see Chapter 10.

Alcohol abuse among the elderly

There is a widely held belief that alcohol abuse is not much of a problem with the elderly. Unfortunately, that is a myth. On the basis of careful studies addressing the problem of chronic alcohol abuse among the elderly, it has been estimated that between 2 and 10 percent of the elderly population have alcohol problems, with the percentage rising to nearly 50 among those residing in nursing homes. A recent analysis of Medicare records has indicated that more people over the age of sixty-five are hospitalized each year for alcohol-related problems than for heart attacks.[32]

One of the reasons for the underreporting of this problem is that we typically use the quantity of alcohol consumed as a primary index of alcoholism, and alcohol consumption does indeed decline with age. Yet, due to the changes in alcohol metabolism over a lifetime, three drinks consumed at age sixty can be equivalent in their effects to four times as many drinks for someone at age twenty. In addition, the indications of social and occupational problems, traditionally part of the criteria for alcoholism, are often irrelevant for an elderly drinker. There is no incidence of drunk driving if the person is no longer driving, no job supervisor to notice a decline in work performance, and frequently no spouse to complain of social difficulties. Finally, the occurrence of blackouts or symptoms of Wernicke-Korsakoff syndrome may be misdiagnosed simply as an indication of senility or the onset of Alzheimer's disease.

A number of problems particularly affect the elderly who chronically abuse alcohol. One problem is the risk of the alcohol interacting with the many medications that the elderly typically take. Another is the risk of complications in already existing medical conditions of heart disease and gastrointestinal disorders. There is growing recognition that treatment programs for alcoholism ought to be tailored to the elderly person's special needs, and frequently the traditional treatment programs for much younger individuals do not work well with older people. Many of these people grew up during the Prohibition Era and have a highly negative attitude toward drinking, so that if they are drinking themselves they feel stigmatized and resist treatment. On a brighter note, however, it has been found that, when treatment programs are designed specifically with the elderly in mind, older alcoholics will often respond better to treatment than younger alcoholics.[33]

The social and family dynamics of alcoholism

Alcoholism, like any form of drug abuse, is an especially traumatizing experience for the families involved. For every one person who has a problem with alcohol, there are, on average, at least four others who are directly affected on a day-to-day basis. It is therefore important to examine some of these effects on particular family members. Since the 1950s, a systems approach has encouraged a look at how the alcoholic and other members of the family interact among one another.[34] We discussed one of these aspects earlier in the chapter in connection with the adverse effects of enabling behavior on the alcoholic. Another important aspect related to an alcoholic's family is the possibility of codependency.

Beginning in the early 1980s, the concept of **codependency** has gained widespread attention as a way of understanding people who have lived with an alcoholic or any individual with a drug dependence. Definitions vary but most identify four essential features. In members of the family of an alcoholic, therapists have observed (1) an overinvolvement with the alcoholic, (2) obsessive attempts to control the alcoholic's behavior, (3) a strong reliance upon external sources of self-worth, through the approval of others, and (4) an attempt to make personal sacrifices in an effort to improve the alcoholic's condition.[35] In the mind of a codependent, it is not OK to have one's own feelings, not OK to have problems of one's own, and not OK to enjoy oneself. If people in a relationship with a codependent act badly, the codependent believes that he or she is responsible for their behavior. Since codependency is considered to be a learned pattern of thinking rather than an innate trait, the goal of therapy is to teach the codependent person to detach himself or herself from the alcoholic and begin to meet his or her needs rather than those needs that are based on the value judgments of others.[36]

There have been questions, however, about the validity of the codependency concept. Some therapists have argued that by labeling a person a codependent, the therapist is promoting feelings of helplessness or victimization in these individuals that might not have existed before. Indeed, the idea of codependency might diminish the person's incentive to begin efforts to take control over his or her life by reinforcing the feeling that he or she is "doomed to suffer." Other critics have pointed out that actual patterns of codependency may not be specific to particular individuals but rather are common to practically everyone. Codependency may reflect simply the problems of living in modern society, only now we have found language to express our own failures by blaming other people.[37]

Children of an alcoholic parent or parents

Considering the immense impact that one's parents have in our lives, it is understandable that an alcoholic family will have distinct negative consequences on the psychological development of the children in that family.

> **codependency**
> A concept that individuals who live with a person having a drug dependence suffer themselves from difficulties of self-image and social independence.

Nonetheless, while the statistical risks of becoming an alcoholic increase if one's parent has been an alcoholic, we should remember that most **children of alcoholics (COAs),** as many as 59 percent according to one major study, do not develop serious adult problems, much less become alcoholics themselves. The question of what factors contribute to the resilience of some COAs, so that their difficulties are not reflected later in life, is a major subject of current research.[38]

The genetics of alcoholism

For centuries, there has been the idea that alcoholism appears to run in families. In the late twentieth century, this casual observation has led to a specific question: To what extent is alcoholism genetically determined (through the genes of the parents) and to what extent is it environmentally determined (through the living conditions in which the offspring have been brought up)? One approach is to examine the inheritance pattern in a family tree. It is impossible, however, to tease out the separate genetic (nature) and environmental (nurture) factors from information of this kind.

For more precise answers, one option is to turn to cases of adoption in which children can be compared to either their biological or adoptive parents. In 1981 an extensive research study in Sweden looked at the adoption records of approximately three thousand children who had alcoholic biological parents but lived with nonalcoholic adoptive parents. The results showed that a larger percentage of these children become alcoholic themselves than would be seen in the general population. The greater incidence was present even when the children had been raised by their adoptive parents immediately after being born, indicating that a strong genetic component was operating.

There were, however, two subgroups within those children who became alcoholic. One subgroup, called *Type 1 alcoholics,* developed problem drinking later in life and gener-

Characteristics	Type 1	Type 2
Usual age at onset (years)	after 25	before 25
Inability to abstain	infrequent	frequent
Fights and arrests when drinking	infrequent	frequent
Psychological dependence (loss of control)	infrequent	frequent
Guilt and fear about alcoholism	frequent	infrequent
Novelty-seeking personality	low	high
Tendency to use alcohol to escape negative feelings	high	low
Tendency to use alcohol to achieve positive feelings	low	high
Gender	male and female	male only
Extent of genetic influences	moderate	high
Extent of environmental influences	high	low

TABLE 11.1

Two types of alcoholics

SOURCE: Adapted from Cloninger, C. Robert (1987). Neurogenetic adaptive mechanisms in alcoholism. *Science, 236,* 410–416.

ally functioned well in society. While there was a genetic predisposition toward alcoholism, there was for this subgroup a strong environmental factor as well. Whether or not the child was placed in a middle-class or poor adoptive family influenced the final outcome. A second subgroup, called *Type 2 alcoholics,* developed alcoholism earlier in life and had significant antisocial patterns of behavior. A strong genetic component was operating in this subgroup, and since the socioeconomic status of the adoptive family made no difference in the outcome, we can conclude that environmental factors played a negligible role. Table 11.1 gives a more complete picture of the characteristics associated with Type 1 and Type 2 alcoholics.[39]

children of alcoholics (COAs)
Siblings who grew up in a family with either one or two alcoholic parents.

The study of twins gives us additional information about the genetic and environmental influences in alcoholism. Probably the most important piece of data is the **concordance rate** for alcoholism in pairs of identical twins, that is, how likely one member of a pair is to be alcoholic if the other one is. The concordance rate has been found to be only 58 percent. If genetics were the whole story in determining the incidence of alcoholism, the concordance rate would have been 100 percent. Once again, however, if we look more closely at the type of alcoholic involved and whether the alcoholic is male or female, the data from twin studies are similar to those found in the adoption research. A study conducted in 1992, for example, found that the concordance rate for identical twins was significantly higher than the concordance rate for fraternal twins when one member of the pair was a male alcoholic whose drinking problems started in adolescence (in other words, a Type 2 alcoholic). For female and male alcoholics whose drinking problems started after adolescence (the Type 1 subgroup), a comparison of concordance rates shows that genetic factors played a lesser role.[40]

The concept of alcoholism as a disease

n contrast to the days when alcoholism was considered a moral failure or worse, there is a growing consensus today that alcoholism is best characterized as a disease and that the alcoholic deserves to be treated rather than punished. This viewpoint has evolved over the years, originating from the writings of E. M. Jellinek in the late 1940s in which he proposed that there was a natural sequence

concordance rate
The likelihood that one member of a twin or family relation will have a condition if the other one has it.

of stages in alcohol dependence much like the development of a physical illness.[41] In more recent interpretations, the disease concept has moved away from the idea that all alcoholics follow a common path (since many of Jellinek's ideas have not been confirmed) to a focus on the biological factors that might differentiate alcoholics from nonalcoholics. In addition, the disease concept has led to the idea that the alcoholics are fundamentally out of control and abstinence is the only answer to their recovery.[42] Since 1957 the American Medical Association has defined alcoholism as a disease, and numerous other health organizations have adopted a similar position. As reasonable as this position might sound, the disease concept has created something of a dilemma among professionals concerned with the treatment of alcohol abuse. It places the burden on physicians to deal with the alcoholic through medical interventions, and unfortunately the medical profession is frequently ill-equipped to help.[43]

There are also important legal considerations. Can we say, for example, that an alcoholic is legally absolved from a crime or a legal obligation because he or she was afflicted with this disease? These issues will be explored in the Point/Counterpoint debate.

Approaches to treatment for alcoholism

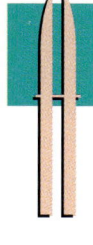

lcoholism, as should be clear at this point, is a study in diversity, and it makes sense that there should be a variety of approaches to treatment according to the circumstances of the individual. Perhaps, in a more perfect world, such variety would prevail. As it is, however, we have to concede that there are not enough individualized treatment programs for alcoholics, that they are forced to fit into rather standard molds, and that we should focus more on individual needs. Different forms of alcoholism treatment fall into two broad areas: biological interventions, which involve medications, and psychosocial interventions such as Alcoholics Anonymous and other self-help programs.

Biologically based treatments

The use of **disulfiram** (brand name: Antabuse) is based on the idea that if you can induce an aversive reaction in alcoholics when alcohol is consumed then they will consume less and the problems of alcoholism will be reduced. Disulfiram, taken orally as a pill once each day, inhibits alcohol dehydrogenase, allowing acetaldehyde to build up in the bloodstream. As a result, individuals who consume alcohol in combination with disulfiram experience a flushing of the face, rapid heart rate and palpitations, nausea, and vomiting. These effects occur not only by consuming alcoholic beverages but by ingesting alcohol in other forms such as mouthwashes, cough mixtures, and even by the absorption of aftershave lotions and shampoos through the skin.

Clearly the symptoms caused by a combination of disulfiram and alcohol are aversive, but the question is whether or not this kind of aversion therapy is an effective treatment. Careful studies in which disulfiram has been administered to large numbers of alcoholics indicate that it is not effective when used alone. One major problem is that alcoholics must take the drug regularly every day, and because disulfiram does nothing to reduce the alcoholic's craving for alcohol, compliance rates are low. The consensus among professionals in this field is that disulfiram can be useful in a subgroup of higher-functioning alcoholics with exceptionally high motivation to quit drinking; for others, disulfiram can be useful as a transitional treatment until other support programs are in place. In the future, a transdermal patch for the slow absorption of disulfiram through the skin, such as the ones currently available for nicotine, may be feasible. Physicians and drug counselors could assure compliance

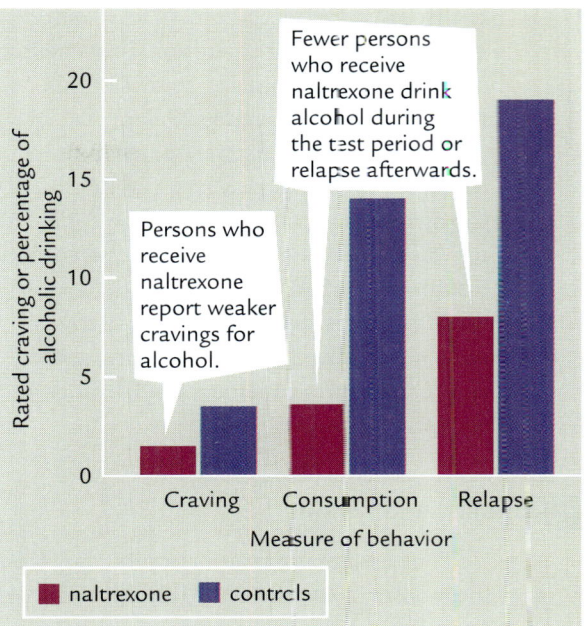

FIGURE 11.3

The effects of naltrexone on the craving, consumption, and relapse rate of alcoholics.
SOURCE: *Robert A. Baron, Psychology 2/E. Copyright © 1992 by Allyn and Bacon. Adapted by permission.*

by checking the continued presence of the patch on the alcoholic's skin, particularly if the patch were designed so that the user could not repeatedly remove and reapply it.[44]

A more direct approach to treatment than aversion therapy is to reduce the actual craving for alcohol on a physiological level. As noted in Chapter 10, there is a strong suspicion that alcohol dependence is related to the same morphine-sensitive receptors in the brain that have been implicated in narcotic addiction. Based on this idea, it makes sense that a drug that inhibits these receptors, such as naltrexone would be useful in the treatment of alcoholism. Research has borne this out. In a 1992 study, naltrexone treatment was shown to reduce the incidence of

disulfiram (deye-SULL-fih-ram)
A medication that causes severe physical reactions and discomfort when combined with alcohol. Brand name is Antabuse.

relapses from sobriety from 54 to 23 percent when combined with traditional counseling, (Fig. 11.3). On the basis of studies of this kind, the FDA approved in 1994 the use of naltrexone for the treatment of alcoholism. Marketed under the new name of ReVia, naltrexone became the first drug to be approved for this purpose since the introduction of disulfiram in 1948.[45]

Other drugs specifically oriented toward reducing craving are currently being tested, either alone or in conjunction with other forms of treatment.

Alcoholics Anonymous

The best-known treatment program for alcoholism is **Alcoholics Anonymous (AA).** Founded in 1935, this organization has been conceived basically as a fellowship of alcoholics who wish to rid themselves of their problem drinking by helping one another maintain sobriety. The philosophy of AA is expressed in the famous "Twelve Steps" (Table 11.2). Members must have acknowledged that they were "powerless over alcohol" and their lives became unmanageable, and to have turned their will and their lives over "to the care of God *as we understood Him.*" As the steps indicate, there is a strong spiritual component to the AA program, though the organization vigorously denies that religious doctrine prevails.

AA functions as a type of group therapy with each member oriented toward a common goal: the maintenance of abstinence from alcohol despite the powerful and continuing craving for it. All meetings are completely anonymous (only first names are used in all communications), and they are dominated by members recounting their personal

Alcoholics Anonymous (AA)
A worldwide organization devoted to the treatment of alcoholism through self-help groups and adherence to its principles.

T A B L E   1 1 . 2
The famous Twelve Steps of Alcoholics Anonymous

1. Admitted we were powerless over alcohol—that our lives had become unmanageable.
2. Came to believe that a Power greater than ourselves could restore us to sanity.
3. Made a decision to turn our will and our lives over to the care of God *as we understood Him.*
4. Made a searching and fearless moral inventory of ourselves.
5. Admitted to God, to ourselves, and to another human being the exact nature of our wrongs.
6. Were entirely ready to have God remove all these defects of character.
7. Humbly asked Him to remove our shortcomings.
8. Made a list of all persons we had harmed and became willing to make amends to them all.
9. Made direct amends to such people wherever possible, except when to do so would injure them or others.
10. Continued to make moral inventory and when we were wrong promptly admitted it.
11. Sought through prayer and meditation to improve our conscious contact with God *as we understood Him,* praying only for knowledge of His will for us and the power to carry that out.
12. Having had a spiritual awakening as a result of these steps, tried to carry this message to alcoholics, and to practice these principles in all our affairs.

SOURCE: The Twelve Steps are reprinted and adapted with permission of Alcoholics Anonymous World Services, Inc. Permission to reprint this material does not mean that AA has reviewed or approved the contents of this publication, nor that AA agrees with the views expressed herein. AA is a program of recovery from alcoholism *only.* Use of Twelve Steps in connection with programs and activities that are patterned after AA, but that address other problems, does not imply otherwise.

struggles with alcohol, their efforts to stop drinking, and their support for fellow alcoholics in their struggles. New members are encouraged to pair up with a sponsor, typically a more experienced AA member who has successfully completed the Twelve Steps and can serve as a personal source of support on a day-to-day basis. According to AA, no alcoholic is ever cured, only recovered, and the process of recovery continues throughout that person's life. Alcoholism, in its view, is a disease, and relapse from sobriety can occur at any moment (Focus 11.3).

Is controlled drinking possible for alcoholics?

ne of the most intensely debated questions in the field of alcoholism treatment has been whether or not it is possible for alcoholics to achieve a level of "controlled drinking" without falling back into a state of alcohol dependence.

On one side are well-entrenched organizations such as Alcoholics Anonymous and the National Institute on Alcohol Abuse and Alcoholism, as well as many other organizations, which assert that alcoholism is an irreversible disease, that abstinence is the only answer, and that even the slightest consumption of alcohol will trigger a cascade of prob-

lems that the alcoholic is constitutionally incapable of handling.

On the other side are groups, represented in greater numbers in Canada and Europe than in the United States, asserting that uncontrolled drinking is a reversible behavioral disorder and that for many alcoholics the promotion of total abstinence as a treatment goal is a serious obstacle to their success in rehabilitation.

Some of the early controlled-drinking studies had enough methodological flaws that the abstinence-only group could be justified in denouncing them. But later research, using carefully randomized assignment of alcoholic

subjects to either an abstinence-oriented treatment or a controlled-drinking one, has shown that long-term results are comparable for either group. This is not to say that the prospects are wonderful for either of them; the odds are still higher *against* long-term recovery from alcoholism than *for* it, no matter what the treatment. But it does appear that controlled drinking can occur.

How many alcoholics can manage to achieve a continued level of non-problem drinking? Percentages vary from 2 to 10 to 15, though the lower figure is probably more accurate for those individuals with severe alcoholic difficulties. Perhaps a more important point is that no one knows how to predict whether or not an alcohol abuser will be one of that small number of successful controlled drinkers. Obviously, most alcoholics are convinced that they will be the lucky ones. How does an alcoholism-treatment coun-

selor handle this? A prominent expert offers one strategy:

My own perspective is that there is little sense in losing a client by a standoff on this issue. . . .It has been my clinical experience that an unsuccessful trial at "controlled drinking" may be a more persuasive confrontation of the need for abstinence than any amount of argumentation between therapist and client.

SOURCES: Goode, Erich (1989). *Drugs in American society* (3rd ed.). New York: McGraw-Hill, pp. 132–134.   Hester, Reid K., and Miller, William R. (1989). Self-control training. In Reid K. Hester and William R. Miller (Eds.), *Handbook of alcoholism treatment approaches*. New York: Pergamon Press, pp. 141–149.   Miller, William R. (1989). Increasing motivation for change. In Reid K. Hester and William R. Miller (Eds.), *Handbook of alcoholism treatment approaches*. New York: Pergamon Press, p. 77. Sobell, Mark B., and Sobell, Linda C. (1978). *Behavioral treatment of alcohol problems: Individualized therapy and controlled drinking*. New York: Plenum.

AA has grown to more than 73,000 groups around the world and more than a million members, though it is difficult to get a precise count since the organization is deliberately structured very loosely. Perhaps more important than its size is the powerful impact it has made not only on the way we deal with alcoholism but also on the way we consider treatment for any compulsive behavior. Over the years, the twelve-step program has become a generic concept, as the precepts and philosophy of AA have

been widely imitated. We now have Al-Anon for the spouses and family of alcoholics going through the AA program and Alateen as a specialized AA program for teenage alcoholics, as well as Gamblers Anonymous, Narcotics or Cocaine Anonymous, and Overeaters Anonymous.

Despite its stature as an approach to treatment, however, there are relatively few scientific appraisals of the overall effectiveness of AA. One of the principal problems is the anonymity that must be insured for all mem-

Bill W. and Dr. Bob— Founders of Alcoholics Anonymous

he backgrounds of William Griffith Wilson and Dr. Robert Smith, when they met in the spring of 1935, could not have been more different, but they shared an important common thread. They were both alcoholics, and their lives had come apart because of it. Wilson had gone from being a successful businessman, whose investments on Wall Street during the 1920s had made him rich, to a penniless failure after losing all his fortune in the 1929 crash. Whether rich or poor, he had been a drunk, but his poverty made the condition worse. In 1934 Wilson was admitted to Towns Hospital in New York City and agreed to subject himself to the "belladonna cure," a treatment based on his receiving morphine and the powerful hallucinogen belladonna. Under the influence of this combination of drugs, Wilson experienced "his spiritual awakening." He later wrote,

In the wake of my spiritual experience there came a vision of a society of alcoholics. If each sufferer were to carry the news of the scientific hopelessness of alcoholism to each new prospect, he might be able to lay every newcomer wide open to a transforming spiritual experience.

For several months following his new-found mission in life, Wilson sought out drunks to "work on" but with little success. On a trip to Akron, Ohio, where he was seeking a new job, he was introduced by mutual friends to a proctologist and surgeon named Dr. Robert Smith.

Smith's alcoholism had wrecked a distinguished medical career, and in 1935 he was in severe financial straits. Wilson's determination combined with Smith's desperation led to their taking on the task of keeping each other sober and helping others do the same. Smith kept on drinking though, until June 10, 1935 (the official date of the founding of Alcoholics Anonymous), when Smith took his last drink. By 1939, Wilson had completed the writing of the Twelve Steps and an extended explanation of the new organization's philosophy, known today as the Big Book. Wilson and Smith had discovered that they were most successful in keeping alcoholics abstinent when they attended meetings on a regular basis and were assured of complete privacy and anonymity. Wilson became Bill W., and Smith became Dr. Bob.

It was not until the 1940s that AA started to be nationally known. The *Saturday Evening Post,* one of the leading magazines at that time, gave them their first real publicity break, publishing an article about the organization that generated an avalanche of responses and a dramatic increase in membership. During this time, a member of a New York branch of AA started to include in its meetings a prayer that would eventually be repeated millions of times in AA meetings throughout the world: "God grant me the serenity to accept the things I cannot change, the courage to change the things I can, and the wisdom to know the difference."

SOURCES: *Alcoholics Anonymous comes of age: A brief history of AA (1959).* New York: Alcoholics Anonymous World Services. Alibrandi, Lucinda A. (1982). The fellowship of Alcoholics Anonymous. In E. Mansell Pattison and Edward Kaufman (Eds.), *The encyclopedic handbook of alcoholism.* New York: Gardner Press, p. 979. Bufe, Charles (1991). *Alcoholics Anonymous: Cult or cure?* San Francisco: See Sharp Press, pp. 34–54.

bers, making it difficult to conduct well-controlled follow-up studies on how well AA members are doing. Nonetheless, AA is widely regarded in the field of alcohol reha-

bilitation as a beneficial self-help approach, particularly when it is combined with other treatments such as individual counseling and medical interventions.

Rational Recovery (RR)
An alcoholism and other drug-abuse-treatment program, emphasizing a nonspiritual philosophy and a greater sense of personal control in the abuser.

Rational Recovery

In contrast to AA, the self-help program **Rational Recovery (RR),** assumes that people do not have to believe they are "power-less over alcohol" or submit to "a Power greater than ourselves" (excerpts taken from the Twelve Steps) in order to recover from alcoholism. Instead, the dominant philosophy is that individuals have the power themselves to overcome anything, including drinking. The strategy is based on Rational Emotive Therapy (RET), developed by the psychologist Albert Ellis, which emphasizes the rooting out of irrational thoughts, emotions, and beliefs that prevent the achieving of personal goals. Another major difference is that RR insists upon professional involvement in its program, with a professional adviser (often a clinical psychologist) assisting members in learning the fundamentals of RET. No reference is made to God or a higher power; in fact, RR points out that the objective is "NHP (no higher power) sobriety." The goal in RR is that within a year and a half members will be able to maintain sobriety without going to RR meetings. In the last decade, there has been increased interest in secular (nonreligious) approaches to self-help alcoholism treatment such as RR. Two other examples of this approach are Women for Sobriety (WFS) and Secular Organization for Sobriety (SOS).[46]

Alcoholism in the workplace

onsidering the negative impact that alcoholism has on worker productivity, it makes sense that corporations, hospitals, the armed services, and many other large organizations should profit by instituting programs of their own for employees needing help. These efforts, referred to as **employee assistance programs (EAPs),** have grown enormously over the past twenty years; today it is estimated that about 40 percent of the U.S. work force is covered by EAPs at their place of employment. EAPs in the context of drug abuse prevention will be examined in Chapter 17.[47]

employee assistance programs (EAPs)
Corporate or institutional programs for workers or employees to help them with alcohol or other drug-abuse problems.

Summary

ALCOHOLISM: STEREOTYPES, DEFINITIONS, AND CRITERIA

- Alcoholism is a multidimensional condition that is typically defined in terms of four major criteria: (1) problems associated with a preoccupation with drinking, (2) emotional problems, (3) vocational, social, and family problems, and (4) physical problems. Not all criteria have to be met, however, for alcoholism to be diagnosed.

A HISTORY OF EFFORTS TO REGULATE CHRONIC ALCOHOL ABUSE

- An appreciation of the adverse consequences of chronic alcohol abuse started in the late 1700s and took root in the United States as a temperance movement. This movement addressed its concerns primarily toward the drinking of distilled spirits.

- The differentiation among forms of alcohol drinking became blurred over the nineteenth century, as temperance advocates began to promote a total ban on alcohol consumption. National Prohibition was the law in the United States from 1920 to 1933.

- Since the end of Prohibition, government regulation has been carried out chiefly through education and the taxation of alcohol.

CHRONIC EFFECTS OF ALCOHOL

- Physical effects of alcoholism include tolerance and withdrawal, liver disease, cardiovascular disease, cancer, and neurological disorders such as Wernicke-Korsakoff syndrome.

- A particular concern is the development of fetal alcohol syndrome (FAS) in the offspring of alcoholic mothers.

- The concept of codependency has helped shed light on the specific effects of alcoholism on spouses and other family members. The children of alcoholics (COAs) have been considered particularly vulnerable, though many appear to be resilient enough to develop fairly normally.

THE GENETICS OF ALCOHOLISM

- Studies of adoptions and twins have provided information about the relative influences of genetics and environment on the development of alcoholism.

- A distinction has been made between a male or female alcoholic with drinking problems occurring late in life (Type 1) and a male alcoholic with drinking problems occurring in adolescence (Type 2). The latter subgroup appears to have a greater genetic component in the inheritance pattern.

APPROACHES TO TREATMENT FOR ALCOHOLISM

- Approaches include biologically based treatments, such as the administration of disulfiram (Antabuse) or naltrexone (ReVia), and psychosocial treatments, such as the self-help programs of Alcoholics Anonymous (AA).

- Objections to certain aspects of the AA philosophy have promoted the growth of other self-help organizations such as Rational Recovery (RR).

- Corporations and other large organizations have instituted employee assistance programs (EAPs) to help workers with problems of alcohol abuse or other forms of drug abuse.

Key Terms

Endnotes

1. Modified from Julien, Robert M. (1992). *A primer of drug action* (6th ed.). New York: Freeman, pp. 86–88.

2. Hoff, Ebbe Curtis (1974). *Alcoholism: The hidden addiction.* New York: Seabury Press, pp. 75–88.

3. Hofmann, Frederick G. (1983). *A handbook on drug and alcohol abuse* (2nd ed.). New York: Oxford University Press, p. 99.

4. Hoff. *Alcoholism,* pp. 78–79.

5. Ludwig, Arnold M. (1988). *Understanding the alcoholic's mind: The nature of craving and how to control it.* New York: Oxford University Press.

6. Schuckit, Marc A. (1989). *Drug and alcohol abuse: A clinical guide to diagnosis and treatment* (3rd ed.). New York: Plenum, pp. 45–76.

7. U.S. Department of Health and Human Services (1990). *Alcohol and health* (Seventh Special Report to the U.S. Congress). Rockville MD: National Institute on Alcohol Abuse and Alcoholism, p. 174

8. Hofmann. *Handbook on drug and alcohol abuse,* pp. 98–99.

9. Goode, Erich (1989). *Drugs in American Society* (3rd ed.). New York: McGraw-Hill, p. 136.

10. American Psychiatric Association (1994). *Diagnostic and statistical manual of mental disorders* (4th ed.). Washington DC: American Psychiatric Association, pp. 181–183, 194–196.

11. U.S. Department of Health and Human Services (1990). *Alcohol and health,* pp. 1–2.

12. Quoted in Sournia, Jean-Charles (1990). *A history of alcoholism.* Cambridge MA: Basil Blackwell, p. 29.

13. Lender, Mark E., and Martin, James R. (1982). *Drinking in America: A history.* New York: Free Press, p. 107.

14. Sournia. *History of alcoholism,* p. 122.

15. *Jobson's liquor handbook 1993.* New York: Jobson Publishing Corp., p 203.

16. Chaloupka, Frank J. (1993). Effects of price on alcohol-related problems. *Alcohol Health and Research World, 17,* 46–53.

17. Schuckit. *Drug and alcohol abuse,* p. 63.

18. Sellers, Edward M., and Kalant, Harold (1982). Alcohol withdrawal and delirium tremens. In E. Mansell Pattison and Edward Kaufman (Eds.), *Encyclopedic handbook of alcoholism.* New York: Gardner Press pp. 147–166.

19. Alcohol and the liver (1993, January). *Alcohol Alert,* No. 19. Rockville MD: National Institute on Alcohol Abuse and Alcoholism. U.S.

Department of Health and Human Services. *Alcohol and health,* pp. 107–114.

20. Moderate drinking (1992, April). *Alcohol Alert,* No. 16. Rockville MD: National Institute on Alcohol Abuse and Alcoholism.

21. Alcohol and cancer (1993, July). *Alcohol Alert,* No. 21. Rockville MD: National Institute on Alcohol Abuse and Alcoholism.   U.S. Department of Health and Human Services. *Alcohol and health,* pp. 121–122.   Garro, Anthony J., Espina, Noel, and Lieber, Charles S. (1992). Alcohol and cancer. *Alcohol Health and Research World, 16,* 81–86.

22. U.S. Department of Health and Human Services. *Alcohol and health,* pp. 123–124.

23. Kalat, James W. (1995). *Biological Psychology* (5th ed.). Pacific Grove CA: Brooks–Cole, pp. 460–461.   McEvoy, Joseph P. (1982). The chronic neuropsychiatric disorders associated with alcoholism. In E. Mansell Pattison and Edward Kaufman (Eds.), *Encyclopedic handbook of alcoholism.* New York: Gardner Press, pp. 167–179.

24. Jones, Kenneth L., and Smith, David W. (1973). Recognition of the fetal alcohol syndrome in early infancy. *Lancet, 2,* 999–1001. Jones, Kenneth L., Smith, David W., Ulleland, Christy N., and Steissguth, Ann P. (1973). Pattern of malformation in offspring of chronic alcoholic mothers. *Lancet, 1,* 1267–1271.

25. U.S. Department of Health and Human Services (1991). *Alcohol research: Promise for the decade.* Rockville MD: National Institute on Alcohol Abuse and Alcoholism, p. 54.

26. Fetal alcohol syndrome (1991, July). *Alcohol Alert,* No. 13. Rockville MD: National Institute on Alcohol Abuse and Alcoholism.   U.S. Department of Health and Human Services. *Alcohol and health,* pp. 139–161.   U.S. Department of Health and Human Services. *Alcohol research,* p. 52.

27. May, Philip A. (1991). Fetal alcohol effects among North American Indians. *Alcohol Health and Research World, 15,* 239–248.

28. Fetal alcohol syndrome.   Serdula, Mary, Williamson, David F., Kendrick, Juliette S., Anda, Robert F., and Byers, Tim. (1991).

Trends in alcohol consumption by pregnant women. *Journal of the American Medical Association, 265,* 876–879.

29. Estimating the economic cost of alcohol abuse (1991, January). *Alcohol Alert* No. 11. Rockville MD: National Institute on Alcohol Abuse and Alcoholism, pp. 1–3.   U.S. Department of Health and Human Services. *Alcohol and health,* pp. 174–176.

30. Cloninger, C. Robert (1987). Neurogenetic adaptive mechanisms in alcoholism. *Science, 236,* 410–416.   Guze, Samuel B., Cloninger, C. Robert., Martin, Ronald, and Clayton, Paula J. (1986). Alcoholism as a medical disorder. *Comprehensive Psychiatry, 27,* 501–510.

31. Caces, M. F., Stinson, Frederick S., Elliott, Steven D., and Noble, John A. (1991). Comparative alcohol-related mortality statistics in the United States by state, 1979–1985. *Alcohol Health and Research World, 15,* 161–168.

32. Maletta, Gabe J. (1982). Alcoholism and the aged. In E. Mansell Pattison and Edward Kaufman (Eds.), *Encyclopedic handbook of alcoholism.* New York: Gardner Press, pp. 779–791.

33. Doweiko, Harold E. (1993). *Concepts of chemical dependency* (2nd ed.). Pacific Grove CA: Brooks–Cole, pp. 230–233.   Muha, Laura (1994, January 12). Alcoholism's heavy toll on the elderly (Part II). *Newsday,* pp. 49, 85.

34. Meeks, Donald E. (1976). Family therapy. In Ralph E. Tarter and A. Arthur Sugerman (Eds.), *Alcoholism: Interdisciplinary approaches to an enduring problem.* Reading MA: Addison-Wesley, pp. 835–852.

35. Doweiko. *Concepts of chemical dependency,* p. 265.

36. Beattie, Melody (1989). *Beyond codependency.* New York: Harper and Row, pp. 15–16, 84–85.

37. Doweiko. *Concepts of chemical dependency,* pp. 269–271, 282–284.

38. Children of alcoholics: Are they different? (1990, July). *Alcohol Alert,* No. 9. Rockville MD: National Institute on Alcohol Abuse and Alcoholism.   Sher, Kenneth J. (1991). *Children of alcoholics: A critical appraisal of theory and research.* Chicago: University of Chicago Press.

39. Cloninger. Neurogenetic adaptive mechanisms.   Cloninger, C. Robert, Gohman, M., and Sigvardsson, S. (1981). Inheritance of alcohol abuse: Cross fostering analysis of adopted men. *Archives of General Psychiatry, 38,* 861–868.

40. McGue, Matt, Pickens, Roy W., and Svikis, Dace S. (1992). Sex and age effects on the inheritance of alcohol problems: A twin study. *Journal of Abnormal Psychology, 101,* 3–17.   Schuckit, Marc A. (1987). Biological vulnerability to alcoholism. *Journal of Counseling and Clinical Psychology, 55,* 301–399.

41. Jellinek, E. M. (1952). Phases of alcohol addiction. *Quarterly Journal of Studies in Alcohol, 13,* 672.   Jellinek, E. M. (1960). *The disease concept of alcoholism.* New Haven CT: Hillhouse Press.

42. George, William H., and Marlatt, G. Alan. (1983). Alcoholism: The evolution of a behavioral perspective. In Marc Galanter (Ed.), *Recent developments in alcoholism* Vol. 1. New York: Plenum, pp. 105–138.

43. Fingarette, Herbert. (1988, November/December). Alcoholism: The mythical disease. *Utne Reader, 30* p. 66.

44. Banys, Peter (1988). The clinical use of disulfiram (Antabuse): A review. *Journal of Psychoactive Drugs, 20,* 243–261.   Schuckit. *Drug and alcohol abuse,* pp. 266–268.

45. Maier, Thomas (1995, February 21). New weapon to battle alcoholism. *Newsday,* pp. B23, B28–29. Schuckit, Marc A. (1993, August). Naltrexone and the treatment of alcoholism. *Drug Abuse and Alcoholism Newsletter.* San Diego CA: Vista Hill Foundation. Volpicelli, Joseph R., Alterman, Arthur L, Hayashida, Motoi, O'Brien, Charles P (1992). Naltrexone in the treatment of alcohol dependence. *Archives of General Psychiatry, 49,* 876–880.

46. Bufe, Charles (1991). *Alcoholics Anonymous: Cult or cure?* San Francisco: See Sharp Press, pp. 123–127.   Ellis, Albert, and Velten, Emmett (1992). *When AA doesn't work for you: Rational steps to quitting alcohol.* Fort Lee NJ: Barricade Press.   O'Brien, Jim (1991, March 26). A new way to treat alcoholism. *Your health,* p. 13.

47. Blum, Terry C., Roman, Paul M., and Martin, Jack K. (1993). Alcohol consumption and work performance. *Journal of Studies on Alcohol, 54,* 61–70.   U.S. Department of Health and Human Service. *Alcohol and health,* pp. 252–254.

Should alcoholism be viewed as a disease?

he following viewpoints on whether or not alcoholism is a disease represent both sides of this controversial issue. Read them with an open mind. Discuss them in your class, with your family, and with your friends. Don't think you have to come up with the final answer, nor should you necessarily agree with the argument you heard last. Many of the ideas in this feature come from sources listed at the end, where more extensive discussions can be found.

POINT

Alcohol abuse has recently been defined by the National Institute of Alcohol Abuse and Alcoholism (NIAAA) as having three criteria: a preoccupation with drinking alcohol, a pattern of compulsive use despite the adverse consequences, and a pattern of relapse to alcohol use.

Alcoholics cannot control their drinking; that is their disease. Give a drink to a person who is genetically vulnerable to alcohol and the consumption of alcohol will make that person an alcoholic, just as a person infected with a type of bacteria might acquire an infectious disease.

COUNTERPOINT

First of all, you're taking considerable liberties with the bacterial infection argument. The research on alcoholism does not show that everyone who acquires the behaviors of alcohol abuse was genetically disposed to it. Controlled drinking is attainable for at least some alcoholics. How do you separate the alcoholics who respond less to genetic factors than to environmental ones and seem to retain some degree of control over their drinking from those individuals who do not? Besides, we are not talking about alcohol as some invisible bacteria floating around, wait-

ing to "infect" people without their knowledge. Alcoholics become alcoholic because they consume a substance that later on they no longer can handle. At one time in their lives, they chose to have that first drink; no one person or thing made them do it.

POINT

We accept the fact that the alcoholic is responsible for "that first drink," but we assert that the consequences are not voluntary. The alcoholic is powerless over alcohol, not over his or her alcoholism. The situation is similar to a diabetic being in control over whether or not a treatment of insulin injections should be taken. The alcoholic can seek treatment.

COUNTERPOINT

You can't have it both ways. Being responsible for the treatment of the disease is not the same as being powerless in the face of alcoholism (one of the main assumptions of Alcoholics Anonymous). Even the Supreme Court has trouble wrestling with the issue. In 1988 it ruled that two alcoholics could not be excluded from claiming educational benefits normally accorded to veterans just because their alcoholism prevented them from applying in the time

allowed. The Veteran's Administration had refused them, claiming that alcoholism, without physical or mental disorders, is an example of "willful misconduct."

POINT

Not exactly. The Court ruled that the source of the "willful misconduct" was the disease of alcoholism. In doing so, they actually reconfirmed the concept of alcoholism as a disease. The courts typically do not excuse the alcoholic from the consequences of the condition. Instead, they give the person a choice of being punished for his or her offenses or accepting a program of rehabilitation. We cannot go back to the days when drinking too much was considered a moral deficiency.

COUNTERPOINT

If alcoholism is a disease, then it's a very strange one. It may be in a category all its own.

SOURCES: Holden, Constance (1987). Is alcoholism a disease? *Science, 238,* 1647. Miller, Norman, and Toft, Doug (1990). *The disease concept of alcoholism and other drug addiction.* Center City MN: Hazelden Foundation.

12

Nicotine and Tobacco

Their roguish tobacco. It is good for nothing but to choke a man and fill him full of smoke and embers.

Ben Jonson
Everyman out of his humours
Act III, Scene 5 (1600)

To cease smoking is the easiest thing I ever did. I ought to know because I've done it a thousand times.

Attributed to Mark Twain
(1835–1910)

n some ways, our attitudes toward tobacco have not changed. Many people still find tobacco smoke and the behavior of smoking as personally objectionable as they did in Ben Jonson's time, and people have as much difficulty as they did in Mark Twain's time in trying to quit. In other ways, however, the times have definitely changed. For almost fifty years, up until the middle 1960s, lighting up and smoking a cigarette was an unquestionable sign of sophistication. It was definitely cool to smoke; the best people seemed to do it often. It was an era before the issuance of reports by the surgeon general, National Smoke-out Days, and no-smoking sections in restaurants.

Today, it is no longer a matter of debate that tobacco smoking is a major health hazard not only to the person doing the smoking but also to society at large. These concerns are based not on public attitudes that can change over time but on solid scientific fact. It is also no longer a matter of debate that the main psychoactive ingredient in tobacco, nicotine, is a major dependence-producing drug. Yet we need to recognize that tobacco products are legally sanctioned commodities with an economic significance, both to the United States and the world, that cannot be ignored. How did we arrive at this point, and what lies ahead? This chapter will explore what we now know about the effects of tobacco smoking and other forms of tobacco consumption, the impact these behaviors have had on U.S. society, and the ways in which society has dealt with the issue of tobacco over the years. It will also consider current approaches toward helping people who choose to stop smoking and preventing the adverse consequences.

Tobacco through history

Shortly after setting foot on the small island of San Salvador on October 12, 1492, Christopher Columbus received from the inhabitants a welcoming gift of large, green, sweet-smelling tobacco leaves. Never having seen tobacco before, Columbus did not know what to make of this curious offering, except to observe in his journal that the leaves were greatly prized by the Indians. In the first week of November, two members of the expedition ventured to the shores of Cuba, searching at Columbus's insistence for the great khan of Cathay (China). They found no evidence of the khan but did return with reports of Indians who apparently were "drinking smoke." They rolled up tobacco leaves in the dried leaves of Indian corn or stuffed them into hollow reeds, lit them with fire, and then inhaled the smoke through the nose and mouth. It was a totally bizarre scene to these European observers; one interpretation was that the Indians were perfuming themselves in some exotic ritual.

It did not take long for Columbus's men to try out "tobacco drinking" themselves. One sailor in particular, Rodrigo de Jerez, became quite fond of the practice. He was, in fact, history's first documented European smoker, though he lived to regret it later on. When Rodrigo returned to Spain, he volunteered to demonstrate the new-found custom to his neighbors, who instead of being impressed thought that anyone who could emit smoke from the nose and mouth without burning had to be possessed by the devil. A parish priest turned Rodrigo over to the Inquisition, which sentenced him to imprisonment for witchcraft. He spent several years in jail, presumably without a supply of tobacco. Rodrigo may therefore also be remembered as the first European smoker to go cold turkey.[1]

In 1560, the year historians mark as the year tobacco was officially introduced to Europe, a Spanish physician brought some tobacco plants back from the New World and presented them to King Philip II of Spain. Meanwhile, in England, both Sir Francis Drake on his return from his voyage around the world and Sir Walter Raleigh on his return from the new colony of Virginia championed the use of tobacco. Suddenly, the practice of smoking tobacco through long, elaborate pipes became fashionable among the aristocracy.

Not everyone, however, was enthusiastic about this new fad of smoking. King James I of England issued a stern pamphlet in 1604 condemning tobacco. "It is like hell in the very substance of it," he wrote, "for it is a stinking, loathesome thing." In the first recorded comment on its potential for causing dependence the king observed that "he that taketh tobacco saith he cannot leave it, it doth bewitch him." Elsewhere in the world, during the early seventeenth century, the condemnation became extreme. In Russia, conservatives in power saw tobacco use as just one more piece of evidence that their country was going "Western" and penalties for smoking included whipping, public torture, exile to Siberia, and death. Turkey, Japan, and China tried similar tactics, but, not surprisingly, tobacco use continued to spread.[2]

Sir Walter Raleigh (1552–1618) relaxes with a long smoking pipe and his servant ready to extinguish the fire with a pail of beer.

Politics, economics, and tobacco

By the end of the seventeenth century, even the fiercest opponents of tobacco had to concede that it was there to stay. A sultan of Turkey in 1648 became a smoker himself, and naturally penalties vanished overnight; Czar Peter the Great in 1689 pledged to open up Russia to the West, and tobacco became a welcome symbol of modernism; Japan and China stopped trying to enforce a prohibition that citizens obviously did not want. Even James I, despite his personal dislike for tobacco, soon recognized the prospect of sizable revenue from taxes on this popular new commodity.[3]

Snuffing and chewing

One of the forms of tobacco use observed by the early Spanish explorers was the practice of taking a mixture of tobacco ground into a fine powder (**snuff**), placing a pinch of it into the nose, and exhaling it with a sneeze. By the 1700s, this custom, called **snuffing,** overtook smoking as the dominant form of tobacco use. Among French aristocrats, both men and women, expensive snuffs, perfumed with exotic scents and carried around in jeweled and enameled boxes, became part of the daily routine at the court in France and then in the rest of Europe. There were snuffs for the morning, snuffs for the afternoon, and others for after dinner; some were designed for the ladies, the aged, novices, and the advanced. Sneezing was considered to clear the head of "superfluous humours," invigorate the brain, and brighten the eyes. In an era when bad smells were constant features of daily living, snuffing

snuff
A quantity of finely shredded or powdered tobacco. Modern forms of snuff are available in either dry or moist forms.

snuffing
The ingestion of snuff either by inhalation or absorption through tissues in the nose.

brought some relief, not to mention a very effective way of sending nicotine to the brain. An additional benefit was the freedom from accidental fires caused by tobacco smoking.

Considering their dominance in the rapidly expanding tobacco market, the English colonies in America, particularly Virginia, prospered greatly. England enjoyed a profitable tobacco trade, but you might say that their development of colonial tobacco growing eventually backfired. In 1777, when Benjamin Franklin was sent as an envoy to France on a mission to gain support in fighting the British in the American War for Independence, a key factor in his success was an offer to deliver prime Virginia tobacco in return for French money. The French agreed, and the rest is history. Had it not been for American tobacco, there might not have been a United States of America at all.[4]

In the United States, snuffing was soon replaced by a more rough-and-ready method for using tobacco: chewing. The practice was not totally new; early Spanish explorers had found the natives chewing tobacco as well as smoking it from the earliest days of their conquest, though North American tribes had stuck exclusively to smoking. On the one hand, chewing tobacco had the advantage of freeing the hands to work, and its low cost made it a democratic custom befitting a vigorous new nation in the nineteenth century. On the other hand, the need to spit out tobacco juices on a regular basis raised the tobacco habit to unimaginable heights of gross behavior. It was enough to make the objections of smoke and possible fire fade into insignificance; now the problem was a matter of public health. Tobacco spitting became a major source for the spread of infectious diseases such as tuberculosis. Adding to the picture was the likelihood that a person's accuracy in targeting the nearest spittoon was inevitably compromised by his level of alcohol consumption, which was setting all-time highs during this period (Chapter 10). Charles Dickens, on his travels through the United States, commented in 1842 that the demise of the once-handsome carpet in the U.S. Senate chamber was personally depressing:

> Washington may be called the head-quarters of tobacco-tinctured saliva. . . . In all the public places of America, this filthy custom is recognized. In the courts of law, the judge has his spittoon, the crier his, the witness his, and the prisoner his, while the jurymen and spectators are provided for.[5]

A present-day baseball dugout seems, by comparison, to be a model of decorum. The growth in the popularity of smokeless tobacco since the 1970s will be examined in a later section.

Cigars and cigarettes

By the time of the American Civil War, the fashion in tobacco use began to shift once more, as its overall popularity continued to soar. Although the plug of tobacco suitable for chewing was still a major seller and would remain so until the early twentieth century, two new trends developed, particularly in the growing industrial cities. One of them was the popularity of smoking **cigars** (commonly known as "seegars"), tight rolls of dried tobacco leaves. New innovations in curing (drying) tobacco leaves had produced a milder and lighter-quality leaf that was more suitable for smoking than the older forms that had been around since the Spaniards. North Carolina, with its ideal soil for cultivating this type of tobacco, began to dominate as the tobacco-growing center of the United States, as it continues to do today. With the advent of cigars, tobacco consumers could combine the feeling of chewing (since the cigar remained in the mouth for a relatively long period of time) and the effects of ingesting tobacco smoke.

The other trend was the introduction of **cigarettes,** rolls of shredded tobacco wrapped in paper. They had become popular among British soldiers returning from the Crimean War in 1856, who had learned of the practice from the Turks. Europeans took to cigarettes immediately, but the United States proved a harder sell. Part of the problem was the opposition of a well-entrenched U.S. cigar industry, which did not look kindly on a new competing product. Cigar makers did not discourage the circulation of stories that cigarettes were being adulterated with opium and that was the reason people were getting hooked on them (obviously nicotine could not possibly have been a factor) or that the paper wrapping in cigarettes was actually soaked in arsenic or white lead. Other accusations were that cigarette factory workers were urinating on the tobacco to give it an extra "bite" or that Egyptian brands were mixed with crushed camel dung.[6]

An even greater problem than unsubstantiated rumors, however, was the image of cigarette smoking itself. A cigarette was looked upon as a dainty, sissy version of the he-man cigar; cigars were fat, long, and dark while cigarettes were slender, short, and light. Well into the beginning of the twentieth century, this attitude persisted. This is what John L. Sullivan, champion boxer and symbol of masculinity, thought of cigarettes in 1904:

> Who smokes 'em? Dudes and college stiffs— fellows who'd be wiped out by a single jab or a quick undercut. It isn't natural to smoke cigarettes. An American ought to smoke cigars. . . . It's the Dutchmen, Italians, Russians, Turks, and Egyptians who smoke cigarettes and they're no good anyhow.[7]

The public image of the cigarette would eventually change dramatically, but until then cigarette manufacturers had to rely upon a distinct marketing advantage: low cost. In 1881 James Bonsack patented a cigarette-making machine that transformed the tobacco

cigars
Tightly rolled quantities of dried tobacco leaves.

cigarettes
Rolls of shredded tobacco wrapped in paper, today usually fitted at the mouth end with a filter.

industry. Instead of producing at most 300 cigarettes an hour by hand, three machine operators could now turn out 200 a minute, or roughly 120,000 cigarettes a day. This is a snail's pace compared to the present state-of-the-art machines capable of producing 10,000 cigarettes a minute, but in those days the Bonsack machine was viewed as an industrial miracle.[8]

By 1889, James B. Duke, later to be the major tobacco mogul of his time as well as benefactor and namesake of a prominent university in North Carolina, had used Bonsack machines to great advantage and was producing almost a billion cigarettes annually. Undercutting his competition by concentrating on a high volume of sales at marginally profitable prices (a practice we would call dumping today), Duke managed to force other tobacco companies to merge with his company into a giant corporation, the American Tobacco Company, with Duke as president. Except for cigars, Duke and his Tobacco Trust enjoyed a virtually complete monopoly over tobacco consumption in the United States for about twenty years: 86 percent of all cigarettes, 85 percent of all chewing tobacco, 76 percent of all pipe tobacco, and 96 percent of all snuff. It was not until 1911 that the trust was broken up, as a result of an enforcement of the Sherman Antitrust Act, into five or so major companies that have controlled the tobacco industry to the present day. In the meantime, cigarette prices by the end of the 1800s were as cheap as twenty for a nickel.[9]

Tobacco in the twentieth century

At the beginning of the twentieth century, Americans had a variety of ways to satisfy their hunger for tobacco. Cigars and pipes were still the dominant form of tobacco use. Plugs of chewing tobacco were still enjoyed by many and spittoons were still in evidence, but with the new emphasis on social manners and crackdowns by public health officials concerned with major epidemics of infectious diseases, their days were numbered in the big cities. Chewing remained popular, however, in rural towns of America, and present-day sales are concentrated in these regions.

The future seemed to favor the cigarette for two basic reasons. First of all, a growing number of women began to challenge the idea of masculine domination and smoking tobacco was one of the privileges of men that women now wanted to share. Not that smoking was met with immediate acceptance; in one famous case in 1904, a New York City woman was arrested for smoking in public. Nonetheless, as smoking among women became more common, the mild-tasting, easy-to-hold cigarette was the perfect option for them. By the 1920s, advertising slogans such as "Reach for a Lucky instead of a sweet" (a clever effort to portray cigarette smoking as an aid in keeping one's weight down) as well as endorsements by glamorous celebrities were being targeted specifically for the women's market. Another factor was World War I, during which time cigarettes were a logical form of tobacco to take along to war. Times of tension were always times in which tobacco use increased. When the war was over, the cigarette was, in the words of one historian, "enshrined forever as the weary soldier's relief, the worried man's support, and the relaxing man's companion."[10]

Cigarettes really came into their own in the 1920s, with the introduction of heavily advertised brand names and the intense competition among newly independent tobacco companies after the breakup of the Tobacco Trust. Camels, introduced in 1913 with an initial advertising campaign budgeted at an unheard-of $3 million, captured the top spot and held it through the end of World War II. Some of the other major brand names introduced during this period were Chesterfield, Lucky Strike, Philip Morris, and Old Gold. Cigarette sales in the United States increased from 45 billion in 1920 to 80 billion in 1925 and 180 billion by 1940.[11]

Health concerns and smoking behavior

A combination of promotion through mass media advertising and the implied endorsement of smoking by glamorous people in the entertainment industry and sports celebrities enabled the tobacco industry, now dominated by cigarettes, to increase its volume of sales from 1940s to the 1980s by a steady 9 billion cigarettes each year. The peak was reached in 1981, when approximately 640 billion were sold. Owing to the increase in population, however, per capita consumption in the United States had peaked in 1963 at approximately 4,300 cigarettes per year. The year of the turnaround in per capita consumption coincided with the first of several reports by the surgeon general that finally asserted publicly in 1964 what had been suspected for decades, that tobacco smoking was linked to cancer and other serious diseases.

From the standpoint of public consumption of tobacco, the surgeon general's report had several effects. First of all, in the month or so immediately after the report came out, there was a dramatic dip (approximately 25 percent) in the per capita consumption levels. Although succeeding months in 1964 showed a bounce upward, reflecting most likely the fact that many people tried to quit for a short while but could not stay away from smoking for long, the general trend from that point on has been downward. As evidence of health risks accumulated, restrictions on public consumption were instituted. In 1971 all television advertising for tobacco was banned, and in 1984 a rotating series of warning labels (already on all packages of tobacco products since 1966) were required on all print advertisements and outdoor billboards From 1980 to 1992, per capita consumption of Americans age eighteen or older declined from approximately 3,800 cigarettes a year to approximately 2,600.[12]

A second major effect has been the change in the types of cigarettes smoked by the average smoker. In the 1950s cigarette smokers chose in increasing numbers to smoke filtered as distinct from unfiltered cigarettes, in an effort to ingest less of the toxins in tobacco. By 1990, about 95 percent of all smokers were using filtered brands.[13]

Unfortunately, the dominance of filtered cigarettes has not improved the health consequences of smoking, only creating the illusion of having done so. The problem is that when filtered cigarettes were introduced, the industry changed the formulation of the cigarette tobacco, substituting a stronger blend of tobacco with an increased tar content. Tar as will be shown, represents a major factor in causing health problems in smokers, but it is also the primary source of a cigarette's flavor. Ironically, a higher-tar blend was needed to

Cigarette advertisements drew upon an association with glamorous women and Hollywood celebrities.

satisfy the consumer, even though it counter-acted the purpose of using a filter in the first place. One additional consequence is that, as a result of a stronger "filter blend" formula in the cigarette, **sidestream smoke,** the smoke directly inhaled by a nonsmoker from a burning cigarette, ends up more toxic when originating from a filtered cigarette than it is from an unfiltered one.

It should be pointed out that, from a standpoint of profits, filtered cigarettes were a boon to the tobacco industry. Filters were only paper and therefore cost considerably less than filling the same space with tobacco. One prominent brand went one step farther by recessing its filter "a neat, clean, quarter inch away," giving the further illusion of filtering away impurities but actually only creating a space of air.[14]

A third consequence was a direct response to the assertion by the surgeon general that tar and nicotine were specifically responsible for increased health risks from smoking. New cigarette brands were introduced that were low in tar and nicotine (T/N), and the Federal Trade Commission began to issue a listing of tar and nicotine levels in major commercial brands. As later surgeon general's reports have indicated, however, smokers can essentially cancel out the benefits of switching to low T/N brands by varying the manner in which they smoke a low T/N cigarette . It is also true that in order to maintain the same amount of nicotine (the same number of nicotine "hits"), a greater number of low T/N cigarettes have to be smoked, a fact that has not gone unnoticed by the tobacco industry.[15]

sidestream smoke
Tobacco smoke that is inhaled by non-smokers from the burning cigarettes of nearby smokers. Also referred to as environmental tobacco smoke.

environmental tobacco smoke (ETS)
Tobacco smoke in the atmosphere as a result of burning cigarettes; also called sidestream or secondary smoke.

Tobacco today: An industry on the defensive

he tobacco industry in the 1990s faces substantial problems, particularly in light of the continuing challenges from federal governmental agencies and Congress. In 1993 the Environmental Protection Agency (EPA) announced its conclusion from available research that **environmental tobacco smoke (ETS),** the sidestream smoke in the air inhaled by nonsmokers as a result of tobacco smoking, causes lung cancer. In the meantime, the U.S. Postal Service has banned smoking at all of its facilities, on the basis of the EPA report, while the U.S. Department of Defense has banned smoking in the offices of all military bases around the world. Several U.S. states and cities have established smoke-free environments in all public and private workplaces, unless specially ventilated "smoking rooms" have been provided.

In 1994 congressional hearings were held on allegations that during the 1970s tobacco companies had suppressed research data obtained in their own research laboratories regarding the dangers of cigarette smoking. The U.S. Food and Drug Administration (FDA) has charged that nicotine levels are being manipulated in certain brands of cigarettes. The tobacco companies contend that they did so to enhance the cigarette's flavor; opponents contend that the motivation was to provide a sufficient level of nicotine so as to produce dependence (to keep smokers "hooked").

The semantics in this argument have become crucial. If the FDA can prove that there was "intent" on the part of tobacco manufacturers to sell a product that affected the structure or function of the body, then nicotine meets the criteria to be defined as a drug. In that case, the agency would then have the authority to regulate the manufacture of all tobacco products, just as it presently does prescription and nonprescrip-

In 1994, tobacco industry executives testified before a congressional committee in defense of cigarette smoking and other tobacco use.

tion drugs. One prominent cigarette manufacturer, the R. J. Reynolds Company, has recently developed a new type of cigarette that delivers nicotine but little or no smoke. Problems associated with ETS are avoided, but whether the FDA judges this product to be simply another cigarette or a "nicotine-delivery device" remains to be seen.[16]

Another concern for the industry is purely economic. It has been proposed that federal excise taxes on cigarettes be increased in order to help finance tobacco-related health costs. Why not increase taxes on cigarettes, the logic goes, when cigarette smoking contributes so substantially to major disease? Besides, it is also argued, an increased price for a pack of cigarettes would discourage youngsters from buying cigarettes, thus reducing the prevalence of underage smoking. This possibility is supported by data from U.S. states and other countries where the tobacco excise tax has been substantially increased. In Canada, tax levies of $3 per pack have helped cut cigarette consumption nearly in half since 1980, and the smoking rate among teenagers has declined by 60 percent. These changes far exceed the declines in the United States over a similar period of time.[17]

In recent years many U.S. corporations have become increasingly involved in economic decisions that have a global impact. The tobacco industry is no exception. In 1993 a federal provision was passed by Congress requiring that all U.S.-made cigarettes contain a minimum of 75 percent U.S.-grown tobacco. The new minimum is more than twice the proportion of American tobacco previously used in most cigarettes, so the domestic tobacco-producing industry is the obvious beneficiary. However, foreign-grown tobacco costs more than 40 percent less than its domestic counterpart, and a shift to a greater proportion of domestic tobacco will inevitably result in a more expensive cigarette. One prospect in the future is the shifting of cigarette manufacturing to foreign countries, as a way of circumventing the new regulation. Giant tobacco companies such as Philip Morris have the financial resources to do this, but smaller tobacco companies cannot easily shift their operations overseas. Through the 1990s and into the next decade, it is likely that the struggle among tobacco companies to maintain their share of the market will intensify.

To make matters more complicated still, we need to consider the fact that cigarettes represent a major factor in U.S. foreign trade policy. In recent years, U.S. exports of tobacco products have exceeded imports by approximately $2 billion. In other words, the exporting of tobacco products helps the overall U.S. trade deficit from being larger than it already is. If foreign countries that have exported unmanufactured tobacco to the United States decide to boycott American cigarettes, major markets will be lost and the U.S. trade deficit will worsen.[18]

What's in tobacco?

hen a smoker inhales from a lit cigarette, the temperature at the tip rises to approximately 1700 degrees Fahrenheit (926 degrees Centigrade), as oxygen is drawn through the tobacco, paper, and other additives. This is the reason for the intense glowing effect as a smoker inhales from a cigarette. At this intense heat, more than four thousand separate compounds are oxidized and released through cigarette smoke. The smoker inhales the result as **mainstream smoke,** usually screened through the cigarette filter and cigarette paper. As mentioned earlier, the sidestream smoke that is released from the burning cigarette tip itself is unfiltered, and because it is a product of a slightly less intense burning process occurring between puffs, more unburned particles are contained in the smoke.

In general, we can speak of two components in tobacco smoke. The **particulate phase,** consisting of small particles (one micrometer or larger in diameter) suspended in the smoke, includes water droplets, nicotine, and a collection of compounds that will be referred to collectively as **tar.** The particles in tar constitute the primary source of carcinogenic compounds in tobacco. The second component is the **gaseous phase,** consisting of gas compounds in the smoke, which includes carbon dioxide, carbon monoxide, ammonia, hydrogen cyanide, acetadehyde, and acetone. Among these gases, carbon monoxide is clearly the most toxic.

This diverse collection of physiologically active toxins is quite unique to tobacco. One way of putting it is that the fifty thousand to seventy thousand puffs per year that a one-pack-a-day cigarette smoker takes in amounts to a level of pollution far beyond even the most polluted urban environment anywhere in the world.[19] The following discussion will focus on three of the most important compounds in tobacco smoke: carbon monoxide, tar, and nicotine.

Carbon monoxide

As most people know, **carbon monoxide** is an odorless, colorless, tasteless but extraordinarily toxic gas. It is formed when tobacco burns because the oxidation process is incomplete. In that sense, burning tobacco is similar to an inefficient engine, like a car in need of a tune-up. The danger in carbon monoxide is that it easily attaches itself to hemoglobin, the pigment inside red blood cells, where it occupies those portions of the hemoglobin molecule normally reserved for the transport of oxygen from the lungs to the rest of the body. Carbon monoxide has about a two hundred times greater affinity for hemoglobin than oxygen has, so oxygen does not have much of a chance. Carbon monoxide is also more resistant to detaching itself from hemoglobin, so there is an accumulation of carbon monoxide over time.

The ultimate result of carbon monoxide is a subtle but effective asphyxiation of the body from a lack of oxygen. Generally, people who smoke a pack a day accumulate levels of carbon monoxide in the blood of 25 to 35 parts per million blood components (p.p.m.), with levels of 100 p.p.m. for short periods of time while actually smoking. Of course, greater use of tobacco produces proportionally higher levels of carbon monoxide. Carbon monoxide is the primary culprit in producing cardiovascular disease among smokers, as well as causing deficiencies in physiological functioning and behavior.[20]

Tar

The quantity of tar in a cigarette varies from levels of 12 to 16 mg per cigarette to

mainstream smoke
The smoke inhaled directly from cigarettes or other tobacco products.

particulate phase
Those components of smoke that consist of particles.

tar
A sticky material found in the particulate phase of tobacco smoke and other pollutants in the air.

gaseous phase
The portion of tobacco smoke that consists of gases.

carbon monoxide
An extremely toxic gas that prevents blood cells from carrying oxygen from the lungs to the rest of the body.

less than 6 mg. It should also be noted that the last third of each cigarette contains 50 percent of the total tar, making the last final puffs far more hazardous than the first ones.

The major problem with tar lies in its sticky quality, not unlike that of the material used in paving roads, which allows it to adhere to cells in the lungs and the airways leading toward them. Normally, specialized cells with small hairlike attachments called **cilia** are capable of removing contaminants in the air that might impede the breathing process. These cilia literally sweep the unwanted particles upward to the throat, in a process called the **ciliary escalator,** where they are typically swallowed, digested, and finally excreted from the body through the gastrointestinal system. Components in tar alter the coordination of these cilia so that they can no longer function effectively. The accumulation of sticky tar on the surface of the cells along the pulmonary system permits carcinogenic compounds that would normally have been eliminated to settle on the tissue. As will be discussed later, the resulting cellular changes produce lung cancer, and similar carcinogenic effects in other tissues of the body produce cancer in other organs.[21]

Nicotine

Nicotine is a toxic, dependence-producing psychoactive drug found exclusively in tobacco. It is an oily compound varying in color from colorless to brown. A few drops of pure nicotine, about 60 mg, on the tongue would quickly kill a healthy adult, and it is commonly used as a major ingredient in insecticides and pesticides of all kinds. Cigarettes, however, contain from 0.5 to 2.0 mg of nicotine (depending on the brand), with about 20 percent being actually inhaled and reaching the bloodstream. This means that 2 to 8 mg of nicotine are ingested per day for a pack-a-day smoker, and 4 to 16 mg of nicotine for a smoker of two packs a day.[22]

Inhaled nicotine from smoking is absorbed extremely rapidly, typically in about seven seconds, and easily passes through the blood-brain barrier, as well as through the blood-placental barrier in pregnant women. The entire effect is over in a matter of minutes. By the time a cigarette butt is extinguished, nicotine levels in the blood have peaked, and its metabolism and excretion from the body are well underway.

The primary effect of nicotine is to stimulate CNS receptors that are sensitive to acetylcholine (Chapter 3). These receptors are called *nicotinic receptors* because they are excited by nicotine. One of the effects of activating them is the release of adrenalin, which increases blood pressure and heart rate. Another effect is to inhibit activity in the gastrointestinal system. At the same time, however, as most smokers will tell you, a cigarette is a relaxing factor in their lives. Part of this reaction may be due to an effect on the brain that promotes a greater level of clear thinking and concentration; another part may be due to the fact that nicotine, at moderate doses, serves to reduce muscle tone so that muscular tightness is decreased. Research has shown that cigarette smoking helps to sustain performance on monotonous tasks and to produce improvements in both the speed and accuracy of tasks requiring the processing of complex information. We can assume that it is the nicotine in cigarettes and other tobacco products that is responsible, since nicotine tablets have comparable behavioral effects.[23]

cilia
Small hair cells.

ciliary escalator
The process of pushing back foreign particles that might interfere with breathing upward from the air passages into the throat, where they can be swallowed and excreted through the gastrointestinal tract.

nicotine
The prime psychoactive drug in tobacco products.

The dependence potential of nicotine

istorically, the dependence potential of nicotine has been demonstrated at times in which the usual availability of tobacco has suddenly been curtailed. In Germany, for example, following the end of World War II, cigarettes were rationed to two packs a month for men and one pack a month for women. This "cigarette famine" produced dramatic effects on the behavior of German civilians. Smokers bartered their food rations for cigarettes, even under the extreme circumstances of chronic hunger and poor nutrition. Cigarette butts were picked out of dirt in the street by people who admitted that they were personally disgusted by their desperation. Some women turned to prostitution to obtain cigarettes, while alcoholics of both sexes testified that it was easier to abstain from drinking alcohol than it was to abstain from smoking.[24]

Several factors surrounding the behavior of smoking tobacco combine with each other, leading to the likelihood that a dependence will be created. One of these factors is the speed with which smoked nicotine reaches the brain. A second factor is the wide variety of circumstances and settings surrounding the act of smoking that later come to serve as learned rewards. A smoker may find, for example, that the first cigarette with a cup of coffee in the morning (a source of another psychoactive drug, caffeine) is strongly reinforcing. A major reseacher on addictions has expressed it in this way:

Smoking . . . comes to be rewarded by the enjoyment of oral, manual, and respiratory manipulations involved in the process of lighting, puffing, and handling cigarettes, the pleasure and relaxation associated with using alcohol, finishing a good meal,. . . and the perceived diminution of unpleasant affective [emotional] states of anxiety, tension, boredom, or fatigue. . . . No other substance can provide so many kinds of rewards, is so readily and cheaply available, and can be used in so many settings and situations.[25]

A third factor is the sheer number of times the smoker experiences a dose of nicotine. When you consider that a smoker will take from one to two hundred puffs each day from the twenty cigarettes that represent a pack-a-day pattern of smoking, you realize that smoking is a highly practiced, overlearned behavior, in addition to being rewarded by both physiological events in the brain and a range of social events that are linked to it.[26]

The titration hypothesis of nicotine dependence

There is considerable evidence that smokers adjust their smoking behavior to obtain a stable dose of nicotine from whatever cigarettes they are smoking, an idea called the **titration hypothesis.** When exposed to cigarettes of decreasing nicotine content, smokers will smoke a greater number of them to compensate and will increase the volume of each puff. When they take more puffs per cigarette, there will be a greater interval of time before they light up another one. If they are given nicotine gum to chew, the intensity of their smoking behavior will decline, even though they have not been told whether the gum actually contains nicotine or is a placebo. All these studies indicate that experienced smokers arrive at a consistent "style" of smoking that provides a relatively constant level of nicotine to enter their bodies.[27]

Tolerance and withdrawal

First-time smokers will often react to a cigarette with a mixture of nausea, dizziness, or vomiting. These effects typically disappear as tolerance develops in the nicotinic receptors in the brain. Other physiological effects, such

titration hypothesis
The idea that smokers will adjust their smoking of cigarettes so as to maintain a steady input of nicotine into the body.

as increases in heart rate, tremors, and changes in skin temperature, show weaker tolerance effects or none at all. The strongest dependence-related effect in cigarette smoking can be seen in the symptoms of withdrawal that follow the discontinuation of smoking. Within about six hours after the last cigarette, a smoker's heart rate and blood pressure will decrease. Over the next twenty-four hours, common symptoms will include headache, an inability to concentrate, irritability, drowsiness, and fatigue, as well as insomnia and other sleep disturbances. Most striking of all is the strong craving for a cigarette. Most, if not all, ex-smokers can attest to the cravings that slowly diminish but nonetheless can continue for months, and in some cases, for years.[28]

Nicotine dependence, as demonstrated, is the central factor in the continuation of smoking behaviors. The level of dependence is significant, even when compared to that for many of the illicit drugs available on the street. In a 1989 study of people who smoked and were also in some form of drug-abuse treatment, 74 percent judged the difficulty of quitting smoking to be at least as great as the difficulty in stopping their drug of choice. One in three considered it "much harder" to quit smoking.[29]

Health consequences from tobacco use

The adverse health consequences of tobacco use can be classified in three broad categories: cardiovascular disease, respiratory disease, and cancer. In addition, there are also special health difficulties that smoking can bring to women and hazards from using smokeless tobacco. The enormous literature on the adverse effects of tobacco use has grown steadily since the original surgeon general's report in 1964, though by that time more than thirty thousand research studies had been conducted on the question.

Beyond all the reports, however, are the sheer numbers of people who are affected. In the United States alone, among the estimated 520,000 deaths each year that are attributed to substance abuse of one kind or another, approximately 419,000 of them (more than the total number of Americans who died in World War II) are specifically tied to cigarette smoking. These deaths are considered, from a medical point of view, as premature deaths because they are entirely preventable; these people would have been alive if their behaviors had been different

Another way to view the situation is to recognize that smoking-related deaths account for at least one out of every five deaths in the United States every year. Unlike alcohol, which presents no significant health hazards when consumed in moderation, tobacco is a dangerous product when used as intended.[30]

Cardiovascular disease

Cardiovascular disease includes a number of specific conditions. Some of these diseases are **coronary heart disease (CHD),** in which damage to the heart is incurred through the restriction of blood flow through narrowed or blocked coronary arteries; **arteriosclerosis,** in which the walls of arteries harden and lose their elasticity; **atherosclerosis,** in which fatty deposits inside arteries impede blood flow; and stroke, in which interruption or reduction in blood flow causes

coronary heart disease (CHD)
Disease that damages the heart as a result of a restriction of blood flow through coronary arteries.

arteriosclerosis (ar-TEER-ee-oh-scluh-ROH-sis)
A disease in which blood flow is restricted because the walls of arteries harden and lose their elasticity.

atherosclerosis (ATH-er-oh-scluh-ROH-sis)
A disease in which blood flow is restricted because of the buildup of fatty deposits inside arteries.

damage to the brain. In all these diseases, cigarette smoking increases the risk dramatically.

We know now that smoking is responsible for approximately 30 percent of all deaths due to CHD. The risk of CHD doubles if you smoke and quadruples if you smoke heavily. Smoking also raises, on average, the risk of a sudden death (such as from a heart attack) by two to four times, with the degree of risk increasing as a direct function of how many cigarettes are smoked per day (Fig. 12.1). To put it even more boldly, it has been estimated that, unless smoking patterns change dramatically in the future, about 10 percent of all Americans now alive may die prematurely from some form of heart disease as a result of their smoking behavior.[31]

These statistics are strengthened by the understanding we have of how cigarette smoking actually produces these dangerous cardiovascular conditions. The major villains are nicotine and carbon monoxide. Nicotine, as a stimulant drug, increases the contraction of heart muscle and elevates heart rate. At the same time, it causes a constriction of blood vessels, leading to a rise in blood pressure, and also increases *platelet adhesiveness* in the blood. As a result of a greater adhesiveness, platelets clump together and increase the risk of developing a blood clot. If a clot forms within coronary arteries, a heart attack can occur, while a clot traveling into the blood vessels of the brain can produce a stroke. Finally, nicotine increases the body's serum cholesterol and fatty deposits, leading to the development of atherosclerosis. While nicotine is doing its

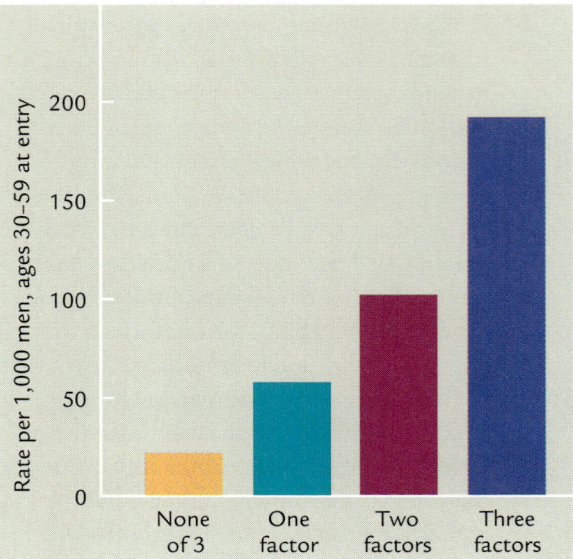

FIGURE 12.1

The cumulative effects of three risk factors (smoking, elevated cholesterol, and hypertension) on coronary heart disease.
SOURCE: *U.S. Department of Health and Human Services, Public Health Service, Office of Smoking and Health (1983). The health consequences of smoking: Cardiovascular disease (A report of the surgeon general). Rockville MD: U.S. Public Health Service.*

dirty work, carbon monoxide makes matters worse. A lack of oxygen puts further strain on the ability of the heart to function under already trying circumstances.[32]

Respiratory diseases

The general term **chronic obstructive lung disease** (COLD) refers to several conditions in which breathing is impaired because of some abnormality in the air passages either leading to or within the lungs. In the United States, 80 to 90 percent of all such cases are due to cigarette smoking. With the exception of a rare genetic defect, cigarette smoking is the only established cause for clinically significant COLD.

Two examples of COLD are **chronic bronchitis**, in which excess mucus builds up in air passages, leading to an inflammation of bronchial tissue, and **emphysema**, in which

chronic obstructive lung disease (COLD)
A group of diseases characterized by impaired breathing due to an abnormality in the air passages.

chronic bronchitis
A respiratory disease involving inflammation of bronchial tissue following a buildup of excess mucus in air passages.

emphysema (EM-fuh-SEE-mah)
An enlargement of air sacs in the lungs and abnormalities in the air sac walls, causing great difficulty in breathing.

air sacs in the lungs are abnormally enlarged and the air sac walls either become inelastic or rupture, leading to extreme difficulty in inhaling oxygen and exhaling carbon dioxide. In the case of advanced emphysema, more than 80 percent of a patient's energy is required merely to breathe. Either disease or a combination of the two causes more than sixty thousand deaths each year, and many additional thousands are forced to lead increasingly debilitating lives, gasping and struggling each day to breathe:

> There are thousands of people alive today with COLD. Many of them are attached to oxygen tanks, imprisoned at home or in the hospital because they are too weak to breathe on their own. Often their friends or family members will pound on their backs, temporarily freeing the lungs of the yellow mucus that impedes their breathing every day.[33]

While it is known that the tar in cigarette smoke produces an oversecretion of mucus in the air passages of the respiratory system and therefore is the likely agent producing chronic bronchitis, it is presently not known what agent in tobacco smoke is responsible for the condition of emphysema.[34]

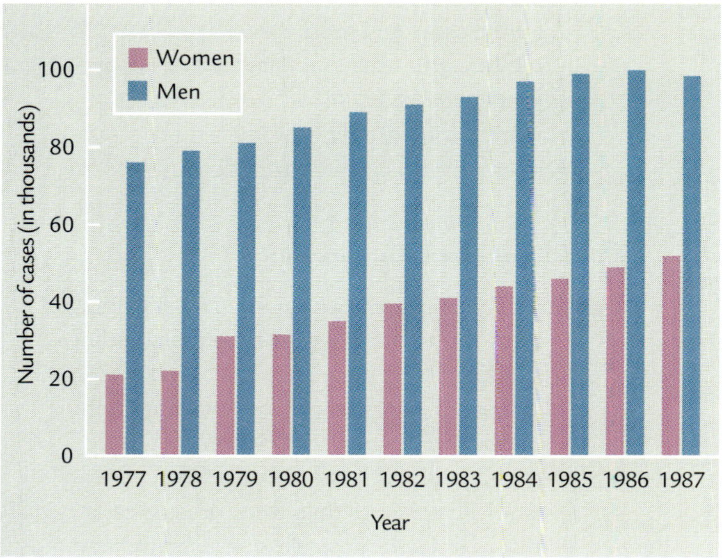

Lung cancer

At the beginning of the twentieth century, lung cancer was a rare disease, and its steady increase in U.S. society since then has been in direct proportion to the availability of cigarettes. Today, nearly 90 percent of the more than 140,000 lung cancer deaths each year have been determined by the American Cancer Society to be due to cigarette smoking. These facts are made even more tragic when you consider that the survival rate for one year after a diagnosis of lung cancer is only approximately 25 percent, and about 87 percent of lung cancer patients will die within five years of initial diagnosis.

Another important change has occurred over the years with respect to this disease. Lung cancer was once looked upon as a "man's disease." In recent years, however, increasing numbers of women have contracted lung cancer as a result of their increased level of cigarette smoking. From 1977 to 1987, for example, the rate of lung cancer for men in the United States rose by 30 percent but for women by 132 percent. Since 1988, lung cancer has exceeded breast cancer as the leading cause of cancer deaths among women (Fig. 12.2).

As discussed earlier in the chapter, the exposure to tar in cigarette smoke disrupts the necessary action of ciliary cells in the bronchial tubes leading to the lungs. In addition, there is an increase in the number of layers of cells lying in the inner surface of these bronchial tubes, a result of the continual irritation from tobacco smoke. The final stage in this process is the formation of cancerous growths, **carcinomas,** on the tissue surface lining the lungs. Of the thousands of compounds that have

FIGURE 12.2

The increasing trend in the rate of lung cancer for men and women, 1977 to 1987
SOURCE: *American Cancer Society*

carcinomas (CAR-sih-NOH-mas)
Cancerous tumors or growths.

been identified in tobacco smoke, several dozen are known carcinogens.[35]

Other cancers

While lung cancer is the best-known and most common example of smoking-related cancers, other organs are affected in a similar way. In the United States, approximately 30 percent of cancer deaths *of all types* have

leukoplakia (LOO-koh-PLAY-kee-ah)
Small white spots inside the mouth and nasal cavity, indicating precancerous tissue.

erythroplakia (eh-RITH-ro-PLAY-kee-ah)
Small red spots inside the mouth and nasal cavity, indicating precancerous tissue.

nitrosamines (nih-TRAW-seh-meens)
A group of carcinogenic compounds found in tobacco.

been linked to smoking. It has been estimated that smokers increase their risk by two to twenty-seven times for cancer of the larynx, thirteen times for mouth or lip cancer, two to three times for bladder cancer, two times for pancreatic cancer, and five times for cancers of the kidney or uterine cervix.[36]

Despite a widespread belief to the contrary, using smokeless tobacco, in the form of chewing tobacco or snuff, does not prevent the user from incurring an increased risk of cancer. Continuing contact with tobacco in the mouth has been shown to produce precancerous cell changes, as revealed by **leukoplakia** (white spots) and **erythroplakia** (red spots) inside the mouth and nasal cavity. While smokeless tobacco obviously avoids the problems associated with tobacco smoke, it does not prevent the user from being exposed to carcinogens, specifically a class of compounds called **nitrosamines** that are present in all tobacco products. As a result of federal legislation in 1986, all forms of smokeless tobacco must contain, on the package, a set of specific warnings that these products may cause mouth cancer as well as gum disease and tooth loss (Focus 12.1). To reinforce the idea that dangers are still present in smokeless tobacco, one of these warnings reads: "This product is not a safe alternative to cigarette smoking."

Special problems for women

The range of health risks to a developing fetus and to the newborn when the mother smokes during pregnancy has been listed in Chapter 2. To these concerns, an important addition is the toxic interaction of tobacco smoke with birth control pills. Women who smoke have more than three times greater risk of dying from stroke due to brain hemorrhaging and almost two times greater risk of dying from a heart attack. If they are using birth control pills as well, the risk increases to twenty-two times and twenty times respectively.[37]

C. Everett Koop— Surgeon general

As surgeon general of the United States from 1981 to 1989, C. Everett Koop earned the reputation of saying what was on his mind, what he believed in, no matter what the political consequences may have been. He has been called the master of the ethically correct, not the politically correct. The image that Koop projected during his tenure as surgeon general and continues to project today as a major spokesman on questions of public health is one of supreme authority. As the journalist Margaret Carlson put it, "There are the Old Testament beard and the preacher's voice that make him seem like Moses come down again from Mount Sinai to deliver commandments 11 through 20."

Koop's two terms as an appointee under the Reagan administration certainly shook things up. His surgeon general's reports on smoking minced no words. There were no "might's" or "could be's." When he found that the tobacco industry had fought hardest over the years against the government's assertion that nicotine was addicting, Koop said that it was indeed addicting, flat out, at the top of his 1988 report to Congress. When the tobacco companies read his report, he said, "They absolutely hated it." When the companies claimed that there was no scientific proof that cigarettes cause cancer, Koop called their assertions "flat-footed lies." When speaking of the selling of cigarettes to developing nations, he said, "I think it is reprehensible for this wealthy nation to export death, disease, and disability to the Third World. I don't think you ought to trade cigarettes for Toyotas."

Domestically, Koop has named cigarette smoking as the "chief preventable cause of death" and has called on the United States to be a smoke-free society by the year 2000. He believes that all tobacco advertising should be banned, urges that all cigarettes be removed from vending machines (where they are available to minors), and in general believes that the distribution of tobacco should be as restricted as that of alcohol.

C. Everett Koop

While conservative in his own personal philosophy, Koop kept an open mind when he had to write a report. His recommendations in 1986 on the prevention of AIDS was a good example of his fairness and adherence to the data. A journalist has observed:

Administration conservatives were stunned by the report's candor. They were particularly outraged that he did not preach abstinence alone and refer euphemistically to body fluids rather than semen. "The White House doesn't like the C word [Koop said]. But if you don't talk about condoms, people are going to die. So I talk."

In January 1989, Koop disappointed conservatives once again when his report concluded that the evidence just wasn't there to condemn the practice of abortion as psychologically harmful to the mother.

First and foremost, as the chief public health officer in the federal government, Koop stayed a doctor and considered medicine his true calling. He went to Washington with a reputation as a pioneering pediatric surgeon, tireless and dedicated to the care of young children. As surgeon general, he extended this caring to the American public.

SOURCES: Carlson, Margaret (1989, April 24). A doctor prescribes hard truth. *Time,* pp. 82–84. Judis, John B. (1989, January 23). An officer and a gentleman. *New Republic,* pp. 19–22. Schlaadt, Richard G. (1992). *Tobacco and health.* Guilford CT: Dushkin Publishing, pp. 7, 99.

The hazards of environmental smoke

In the early days of developing methods for detecting nicotine in the bloodstream, scientists were puzzled to find traces of nicotine in nonsmokers. They suspected at first that there was some flaw in their analysis but later had to conclude that their measurements were indeed accurate. Nonsmokers testing positive had shared car rides or workplaces with smokers shortly before their test. Today, there is a large body

Who has the right: Smokers or nonsmokers?

Since the 1980s, an increasingly thorny issue that divides worker against worker, restaurant patron against restaurant patron, and nearly anyone who ventures out of his or her home is the question of smokers' rights versus nonsmokers' rights. On the one hand, smokers will argue that smoking is a personal freedom and that nonsmokers are restricting that freedom. On the other hand, nonsmokers, armed with increasing facts to back them up, will argue that we are talking about a genuine hazard to the public health, not merely an objection based on the smell of smoke or the cleanliness of ashtrays. To quote a line from the self-styled Nonsmoker's Bill of Rights, "Nonsmokers have the right to breathe clean air, free from harmful and irritating tobacco smoke. This right supersedes the right to smoke when the two conflict."

As we are all aware, the balance of public sentiment has tilted increasingly toward the side of the nonsmoker. Anyone in an airport will have no difficulty observing the feverish last-minute smokers, getting in that last cigarette before the start of a nonsmoking flight, or the pained look on their faces when confronted by the ubiquitous no-smoking sign. Perhaps the most concrete development has been the decision by the Chrysler Corporation to design the 1995 and subsequent Chrysler Cirrus and Dodge Stratus automobiles without ashtrays or cigarette lighters. Smokers are able to order these items on these models only as an option. Smoking is no longer standard.

SOURCE: Bennet, James (1994, January 5). In new Chrysler, ashtrays will be just an option. *New York Times*, pp. A1, D26.

of evidence indicating not only the presence of tobacco smoke compounds in the bodies of nonsmokers but also the significant health risks that such "involuntary smoking" can bring. In other words, environmental tobacco smoke is a hazard to the health of people even though they are not actively smoking.

Approximately 85 percent of the smoke in an average room where people are smoking cigarettes is generated by sidestream smoke, and about three fourths of the nicotine originating from these cigarettes ends up in the atmosphere. How much of this nicotine is ingested depends on several factors. Any compound released in this way is diluted in the air, so the size of the interior space, the number of smokers and nonsmokers in it, and the degree of ventilation are important considerations. In some cases, however, the carcinogens released in ETS are so potent that they are dangerous even in their diluted state. For example, N-nitrosamine (an example of a group of carcinogens mentioned earlier in connection with smokeless tobacco) is so much more concentrated in sidestream smoke than it is in mainstream smoke that nonsmokers will inhale as much of it after one hour in a very smoky room as will a smoker after smoking ten to fifteen cigarettes.[38]

In the words of former Surgeon General C. Everett Koop (see Portrait); "It is now clear that disease risk due to inhalation of tobacco smoke is not limited to the individual who is smoking."

Most of the studies on this question support his position. Overall, nonsmoking wives of husbands who smoke have a 30 percent increased chance of lung cancer compared with women whose husbands do not smoke; if the husband is a heavy smoker, then the wife's risk increases by two to three times. If both spouses smoke, of course, they are susceptible to the effects of both ETS and their own mainstream smoke. Children are also vulnerable, with a greater chance of developing colds, asthma, bronchitis, chronic coughs, ear infections, and reduced lung functioning if they are the children of smokers. Overall, an estimated 53,000 deaths annually in the United States alone are considered to be caused by ETS, including 4,000 deaths from lung cancer (Focus 12.2).[39]

Patterns of smoking behavior and use of smokeless tobacco

n 1965 about 40 percent of all American adults smoked cigarettes, and in the 1940s it is estimated that more than 50 percent did. By 1987, however, the proportion had declined substantially to roughly 29 percent, largely as a result of the publicity about the health risks of smoking. In 1992, according to the National Household Survey on Drug Abuse, approximately 26 percent smoked a cigarette within the past month, qualifying as regular smokers. Though this percentage is significantly less than it had been, we are still considering a very large number of people. Extrapolating to the entire adult U.S. population, a 26 percent prevalence rate corresponds to approximately 54 million people. Unfortunately, the steady decline in the percentage of American smokers stopped around 1991 and the prevalence rate has been inching upward since then. This reversal is largely due to the increasing numbers of smokers among young, white women.[40]

To look at prevalence rates among younger populations, we turn to the results of the 1993 University of Michigan survey. Among young adults age nineteen to thirty-two, the percentage of those who reported having smoked in the previous month was approximately the same as the overall population. In addition, about 21 percent of them had smoked on a daily basis and about 16 percent had smoked at least half a pack a day. Men and women were represented in virtually equal numbers, except for a slightly greater percentage of males who had smoked at least a half pack a day. Among high school seniors, about 19 percent had smoked on a daily basis and 11 percent had smoked at least half a pack a day. In this age group, there was a slightly greater percentage of boys who had smoked one or more cigarettes or at least a half pack a day.[41]

The youngest smokers

The University of Michigan survey also gives us an idea of the patterns of smoking among students at the junior high school level. In 1993 nearly half of eighth graders reported that they had tried cigarettes in their lifetime, and about 17 percent, approximately one in six, said that they had smoked at least once in the prior month. Approximately 8 percent of all eighth graders smoked on a daily basis, and 4 percent smoked at least a half pack a day. As with high school seniors, cigarette smokers in the eighth grade were more likely to be boys than girls.

The peak years for starting to smoke were reported to be in the sixth and seventh grade, but a large number said that they had started earlier. Nearly 30 percent reported that they had begun prior to the seventh grade, while more than 10 percent reported that they had started in the fourth grade.[42]

Cigarette smoking among minors is a continuing social problem.

Social differences and attitudes: Disturbing signs

Few other forms of drug-taking behavior show as great a difference in prevalence as a result of social and economic factors as does cigarette smoking. Whether we are considering high school seniors, young adults, or members of the general population, the likelihood of cigarette smoking decreases as the number of years of education goes up, the level of income goes up, or occupational status goes up. Among high school seniors, individuals who are not going to college are three times more likely to smoke half a pack a day or more than those who are college bound. High school dropouts are four times as likely to be smoking cigarettes daily than high school students who are graduating. Therefore, it is not surprising that there is a substantially lower rate of smoking among college students than among noncollege individuals of the same age.

There are also marked differences in prevalence rates among racial groups. In the late 1970s, white and African American high school seniors showed about the same level of smoking. Since then, the smoking rate among African American seniors has declined steadily, while the rates among white students have changed relatively little. As a result, the smoking rates for African

American seniors are about one fifth to one third those for whites. A striking difference is also seen in white and African American women between eighteen and twenty-four. Between 1987 and 1992, the percentage of smokers among African American women in this age group declined from 22 to 6, while the percentage among white women remained unchanged at about 27. Considering that risks of low-birth-weight infants and infant mortality are increased with cigarette smoking during pregnancy, the prevalence rate for white women during a significant portion of their reproductive years is of great concern.[43]

Perhaps the most discouraging aspect of statistics about smoking is not the prevalence rates but rather the relatively low percentage of people reporting that cigarette smoking presents a great risk to their health. The National Household survey showed that only 68 percent of individuals over the age of thirty-five thought that smoking one pack a day or more presented "great risk." In the University of Michigan survey, the percentage of high school seniors who thought the same way was about the same.

The percentage of eighth graders concerned with the health risks of smoking was substantially lower. Slightly more than one out of every two eighth graders (53 percent) considered smoking one pack a day to be presenting a great risk. This finding is particularly troubling, given the high potential for nicotine dependence, the consistent finding that most adult smokers began to smoke at this time in their lives, and the quantity of public information available on the risks of cigarette smoking.[44] Focus 12.3 will look at a current controversy over a popular youth-oriented cigarette advertising campaign and concerns about its impact on teenage smoking.

Use of smokeless tobacco

Smokeless tobacco is ingested, as the name implies, by absorption through the

The controversial Camel advertising campaign

Most of us know Joe Camel, the cartoon character featured since 1988 in the R. J. Reynolds Company's advertising campaign for Camel cigarettes. He's the symbol of cool in his leather jacket, astride a motorcycle or driving his race car, enjoying the glamorous life, a "smooth character with smooth moves." Evidently, young children know about him too. A study published in the *Journal of the American Medical Association* in 1991 showed that a majority of children as young as three to six were able to recognize Joe Camel and associate the character with cigarettes; by the age of six they were almost as familiar with Joe Camel as they were with the Mickey Mouse logo for the Disney Channel on cable TV.

The marketing statistics support the success of the Reynolds campaign in reaching young smokers. Between 1987 and 1990, illegal sales of Camel cigarettes to minors increased from $6 million to $476 million, and the market share for children went from less than 1 percent (seventh place) to about 33 percent (third place). In fact, illegal Camel sales accounted for about one fourth of all Camel sales in 1990. Concern about childhood nicotine addiction and its health consequences, and the knowledge that nearly all adult smokers start as teenagers purchasing cigarettes illegally, have led to a call by the surgeon general and the American Medical Association to discontinue the Joe Camel campaign, citing it as a threat to public health.

To these charges, the tobacco industry maintains that "no linkage has been made between advertising and the consumption of cigarette products." But the evidence supports the opposite view. A study of children age eleven to fourteen in Scotland found that those who were more aware of cigarette advertising were more likely to have positive attitudes toward smoking. They also were more likely to say a year later that they intended to start smoking. Another study with children of the same age in Fitchburg, Massachusetts, showed that those who smoked were three times more likely than their nonsmoking peers to believe that smoking would make them popular or attractive, though the two groups were equally aware of the health hazards. The young smokers were also less likely to believe that cigarette advertisements are deceptive.

Countercampaigns have begun to become popular as a way of controlling the appeal of cigarette advertising. One bumper sticker in California reads "Say no to Cancer Joe." The tobacco industry proclaims its innocence and cites the First Amendment regarding free speech. While the Federal Trade Commission, in charge of maintaining advertising standards in the United States, ruled in 1994 that the Joe Camel campaign could continue, the dust has not yet settled on the question of cigarette advertising and its impact on recruiting new generations of future smokers. Or, perhaps we should say, the smoke has not yet cleared.

SOURCES: Berkowitz Harry (1994, June 2). It's a go for Joe. *Newsday*, p. A3. Kong, Dolores (1992, April 27). Do ads lure youngsters to drink, smoke? *Boston Globe*, p. 41. Lane, Stuart M. (1993). *Marketing cigarettes to kids: A consumer guide to the harmful tactics of tobacco companies.* New York: American Council on Science and Health. Rustin, Terry A. (1993, winter). Death and disease for sale. *Priorities,* pp. 37–41.

Doonesbury

BY GARRY TRUDEAU

TABLE 12.1

Forms of smokeless tobacco

Type	Description
Chewing tobacco	
Loose-leaf	Made of cigar-leaf tobacco, sold in small packages, heavily flavored or plain
Fine-cut	Similar to loose-leaf but more finely cut so that it resembles snuff
Plug	Leaf tobacco pressed into flat cakes and sweetened with molasses, licorice, maple sugar or honey
Twist	Made of stemmed leaves twisted into small roles and then folded

(Chewing tobacco is not really chewed but rather held in the mouth between the cheek and lower jaw.)

Snuff	
Dry	
Moist	
Sweetened	
Flavored	
Salted	
Scented	

(A pinch of snuff, called a quid, is typically tucked between the gum and the lower lip. Moist varieties are currently the most popular.)

SOURCE: Adapted from Popescu, Cathy (1992). The health hazards of smokeless tobacco. In Kristine Napier (Ed.), *Issues in tobacco*. New York: American Council on Science and Health, pp. 11–12.

membranes of the mouth rather than by inhalation into the lungs (Table 12.1). The two most common forms are the traditional loose-leaf chewing tobacco (brand names include Red Man and Beech Nut) and moist, more finely shredded tobacco called **moist snuff** or simply snuff (brand names include Copenhagen and Skoal). Snuff, by the way, is no longer sniffed into the nose, as in the eighteenth century, but rather placed inside the cheek or alongside the gum under the lower lip. Some varieties of snuff are available in a small absorbent-paper sack (like a tea bag), so

moist snuff
Damp, finely shredded tobacco, typically placed against the gum under the lower lip.

that the tobacco particles do not get stuck in the teeth. The practice is called "dipping."

Since the 1970s, smokeless tobacco has enjoyed an increase in popularity, particularly among young people in the South and West. Prevalence rates for smokeless tobacco still distribute themselves along regional lines. In the 1993 University of Michigan survey, about 4 percent of high school seniors in the South and West reported using smokeless tobacco on a daily basis, approximately twice the rate of seniors in the Northeast. A similar difference was seen in terms of population density. Seniors living in rural communities had a prevalence rate approximately three times that of seniors living in large cities.

Currently, the form of smokeless tobacco showing the most consistent gains in recent sales is moist snuff, with some brands sold in cherry or wintergreen flavors. Variations in the alkalinity of different brands of moist snuff allow for different percentages of the nicotine in the tobacco to be absorbed through the membranes of the mouth. Thus, snuff users typically start with brands that release relatively low levels of nicotine, then "graduate" to more potent brands. The most potent brand on the current market, Copenhagen, is also the best-selling snuff in the United States, representing 42 percent of the total snuff market.[45]

Use of tobacco around the world

Tobacco smoking has never been limited to North America, but until recently much of that smoking has been independent of American tobacco companies. Today, the picture has changed; a few statistics illustrate this new relationship. Overall, U.S. cigarette exports in 1991 have increased about 200 percent since 1985. In two countries alone, the increase has been particularly dramatic. Cigarette exports have increased more than 700 percent to Japan, from 6.5 billion cigarettes in 1985 to 54 billion in 1991, and more than 1200 percent to South Korea, from 300 million cigarettes to 4 billion in 1991.

Yet we have to recognize that while the percentage of imported cigarettes into Asian countries has risen, the American presence represents only a relatively small percentage of total cigarette sales. The prevalence rate of smoking in these countries far exceeds that of the United States, coupled with substantially less public concern for the consequences of smoking on health. In Japan, for example, more than 60 percent of all adult men smoke cigarettes as do 44 percent of all doctors (Fig. 12.3). No-smoking sections in restaurants and offices are uncommon; approximately half a million outdoor vending machines allow minors to purchase cigarettes easily, though officially such sales are illegal, and there is little or no governmental opposition to smoking in general. While the Japanese currently enjoy the longest life expectancy in the world, health officials are concerned that this status is certain to change over the next twenty years. Deaths from lung, tracheal, and bronchial cancer among the Japanese have risen approximately 66 percent from 1930 to 1990, and there is no indication that this trend will moderate.[46]

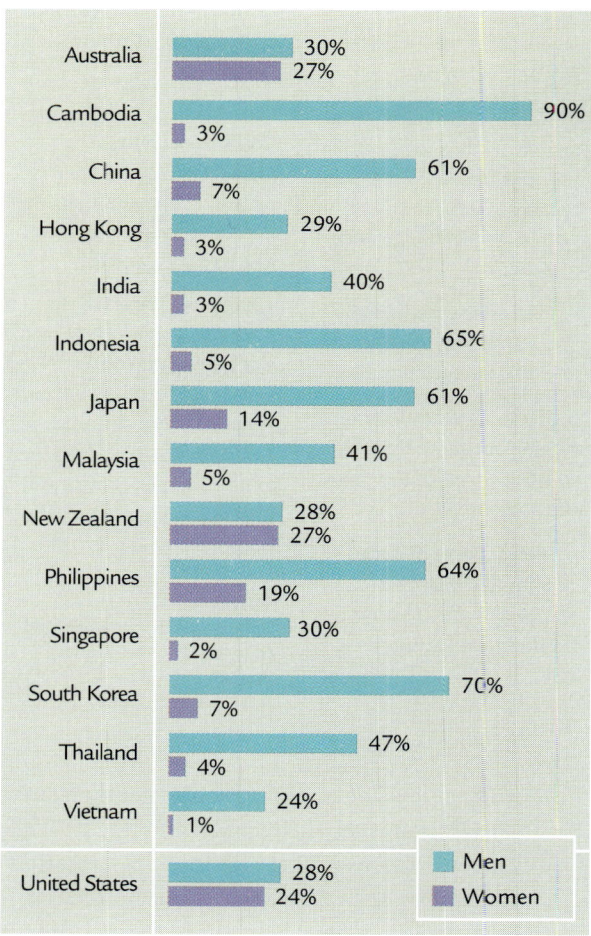

FIGURE 12.3

The percentage of smokers among men and women in the United States and fourteen other nations
SOURCE: *Copyright 1994 by the New York Times Company. Reprinted by permission.*

Quitting smoking: The good news and the bad

Given the grim story of all the documented health risks associated with tobacco, it is at least reassuring to know that if a smoker does succeed in quitting, some of the damage can be undone. The 1990 surgeon general's report issued five principal conclusions on smoking cessation:

1. When smokers quit smoking, there are major and immediate health benefits for men and women of all ages, and these benefits can be gained by people who have not yet developed any smoking-related disease and by people who have.

2. Former smokers live longer than continuing smokers, and the benefits of quitting extend to those who quit at older ages. For example, individuals who quit smoking before the age of fifty have half the risk of dying in the next fifteen years compared to continuing smokers. After ten to fifteen years of abstinence from smoking, the risk of dying from any cause returns nearly to that of individuals who have never smoked in their lives.

3. Smoking cessation reduces the risk of lung cancer, other cancers, coronary heart disease, stroke, and chronic lung disease. For lung cancer, the risk declines by 30 to 50 percent after ten years of abstinence; for coronary heart disease, the risk declines by 50 percent after one year of abstinence.

4. Women who stop smoking before pregnancy or during the first three to four months of pregnancy reduce their risk of have a low-birth-weight baby to that of women who never smoked.

5. The health benefits of smoking cessation far exceed any risks from an average five-pound weight gain or any other adverse psychological effects that may follow quitting.[47]

The bad news: How hard it is to quit

The advantages of quitting are there and most people are aware of them, but the fact remains that, in the words of the surgeon general's report in 1988, "The pharmacologic and behavioral processes that determine tobacco addiction are similar to those that determine addiction to drugs such as heroin and cocaine."[48] On the one hand, it may be easy to quit smoking for a short while but it is very difficult to avoid a relapse, as any former or present smoker will tell you. Approximately 80 percent of smokers who have initially succeeded in stopping smoking return to smoking over a twelve-month period.[49]

On the other hand, millions of people do manage to quit and remain abstinent from smoking for at least a year. From 1964 to 1987, the estimated number of Americans who have done so exceeds 38 million, nearly half of all living adults who have ever smoked in their lives. Figures are not available through the 1990s, but it is highly likely that the number presently exceeds 50 million. Research studies on smoking cessation indicate that there are no gender differences with regard to the likelihood that a person will quit smoking for one to four years, though men are more likely than women to have been abstinent for five years or more. African American smokers are in general less likely than white smokers to have been abstinent for one year or more, and those smokers with less education are not as successful as those with more education. The fact that a higher level of smoking is consistently related to a lower level of education and family income makes it vital that smoking-cessation programs be available to those who ordinarily would not be able to afford them. Unfortunately, smoking rates among people who did not complete high school have decreased more slowly since the 1970s than those among college graduates.[50]

F O C U S 12.4

Ten tips on how to succeed when trying to quit smoking

1. Choose a quit date and stick to it.

2. Remember that you are dependent, physiologically and psychologically, on nicotine and that the first few days without cigarettes will be the hardest.

3. Change the habits that are associated with smoking. If you have had a cigarette with your morning coffee, drink orange juice instead.

4. Tell all the people you know that you are quitting and ask for their support.

5. Drink lots of water and brush your teeth frequently to rid yourself of the taste of tobacco.

6. Never carry matches or a lighter with you. Put away your ashtrays or fill them with something else.

7. Spend time with people who don't smoke.

8. Keep a supply of sugarless gum, celery sticks, cinnamon sticks, or hard candy on hand to use as a cigarette substitute.

9. If you have an uncontrollable urge to light up, take ten deep breaths instead. Hold the last breath, then exhale slowly, and tell yourself you have just had a cigarette.

10. Think about all the money you are saving by not buying cigarettes. A simple calculation will convince you that the amount saved in five years from just a moderate level of smoking (say half a pack a day) is approximately $2,000.

SOURCE: American Cancer Society (1986). *Breaking free.* Atlanta: American Cancer Society, p. 9.

The options available to smokers who want to quit range from behaviorally oriented social support groups (Smokers Anonymous, SmokEnders, Smoke-Stoppers are some examples) to hypnosis, acupuncture, and nicotine-containing substitutes. The next section will focus on this last alternative.

Nicotine gums, patches, and sprays

Because nicotine is the agent that produces the dependence on cigarette smoking and other forms of tobacco use, it is logical to assume that an alternative ingestion route for nicotine, avoiding the simultaneous ingestion of carbon monoxide and tars, would be useful in helping people who want to quit smoking. The long-term goal would be to do without the nicotine all together and be totally free of any hazard associated with tobacco. Prescription chewing gums containing nicotine (brand name: Nicorette) have been available since the early 1970s and, when combined with behavioral counselling, have been a viable option for smokers seriously wanting to quit. More recently, transdermal nicotine patches (see Chapter 3) have become very popular as an alternative

route for nicotine, and nicotine sprays are presently under development.[51]

A final word on quitting

It should be emphasized, however, that approximately 90 percent of all smokers who quit do so on their own, without any professional or outside help, by simply going cold turkey and deciding to forgo all cigarettes in the future. Abrupt and total withdrawal from nicotine produces withdrawal symptoms that subside more quickly and are no worse than those experienced after a gradual withdrawal.[52] It is when these efforts have failed that alternative approaches need to be considered. Health professionals emphasize that if one treatment strategy does not work out, the smoker should try another. The long-term consequences of failure are just too great (Focus 12.4). The best option, of course, is never to have started in the first place, which brings us back to the teenage years when virtually all adult smokers begin. The issues of education and prevention in smoking, as well as in other forms of drug-taking behavior, will be discussed in Chapter 17.

Summary

TOBACCO THROUGH HISTORY

- Tobacco use originated among the original inhabitants of North and South America, and its introduction to Europe and the rest of the world dates from the first voyage of Columbus. Europeans used tobacco initially in the form of pipe smoking and later in the form of snuff.

- In the nineteenth-century United States, the most popular form was tobacco chewing and later cigar smoking. It was not until the late nineteenth century and early twentieth century that cigarette smoking became popular.

HEALTH CONCERNS AND SMOKING BEHAVIOR

- The 1964 surgeon general's report, which was the first official statement on the connection between smoking and adverse health consequences, produced a general reversal in the previously climbing per capita consumption of cigarettes.

- Since 1964 the surgeon general's reports have solidified the position that nicotine is a clearly addicting component of tobacco and that tobacco use, whether in a smoked or smokeless form, causes significant health risks.

- Since 1964 there has been a trend toward filtered, low-tar and low-nicotine cigarettes.

TOBACCO TODAY: AN INDUSTRY ON THE DEFENSIVE

- The tobacco industry is currently under considerable pressure by efforts to establish smoke-free environments.

- An additional pressure has come from proposals to increase the federal excise tax on tobacco products.

WHAT'S IN TOBACCO?

- The principal ingredients consumed during the smoking of tobacco are nicotine, tar, and carbon monoxide.

- The smoker inhales smoke in the form of mainstream smoke (through the cigarette itself) and sidestream smoke (released from the cigarette tip into the air).

THE DEPENDENCE POTENTIAL OF NICOTINE

- Nicotine ingestion produces both tolerance effects and physical withdrawal symptoms.

- Smokers adjust their smoking behavior to obtain a stable dose of nicotine.

HEALTH CONSEQUENCES FROM TOBACCO USE

- Tobacco smoking produces an increased risk of cardiovascular disease such as coronary heart disease and stroke, lung cancer and other forms of cancer, and respiratory diseases such as chronic bronchitis and emphysema.

- In addition to the hazards to the smoker through the inhalation of mainstream smoke, there are hazards to the developing fetus when the mother is smoking and hazards to nonsmokers who inhale sidestream smoke.

PATTERNS OF SMOKING BEHAVIOR AND USE OF SMOKELESS TOBACCO

- In the early 1990s the prevalence rate for smoking in the United States was approximately 26 percent.

- The peak years for smokers to start are in the sixth and seventh grades of school; by the time of graduation approximately 17 percent of high school seniors are smoking on a daily basis and 10 percent are smoking at least half a pack a day.

- A disturbingly low percentage of students think that cigarette smoking presents "great risk" to their health, despite well-publicized information regarding adverse affects.

- Equally discouraging is the global trend of increased smoking rates in Japan, South Korea, and other countries in Asia and elsewhere.

QUITTING SMOKING: THE GOOD NEWS AND THE BAD

- Research has clearly shown that when people quit smoking the health risks diminish rapidly. Unfortunately, nicotine dependence is very strong, and it is difficult to quit smoking permanently.

- Present-day approaches toward smoking cessation include behavioral treatment programs, hypnosis and acupuncture, and pharmacological approaches such as nicotine substitutes.

Key Terms

arteriosclerosis, p. 295
atherosclerosis, p. 295

carbon monoxide, p. 292
carcinomas, p. 297

Endnotes

1. Brooks, Jerome E. (1952). *The mighty leaf: Tobacco through the centuries.* Boston: Little, Brown, pp. 11–14.   Fairholt, Frederick W. (1859). *Tobacco: Its history and associations.* London: Chapman and Hill, p. 13.

2. Ibid., pp. 82–83, 121.   White, Jason M. (1991). *Drug dependence.* Englewood Cliffs NJ: Prentice Hall, pp. 32–33.

3. Austin, Gregory A. (1978). *Perspectives on the history of psychoactive substance use.* Rockville MD: National Institute on Drug Abuse, pp. 1–12.

4. Brooks. *The mighty leaf,* p. 181.   Lehman Brothers (1955). *About tobacco.* New York: Lehman Brothers, pp. 18–20.

5. Quotation from Dickens, Charles (1842). *American notes.* Cited in Brooks. *The mighty leaf,* pp. 215–216.

6. Tate, Cassandra (1989). In the 1800s, anti-smoking was a burning issue. *Smithsonian, 20* (4), p. 111.

7. Quotation originally in Bain, John, and Werner, Carl (1905). *Cigarettes in fact and fancy.* Boston: H. M. Caldwell. Cited in Brooks. *The mighty leaf,* p. 259.

8. Slade, John (1992). The tobacco epidemic: Lessons from history. *Journal of Psychoactive Drugs, 24,* 99–109.

9. Lehman Brothers. *About tobacco,* pp. 24–27.

10. Ibid., p. 30.

11. Ibid., p. 31.

12. U.S. Department of Health and Human Services (1991). *Strategies to control tobacco use in the United States: A blueprint for public health action in the 1990s* (NIH Smoking and Tobacco Control Monograph No. 1). Bethesda MD: National Cancer Institute.

13. Federal Trade Commission Report to Congress (1992). Pursuant to the Federal Cigarette Labeling and Advertising Act, p. 31.

14. Short, J. Gordon (1990, fall). The golden leaf. *Priorities,* p. 10.

15. Gerstein, Dean R., and Levison, Peter K. (Eds.) (1982). *Reduced tar and nicotine cigarettes: Smoking behavior and health.* Washington DC: National Academy Press.   Mann, Charles K. (1975). *Tobacco: The ant and the elephants.* Salt Lake City UT: Olympus Publishing, pp. 91–109.

16. Hilts, Philip J. (1994, November 27). Little smoke, little tar, but full dose of nicotine. *New York Times,* pp. 1, 38.   Manegold, Catherine S. (1994, March 22). Becoming a land of the smoke-free, ban by ban. *New York Times,* pp. A1, A16.   Mostly smoke (1994, July 4). *Newsweek,* p. 45.   Nowak, Rachel (1994). Regulatory policy: Nicotine scrutinized as FDA seeks to regulate cigarettes. *Science, 263,* 1555–1556.   Should cigarettes be outlawed? (1994, April 18). *Newsweek,* pp. 32–38.

17. Cowley, Geoffrey, and Hager, Mary (1994, March 28). Taxes as an antidote to addiction. *Newsweek,* pp. 26–27.

18. Food, beverages, and tobacco, current analysis. (1993, December 2). *Standard and Poor's Industry Surveys* Vol. 161, No. 48, pp. F5-F7.

19. Payne, Wayne A., and Hahn, Dale B. (1992). *Understanding your health.* St. Louis: Mosby Year Book, p. 270.

20. Schlaadt, Richard G. (1992). *Tobacco and health.* Guilford CT: Dushkin Publishing, p. 41.

21. Gahagan, Dolly D. (1987). *Switch down and quit: What the cigarette companies don't want you to know about smoking.* Berkeley CA: Ten Speed Press, p. 44.   Payne and Hahn. *Understanding your health,* pp. 273–275.   Terry, Luther L., and Horn, Daniel. *To smoke or not to smoke.* New York: Lothrop, Lee, and Shepard, p. 24.

22. Jacobs, Michael R., and Fehr, Kevin O'B. (1987). *Drugs and drug abuse: A reference text* (2nd ed.). Toronto: Addiction Research Foundation, pp. 417–425.   Julien, Robert M. (1995). *A primer of drug action* (7th ed.). New York: Freeman, pp. 166–168.

23. American Lung Association (1989). *Facts about . . . nicotine addiction and cigarettes.* New York: American Lung Association.   Julien. *A primer of drug action,* p. 168–169.   Schuckit, Marc A. (1989). *Drug and alcohol abuse: A clinical guide to diagnosis and treatment* (3rd ed.). New York: Plenum, p. 217.   Wesnes, K., and Warburton, D. M. (1983). Smoking, nicotine, and human performance. *Pharmacological Therapy, 21,* 189–208.

24. Brecher, Edward M., and the editors of Consumer Reports (1972). *Licit and illicit drugs.* Boston: Little, Brown, pp. 220–228.

25. Lichtenstein, Edward, and Brown, Richard A. (1980). Smoking cessation methods: Review and recommendations. In William R. Miller (Ed.), *The addictive behaviors: Treatment of alcoholism, drug abuse, smoking, and obesity.* New York: Pergamon Press, pp. 169–206.

26. Ibid., pp. 172–173.

27. Herning, Ronald I., Jones, Reese T., and Fischman, Patricio (1985). The titration hypothesis revisited: Nicotine gum reduces smoking intensity. In John Grabowski and Sharon M. Hall (Eds.), *Pharmacological adjuncts in smoking cessation* (NIDA Research Monograph 53). Rockville MD: National Institute on Drug Abuse, pp. 27–41.   Jarvik, Murray E. (1979). Biological influences on cigarette smoking. In Norman A. Krasnegor (Ed.), *The behavioral aspects of smoking* (NIDA Research Monograph 26). Rockville MD: National Institute on Drug Abuse, pp. 7–45.

28. Ibid., pp. 25–29.   Schuckit. *Drug and alcohol abuse,* pp. 217–221.

29. Koslowski, Lynn T., Wilkinson, Adrian, Skinner, Wayne, Kent, Carl, Franklin, Tom, and Pope, Marilyn. (1989). Comparing tobacco cigarette dependence with other drug dependencies. *Journal of the American Medical Association, 261,* 898–901.

30. Substance abuse toll (1993, October 22). *Newsday,* p. 17.   Roper, W. L. (1991). Making smoking prevention a reality. *Journal of the American Medical Association, 266,* 3188–3189.

31. U.S. Department of Health and Human Services, Public Health Service, Office of Smoking and Health (1983). *The health consequences of smoking: Cardiovascular disease* (A report of the surgeon general) Rockville MD: U.S. Public Health Service, pp. 63–156.

32. Payne and Hahn. *Understanding your health,* pp. 272–273.

33. Schlaadt. *Tobacco and health,* p. 52.

34. U.S. Department of Health and Human Services, Public Health Service, Office of Smoking and Health (1984). *The health consequences of smoking: Chronic obstructive lung disease* (A report of the surgeon general). Rockville MD: U.S. Public Health Service, pp. 329–360.

35. Carroll, Charles R. (1993). *Drugs in modern society* (3rd ed.). Dubuque IA: Brown and Benchmark, pp. 253–255.

36. Schuckit. *Drug and alcohol abuse,* p. 222.

37. U.S. Department of Health and Human Services, Public Health Service, Office of Smoking and Health (1980). *The health consequences of smoking for women* (A report of the surgeon general). Rockville MD: U.S. Public Health Service, pp. 98–101

38. Fielding, Jonathan E., and Phenow, Kenneth J. (1989). Health effects of involuntary smoking. Atlanta: American Cancer Society, pp. 2   Ginzel, K. H. (1992). The ill-effects of second hand smoke. In Kristine Napier (Ed.), *Issues*

in tobacco. New York: American Council on Science and Health, pp. 6–7.   Public Citizen Health Research Group (1987, May). Warning: Cigarettes may give you cancer even if you don't smoke. *Health Letter,* 3 (5), p. 9.

39. American Cancer Society (1987). *The smoke around you: The risks of involuntary smoking.* Atlanta: American Cancer Society.   "Secondhand smoke, is it a hazard? The tobacco merchants claim there's still a controversy. We don't buy it." *Consumer Reports* (1995, January), pp. 27–33.

40. Substance Abuse and Mental Health Services Administration (1993). *National household survey on drug abuse: Population estimates 1992.* Rockville MD: Substance Abuse and Mental Health Services Administration, Office of Applied Studies, Table 14A.

41. Johnston, Lloyd D., O'Malley, Patrick M., and Bachman, Jerald G. (1994). *National survey results on drug use from the Monitoring the Future study, 1975–1993.* Vol. 1. Rockville MD: National Institute on Drug Abuse, Tables 1 and 9.   Ibid. Vol. 2, Table 6.

42. Ibid. Vol. 1, Tables 1, 9, and 18a.

43. Cigarette smoking among women of reproductive age—United States, 1987–1992 (1994). *Journal of the American Medical Association, 272,* 1649–1650.   Johnston, O'Malley, and Bachman. *National survey results.* Vol. 1, Table 10.   U.S. Department of Health and Human Services, Public Health Service (1993, April 2). Cigarette smoking among adults—United States, 1991. *Morbidity and mortality weekly report,* 230–233.   Wynder, Ernst L. (1993). Toward a smoke-free society: Opportunities and obstacles. *American Journal of Public Health, 83,* 1204–1205.

44. Johnston, O'Malley, and Bachman. *National survey results.* Vol. 1, Table 19.   U.S. Department of Health and Human Services. *Cigarette smoking among adults,* p. 144.

45. Freedman, Alix M. How a tobacco giant doctors snuff brands to boost their "kick." (1994, October 26). *Wall Street Journal,* pp. A1, A14.   Industry confronts legal and social challenges (1993, August 28). *Standard and Poor's Industry surveys,* p. F33.   Johnston, O'Malley,

and Bachman. *National survey results.* Vol. 1, Table 9.

46. American Cancer Society (1993). *Cancer facts and figures 1993.* Atlanta: American Cancer Society, p. 22.   Sterngold, James (1993, October 17). When smoking is a patriotic duty. *New York Times,* Sect 3, pp. 1, 6.

47. U.S. Department of Health and Human Services, Public Health Service, Office of Smoking and Health (1990). *The health benefits of smoking cessation* (A report of the surgeon general). Atlanta: Office of Smoking and Health, p. 8.

48. U.S. Department of Health and Human Services, Public Health Service, Office of Smoking and Health (1988). *The health consequences of smoking: Nicotine addiction* (A report of the surgeon general). Rockville MD: Public Health Service, p. 9.

49. Carmody, Timothy P. (1992). Preventing relapse in the treatment of nicotine addiction: Current issues and future directions. *Journal of Psychoactive Drugs, 24,* 131–158.

50. U.S. Department of Health and Human Services. *The health benefits of smoking cessation,* pp. 610–611.   Ehrich, Beverly and Emmons, Karen M. (1994). Addressing the needs of smokers in the 1990s. *The Behavior Therapist, 17* (6), 119–122.

51. Hall, Sharon M., and Killen, Joel D. (1985). Pharmacological and psychological approaches to smoking relapse prevention. In John Grabowski and Sharon M. Hall (Eds.), *Pharmacological adjuncts in smoking cessation* (NIDA Research Monograph No. 53) Rockville MD: National Institute on Drug Abuse, pp. 131–143.   Russell, M. A. H., and Jarvis, M. J. (1985). Theoretical background and clinical use of nicotine chewing gum. In John Grabowski and Sharon M. Hall (Eds.), *Pharmacological adjuncts in smoking cessation* (NIDA Research Monograph No. 53). Rockville MD: National Institute on Drug Abuse, pp. 110–130.   Waite, Teresa (1992, August 25). Nicotine spray may help heavy smokers quit. *New York Times,* p. C3.

52. Jarvik. Biological influences, p. 32.

Debate has been suspended, this time

rdinarily, this feature has highlighted a controversial issue and presented a debate based on opposing viewpoints. On the question of the advisability of tobacco smoking, however, this author believes there is no debate. So instead, the following editorial is presented, eloquently expressed by Dr. Elizabeth M. Whelan, president of the American Council on Science and Health. It appeared as a newspaper column on January 11, 1994, thirty years to the day after the first surgeon general's report on smoking and health.

SMOKING AND HEALTH: THREE DECADES LATER

Today marks the 30th anniversary of the release of the first surgeon general's report linking cigarette smoking and disease. Yet, a quarter of the American population still smokes cigarettes regularly, and people are still dying at a rate of a half million a year from cigarette-induced causes.

Our current policies to curb smoking simply are not working.

It's time to remove the warning label from cigarette packs.

I know that sounds odd. But the warning label has not only done nothing to discourage smoking, but it has provided extraordinary legal protection for the tobacco industry.

During the mid-1980s, when the hazards of smoking finally became undeniable to policy makers—nearly 30 years after the scientific community had reached consensus on the issue—public health activists and the tobacco industry both lobbied Congress for warning labels. Health advocates thought they were "doing good."

The industry acted to ensure survival. First, because as more states proposed different warning labels, the chaos in interstate commerce loomed as a nightmare. Better to have a single standard label, they reasoned. Second, because by agreeing to the labels, they were buying immunity from the lawsuits that would be brought by the families of people who

became ill and died from smoking cigarettes.

In other words, as a direct result of the 1965 congressionally mandated "health" label (which was extended to include advertisements in 1969), the industry was given a Teflon coating protecting it from liability claims. As a result, the cigarette industry has never paid a cent in liability damages.

Indeed, in 1992 the Supreme Court agreed that the government warning label pre-empted lawsuits—although it did leave a window open if an industry disinformation conspiracy could be established.

The threat of litigation is a clear and powerful incentive for an industry to keep its products safe—or to be very, very specific about the dangers associated with their use. However, given their litigation shield, cigarette manufacturers have no incentive to be honest about the consequences of smoking. Thus, despite 60,000 medical citations to the contrary, the industry spokesmen continue to maintain that there is no evidence that smoking adversely affects health. Tobacco companies spend $4 billion annually promoting cigarettes as healthy, invigorating and part of the good life, a clear distortion of the grim medical realities. And only an industry that perceives itself as immune from lawsuits would have the gall to offer "free" designer clothing in return for proof of purchase of 975 packs of cigarettes in six

months—more than five packs a day.

Advocates for tobacco control frequently contend that the solution to our nation's pandemic of cigarette-related diseases is more government intervention: a ban on advertising, a hike in the excise tax and restrictions on smoking in public places. Recently, five U.S. representatives have, with the endorsement of President Bill Clinton, proposed legislation that would strengthen the warning label to include "Smoking can kill you."

But the solution lies in the opposite direction. If government had not meddled in the first place, cigarette companies would conduct business on the same legal turf as every other industry. They would have been sued by smokers made ill by their deadly products and by the loved ones of people who had died from their use. The industry would have paid, and paid big, because it markets an inherently hazardous product without full disclosure.

So Congress should repeal the Cigarette Labeling Act of 1965 and abolish the label entirely. This would leave the cigarette manufacturer at the mercy of free-market forces and an unfettered judicial system. It may well turn the white cylinder into an anachronism, because it would be too expensive to buy and too unprofitable to produce.

Reprinted with permission of Dr. Elizabeth M. Whelan.

13

Caffeine

f you enjoy a cup of caffeinated coffee or caffeinated tea, a wedge of chocolate, or a glass of some cola drink, you may be surprised to know that you are engaging in the most popular form of drug-taking behavior in the world. To varying degrees, all these products contain caffeine, a psychoactive stimulant drug. It should be added, however, that you need not be overly concerned. Among the range of psychoactive stimulants that exist (the major ones were examined in Chapters 4 and 12), caffeine is considerably weaker and the research shows that it is relatively benign. Nonetheless, as will be shown, caffeine is a dependence-producing drug, and there are precautions against its use that should be heeded.

Caffeine is an example of a family of stimulant drugs called **xanthines.** Two other major xanthine compounds, **theobromine** (found in chocolate) and **theophylline** (found in small amounts in tea), also have stimulating effects. In general, theophylline and caffeine have approximately equal stimulatory effects, and theobromine is only about one-tenth as strong. The focus of this chapter will be on what we know about caffeine itself, beginning with a look at three natural sources of caffeine: coffee, tea, and chocolate.

Coffee

e do not know just when coffee drinking began, but we do know that the plant ***Coffea arabica,*** from which coffee beans were first harvested, originated in Ethiopia, and its cultivation spread to Yemen and Arabia at some time between the eleventh and the fifteenth century. Coffee has been called "the wine of

> Hail, hail, hail to thee coffee
> Hail, hail best of blisses
> Ah coffee, ah sweet coffee
> Coffee, if my Pa would please me
> Only coffee will appease me.
>
> from the satirical *Coffee Cantata*
> by Johann Sebastian Bach (1732)

> There are few hours in life more agreeable than the hour dedicated to the ceremony known as afternoon tea.
>
> Henry James
> *Portrait of a Lady* (1881)

Islam," suggesting that it was viewed as a substitute for wine, which had been forbidden by the Koran. One legend concerning the beginnings of coffee drinking has it that a young Yemenite or Ethiopian goatherd named Khaldi, while tending his flock, noticed that his goats were unusually hyperactive and unable to sleep after nibbling some red berries in the field. Khaldi tried some himself and, on feeling as exhilarated as his goats, took the berries to the local Islamic monastery. The chief holy man there prepared a beverage from these berries and found the effect to be so invigorating that he was able to keep awake during a long night of prayers in the mosque. According to this legend, the fame of the "wakeful monastery" and the reason for it spread through the whole kingdom and to other countries of the region.[1]

At first, coffee was banned on religious grounds because some Islamic clerics considered it to be as much an intoxicant as wine, but the disputes were eventually settled and coffee drinking became a fixture of daily life. In the words of one historian, "The growth of coffee and its use as a national beverage became as inseparably connected with Arabia as tea is with China."[2]

Coffee in Britain and North America

The practice of coffee drinking reached England in the seventeenth century, just in time for one of the most turbulent periods of political, social, economic, and religious unrest in its history. Establishments specializing in the sale of coffee, known as coffee houses, became the sites of heated debates about the great issues of the day. The idea of constitutional self-government, the divine right of the king to rule his country, and religious tolerance between English Catholics and Protestants were some of these social questions.

Coffee houses were the places where the intellectuals met and argued their respective points of view. Until the end of the eighteenth century, when tea began to replace coffee as

the dominant British drink, coffee was the principal alternative social beverage to alcohol. The British coffee house enjoyed the reputation of being a place where men (women rarely frequented them, though they often managed them) could socialize with one another and enjoy a nonintoxicating beverage while keeping a clear head. The emphasis was on keeping a clear head, which was certainly not likely after an hour at the local tavern. In fact, historians have credited coffee houses with helping to moderate the widespread drunkenness that was going on as a result of the "gin epidemic" in England during the 1700s (see Chapter 10). A popular nickname for coffee houses was penny universities, since the conversation there was considered to be as stimulating as a university education and a lot cheaper.[3]

Coffee houses in colonial America served a similar purpose. One such political gathering place, the Green Dragon in Boston, was the setting for the meetings of John Adams, Paul Revere, and their compatriots as they planned their strategy against the British. After the Revolutionary War, coffee emerged as the American national drink, especially after 1830 when alcohol consumption began to decline (Chapter 10). During the settling of the American frontier, coffee was an important part of the provisions necessary for the long trek

---

caffeine
A xanthine stimulant found in coffee, tea, chocolate, cola drinks, and several medications.

xanthines (ZAN-theens)
A family of CNS stimulant drugs that includes caffeine, theophylline, and theobromine.

theobromine (THEE-oh-BROH-meen)
A xanthine stimulant found in chocolate.

theophylline (THEE-oho-FILL-lin)
A xanthine stimulant found in small amounts in tea. It is used as an anti-asthma medication.

Coffea arabica
A type of coffee bean native to the Middle East but now grown principally in South America.

westward. By 1860, Americans were consuming three fourths of the world's entire production of coffee.

Today, the United States remains the top importer of coffee among countries in the world, though U.S. per capita coffee consumption ranks only in the top ten, behind most countries in Western Europe and Scandinavia. Two thirds of the total U.S. coffee bean imports come from five nations (in descending order of dominance): Brazil, Colombia, Mexico, Guatemala, and El Salvador. Since roughly 1960, however, coffee consumption has gradually declined as American drinking habits have shifted to an increased consumption of colas, particularly among young adults. Overall, cola drinks are coming close to surpassing coffee as the country's primary source of caffeine.[4]

Expert coffee tasters in a German coffee company sample the possibilities before deciding on a particular blend.

Major sources of coffee

Two species of coffee beans dominate the world market. *Coffea arabica,* the original coffee bean as far as Westerners are concerned, is grown mostly in Brazil and Colombia, having been brought to South America by the French in the early 1700s. Another major species, **Coffea robusta,** is grown primarily in formerly Dutch plantations in the Indonesian island of Java (hence, the popular phrase "a cup of Java" for a drink of coffee); some of it is also produced in Brazil and the Ivory Coast and other countries in Africa.

Coffee blends are generally combinations of these two types of beans, with the ratio dictated by local tastes. Robusta beans are considered by coffee experts to be inferior to arabica beans because of their relatively harsher taste, but robusta beans have approximately twice the caffeine content and are cheaper to buy. Pure arabica beans are too expensive to be used exclusively for commercial brands of coffee.

Coffea robusta
A type of coffee bean grown principally in Indonesia, South America, and Africa.

How coffee is made

The preparation of today's coffee begins by separating the coffee bean from the ripened berry of the coffee plant, which is accomplished in two basic ways. The dry method is a variation of the most ancient and primitive tradition; freshly picked berries are spread out to dry in the sun for two to three weeks or dried in special heating machines. Afterward, the dried husks are removed mechanically or by hand to yield green coffee beans. Brazilian arabica beans are prepared by the dry method, as are almost all robusta beans. According to the wet method, coffee berries are soaked in water for about twenty-four hours, later washed and then dried in the sun. All arabica beans, except for those grown in Brazil, are prepared by the wet method.

Which of the two methods yields better-tasting coffee is frequently debated among coffee lovers, but no one questions the fact that more can go wrong with the dry method. When the berries are dried immediately after picking, the whole process takes much longer;

there is a chance, for example, that a few rotting berries can impart a foul taste to other berries and ruin the crop. It is less expensive, however, and is tailored to the conditions of a less industrialized nation.

Whether it is prepared wet or dry, the result is a green coffee bean, with a shelf life of a year or more. Assuming these beans are not to be decaffeinated, the next step is roasting, where the beans are heated to approximately 400 to 500 degrees Fahrenheit for five minutes or so. The longer the roasting time, the darker the roasted bean and the stronger the flavor once the beans are ground. According to coffee experts, roasted coffee beans reach the peak of flavor from twenty-four to seventy-two hours after roasting, depending on the variety of bean. After a week or two, roasted beans are no longer considered fresh. It is important to grind and consume the coffee, they say, within a week for optimal results.[5] These guidelines apply, of course, to coffee from beans that are sold by specialty stores; most U.S. consumers buy their coffee in vacuum-packed cans that prolong the freshness.

Instant coffee, a form of coffee that represents about a third of total U.S. coffee consumption, is made either by the spray-dried method, in which brewed coffee is dried by hot air, or by the freeze-dried method, in which brewed coffee is frozen and the water separates itself from the solids in the coffee upon freezing. These solids are later granulated or converted into flakes. The freeze-dried method is the more expensive of the two, but the consensus is that it yields a better-tasting instant coffee.[6]

The caffeine content in coffee

A caffeine content in a "standard" five-ounce cup of coffee can range from about 29 to 176 milligrams (mg) depending on the method of brewing, the amount of coffee used, the brand of coffee, and the brewing time. Roughly speaking, the caffeine content in coffee can be estimated to be

about 100 mg. Comparable amounts of instant coffee have about 60 mg of caffeine, percolated coffee has about 85 mg, and drip-brewed coffee has about 112 mg. Caffeine is the only xanthine found in coffee (Focus 13.1).[7]

Tea

y the standard of historical records, tea is the world's oldest caffeine-containing beverage. The legendary Chinese emperor Shen Nung is credited with its discovery in 2737 B.C., along with other stimulants such as the antiasthma medication we now know as ephedrine (Chapter 4) and marijuana (Chapter 9). Tea is a brew of leaves from the ***Camellia sinensis*** (tea plant), a large evergreen tree that is typically trimmed back to look more like a bush. The word *sinensis* refers to its origin in China.[8]

Dutch traders brought tea from Asia to Western Europe in the early 1600s, where it met with mixed reviews. The Germans tried tea drinking for a while but then returned to beer; the French also tried it but then returned to coffee and wine. The Chinese traded directly with the Russians, who loved it and made tea drinking a national pastime, sipping hot tea from glasses through a sugar cube held between the teeth. Giant tea urns, called samovars, kept tea available for drinking throughout the day.

Tea in Britain and North America

The principal Dutch success with tea in Europe was in Britain, where it eventually became the national drink. Chinese tea, as noted in Chapter 7, was in such great demand by the British that the Chinese were forced to trade their tea in exchange for opium imported by the British into their own country. By 1842, the problems with such an arrangement escalated into the Opium War, pitting China against Britain and later France and the United States.

By the end of the nineteenth century, however, China was no longer the principal source for British tea. Tastes had changed, away from the subtle flavor of Chinese green tea leaves and toward a stronger, blacker tea that was being grown in India and Ceylon (now Sri Lanka). It also did not hurt that a greater number of cups could be made from a pound of Indian or Ceylonese tea, making it more economical for the average consumer. Today's teas are blends of black tea leaves, chiefly from India, Sri Lanka, and Indonesia, though there is a growing market for tea from China and Kenya.[9]

We do not know whether the gentlemen at the Green Dragon coffee house in Boston were drinking coffee or tea during the months of growing unrest and resentment against the British prior to the beginning of the Revolutionary War, but it is quite likely that many of the conversations were about tea. In 1773 the British government had decided to allow British agents to sell cheap tea directly to the American colonies, bypassing American tea merchants in the process. It was, in the eyes of the Americans, another instance of British insensitivity and one more reason why the colonies should be independent.

We do know what happened next. On the night of December 16, 1773, while three British ships loaded with chests of British tea lay at anchor in Boston harbor, fifty to sixty colonists, supposedly dressed up as Indians (this part is disputed), boarded the vessels and proceeded to break open the tea chests and dump the contents into the water. Thus, the "Boston tea party." Strangely enough, the initial reaction to this event in British newspapers did not focus on the political ramifications but rather on the pharmacological effect of the tea on the unfortunate fish in Boston harbor. One report said that the fish "had contracted a disorder not unlike the nervous complaints of the body." Assuming this story is true, we can only

An engraving depicting American colonists at the Boston Tea Party, 1773.

Camellia sinensis
The plant from which tea leaves are obtained.

conclude that all that tea had given the fish a large dose of caffeine.[10]

Largely as a result of continuing anti-British sentiment during the early history of the United States, drinking tea was viewed as unpatriotic, and coffee became the preferred beverage. Today, American consumption of tea is only approximately one eighth that of Great Britain and Ireland, who lead the world as you might suspect in per capita tea drinking. More than 80 percent of all tea consumed in the United States is in the form of iced tea, a beverage that was introduced at the Louisiana Purchase Exposition in St. Louis in the summer of 1904.

The xanthine content in tea

Tea contains two xanthines, caffeine and theophylline. The caffeine content of a five-ounce cup of tea is approximately 60 mg, the same level as a comparable cup of instant coffee. This comparison, however, applies to a medium brew of tea. If the tea is a strong brew, the caffeine content approaches that of regular coffee, especially if the tea is produced in Britain rather than the United States. A strong brew of Twining's English Breakfast tea, for example, contains approximately 107 mg of caffeine, a larger dose than many regular brewed coffees and certainly greater than instant coffee.[11]

The other xanthine found in tea, theophylline, is found in much smaller concentrations than those of caffeine. As will be noted later, its bronchodilating effect is clinically useful for the treatment of asthma and other respiratory problems.

Chocolate

Chocolate comes from **cocoa bean pods** growing directly on the trunk and thick main branches of cacao trees. Cacao trees are native to Mexico and Central America, but now they are grown in tropical regions of the Caribbean, South America, Africa, and Asia.

In 1992 the leading exporters of cocoa beans to the United States were Indonesia, Ivory Coast, Brazil, Dominican Republic, and Malaysia, in that order.[12]

According to a popular legend, chocolate was a gift from the Aztec god Quetzalcoatl to give humans a taste of paradise. At the time of Hernando Cortés's expedition to Mexico in 1519, chocolate (*xocoatl* or *cuocolatl* as the Aztecs called it) was a prized beverage, to be enjoyed only by the rulers and the upper classes of society. The Aztec emperor Montezuma II drank a cocoa-derived mixture flavored with spices and presumably liked it so much that he consumed fifty cups daily. But it was very different from the chocolate we know today. The original version was a cold, thick, frothy, souplike concoction that was eaten with a spoon. Most significant, it was bitter in taste because the Aztecs had no knowledge of sugarcane and therefore no way to sweeten it. Nonetheless, Cortés took some cocoa bean pods back to Spain in 1528.

Once he was home, Cortés prepared chocolate as he had learned it from the Aztecs. First, the cocoa beans were removed from inside the pods and spread in the sun to dry. Then they were roasted over a fire and ground into a paste. When mixed with water, the beans became a beverage. The Spanish emperor Charles V enjoyed the result especially when it was sweetened with sugar. As a result, chocolate, called *molinet* by the Spaniards, began to be enjoyed by the royal court. Meanwhile, back in the New World, Spanish colonization in the Caribbean resulted in the establishment of cacao tree plantations and new sources of supply for chocolate.

The Spanish were able to keep chocolate a closely guarded secret and chocolate consumption to themselves until the beginning of

cocoa bean pods
(COH-coh, as opposed to coca,
which is the source of cocaine)
Parts of the cacao tree that are the raw material for cocoa and chocolate.

the 1600s. Inevitably, word leaked out to the royal courts of Europe that the Spanish were enjoying an exotic new drink that had come from the New World. Realizing that it was futile to keep chocolate to themselves forever, the Spanish decided to let it go public with a highly visible event: a royal wedding. When the fourteen-year-old Spanish princess arrived in Paris to marry the fourteen-year-old Louis XIII of France in 1615, she carried with her a betrothal gift of Spanish chocolate. It was the beginning of the tradition of chocolate as connected with romance. Later, in 1660, a similar betrothal gift at the wedding of another Spanish princess and Louis XIV of France sealed its fate as the gift of love. It also has not hurt chocolate's image that the eighteenth-century Italian lover Casanova credited his habit of drinking chocolate each morning with his considerable sexual prowess.

Chocolate took its place in England not so much as a symbol of romance but as simply another good-tasting beverage that could be sold in the growing number of coffee houses in English cities. From the beginning, chocolate was sold in shops rather than hidden away behind palace walls. It was not cheap, but at least it was available to all who could afford to buy it. By 1700, the specialty chocolate house rivaled the coffee house as the place to gather and talk about the events of the day.

How chocolate is made

From the days of pre-Columbian America to the early part of the nineteenth century, the method for preparing chocolate did not fun-

damentally change, except for the addition of such ingredients as sugar. In 1828, however, something did change. To appreciate what transpired, it is important to know, first of all, the nature of chocolate itself and the ways it can be processed.

Once cocoa beans are roasted, they can be heated in a machine to such temperatures that the natural fat within the beans, called **cocoa butter,** melts. The result is a deep-colored chocolaty-smelling paste called **chocolate liquor.** When it later cools and hardens, the paste is often called **baking chocolate.** As chocolate, it is as pure as you can get, but since it has an "extrabittersweet" flavor, it is not yet good enough to eat. The real innovation in chocolate processing came in 1828, when a Dutch chemist, Coenraad van Houten, invented a screw press to squeeze the cocoa butter out of the hardened chocolate liquor. If you saw pure cocoa butter, it would be white in color; in fact, "white chocolate" is essentially pure cocoa butter with added ingredients. What is left after the cocoa butter has been removed from the chocolate liquor is a dry, dark-colored, cake-like substance that can be crushed into a powder. This powder can be mixed with sugar and other flavorings and hot milk or water can be added to make cocoa.

To make chocolate as we know it, we have to take several additional processing steps, many of which were developed by the Swiss chocolatier Rodolphe Lindt in 1879. A ratio of cocoa liquor and cocoa butter is combined with milk, sugar, and vanilla to make milk chocolate. Just how much cocoa butter is added depends on the type of chocolate that is wanted—the more cocoa butter, the sweeter the result. Fortunately, unlike other fats, cocoa butter almost never goes rancid. In other words, milk chocolate keeps. It might turn white after a while, but that simply means that the cocoa butter is starting to separate from the mixture. It is all right to eat, though chocolate connoisseurs will surely disagree. All that is needed to produce commercial chocolate is to refine the texture to

cocoa butter
The fat content of the cocoa bean.

chocolate liquor (lih-KOOR)
A deep-colored paste made when roasted cocoa beans are heated so that the cocoa butter in the beans melts.

baking chocolate
A hardened paste, consisting of chocolate liquor, produced by heating roasted cocoa beans.

Milton S. Hershey and the town built on chocolate

When Milton Hershey made a decision in 1893 to go into the chocolate business, he was already an experienced confectioner with a prosperous caramel company in Lancaster, Pennsylvania, to his credit. But he could see that the future was in chocolate. Imports of cocoa beans into the United States had grown from 9 million pounds to 24 million pounds in the previous decade; new German-built machinery was now available to mass-produce milk chocolate. Hershey wanted to be in the business on the ground floor.

He bought the equipment and started to experiment on a special recipe, using fresh milk from the local dairy farms instead of powdered milk. The proportion of milk and sugar, the blend of cocoa beans, and the roasting time are secrets to this day. All we know is that somehow Hershey figured out a recipe that was a winner. The new Hershey bar was an instant hit, and in the process Hershey had another salable product as well. Just as cocoa makers end up with leftover cocoa butter, chocolate makers who extract cocoa butter for the chocolate end up with leftover cocoa. Hence, Hershey's cocoa.

By 1903, the Hershey chocolate business had been so successful that it needed a new factory. With the application of mass-production technology to chocolate making, Hershey was able to manufacture his products in such volume that the Hershey bar became affordable enough for every man, woman, and child in the country. Defying conventional wisdom, however, Hershey did not look for a town or city for the factory but rather went into the surrounding countryside. He bought a thousand acres of prime Pennsylvania Dutch farmland, built his factory, then decided to build a town around it.

By 1930, the town of Hershey had grown to include residents beyond the six thousand factory workers. The Hershey business was now worldwide, with its chocolate kisses and chocolate syrup in addition to other products. During hard economic times, Hershey would say with pride, "No man in Hershey was dropped by reason of the Depression. And no salaries were cut." In order to maintain employment, Hershey went on a construction spree. He built the famous Hershey Hotel, Hershey Gardens, a football stadium and sports arena, and a convention center. Because he was childless, he turned

Milton Hershey

his attention to building a Milton Hershey school for orphaned boys and girls.

Milton Hershey died in 1945 at the age of eighty-eight, but his corporate heirs continued in his spirit. Today, there is the Milton S. Hershey Medical Center of the Pennsylvania State University, endowed by the Hershey Company. And of course there is Hersheypark, a continuation of the old amusement park Hershey had built in 1905, all powered by a best-selling chocolate bar and a man with a very sweet dream.

SOURCE: Morton, Marcia, and Morton, Frederic (1986). *Chocolate: An illustrated history.* New York: Crown Publishers, pp. 89–125.

achieve that degree of smoothness we have come to know and love (Focus 13.2) [13]

The chocolate industry today

Present-day domestic sales of chocolate bars in the United States are dominated by Hershey Chocolate USA and M&M/Mars, together holding 80 percent of the market. Overall, the per capita consumption of chocolate in the United States, according to 1992 statistics, was 10.6 pounds, which put the country about tenth among chocolate-loving nations of the world. The champion, not surprisingly, was Switzerland, where the per capita consumption of chocolate was approximately 22 pounds a year. Norway and Belgium/Luxembourg were runners-up with per capita consumptions of approximately 17 pounds a year. Incidently, the three countries consuming the least chocolate a year (4 pounds or less) were Italy, Japan, and Spain. [14]

Chocolate and heart disease: No cause for alarm

Are we running any risk to our health by indulging in our obvious love for chocolate? It is true that chocolate is rich in saturated fatty acids, the villains when it comes to raising cholesterol and clogging our coronary arteries. Yet, the particular saturated fatty acid in the cocoa butter of chocolate turns out to be quite benign. The main component of cocoa butter is a fatty acid known as stearic acid, which is rapidly converted in the liver to oleic acid, a monounsaturate that neither raises nor lowers serum cholesterol. A recent study found that healthy young men on a twenty-six-day diet in which a total of 37 percent of calories came from fat and 81 percent of those fat calories came from cocoa butter had no increase in their serum cholesterol, and their cholesterol levels were no higher than if they had been on a comparable diet in which the fat came from olive oil.

Is chocolate completely blameless? Not exactly. Dark chocolate is better than milk chocolate, since by definition (and by law) the latter must contain a minimal amount of milk-derived butterfat in addition to cocoa butter. Some chocolates contain added ingredients such as palm oil or coconut oil, two saturated fats that do raise cholesterol levels. And no one should expect to lose any weight on a chocolate diet. Even so, nutritionists are concluding that there is not much of a problem in eating two or three chocolate bars a week, which is good news for chocolate lovers everywhere.

SOURCE: Brody, Jane E. (1994, February 14). Hearts may safely flutter over valentine chocolates. *New York Times*, A1, A15.

The xanthine content in chocolate

The amounts of xanthines are much smaller in chocolate than in coffee or tea. A typical 1-ounce piece of milk chocolate, for example, contains about 6 mg of caffeine and about 44 mg of theobromine. Since theobromine has about one tenth the stimulant power of caffeine, we can approximate the total effect in chocolate to be roughly equivalent to 10 mg of caffeine. Of course, eating more than 1 ounce of chocolate will change these figures (a typical chocolate bar is approximately 1.5 ounces), but even so, it is unlikely that chocolate will keep you up at night.[15]

Cola drinks

The fourth and final major source of caffeine in our diet comes from soft drinks, predominantly of the cola type. Table 13.1 shows the caffeine content of major soft-drink brands. Except for Mountain Dew and Mello Yello, the caffeinated brands are all colas. The reason why even a noncola can be a caffeinated beverage is that more than 95 percent of the caffeine in caffeinated soft drinks is added by the manufacturer during production. Less than 5 percent actually comes from the West African kola nut, from which colas get their name. As indicated in Table 13.1, the caffeine content of a twelve-ounce serving of Coca-Cola or Pepsi-Cola is about three fourths the caffeine content of a five-ounce cup of tea, and in the case of Mountain Dew the stimulating effect is approximately the same.

Caffeine from medications

Caffeine is sold purely as a stimulant in over-the-counter (OTC) drugs such as NoDoz and Vivarin tablets and as one of several ingredients in a number of other products ranging from pain relievers and cold remedies to diuretics and weight-control aids. As Table 13.2 shows, the equivalent caffeine level in these products ranges approximately from that of one third of a cup to two cups of regular coffee.

TABLE 13.1

Caffeine levels and market share of leading brands of soft drink

Brand name	Percentage of market (1992)	Caffeine content (mg/12 oz.)
Coca-Cola Classic	20.0	45.6
Pepsi-Cola	18.0	38.4
Diet Coke	9.1	45.6
Diet Pepsi	6.1	38.4
Dr. Pepper	5.9	40.0
Mountain Dew	4.1	54.0
Sprite	4.0	none
7UP	2.8	none
Caffeine-free Diet Coke	2.3	none
Caffeine-free Diet Pepsi	1.6	none
Others (root beers, orange sodas, etc.)	26.1	

Note: Jolt Cola, a widely available beverage, contains 72 milligrams of caffeine per 12 ounces (the highest amount allowed by the FDA to be added to soft drinks), a little less than twice the level found in the leading cola brands.

SOURCES: *Market Share Reporter 1995*. Detroit MI: Gale Research, p. 101.   Gilbert, Richard M. (1992). *Caffeine: The most popular stimulant*. New York: Chelsea House Publishers, p. 41.

TABLE 13.2

Caffeine content in common over-the-counter medications

Medication	Caffeine per tablet or capsule (in milligrams)	Caffeine per recommended dosage (in milligrams)
Stimulants		
NoDoz	100	200
Vivarin	200	200
Pain relievers		
Anacin	32	64
Excedrin	65	130
Midol	32	64
Vanquish	33	66
Cold remedies		
Coryban-D	30	30
Dristan	16	32
Triaminicin	30	30
Diuretics		
Aqua-Ban	100	200

Note: Caffeine is also found in prescription remedies for migraine (Cafergot and Migral) and in pain relievers (Darvon Compound and Fiorinol).

SOURCE: Updated from Gilbert, Richard J. (1986). *Caffeine: The most popular stimulant*. New York: Chelsea House Publishers, p. 51.

The era of decaffeination

Public concerns about adverse effects of caffeine and a general increase in consciousness about health have led to a steady increase in decaffeinated consumer products, particularly coffee. From 1962 to 1990, the percentage of decaffeinated coffee in total coffee sales rose from scarcely 3 to more than 20. Unfortunately, as most coffee lovers know, decaffeination greatly reduces coffee flavor.

One of the reasons for the loss in flavor is the choice of beans being decaffeinated. Typically, only the robusta species of coffee bean is decaffeinated, not only because it costs less but also because its harsher flavor can better withstand the decaffeination process.[16]

Another reason is the decaffeination method typically used. In general, there are two techniques used to decaffeinate coffee beans. The first, called the direct method, begins by steaming the beans to loosen the chemical bonds that normally hold caffeine to them. Then, a chemical solvent, typically methylene chloride, is circulated through the beans, which are resteamed to remove any residual solvent and later dried. The solvent is later mixed with water and the caffeine extracted. The extracted caffeine, now separated from the coffee bean, is recycled by being shipped to soft-drink bottlers so it can be added to the basic formula for caffeinated soft drinks.

The direct method preserves the flavor of the coffee bean, but concerns have been raised as to the health risks of consuming methylene chloride residue in decaffeinated coffee. Just how much we should be concerned is debatable. Since 1985, methylene chloride has been banned from hair sprays after it was demonstrated from animal studies that it could be dangerous if inhaled. When orally consumed, however, methylene chloride is apparently harmless. Even when mice are fed methylene chloride in their drinking water equivalent to 4.4 million cups of decaffeinated coffee a day, there are no

to soak the still-wet beans, in an effort to give them back some of the lost flavor. Most coffee experts consider the coffee bean that has been "naturally decaffeinated" in this way to be a pale resemblance of its former self. Coffee manufacturers tend to roast the decaffeinated beans longer (some say that they are then overroasted) to produce extra body and flavor.

Is there a middle ground for coffee lovers who need to have decaffeinated coffee? Recently, a new technique of using carbon dioxide instead of methylene chloride has been developed, and decaffeinated coffees produced in this way are available in a few selected brands. The flavor is significantly superior to coffee decaffeinated by the water method and avoids the concerns people may have (despite the evidence to the contrary) about methylene chloride.[17]

Caffeine as a drug

hen ingested orally, caffeine is absorbed in about thirty to sixty minutes. Caffeine levels peak in the bloodstream in one hour, and reactions in the central nervous sytem peak in about two hours. Many coffee drinkers notice a boost of energy, or "buzz," almost immediately, but this effect is due either to the sugar in the coffee or a conditioned learning effect, not to the caffeine itself. From three to seven hours after caffeine is consumed, approximately half of it still remains in the bloodstream. The metabolism of caffeine and the time it takes to eliminate it vary according to a number of factors. For example, women in late stages of pregnancy and those using oral contraceptives eliminate caffeine from their systems more slowly than either men or women in general. Infants and the elderly also show a slower elimination of caffeine. In contrast, smokers eliminate caffeine about 100 percent more quickly than nonsmokers. As a result, smokers on average experience the effect of the caffeine they consume for a relatively shorter period of time; it is possible that

toxic or carcinogenic reactions. Besides, the solvent evaporates at a temperature of between 100 to 120 degrees Fahrenheit, far below the roasting temperature of coffee beans or even the brewing temperature of coffee itself. As a result, the FDA has pronounced the risks involved to be so low "as to be essentially nonexistent." Yet the public reaction and its fear of chemical contaminants in general have driven major coffee manufacturers to avoid using the direct methylene chloride procedure in decaffeinating their coffee brands.

The major alternative to the direct method of decaffeination is the water method. In this technique, the beans are first steamed as before, but then they are soaked in water. The soaking removes the caffeine but also all the other solids in the coffee beans that give them a rich flavor. The water is removed, the caffeine is removed from the water, and the remaining water is returned

smokers tend to drink more caffeinated coffee than nonsmokers in order to compensate for a faster elimination of caffeine.[18]

Effects of caffeine on the body

The stimulant effects of caffeine, as well as those of the other xanthines, are a result of its ability to block the effects of an inhibitory neurotransmitter called **adenosine.** Normally, adenosine binds to receptors on the surface of cells and, consequently, produces sleepiness, dilation of blood vessels, and constriction of bronchial passageways. It also protects the body against seizures, slows down the body's reaction to stress, and lowers heart rate, blood pressure, and body temperature.

By inhibiting the effects of adenosine, caffeine and other xanthines cause the opposite responses to occur, though the actual results are complex. In general, peripheral blood vessels are dilated, while cerebral blood vessels in the head are constricted. Since dilated blood vessels in the head can frequently result in headache pain, caffeine can help headache sufferers, and that is the reason why it can be found in many OTC pain relievers. Heart rate is slightly elevated when caffeine is consumed, but the effect is dose dependent and often is not observed at all. The fact that caffeine has a bronchodilating effect makes it helpful in treating asthmatic conditions in which the bronchial passageways are abnormally constricted. Theophylline, however, has a stronger bronchodilating effect than caffeine and as a result can be prescribed at lower doses. Caffeine is effective, but patients often report unpleasant side effects of "jitteriness" before their asthmatic condition improves.[19]

Effects of caffeine on behavior

A major effect of caffeine as well as other xanthines is to excite neuronal activity in the brain. As the dose increases, the effects expand from the cerebral cortex downward to lower systems in the brain and finally to the spinal cord. The behavioral consequence of this excitation is a feeling of mental alertness and lack of fatigue. On the basis of these effects, you might expect that caffeine would also improve human performance, but reports in this regard are quite mixed. Subjects in controlled experimental settings feel stimulated and more alert, but whether or not they improve their performance after caffeine depends on the type of task, their personal characteristics, and even the time of day when the experiment is conducted.

Nonetheless, it is possible to make some generalizations about caffeine's effect on performance. In general, caffeine increases vigilance and attentiveness in tasks where subjects become easily bored, and it decreases the response time to simple visual or auditory signals. For more complex tasks in which subjects need to decide which responses to make or in situations that require motor coordination, however, caffeine either has little effect or can be disruptive. Most reports of improvements under caffeine involve conditions in which the subject is already either bored or fatigued. In these circumstances, caffeine helps either to maintain a level of performance that would otherwise have declined or to restore performance from a state degraded by boredom or fatigue.[20]

There is less disagreement as to the impact of caffeine on sleep. The most obvious effect is a lengthening of the time it takes to fall asleep and a decrease in the quality of sleep once it comes. Generally, studies investigating caffeine effects have involved coffee drinking, and the sleep effects are seen more strongly in nondrinkers of coffee than in habitual heavy coffee drinkers.[21]

As a final note, it is important to emphasize an effect that caffeine does *not* produce:

adenosine (a-DEN-oh-seen)
An inhibitory neurotransmitter that is inhibited by caffeine and other xanthines. The action upon adenosine receptors in the body is the basis for the stimulant properties of these drugs.

Caffeine is typically most effective to ward off sleep and improve the performance of tedious tasks.

the supposed ability to sober you up after being intoxicated with alcohol. Despite the widespread notion that a cup of strong black coffee will help you if you are drunk, the evidence is simply not there. The only result is that you will be a more alert drunk than before; the behavioral consequences of alcohol intoxication (Chapter 10) will remain the same.

Health risks

studies investigating the health consequences of caffeine consumption have been conducted for more than a century, and the conclusions have varied considerably.

Cardiovascular effects

Because it is known that caffeine stimulates cardiac muscle as well as skeletal muscle throughout the body, it is only natural to be concerned with the possibility that caffeine consumption would be a risk factor for a heart attack or cardiac arrhythmia (irregular heart beat). In 1973 a great deal of publicity was generated by a study called the Boston Collaborative Drug Surveillance Program in which a large number of individuals at Boston metropolitan hospitals were surveyed as to

their use of many different drugs, including caffeine, and the incidence of various disease states. The researchers reported that the consumption of more than six cups of caffeinated coffee a day more than doubled the risk of a heart attack.[22] Further studies, however, have failed to find any connection at all between caffeine and heart attacks.

What do we do when the medical literature is so inconclusive and contradictory? First of all, in caffeine studies that show some cardiovascular health risk, the consumption levels are rather high (five to six cups or more a day). Drinking less caffeine has not been identified as a risk factor. Nonetheless, perhaps a cautious approach is needed here:

A conservative view is that caffeine should be used in moderation in people who are at risk (that is, males, smokers, and people who have a family history of heart disease, obesity, hypertension, or elevated blood cholesterol levels).[23]

We should also be aware that a four-year-old child drinking a twenty-ounce cola drink is consuming a high dose of caffeine, and we should not be surprised that marked behavioral and physiological effects will be observed.

Osteoporosis and bone fractures

A 1990 study analyzing caffeine consumption and incidence of hip fractures among more than three thousand elderly men and women found that those who reported drinking 2.5 to 3 cups of caffeinated coffee or 5 to 6 cups of caffeinated tea per day had a 69 percent greater risk of osteoporosis (bone loss and brittleness) than caffeine abstainers. Those who reported drinking more than 3.5 cups of caffeinated coffee or 7 cups of caffeinated tea had an 82 percent greater risk. Because one of the effects of caffeine is to increase the urinary excretion of calcium and to inhibit the absorption of calcium from the diet in the elderly, it makes sense that there might be an adverse effect on bone tissue in this age group.[24]

Breast disease

A 1981 report indicated a relationship between caffeine consumption and the formation of benign (that is, noncancerous) lumps in the breasts called fibrocystic lesions. However, the study was severely criticized as not being based on randomized sampling nor having methodological controls that would shield the researchers from imposing their bias in observing fibrocystic lesion cases. More recent and carefully executed studies show no relationship between the incidence of this frequently painful condition and caffeine consumption.[25] There is disagreement about whether women who already have fibrocystic lesions might show improvement by abstaining from caffeinated products; a 1985 report indicates that abstinence is helpful, while subsequent reports indicate that there is no benefit.[26]

Cancer

A 1971 study indicated an association between caffeine consumption and urinary-tract cancer, and a 1981 study indicated an association with pancreatic cancer. In both studies, the conclusions were based on methodologically flawed designs, and presently the medical consensus is that caffeine consumption is not causally related to these or any other types of cancer.[27]

Effects during pregnancy and breastfeeding

Though the evidence is not entirely conclusive, caffeine is suspected to be linked to infertility. In general, the greater the quantity of caffeine a woman ingests, the longer it takes her to get pregnant. In one study, women who consumed three cups of coffee a day reduced their chances of conceiving by 25 percent.[28]

In addition, caffeine consumption (more than three or four cups of coffee a day) during the first three months of pregnancy is related to a greater incidence of low birthweight in the newborn, though the incidence of premature birth or birth defects is not increased. There is also a relationship between caffeine consumption at any time during pregnancy and an increased risk of miscarriage. Therefore, the cautionary advice of the FDA is warranted: Women should abstain from caffeine if at all possible during pregnancy.[29]

Afterward, in the case of breastfeeding, it is also a good idea to continue a caffeine-free diet. Enzymes that normally metabolize caffeine in the liver are not present in the liver of a newborn baby, and as a consequence the half-life of caffeine is much longer than in the adult, up to eighty-five hours. While there is no evidence of specific harm from having a stimulant like caffeine in the nervous system for such intervals of time, it seems to be a situation that might well be avoided.[30]

Panic attacks

Consumption of caffeine equivalent to about four to five cups of coffee a day has been associated with the onset of panic attacks in those individuals suffering from a panic disorder. This finding is consistent with the known effects of caffeine as a CNS stimulant. As a result, any person with a history of panic attacks should be careful to avoid caffeine, and mental-health professionals should be aware of the possibility that caffeine consumption could trigger a panic episode.[31]

Dependence: Tolerance and withdrawal

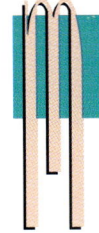

ore than 85 percent of people in the United States consume caffeine in one form or another each day. In 1935, 401 men and women, all employees of the state of New York, were asked about their caffeine consumption over the previous seventy-two-hour period, including all foods, beverages, and medications that might contain caffeine.

Only 11 of them did not consume any caffeine at all, and the average caffeine consumption level was about 400 mg.[32] This was neither a random nor a very large sample, but the results nonetheless illustrate the basic point made at the opening of this chapter: caffeine consumption is a cultural norm in the United States and the rest of the world. The fact that caffeinated beverages in particular are embedded in the diet of this country makes it difficult to think of caffeine as a drug, much less one that could cause dependence. "People say they're addicted to caffeine and laugh," a prominent caffeine researcher has said: "they wouldn't say the same thing about heroin."[33]

Tolerance

When individuals who do not usually use caffeine are administered repeated doses equivalent to amounts that would ordinarily be acquired from the diet, the initial increases in heart rate and blood pressure start to decline after approximately seventy-two hours.[34] In other words, with respect to the cardiovascular effects of caffeine, a classic tolerance effect, as defined in Chapter 2, can be observed.

With respect to the behavioral and psychological effects of caffeine, tolerance effects are more difficult to evaluate, despite the fact that most of us have noticed at some time in our lives that caffeine was having a progressively smaller effect on us as we started to be habitual caffeine consumers. The problem appears to be that once we are in a laboratory setting most of us are already tolerant to the effects of caffeine. Recent studies that have specifically controlled for variations in the subject's recent dietary intake of caffeine have shown tolerance effects for dosage levels as low as 100 mg, the equivalent of one to two cups of coffee.

caffeinism
A dangerous state of overstimulation from a very large dose of caffeine.

Withdrawal

A stronger case for caffeine being a drug that produces physical dependence is the research findings concerning withdrawal. As you may have encountered yourself, a sudden cessation in the intake of coffee or other caffeinated products results in symptoms of headache, impaired concentration, drowsiness, irritability, muscle aches, and other flu-like symptoms. A headache is a typical withdrawal symptom, usually appearing from twelve to eighteen hours after the last dose of caffeine, peaking over the next two days or so, and persisting in some individuals for up to a week. As you would expect, a reintroduction of caffeine causes the withdrawal symptoms to disappear. One study on the pattern of withdrawal symptoms from caffeine found significant symptoms even when subjects had been consuming as little as 100 mg per day.[35]

Craving

While the case for physical dependence is clear, the case for psychological dependence is presently uncertain. We do not know if the tendency to have that next cup of coffee or other caffeinated product is a matter of desiring to have it or an effort to avoid withdrawal symptoms that would ensue if we did not have it.

Acute toxicity of caffeine

Too much caffeine can produce toxic effects on the body, but the amount that might do so is substantial and generally beyond what we typically consume. Approximately 1,000 mg of caffeine (equivalent to about ten cups of caffeinated coffee), consumed over a short period of time, results in extreme nervousness and agitation, muscle hyperactivity and twitching, profound insomnia, heart palpitations and arrhythmias, gastrointestinal upset, nausea, and diarrhea. The condition is referred to as **caffeinism.** In a few individuals, particularly those who do not typically ingest caffeine, these symptoms might arise from a much lower dose level. The DSM-IV criterion for symptoms of acute caffeine intoxication (a term equivalent to caffeinism) is a caffeine intake in excess of 250 mg. Naturally, as the dose rises above this level, the probability of observing a toxic reaction increases.[36]

The adult lethal dose is approximately 5 to 10 grams (5,000 to 10,000 mg), which is equivalent roughly to somewhere between forty and eighty cups of caffeinated coffee. The lowest caffeine dose known to have been fatal in an adult is 3.2 grams, administered mistakenly by a nurse who believed the syringe contained another drug. Lethal doses for children are lower, and a number of accidental deaths have resulted from eating large quantities of caffeine-containing medications.[37]

Medications based on xanthines

Owing to the superiority of theophylline over caffeine in its ability to relax smooth muscle, theophylline has been used medically to treat a number of clinical conditions. The application as a bronchodilator for asthmatics has been mentioned earlier. One particular medication, aminophylline, combines theophylline with methylediamine, an inert compound that increases the absorption of theophylline and enhances its clinical benefit. Since theophylline also stimulates cardiac muscle, it is sometimes prescribed for patients with congestive heart disease (Table 13.3).

TABLE 13.3
Some examples of xanthine-based medications

Medication	Brand name	Manufacturer
theophylline	Asbron G	Sandoz
	Choledyl	Parke-Davis
	Quibron-T	Bristol
	Slo-Bid	Rhone-Poulenc Rorer
	Theo-Dur	Key Pharmaceuticals
	Theolair tablets	3M Pharmaceuticals
aminophylline	Aminophylline injection	Elkins-Sinn
	Aminophylline tablets and oral solution	Roxane
	Mudrane	ECR

SOURCE: *Physician's desk reference* (1994). Montvale NJ: Medical Economics Data.

Summary

- Caffeine belongs to a family of stimulant drugs called xanthines. It is found in coffee, tea, chocolate, many soft drinks, and many medications.

- Other xanthines are theophylline (found in tea) and theobromine (found in chocolate).

COFFEE

- Coffee drinking originated in the Middle East and later was introduced to England in the seventeenth century. Coffee houses in Britain and in colonial America sprang up as establishments where political and social discussions could be held.

- Today's coffee comes from a mixture of arabica and robusta beans, imported largely from Brazil, Colombia, Indonesia, and several nations in Africa.

- On average, a five-ounce cup of coffee contains roughly 100 mg of caffeine, with the actual level determined by the type of coffee beans used and the method of brewing

TEA

- Tea drinking originated in China and later was introduced to Europe by Dutch traders in the early seventeenth century. It became most popular in Britain and Russia. Today, tea consumption is greatest in Britain and Ireland.

- On average, a five-ounce cup of tea contains roughly 60 mg of caffeine, with the actual level determined by the method of brewing and brand.

CHOCOLATE

- Chocolate originated in pre-Columbian America and was introduced to Europe by the return of Cortés to Spain in 1528. Its popularity spread across Europe in the seventeenth century. By the 1880s, techniques for present-day milk chocolate had been perfected.

- The caffeine level in chocolate is relatively low, roughly 6 mg per ounce.

COLA DRINKS

- Caffeinated colas have most of the caffeine content added to the beverage during production. Levels of caffeine in these beverages are approximately 40 mg per 12 ounces.

CAFFEINE FROM MEDICATIONS

- As a drug, caffeine and other xanthines are stimulants of the CNS and of peripheral mus-culature. Theophylline, in particular, has a strong bronchodilating effect and is useful for treating asthmatic conditions.

CAFFEINE AS A DRUG

- The behavioral effects of caffeine can be characterized principally as a reduction in fatigue and boredom, as well as a delay in the onset of sleep.

- Health risks from moderate consumption of caffeine are not clinically significant, except for the adverse effects of fetal development during pregnancy, the development of bone loss among the elderly, possibly an adverse effect on cardiac condition of patients already suffering from cardiovascular disease, and the aggravation of panic attacks among patients with this disorder.

- Continued consumption of caffeine produces tolerance effects; when caffeine consumption ceases, withdrawal symptoms are observed. High levels of caffeine consumption can produce toxic effects, though deaths are extremely rare.

Key Terms

Endnotes

1. Austin, Gregory A. (1978). *Perspectives on the history of psychoactive substance use.* Rockville MD: National Institute on Drug Abuse, p. 50.   Jacob, Heinrich E. (1935). *Coffee: The epic of a commodity.* New York: Viking Press, pp. 3–10.

2. Robinson, Edward F. (1893). *The early history of coffee houses in England.* London: Kegan Paul, p. 26. Cited in Edward M. Brecher, and the editors of Consumer Reports (1972), *Licit and illicit drugs.* Boston: Little Brown, p. 197.

3. Ukers, William H. (1935). *All about coffee.* New York: Tea and Coffee Trade Journal Co., p. 61. Wellman, Frederick L. (1961). *Coffee: Botany, cultivation, and utilization.* New York: Interscience Publishers, p. 22 or 23.

4. Brooke, James (1994, June 29). Grim view from Brazil coffee fields. *New York Times,* pp. D1, D3. Gilbert, Richard J. (1986). *Caffeine: The most popular stimulant.* New York: Chelsea House, pp. 24–25, 55, 60. Starbird, Ethel A. (1981, March). The bonanza bean: Coffee. *National Geographic Magazine,* pp. 398–399.

5. Svicarovich, John, Winter, Stephen, and Ferguson, Jeff (1976). *The coffee book: A connoisseur's guide to gourmet coffee.* Englewood Cliffs NJ: Prentice-Hall, pp. 21–31.

6. Davids, Kenneth (1976). *Coffee: A guide to buying, brewing, and enjoying.* San Francisco: 101 Productions, pp. 161–166. Gilbert *Caffeine,* pp. 31–35. International Coffee Organization (1985). *United States of America, coffee drinking study—Winter 1984.* London: International Coffee Organization.

7. Barone, J. J., and Roberts, H. (1984). Human consumption of caffeine. In Peter B. Dews (Ed.), *Caffeine: Perspectives from recent research.* Berlin: Springer-Verlag, pp. 60–63.

8. Shalleck, Jamie (1972). *Tea.* New York: Viking Press.

9. Maitland, Derek (1982). *5000 years of tea: A pictorial companion.* Hong Kong: CFW Publications Limited, pp. 80–89.

10. Gilbert. *Caffeine,* p. 23.

11. Groisser, Daniel S. (1978). A study of caffeine in tea. *American Journal of Clinical Nutrition, 31,* 1727–1731.

12. U.S. Department of Agriculture, Foreign Agricultural Service, 1992 data. Information courtesy of the Chocolate Manufacturers Association, McLean, Virginia.

13. Morton, Marcia, and Morton, Frederic (1986). *Chocolate: An illustrated history.* New York: Crown Publishers, pp. 77–87.

14. Brody, Jane E. (1994, February 14). Hearts may safely flutter over valentine chocolates. *New York Times,* A1, A15. International Office of Cocoa, Chocolate, and Sugar Confectionery,

1992 data. Information courtesy of the Chocolate Manufacturers Association, McLean, Virginia. *The market share reporter 1992* (1993). Detroit MI: Gale Research, p. 417.

15. Spiller, Gene A. (1984). *The methylxanthine beverages and foods: Chemistry, consumption, and health effects.* New York: A. R. Liss, pp. 171–172.

16. Kummer, Corby (1990, July). Is coffee harmful? *Atlantic, 266,* pp. 92–96.

17. DeMers, John (1986). *The community kitchen's complete guide to gourmet coffee.* New York: Simon and Schuster, pp. 85–89. Kummer. Is coffee harmful? pp. 92–96.

18. Gilbert. *Caffeine,* pp. 76–79. Julien, Robert M. (1995). *A primer of drug action* (7th ed.). New York: Freeman, p. 159.

19. Ibid., pp. 133–134. Schiwall, S. I. (1986, November). Asthma relief that's brewed by the cup. *Prevention, 38,* 127.

20. Curatolo, Peter W., and Robertson, David (1983). The health consequences of caffeine. *Annals of Internal Medicine, 98,* 641–653. Dews, Peter B. (1984). Behavioral effects of caffeine. In Peter B. Dews (Ed.), *Caffeine: Perspectives from recent research.* Berlin: Springer-Verlag, pp. 86–103. Sawyer, Deborah A., Julia, Harry L., and Turin, Alan C. (1982). Caffeine and human behavior: Arousal, anxiety, and performance effects *Journal of Behavioral Medicine, 5,* 415–439.

21. Curatolo and Robertson Health consequences of caffeine, p. 644.

22. Jick, Hershel, Miettinen, Olli S., Neff, Raymond K., Shapiro, Samuel, Heinonen, Olli, and Slone, Dennis (1973). Coffee and myocardial infarction. *New England Journal of Medicine, 289,* 63–67.

23. Julien. *A primer of drug action,* p. 163.

24. Kiel, Douglas P., Felson, David T., Hannan, Marian T., Anderson, Jennifer J., and Wilson, Peter W. F. (1990). Caffeine and the risk of hip fracture: The Framingham study. *American Journal of Epidemiology, 132,* 675–684.

25. Levinson, Wendy, and Dunn, Patrick M. (1986). Nonassociation of caffeine and fibrocystic breast disease. *Archives of Internal Medicine, 146,* 1773–1775. Minton, John P.,

Foecking, M. K., Webster, J. T., and Matthews, R. H. (1979). Caffeine, cyclic nucleotides, and breast diseases. *Surgery, 86,* 105–109.   Russell, Linda C. (1989). Caffeine restriction as initial treatment for breast pain. *Nurse Practitioner, 14,* 36–37.

26. Julien. *A primer of drug action,* p. 162.

27. Curatolo and Robertson. Health consequences of caffeine, p. 647.

28. Joesoef, M. Riduan, Beral V., Rolfs, Robert T., Aral, Sevgio O., and Cramer, Daniel W. (1990). Are caffeinated beverages risk factors for delayed conception? *Lancet, 335,* 136–137. Coffee and health (1994, October). *Consumer Reports,* pp. 650–651.

29. Fenster, Laura, Eskenazi, Brenda, Windham, Gayle C., and Swan, Shanna H. (1991). Caffeine consumption during pregnancy and fetal growth. *American Journal of Public Health, 81,* 458–461.   Infante-Rivard, Claire, Fernandez, Alberto, Gauthier, Robert, David, Michele, and Rivard, Georges-Etienne (1993). Fetal loss associated with caffeine intake before and during pregnancy. *Journal of the American Medical Association, 270,* 2940–2943.

30. Gilbert. *Caffeine,* pp. 78–79.

31. Charney, Dennis S., Heniger, George R., and Jatlow, Peter L. (1985). Increased anxiogenic effects of caffeine in panic disorders. *Archives of General Psychiatry, 42,* 233–243.

32. Weidner, Gerdi, and Istvan, Joseph (1985). Dietary sources of caffeine. *New England Journal of Medicine, 313,* 1421.

33. DeAngelis, Tori (1994, February). People's drug of choice offers potent side effects. *APA Monitor* (American Psychological Association, Washington DC), p. 16. Quotation by Dr. John Hughes.

34. Robertson, David, Wade, Dawn, Workman, Robert, and Woosley, Raymond L. (1981). Tolerance to the humoral and hemodynamic effects of caffeine in man. *Journal of Clinical Investigation, 67,* 1111–1117.

35. Griffiths, Roland R., and Woodson, Phillip P. (1988). Caffeine physical dependence: A review of human and animal laboratory studies. *Psychopharmacology, 94,* 437–451.   Silverman, Kenneth, Evans, Suzette M., Strain, Eric C., and Griffiths, Roland R. (1992). Withdrawal syndrome after the double-blind cessation of caffeine. *New England Journal of Medicine, 327,* 1109–1114.

36. American Psychiatric Association (1994). *Diagnostic and statistical manual of mental disorders (DSM-IV)* (4th ed.). Washington DC: American Psychiatric Association, pp. 212–215.

37. Gilbert. *Caffeine,* pp. 108–109.

14

Anabolic Steroids and Drug Abuse in Sports

n a world where running one hundredth of a second faster can mean the difference between a gold medal or a silver, where throwing a javelin a few centimeters farther or lifting a kilogram or two more can make you either the champion or an also-ran, temptations abound. In this high-pressure world, athletes are continually on the lookout for a "winning edge." It may involve an unusual technique in training, a new attitude toward winning, or a special diet. Or it could involve the use of drugs. This chapter takes up the problem of drug abuse in the world of sports, and, in particular, the abuse of anabolic steroids.

The use of anabolic steroids to achieve that "winning edge" is not only a problem among athletes who are in the public eye but also among a growing number of young people who simply want to look better by developing the musculature of their bodies. The serious dangers in such drug-taking behavior, whether the motivation lies in the desire for some athletic advantage or in personal vanity, is a major problem that needs to be examined closely. It is instructive to look first at how drugs in general have affected competitive sports over the centuries.

Drug-taking behavior in sports

he first recorded athletic competition, the ancient Olympic Games in Greece, is also the place where we find the first recorded application of psychoactive drugs. As early as 300 B.C., Greek athletes ate hallucinogenic mushrooms, either to improve their perfor-

Swifter, higher, stronger
(*Citius, altius, fortius*)

The official motto of the International Olympic Committee (1896)

I don't call it cheating. My definition of cheating is doing something nobody else is doing.

Charlie Francis, former coach of Canadian sprinter Ben Johnson
Sports Illustrated (1990)

mance in the competition or to achieve some kind of mystical connection to the gods. Later, Roman gladiators and charioteers used stimulants to sustain themselves longer in competition, even when injured by their opponents.

In the modern era, drugs have continued to be a factor in athletic competitions. By the end of the nineteenth century, world-class athletes were experimenting with a variety of stimulant and depressant drugs, including cocaine, caffeine, alcohol, nitroglycerine, opiates, strychnine, and amphetamines. In 1886, while competing in a cross-country race, a Welsh cyclist died of a combination of heroin and cocaine (commonly referred to as a speedball), the first drug-related death ever recorded in sports. During the 1904 Olympics, Tom Hicks, a U.S. marathoner, collapsed after winning the race and lost consciousness. When he was revived, doctors were told that he had taken a potentially lethal mixture of strychnine (a CNS stimulant when administered in low doses) and brandy.[1]

With the introduction of anabolic steroid drugs, specifically patterned after the male sex hormone, testosterone, a new element entered the world of competitive sports. Here was a class of drugs that did more than temporarily alter the behavior of the athlete; these drugs actually altered the physical structure of the athlete. Anabolic steroid drugs had been studied since the 1930s as a treatment for anemia and conditions that caused the wasting away of muscles. After World War II, steroid drugs were administered to people who were near death from starvation and weight loss. It quickly became apparent, however, that steroids could be useful when given to otherwise healthy individuals as well. As pharmaceutical companies began to introduce dozens of new drugs, all based on the testosterone molecule, it was natural that information about anabolic steroids would come to the attention of athletes, as well as their coaches and trainers.[2]

Why take anabolic steroids?

To understand how testosterone-based steroids produce **ergogenic** (performance-enhancing) changes, we first have to recognize that testosterone itself has two primary effects on the human body. The first and most obvious effect is **androgenic** (man-producing), in that the hormone promotes the development of male sex characteristics. Due to increased levels of testosterone, boys acquire during puberty an enlarged larynx (resulting in a deeper voice), body hair, and an increase in body size, as well as genital changes that make them sexually mature adults. The second effect is **anabolic** (upward-changing), in that it promotes the development of protein and, as a result, an increase in muscle tissue. Muscles in men are inherently larger than muscles in women due to the anabolic action of testosterone in the male body.

Steroid drugs based on alterations in the testosterone molecule are therefore called **anabolic-androgenic steroids.** The goal, however, has been to develop drugs that emphasize the anabolic function while retaining as little of the androgenic function as possible. For that reason, they are most often called simply **anabolic steroids.** Unfortunately, as we will see, it has not been possible to develop a testosterone-derived

ergogenic
Performance-enhancing.

androgenic (AN-droh-JEN-ik)
Acting to promote masculinizing changes in the body.

anabolic (AN-ah-BALL-ik)
Acting to promote protein growth and muscular development.

anabolic-androgenic steroids
Drugs that promote masculine changes in the body and increased muscular development.

anabolic steroids
Drugs patterned after the testosterone molecule that promote masculine changes in the body and increased muscular development. The full name is anabolic-androgenic steroids.

TABLE 14.1

Currently available anabolic steroids

Type of steroid	Generic name	Brand name
Oral	danazol	Danocrine capsules
	fluoxymesterone	Halotestin tablets
	methyltestosterone	Android-10 and Android-25 tablets, Estratest tablets, Mediatric capsules, Metandren linguets and tablets, Premarin with methyltestosterone, Virion
	oxymetholone	Anadrol-50 tablets
	stanozodol	Winstrol tablets
Intramuscular injectable	nandrolone decanoate	Deca-Durabolin injectable
	nandrolone phenproprionate	Durabolin injectable
	testosterone cypionate	DEPO-Testosterone injectable, Virion IM

Note: Several brands of anabolic steroids (e.g., Anabol, Dianabol, Maxibolin, and Testomet) that have been used in the past are no longer available through legitimate commercial sources.

SOURCE: *Physicians' desk reference* (48th ed.) (1994). Montvale NJ: Medical Economics Data.

drug without at least some androgenic effects (Table 14.1).

As a final point, it is important that anabolic steroids not be confused with **adrenocortical steroids,** drugs that are patterned after glucocorticoid hormones secreted by the adrenal glands. The major drug of this latter type is cortisone (brand name among others: Hydrocortone injection). The molecular shape of these drugs qualifies them to belong to the steroid family, but there is no relationship to testosterone or any testosterone-like effects. In sports, adrenocortical steroids are used to reduce inflammation associated with muscular injuries. Their effect on muscular development can be viewed as catabolic (downward-changing) in that muscles tend to atrophy, so its long-term use is unlikely to be a desirable alternative for athletes.[3] In this chapter, any mention of steroids will refer to anabolic or anabolic-androgenic steroids, exclusively.

adrenocortical steroids
A group of hormones secreted by the adrenal glands. Their anti-inflammatory action makes them useful for treating arthritis and muscular injuries.

Anabolic steroids at the modern Olympics

By the time of the 1952 Olympic Games in Helsinki, athletes were well acquainted with ergogenic drugs. Legally available amphetamines (see Chapter 4), in particular, were commonplace, particularly in events that emphasized speed and endurance. Among events where strength and size were important, anabolic steroids were seen to be perfectly suited for gaining a competitive advantage.

It is debatable which country first used anabolic steroids. U.S. athletic officials have claimed that Soviet weight-lifting champions were using steroids in international competitions in 1954; British officials have claimed that an American hammer thrower used steroids prior to 1954. Whoever has the dubious honor of being first, steroid use became the norm by the 1956 Olympic Games in Melbourne for both men and women athletes.

Steroid use was clearly out in the open during the 1968 Olympic Games in Mexico City. An estimated one third of the entire U.S. track-and-field team, not merely the strength-event and field-event competitors but the

Russian pentathlon champion Nadezhda Tkachenko was one of several world-class female athletes who later tested positive for anabolic steroids.

sprinters and middle-distance runners as well, were using anabolic steroids. The controversy did not concern the appropriateness or morality of taking steroids, only which particular steroids worked best. Strength-event athletes were taking at least two to five times the therapeutic recommendations (based on the original intent of replacing body protein). The taking of multiple steroids (a practice called stacking), as well as the simultaneous use of injectable and oral forms, were becoming popular. The following year, an editor of *Track and Field News* dubbed anabolic steroids "the breakfast of champions." In 1971 an American weight lifter commented in reference to his Soviet rival:

Last year the only difference between me and him was I couldn't afford his drug bill. Now I can. When I hit Munich [in 1972] I'll weigh in at about 340, or maybe 350. Then we'll see which is better, his steroids or mine.[4]

In the meantime, the masculine features of many women athletes from Eastern European countries in the 1950s and 1970s, not to mention the number of Olympic records that were suddenly broken, made it reasonable to ask whether they were either men disguised as women or genetic "mistakes." Questions about the unusually deep voices of East German women swimmers prompted their coach, at one point, to respond: "We came here to swim, not to sing." From information that has come to light since then, we now know that the effects were chiefly due to large doses of steroids and that the East German government was conducting, until the late 1980s, a specific scientific program to develop new steroid formulations that would benefit their national athletes and, at the same time, be undetectable by standard screening procedures. As recently as the 1992 Olympic Games in Barcelona, athletes were being expelled from competition after failing screening tests for anabolic steroids.[5]

Anabolic steroids in professional and collegiate sports

The wholesale use of anabolic steroids in the world of international athletics soon filtered down to sports closer to home. Beginning in the early 1960s, trainers in the National Football League began to administer anabolic steroids to their players. By the 1970s and 1980s, virtually all of the NFL teams were familiar with these drugs. Estimates of how many players were on anabolic steroids varied from 50 percent to 90 percent. We will never know precisely the full extent of the practice, except to say that it was certainly substantial.

Several of the professional football players remarked that their steroid use had begun while they were playing on collegiate teams, and indeed football players in several colleges and universities during the 1980s were implicated in steroid use. Football players were not alone in this regard. Use of anabolic steroids had found its way into other collegiate and high school sports, such as track and field, baseball, basketball, gymnastics, lacrosse, swimming, volleyball, wrestling, and tennis.

It is fair to say that until the late 1980s, when screening procedures became commonplace, there was no sport in either professional or amateur categories for which the use of anabolic steroids was not an accepted element in training.[6]

A milestone year in the history of anabolic steroids

Two events in 1988 made that year a turning point in the history of anabolic steroids in sports. Magazine articles and news accounts had exposed the widespread use of steroids since 1969, but public interest was only briefly aroused and media coverage would dwindle in a month or so. In September 1988, however, in a dramatic and highly publicized moment in the Seoul Olympic Games, the Canadian sprinter Ben Johnson won the gold medal in the men's one hundred-meter dash in the world-record-breaking time of 9.79 seconds, only to be denied his achievement shortly afterward when it was determined that he had tested positive for anabolic steroids. The world was stunned and suddenly had to confront the pervasiveness of the practice as well as its consequences once and for all (see Portrait).

About a month later, another dramatic development emerged when a major study published in the *Journal of the American Medical Association* reported the outcome of the first nationwide survey on use of anabolic steroids among adolescent boys in the United States. The survey found that approximately 7 percent of all high school seniors were using or had used anabolic steroids. More than 77 percent of the users were white and middle class; more than 52 percent had parents who were college graduates; nearly 50 percent had started using

steroids before they were fifteen years old. More than 47 percent said that their motivation was to improve their athletic performance, but almost 27 percent said that the motivation was completely outside the realm of organized sports: they simply wanted to look better.[7]

The hazards of anabolic steroids

One of the great problems in looking at the adverse effects of steroid abuse is that the dosage levels vary over an enormous range, and it is virtually impossible to know the exact dosage levels or even the exact combinations of steroids a particular individual may be taking. It is estimated that a "typical" body builder on anabolic steroids may be taking in a minimum of three to ten times the therapeutic doses recommended for the medical use of these drugs, but in some cases, the estimates have gone as high as a hundred to a thousand times the recommended therapeutic dose.[8]

Effects on hormonal systems

At these huge dosages, anabolic steroids are literally flooding into the body, upsetting the delicate balance of hormones and other chemicals that are normally controlled by testosterone. The primary effect in men is for the testes gland to react to the newly increased testosterone levels in the blood by producing less testosterone on its own. In other words, the gland is getting the incorrect message that its services are no longer needed. As a result, the testicles shrink, and a lower sperm count leads to sterility that is reversible for most men but irreversible in a small number of cases. Paradoxically, the male breasts enlarge (a condition called **gynecomastia**) because steroids break down eventually into estradiol, the female sex hormone. Other related consequences include frequent, sustained, and often painful erections (a condition called **priapism**), and an enlargement

gynecomastia (GEYE-neh-coh-MAST-ee-ah) An enlargement of the breasts.

priapism (PREYE-ah-pih-zem) A condition marked by persistent and frequently painful penile erections.

Ben Johnson, Charlie Francis, and the gold medal

t would be an understatement to say that Ben Johnson returned home to Canada from the 1988 Olympic Games in disgrace. While some newspapers spoke of the country's disappointment in a question, "How could Ben do this to us?" others were more direct in their indignation. One column in the *Ottawa Citizen* carried the angry headline, "Thanks a lot, you bastard." Johnson's world record had been taken away in Seoul, and the first Canadian gold medalist in a hundred-meter event since 1928 was now not only denied his achievement but also forbidden to participate in any competition for two years. Johnson's agent estimated that the total financial loss from the cancellation of major endorsement deals would approach $10 million for 1989 alone and probably $25 million over his career.

Charlie Francis, Johnson's Olympic coach, had been shocked when he first heard of the positive drug test but for a different reason from what you might suspect:

I felt spinning with confusion. I assumed that Ben had been nailed for an anabolic steroid, but it made no sense to me. For the past three years, some of my sprinters had been using an injectable form of the steroid furazabol, which we referred to as Estragol. I knew that it couldn't be detected, since the IOC's [International Olympic Committee's] lab equipment hadn't been programmed to identify furazabol's metabolites, the breakdown substances produced in the body. . . . Just what was going on here?

The test, as Francis found out shortly afterward, was positive for stanozolol, a chemical cousin to furazabol:

I was floored. To my knowledge, Ben had never injected stanozolol. He occasionally used Winstrol, an oral version of the drug, but for no more than a few days at a time, since it tended to make him stiff. He'd always discontinued the tablets at least six weeks before a meet, well beyond the accepted "clearance time"—the number of days required for a given drug to clear an athlete's system and become undetectable.

Interestingly, nowhere in his reaction was a denial that steroids had been a part of Johnson's training, as well as the training of others on the Canadian team, only that they had been caught.

Ben Johnson

In a special investigation into the scandal, conducted six months after the Seoul Olympics, a Canadian panel heard testimony from Johnson, Francis, and a large number of athletes, coaches, and trainers involved in competitive sports. Johnson had stonewalled the question up until that point, denying that he had taken any steroids in his career. Now the truth was revealed. At the hearing Francis's testimony alone lasted twenty-nine hours. Determined to set the record straight about the state of international sports, he testified that the standards, and the majority of world records, were steroid dependent. As he later wrote in his 1990 autobiography, of steroids in world-class athletics during the previous two decades or more, "The IOC and the IAAF [International Amateur Athletics Federation] refused to admit that most of the best athletes were already using the drugs."

Today, with the increasingly sophisticated techniques for drug testing, no one is surprised at the difficulty of breaking many of the historic performance records of the 1970s and 1980s.

Postscript: In 1993 Ben Johnson tested positive again for steroid use after a short-lived return to competitive running. He is now banned from competitive track and field events for life.

SOURCE: Cohen, Roger (1993, March 6). Johnson is banned for life after testing positive for drugs. *New York Times*, p. 32. Francis, Charlie, with Coplon, Jeff (1990). *Speed trap: Inside the biggest scandal in Olympic history.* New York: St. Martin's Press. Quotations on pp. 2, 3, and 91.

of the prostate gland. Severe acne, particularly on the shoulders and back, results from an increase in the secretions of the sebaceous glands in the skin. Other testosterone-related effects include changes in hair growth patterns: Facial hair growth is increased, while balding on the top of the head is accelerated.

Some athletes attempt to counter these undesirable hormonal effects by combining anabolic steroids with human chorionic

Anabolic steroids produce massive development of musculature, a prized asset in competitive bodybuilding.

gonadotropin (HCG), a hormone that ordinarily stimulates the testes to secrete testosterone. In theory, this strategy may work, but the dosages have to be carefully controlled, something that self-medicating athletes are unlikely to do. Repeated HCG treatments can actually have the opposite effect from the one that is intended, making matters worse rather than better. In addition, HCG itself has its own adverse effects, including headache, mood swings, depression, and retention of fluids.[9]

Among women taking anabolic steroids, the dramatically increased levels of testosterone in bodies that normally have only trace amounts produce major physiological changes, only some of which return to normal when steroids are withdrawn. Table 14.2 lists the major reversible and irreversible effects among women.

Effects on other systems of the body

Since the liver is the primary means for clearing drugs from the body, it is not surprising that large doses of anabolic steroids should take their toll on this particular organ. The principal result is a greatly increased risk of developing liver tumors. The type of liver

tumors frequently seen in these circumstances are benign (noncancerous) blood-filled cysts, with the potential for causing liver failure. In addition, a rupture in these cysts can produce abdominal bleeding, requiring life-saving emergency treatment. Fortunately, these liver abnormalities are reversible when steroids are withdrawn from use.[10]

There is evidence from animal studies that increased steroid levels in the body can produce high blood pressure and high cholesterol levels, as well as heart abnormalities. Whether cardiovascular effects present a problem for steroid abusers, however, is not well established, and some researchers consider the often publicized cardiovascular risks associated with anabolic steroids to be highly exaggerated. The one or two documented cases of heart-disease-related deaths

TABLE 14.2

Reported side effects of anabolic steroids in ten women

Effect	Number reporting the effect	Reversible after end of use
Lower voice	10	no
Increased facial hair	9	no
Enlarged clitoris	8	no
Increased aggressiveness	8	yes
Increased appetite	8	unknown
Decreased body fat	8	unknown
Diminished or stopped menstruation	7	yes
Increased sexual drive	6	yes
Increased acne	6	yes
Decreased breast size	5	unknown
Increased body hair	5	no
Increased loss of scalp hair	2	no

Note: The ten women were all weight-trained athletes.

SOURCES: Strauss, Richard H., and Yesalis, Charles E. (1993). Additional effects of anabolic steroids in women. In Charles E. Yesalis (Ed.), *Anabolic steroids in sport and exercise.* Champaign IL: Human Kinetics Publishers, pp. 151–160. Strauss, Richard H., Ligget, M. T., and Lanese R. R. (1985). Anabolic steroid use and perceived effects in ten weight-trained women athletes. *Journal of the American Medical Association, 253,* 2871–2873.

among abusers have been tied to factors other than the chronic intake of steroid drugs.[11]

Psychological problems

Stories abound of mood swings and increased aggressiveness, often referred to by athletes as " 'roid rage," when taking anabolic steroids. The relationship between increased testosterone and emotionality is not well understood, but the numerous anecdotal reports force us to consider the possibility that real psychological changes are going on.[12] As an example, this is how one sports writer recalled the unusual behavior of the professional football player Lyle Alzado:

I was covering the Los Angeles Raiders when Alzado, who had played previously with the Denver Broncos and Cleveland Browns, joined [the team] in 1982. He had acne on his back and upper arms, classic signs of steroid use. And his moods? One minute, he was the greatest guy in the world; the next minute, he was an erupting volcano for seemingly no reason. In 1984, I was talking to one of his teammates across the Raiders' dressing room, when Alzado, with no provocation, picked up his gray metal stool and threw it in my direction, shouting something about "reporters in the locker room." Shaken, I asked several players who knew him best what was bugging him. They said Alzado probably just had a steroid injection and to stay out of his way. Good advice.[13]

Special problems for adolescents

During puberty, a particularly crucial process among boys is the growth of the long bones of the body, which results in an increase in height. Anabolic steroids suppress growth hormone; as a result, muscular development is enhanced but overall body growth is stunted. Among girls, testosterone-related drugs delay the onset of puberty, making the body shorter, lighter, and more "girl-like" while enhancing their overall strength[14]

QUICK CONCEPT CHECK 14.1

Understanding the effects of anabolic steroids

heck your understanding of the effects of anabolic steroids by answering whether or not the following conditions can be attributed to steroid use.

1. severe acne on the lower extremities of the body

2. increased aggressiveness and mood swings

3. premature balding in men

4. increased development of the testicles

5. enlarged breasts (gynecomastia) among women

6. accelerated growth among adolescents around the time of puberty

ANSWERS: 1. no 2. yes 3. yes 4. no 5. no 6. no

Patterns of abuse of anabolic steroids

n 1990, as a response to the increasing awareness of the abuse of anabolic steroids both in and out of competitive sports, Congress passed the Anabolic Steroids Control Act, reclassifying anabolic steroids as Category III controlled substances, on a par with codeine preparations and barbiturates. Jurisdiction was transferred from the Food and Drug Administration (FDA) to the Drug Enforcement Administration (DEA). As a result of this legislation, pharmacies are permitted to fill prescriptions up to a maximum of five times, but penalties can result in a five-year prison term and a $250,000 fine for illegal nonmedical sales and a one-year term and a $1,000 fine for nonmedical possession. Penalties are doubled for repeated offenses or for selling these drugs to minors.

Despite the new regulations in effect, as you might expect, steroid abuse today continues to be a problem. Its distribution is now a black-market enterprise. Commonly referred to as 'roids, these drugs are channeled principally through people associated with body-building gyms and through mail-order companies that frequently change their location and identities to stay one step ahead of the law. It is estimated that the illicit anabolic steroid market is valued at between $300 million to $400 million each year, with the drugs smuggled into the United States from Europe, Canada, and Mexico.

The potential for steroid dependence

While anabolic steroids can be taken orally and through intramuscular injections, abusers often administer a combination of both types in a practice called stacking. Hard-core abusers may take a combination of three to five different pills and injectables simultaneously, or they may consume any steroid that is available ("shotgunning"), with the total exceeding a dozen. In addition to the complications that result from so many different types of steroids being taken at the same time, multiple injections into the buttocks or thighs, with 1.5 inch needles (called darts or points), are painful and inevitably leave scars. If these needles are shared, as they frequently are, there is the significant risk of hepatitis or HIV contamination.

A typical approach among steroid abusers is to follow a cyclical pattern of taking steroids for periods lasting from four to eighteen weeks, each separated by an "off" period of abstention. Unfortunately, when the drugs are withdrawn, the newly developed muscles tend to "shrink up," throwing the abuser into a panic that his or her body is losing the gains that have been achieved. In addition, absten-

tion from steroids can lead to signs of depression, such as problems in sleeping, lack of appetite, and general moodiness. All these effects encourage a return to steroids, frequently in even larger doses, and a craving for the euphoria that the person felt while on steroids.

Another problem associated with steroid abuse is the general attitude that no physique is ever perfect. In a kind of "reverse anorexia" that some call **megorexia,** body builders continue to see their bodies as weak and small when they look at themselves in a mirror, despite their greatly enhanced physical development. Peer pressure at the gyms and clubs is also a factor in never being satisfied with the size of one's muscles. It has been estimated that between 13 and 18 percent of those who have taken steroids show signs of physical and psychological dependence, in that they are unable to control or cut down on them, take more steroids than they intended, develop a tolerance to them, or take them to relieve or avoid undesirable withdrawal symptoms (Focus 14.1).[15]

Counterfeit steroids and the placebo effect

As with any form of use of illicit drugs, there are products marketed that look like anabolic steroids but are not the real thing. The problem here is that athletes are notoriously superstitious and easily leave themselves open to placebo effects. On the one hand, in the case of anabolic steroids, the effects on muscle development are usually so dramatic that it is difficult to mistake the response as simply a result of a placebo effect. On the other hand, there are several other forms of ergogenic drugs out there that have more subtle effects, and psychological factors can end up playing a greater role. Consider the clever strategy a baseball trainer claims to have used for the St. Louis Cardinals in the 1960s:

In 1964, I devised a yellow RBI pill, a red shutout pill, and a potent green hitting pill. Virtually every player on the team took them, and some

megorexia
The perception of one's own body as small and weak, despite evidence to the contrary.

wouldn't go out on the field until they took my pills. They worked so well that we won the pennant. We used them again in 1967 and 1968 and also won the pennant. They worked because I never told them that the pills were placebos.[16]

In other cases, however, the contents of pills and injectables supplied to unsuspecting customers may not be so benign. As with any illicit drug, you can never be sure of what you are getting. Frequently, a bogus drug can achieve enormous popularity simply by word of mouth. A former steroid "customer" relates the following story:

Bolasterone. It swept the country. They made millions. Millions, those California guys. All it was, was vegetable oil, a little bit of testosterone, and liquid aspirin. And they called it Bolasterone. And they hyped it up so much. It was selling for $250 to $275 a bottle. You would do anything to get this stuff. [They said] "Mr. Olympia used it! Secretly." I tell you, Madison Avenue could not have come up with a better campaign to sell this stuff. . . . If you had a bottle of it, I mean you could sell it for anything. . . . [It was hyped] through the grapevine. Underground. The network was incredible. From gym to gym to gym. . . . They'll say, "Did you see M.? He put on 15 pounds in a week." "What the hell is he using?" "Don't say anything. He's using Bolasterone!" "Wow. What the hell is it? Can you get it?" "Yeah, I can."[17]

Other ergogenic drugs of abuse

While anabolic steroids have dominated the ergogenic drug scene, other illicit drugs continue to be available for performance-enhancing purposes. One alternative, **human growth hormone (hGH),** has been increasingly popular, according to experts in this field, because it is more widely available and cheaper than in previous years, in contrast to illicit steroids that have become more expensive. An athlete can reportedly buy an eight- to ten-week cycle of hGH for less than $1,000. Those who take this pituitary hormone, however, have the increased

F O C U S   14.1
DRUG ABUSE ALERT
The signs of steroid abuse

OR BOTH SEXES

1. Rapid increases in strength and/or size beyond what you would expect in a relatively short time. Putting on ten to twenty pounds of solid muscle within a period of a few weeks or so should be a strong warning.

2. Involvement in activities where steroid abuse is known to be condoned or encouraged

3. Sudden increases in appetite and preoccupation with changes in one's physical condition

4. Recent appearance of acne, particularly on the upper back, shoulders, and arms

5. Premature male-pattern baldness, including a rapidly receding hairline or loss of hair from the top rear of the head

5. A puffy appearance in the face as if the individual is retaining water

6. An increase in moodiness or unusual shifts in mood

7. A reddening of the face, neck, and upper chest, appearing as if one is constantly flushed

8. A yellowing of the skin or the whites of the eyes, stemming from a disturbance in liver functioning

FOR MEN

1. An enlargement of the breasts, often accompanied by protruding nipples

2. An increase in sexual interest and a tendency to display that interest more aggressively

FOR WOMEN

1. A lowering of the vocal range

2. Smaller or flatter breasts. (See Table 14.2)

SOURCE: Wright, James E., and Cowart, Virginia S. (1990). *Anabolic steroids: Altered states.* Carmel IN: Benchmark Press, pp. 71–91.

human growth hormone (hGH)
A naturally occurring hormone promoting growth, particularly in the long bones of the body.

risk of developing a significant side effect called **acromegaly,** a condition resulting in a coarse and misshapen head, enlarged hands and feet, and damage to various internal organs. Prior to 1985, hGH was obtained from the pituitary glands of human cadavers, but now genetically engineered hGH (brand names: Protropin and Humatrope) is available, approved by the FDA for the treatment of rare cases of stunted growth. While the distribution of these drugs is controlled by their manufacturers as carefully as possible, supplies manage to get diverted for illicit use. Since hGH has a very short half-life, no screening procedure has yet been developed to detect it, so long as the individual abstains from it prior to the test.[18]

Some of the other ergogenic drugs and aids presently used for illicit athletic or body-building purposes are listed in Table 14.3.

Present-day drug-testing procedures and policies

Since the mid-1960s, organizers of major athletic competitions have attempted to develop effective screening procedures to prevent the use of ergogenic drugs from resulting in an unfair advantage of one competitor over another. Needless to say, neither have these procedures proved perfect nor have they served as an effective deterrent for drug use among athletes. It is a rare occasion when you fail to read about some athlete who has been disqualified from competing or who has been denied the honor of winning because he or she tested positive for a particular banned substance. Disputes about positive findings are argued all the time.

It is ironic that the present status of drug testing as a fact of life in modern sports has brought with it a new form of contest, pitting the skill and ingenuity of the laboratory scientist whose job it is to detect the presence of ergogenic drugs against the skill and ingenuity of the athlete in devising ways to get away with using these drugs without detection.

This section will look at drug-testing techniques designed not only to detect performance-enhancing drugs that are relevant to sports but also a wider range of illicit drugs, such as heroin, cocaine, and marijuana. As you might already be aware, drug testing goes on for individuals in selected industries affecting public safety such as airline pilots and railroad engineers (see Chapter 17), but the largest proportion of tests are conducted among athletes. Within some sports organizations, such as the National Collegiate Athletic Association (NCAA), drug tests are conducted not only for the presence of ergogenic drugs but also for the presence of drugs that have no particular ergogenic benefits. In the case of marijuana, for example, the proper description for its effects might be ergolytic (performance-hampering) with regard to athletic competitions. The policy is defended on the premise that athletes have the potential for exposure to illicit substances, and no collegiate athlete should be permitted to compete while engaging in illegal activity.

Techniques for drug testing

Present-day drug-testing procedures begin with a urine sample from the individual in question. The advantages lie in the ease and noninvasiveness of collecting urine, the ease with which urine can be analyzed for specific factors, and the fact that drugs or their metabolites (by-products) are usually very stable in frozen urine. Therefore, it is possible to provide long-term storage of positive samples, in the event that the results are disputed. The disadvantages are that many perceive urine collection to be a humiliating experience, a dehydrated athlete immediately after competing may find it difficult to urinate, and there may be ways to tamper with the urine sample

acromegaly (A-kroh-MEG-ah-lee)
A condition resulting in structural abnormalities of the head, hands, and feet, as well as damage to internal organs.

Nonsteroid ergogenic drugs and aids in sports and bodybuilding

Drug or aid	Licit use or natural origin	Illicit application
Zeranol	Drug to fatten cattle	Anabolic agent
Carnitine	Nonprotein amino acid	Anabolic agent
Clenbuterol	Drug to treat asthma in Europe; not approved for any purpose in the U.S.	Anabolic agent
Deprenyl	Drug to treat Parkinson's disease; inhibitor of monoamine oxidase (MAO)	Amphetamine-ike stimulant for endurance events
orotic acid	Vitamin, benefits unknown	Anabolic agent
erythropoietin (EPO)	Naturally occurring hormone, to treat anemia	Increases red blood cells; enhances oxygen-carrying capacity of the blood
beta blockers	To treat high blood pressure, cardiac arrhythmias, and social anxiety	Increases steadiness in archery and other shooting events
diuretics	To reduce water retention	Causes rapid weight loss by wrestlers, jockeys, and gymnasts as well as dilution of the urine to minimize detection in drug testing
blood doping (infusion with red blood cells from one's own blood)	No medical application	Increases oxygen-carrying capacity of the blood
soda doping* or buffer boosting	Liquid of bicarbonate soda drunk before an event; no medical application	Prevents lactic acid buildup in order to delay muscle fatigue

*Note: The word *dope* originates from the practice of Kaffir tribesmen in South Africa, who drank a mixture of alcohol and cola called *dop*, to gain increased energy and stamina. The Boer settlers in South Africa added an "e" at the end, giving the world the word that is frequently taken to mean illicit drugs in general.

SOURCES: Dolan, Edward F. (1992). *Drugs and sports* (rev. ed.). New York: Franklin Watts, p. 17.   Kammerer, R. Craig (1993). Drug testing and anabolic steroids. In Charles E. Yesalis (Ed.), *Anabolic steroids in exercise and sport*. Champaign IL: Human Kinetics Publishers, pp. 283–308. Wadler, Gary I., and Hainline, Brian. *Drugs and the athlete*. Philadelphia: F. A. Davis, pp. 159–177.

prior to testing. Despite these problems, however, this procedure is considered to be the most practical way of testing for drugs. Testing procedures based upon saliva, blood, or hair samples are available but not widely used.

The two major urinanalysis methods are the **enzyme immunoassay (EIA)** technique and a procedure combining **gas chromatography and mass spectrometry (GC/MS).** In both these methods, the collected urine is divided into two samples prior to being sent off to the laboratory, so that if the analysis of one sample yields a positive outcome the analysis can be repeated on the other sample. This reanalysis procedure is often required if an individual appeals the original test result.[19]

With the EIA method, a separate test must be run on each particular drug that is being screened. First, at an earlier time, the substance to be tested for (THC or cocaine, for example) has been injected into an animal, eliciting specific immunological antibodies to that substance. The antibodies are then purified into a testing substrate. The combination of the collected urine and the testing substrate will yield a specific reaction if the urine contains the banned substance. A popular

enzyme immunoassay (EIA)
One of the two major drug-testing techniques for detecting banned substances or drugs.

gas chromatography/mass spectrometry (GC/MS)
A drug-testing technique based on the combination of gas chromatography and mass spectrometry.

commercial testing kit for screening major banned substances, called **EMIT (Enzyme Multiplied Immunoassay Technique),** has been marketed by Syva Laboratories, a subsidiary of Syntex Corporation in Palo Alto, California, since the early 1970s. This kit is relatively inexpensive and can be used to screen large numbers of urine samples. It is so widely available that the trademark name, EMIT, is often used to mean any form of EIA method.

With the GC/MS method, the urine is first vaporized and combined with an inert gas, then passed over a number of chemically treated columns. Through the process of gas chromatography, technicians are able to identify the presence of a banned substance by the different colorations that are left on the columns. After this has been done, the gas is then ionized (converted into an electrically active form) and sent through an electric current and magnetic field that separates out each of the different ions (electrically charged particles) in the gas. Through the process of mass spectrometry, a particular "fingerprint," or "signature," of each chemical substance can be detected and measured. The GC/MS technique is considered more definitive than the EIA technique, but it is considerably more expensive and time-consuming. It is also the only testing procedure adequate to screen for anabolic steroids.[20]

Sensitivity and specificity

As you might imagine, the two principal questions surrounding drug-testing methods are (1) how much of the banned substance needs to be in the urine before it is picked up as a positive test (the sensitivity of the test) and (2) whether it is possible to yield a false-positive result in which the test comes out positive but the urine is in actuality "clean" (the specificity of the test). In this regard, the

---

Enzyme Multiplied Immunoassay Technique (EMIT)
Brand name for a commercial EIA testing kit.

GC/MS test is more sensitive and specific than the EIA test. Frequently, the GC/MS analysis is performed as a confirmation of a positive EIA test. Nonetheless, false positives can occur even with the GC/MS test. Eating a poppy seed roll prior to drug testing, for example, has resulted in false-positive indications of opiate use; therapeutic levels of ibuprofin (brand names: Advil, Motrin, and Nuprin, among others) have resulted in false-positive indications of marijuana smoking. In addition, the passive inhalation of marijuana smoke can leave sufficient levels of THC metabolites to result in false-positive indications of marijuana smoking, though the density of smoke that needs to be experienced for this to happen makes it unlikely that individuals would be completely unaware that they were being exposed to marijuana.[21]

Masking drugs and chemical manipulations

Two specific ways have been attempted to disguise the prior use of anabolic steroids so that the outcome of a drug test is a false-negative. The first was to take the antigout drug probenecid (brand name: Benemid). Available since 1987, it does mask the presence of anabolic steroids, but it is now on the list of banned substances for competitive athletes and is easily detected by GC/MS techniques. The second way was to increase the level of epitestosterone in the body. The standard procedure for determining the present or prior use of anabolic steroids is to calculate the ratio of testosterone against the level of epitestosterone, a naturally occurring hormone that is usually stable at relatively low levels in the body. International athletic organizations have agreed that a ratio of 6:1 or higher be the standard for indicating steroid use. If epitestosterone is artificially elevated, the ratio can be manipulated downward, so as to indicate a false-negative result in drug testing. However, suspiciously high levels of epitestosterone can now be detected by GC/MS techniques, so this form of manipulation is no longer successful.[22]

Pinpointing the time of drug use

It is important to remember that a positive result in a drug test indicates merely that the test has determined a minimal level of a drug or its metabolite. It has not determined when that drug was introduced into the body or the length of time drug-taking behavior was going on. The time it takes for the body to get rid of the metabolites of a particular drug varies considerably, from a few hours to a few weeks. Table 14.4 shows the variations for major drugs of abuse.

An additional point to remember is that the possibility of a positive drug test cannot be an effective deterrent against the abuse of drugs. For example, an athlete can easily manipulate the result of a scheduled drug test by planning to be off the drug long enough prior to testing for the metabolites to be relatively low. Only through a random testing program can the test results adequately reflect the level of drug-taking behavior. Unfortunately, random drug testing is costly. Relatively few colleges and considerably fewer high schools can afford a random schedule of drug testing; most high schools cannot afford drug testing at all. And it is worth considering the following fact: For all those individuals who are abusing anabolic steroids or other ergogenic drugs outside of organized athletic activities, no fear of a positive drug test exists because they will never be required to undergo any form of drug testing.

TABLE 14.4
Detection periods for various drugs

Drug	Detection period
alcohol	1/2 to 1 day
amphetamines and derivatives	1–7 days
barbiturates	
amobarbital, pentobarbital	2–4 days
phenobarbital	Up to 30 days
secobarbital	2–4 days
benzodiazepines	Up to 30 days
cocaine	
Occasional use	6–12 hours
Repeated use	Up to 48 hours
marijuana (THC)	
Casual use up to 4 joints per week	5–7 days
Daily use	10–15 days
Chronic, heavy use	1–2 months
opiates and opiate-like drugs	
Dilaudid	2–4 days
Darvon	6–48 hours
heroin or morphine	2–4 days
methadone	2–3 days
phencyclidine (PCP)	
Casual use	2–7 days
Chronic, heavy use	Several months
Quaalude	2–4 days
anabolic steroids	
Fat-soluble injectables	6–8 months
Water-soluble oral types	3–6 weeks
over-the-counter cold medications containing ephedrine derivatives as decongestants	48–72 hours

SOURCES: *Allen and Hanbury's Athletic drug reference* (1994). Durham NC: Clean Data, p. 19. Inaba, Darryl S., and Cohen, William E. (1989). *Uppers, downers, all arounders.* Ashland OR: Cinemed, p. 206.

What can be done about drug abuse in sports?

nabolic steroids and other ergogenic drugs are quite different from many of the abused drugs covered in previous chapters in that they affect the way we look and how we compare to others rather than the way we feel. Charles E. Yesalis, one of the leading experts in steroid abuse, has put it this way:

If you were stranded on a desert island, you might use cocaine if it were available, but nobody would use steroids. On a desert island, nobody cares what you look like and there is nothing to win. We are the ones who have made the determination that appearance and winning are all important. We're telling kids in our society that sports is more than a game. Until we change those signals, for the most part, we might as well tell people to get used to drug use.[23]

Understanding drug testing

heck your understanding of present-day drug-testing results by answering whether or not the following statements are true.

1. EMIT results are more sensitive than GC/MS results.　❑ yes　❑ no

2. Benemid is an effective way of achieving a false-negative result.　❑ yes　❑ no

3. The time of marijuana smoking is one conclusion that drug testing has great difficulty in determining.　❑ yes　❑ no

4. Athletes are generally very cooperative in achieving the least number of false-negative outcomes.　❑ yes　❑ no

5. Anabolic steroid screening is presently mandated by the International Olympic Committee for winners of Olympic events.　❑ yes　❑ no

ANSWERS: 1. no　2. no　3. yes　4. no　5. yes

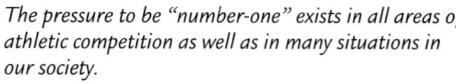

The pressure to be "number-one" exists in all areas of athletic competition as well as in many situations in our society.

The future in fighting abuse of anabolic steroids lies in the likelihood that we can change the winner-take-all mentality of our culture. Unfortunately, there seems to be little cause for optimism. Numerous surveys taken among young athletes and nonathletes alike indicate that the social signals are crystal clear and they are more than willing to take up the challenge, despite the risks. They have typically been asked variations on the following question: "If you had a magic drug that was so fantastic that if you took it once you would win every competition you would enter, from the Olympic decathlon to Mr. Universe, for the next five years, but it had one minor drawback—it would kill you five years after you took it—would you still take the drug?" More than half of those polled have said yes to this question.[24]

Summary

DRUG-TAKING BEHAVIOR IN SPORTS

- The use of ergogenic (performance-enhancing) drugs in athletic competition has a long history, dating from the original Olympic Games in ancient Greece.

- In the modern era, the principal type of ergogenic drugs has been anabolic steroids.

These synthetic drugs, all based on variations of the testosterone molecule, have been available and used in international sports competitions since the 1950s.

- Since the late 1980s, it has also been recognized that anabolic steroids have been popular with body builders as well as competitive athletes. This latter group typically take steroids in enormous quantities and administer them in a largely unsupervised fashion.

THE HAZARDS OF ANABOLIC STEROIDS

- The hazards of steroids derive from the adverse consequences of high levels of testosterone in the body. The health consequences include liver tumors, mood swings, and increased aggressiveness.

- For men, the effects include lower sperm count, enlargement of the breasts, atrophy of the testicles, baldness, and severe acne. For women, masculinizing changes occur, only some of which are reversible if steroids are withdrawn.

PATTERNS OF ABUSE OF ANABOLIC STEROIDS

- Since 1990, possession and sales of anabolic steroids have been illegal without specific medical prescriptions. These drugs are now distributed through illicit black market channels.

- It is now known that a proportion of individuals taking large doses of steroids develop both physical and psychological dependence.

PRESENT-DAY DRUG-TESTING PROCEDURES AND POLICIES

- Drug-testing procedures, chiefly for those in organized athletics, have become increasingly sophisticated in their ability to detect the presence of banned substances.

- Two major techniques, both based on urine samples, are enzyme immunoassay (EIA) and a combination of gas chromatography and mass spectrometry (GC/MS).

- The ultimate goal of drug-testing procedures is to make it impossible to yield either a false-negative or false-positive result.

Key Terms

acromegaly, p. 344
adrenocortical steroids, p. 336
anabolic, p. 335
anabolic-androgenic steroids, p. 335
anabolic steroids, p. 335
androgenic, p. 335
enzyme immunoassay (EIA), p. 345
enzyme multiplied immunoassay technique (EMIT), p. 346

ergogenic, p. 335
gas chromatography/mass spectrometry (GC/MS), p. 345
gynecomastia, p. 338
human growth hormone (hGH), p. 343
megorexia, p. 342
priapism, p. 338

Endnotes

1. Dolan, Edward F. (1986). *Drugs in sports* (rev. ed.). New York: Franklin Watts, pp. 17–18.   Meer, Jeff (1987). *Drugs and sports.* New York: Chelsea House, p. 21. Wadler, Gary I., and Hainline, Brian (1989). *Drugs and the athlete.* Philadelphia: F. A. Davis, pp. 3–17

2. Meer. *Drugs and sports,* pp 61–75.   Taylor, William N. (1991). *Macho medicine: The history of the anabolic steroid epidemic.* Jefferson NC McFarland and Co., pp. 3–16.

3. Lombardo, John (1993). The efficacy and mechanisms of action of anabolic steroids. In Charles E. Yesalis (Ed), *Anabolic steroids in*

sport and exercise. Champaign IL: Human Kinetics Publishers, p. 100.

4. Scott, Jack (1971, October 17). It's not how you play the game, but what pill you take. *New York Times Magazine,* p. 41.

5. Dickman, Steven (1991). East Germany: Science in the disservice of the state. *Science, 254,* 26–27.   Drozdiak, William (1992, July 31). Three Olympians fail drug tests. *Washington Post,* pp. A1, A12.   Janofsky, Michael (1991, December 3). Coaches concede that steroids fueled East Germany's success in swimming. *New York Times,* pp. B11, B18, quotation on p. B11.   Yesalis, Charles E., Courson, Stephen P., and Wright, James (1993). History of anabolic steroid use in sport and exercise. In Charles E. Yesalis (Ed.), *Anabolic steroids in sport and exercise.* Champaign IL: Human Kinetics Publishers, pp. 1–33.

6. W.W.F.'s McMahon indicted (1993, November 19). *New York Times,* p. B12.   Yesalis, Courson, and Wright. History of anabolic steroid use, pp. 40–42.

7. Buckley, William E., Yesalis, Charles E., Friedl, Karl E., Anderson, William A., Streit, Andrea L., and Wright, James E. (1988). Estimated prevalence of anabolic steroid use among male high school seniors. *Journal of the American Medical Association, 260,* 3441–3445. Yesalis, Charles E. (1993). Introduction. In Charles E. Yesalis (Ed.), *Anabolic steroids in sport and exercise.* Champaign IL: Human Kinetics Publishers, pp. xxxi–xxxii.

8. Brower, Kirk J., Catlin, Donald H., Blow, Frederic C., Eliopulos, George A., and Bereford, T. P. (1991). Clinical assessment and urine testing for anabolic-androgenic steroid abuse and dependence. *American Journal of Drug and Alcohol Abuse, 17,* 161–172.   Council on Scientific Affairs (1990). Medical and nonmedical uses of anabolic-androgenic steroids. *Journal of the American Medical Association, 264,* 2923–2927.

9. Friedl, Karl E. (1993). Effects of anabolic steroids on physical health. In Charles E. Yesalis (Ed.), *Anabolic steroids in sport and exercise.* Champaign IL: Human Kinetics Publish-
ers, pp. 107–150.   Hunt, Liz (1991, August 17). Steroid use may cause sterility: Long-term effect seen in some men. *Washington Post,* pp. A1, A14.   Wadler, Gary I., and Hainline, Brian (1989). *Drugs and the athlete.* Philadelphia: F. A. Davis, pp. 55–69.

10. Friedl. *Effects of anabolic steroids,* pp. 121–131.

11. Ibid., pp. 116–121.

12. Su, Tung-Ping, Pagliaro, Michael, Schmidt, Peter J., Pickar, David, Wolkowitz, Owen, and Rubinow, David R. (1993). Neuropsychiatric effects of anabolic steroids in male normal volunteers. *Journal of the American Medical Association, 269,* 2760–2764.

13. After bodybuilder is accused of murder, many point finger at steroid use (1993, July 3). *New York Times,* p. 27.   Greenberg, Alan (1991, June 29). Alzado has a serious message to kids about steroids—Don't use them. *Hartford (CT) Courant,* Cited in Jim Ferstle (1993), Evolution and politics of drug testing. In Charles E. Yesalis (Ed.), *Anabolic steroids in sport and exercise.* Champaign IL: Human Kinetics Publishers, p. 276.

14. Bahrke, Michael S. (1993). Psychological effects of endogenous testosterone and anabolic-androgenic steroids. In Charles E. Yesalis (Ed.), *Anabolic steroids in sport and exercise.* Champaign IL: Human Kinetics Publishers, pp. 161–192.

15. Bower, Bruce (1991). Pumped up and strung out. *Science News, 140,* 30–31.   Schrof, Joanne M. (1992, June 1). Pumped up. *U.S. News and World Report,* pp. 55–63.

16. Quotation by Bob Bauman (1992). In Bob Goldman and Ronald Klatz, *Death in the locker room II: Drugs and sports.* Chicago: Elite Sports Medicine Publications, pp. 10–11.

17. Goldstein, Paul J. (1990). Anabolic steroids: An ethnographic approach. In Geraline C. Lin and Lynda Erinoff (Eds.), *Anabolic steroid abuse* (NIDA Research Monograph 102). Rockville MD: National Institute on Drug Abuse, p. 84.

18. Catlin, Don, Wright, Jim, Pope, Harrison, and Liggett, Mariah (1993). Assessing the threat of anabolic steroids: Sportsmedicine update. *The*

physician and sportsmedicine, 21, 37–44. Wadler and Hainline. *Drugs and the athlete,* pp. 70–74.

19. Ibid., pp. 201–202.
20. Meer. *Drugs and sports,* pp. 92–95.
21. *Allen and Hanbury's Athletic drug reference* (1994). Durham NC: Clean Data, pp. 65–66. Struempler, Richard E. (1987, May/June). Excretion of codeine and morphine following ingestion of poppy seeds. *Journal of Analytical Toxicology, 11,* 97–99. Wadler and Hainline. *Drugs and the athlete,* pp. 208–209.
22. Catlin, Wright, Pope, and Liggett. Assessing the threat, p. 39.
23. Quotation of Charles E. Yesalis. In Wright and Cowart. *Anabolic steriods,* p. 196.
24. Goldman, Bob, and Klatz, Ronald (1992) *Death in the locker room II: Drugs and sports.* Chicago: Elite Sports Medicine Publications, pp. 23–24.

15

Prescription and Over-the-Counter Drugs

THIS CHAPTER WILL INTRODUCE YOU
TO THE FOLLOWING SUBJECTS:

- The distinction between prescription and OTC drugs

- The evolution of U.S. drug regulations

- FDA guidelines for approving new drugs

- Prescription drugs changing to OTC drugs

- Analgesics, as well as weight-loss, sleep-aid, and cough-and-cold remedies

- The pharmaceutical industry today

Here lies the body of Mary Ann Waters,
Died of drinking Cheltenham waters, If she
had stuck to Epsom salts, She wouldn't be
lying in these here vaults.

Epitaph from an English country
churchyard (date unknown)

Medicines are nothing in themselves,
if not properly used, but the very hands
of the gods, if employed with reason
and prudence.

Herophilius (300 B.C.)
Greek physician

he next time you are in a pharmacy or drug store, take a minute to look around you. Besides the overwhelming variety of cosmetics, shaving creams, toothpastes, deodorants, and all the other products that have become part of our daily lives, two broad categories of products are available for purchase as medicines.

The first group of medicinal products, roughly 2,500 of them, placed mostly out of view and behind the pharmacist's counter, are **prescription drugs.** Their purchase and use requires the submission of a written prescription form with an appropriate signature (or a doctor's phone call) that certifies that you are taking one of these drugs for a medical condition and at a dosage level appropriate for that condition. The amount of the drug that you are allowed to purchase at any one time is specified, and a limit on the number of prescription renewals offers some control over that drug's use over an extended period of time. By law, only licensed physicians or dentists are permitted to write (or call in) prescriptions for their patients, and only registered pharmacists are permitted to fill these prescriptions and dispense the drugs to the consumer.

The second group of medicinal products, roughly 300,000 of them, are **over-the-counter (OTC) drugs.** In contrast to prescription drugs, OTC drugs are available to you right off the shelves that line the aisles of the store, and their use is limited only by your ability to pay for them. With OTC drugs, you are your own physician. In most cases, you have diagnosed the ailment yourself and decided on the course of treatment. While the recommended doses are clearly printed on the label and you may get some

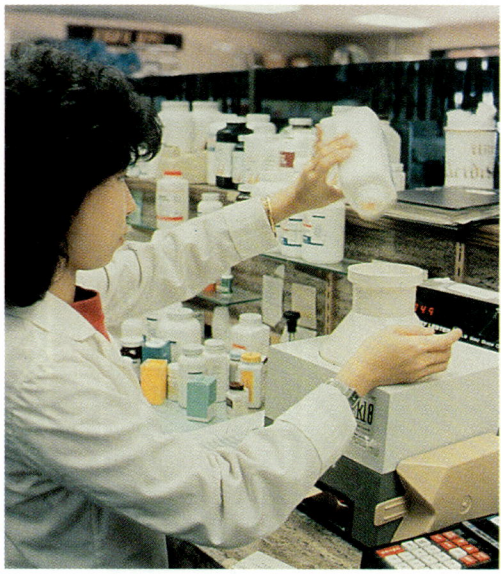

Pharmacists are specially trained to dispense approximately 2500 different prescription drugs.

drug should continue to be available for public use and whether a newly developed drug can pass the standards of safety and effectiveness to be marketed as a prescription drug. It also oversees the safety and effectiveness of OTC drugs. By necessity, according to FDA standards, the strength and concentration of active ingredients in OTC drugs must have a greater margin of safety than active ingredients in prescription drugs to justify their wide availability to the general public under such unsupervised circumstances.

This chapter will look at the governmental policies and procedures that have evolved over the last century to protect us from unsafe and ineffective medications. No drug, however, is totally free of potentially toxic effects, despite our best efforts to assure the safety of prescription and OTC drugs. The potential for misuse of OTC drugs is a particular concern. It is important, therefore, to cover four major classes of OTC drugs for which a potential for misuse exists: analgesics, weight-loss aids, sleep aids, and cough-and-cold remedies.

guidance from the pharmacist, there is no direct medical supervision over the dosage level that you actually consume at any given time. No one will tell you when to stop using these drugs or whether they were appropriate to take in the first place. Given the almost total absence of supervision over the personal use of OTC drugs, some basic safeguards are needed. Are the drugs safe to use, if taken at the dosage levels listed on the package? Are they effective in helping you in the way they are advertised?

In the United States, the regulation of both prescription and OTC drugs has been assigned to the U.S. Food and Drug Administration. The FDA has the responsibility for determining whether an existing prescription

How the regulation of prescription and OTC drugs began

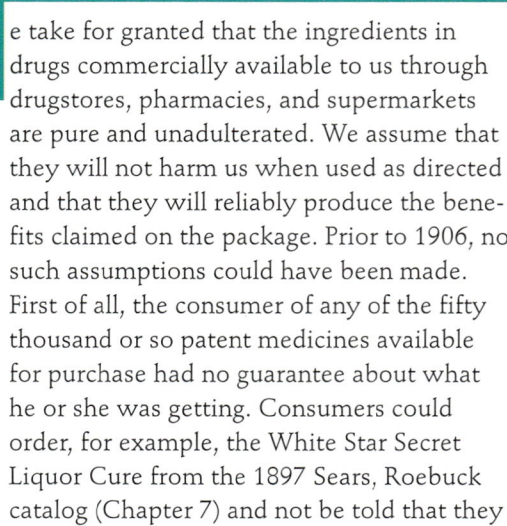

e take for granted that the ingredients in drugs commercially available to us through drugstores, pharmacies, and supermarkets are pure and unadulterated. We assume that they will not harm us when used as directed and that they will reliably produce the benefits claimed on the package. Prior to 1906, no such assumptions could have been made. First of all, the consumer of any of the fifty thousand or so patent medicines available for purchase had no guarantee about what he or she was getting. Consumers could order, for example, the White Star Secret Liquor Cure from the 1897 Sears, Roebuck catalog (Chapter 7) and not be told that they

prescription drugs
Drugs available to the public only when approved by a medical professional and dispensed by a licensed pharmacist.

over-the-counter (OTC) drugs
A class of medicinal drugs available to the public without the requirement of a prescription.

would be consuming opium. The manufacturer was under no obligation to tell buyers that fact (or anything else for that matter) on the label.

As a response to public outcry about all the unregulated patent medicines on the market as well as publicity about the terrible conditions in the meatpacking industry, Congress enacted the Pure Food and Drug Act in 1906. This legislation set out to assure that all food and drugs in the United States would be inspected for purity and consistency. In addition, all active ingredients in drugs had to be clearly and accurately identified. The 1906 act did not, however, guarantee any more protection than that. Until 1938, drugs could still be useless and dangerous so long as the label listed the ingredients in a correct manner.

By the early 1930s, proposals to strengthen food and drug regulations were introduced in Congress, but the legislative process was at a virtual standstill as drug manufacturers and advertising lobbyists fought successfully to maintain the status quo, and attention was focused principally on the economic problems facing the nation.

As often happens, it took a national crisis before action was finally taken. In September 1937 a syrup for sore throats called Elixir Sulfanilamide, manufactured in a small factory in Tennessee, was found to be the cause of 107 deaths throughout the United States. Many of those affected were children. The reason for the tragic results was quickly determined to be the fact that the sulfanilamide component (in itself a useful antibiotic) had been dissolved in a solution containing diethylene glycol, a close relative to present-day antifreeze. Obviously, the drug had not been adequately tested for safety.

Luckily, the FDA was able to seize the entire stock of the medicine, and it was taken off the market before any more deaths occurred. But the FDA acted not because the Elixir had been judged unsafe (under the 1906 law the FDA would not have been able to act on these grounds) but because the preparation had been mislabeled. Technically, an elixir had to contain some quantity of ethyl alcohol (see Chapter 10), and Elixir Sulfanilamide had none. Hence, the law had been broken![1]

After the incident, the American public sent a clear message to Washington that they would no longer tolerate the marketing of unsafe drugs. By December 1937, Congress finally passed the legislation that had been stalled for years. President Roosevelt signed into law the Federal Food, Drug, and Cosmetic (FDC) Act, which has served to the present-day as the basic food and drug law in the United States. Taking effect in 1938, this law mandated that all ingredients in cosmetic products had to be accurately identified, and drug companies were henceforth required to demonstrate by research studies that new drugs were safe (when used as directed) before they could be marketed commercially. A 1951 amendment to the FDC Act established the clear distinction between prescription and OTC drugs. By that point, the FDA had grown in stature and power as the official guardian of the public interest with regard to food, drugs, and cosmetics.

The final element of governmental control took effect in 1962, once again as a reaction to a well-publicized health emergency. In the late 1950s, a drug called **thalidomide** had been marketed by a West German pharmaceutical company and used by thousands of pregnant women in Europe, Canada, Australia, and South America as a sedative and treatment for the discomforts of morning sickness. In 1960 a U.S. pharmaceutical company applied to the FDA for approval to market thalidomide in the United States. Despite pressures to do so, the FDA refused the application. Scattered reports had been noticed of the incidence of deformities among babies of mothers who had been taking thalidomide (see Portrait). Thousands of babies around the world were born armless, legless, or both because of this drug. By 1962, Americans

thalidomide (tha-LID-oh-meyed)
A highly teratogenic (birth-defect producing) drug.

PORTRAIT

Frances Kelsey— Saving a generation of American babies

n October 1961 a new medical officer at the FDA's Division of New Drugs, Dr. Frances Kelsey, was assigned the task of supervising the approval for a new drug called thalidomide. Introduced by a German pharmaceutical company in 1958, the drug had been hailed as "the tranquilizer of the future." Even massive doses of thalidomide couldn't kill you. Of all the countries of the world that had accepted thalidomide for marketing within their own borders, only France, Israel, and the United States were holding out. At that time, the FDA had to reject the application for a new drug in sixty days or automatically allow it to be approved and marketed. Merrell Pharmaceuticals had sponsored the application for thalidomide and was anxiously awaiting the results. But Kelsey kept on stalling; after each sixty-day period, she would rou-

tinely reject the application as "incomplete."

As Kelsey studied the data, something seemed wrong about thalidomide. One of its side effects, of minor importance by itself, was a mild neuritis, or "tingling of the nerves." It reminded her of research she had conducted fifteen years earlier where she had observed that neuritis of this type in pregnant animals resulted in deformed offspring. None of the experimental animal data, however, had shown anything even resembling birth defects. It remained simply her gut instinct to wait a little longer, just to be sure.

In retrospect, seldom had a wait been more worthwhile. Within a year of thalidomide's introduction in Germany, an extremely rare birth deformity began to appear. Babies were born with short, finlike appendages instead of normal arms and legs, victims of a disorder called phycomelia. The

number of cases of phycomelia had mysteriously increased from 12 in 1959, to 83 in 1960, to 302 in 1961. A German pediatrician offered the theory that these horrible deformities were tied to the taking of thalidomide by pregnant women. By 1962, it was clear that the drug was indeed the culprit.

Frances Kelsey

It has been estimated by the FDA that ten thousand babies in twenty countries were victims of thalidomide. But American children never had to experience this tragedy, thanks to one woman who had her suspicions and was brave enough to say no. In 1962 President John F. Kennedy awarded Kelsey the President's Gold Medal for Distinguished Service, in honor of her heroic stance. In 1995, at the age of 80, Kelsey remains active in protecting the public from the possible dangers of new drugs, as the Director of

Scientific Investigations at the FDA.

Today, thalidomide is used only in extremely restricted applications and is never given to fertile women on the off chance that they might be pregnant. Ironically, this highly teratogenic (birth defect-causing) drug is one of the few treatments available for leprosy. It is also valuable for cancer patients who have undergone bone-marrow transplants. For some reason that is presently unknown, thalidomide stops the graft-versus-host reaction following such procedures that has the potential for killing the patient.

SOURCES: Adler, Tina (1994). The return of thalidomide. *Science News, 146,* 424–425. Fredman, Steven, and Burger, Robert E. (1976). *Forbidden cures: How the FDA suppresses drugs we need.* New York: Stein and Day, pp. 13–15. Friedman, Saul (1995, February 23). Medicine may be hard to swallow. *Newsday,* pp. A39, A41. Patrick, William (1988). *The Food and Drug Administration.* New York: Chelsea House, pp. 41–42. Squires, Sally (1989, April 25). Leprosy's legacy. *Washington Post,* p. 13.

learned of the enormity of the tragedy and how close they had come to being affected themselves.

Though the Kefauver-Harris Amendment of 1962 was a direct consequence of the

thalidomide crisis, the FDA had in fact been acting on the basis of statutes that were already existing. The safety of new drugs had to be assured by an FDA approval process, which is precisely what the FDA carried out. Nonetheless, the American public, anxious because it had just barely avoided a major catastrophe, was insistent that the FDA be given broader powers. As a result of the 1962 amendment, drug companies were required to prove that new drugs were *effective* as well as safe. The concern up to then had been only the matter of safety. An important additional feature of the new regulations, however, did affect the maintenance of drug safety. Once new drugs were approved, drug companies were required to send reports to the FDA on a regular basis, informing the agency of any adverse reactions experienced by their users. As a result, any unforeseen difficulties with FDA-approved drugs could be recognized and appropriate measures could then be taken.

While the FDA continues to prosecute violators of the drug laws, regulations since 1938 have allowed the FDA a more active role in preventing problems from arising in the first place (Table 15.1).[2] A major part of this preventive approach is the set of procedures required for the approval of new prescription drugs and the setting of standards for OTC drugs.

TABLE 15.1

Major regulatory laws of the FDA since 1938

Act or amendment	Year	Effect
Color Additive Amendment	1960	Regulated the safe use of color additives in drugs and food
Hazardous Substances Labeling Act	1960	Required warning labels on all products intended for home use
Kefauver-Harris Amendment	1962	Required that new drugs be effective as well as safe
Child Protection Act	1966	Regulated the safety of toys sold across state lines
Medical Device Amendment	1976	Required that any health-care product or device be effective and safe
Instant Formula Act	1980	Regulated the contents of baby-formula preparations
Antitampering Act	1983	Required tamper-resistant packaging for all OTC products
Orphan Drug Act	1983	Allowed drug companies to take tax credits for developing new drugs with low potential for profits

SOURCE: Patrick, William (1988). *The Food and Drug Administration.* New York: Chelsea House Publishers, pp. 37–49.

Procedures for approving prescription and OTC drugs

The current process for introducing a new prescription drug on the market consists of a number of stages or phases of approval required by the FDA. It begins in the laboratories of the drug companies themselves, with the identification of the composition of a new compound, a purification of its active ingredients, and a preliminary determination of any possible toxic effects. Extensive tests in two or more species of laboratory animals are carried out to establish the LD50 dosage of the compound, the concentration that leads to death in 50 percent of the animals studied (Chapter 2). Specific tests are also made on pregnant animals to determine

whether administration of the compound might produce birth defects. If the intention is to market the compound as a drug for chronic disorders, the toxicity studies need to be extended over a period of time that simulates the projected duration that the drug would be used by human patients. After these preliminary studies are completed and the new drug has been determined to be safe with animals, the drug company then notifies the FDA through an application known as a Notice of Claimed Investigational Exemption for a New Drug (IND) that this compound has promise as a new prescription drug and permission is now requested to conduct testing in humans.

Phases of clinical studies for prescription drugs

At this point, the testing procedure focuses on the question of whether or not the compound will be effective as a medicinal drug, though safety considerations are noted as well (Focus 15.1). In the first stage of clinical studies, called *Phase 1 trials*, healthy volunteers (frequently prison inmates or medical students) are administered the drug, and certain pharmacological questions are answered. How quickly is the new drug absorbed and excreted? Are there any side effects? What is the range of dosages that are safe for use? Are there any specific schedules for administration (one large dose per day or three smaller ones distributed through a day) that minimize any adverse effects?

In the second major stage of clinical investigations, called *Phase 2 trials*, the new drug is tested on a small number of human patients who have the medical condition or illness for which the drug is intended as the treatment. Researchers are careful to select only those patients who are free of any other health problems, so that any improvement in their health will be identified as a genuine effect on the illness in question. It should not be surprising that all these clinical studies are conducted in a double-blind fashion. Neither the researchers nor the patients are aware of whether the new drug or a look-alike placebo is being administered. As a result, positive effects (if any) are attributed to the therapeutic properties of the drug, free of any expectations or biases that the researcher or the patient may have.

Phase 2 trials are conducted on a population of up to several hundred patients. If successful, the third and last clinical stage, called *Phase 3 trials*, is begun. At this point, the safety, effectiveness, and proper dosage levels are investigated in a population of several thousand patients. A closer examination of

---

FOCUS 15.1

Widening the population during drug testing

raditionally, clinical trials for potential new drugs have been conducted on young men. In 1977 the FDA banned women from taking part in most of the clinical trials for new drugs on the grounds that there might be harm to the fetus if a woman became pregnant during testing. Since 1993, however, the ban has been lifted. Possible risks for pregnant women are still a matter of great concern, but equal consideration is now directed to the need for gender-specific data on a future drug. As a result, it is possible to know about any adjustment in dosage or administration that might optimize the drug's effect for women, as well as men.

A related matter is the smaller amount of attention that has been paid to the possibility that either elderly or very young patients would have responses to a prescription drug substantially different from those of young adults. It is not simply a matter of giving a lower level of the recommended "adult dose" to these populations. The elderly and children often metabolize drugs in unique ways, so that some prescription drugs may not be appropriate for them at any dose level. Conversely, an orientation toward diverse populations in the clinical trials of new drugs can help foster the development of drugs that will be useful for illnesses specific to those populations. New drugs, for example, are now available that help the survival of premature infants whose lungs have not yet fully developed, in addition to others that are used to treat geriatric illnesses.

SOURCES: Is there gender bias in drug testing? (1991, April). *FDA Consumer*, pp. 9–13. Testing drugs in older people (1990, November). *FDA Consumer*, pp. 24–27. Why FDA is encouraging drug testing in children (1991, July-August). *FDA Consumer*, pp. 14–17. Health Front: Women on trial (1993, November). *Prevention*, pp. 30–31.

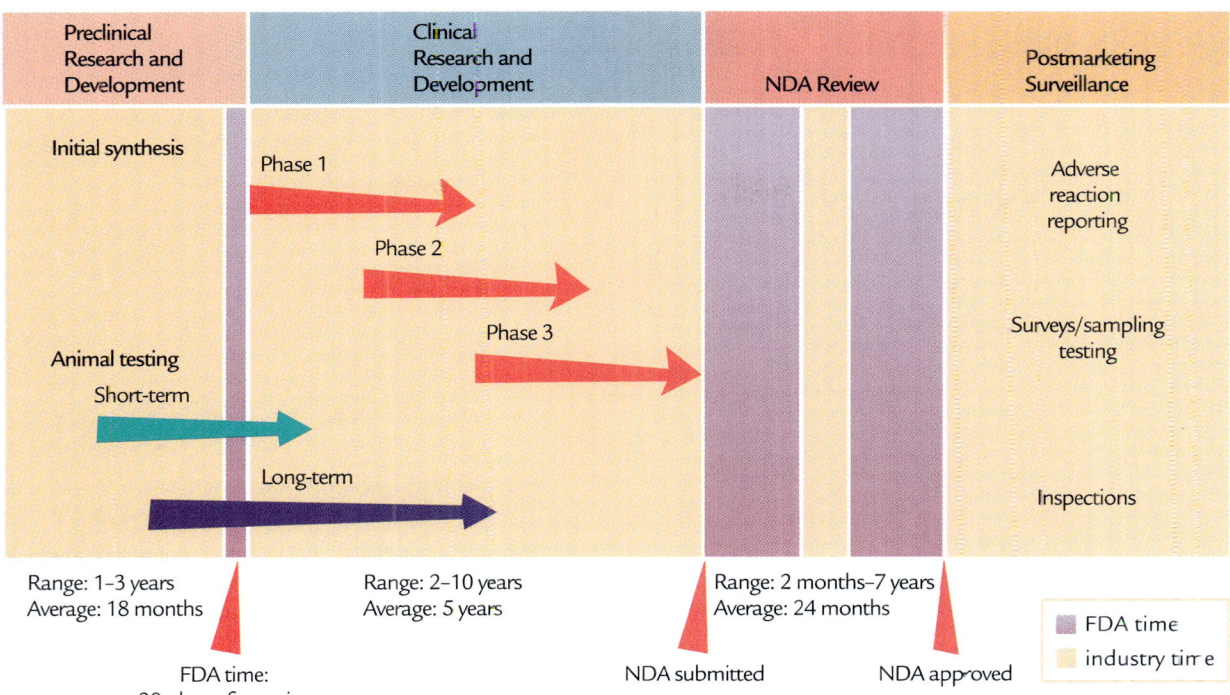

Preclinical Research and Development	Clinical Research and Development	NDA Review	Postmarketing Surveillance
Initial synthesis	Phase 1		Adverse reaction reporting
	Phase 2		
	Phase 3		Surveys/sampling testing
Animal testing			
Short-term			
Long-term			Inspections
Range: 1–3 years Average: 18 months	Range: 2–10 years Average: 5 years	Range: 2 months–7 years Average: 24 months	

FDA time: 30–day safety review

NDA submitted

NDA approved

☐ FDA time
☐ industry time

FIGURE 15.1

Development of new prescription drugs and the FDA approval process
SOURCE: *Young, Frank E., (1990). The reality behind the headlines.* New drug development in the United States. *Rockville MD: U.S. Food and Drug Administration, p. 3.*

possible side effects is carried out and further fine-tuning is made in the recommended usage of the drug.

After all three phases of clinical trials have been completed, a process that takes five years or more (Fig. 15.1) and the drug company considers the results satisfactory, a New Drug Application (NDA) is submitted for approval by the FDA. This application includes all the data on the animal testing and clinical trials. Less than 30 percent of all compounds that drug companies consider worthy of human trials will have made it this far. The FDA then has six months to review the application and either accept or reject the new drug for commercial marketing.

By the time a new drug is FDA approved for prescription use, it is likely that seven to ten years will have elapsed since a com-

pound was first synthesized and considered promising enough to begin testing. The development costs to the drug company range between $25 million and $125 million for each drug that makes it through the approval process. These figures include the expense associated with "dry holes," compounds that never proceed even to clinical trials. Approximately thirty new drugs are FDA approved each year, a small fraction of the original number that are subject to testing.[3]

Even after release for commercial use, as mentioned before, a new drug is still monitored for any unforeseen side effects or toxic reactions, in a stage called *Phase 4 trials*. At this point, physicians around the country are instructed to report to the FDA any instances of adverse effects resulting from the use of the new drug by their patients.

Patents and generic forms of prescription drugs

Approval by the FDA gives the drug company exclusive rights to manufacture and sell the new drug under its own brand name (with a capitalized letter). All other companies are

> **patent**
> The exclusive right of a drug company to market a particular drug. The duration of a patent is seventeen years.
>
> **bioequivalency**
> A characteristic of two drugs in which all pharmacological and physiological effects are identical.

forbidden by law to sell the compound under that brand name or any other name. These rights, called a **patent,** have a fixed duration of seventeen years. The clock starts, however, from the time the original IND has been submitted to the FDA, not when it hits the market. Consequently, the drug company may, in reality, have patent protection for a prescription drug for only seven to ten years. After that, the drug "goes off patent" and generic forms of it can be manufactured and sold to the public. The original drug company frequently continues to market the drug under its brand name, but now the consumer has the option of having it prescribed and purchased either as a brand drug or as a generic (and much less expensive) version. Since 1984 the FDA requires that all generic drugs demonstrate **bioequivalency** with respect to the original, brand-name drug, meaning that both versions must be shown to be chemically and pharmacologically identical.[4]

Speeding up the FDA approval process

Considering the long and arduous road that a drug must travel to reach the marketplace in the 1990s, it is important to examine special circumstances under which the process can be made faster. In 1987 the FDA authorized the use of a "treatment IND" application, specially designed for new drugs that show promise for certain seriously ill patients. Without compromising the standards for safety and effectiveness, a streamlined approval procedure now makes it possible for a novel drug treatment to reach patients who can benefit from it in a matter of months instead of years. Medical conditions for which such drugs have been approved in this way include AIDS, infection associated with kidney transplants, Alzheimer's disease, Parkinson's disease, and forms of advanced cancers.

Ultimately, the limiting factor in much of the approval process is the number of scientists and administrators assigned to examine test data from the thousands of new drugs evaluated each year. Since 1992 the FDA has been permitted to charge "user fees" from drug companies to support the hiring of chemists, microbiologists, and pharmacologists, as well as other professionals and support staff at the agency. In this way, larger numbers of new drugs can be evaluated (Table 15.2).[5]

Procedures for approving OTC drugs

When the Kefauver-Harris Amendment took effect in 1962, with the aim of insuring that all drugs sold in the United States were both safe and effective, the challenge with regard to prescription drugs was ambitious,

but the challenge with regard to OTC drugs was even more difficult. The number of OTC drugs, as mentioned earlier, is roughly a hundred times the number of prescription drugs, and the same approximate ratio existed in 1962. Besides, most OTC drugs on the market at that time contained compounds that had been available to the public for decades or more. The FDA's solution to these difficulties was to set up two separate studies. The Drug Efficacy Study Investigation (DESI) was established to examine all existing prescription medicines, and the Over-The-Counter Review (OTC Review) was established for existing nonprescription medicines.

TABLE 15.2

The leading brands of prescription and nonprescription drugs

Prescription drugs in terms of sales for 1992

Brand name (manufacturer)	Medical application	Sales (in millions of dollars)
1. Zantac (Glaxo Pharmaceuticals)	Stomach ulcers	1,018.6
2. Procardia (Pratt/Pfizer)	Angina pain	608.3
3. Mevacor (Merck & Co.)	Elevated cholesterol	565.4
4. Cardizem (Marion Merrell Dow)	Hypertension and angina pain	512.4
5. Prozac (Lilly)	Depression	468.0
6. Vasotec (Merck & Co.)	Hypertension and congestive heart failure	441.9
7. Ceclor (Lilly)	Bacterial infections	417.3
8. Xanax (Upjohn Co.)	Anxiety and panic disorder	371.7
9. Premarin (Wyeth-Ayerst Labs.)	Abnormal uterine bleeding	357.4
10. Tagamet (SmithKline Beecham)	Stomach and duodenal ulcers	354.2

Nonprescription drugs in terms of sales for 1993

Brand name (manufacturer)	Medical application	Sales (in millions of dollars)
1. Tylenol (McNeil/Johnson & Johnson)	Pain	855
2. Advil (American Home Prods.)	Pain	360
3. Vicks (Richardson-Vicks)	Colds and coughs	350
4. One Touch II Glucose Monitor (LifeScan)	Diabetes diagnosis	220
5. Robitussin (American Home Prods.)	Colds and coughs	205
6. Bayer products (Sterling Winthrop)	Pain	170
7. Alka-Seltzer (Miles Consumer)	Pain and indigestion	160
8. Centrum (Lederle)	Multivitamin	150
9. Mylanta (J & J/ Merck)	Antacid/anti-gas	135
10. Tums (SmithKline/Beecham)	Antacid/anti-gas	135

SOURCES: *Drug Topics* (1993, April 5), p. 73. Freudenberg, Milt (1994, September 27). Rearranging drugstore shelves. *New York Times*, pp. D1, D5. *Physicians' desk reference (48th ed.)* (1994). Montvale NJ: Medical Economics Data.

Whether it was in a prescription or nonprescription category, every drug was to be judged as GRAS (generally regarded as safe), GRAE (generally regarded as effective), and GRAHL (generally regarded as honestly labeled). If a drug failed to meet any one of these criteria, the drug manufacturer had six months to convince the FDA otherwise or else the drug would not be permitted to be marketed across state lines within the United States.

When the DESI was completed in 1984, twenty-two years after the enactment of the legislation, 1,092 prescription drugs out of approximately 3,000 that were reviewed were found to have failed the GRAE requirement. The OTC Review, understandably, has taken longer, especially since it took ten years after the Kefauver-Harris Amendment even to get started. As of the mid-1990s, the FDA has still not finished its work. Perhaps the dawning of the twenty-first century will see a final resolution as to the safety and effectiveness of OTC drugs.

In the meantime, however, the OTC Review has produced two important changes in OTC drugs available to the consumer. First, the professional committees examining present-day OTC drugs have recommended and the FDA has approved an increase in the recommended dosage for certain OTC drugs. OTC-type antihistamines, for example, are stronger than in previous years as a result. Second, several prescription drugs have been determined to be safe enough to warrant use on an OTC basis, and consequently a growing number of prescription drugs can now be purchased on a nonprescription basis. Table 15.3 lists some of these new OTC drugs.[6]

Are FDA-approved drugs safe?

The answer to the safety question for FDA-approved drugs, unfortunately, is yes and no. On the one hand, the FDA approval process is designed to prevent the introduction of any new drug or the continued availability of any present drug if there is a serious question about its safety when consumed in the recommended dosage for the treatment of cer-

T A B L E   1 5 . 3

A partial list of former prescription drugs now sold over the counter

OTC brand name	Generic name	Application
Actifed	triprolidine	Antihistamine
Aleve	naproxen	Analgesic and anti-inflammatory
Bactine, Cortaid	hydrocortisone	First aid ointment
Benadryl	diphenhydramine	Antihistamine
Coricidin Nasal Mist	oxymetazoline	Allergy treatment
Dimetane, Dimetapp	brompheniramine	Antihistamine
Gyne-Lotrimin, Mycelex	clotrimazole	Treatment for vaginal yeast infections
Monistat	miconazole	Treatment for vaginal yeast infections
Motrin, Advil, Nuprin	ibuprofen	Analgesic and anti-inflammatory
OcuClear	oxymetazoline	Treatment for allergic eyes
Sominex	diphenhydramine	Sleep aid
Tavist-D	clemastine, fumerate, and phenylpropanolamine	Antihistamine

SOURCES: Information courtesy of the Nonprescription Drug Manufacturers Association, Washington DC, January 14, 1994.   *Physicians' desk reference* (48th ed.) (1994). Montvale NJ: Medical Economic Data. *Physicians' desk reference for nonprescription drugs* (13th ed.) (1992). Montvale NJ: Medical Economic Data. Segal, Marian (1991, March). Rx to OTC: The switch is on. *FDA Consumer,* pp. 9–11.

DRUG USE ALERT

Side effects of common medications

his Focus is not a Drug Abuse Alert or a Drug Misuse Alert but rather a cautionary note on the side effects that may occur from the *use* of medicinal drugs at recommended dosages. Physicians often warn their patients that a stimulant drug might cause some sleep disturbance, or another might produce some gastrointestinal distress or sexual potency problems, but few of them routinely mention possible effects on the mouth, eyes, ears, or skin. Here are some common prescription and OTC drugs that can produce these types of side effects.

A DRYING OF THE MOUTH OR REDUCTION IN SALIVA, AS WELL AS A REDUCTION IN TEAR FLOW IN THE EYES

- Lasix, Hydrodiuril, Dyrenium (diuretic drugs)
- Aldomet, Catapres, Minipress (antihypertensive drugs)
- Tofranil, Elavil (antidepressant drugs)

- Compazine, Haldol, Thorazine (antipsychotic drugs)
- Artane, Larodopa (anti-Parkinson's disease drugs)

EYE PROBLEMS

- corticosteroids, which can trigger the growth of a cataract
- digitalis (a heart stimulant), which can disrupt color vision
- sulfa drugs and diuretics, which can cause blurred vision
- antipsychotic drugs, which can cause a feeling of burning
- oral contraceptives, which can cause bleeding in the eye

HEARING AND EQUILIBRIUM PROBLEMS

- aspirin, which can cause a ringing in the ears and deafness

- neomycin (antibiotic), which can cause auditory damage

INCREASED SKIN SENSITIVITY TO THE SUN

- many antipsychotic drugs and antidepressant drugs
- tetracycline, sulfa drugs (antibiotics)
- Lasix, thiazides (diuretic drugs)
- oral contraceptives

SOURCES: Brody, Jane E. (1992, February 26). Personal health: Unsuspected common drugs can wreak havoc. *New York Times*, p. C13. *Drug interactions and side effects index to the Physicians' desk reference* (46th ed.) (1992). Montvale NJ: Medical Economics Data, pp. 1061–1253.

---

tain specified medical disorders. If anything, the FDA is often criticized for being overly cautious and delaying the availability of new drugs to people who need them until it is virtually certain there are no problems. On the other hand, no drug is without side effects. Some of these side effects are quite minor, but others can be serious if the drug is taken by individuals with specific health problems. A quick look at the full disclosure statement that is packaged with commercial drugs will indicate to you the wide range of possible adverse effects (Focus 15.2). In addition, there is the significant problem of misusing the prescription or nonprescription drug by either ignoring the precautionary advice by the manufacturer or exceeding the recommended dosage levels.

The Drug Abuse Warning Network (DAWN) reports, discussed in Chapter 2, give us an idea of the prevalence of emergency room incidences and fatalities that involve the misuse of either prescription or nonprescription drugs, as well as the abuse of illicit drugs. The incidence of nonprescription drugs (specifically analgesics) will be discussed in a later section. Prescription drugs will be the focus here.

Several prescription drugs rank prominently among the causes for serious health emergencies. Among the drugs most frequently reported as ER mentions, benzodiazepines such as alprazolam (brand name: Xanax) and diazepam (brand name: Valium) rank seventh and ninth respectively. The antidepressant amitriptyline (brand names:

Elavil and Endep) is tenth. In terms of ME mentions, diazepam is fifth in the rankings, the antidepressants amitriptyline and nortriptyline (brand name: Pamelor) are seventh and tenth respectively. Diphenhydramine (an antihistamine in several prescription and OTC cold medications as well as OTC sleep aids) is eleventh.

Three important points should be made, however, when considering these statistics. First, the rankings for these drugs are high, but their overall occurrence is low when compared to the top-ranked drugs in both ER and ME categories: cocaine, heroin and morphine, and alcohol-in-combination. Second, in 40 percent to almost 60 percent of the situations involving these prescription drugs as either an ER or ME mention, the individual had attempted suicide or succeeded in doing so. Obviously, the doses ingested far exceeded recommended levels. Third, more than two thirds of such DAWN-report incidences involve the combination of multiple drugs along with the drug in question. As noted in Chapter 5, for example, diazepam overdose is unlikely to prove fatal when ingested by itself. A combination of diazepam with alcohol, however, can produce serious life-threatening conditions. The tendency to combine drugs with alcohol and end up with serious medical problems accounts for the "alcohol-in-combination" incident being ranked first in cases seen in hospital emergency rooms (ER mentions) and second in cases in which a patient has died (ME mentions).[7]

salicylic acid (SAL-ih-SIL-ik ASS-id)
A drug developed in the nineteenth century to treat mild to moderate pain, though it was extremely irritating to the stomach.

acetylsalicylic acid (ASA)
(a-SEE-til-SAL-ih-SIL-ik ASS-id)
A modification of salicylic acid that made the drug less irritating to the stomach without lessening its analgesic powers.

aspirin
Any analgesic drug containing acetylsalicylic acid (ASA).

Major OTC analgesic drugs

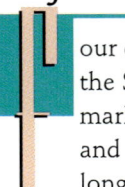 our classes of OTC drugs currently represent the $2.7 billion nonprescription analgesic market: aspirin, acetaminophen, ibuprofen, and naproxen. Of these, aspirin has the longest history of usage, though its commercial availability spans barely a century.

Aspirin

When American pioneers traveled west in the nineteenth century, they encountered Indian tribes that were treating pain and fever by chewing willow bark, reminiscent of a remedy that had been popular in Europe from as early as 400 B.C. It turns out that willow bark contains an analgesic compound called **salicylic acid,** named from *Salix,* the botanical name for willow. The beneficial effect of pure salicyclic acid on pain, however, was for a long time limited by the fact that most digestive systems could not handle it easily. In 1898 Felix Hoffman, a chemist at the Bayer Company in Germany, found that by adding an acetyl group (making the result **acetylsalicylic acid,** or **ASA**), this side effect was reduced without lessening its therapeutic power. To arrive at a name that was easier to say, company officials recalled that salicylic acid also came from spirea plants: thus the name **aspirin** was born.[8]

In 1918, following World War I, Sterling Products (now Sterling Winthrop) bought the trademark rights to the name aspirin, from confiscated property belonging to the Bayer Company of New York. Later, a U.S. federal judge ruled that the name was common enough to be treated generically. To this day, Sterling Winthrop markets its aspirin as "Genuine Bayer Aspirin," though the ASA contained in it is identical to that in any other ASA product. In the United States, Britain, and France, aspirin is the common name for ASA, and any company marketing ASA can use the name to describe its product. In approximately seventy other countries, aspirin is a registered trademark of Bayer AG, Germany. In Canada, aspirin is a registered trademark name used exclusively to identify ASA manufactured and distributed by Sterling Winthrop. This chapter will use the terms aspirin and ASA interchangeably.[9]

The three principal medical applications of aspirin are well known. It is an effective analgesic drug for mild to moderate pain (hence, its use in treating headaches), an **anti-inflammatory** drug in that it relieves inflammation and tenderness in joints of the body (hence, its use in treating rheumatoid arthritis), and an **antipyretic** drug in that it lowers elevated body temperature when the body is fighting infection (hence, its use in treating fever). A recommended adult dosage of 325 to 650 mg (one to two tablets or capsules), taken every four hours, is considered to be adequate for these purposes, with a recommended limit of 3,900 mg (12 tablets or capsules) per day.[10]

Until the early 1970s, the therapeutic effects of aspirin were largely a mystery. A prominent magazine had even called aspirin "the wonder drug nobody understands."[11] The answer came in a surprising way. Aspirin was found to work as an analgesic, not on a CNS level (like morphine or other opiate drugs) but rather on a peripheral level by blocking the synthesis of **prostaglandins,** a group of hormone-like chemicals normally produced by every body cell when some injury to that cell has occurred. Prostaglandins, when released following injury, also encourage inflammation in the joints. Finally, prostaglandins act on the hypothalamus of the brain to elevate body temperature, so a blocking of prostaglandins here has a fever-reducing effect. Therefore, a combination of antiprostaglandin effects, both in the CNS and peripheral to it, explains the three therapeutic actions of aspirin.

Other physiological effects of aspirin can produce serious problems, however, and as a result three specific cautions about the use of aspirin must be made:

First, aspirin-treated patients have a higher risk of developing gastric bleeding because the drug has a direct erosive effect on the stomach wall. Anyone with a history of stomach ulcers or related stomach problems should avoid taking aspirin. Even individuals without such a history frequently suffer some degree of aspirin-related stomach discomfort. In one study, approximately 15 percent of those who took 1,000 mg of aspirin reported stomach pain, 12 percent reported heartburn, and 8 percent reported nausea or vomiting or both. The aspirin taken in these instances, however, was "uncoated." In order to reduce these symptoms, some forms of aspirin are either buffered with a coating of an antacid or "enteric-coated" so that absorption is delayed until the aspirin is past the stomach and in the upper intestine. While these forms of aspirin reduce the gastric problems, the pain-reducing and other therapeutic effects are delayed.[12]

The second caution is that aspirin increases the time it takes for blood to clot. Ordinarily, prostaglandins promote the clumping of blood platelets that is part of the normal clotting process. Therefore, when there is a reduction in the action of prostaglandins, the ability for blood to clot is reduced as well. Surgical patients should not have their bleeding time increased, so they are frequently recommended not to take aspirin a week to ten days prior to surgery. A reduction of clotting can be beneficial, however, for individuals who are susceptible to small clots either in the brain or in coronary arteries, as discussed in Focus 15.3.

> **anti-inflammatory**
> Having an effect that reduces inflammation or soreness.
>
> **antipyretic**
> Having an effect that reduces body temperature and fever.
>
> **prostaglandins**
> **(PROS-tah-GLAN-dins)**
> Hormone-like substances that are inhibited by OTC analgesic drugs.

New medical applications for aspirin

he anticlotting action of aspirin has led to two new applications for patients with cardiovascular disease. The first application is for the prevention of a second myocardial infarction (heart attack) among men who have previously suffered one. In addition, there is evidence that, for men over the age of fifty, a substantially lowered risk of having a heart attack in the first place could be achieved by taking a single aspirin tablet (325 mg) every other day. These benefits, by the way, do not apply to women. It is advisable to consult your doctor if you think that aspirin therapy is appropriate.

The second application is for the treatment of recurrent episodes of potentially dangerous clotting in the brain or the retina *(transient ischemic attacks, TIAs)*. These mini-strokes can frequently be preliminary events to a larger stroke that causes long-lasting brain damage. The present FDA recommendation is that 1,300 mg of aspirin a day (four tablets) can be effective in reducing the chances of future TIAs or strokes in men with a history of TIAs. Once again, these benefits do not apply to women.

Though less solid evidence is available for other medical applications of aspirin, it is suspected that aspirin might be useful in preventing the severity of migraine headaches, enhancing the circulation of blood to the gums, preventing certain types of cataracts, lowering the risk of a recurrence of colorectal cancer, and lowering high blood pressure that occurs in 5 to 15 percent of all pregnancies.

SOURCES: Flieger, Ken (1994, January-February). Aspirin: A new look at an old drug. *FDA Consumer,* pp. 19–21. Lewis, H. D., et al. (1983). Protective effects of aspirin against acute myocardial infarction and death in men with unstable angina (Results of a Veterans Administration cooperative study). *New England Journal of Medicine, 309,* 396–403. Steering Committee of the Physicians' Health Study Research Group (1988, January 28). Preliminary report: Findings from the aspirin component of the Ongoing Physicians' Health Study. *New England Journal of Medicine, 318* (4), 262–264.

Aspirin can also have serious adverse effects for women in the late stages of pregnancy. The anticlotting action of aspirin can prolong labor and produce bleeding during delivery. In addition, a reduction in clotting can occur in their babies. As a result of these significant concerns, this warning is included on the label of all aspirin products:

IT IS ESPECIALLY IMPORTANT NOT TO USE ASPIRIN DURING THE LAST 3 MONTHS OF PREGNANCY UNLESS SPECIFICALLY DIRECTED TO DO SO BY A DOCTOR BECAUSE IT MAY CAUSE PROBLEMS IN THE UNBORN CHILD OR COMPLICATIONS DURING DELIVERY.

Reye syndrome (RYE SIN-drohm)
A rare but highly dangerous childhood disorder that has been associated with the administration of ASA-type analgesic drugs for the treatment of certain viral infections.

The third caution involves children who have contracted a viral infection such as chicken pox or the flu. Aspirin has been found to be related to the development of **Reye syndrome,** a rare but highly dangerous condition marked by lethargy, nausea and severe vomiting, disorientation, and coma. Approximately 26 percent of Reye syndrome cases are fatal. Since 1985 it has been required that warnings on the labels of all aspirin products indicate that "children and teenagers should not take aspirin for chicken pox or flu symptoms before a doctor is consulted." Because it is difficult to tell if even a common cold may be the beginning of the flu, it is advisable to refrain from giving aspirin to anyone under the age of twenty. There has been a drop in the incidence of Reye syndrome in the United States since these warnings have been issued.[13]

Acetaminophen

Since the 1950s **acetaminophen** (brand names: Tylenol, Datril, Anacin-3, and Panadol, among others) has been available as an OTC drug, but it is only since the 1970s that it has been a popular alternative to aspirin for analgesic and antipyretic purposes. You may notice that an anti-inflammatory purpose has been left out. On the one hand, acetaminophen does not reduce inflammation and, except for reducing the associated pain, does not help in the treatment of arthritis. On the other hand, acetaminophen does not produce gastric distress nor does it interfere with the clotting process, so there are significant benefits for those individuals adversely affected by aspirin.

The fact that acetaminophen has an effect on pain equivalent to that of aspirin without some of the prominent aspirin-related side effects has made acetaminophen the leading form of OTC pain reliever in the United States. In 1993 acetaminophen products represented approximately 45 percent of the pain-relief market, with aspirin and ibuprofen accounting for 27 percent and 28 percent respectively.[14]

Safety-sealed, tamper-resistant packaging became a fact of life for consumers of OTC drugs following the 1982 Tylenol poisoning crisis.

This is not to say, however, that acetaminophen is totally benign. A serious problem is its relatively high potential for producing liver damage. About 7,500 mg of acetaminophen (equivalent to fifteen 500-mg tablets of Extra-Strength Tylenol) can produce liver damage, and the combination of acetaminophen with alcohol greatly increases the risk of such a toxic reaction. In 1993 an FDA advisory panel recommended that warnings on acetaminophen labels refer to the particular risk of combining acetaminophen with alcohol. It has been recommended that individuals having more than two drinks a day restrict their intake of acetaminophen to two grams per day (equivalent to four extra-strength tablets or about six regular-strength tablets). The normal maximal recommended dose per day is four grams. Anyone who has taken acetaminophen in this dosage range in combination with alcohol should seek medical attention immediately, prior to the appearance of symptoms related to liver disease. As an emergency medical procedure, an injection of acetycysteine (brand name: Mucosil) can be used as an antidote for acetaminophen overdose, but this treatment is successful only if begun immediately. It may take as much as forty-eight to ninety-six hours before the symptoms of acetaminophen overdose appear, and by this time liver damage will have reached an advanced stage.[15]

Another concern is the risk of kidney damage as a result of heavy average use or moderate cumulative use of acetaminophen. A 1994 study found that the risk of kidney failure doubled in people who had taken more than 365 acetaminophen pills over a year's time (averaging one per day) or 1,000–5,000 pills over a lifetime. Aspirin use was not found to

acetaminophen
(a-SEE-tuh-MIN-oh-fen)
A type of OTC analgesic drug. A major brand name is Tylenol.

increase the chances of kidney damage though, as noted earlier, aspirin has its own health risks.[16]

Ibuprofen

From 1968 to 1984, **ibuprofen** was available only as a prescription analgesic (brand name: Motrin), but in 1984 it was approved as an OTC drug. Presently, ibuprofen is marketed under a variety of brand names, most prominently as Advil, Mediprin, Midol, Motrin, and Nuprin. It is effective in reducing pain, inflammation, and elevated temperature due to fever. In addition, ibuprofen has been found to be particularly effective in the treatment of menstrual cramps. The mechanism behind ibuprofen's effects is to block the production of prostaglandins, in a similar way to the effects of aspirin.

The recommended adult dosage of ibuprofen is 200 mg (one tablet) every four to six hours. Two tablets may be used but no one should exceed 1,200 mg (six tablets) in a twenty-four-hour period. There is less gastric irritation in taking ibuprofen than in taking aspirin, though some discomfort can be experienced and the warning label suggests that milk or food be consumed when taking the drug. In general, since the mechanism behind the action of ibuprofen is so similar to that of aspirin, ibuprofen shares the anticlotting feature associated with aspirin.

A serious concern, specific to ibuprofen, is the potential for kidney damage or kidney failure. It is not advisable for individuals to take ibuprofen if they have a history of kidney disease.[17]

---

ibuprofen (EYE-boh-PRO-fin)
A type of OTC analgesic drug. Major brand names include Advil, Motrin, and Nuprin.

naproxen (na-PROX-sin)
An analgesic drug, formerly available only as a prescription drug (brand names: Naprosyn and Anaprox). It is now available as an OTC drug under the brand name Aleve.

Naproxen

The newest OTC analgesic drug, **naproxen,** is actually a well-known prescription drug that has been FDA approved since 1994 for nonprescription use. When it was marketed as a prescription drug, it was known under the brand names Naprosyn and Anaprox. As an OTC drug, naproxen is available at a slightly lower dosage under the brand name Aleve.

Naproxen has analgesic, anti-inflammatory, and antipyretic effects, with a duration of action of eight to twelve hours, substantially longer than the other types of OTC analgesic drugs. As a prescription drug, naproxen has been the number one antiarthritic medication on the market, and as an OTC drug it is likely to remain a leader in this category. The principal problem with naproxen is gastrointestinal irritation. Chronic naproxen treatment runs the risk of causing gastric bleeding, ulceration, or perforation. It is important to be aware of signs of these problems while taking naproxen and discontinue its use if any difficulties arise.[18]

Analgesic drugs and attempted suicide

In 1992 acetaminophen, aspirin, and ibuprofen were listed fourth, sixth, and eighth respectively in terms of drugs associated with ER mentions in the DAWN reports. In more than 90 percent of these cases the cause was classified as a drug overdose, and in more than 75 percent of the cases the patient reported that a suicide had been attempted. Breaking down the data into demographic groups yields an approximate profile of a high-risk individual with respect to an attempted suicide by an overdose of OTC analgesics: white, female, and between the ages of six and seventeen years. These statistics do not include those cases in which an analgesic drug had been combined with alcohol or a second drug. Fortunately, relatively few suicide attempts involving analgesics alone (without alcohol) were successful.[19]

Other major classes of OTC drugs

n addition to analgesic products, a number of other OTC drug categories play a major role in the overall OTC market. Three of them will be considered: weight-loss aids, sleep aids, and cough-and-cold remedies.

Weight-loss aids

Most of us can relate to the desire to lose weight with as little pain or inconvenience as possible. One option is to suppress one's appetite, which a group of OTC drugs are designed to do. The only FDA-approved active ingredient in such products (brand names: Acutrim and Dexatrim) is **phenylpropanolamine (PPA),** a mild stimulant and nasal decongestant. A 75-mg dosage per day is the maximum allowed by law, with the entire amount in one pill, one half of the daily dosage taken twice a day, or one third of the daily dosage taken three times a day. There is some question as to whether PPA works as an appetite suppressant for everyone or whether it is successful in producing long-term weight loss. Research studies show that there is a greater effect with PPA than with a placebo, but the total weight loss averages only one pound or so a week. There is also a concern that even a mild CNS stimulant can be a problem for people who have elevated blood pressure or cardiovascular disorders. Caffeine used to be included as an additional ingredient in these appetite suppressants, but the FDA has now prohibited the practice. When such products advertise that they are "caffeine-free," the impression is given that the action has been voluntary when, in fact, it is simply against the law.[20]

Sleep aids

The only FDA-approved active ingredients in OTC sleep aids are **diphenhydramine,** an

antihistamine to be taken in either a 25-mg or 50-mg dosage once a day (also available in various types of Benadryl), and **doxylamine succinate,** another antihistamine to be taken

phenylpropanolamine (PPA)
(FEN-il-pro-PAN-oh-la-meen)
The only FDA-approved active ingredient in OTC appetite-suppressant, weight-loss aids.

diphenhydramine
(DEYE-fen-HEYE-druh-meen)
One of two FDA-approved active ingredients in OTC sleep-aid products, such as Nytol, Sleep-Eze, and Sominex.

doxylamine succinate
(DOX-il-a-meen SUK-ih-nate)
One of two FDA-approved active ingredients in OTC sleep-aid products, such as Unisom.

in a 25-mg dosage once a day. Brand names of such sleep aids containing diphenhydramine include Miles Nervine Nighttime Sleep Aid, Nytol, Sleep-Eze, and Sominex; Unisom is the brand name for a sleep aid containing doxylamine succinate. Some of these products are also marketed in combination with acetaminophen as a "sleep-aid pain-relief formula" medication. Individuals taking this kind of medication should be aware that they are dealing with a CNS depressant, and any combination with other depressants, such as alcohol or antihistamines contained in cough-and-cold remedies, can inadvertently enhance the overall effect.[21]

Cough-and-cold remedies

As we all know, a cold can be a miserable experience. It can be frustrating as well, because it is a viral infection and no antibiotic drug or any other drug for that matter has yet been discovered that can prevent a cold, cure it, or even reduce the length of time that we have it. All we can do is attempt to reduce the symptoms of a cold. This is where OTC remedies come into the picture. About 21 percent of all OTC drugs are marketed specifically for the control of cold symptoms, comprising the second largest category of such products.[22]

Choosing a cough-and-cold remedy (along with similar medications that treat allergic symptoms, which are often very similar) depends on the symptoms that are present. Basic ingredients can include an *antitussive agent,* or cough suppressant, for the control of a cough; an *expectorant* to reduce the thickness of mucus in the throat and pharynx (making it easier to cough it up); a *decongestant* to widen blocked nasal passages and sinuses; an *antihistamine* to relieve the itching, sneezing, teary eyes, and runny nose; and finally an analgesic and antipyretic drug to reduce the sinus pain, headache, or fever. Most cough-and-cold medications combine these ingredients in various proportions, so it is important to read the labels carefully to find out if the particular product is the best one for the symptoms.

Potential problems can occur as a result of two factors in current cough-and-cold remedies. The first problem is inherent in the depressant character of antihistamines. While antihistamines can frequently act paradoxically as stimulants in young children, they produce drowsiness and sleep for most adults. This effect might be fine for bedtime, but it is very important to refrain from driving a car or engaging in any task that requires full attention while taking an antihistamine product.

The second problem concerns the quantity of alcohol in several cough-and-cold remedies. With levels of alcohol sometimes reaching 25 percent, these cough-and-cold remedies can function essentially as alcoholic beverages. This factor will combine additively to the antihistamine effect and make a person even drowsier than he or she would have been with the antihistamine alone. A person should take care not to consume alcoholic beverages while being treated with an antihistamine medication.

Many cough-and-cold products include specific warnings on the labels that refer to potential difficulties that might arise if the individual is diabetic, has high blood pressure, or suffers from heart or thyroid disease. Women who are pregnant or nursing should consult their physician or other health professional before taking any cough-and-cold remedy.[23]

The pharmaceutical industry today

ike most other giant corporations in the 1990s, pharmaceutical companies have had to diversify in order to survive in an extremely competitive marketplace, sometimes in surprising ways. It is a little-known fact, for example, that a pharmaceutical company best known for a particular type of analgesic drug more than likely manufactures and distributes other types as well. McNeil Consumer Products (a division of Johnson and Johnson) is best identified with Tylenol, but the company also markets an ibuprofen product (Medipren). Sterling Health (a division of Sterling Winthrop) is best identified with Bayer Aspirin, but the company also markets an acetaminophen product (Panadol) as well as an ibuprofen product (Midol). It is quite likely that a number of the above companies will introduce an OTC version of naproxen in the future, competing with the present brand Aleve. It is a strategy for insuring that a given company maintains a significant share of the overall market.

As they enter the late 1990s, major pharmaceutical companies are facing increasing strains and pressures from a number of sources. They have been criticized for runaway prescription drug prices, excessive corporate profits, and an apparent willingness to spend more on advertising and promotion than on research and development. In addition, the prices they charge for identical drugs vary widely from country to country, depending on "what the market will bear." There are numerous examples where the price charged for a prescription drug is three to eight times higher in the United States than in Canada.

The relatively higher prices for prescription drugs in the United States is a particular

The elderly often have to contend with a multitude of medications, some of which may interact with one other.

concern when viewed in terms of the economic burden placed on elderly Americans. Not only do the elderly typically consume a substantially greater proportion of drugs than do younger subpopulations, but, to make matters worse, the elderly are frequently ineligible for receiving reimbursements for outpatient pharmaceutical expenses. In 1992 the U.S. Senate Special Committee on Aging reported that older Americans on average pay three quarters of their outpatient drug bills out of pocket. The fight to contain the high cost of prescription drugs, sometimes called "the other drug war," as well as the high cost of health care in general, is certain to escalate in the years ahead.[24]

Summary

- Two categories of medicinal drugs are available to us: prescription drugs, which require medical approval, and over-the-counter (OTC) drugs, which can be purchased without any restrictions.

- In either case, the U.S. Food and Drug Administration (FDA) is responsible for setting the standards of safety, effectiveness, and honesty in labeling.

HOW THE REGULATION OF PRESCRIPTION AND OTC DRUGS BEGAN

- A series of federal laws, put into effect since 1906, have established the FDA as the authority for safeguarding the public health with regard to prescription and OTC drugs, as well as food products, cosmetics, and medical devices.

PROCEDURES FOR APPROVING PRESCRIPTION AND OTC DRUGS

- The FDA process for the approval of new prescription drugs begins with animal studies to determine the safety limits and relative toxicity. If these standards are met, clinical trials, first with healthy human volunteers and later with actual patients, are conducted to identify the optimal dosage levels and degree of effectiveness.

- Only a small proportion of new compounds developed by drug companies make it successfully through these clinical trials and are eventually approved by the FDA for marketing as a new prescription drug. The process often takes several years, and the company responsible for a new drug has an exclusive patent on its commercial sale for a period of seventeen years.

- Since 1962, all prescription and OTC drugs have been required by the FDA to be generally recognized as safe (GRAS), effective (GRAE), and honestly labeled (GRAHL).

ARE FDA-APPROVED DRUGS SAFE?

- There is considerable concern that although prescription and OTC drugs are FDA approved for use when taken in the recommended dosages and under the recommended circumstances, misuse can result in medical emergencies and fatalities.

- The DAWN reports show that the misuse of analgesic OTC drugs, in particular, can present significant health risks.

MAJOR OTC ANALGESIC DRUGS

- Acetylsalicylic acid (aspirin), acetaminophen, ibuprofen, and naproxen are four types of OTC analgesic drugs available to the public.

- Since each of these types has its benefits and hazards, it is strongly urged that recommended dosage levels be observed and anyone with specific health problems be aware that analgesic drugs may be harmful.

OTHER MAJOR CLASSES OF OTC DRUGS

- Three other classes of OTC drugs can be highlighted in terms of their use and potential for misuse. The first is the variety of weight-loss aids, all of which contain the active ingredient phenylpropanolamine (PPA). The second is the variety of sleep aids, with the active ingredient of either diphenhydramine or doxylamine succinate. The third is the variety of cough-and-cold remedies that generally contain some combination of antihistamine and decongestant.

- Careful use of all of these products is advised.

THE PHARMACEUTICAL INDUSTRY TODAY

- In the present-day pharmaceutical industry, companies have diversified their prescription and OTC products to maintain their share of a highly competitive market.

- Pharmaceutical companies are also under pressure to reduce the prices of their products as a component of controlling overall health-care costs.

Key Terms

Endnotes

1. Patrick, William (1988). *The Food and Drug Administration.* New York: Chelsea House, pp. 29–49.

2. Burkholz, Herbert (1994). *The FDA follies.* New York: Basic Books.   Patrick. *The Food and Drug Administration,* p. 40.

3. Janesh, Barbara J. (1989, January). How these little pills went to market. *Everyday Law,* pp. 40–44.   Julien, Robert M. (1995). *A primer of drug action* (7th ed.). New York: Freeman, p. 47   Payne, Wayne A., Hahn, Dale B., and Pinger, Robert R. (1991). *Drugs: Issues for today.* St. Louis: Mosby Year Book, pp. 95–98.

4. Yorke, Jeffrey (1992, September). FDA ensures equivalence of generic drugs. *FDA Consumer,* pp. 11–15.

5. Carey, John (1993, October 25). Getting the lead out at the FDA. *Business Week,* pp. 96–98. Flieger, Ken (1993, October). FDA finds new ways to speed treatments to patients. *FDA Consumer,* pp. 15–18.   Henkel, John (1993, October). User fees to fund faster reviews. *FDA Consumer,* pp. 19–21.

6. Segal, Marian (1991, March). Rx to OTC: The switch is on. *FDA Consumer,* pp. 9–11.

7. Substance Abuse and Mental Health Services Administration (1994a). Annual emergency room data 1992. Data from the Drug Abuse Warning Network (DAWN). Series 1, No. 12A. Rockville MD: Substance Abuse and Mental Health Services Administration, Office of Applied Studies, pp. 32 and 52. Substance Abuse and Mental Health Services Administration (1994b). Annual medical examiner data 1992. Data from the Drug Abuse Warning Network (DAWN). Series 1, No. 12B. Rockville MD: Substance Abuse and Mental Health Services Administration, Office of Applied Studies, pp. 16 and 33.

8. Krantz, John C. (1974). Felix Hoffman and aspirin. *Historical medical classics involving new drugs.* Baltimore: Williams and Wilkins pp. 37–41.   Levinthal, Charles F. (1988). *Messengers of paradise: Opiates and the brain.* New York: Anchor Press/Doubleday, p. 112.

9. Ibid., p. 211.   Mann and Plummer. *Aspirin wars,* p. 4.

10. *Physicians' desk reference for nonprescription drugs* (13th ed.). (1992). Montvale NJ: Medical Economics Data, pp. 724–725.

11. Boehm, George A. W. (1966, September 11). Aspirin doesn't cure disease—It is the wonder drug nobody understands. *New York Times Magazine,* p. 56.

12. Lewis, H. Daniel, et al. (1983). Protective effects of aspirin against acute myocardial infarction and death in men with unstable angina. Results of a Veterans Administration Cooperative Study. *New England Journal of Medicine, 309,* 396–403.   *Physicians' desk reference for nonprescription drugs,* p. 725.

13. Kolata, Gina (1985). Study of Reye's-aspirin link raises concerns. *Science, 227,* 391–392. *Physicians' desk reference for nonprescription drugs,* p. 724.   Zamula, Evelyn (1990, November). Reye syndrome: The decline of a disease. *FDA Consumer,* pp. 21–23.

14. DeNitto, Emily (1993, September 29). 100 leaders monopolize pain relievers. *Advertising Age,* p. 2.

15. Acetaminophen warning (1993, June 30). *New York Times,* p. C14.   Morgenroth, Lynda (1989, December). High-risk pain pills. *Atlantic,* pp. 36–42.

16. Perneger, Thomas V., Whelton, Paul K., and Klag, Michael J. (1994). Risk of kidney failure associated with the use of acetaminophen, aspirin, and nonsteroidal antiinflammatory

drugs. *New England Journal of Medicine, 331,* 1675–1679.

17. U.S. Department of Health and Human Services (1984, August). *FDA Drug Bulletin,* pp. 19–20.   *Physicians' desk reference for nonprescription drugs,* p. 761.   Whelton, Andrew, Stout, Robert, Spilman, Patricia, and Klassen, David (1990). Renal effects of ibuprofen, piroxicam, and sulindac in patients with asymptomatic renal failure. *Annals of Internal Medicine, 112,* 568–576.

18. Darnay, Arsen J., and Reddy, Marlita A. (1994). *Market Share Reporter.* Detroit: Gale Research, p. 195.   *Physicians' desk reference* (48th ed.) (1994). Montvale NJ: Medical Economic Data, pp. 2363–2365.

19. Substance Abuse and Mental Health Services Administration. Annual emergency room data, pp. 32, 34, 36, 43, and 44.   Substance Abuse and Mental Health Services Administration. Annual medical examiner data, pp. 16, 18, and 19.

20. The new diet pills (1982, January). *Consumer Reports,* pp. 14–16.

21. *Physicians' desk reference for nonprescription drugs,* pp. 718–719.

22. Rx-to-OTC conversions to boost market (1993, September 9). *Standard and Poor's Industry surveys,* pp. H31-H32.

23. *Physicians' desk reference for nonprescription drugs.*   Willis, Judith L. (1991, November). Using over-the-counter medications wisely. *FDA Consumer,* pp. 35–37.

24. Health care products and services: Basic analysis (1993, September 9). *Standard and Poor's Industry Surveys,* pp. H18-H32.   Unger, Michael (1992, October 4). The other drug war. *Newsday,* pp. 82, 76.   Earning a failing grade: A report card on 1992 drug manufacturer price inflation (1993) (Staff report to the Special Committee on Aging, United States Senate). Washington DC: U.S. Government Printing Office.

POINT / COUNTERPOINT

How do we get orphan drugs adopted?

he following discussion of viewpoints represents the opinions of people on both sides of the controversial issue of adopting orphan drugs. Read them with an open mind. Discuss them in your class, with your family, and with your friends. Don't think you have to come up with the final answer, nor should you necessarily agree with the argument you heard last. Many of the ideas in this feature come from sources listed at the end, where more extensive discussions can be found.

POINT
The issue should be pretty clear. We have people out there who are very sick; some are dying. But according to the pharmaceutical industry they don't count because there are too few of them to service and still make a profit. We need more effort on the part of drug companies to help these people, the true "orphans" in the world of pharmaceutical treatment.

COUNTERPOINT
Now hold on. Before you start painting the drug industry as a bunch of Simon Legrees, let's look at the facts, not the rhetoric. Since 1983 we have the Orphan Drug Act, which has been responsible for providing dozens of new drugs for patients with AIDS, rare blood and metabolic disorders, and unusual forms of cancer. These are disorders for which there are fewer than 200,000 patients worldwide. As a result of the act, new products that would not have been developed before are now being marketed to these people, and as a result lives are being saved. If it hadn't been for the Orphan Drug Act, for example, we probably would not have today drugs such as AZT, which prolongs the lives of AIDS patients, or pentamidine isethionate, which treats the pneumonia that strikes many people with AIDS.

POINT
True, up to a point. Let's review exactly what this Orphan Drug Act has been doing. First of all, the government has given the drug companies a tax credit of 50 percent of all costs incurred in conducting human clinical trials for these orphan drugs in any given year, and the remain-

ing 50 percent of the costs can be a tax-deductible business expense. You're talking about a total reduction of 73 percent in taxes that might have been paid. Not a bad deal at all. It's not as if the drug companies are doing the public a favor.

COUNTERPOINT

These tax concessions have been necessary. Otherwise, drug companies could not have afforded the enormous expenses incurred in developing a new drug when the market for that drug is so small. Like it or not, it's a matter of economic reality.

POINT

Let's talk a little economic reality. There's a drug called Ceradase that is marketed by Genzyme Corporation, a biotechnology company. For severe cases of Gaucher's disease, an inherited enzyme disorder, it costs as much as $300,000 a year to treat the disease with Ceradase. This drug is considered the world's most expensive drug. Is it necessary to charge such a high price when the development was subsidized in part by the taxpayer?

COUNTERPOINT

Genzyme says that the cost of Ceradase treatment is soon to come down. Besides, the company has been losing money for at least the first ten years of its history, despite its success with Ceradase. Given the costs of research into drugs that never reach the market (the "dry holes"), the rewards of a successful drug are justified.

POINT

We are still faced with a situation in which companies are reaping huge annual sales from orphan drugs, in some cases two to three times the research costs that were incurred in developing them. And they are enjoying a seven-year exclusive monopoly on their sales, all thanks to the Orphan Drug Act.

COUNTERPOINT

The seven-year patent is necessary to recoup the expenses of other orphan drugs that don't make the headlines like Ceradase.

POINT

What about having a ceiling of $200 million in sales from an orphan drug, after which the company relinquishes its monopoly? At least, this limit would encourage competition for those blockbuster drugs that more than likely would have been developed without the act. Besides, "true" orphan drugs would never reach this sales trigger level anyway.

COUNTERPOINT

Any change in the law would essentially kill orphan-drug research. It would eliminate any incentive to get these drugs out to the people who need them. The law is working for now. Let's not tamper with it.

SOURCES: Asbury, Carolyn H. (1985). *Orphan drugs: Medical versus market value.* Lexington MA: Lexington Books. Cushman, John R. (1992, January 22). Incentives for research on drugs are debated. *New York Times*, p. A13. Hamilton, Robert A. (1990, November). Rare disease treatments: "Orphans" saving lives. *FDA Consumer*, pp. 7–10.

16

Psychiatric Drugs: Treating Schizophrenia and Mood Disorders

THIS CHAPTER WILL INTRODUCE YOU
TO THE FOLLOWING SUBJECTS:

- The development of antipsychotic drugs

- How antipsychotic drugs work in the brain

- Types of antidepressant medication

- How antidepressants work in the brain

- Treatment for mania and bipolar disorder

- Social policies regarding psychiatric drug treatment

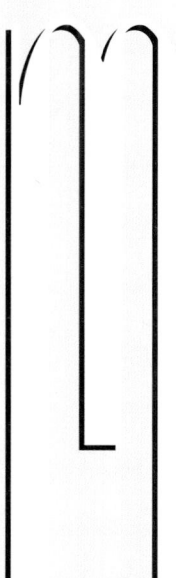

I have been extremely nervous. That's why my thoughts were completely paralyzed. I suppose the medicine has killed off my unhealthy thoughts, as I'm a lot calmer inside now. That's how it seemed to me. . . . I reckon the medicine has taken the bad thoughts away.

A schizophrenic patient under treatment (1965)

It was as if I woke up this morning [after taking antidepressants] and the curtain rose, and there was color in the world and I could think of at least three reasons to live.

Dick Cavett (1992)

any drugs have the potential to liberate the mind from mental illness. This chapter will look at a special class of psychoactive drugs that can relieve emotional distress, reduce personal suffering, and enable deeply troubled people to lead normal lives. Chapter 5 reviewed the types of antianxiety drugs used in treating panic disorders and generalized stress. The focus here will be on medications used for the treatment of two major forms of mental illness: schizophrenia and mood disorders such as depression or mania. These drugs are often referred to as **psychiatric drugs,** because they are prescribed and supervised by psychiatrists. An alternative term, **psychotropic medication,** refers to the fact that the effects move the patient closer to a normal state of mind (*trop,* meaning "to turn toward").

These drugs are something like a two-edged sword. On the one hand, the development of psychiatric drugs has brought about nothing short of a revolution in the quality of mental-health care, as well as a major insight into the biochemical nature of mental illness. Millions of schizophrenic and depressed people have benefited from psychiatric drugs. On the other hand, these medications frequently have significant side effects, and whether or not they should be used as extensively as they are is a matter of controversy among many mental-health professionals.

The biomedical model

U sing the term *mental illness* to describe the symptoms of disorders such as schizophrenia, depression, or mania implies that we are viewing abnormal psychological and behavioral symptoms as being no different from symptoms arising from a physical disease such as pneumonia or a stroke. This viewpoint, commonly referred to as the **biomedical model,** holds that abnormal thoughts and behaviors are results of biochemical processes in the brain. According to this model, the effectiveness of psychiatric drugs in changing such symptoms is a function of altering these biochemical processes toward a more normal state.

Not everyone believes wholeheartedly in the biomedical model, and some mental-health professionals have considered alternative points of view. It is possible that adverse sociological factors, psychodynamic factors, or behavioral factors also play a role in producing abnormal thoughts and behaviors. The fact remains, however, that for many patients the administration of psychiatric drugs is an effective means for treating schizophrenia and mood disorders. Since these drugs are affecting the brain, the inference is inescapable that the improvements observed in such patients are directly related to the biochemical changes that the drugs produce. In other words, from the perspective of developing therapeutic approaches toward these patients, the biomedical model seems to work.

We can find support for the biomedical model in other ways as well, particularly when we look at patterns of schizophrenia in the general population. For example, the concordance rate for schizophrenia in pairs of identical twins (corresponding to the probability of one twin becoming schizophrenic if the other twin already is) has been estimated to be 46 percent, compared to a concordance rate of 15 percent in pairs of fraternal twins. Since the environmental influences on identical and fraternal twins are highly similar, the difference in the two concordance rates indicates a strong genetic component. In addition, the incidence of schizophrenia shows a remarkable stability throughout the world, across such widely separated cultures and societies as those of Swedes, Eskimos, and West African tribal peoples. If a common biological factor were not operating, it is unlikely that we would be seeing such a consistent pattern.[1]

Antipsychotic drugs and schizophrenia

D rugs specifically intended to treat schizophrenia are traditionally referred to as **antipsychotic drugs.** Before considering these drugs in detail, however, it is helpful first to take a careful look at the often misunderstood symptoms of schizophrenia itself.

The symptoms of schizophrenia

The name **schizophrenia** literally means "split-mind," a term that unfortunately has led to an erroneous expectation about how schizophrenic patients typically think and behave. Schizophrenic patients do not have a split or multiple personality. Such psychiatric conditions exist, but they are referred to as dissociative disorders. The accurate way of viewing a schizophrenic is in terms of an

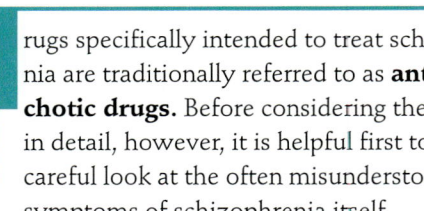

psychiatric drugs
Medications used to treat forms of mental illness.

psychotropic medication
An alternative term for psychiatric drugs.

biomedical model
A theoretical position that mental disorders are caused by abnormal biochemical processes in the brain.

antipsychotic drugs
Medications used to treat symptoms of schizophrenia.

schizophrenia
A major mental illness, characterized by being "cut off" from reality.

individual being "split-off" or "broken-off" from a firm sense of reality. The presence of **delusions** (beliefs not rooted in reality) leading to feelings of persecution or paranoia and the presence of auditory hallucinations commonly in the form of "voices," often torment the patient.

Not all schizophrenics, however, have delusions or hallucinations. Some may display a significant "split" in the connections that normally exist among the processes of thinking, emotion, and action. The expression of emotion may be dulled or altogether absent; verbal expressions or mannerisms may be entirely inappropriate to a given situation; odd postures may be assumed for long periods of time (a condition called **catatonia**). Given the wide diversity in schizophrenic behaviors, it is possible that we may be dealing with a cluster of disorders collectively known as schizophrenia rather than simply one singular psychiatric condition.

A catatonic schizophrenic woman displays the classic symptoms of immobility and unusual body posture.

Overall, the prevalence of schizophrenia is approximately 1 percent of the general U.S. population, representing a total of 2.5 million people. Schizophrenic patients, however, constitute between 40 and 50 percent of all patients in U.S. psychiatric hospitals.[2]

The early days of antipsychotic drug treatment

To appreciate the difference antipsychotic drugs have made in the treatment of schizophrenia, we have to go back to the mid-1950s. Prior to that time, the principal methods of dealing with schizophrenic patients included the heavy administration of barbiturates and surgical interventions such as prefrontal lobotomies. These treatments produced severely apathetic and sedated patients. By 1955, the total population of hospitalized psychiatric patients in the United States (of which schizophrenics represented the majority) had risen to about 560,000, roughly 50 percent of all those hospitalized for any reason. The demand for facilities to house psychiatric patients was quickly reaching crisis proportions.[3]

With the introduction of antipsychotic drugs around 1955, the tide turned. For the first time, symptoms of a major mental disorder such as schizophrenia were genuinely alleviated. Many schizophrenic patients could be treated on an outpatient basis:

While virtually all symptoms decreased with use of antipsychotics, the decrease in symptoms of confusion and disorganization was the greatest. For example, incoherent speech became coherent. Personal hygiene improved, patients dressed themselves, washed, combed their hair, and used the toilet. Patients who had not spoken or responded to others became responsive to questions and

delusions
Ideas that have no foundation in reality.

catatonia (CAT-ah-TONE-yah)
A symptom displayed by some schizophrenic patients, characterized by a rigid, prolonged body posture.

requests. . . . Antipsychotics do not always eliminate delusions and hallucinations, but the drugs usually permit the patient to recognize hallucinations and delusions as such and to know that they are symptoms of disease.[4]

Over the next thirty years, the resident population in U.S. mental hospitals decreased by 80 percent, a result of two principal factors. The first was the beneficial effect of antipsychotic medications on approximately half the schizophrenic population, allowing them to lead relatively normal lives outside a mental hospital. The second was a policy of deinstitutionalization, in which psychiatric patients of all types were admitted to mental hospitals only for limited periods of time. The social consequences of deinstitutionalization will be considered later in this chapter.[5]

The nature of antipsychotic drug treatment

For most schizophrenic patients, antipsychotic drugs are administered orally in daily doses. In a few cases, i.v. or i.m. injections are given when a highly agitated patient has to be subdued quickly. When administered orally, the benefits appear slowly over a period of a few weeks. During the initial days of treatment, patients usually feel sedated, but the degree of sedation generally declines as the antipsychotic effects begin to appear. In general, activity levels tend to

become normal, with agitated patients becoming more relaxed and withdrawn patients becoming more sociable. When receiving the proper dosage, patients remain reasonably alert. Since they do not produce euphoria, tolerance, or psychological dependence, antipsychotic drugs have a low potential for abuse. They also are quite safe from the risks of accidental overdose, because even massive doses do not impair breathing.[6] This chapter's Portrait offers a look at the personal experiences of a patient recovering from schizophrenia through antipsychotic drug therapy.

In order to minimize side effects, the customary practice is to administer gradually increasing doses of antipsychotic medication until symptoms appear to moderate. Once the patient is responding well to a particular level of the drug, it is then customary to lower the dose to determine the least amount of drug required to achieve a beneficial effect. Until recently, schizophrenic patients were eventually placed on a maintenance drug dose indefinitely. Today, many psychiatrists no longer keep their patients on antipsychotic medications for long periods of time. Instead, the drugs are administered only when severe symptoms arise and are withdrawn completely when the symptoms are eliminated. This practice is called **target dosing.**[7]

Among the medications currently on the market for the treatment of schizophrenia (Table 16.1), most are highly similar to each other both in terms of their benefits and side effects. These drugs are referred to as **typical antipsychotic drugs;** they include chlorpromazine (brand name: Thorazine), haloperidol (brand name: Haldol), thiothixene (brand name: Navane), and thioridizine (brand name: Mellaril). Two major exceptions are clozapine (brand name: Clozaril), available since 1989, and risperidone (brand name: Risperdal), available since 1994. Clozapine and risperidone are considered **atypical antipsychotic drugs,** with their own pharmacological "profiles."

target dosing
A strategy of drug treatment in which only minimal dosage levels are administered to control symptoms and drug treatment is withdrawn when symptoms subside.

typical antipsychotic drugs
A majority of available antipsychotic medications, all of which are associated with the possibility of extrapyramidal motor side effects.

atypical antipsychotic drugs
Relatively new antipsychotic medications that fail to produce extrapyramidal side effects. Clozapine (brand name: Clozaril) is an example.

Presently available antipsychotic medications

Generic name	Brand name	Daily recommended oral dosage in milligrams
Phenothiazines		
chlorpromazine	Thorazine	100–500*
fluphenazine	Prolixin	5–20*
mesoridizine	Serentil	100–300*
perphenazine	Trilafon	12–24*
prochlorperazine	Compazine	50–150*
thioridizine	Mellaril	150–600
trifluoperazine	Stelazine	10–30*
Butyrophenones		
haloperidol	Haldol	1–12*
Thioxanthenes		
thiothixene	Navane	10–30*
chlorprothixene	Taractan	50–300*
Dibenzoxazepines		
clozapine	Clozaril	300–900
loxapine	Loxitane	20–60*
Dihydroindolones		
molindone	Moban	100–225
Benzisoxasoles		
risperidone	Risperdal	1–3

*Also available in injectable forms

SOURCES: Julien, Robert M. (1995). *A primer of drug action* (7th ed.). New York: Freeman.   *Physician's desk reference* (48th ed.). (1994). Montvale NJ: Medical Economics Data.

Typical antipsychotic drugs: side effects and risks

The side effects of typical antipsychotic drugs range from relatively minor inconveniences to severe neurological difficulties. Patients may develop a dry mouth, blurred vision, dizziness, or weight gain. The skin can become oversensitized to the sun, so that burning occurs even after a minimum of exposure. More significant reactions, however, include a severe disturbance in motor systems in the brain (Chapter 3). Patients may develop a stiff, shuffling walk, a lack of spontaneity, restlessness, a fixed facial expression, and loss of coordinated movements such as the free swinging of the arms during walking. These problems are called **Parkinson's-like symptoms** because they resemble many of the features of Parkinson's disease. In fact, some types of anti-Parkinson's medication, such as trihexyphenidyl (brand name: Artane), benztropine (brand name: Cogentin), and procyclidine (brand name: Kemadrin), are frequently given along with antipsychotic drugs to reduce the incidence of these particular side effects. Strangely, administration of the original drug developed to relieve Parkinson's disease symptoms, L-Dopa, makes matters worse rather than better.[8]

The side effects listed here that are associated with typical antipsychotic drugs disappear when the medication is either reduced in dosage or withdrawn. An exception to this rule, however, is the development of **tardive dyskinesia,** a neurological syndrome that may appear after two or more years of continual drug treatment. Tardive dyskinesia, which literally means "a movement disorder arriving late," consists of jerky, tic-like movements of the lips, tongue, jaw, and face. Patients may smack their lips or flick their tongues in and out as frequently as twenty times in thirty seconds; their walking may become progressively unsteady, or they may rock back and forth while seated. It has been estimated that the likelihood of developing tardive dyskinesia as a result of treatment with typical antipsychotic drugs is about 15 to 20 percent. Women and elderly patients show a higher incidence than men and younger patients in general.[9]

Parkinson's-like symptoms
Side effects of typical antipsychotic drugs involving a fixed facial expression and difficulties in walking.

tardive dyskinesia (TAR-div DIS-keh-NEEZ-ee-ah)
A serious side effect affecting approximately 15 percent of schizophrenic patients who have undergone chronic treatment with typical antipsychotic drugs.

Although it is true that many patients who acquire tardive dyskinesia display only mild symptoms, the fact that it may occur at all is a source of great concern both among psychiatrists and the families of schizophrenic patients who have to confront the possibility of an irreversible side effect as socially debilitating as schizophrenia itself. Withdrawal from drug treatment frequently has little impact on the symptoms of tardive dyskinesia. Increasing the dose can block tardive dyskinesia but also increases the potential for more severe reactions if and when the dosage levels are reduced. Unfortunately, the prospect of this Catch-22 situation leads many unhospitalized patients to forego their medication and relapse into schizophrenia.[10]

Clozapine and risperidone: atypical antipsychotic drugs

Clozapine is quite unlike typical antipsychotic medications in that Parkinson's-like side effects and tardive dyskinesia are rare. In

---

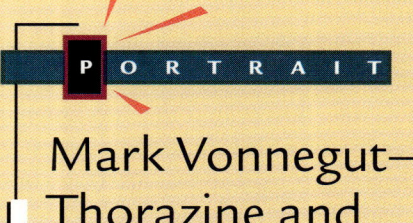

PORTRAIT

Mark Vonnegut— Thorazine and recovery

n his eloquent autobiography *Eden Express*, Mark Vonnegut wrote of his battle with the demons of schizophrenia, his love-hate feelings about Thorazine, and his growing recognition that the biochemistry of his brain was responsible for his deeply troubled life. A child of the sixties, follower of the countercultural movement of that era, and son of the famous writer Kurt Vonnegut, Mark Vonnegut began to experience hallucinations and feel his personality coming undone. In his words:

By this time the voices had gotten very clear. At first I'd had to strain to hear or understand them. They were soft and working with some pretty tricky codes. Snap-crackle-pops, the sound of the wind with blinking lights and horns for punctuation. I broke the code and somehow was able to internalize it to the point where it was just like hearing words. . . . The voices weren't much fun in the beginning. Part of it was simply my being uncomfortable about hearing voices no matter what they had to say, but . . . later the voices could be very pleasant.

For years of his life, Vonnegut was a hospitalized schizophrenic. His treatment with ordinary psychotherapy was fruitless. When he was administered Thorazine and the drug took hold, he would become ambivalent about its effects:

Taking Thorazine was part of doing things right. I hated Thorazine but tried not to talk about hating it. Hating Thorazine probably wasn't a healthy sign. . . . On Thorazine everything's a bore. Not a bore, exactly. Boredom implies impatience. You can read comic books and Reader's Digest forever. You can tolerate talking to jerks forever. . . . The weather is dull, the flowers are dull, nothing's very impressive. . . . When I did manage to get excited about some things, impatient with some things, interested in some things, it still didn't have the old zing to it.

Nonetheless, he knew that Thorazine was helping him. When he first entered a hospital, he was totally disoriented. With Thorazine, things started to clear:

It took a while before I was able to pay much attention to the fact [that I was in a hospital]. . . . Little by little, with the help of massive doses of Thorazine in the ass and in my milkshakes (which was all they could get me to eat), little by little it started mattering to me where I was and what was going on.

Eventually, Vonnegut recovered and could look back on those years:

The only decent answers I've been able to come up with are biochemical ones. Admittedly biochemistry is boring as mud next to psychology, religion, and politics, but the object evidence for schizophrenia's being biochemical is overwhelming.

And yet, he recognized the treatment he had undergone would be only a primitive first step toward understanding the process of schizophrenia:

While I very likely owe my life to Thorazine, I doubt if I will ever develop much affection for it. . . . There are great insights to be gained from schizophrenia, but remember that they won't do you or anyone else much good unless you recover.

SOURCE: Vonnegut, Mark (1975). *Eden express.* New York: Praeger, quotations pp. 106, 195–196, 197, 127, 210–211, 213, and 214. Copyright © 1975 by Mark Vonnegut. Reprinted by permission of Knox Burger Associates.

addition, clozapine is effective in reducing a wide range of schizophrenic symptoms in many patients who have not been helped by chlorpromazine or other medications in the typical antipsychotic drug category. This medication obviously offers significant advantages over typical antipsychotic drugs. However, a unique feature of clozapine is the 1 percent to 2 percent chance of developing a potentially lethal blood disease called **agranulocytosis,** a condition involving the loss of white blood cells and a decline in the immune system as a result. If early signs of agranulocytosis are detected, clozapine can be withdrawn and the patient will recover. Therefore, clozapine-treated patients must undergo weekly blood tests for the entire time they are under treatment. The need for regular blood testing has made clozapine treatment far more expensive than traditional treatment with typical antipsychotic drugs.

Risperidone (brand name: Risperdal) is the newer of the two atypical antipsychotic drugs currently available for treating schizophrenia. Like clozapine, it reduces schizophrenic symptoms while maintaining a low incidence of Parkinson's-like side effects and tardive dyskinesia. Possible side effects of risperidone include agitation, anxiety, insomnia, nose stuffiness, and nausea. Unlike clozapine, however, agranulocytosis has not been reported to be a problem with risperidone treatment.[11]

Effects of antipsychotic drugs on the brain

When the first antipsychotic drugs were introduced in the 1950s, the question of how they work at a neuronal level in the brain was a total mystery. In those days, drugs were "discovered" quite accidentally. Chlorpromazine, for example, was first administered as a treatment for severe vomiting (which remains one of its applications today) and a sedative for presurgical patients. Only later was it recognized as having beneficial effects on schizophrenia.

As haphazard as the development of psychiatric drugs was at that time, however, there was frequently a common thread that connected them, suggesting that a common mechanism might be responsible for their actions. In the case of antipsychotic drugs, there was an unmistakable connection between the improvement in schizophrenic symptoms and the often observed signs of Parkinson's-like motor problems. Could this connection provide a clue as to the underlying biochemistry of schizophrenia?

Fortunately, by 1963, the biochemical nature of Parkinson's disease was beginning to be understood. Essentially, its symptoms were found to be a result of a deficiency in dopaminergic (dopamine-using) neurons in an area of the midbrain called the substantia nigra (Chapter 3).[12] One result was the development of new treatment drugs that helped Parkinson's patients by boosting the level of dopaminergic activity in the brain.

The second result was an insight into the mechanism behind antipsychotic drugs. The reasoning was that if Parkinson's-like symptoms were appearing when patients' schizophrenic symptoms were improving and if Parkinson's disease was due to a dopaminergic deficiency, then perhaps the antipsychotic drugs were actually reducing the activity level of dopamine in the brain. By implication, schizophrenia would be tied to an excessively high level of dopaminergic activity, and treating it would be a matter of bringing that level down.

Evidence for a dopaminergic involvement in schizophrenia comes from a variety of sources. You would predict that an overdose of L-dopa, an anti-Parkinson's drug that elevates dopaminergic activity in the brain, would produce schizophrenic-like behavior, and it does. Parkinson's patients need to be careful about the dose levels of their medication to avoid displaying signs of disorientation, disturbed

**agranulocytosis
(A-GRAN-yoo-loh-seye-TOH-sis)**
A potentially lethal blood disorder associated with atypical antipsychotic drugs.

thinking, paranoia, or catatonia. Another prediction is that the mechanism behind the action of antipsychotic drugs would be specifically associated with a decline in dopaminergic activity. It turns out that all the typical antipsychotic drugs block the stimulation of dopaminergic receptor sites. In fact, the degree to which these drugs are effective in treating schizophrenia is highly correlated with their effectiveness in blocking dopamine (Fig. 16.1).

Other evidence, however, points to the possibility that a dopaminergic connection might be only a first step toward understanding schizophrenia. Researchers know that dopaminergic receptors in the brain can be broken down into subtypes. At least six subtypes have been identified so far. Typical antipsychotic drugs block a particular receptor subtype called D_2 receptors. Atypical antipsychotic drugs, however, operate in a

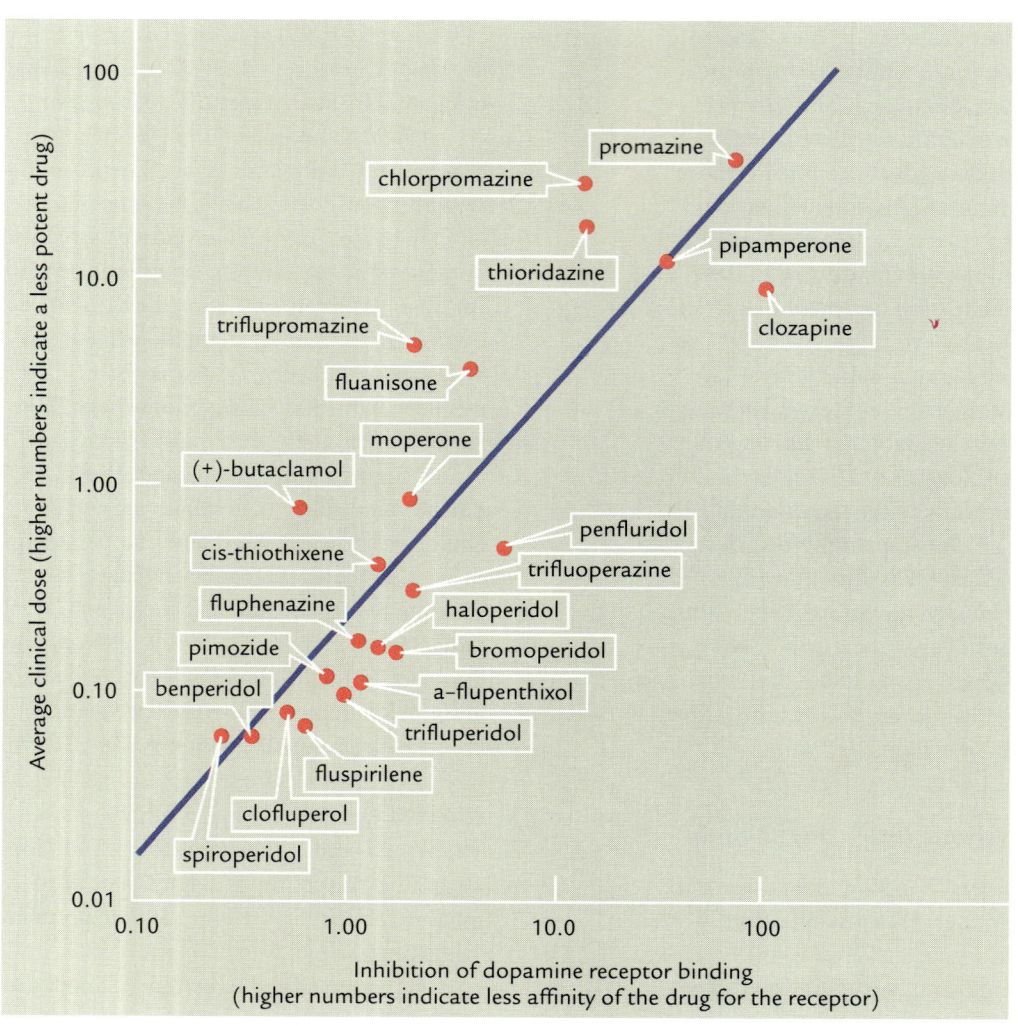

FIGURE 16.1

The association between the strength of an antipsychotic drug in reducing schizophrenic symptoms and the degree to which dopaminergic receptors are blocked in the brain. The relationship would be perfect if all the data points were exactly on the line.
SOURCE: *Adapted from Snyder, Solomon H. Neuroleptic drugs in neurotransmitter receptors.* Journal of Continuing Education in Psychiatry, *1978, 39, p. 25.*

somewhat different way. For example, clozapine appears to block a subtype called D_4 receptors, and risperidone appears to block D_2 and S_2 (a subtype sensitive to serotonin) receptors simultaneously. The absence of Parkinson's-like side effects during clozapine or risperidol treatment appears to be related to the particular set of receptor subtypes that are affected. The development of future antipsychotic drugs will depend upon understanding the complexity of receptor subtypes in the brain.[13]

Drugs used to treat mood disorders

Severe and debilitating depression, usually referred to as major depression, is the most common form of mood disorder. It has been estimated that about 5 percent of the U.S. population will have suffered an episode of major depression at some time in life. A large number of famous men and women in history ranging from the Roman emperor Tiberius and Queen Victoria to Peter Ilich Tchaikovsky, Fyodor Mikhaglovich Dostoevski, Abraham Lincoln, and Sigmund Freud were depressed during prolonged periods of their lives.

We are dealing with an emotional state far beyond ordinary feelings of sadness, grief, or remorse. Many depressed individuals have turned to alcohol as the answer. As we know, however, the depressant action of alcohol on the nervous system not only makes matters worse but also sets the stage for alcohol dependence and alcoholism (Chapter 11). Naturally, as a more immediate concern, there is the risk of suicide. Although not all people who either attempt or actually commit suicide are depressed, the inclination toward depression increases the risk substantially. One way of looking at it is that only about 15 percent of depressed people are suicidal but most suicide-prone people are or have been depressed. Ironically, the risk of a suicide attempt is highest in the initial phase of an upswing in mood after a deep period of depression. When the depression is at its most intense, the depressed individual has little energy to carry out suicidal feelings and thoughts.[14]

Drugs used to treat major depression are referred to as **antidepressants.** Such drugs fall into three general categories: MAO inhibitors, tricyclic types, and the recently introduced atypical antidepressants.

MAO inhibitors

Like the earliest antipsychotic medications, the earliest antidepressants were discovered accidentally, with their applications frequently having little to do with psychological disorders. One early antidepressant was originally intended for the treatment of tuberculosis. It was soon recognized that the improvement in the patient's spirits was not merely a matter of reduced symptoms of this disease. When depressed but otherwise healthy individuals were given the drug, a significant improvement in mood was observed. Eventually, it was discovered that other chemically similar drugs were also effective antidepressants. The key factor connecting them all was their ability to inhibit the enzyme **monoamine oxidase (MAO),** hence their classification as **MAO inhibitors.** There are three MAO inhibitors currently marketed for the treatment of depression: isocarboxazid (brand name: Marplan), phenelzine (brand name: Nardil), and tranylcypromine (brand name: Parnate).

effects of excessive tyramine. Ordinarily, this action would not be a problem, except for the fact that tyramine is contained in many foods and drinks. Any food product or drink that involves fermentation or aging in its processing contains high levels of tyramine, and combining them with an MAO inhibitor can be highly dangerous. Therefore, they must be avoided by patients on MAO-inhibitor antidepressants. While MAO inhibitors continue to be an option in the treatment of depression, the difficulty in maintaining this kind of restricted diet for long periods of time has made other drug approaches more desirable. One of the alternative options is the administration of tricyclic antidepressant drugs.

Tricyclic antidepressants

Tricyclic antidepressants all have a three-ring portion in their molecular structure, hence their name. Of the dozen or so tricyclic drugs on the market, three of the most prominent are amitriptyline (brand names: Elavil or Endep), desipramine (brand name: Norpramin), and imipramine (brand name: Tofranil). Since tricyclic drugs do not operate specifically upon MAO, the problems inherent in a potentially high level of tyramine are not an issue and there is no need for restrictions in the diet. As a result, depressed patients being treated on an outpatient basis can be more safely given these types of antidepressants. Those patients with cardiovascular problems, however, need to be monitored regularly, because high doses of tricyclic drugs can produce an irregular or elevated heart rate. Some patients with cardiovascular disease cannot be treated with tricyclic drugs at all.

Despite their benefits in the treatment of depression, MAO inhibitors are safely administered only to patients whose dietary habits can be carefully supervised or patients who can be relied upon to observe certain specific dietary restrictions. The problem is that MAO inhibitors inhibit MAO not only in the brain but elsewhere in the body as well. In the liver, MAO serves a useful function in breaking down a chemical called tyramine. Too high a level of tyramine produces a highly toxic reaction by elevating the blood pressure and increasing the chances of a stroke. Therefore, although MAO inhibitors are useful at the level of the brain, they also remove the safety barrier we normally have against the harmful

Atypical antidepressants

The newest forms of antidepressant drugs bear no chemical similarity either to MAO inhibitors or tricyclic types. Hence, for lack of a better description, they are referred to as **atypical antidepressants.** Although there are three drugs of this type currently on the

tricyclic antidepressants
A class of antidepressant drugs. Brand names include Elavil, Norpramin, and Tofranil.

atypical antidepressants
Relatively new antidepressant drugs that bear no chemical similarity to either MAO inhibitors or tricyclic drugs. Fluoxetine (brand name: Prozac) is an example.

market, their enormous popularity as antidepressants makes it virtually certain that there will be a greater number in the near future. They include fluoxetine (brand name: Prozac), paroxetine (brand name: Paxil), sertraline (brand name: Zoloft), venlafaxine (brand name: Efflexor), and nefazodone (brand name: Serzone). Of these, Prozac is the best known and has attracted most of the attention, as well as controversy.

By all accounts, Prozac (along with other atypical antidepressants) has been viewed as a genuine breakthrough in the treatment of major depression. Introduced in 1987, it has quickly become the number one antidepressant medication on the strength of its effectiveness in reducing depressive symptoms with fewer side effects. In particular, Prozac is safe for cardiovascular patients who would have difficulty with tricyclic medications, and many patients whose feelings of depression have not been reduced by other antidepressants respond well to Prozac. Also, unlike tricyclic antidepressants, the risk of overdose with Prozac is extremely remote.

Personal testimonials to the benefits of Prozac treatment abound. One pharmacist has offered this observation on his Prozac customers:

Most of these people used to come in here and complain. . . . Now they're saying, "I never felt better". . . . I can't tell when someone's on medication but I sure can tell when they're off.[15]

Are there significant drawbacks to Prozac treatment? The answer, unfortunately, is yes. Some patients report agitation and feelings of nausea, sexual problems, and in a few cases, an increase in suicidal thoughts after taking Prozac (Focus 16.1). There is an increased risk of seizures, though this side effect can be controlled either by lowering the dose or combining the drug with anti-seizure medication. Another source of concern is the tendency for such a popular drug as Prozac to be overprescribed (more than 4.5 million prescriptions were filled in 1993

FOCUS 16.1

Is there a dark side to Prozac?

Few psychiatric medications, with the exception of Valium, have met with more controversy than Prozac.

Despite its enormous popularity as an antidepressant, Prozac has also been a subject of scorn and fear. In 1990 one psychiatrist reported that his Prozac-treated patients developed intense, violent suicidal thoughts, a phenomenon that has since been estimated to occur anywhere from 3 to 15 percent of the time. Yet a careful examination of patients affected this way has shown that such instances have also been observed in severely depressed patients. It is not clear whether thoughts of suicide are tied to the specific effects of the drug or to the emotional aspects of the disorder itself. In a 1991 review of this issue, the FDA concluded that Prozac was still safe to use as directed, though physicians are warned that "the possibility of a suicide attempt is inherent in depression and may persist until significant remission occurs. Close supervision of high risk patients should accompany initial drug therapy."

Accusations that Prozac can induce violent behavior, including homicide, form the basis of several pending lawsuits. Some defense attorneys have adopted the "Prozac defense," claiming that their clients were not responsible for a homicidal act while under Prozac treatment. So far, however, the results in the courts have been mixed. There have been no instances of acquittal based on this line of reasoning, though in a few cases the terms of sentences have been reduced. In the meantime, the FDA has officially ruled that no evidence exists for violent behavior as a direct result of taking Prozac and has approved its use for the treatment of bulimia.

SOURCES: Colwell, Carolyn (1992, January 22). "Prozac defense" set in LI slaying. *Newsday*, pp. 7, 26. FDA backs use of prozac for bulimia (1994, November 13). *New York Times*, p. 19. Kramer, Peter D. (1993). *Listening to Prozac*. New York: Viking Press. *Physicians' desk reference* (48th ed.). (1994). Montvale NJ: Medical Economics Data, p. 878. Talan, Jamie (1990, July 3). Worries over an antidepressant. *Newsday*, pp. D1, D5.

alone), not only as a treatment for major depression but also for milder episodes of depression and related ailments that might have been better treated by traditional psychotherapy or counseling.

Long-term effects of taking Prozac are unknown. A potential problem is that Prozac may simply be too good; patients may be reluctant to withdraw from it on the grounds that they anticipate the return of depressive feelings. The potential for this form of psychological dependence remains an important question with Prozac as well as other psychiatric drugs. There is, however, no evidence for tolerance or physical withdrawal symptoms with Prozac.

The bottom line to the Prozac story, given our experience with the introduction of new psychoactive drugs over more than a century, should by now be familiar. New drugs, even those like Prozac that are recognized as having great promise, should always be administered with caution. Prozac may certainly be an advance in the treatment of depression, but it is far from a "wonder drug."[16]

Effects of antidepressant drugs on the brain

When MAO inhibitors were discovered as being effective in reducing symptoms of depression, theories concerning the mechanism behind the action of these drugs turned to the properties of MAO itself. As enzymes, MAO molecules were known to inactivate dopamine, norepinephrine, and serotonin (collectively referred to as monoamines) at the synapses where these neurotransmitters were active. We can think of a drug as producing a double-negative effect on these neurotransmitters. By inhibiting MAO, we are inhibiting an inhibitor, and the net result will be a rise in the activity level of dopamine,

serotonin-specific reuptake inhibitors (SSRIs)
A group of atypical antidepressants that slow down the reuptake of serotonin at synapses in the brain.

norepinephrine, or serotonin. If so, then it would be logical to theorize that depression is associated with a lower-than-normal level of any one of these neurotransmitters or some combination of the three.

With the discovery of tricyclic antidepressants, it has been possible to focus on a more specific biochemical theory. Unlike MAO inhibitors, tricyclic drugs do not act upon enzymes in the synapse. Instead, they slow down the reuptake of norepinephrine and serotonin at their respective synapses. Since the reuptake process allows neurotransmitter molecules to be reabsorbed from the receptor sites back to the neuron that released them in the first place (Chapter 3), a slowing down means that these neurotransmitter molecules now remain in the receptor site for a longer period of time. When the neurotransmitter stays in the receptors longer, the receptors are stimulated more intensely. In other words, the effect of tricyclic drugs is to increase the activity level of norepinephrine and serotonin. By a similar line of reasoning from the argument made earlier, depression would be associated with a lower-than-normal level of activity with respect to these neurotransmitters.

Prozac was unique in that it was not "discovered" as much as it was designed with a specific purpose in mind. The intent was to identify a chemical that slowed down the reuptake of serotonin alone. Prozac did precisely that. It became the first of a group of atypical antidepressants called **serotonin-specific reuptake inhibitors (SSRIs).** On a theoretical level, the successful development of Prozac and other SSRIs as effective antidepressants has provided strong evidence for the involvement of serotonin in providing the optimal level of mood in a person's life. This fact does not necessarily mean, however, that serotonin is the exclusive neurotransmitter system in the regulation of mood. As noted earlier, a sizable proportion of depressive patients benefit from the administration of tricyclic drugs, implying that a norepinephrine system is involved as well. It may well be that there are two different forms of depression with similar enough behavioral symptoms to be clinically indistinguishable but with one related to an abnormal serotonin system and one related to an abnormal norepinephrine system in the brain.[17]

Mania and bipolar disorder

mood disorder can encompass forms other than simple depression. Some individuals may display symptoms of **mania** that are as disruptive to themselves and their families as depression. Symptoms of mania include sleeplessness, impulsiveness (a manic patient with a credit card is a dangerous combination), irritability, and feelings of grandeur. Others may display states of mood that swing back and forth between depression and mania (a condition referred to as **bipolar disorder,** formerly known as manic-depression). Until recently, the primary psychiatric drug for the treatment of either mania or bipolar disorder has been **lithium.** Unfortunately, lithium is effective for only 50 percent of patients showing these symptoms, and those who respond well to lithium must undergo periodic blood testing to avoid potential toxic effects to the thyroid gland and kidneys.[18] Two new drugs, valproate (brand name: Depakote) and carbamazepine (brand name: Tegretol), have now been found to help patients suffering from either mania or bipolar disorder, as an alternative to lithium. These medications were originally introduced for the treatment of epilepsy, for which they continue to be prescribed. The mechanism by which they influence levels of mood is presently unclear. Drawing from the understanding we have about depression, however, a good possibility is that the beneficial effects of these drugs will be found to be linked to an alteration in the activity level of either serotonin or norepinephrine.[19]

QUICK CONCEPT CHECK 16.1

Understanding the biochemistry of mental illness

heck your understanding of the current biochemical theories of schizophrenia or mood disorders by associating each of the following psychiatric drug actions with the most likely clinical outcomes that you would predict to occur.

PSYCHIATRIC DRUG ACTIONS

1. Drug W reduces the level of dopamine in the brain.

2. Drug X increases the level of serotonin in the brain.

3. Drug Y increases the level of norepinephrine and serotonin in the brain.

4. Drug Z increases the level of dopamine in the brain.

5. Drug Q increases the activity of monoamine oxidase (MAO).

PREDICTED CLINICAL OUTCOMES

a. Schizophrenic symptoms will improve.

b. Schizophrenic symptoms will get worse.

c. Depressive symptoms will improve.

d. Depressive symptoms will get worse.

ANSWERS: 1.a 2.c 3.c 4.b 5.d

mania
A mood disorder characterized by agitation, bursts of energy, and impulsiveness.

bipolar disorder
A mood disorder in which the patient swings back and forth between feelings of depression and mania

lithium (LITH-ee-um)
A psychiatric drug used in the treatment of mania or bipolar disorder.

Psychiatric drugs, social policy, and deinstitutionalization

Prior to the 1960s, the dominant approach in treating severely impaired psychiatric patients was institutionalization in large state-supported mental hospitals. In such places, medications could be controlled by psychiatrists and hospital staff. During the 1960s, the policy toward treating the mentally ill started to change. Responsibility for treatment shifted from centralized institutions to decentralized community mental-health clinics. A major argument was that these smaller centers could provide a more humane setting for psychiatric patients, closer to their homes and families.

Where has this policy left psychiatric patients? With an increase in court cases that supported the illegality of involuntary commitment (requiring a patient to be hospitalized against his or her will) unless there was a clear danger to society, many patients have ended up drifting in and out of mental-health facilities, no longer supervised carefully enough to take their medication regularly or attend to their personal needs. As a result, many of them have become rootless, without homes or sources of social support. It has

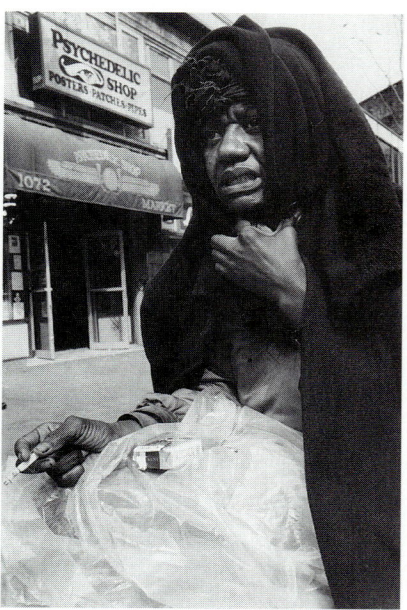

The plight of the homeless is sometimes the plight of deeply troubled individuals adrift from the protection and aid of mental health professionals.

been estimated that 80 percent of all homeless adults have a chronic psychiatric illness, with most of them exhibiting schizophrenic symptoms or drug dependence. The problems of such individuals continue to present a major challenge to our society (Focus 16.2).[20]

Summary

- The development of psychiatric drugs to treat major mental illnesses such as schizophrenia and mood disorders has both revolutionized the field of mental health and provided insights into the biochemical basis for mental illness.

- As effective as psychiatric drugs might be for the mentally ill, none are without side effects. The perfect drug has yet to appear on the scene.

THE BIOMEDICAL MODEL

- The biomedical model, a prevalent viewpoint among mental-health professions, asserts that abnormal thoughts and behaviors are results of biochemical processes in the brain.

ANTIPSYCHOTIC DRUGS AND SCHIZOPHRENIA

- Antipsychotic drugs for schizophrenic patients fall into two broad categories: typical and atypical.

- The typical antipsychotic drugs are effective in reducing symptoms for many patients, but they also carry with them the potential for the development of severe movement-related motor problems.

Psychiatric drugs and the civil liberties debate

et's imagine that you are a hospitalized psychiatric patient, either voluntarily or involuntarily committed to a mental-health facility on the basis of a diagnosis of schizophrenia. You are handed your daily medication that has been prescribed by a staff psychiatrist. There has been a careful diagnosis of your mental illness and a determination that the medication is appropriate and effective in reducing your symptoms. Can you refuse to take it? Do you even have to give a reason for your refusal? If you are asked to participate in a study in which a new experimental drug is being tested against a placebo, should you be required to do so? If you signed an informed consent, are you mentally competent to know what you are agreeing to do? If you state that you are mentally competent but have been diagnosed as a schizophrenic, would your self-assessment be considered valid?

These are a few of the difficult questions presently being faced in mental-health treatment facilities and in the development of new therapeutic drugs. Few of them have been totally resolved. In the late 1960s in Minnesota and New York, physicians were successfully sued for *not* medicating committed, drug-refusing patients. However, in 1975 in Massachusetts, physicians were successfully sued *for* medicating drug-refusing patients. Court decisions since 1979 regarding a patient's right to refuse medication have generally been in the patient's favor, though the decision as to the mental competence of an individual patient is frequently left to a judge's ruling.

Another controversy has arisen surrounding the rights of patients in the development of new drugs, particularly with regard to the treatment of schizophrenia. Should these patients participate in clinical testing trials for experimental antipsychotic medications? On the one hand, as a research psychiatrist has put it, "We must figure out this disease. . . . Unfortunately, there are no animal models for hallucinations and thought disorders. There is no substitute for studying humans." On the other hand, as a civil rights attorney has said, "Persons with severe psychiatric disabilities cannot be made guinea pigs for the greater good of humanity."

What do you think?

SOURCES: Amarasingham, Loma R. (1980). Social and cultural perspectives on medication refusal. *American Journal of Psychiatry, 137,* 353–358. Guthei l, Thomas G. (1980). In search of true freedom: Drug refusal, involuntary medication, and "Rotting with your rights on." *American Journal of Psychiatry, 137,* 327–328. Talan, Jamie (1994, July 5). Schizophrenia: Putting testing on trial. *Newsday,* pp. B25, B23–29, B31.

- A newer class of drugs, called atypical antipsychotic medications, do not produce this particular side effect. One of these drugs, however, can produce a potentially lethal blood disorder in some patients.

- In general, antipsychotic medications are believed to be clinically effective on the basis of their acting upon dopaminergic systems in the brain.

DRUGS USED TO TREAT MOOD DISORDERS

- Antidepressant drugs can be classified in three groups: MAO inhibitors, tricyclic antidepressants, and atypical antidepressants.

- The MAO inhibitors were the first group to be developed for the treatment of depression. Although they are effective, patients need to be on a restricted diet to avoid serious adverse side effects.

- Tricyclic antidepressants do not require dietary restrictions, but their effects on the cardiovascular system make them undesirable for certain patients.

- The newest group, atypical antidepressants, include the popular drug fluoxetine (brand name: Prozac). Despite the advantages of Prozac as an antidepressant, concerns have been raised as to its overuse.

- The effectiveness of antidepressants has been linked to an alteration in either serotonin or norepinephrine systems in the brain.

- Since the 1960s, a growing number of psychiatric patients are treated outside a centralized

hospital or institution and are placed in treatment-care clinics in the community.

- The question of psychiatric patients' rights is a present-day issue of great concern.

Key Terms

agranulocytosis, p. 383
antidepressants, p. 385
antipsychotic drugs, p. 378
atypical antidepressants, p. 386
atypical antipsychotic drugs, p. 380
biomedical model, p. 378
bipolar disorder, p. 389
catatonia, p. 379
delusions, p. 379
lithium, p. 389
mania, p. 389
MAO inhibitors, p. 385

monoamine oxidase (MAO), p. 385
Parkinson's-like symptoms, p. 381
psychiatric drugs, p. 378
psychotropic medication, p. 378
schizophrenia, p. 378
serotonin-specific reuptake inhibitors
  (SSRIs), p. 388
tardive dyskinesia, p. 381
target dosing, p. 380
tricyclic antidepressants, p. 386
typical antipsychotic drugs, p. 380

Endnotes

1. Murphy, Jane M. (1976). Psychiatric labeling in cross-cultural perspective. *Science, 191,* 1019–1028.   Nicol, Susan E., and Gottesman, Irving I. (1983). Clues to the genetics and neurobiology of schizophrenia. *American Scientist, 71,* 398–404.

2. American Psychiatric Association (1994). *Diagnostic and statistical manual* (4th ed.). Washington DC: American Psychiatric Association, pp. 278–290.   Benjamin, Ludy T., Hopkins, J. Roy, and Nation, Jack R. (1994). *Psychology* (3rd ed.). New York: Macmillan, p. 660.

3. Levinthal, Charles F. (1988). *Messengers of paradise: Opiates and the brain.* New York: Anchor Press/Doubleday, pp. 60–61.   Snyder, Solomon H. (1974). *Madness and the brain.* New York: McGraw-Hill, pp. 19–21.

4. Lickey, Marvin E., and Gordon, Barbara (1991). *Medicine and mental illness: The use of drugs in psychiatry.* New York: Freeman, p. 92.

5. Hollister, Leo E. (1983). *Clinical pharmacology of psychotherapeutic drugs* (2nd ed.). New York: Churchill Livingston, pp. 110–171.

6. Davis, John M. (1980). Antipsychotic drugs. In Harold I. Kaplan, Arnold M. Freedman, and Benjamin J. Saddock (Eds.), *Comprehensive textbook of psychiatry.* Vol. 3. Baltimore: Williams and Wilkins, pp. 2257–2289.

7. Baron, Robert A. (1992). *Psychology* (2nd ed.). Boston: Allyn and Bacon, p. 593.

8. Honigfeld, Gilbert, and Howard, Alfreda (1973). *Psychiatric drugs: A desk reference.* New York: Academic Press, p. 37.   Silverstone, Trevor, and Turner, Paul (1978). *Drug treatment in psychiatry* (2nd ed.). London: Routledge and Kegan Paul, pp. 106–108.

9. Lickey and Gordon. *Medicine and mental illness,* pp. 132–133.

10. Palfai, Tibor, and Jankiewicz, Henry (1991). *Drugs and human behavior.* Dubuque IA: W. C. Brown, p. 259.

11. Julien, Robert M. (1995). *A primer of drug action* (7th ed.). New York: Freeman, pp. 288–292. Wallis, Claudia, and Willworth, James (1992, July 6). Awakenings: Schizophrenia. A new

drug brings patients back to life. *Time*, pp. 52–57.

12. Duvoisin, Roger C. (1991). *Parkinson's disease: A guide for patient and family* (3rd ed.). New York: Raven Press.   Hornykiewicz, Oleh (1974). The mechanisms of L-dopamine in Parkinson's disease. *Life Sciences, 15,* 1249–1259.

13. Healy, D. (1991). D_1 and D_2 and D_3. *British Journal of Psychiatry, 159,* 319–324.   Van Tol, Hubert M., Bunzow, James R., Guan, Hong-Chang, Sunahara, Roger K., Seeman, Philip, Niznik, Hyman B., and Civelli, Olivier (1991). Cloning of the gene for a human dopamine D_4 receptor with high affinity for the antipsychotic clozapine. *Nature, 350,* 610–614.

14. Lefton, Lester A. (1994). *Psychology* (5th ed.). Boston: Allyn and Bacon, p. 481.

15. Quoted in Geoffrey Cowley (1990, March 26), The promise of Prozac. *Newsweek,* p. 39.

16. Angier, Natalie (1990, March 29). New antidepressant is acclaimed but not perfect. *New York Times,* p. B9.   Kramer, Peter D. *Listening to Prozac.* New York: Viking, 1993.

17. Levinthal, Charles F. *Introduction to physiological psychology* (3rd ed.). Englewood Cliffs NJ: Prentice-Hall, pp. 174–177.   Maas, James W. (1975). Biogenic amines of depression. *Archives of General Psychiatry, 32,* 1357–1361.

18. Bower, Bruce (1991). Manic depression: Success story dims. *Science News, 139,* 324–325.

19. Goleman, Daniel (1994, July 13). Two drugs get a new use: Soothing mania. *New York Times,* p. C12.   Johnson, F. Neil (1984). *The history of lithium therapy.* New York: Macmillan. Treiser, Susan L., Cascio, Caren S., O'Donohue, Thomas L., Thoa, Nguyen B., Jacobowitz, David M., and Kellar, Kenneth J. (1981). Lithium increases serotonin release and decreases serotonin receptors in the hippocampus. *Science, 213,* 1529–1531.

20. Heston, Leonard L. (1992). *Mending minds: A guide to the new psychiatry of depression, anxiety, and other serious mental disorders.* New York: Freeman, pp. 80–82.

17

Prevention Strategies: Schools, Community, and Family

THIS CHAPTER WILL INTRODUCE YOU TO
THE FOLLOWING SUBJECTS:

- Three types of interventions in drug-abuse prevention

- Which approaches seem to work and which ones do not

- School-based prevention programs

- Community-based prevention and the mass media

- The family in drug-abuse prevention

- Drug-abuse prevention in the workplace

- Multicultural issues in drug-abuse prevention

- Special concerns with regard to college students

onsider for a moment the goal of preventing the misuse and abuse of psychoactive drugs in our society. Everyone is obviously for prevention; no one questions the personal damage and social havoc that the sale, distribution, and consumption of illicit drugs bring to us today. As political leaders continually remind us, we have to "do something" if this monster is to be slain. Nor can we question the magnitude of preventable disease and death that are associated with licit drugs such as alcohol and nicotine. The risks to our health and the health of our families and friends have to be reduced; it is a public-health imperative. Yet as unanimous as we may be in the necessity for some strategy for preventing drug misuse and abuse, the issues are complex and the answers elusive. So far, we have enjoyed only partial success in this area. Health professionals have yet to find the ingredients for a program that makes a significant and long-lasting impact on an individual's inclination to use drugs.

Ways to approach drug-abuse prevention

raditionally, efforts to prevent the abuse of drugs have been divided into three types of intervention: primary, secondary, and tertiary. Each has its own target population and goals.

In **primary prevention**, efforts are directed to those who have not had any experience with drugs or who have been only minimally exposed. The objective is to prevent drug abuse from starting in the first place. Targets in primary-prevention programs are most frequently elementary school or junior high school students, and intervention is typically within a school-based curriculum or special educational program. For example, a primary-prevention program would include the teaching of peer-refusal skills (that is, ways to "say no") to students when they are offered marijuana, alcohol, or cigarettes.

In **secondary prevention,** the target population has already had some experience with drugs. The objective is to limit the extent of drug abuse (reducing it if possible), prevent the spread of drug abuse to other substances beyond the drugs already encountered, and teach strategies for the responsible use of licit drugs such as alcohol. Ordinarily, those receiving secondary-prevention efforts are older than those involved in primary-prevention programs. High school students who are identified as alcohol or drug users may participate in a program that emphasizes social alternatives to drug-taking behavior. College students may focus on the skills necessary to restrict their behavior to the moderate use of alcohol, the dangers of combining drinking and driving, and the signs of chronic alcohol abuse.

In **tertiary prevention,** the objective is to ensure that an individual who has entered treatment for some form of drug abuse stays drug free, without relapsing to former patterns of drug-taking behavior. Successful prevention of future relapse is the ultimate

indication that the treatment has taken hold.[1] Since treatment issues have been already addressed in earlier chapters specific to a particular class of drug, the prevention programs reviewed in this chapter will be limited to the primary and secondary types.

Learning from the past: Prevention strategies that have not worked

 good place to begin is a survey of efforts that have been considered, in the general opinion of health professionals, to have been largely unsuccessful with regard to either primary or secondary prevention. A careful look at the following six prevention programs and policy strategies teaches us something about what to avoid.

Reducing the availability of drugs

On the one hand, it is reasonable to expect that we could avoid the problems of drug abuse if the availability of drugs were reduced or eliminated altogether. This is essentially the "supply/availability argument" in drug prevention. As noted in Chapter 2, a huge amount of governmental resources has been spent on preventing the influx of illegal drugs into this country. On the other hand, according to the economic principle of supply and demand, as supply or availability declines, the product becomes more valuable in the eyes of the consumer and therefore demand goes up. If one accepts the first viewpoint, then reductions in supply or availability should help prevent drug-taking behavior; if one accepts the second viewpoint, then such reductions should exacerbate the situation. Which theoretical viewpoint is operating with respect to drugs is a point of controversy among health professionals both inside and outside the government.

primary prevention
A type of intervention in which the goal is to forestall the use of drugs by an individual who has had little or no previous exposure to them.

secondary prevention
A type of intervention in which the goal is to reduce the extent of drug use in individuals who have already had some exposure to drugs.

tertiary (TER-shee-eh-ree) prevention
A type of intervention in which the goal is to prevent the relapse in a individual following recovery in a drug treatment program.

Given the fact that the country has adopted the policy of reducing the supply or availability of drugs, how successful have we been? Specifically, have we been able to reduce the production of illegal drugs around the world? Unfortunately, drug cultivation (such as the harvesting of opium, cocaine, or marijuana) and exportation of these products from their points of origin is so deeply entrenched in many regions of the world and the resourcefulness of drug producers is so great that our efforts to reduce the production of drugs have been frustratingly inadequate. For example, when Turkish farmers were persuaded in the 1970s to shift their predominant cash crop from opium to wheat and barley, there was a temporary halt in Turkish opium production but no basic change on a global level. Southeast Asia and Afghanistan quickly became the new harvesters of raw opium and sources of heroin. A similar sequence occurred when huge fields of cannabis in Mexico were destroyed in a U.S.-sponsored program to reduce the availability of marijuana. Filling in the vacuum, Colombia and Jamaica became the new sources of marijuana in the Western Hemisphere.

Moreover, the effort to control international drug smuggling and reduce the influx of illegal drugs in this country has been embarrassingly unsuccessful, despite well-publicized busts and seizures. It is estimated that only a very small fraction of illegal drugs are interdicted at our borders.[2]

In recent years, a strategy to reduce the availability of drugs has been attempted with respect to alcohol, in the form of restricting alcohol sales to young people under the age of twenty-one (Chapter 10). Although it was successful in certain areas, the results of this policy indicate that the effects are weaker than we had hoped. For example, in one study, the percentage of teenage, nighttime, single-vehicle, accident fatalities in Massachusetts was found to have declined in 1979 (when the legal drinking age in that state was raised to twenty-one) to a significantly greater degree than in New York, which at that time still had a minimum drinking age of eighteen. This was the good news. The bad news was that the relative levels of alcohol use in this age range stayed the same. Therefore, while we may have been able to reduce one particular consequence of immoderate use of alcohol (drunk driving), we have not been able to affect the incidence of alcohol use itself. As we are all aware, under-age drinking still is prevalent; minors still find opportunities and ways to drink and to drink in excess. The fact that minimum-age requirements have only a limited effect on drinking among minors reinforces the complexity of dealing with primary prevention, whether we are considering legal or illegal drugs.[3]

Punitive measures for drug addicts

A similar question can be asked about the preventive role of law-enforcement and judicial policies with regard to drug offenders. The expectation from such policies is that an individual would be less inclined to use illegal drugs for fear of being arrested, convicted, and sent to jail. The statistics show, however, that this strategy has not worked out. The enticements of many psychoactive drugs are evidently too great for deterrence to work, and the implementation of harsh sentences has frequently been delayed or inconsistent. Mandatory minimum-sentencing laws, on a federal level and in many states, have left more than 300,000 in U.S. prisons for drug offenses, with one in five federal prisoners being first-time offenders. From 1980 to 1993, the percentage of the 87,000 people in federal (as distinct from state) prisons serving time for drug convictions has risen from 22 in 1980 to 60, with half of these prisoners being first-time offenders. The result has been a clogged judicial system and vastly overcrowded prisons, without any noticeable dent in the pattern of consumption of or trafficking in illegal drugs. Although the enforcement of penalties for drug possession and drug dealing may be defended in terms of an overall social policy toward illegal drugs, it has evidently failed

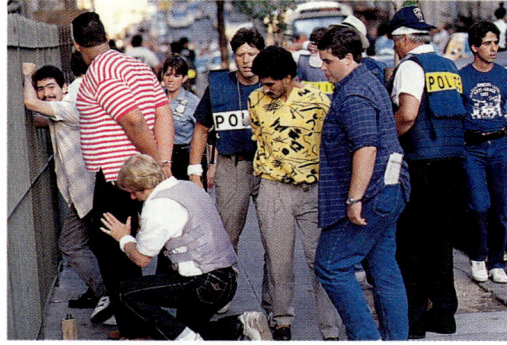

Police officers arrest drug offenders in a drug bust.

as a means for either primary or secondary prevention.[4]

Scare tactics and negative education

In the late 1960s the suddenly widespread use of marijuana, amphetamines, barbiturates, LSD, and other hallucinogens, first among students on college campuses and later among youth at large, spawned a number of hastily designed programs based on the arousal of fear and exaggerated or blatantly inaccurate information about the risks involved. As might be imagined, such efforts turned young people off precisely at a time when they were themselves turning on to an array of exotic and seemingly innocuous drug-taking experiences. Professionals have called it the "reefer madness approach," an allusion to the government-sponsored movie of the 1930s that attempted to scare people away from experimenting with marijuana (Chapter 9). These programs accomplished little, except to reduce even further the credibility of the adult presenters in the eyes of youths who often knew (or thought they knew) a great deal more about drugs and their effects.[5]

Objective-information approaches

At the opposite end of the emotional spectrum are programs designed to present information about drugs and their potential dangers in a straightforward, nonjudgmental way. Unfortunately, evaluations of this "just the facts, ma'am" approach have found that youths exposed to such primary-prevention programs are no less likely to use drugs later in their lives and sometimes are *more* likely to use them. These programs tend to increase their curiosity about drugs in general, obviously something the program planners would want to avoid.[6] Despite these failures, however, it would be a mistake to dismiss the informational aspect of any drug-abuse prevention program completely out of hand. The value of an informational approach appears to depend on whether the target population consists of high-risk or low-risk children:

> Providing information to low-risk youth on the health and legal implications of using illegal drugs often is enough incentive for them to avoid using drugs. When low-risk young people really understand the dangers of drugs, they choose to remain drug free. High-risk youth may not be so easily dissuaded from using drugs, and for them additional intervention is necessary.[7]

Magic bullets and promotional campaigns

A variety of antidrug promotional materials such as T-shirts, caps, rings, buttons, bumper stickers, posters, rap songs, school assembly productions, books, and brochures are frequently seen as "magic bullets" that can insure success in a drug-abuse-prevention program. Their appeal lies in their high visibility; these items give a clear signal to the public at large that something is being done. Yet, although they may be helpful in deglamorizing drug use and providing a forum for young people to express their feelings about drugs, promotional items are inadequate by themselves to reduce drug abuse overall. They do, however, remain components of more comprehensive programs that will be examined later in the chapter.[8]

Self-esteem enhancement and affective education

Several prevention programs in the early 1970s were developed to focus on the "affective component" of drug-taking behavior rather than on specific information about drugs. Since some research had shown a relationship between drug abuse and psychological variables such as low self-esteem, poor decision-making skills, and poor interpersonal-communication skills, programs were instituted that incorporated role-play-

ing exercises with other assignments designed to help young people feel better about themselves. This effort, called **affective education,** was an attempt to deal with underlying emotional and attitudinal factors rather than specific behaviors related to drug use (in fact, drugs were seldom mentioned at all). Affective education was based on the observation that drug users had difficulty identifying and expressing feelings such as anger and love. In a related set of programs, called **values clarification,** moral values were actively taught to children, on the grounds that drug users frequently have a poorly developed sense of where their life is going and lack moral "yardsticks" to guide their behavior.

Difficulties arose, however, when parents, community leaders, and frequently educators themselves argued that the emphasis of affective education was inappropriate for public schools. In regard to values clarification, there was concern that a system of morality was being imposed on students without respecting their individual backgrounds and cultures. Beyond these considerations, the bottom line was that neither affective education nor values clarification was effective in preventing drug use. Some researchers have recently questioned the basic idea that self-esteem is a major factor at all. As a result, affective issues are no longer viewed as central considerations in primary or secondary prevention. Nonetheless, they can be found as components in more comprehensive prevention programs, discussed later, that have been more successful.[9]

affective education
An approach in drug prevention programs that emphasizes the building of self-esteem and an improved self-image.

values clarification
An approach in drug prevention programs which teaches positive social values and attitudes.

Hope and promise: Current school-based prevention programs

ne of the lessons we have learned from evaluations of previous drug-abuse-prevention efforts is that there is a greater chance for success when the programs are multifaceted than when they focus on only a single aspect of drug-taking behavior. We need to remember that success can be measured in various ways. A school-based program, for example, might be considered successful if it enjoys support from parents, administrators, and teachers. It might be considered successful if there is evidence of a change in a child's view toward drugs or in the child's stated inclination to use drugs in the future.

The ultimate goal of any prevention program, however, is to achieve some reduction in actual drug-taking behavior. This last objective is often difficult to measure. The prevention program may lack a "control group" that did not receive the intervention, making it impossible to determine whether the effect of the program itself was greater than doing nothing at all. Evaluations of drug-abuse-prevention programs frequently look at the "exit results" in the form of short-term effects such as changes in how young people feel after the program has ended or think they will act in the future, rather than long-term effects such as reduced drug usage over an extended period of time. With these considerations in mind, it is useful to examine two primary-prevention approaches currently being implemented in the schools. Community-based prevention efforts will be considered later in the chapter.

peer-refusal skills
Techniques by which an individual can resist peer pressure to use drugs.

Peer-refusal and life-skills training

A number of school-based programs, developed during the 1980s, have focused on teaching the personal and social skills and knowledge necessary to resist the various forms of social pressure to smoke, drink, and use drugs (often referred to as **peer-refusal skills**). The emphasis is directed toward an individual's relationships among his or her peers and the surrounding social climate. Rather than simply encouraging adolescents to "just say no," these programs teach them *how* to do so when placed in often uncomfortable social circumstances. Prominent examples of programs designed around this philosophy include Project STAR developed in Kansas City, Project SMART developed in North Carolina, Project ALERT developed in California and Oregon, and Life Skills Training (LST) developed in New York City. In 1993 approximately 50 percent of federally funded substance-abuse-prevention grants went to programs that emphasized social and life skills.[10] The Life Skills Training program will be examined here in detail, as an example of this general approach.

Designations of drug-free school zones are prominent features of many school-based drug prevention programs.

The LST program, under the direction of Gilbert Botvin at the Cornell University Medical College in New York City, is directed toward seventh-grade students in a fifteen-session curriculum, with ten additional "booster" sessions in the eighth grade and five in the ninth grade. The major elements of the program include the following:

1. A cognitive component designed to provide information concerning the short-term consequences of alcohol or other drug use. Students learn about the process of drug abuse and commonly held myths about it.

2. A decision-making component designed to facilitate critical thinking and independent decision making. Students learn to analyze and evaluate the role of media in behavior as well as to formulate counterarguments and use other cognitive strategies to resist advertising pressures.

3. A component designed to help students develop ways to reduce anxiety. Students learn techniques of self-relaxation and stress management and the application of these techniques to everyday situations.

4. A component designed to teach social skills and assertiveness skills, including specific techniques for resisting peer pressure to engage in drug-taking behavior. Students learn to express their feelings, needs, preferences, and opinions directly and honestly and are especially encouraged to apply these newly developed skills in situations in which they may experience social pressure to take drugs.

5. A self-directed behavior-change component designed to facilitate self-improvement and encourage a sense of personal control and self-esteem. Students are assigned to identify a skill or behavior that they would like to change or improve and to develop a long-term goal over an eight-week period and short-term objectives that can be met once a week.[11]

Originally designed as a smoking-prevention program, LST has since been expanded toward alcohol and marijuana. During the program, students engage in peer interactions, demonstrations, exercises, and extended practice through behavioral "homework" assignments. Unlike traditional prevention approaches, LST includes only minimal information concerning long-term health consequences of drug use. Instead, information is provided concerning immediate negative consequences of use, the decreasing social acceptability of use, and actual prevalence rates among adults and adolescents.[12]

The research concerning the effectiveness of LST as an agent for primary prevention has concentrated principally on the prevention of smoking, though the impact on alcohol and marijuana use has also been evaluated. With respect to smoking, Botvin and his associates found in two studies that the proportion of pretest nonsmokers becoming regular smokers (defined as smokers of one or more cigarettes per week) one year later could be reduced 56 to 67 percent without additional booster sessions; in one study in which booster sessions had been held the reduction could be increased to 87 percent. In a three-year follow-up evaluation of LST, statistically significant reductions were found in alcohol and marijuana use, though none were as great as the effects on smoking.[13]

It is important here to note that the success of LST programs, and the success of other programs similar to them, in reducing the incidence of drug use (whether of tobacco, alcohol, or marijuana) declines substantially over time. In other words, the effects are impressive in the short term, but they erode as time passes. While Botvin has reported effects on drug use as late as the twelfth grade, as long as booster sessions are carried out in the eighth and ninth grades, the effects tend to be considerably smaller by that time.[14] Unfortunately, the research indicates that no presently existing school-based program produces behavioral changes that sustain themselves over time.

Drug Abuse Resistance Education (DARE)

In 1983 the Los Angeles Police Department and the Los Angeles Unified School District began a collaborative effort in which uniformed police officers came to kindergarten and to junior high school classrooms to teach basic drug information, peer-refusal skills, self-management techniques, and alternatives to drug use in a program called Drug Abuse Resistance Education (DARE). Quite rapidly, the DARE program spread beyond Los Angeles until today it has been established in all fifty states, in all Native American schools administered by the Bureau of Indian Affairs, and in U.S. Department of Defense schools worldwide, as well as in twelve foreign countries. More than 10 million students participate in DARE each year, making the program the largest drug-education program in the world. While DARE programs extend from kindergarten to the senior year in high school, they typically concentrate on a target population of late elementary school children. Beyond the education in the classroom, the DARE programs arrange teacher-orientation sessions and officer-student interactions on playgrounds and cafeterias. In addition, there are parent-education evenings during which DARE officers explain the curriculum to the parents and provide information about symptoms of drug use and ways to increase family communication.[15]

Responses to Project DARE from teachers, principals, students, and police officers are typically enthusiastic, and it is clear that the program has struck a responsive chord in the eyes of the public who have pushed for active prevention programs in the schools. This enthusiasm can be seen as coming in large part from the image of police departments shifting their emphasis from an exclusive role in "supply reduction" (arresting drug offenders and dealers, and seizing drugs) to a larger social role in "demand reduction."

Yet despite its success in the area of public relations, evidence supporting the effectiveness of DARE has been relatively weak. Studies on drug-related attitudes show positive changes on the part of students in the DARE programs as well as the parents of these students. For example, the percentage of fifth grade students who reported equating drug use with having more friends has been shown to decline from 51 to only 8. Approximately 94 percent of DARE graduates have indicated that they now know how to respond when a friend or friends ask them to do something they do not want to do. Before DARE training, 61 percent of parents thought there was nothing they could do about their children's use of drugs; only 5 percent reported this view after the program. There is also evidence that the program produces a more positive attitude toward the police in general.

However, there is little evidence that DARE has made an impact on actual drug use. A 1991 evaluation in Lexington, Kentucky, showed no significant differences in the percentage of new users of cigarettes, smokeless tobacco, alcohol, or marijuana between sixth grade students receiving DARE instruction and those in a control group. An interesting sidelight of this research, however, was the observation that in several schools participating in the study, only 44 to 60 percent of the sixth grade students had *not* smoked cigarettes anytime in their lives and only 86 to 89 percent of them had *not* smoked marijuana. In other words, if the intention of the program in the first place was to prevent or delay the initial use of these drugs, then a sizable proportion of the children were ineligible for this intervention. A clear implication of the Lexington data and similar evaluations in other parts of the United States is that primary-prevention programs may be starting too late in a child's drug-taking history.[16]

When should we intervene?

A continuing theme in the evaluation of school-based programs is the question of who the target population should be and how long the intervention should last. We may feel more comfortable with the introduction of peer-refusal-skill training in the junior high school or somewhat earlier in the last grades of elementary school, but the reality of present-day drug-taking behavior is that many children have already been introduced to drugs by that time, and for them, primary-prevention programs designed to forestall the initial use of drugs are largely irrelevant. But would such interventions be appropriate for younger students?

There is no controversy, however, about the need to sustain school-based programs through the senior year in high school, although we must be mindful of course that at that point primary prevention has shifted for the most part to secondary prevention.

Community-based prevention programs

Community-based prevention programs offer several obvious advantages over those restricted to schools. The first is the greater opportunity to involve parents and other family members, religious institutions, and the media as collaborative agents for change. The most important factor here is the comprehensive nature of such programs. They draw upon multiple social institutions such as the family, corporations and businesses, media, governmental institutions, and community organizations. They are also in a better position to use multiple strategies rather than a single approach.

Typically, many of the prevention components that have been incorporated in the schools are also components in community-based programs, such as the dissemination of information, stress management, and training in life skills. Other approaches can be handled better in a community setting. For example, although schools can promote the possibility of alternative student

activities that provide positive and constructive means for addressing feelings of boredom, frustration, and powerlessness (activities such as Midnight Basketball and Boys and Girls Clubs), the community is in a better position than the schools actually to provide these activities. There is also a greater opportunity in the community to elicit the involvement of significant individuals (**impactors**) to act as positive role models and to enlist the help of the mass media to promote antidrug messages in the press and on television. Finally, it is possible for community-based programs to be more influential in promoting changes in public policy that foster opportunities for education, employment, and self-development.[17] Two prominent aspects of community-based prevention programs, the development of alternative-behavior programming and the role of the mass media, will be examined in detail.

Alternative-behavior programming

It should not be surprising that it is easier to say no to drugs when you can say yes to something else. In community-based prevention programs, a major effort is made to provide the activities and outlets that steer people away from situations associated with drug use. Owing to the fact that adolescents spend a majority of their time outside school, and it is outside school that most drug use occurs, community programs have the best chance of providing the necessary interventions. In fact, adolescents at highest risk of using drugs are the least likely even to be attending school on the days that prevention efforts are delivered.[18]

Table 17.1 gives a sampling of alternative behaviors corresponding to a particular indi-

impactors
Individuals who function as positive role models to children and adolescents in drug prevention programs.

Alternative behaviors to drug use: Needs and motives

Level of experience	Needs and motives	Alternatives
Physical	Physical satisfaction, more energy	Athletics, dance/exercise, hiking, carpentry, or outdoor work
Sensory	Stimulation of sensory experience	Sensory awareness training, sky diving, experiencing
Emotional	Relief from anxiety, mood elevation, emotional relaxation	Individual counseling, group therapy
Interpersonal	Peer acceptance, defiance of authority figures	Confidence training, sensitivity groups, helping others in distress
Social/Environmental	Promotion of social change or identification with a subculture	Social service; community action; helping the poor, aged, handicapped; environmental activism
Intellectual	Escape from boredom, curiosity, or inclination to explore one's own awareness	Reading, creative games, memory training, discussion groups
Creative/aesthetic	Increase in one's creativity or enjoyment of images and thoughts	Nongraded instruction in visual arts, music, drama, crafts, cooking, gardening, writing, singing
Philosophical	Discovery of the meaning of life, organization of a belief system	Discussions, study of ethics or other philosophical literature
Spiritual/mystical	Transcendence of organized religion, spiritual insight or enlightenment	Study of world religions, meditation, yoga
Miscellaneous	Adventure, risk-taking, "kicks"	"Outward Bound" survival training, meaningful employment

SOURCE: Adapted from Cohen, Allan Y. (1972). The journey beyond trips: Alternatives to drugs. In David E. Smith and George R. Gay (Eds.), *It's so good, don't even try it once: Heroin in perspective.* Englewood Cliffs NJ: Prentice Hall, pp. 191–192.

vidual's needs and motives. One way of thinking about alternative-behavior programming is that the person is trading a negative dependence (on drugs) that causes harm to the body or the mind for a positive dependence that causes no harm and taps into pleasure from within.

How effective is alternative-behavior programming with regard to drug-abuse prevention? An extensive analysis was reported in 1981 in a review of 127 studies of different types of prevention programs. Of these, only 12 studies involved alternative behaviors, and 7 of the 12 reported no significant impact upon program partici-

pants. The other 5 studies, however, had positive outcomes, which resulted in alternative-behavior programming being ranked second in positive effects among ten other approaches to drug-use prevention. In a later 1986 review, alternative-behavior programming was identified as being highly successful for at-risk adolescents such as users of alcohol and other drugs, juvenile delinquents, and students having problems in school. On the basis of these evaluations, the general view (though not a unanimous one) is that alternative-behavior programming can work and deserves to have a place in comprehensive prevention programs.[19]

The role of the media

Consider the fact that many adolescents spend a very large portion of their time watching TV (averaging around 4 to 6 hours a day) and that by the time of graduation from high school, an average teenager has watched an estimated 22,000 hours of TV.[20] It makes sense that the medium of TV should have a major role in drug-abuse-prevention efforts.

Unfortunately, antidrug messages have been largely confined to public-service announcements, brief commercials, and limited program series. Even so, the impact can be substantial. A prominent example is a recent series of TV segments sponsored by the Partnership for a Drug-Free America (PDFA), a volunteer coalition of advertising agencies and media companies, designed to deglamorize drug-taking behavior and reinforce behaviors associated with persuasive and memorable ways to refuse to use drugs. A recent number of segments have targeted inner-city children living in high-risk, drug-use environments, based specifically on studies concerning their attitudes toward drugs and drug dealing. In a 1994 PDFA report of responses from more than fifteen thousand New York City school children, many of whom every day face pressures and decisions about taking drugs, there are indications of an increasingly strong antidrug position, particularly among African American respondents and children attending schools in below-poverty-line areas.[21] This is in contrast to the indications of increased drug use and a softening of antidrug attitudes across the nation as a whole since 1992 (Chapter 1).

In late 1980s a TV campaign designed by the Harvard School of Public Health centering on the concept of designated drivers as part of an overall strategy to reduce alcohol-related automobile accidents indicated the extent to which the media could influence social behavior. A Gallup poll in 1989 found that 78 percent of U.S. adults who attended social functions where alcohol is served had seen a TV message promoting the designation of a nondrinking driver during the previous three months. The percentage of individuals using a designated driver has risen by 10 in barely nine months time. By the time of testing, 72 percent of those polled had accepted the designated-driver concept.[22]

(SFX)

Drug Dealer: Yeah,

I like kids.

Couldn't run my business

without 'em. I look for someone smart,

then just bring him along. If you buy him some sneakers, he'd do anything

for you.

Be a lookout, hold your stash...

So what if he gets caught,

I'll just get me another one.

Project's full of kids.

Announcer: Now that you know what a drug dealer thinks of you, what do you think of him?

Scene segments from an antidrug media message on television. (Courtesy of the Partnership for a Drug-Free America, New York.)

The family and prevention

t can be argued that family influences form the cornerstone of any successful drug-abuse-prevention program. Reaching the parents of youths at greatest risk, however, is a difficult task. Too often drug-abuse-prevention programs are attended by those parents who do not really need the information; the ones that need the information the most, those who are either in denial, too embarrassed, or too out of control, are absent. Other parents may need and genuinely want to participate, but they may have difficulty attending because of lack of child care, lack of transportation, scheduling conflicts in their employment, or language differences. Several of the factors that prevent their attendance are the same factors that increase the risk of drug use among their children.[23]

Although obstacles exist, comprehensive prevention programs strive to incorporate parents and other family members into the overall effort. The reason lies in the variety of special roles that parents play in influencing their children with regard to drug-taking behavior. The following are five basic parenting roles. The ways in which parents play these roles can have a significant impact on their children's inclination to use drugs:

1. Parents as role models. Parents may drink alcoholic beverages, smoke, or drink excessive amounts of caffeinated coffee, not thinking of these habits as drug-taking behaviors. They must avoid sending their children signals about drug abstinence that are inconsistent at best or hypocritical at worst.

2. Parents as educators or resources for information. Verbal messages by which parents help to shape children's behavior with regard to future use of alcohol and other drugs must convey accurate information about health risks.

3. Parents as family policymakers and rule setters. Rules about drug use should reflect a clear understanding of drug-taking consequences. If a parent cannot back up a family rule with log-ical and consistent information, the risk that rules will be broken is increased.

4. Parents as stimulators of enjoyable family activities. Alternative behaviors to taking drugs can arise from family-inspired activities as well as from the community at large.

5. Parents as consultants against peer pressure. Children and adolescents frequently report that their parents' negative reaction was the single most important reason for the offsprings' refusing alcohol or other drugs from their peers.[24]

One further aspect of parenting deserves particular mention as it pertains to drug abuse, namely the type of behaviors referred to as enabling. As discussed in Chapter 11, enabling behaviors on the part of a spouse, family member, or friend can inadvertently exacerbate an alcoholic's drinking problems and serve as a major obstacle to recovery. In the context of primary and secondary prevention, enabling behaviors on the part of a parent have an equally detrimental influence. Either enabling behaviors give children the message that it is all right to use drugs, or they make it easier for children to use drugs by protecting them from the negative consequences of drug use. Justifiably, recent antidrug media campaigns have focused on parent-child communication skills, specifically on the difficulty many parents have in talking to their children about drugs (Focus 17.1).

Drug-abuse prevention in the workplace

he Drug-Free Workplace Act of 1988 established federal statutes requiring that any company or business receiving a single federal contract of $25,000 or more or receiving a grant from the U.S. government of any amount be certified as a drug-free workplace. It must also publish a statement notifying employees that the distribution, possession, or use of controlled substances is prohibited in that workplace and that actions will be taken against employees for

FOCUS 17.1

A test kit for drugs in the home: Who can you trust?

n 1995 a drug detection company introduced a commercial kit capable of testing for illicit drugs in the home. Marketed for parents who wish to check for possible drug abuse among their children, the kit consists of a three-inch premoistened pad that can be wiped across desk tops, telephones, books, clothing, or other items. The pad is mailed to the company where an analysis for the presence of cocaine, crack cocaine, heroin, methamphetamine, LSD, marijuana, and PCP is performed. The testing destroys the sample so it cannot be later used in any court proceedings. The results of the analysis are then mailed to the parents.

The fact that the test kit is designed to be used by parents with or without their children's knowledge has raised a number of controversial issues. On the one hand, the kit is promoted as a potent new weapon in the battle against the increased levels of drug abuse among young people. From this point of view, parents are now able to get early help for their children before drug abuse problems become too great. On the other hand, the kit can also be viewed as a new weapon in the battle of the generations. Detractors argue that it sets up an atmosphere of distrust between parents and their children.

What do you think? If you were a parent, would you consider this new testing kit as a step forward or a step backward in the effort to prevent drug abuse in your family?

SOURCES: Kit to test for drugs at home (1995, March 29). *Newsday*, p. A8. Winslow, Olivia and Lam, Chau (1995, March 30). Test fuels drugs debate. *Newsday*, pp. A6, A51.

---

tion of a drug-testing program, although these components are frequently included in an overall prevention effort.[25]

Although the concept of a drug-free workplace is applicable in all places of business, it is in the transportation industry that drug-abuse-prevention programs have had their greatest impact, owing for the most part to the close linkage between drug-related impairments of performance and the incidence of industrial accidents. One workplace program, instituted by the Southern Pacific Railroad Company, required extensive drug testing for all company accidents or rule violations; as a result of this policy, the annual number of accidents decreased from 911 to 168 in three years and the financial losses from such accidents decreased from $6.4 million to $1.2 million. During the first few months of the new testing program, 22 to 24 percent of employees involved in human-factor-related accidents tested positive for alcohol or other drugs, a figure that declined to 3 percent three years later. Since the enactment of the Transportation Employees Testing Act of 1991, tests for alcohol and other drugs are now required for workers involved in the operation of any form of public transportation. Such workers include bus drivers, railroad engineers, airline pilots, and even drivers of snowplows, dump trucks, and airport runway sweepers.[26]

Multicultural issues in drug-abuse prevention

n the case of drug-abuse-prevention efforts, it is important to remember that information intended to reach individuals of a specific culture must pass through a series of **sociocultural filters.** Understanding this filtering process is essential if we are to maximize the

> **sociocultural filters**
> A set of considerations specific to a particular culture or community which can influence the reception of public information.

violations. There is also the requirement that an ongoing, drug-free, awareness program be created for drug information and counseling opportunities. What is not required, however, is the establishment of an employee-assistance program (see Chapter 11) or the implementa-

reception and acceptance of drug-abuse-prevention information.

Prevention approaches among Latino groups

A good example of the need to recognize sociocultural filters is the set of special concerns associated with communicating drug-related information to Latinos, a diverse group of approximately 20 million people living throughout the United States.[27] The following are three principal insights concerning sociocultural factors in these communities that bear upon the chances of succeeding in drug-abuse-prevention programs:

First, because of the importance Latinos accord to the family and religious institutions, prevention and intervention efforts should be targeted to include the entire family, and if possible, its religious leaders. Prevention efforts will be most effective when counselors reinforce family units and value them as a whole.

Second, prevention programs are needed to help Latino fathers recognize how important their role or example is to their sons' self-image regarding alcohol and other drug use. Because being a good father is a part of machismo, it is important that the men become full partners in parenting. Mothers should be encouraged to learn strategies for inclusion of their husbands into family interactions at home.

Third, because a Latina woman with alcohol or other drug problems is strongly associated with a violation of the womanly ideal of purity, discipline, and self-sacrifice, educational efforts should be concentrated on reducing the shame associated with her reaching out for help.

Prevention approaches among African American groups

Another set of special concerns exist with regard to communicating drug-related information to African American communities.[28] Some basic generalizations have proved helpful in optimizing the design of drug-abuse-prevention programs for these groups of people:

First, African American youths tend to use drugs other than alcohol after they form the attitudes and adopt behaviors associated with delinquency. The most common examples of delinquency include drug dealing, shoplifting, and petty theft. As noted earlier in the media campaigns of the Partnership for Drug-Free America, it is the deglamorization of the drug dealer that appears to be most helpful in primary-prevention efforts among African American youths.

Second, drug use and social problems are likely to be interrelated in African American neighborhoods. The effects of alcohol and other drug use are intensified when other factors exist, such as high unemployment, poverty, poor health care, and poor nutrition.

Third, several research studies have shown that most African American youths, even those in low-income areas, do manage to escape from the pressures toward alcohol and other drug use. Some of the protective factors with regard to drug use are remaining in school, strong family bonds, strong religious beliefs, high self-esteem, adequate coping strategies, social skills, and employment. Prevention programs building upon these positive factors have the greatest chance for success.

Yes, you: Drug-abuse prevention and the college student

In turning to the subject of what we can do about the abuse of alcohol and other drugs among college students, we need to recognize that we are not speaking of a homogenous population. U.S. college students comprise all racial, ethnic, and socioeconomic groups and are likely to come from all parts of the world. They include under-

PORTRAIT

Meredith Poulten— On the front lines

Meredith Poulten

Since 1987, in the high school in Medway, Massachusetts, a quiet suburban town outside Boston, young people have had a place to go for help, for a referral, for a sympathetic ear, or just to sit and relax for a few minutes from the pressures of school, parents, and peers. It is called a Walk-in Center, with entrances both within the school and directly from the outside, and Meredith Poulten, its director and counselor, has been its driving force since its inception. The center deals with contemporary issues of teen suicide, depression, family conflicts, sexuality, alcohol and other drugs, selfesteem, physical health, and personal hygiene—not from a distance but as the daily reality of today's adolescents. Out of an average of 150 student contacts per week in this center,

more than half concern alcohol or other drug involvement at some level. Before the center was established, such students were essentially on their own, "self-medicating" their problems, in the words of Poulten, rather than learning to handle the stresses of their lives. The school guidance department was oriented toward academic needs rather than day-to-day student problems, and many students have said that there was too great a stigma attached to talking to the school psychologist. As one student has expressed it, "I talk to Mrs. P. every day. She's more of a friend than a counselor. I can talk to her about anything." Another student admitted that were it not for the center, he would have been dead in less than a month.

The functioning of Poulten's Walk-in Center illustrates that the prob-

lems of today's youth do not fit into neat categories. They live in a world where drugs and sex are readily available and the pressure to indulge in both is high. At the same time, society equates success with being first and being second best with failure. For many students, communication with parents is next to impossible. Even when parents are open-minded about their child's circumstances, "You don't want to talk to your parents about your problems," says a student, "because you always want to please them."

The story of the center itself is a history of stresses and challenges, not unlike the lives of the students the center serves. For neither has life been easy. In June 1991, when state funding was curtailed and the school district, undergoing financial difficulties, could not assume its support, the center had to close down. By that time, however, a grass-roots organization, Citizens for the Medway Walk-in Center, had rallied to Poulten's side. Fortunately, later that year, a five-year grant from the federal Office of Substance Abuse Prevention came through and saved the day.

No one can predict what will happen when the grant runs out in 1996. Like many community prevention programs, the center relies on outside funding for its existence. All we can say is that in the meantime, the Walk-in Center at Medway High is open for business ready on the front lines to deal with the many tough problems that young people face today. At the center, they are finding some of the solutions in an atmosphere of caring and unconditional support.

SOURCES: Hudson, Ted (1991, February 20) Letter to the Editor: Medway High Walk-in Center must be spared. *The Country Gazette* (Medway MA), p. 3. Graham, Fiona (1989, October 11). A place to call their own. *The Country Gazette* (Medway MA), pp. 1, 14. Meredith Poulten, personal communication, 1994.

---

graduates and graduates, full-time and part-time students, residential students and commuters, students of traditional age and students older than twenty-two. In particular, there are marked differences in drug-abuse-prevention objectives between those under twenty-one and those who are older.

In the former group, the goal may be "no use of" (or abstinence from) alcohol and other drugs, while in the latter group the goal may be the low-risk (that is, responsible) consumption of alcohol and no use of nicotine products and illicit drugs. The term "low-risk consumption" refers to a level of use restricted by considerations of physical health, family background, pregnancy risk, the law, safety, and other personal concerns. As an example of how these considerations would be applied, pregnant women, recovering alcoholics or those with a family history of alcoholism, people driving cars or other machinery, people under medication, or those under the age of twenty-one should not drink alcohol at all. Although the distinction between under-twenty-one and over-twenty-one preventive goals is applicable in many community-oriented programs, it is an especially difficult challenge for drug-abuse-prevention efforts when the target population on a college campus contains both subgroups so closely intermingled.[29]

A second challenge comes from the widely held expectation that heavy alcoholic drinking, as well as some illicit drug use, during the college years represents something of a rite of passage. College alumni (and potential benefactors) frequently impede the implementation of drug-and-alcohol crackdowns, arguing that "we did it when we were in school."[30]

National surveys indicate that by the end of high school about 87 percent of all students have drunk alcohol and 35 percent have smoked marijuana. Therefore, we cannot say that use of these drugs for many college students is a new experience.[31] Given this base of prior exposure, it is not surprising that further experimentation and more extensive patterns of drug taking will occur. With the emphasis on the prevention and control of alcohol, however, it is less common for college administrations to focus on the problems associated with drugs other than alcohol. Although programs for alcohol education are virtually certain to be present on college campuses, attention directed toward comparable activities related specifically to drugs other than alcohol lags behind.

A third challenge relates to the earlier discussion in this chapter on alternative-behavior programming. Frequently there is a lack of recreational and social activities and facilities available to college students on campuses during periods of time when classes are not in session.

Strategies for prevention

On the positive side, college campuses have the potential for being ideal environments for comprehensive drug-abuse-prevention programs because they combine features of school and community settings. Here are some strategies for drug prevention on the college campus:

1. Develop a multifaceted prevention program of assessment, education, policy, and enforcement. Involve students, faculty, and administrators together to determine the degree of availability and demand for alcohol and other drugs on campus and in the surrounding community and initiate public information and education efforts.

2. Incorporate drug education into the curriculum. Faculty members can use drug-related situations as teachable moments, include drug topics in their course syllabus, and develop courses or course projects on drug issues.

3. Ensure that hypocrisy is not the rule of the day. Drug prevention is not a goal for college students only but is a larger issue that affects all members of the academic community.

4. Encourage environments that lessen the pressures to engage in drug-taking behavior. Foster more places where social and recreational activities can take place spontaneously and at hours when the alternative may be the consumption of alcohol and other drugs. A recent encouraging sign is the growing popularity of drug-free dormitories on many college campuses, where the residents specifically choose to refrain from alcohol, smoking, and other drugs.[32]

Where you can go for help

As has been pointed out, drug-abuse prevention is complex and difficult, and progress has been painfully slow. On both a societal and personal level, the goal of living drug free in a world where drugs are all around us remains a continuing challenge. We need all the help we can get. Fortunately there are health professionals waiting to help. But the decision to seek them out has to come from you. Here are some toll-free numbers that will connect you to them:

1-800-622-2255. National Council on Alcoholism. Seven days a week, twenty-four hours a day. You will receive a recording asking you to enter your zip code in order to get a local number in your calling area.

1-800-COCAINE. Cocaine help line. Seven days a week, twenty-four hours a day. You will also be referred to a help line in your local calling area.

1-800-448-3000. Boys' Town National Hotline. Seven days a week, twenty-four hours a day. Information materials and referrals for problems of substance abuse are available.

1-800-843-4971. The Center for Substance Abuse Prevention (CSAP) workplace help line. Information will refer to employers establishing workplace drug-abuse-prevention programs. Monday through Friday, 9:00 A.M. to 8:00 P.M. (Eastern time).

1-800-729-6686. National Clearinghouse for Alcohol and Drug Information. Resource material and referral information. The Center for Substance Abuse Treatment (CSAT) treatment referral hot line is available seven days a week, 8 A.M. to 7 P.M. (Eastern time). Emergency information is also available.

For local referral sources, the best place to look is in the Yellow Pages of your telephone book under "Alcoholism Information" or "Drug Abuse and Addiction Information."

Summary

WAYS TO APPROACH DRUG-ABUSE PREVENTION

- Drug-abuse-prevention efforts fall into three basic categories of intervention: primary, secondary, and tertiary.

- Primary prevention focuses on populations that have had only minimal exposure to drugs or none at all.

- Secondary prevention focuses on populations whose drug experience has not yet been associated with serious problems.

- Tertiary prevention focuses on populations who have entered specific drug-treatment programs and concerns itself with the prevention of relapse.

LEARNING FROM THE PAST: PREVENTION STRATEGIES THAT HAVE NOT WORKED

- Several strategies have been unsuccessful in meeting the goals of drug-abuse-prevention.

They include the reliance upon supply/availability reduction, punitive judicial policies, scare tactics, objective information, and affective education including values clarification.

HOPE AND PROMISE: CURRENT SCHOOL-BASED PREVENTION PROGRAMS

- Current school-based programs, such as Botvin's Life-Skills Training and Project DARE, are typically a mixture of several approaches.

- A particularly prominent component of current programs is the emphasis on learning assertiveness and other interpersonal skills needed to resist peer pressure to use drugs (peer-refusal skills).

COMMUNITY-BASED PREVENTION PROGRAMS

- Community-based programs make use of a broader range of resources, including community leaders and celebrities as positive role models, opportunities for alternative-behavior programming (activities that serve as alternatives to drug-taking behavior and environments associated with drug use), and the mass media.

- Recent efforts by the media have made a major impact on the image of drug-taking behavior in both high-risk populations and others in the community.

THE FAMILY AND PREVENTION

- Community-based drug-use-prevention programs are also increasingly mindful of the important role of the family, particularly of parents, in setting the stage for attitudes toward drugs in general.

DRUG-ABUSE PREVENTION IN THE WORKPLACE

- Programs in drug-abuse prevention have turned to the concerns of drug-taking

behavior in the workplace not only to improve the worker's quality of life but also to reduce the incidence of industrial accidents.

MULTICULTURAL ISSUES IN DRUG-ABUSE PREVENTION

- Attention has been directed toward special cultural considerations when communicating with specific subgroups in the community such as Latino and African American individuals.

YES, YOU: DRUG-ABUSE PREVENTION AND THE COLLEGE STUDENT

- On college campuses, drug-abuse-prevention programs are incorporating features of both school-based and community-based approaches in their efforts to reduce the use of alcohol and other drugs.

Key Terms

affective education, p. 399
impactors, p. 403
peer-refusal skills, p. 400
primary prevention, p. 396

secondary prevention, p. 396
sociocultural filters, p. 407
tertiary prevention, p. 396
values clarification, p. 399

Endnotes

1. Swisher, John D. (1979). Prevention issues. In R. L. DuPont, A. Goldstein, and J. O'Donnell (Eds.), *Handbook on drug abuse.* Washington DC: National Institute on Drug Abuse, pp. 423–435.
2. Goode, Erich (1989). *Drugs in American society* (3rd ed.). New York: McGraw-Hill, p. 270.
3. Hingson, Ralph W., Scotch, Norman, Mangione, Thomas, Meyers, Allan, Glantz, Leonard, Heeren, Timothy, Lin, Nan, Mucatel, March, and Pierce, Glenn (1983). Impact of legislation raising the legal drinking age in Massachusetts from 18 to 20. *American Journal of Public Health, 73,* 163–170.
4. Goode. *Drugs in American society,* pp. 261–287. Nadelmann, Ethan, and Wenner, Jann S. (1994, May 5). Toward a sane national drug policy. *Rolling Stone,* pp. 24–26. Steinberg, Neil (1994, May 5). The law of unintended consequences. *Rolling Stone,* pp. 33–34.
5. Funkhouser, Judith E., and Denniston, Robert W. (1992). Historical perspective. In Mary A. Jansen (Ed.), *A promising future: Alcohol and other drug problem prevention services improve-*

ment (OSAP Prevention Monograph 10). Rockville MD: Office of Substance Abuse Prevention, pp. 5–15.

6. Flay, Brian R., and Sobel, Judith L. (1983). The role of mass media in preventing adolescent substance abuse. In Thomas J. Glynn, Carl G. Leukenfeld, and Jacqueline P. Ludford (Eds.), *Preventing adolescent drug abuse.* Rockville MD: National Institute on Drug Abuse, pp. 5–35. Swisher, John D., Crawford J., Goldstein, R., and Yura, M. (1971). Drug education: Pushing or preventing. *Peabody Journal of Education, 49,* 68–75.

7. Meeks, Linda, Heit, Philip, and Page, Randy (1994). *Drugs, alcohol, and tobacco: "Totally awesome" teaching strategies.* Blacklick OH: Meeks Heit Publishing, p. 201.

8. Ibid., p. 202.

9. Funkhouser and Denniston. Historical perspective, p. 9. Schaps, Eric, DiBartolo, Russell, Moskowitz, Joel, Palley, Carol S., and Churgin, Shoshanna (1981). A review of 127 drug abuse prevention program evaluations. *Journal of Drug Issues, 11,* 17–43. Schroeder, Debra S., Laflin, Molly T., and Weis, David L. (1993). Is there a relationship between self-esteem and drug use?: Methodological and statistical limitations of the research. *Journal of Drug Issues, 22,* 645–665.

10. Center for Substance Abuse Prevention (1993). *Signs of effectiveness in preventing alcohol and other drug problems.* Rockville MD: Substance Abuse and Mental Health Services Administration.

11. Botvin, Gilbert J., Dusenbury, Linda, Baker, Eli, James-Ortiz, Susan, Botvin, Elizabeth M., and Kerner, Jon (1992). Smoking prevention among urban minority youth: Assessing effects on outcome and mediating variables *Health Psychology, 11,* 290–299. Botvin, Gilbert, and Tortu, Stephanie (1988). Preventing adolescent substance abuse through life skills training. In Richard M. Price, Emory L. Cowen, Raymond P. Lorion, and Julia Ramos-McKay (Eds.), *Fourteen ounces of prevention: A casebook for practitioners.* Washington DC: American Psychological Association, pp. 98–110.

12. Botvin, Gilbert J., Baker, Eli, Dusenbury, Linda, Tortu, Stephanie, and Botvin, Elizabeth M. (1990). Preventing adolescent drug abuse through a multimodal cognitive-behavioral approach: Results of a 3-year study. *Journal of Clinical and Counseling Psychology, 58,* 437–446.

13. Botvin, Gilbert J., and Botvin, Elizabeth M. (1992). Adolescent tobacco, alcohol, and drug abuse: Prevention strategies, empirical findings, and assessment issues. *Developmental and Behavioral Pediatrics, 13,* 290–301.

14. Resnicow, Ken, and Botvin, Gilbert J. (1993). School-based substance use prevention programs: Why do effects decay? *Preventive Medicine, 22,* 484–490.

15. Cavazos, Lauro F. (1989). *What works: Schools without drugs.* Washington DC: U.S. Department of Education, p. 38.

16. Clayton, Richard R., and Cattarello, Anne (1991). Prevention intervention research: Challenges and opportunities. In Carl G. Leukefeld and William J. Bukoski (Eds.), *Drug abuse prevention intervention research: Methodological issues* (NIDA Research Monograph 107). Rockville MD: National Institute on Drug Abuse, pp. 29–56. Gallup survey revealed that students believe drug abuse resistance education (D.A.R.E.) helps them avoid problems (1993, July 7) (Press release). DARE America, Los Angeles. Ten years later, DARE is still controversial (1993, October). *Law Enforcement News,* p. 5.

17. Benard, Bonnie (1990). An overview of community-based prevention. In Ketty H. Rey, Christopher L. Faegre, and Patti Lowery, *Prevention research findings: 1988* (OSAP Prevention Monograph 3). Rockville MD: Office of Substance Abuse Prevention, pp. 126–147.

18. Rhodes, Jean E., and Jason, Leonard A. (1991). The social stress model of alcohol and other drug abuse: A basis for comprehensive community-based prevention. In Ketty H. Rey, Christopher L. Faegre, and Patti Lowery (Eds.), *Prevention research findings: 1988* (OSAP Prevention Monograph 3). Rockville MD: Office of Substance Abuse Prevention, pp. 155–171.

19. Schaps, DiBartolo, Moskowitz, Palley, and Churgin. A review of 127 drug abuse prevention program evaluations. Tobler, Nancy S. (1986). Meta-analysis of 143 adolescent drug prevention programs: Quantitative outcome results of program participants compared to a control group. *Journal of Drug Issues, 16,* 537–567.

20. Zeuschner, Raymond (1993). *Communicating today.* Boston: Allyn and Bacon, p. 377.

21. Partnership for a Drug-Free America (1994, July 12). New study shows children in NYC becoming more anti-drug, bucking national trends (Press release). Partnership for a Drug-Free America, New York.

22. Delong, William, and Winsten, Jay A. (1990, Summer). The use of mass media in substance abuse prevention. *Health Affairs,* pp. 30–46.

23. Kumpfer, Karol L. (1991). How to get hard-to-reach parents involved in parenting programs. *Parent training is prevention: Preventing alcohol and other drug problems among youth in the family.* Rockville MD: Office of Substance Abuse Prevention, pp. 87–95. Resnick, Hank, and Wojcicki, Marba (1991). Reaching and retaining high risk youth and their parents in prevention programs. In Eric N. Goplerud (Ed.), *Preventing adolescent drug use: From theory to practice* (OSAP Prevention Monograph 8). Rockville MD: Office of Substance Abuse Prevention, pp. 91–126.

24. *Parent training is prevention: Preventing alcohol and other drug problems among youth in the family* (1991). Rockville MD: Office of Substance Abuse Prevention.

25. U.S. Department of Labor (1990). *An employer's guide to dealing with substance abuse.* Washington DC: U.S. Department of Labor.

26. Funkhouser, Judith E., Goplerud, Eric N., and Bass, Rosalyn O. (1992). Current status of prevention strategies. In Mary A. Jansen (Ed.), *A promising future: Alcohol and other drug problem prevention services improvement* (OSAP Prevention Monograph 10). Rockville MD: Office of Substance Abuse Prevention, pp. 47–48. National Transportation Safety Board (1988). *Alcohol/drug use and its impact on railroad safety: Safety study.* Washington DC: U.S. Department of Transportation. Wald, Matthew L. (1994, September 20). Transportation workers face more frequent tests for drugs. *New York Times,* p. B5.

27. Office of Substance Abuse Prevention (1990). *The fact is . . . reaching Hispanic/Latino audiences requires cultural sensitivity.* Rockville MD: National Clearinghouse for Alcohol and Drug Information.

28. Office of Substance Abuse Prevention (1990). *The fact is . . . alcohol and other drug use is a special concern for African American families and communities.* Washington DC: U.S. Department of Health and Human Services.

29. Office of Substance Abuse Prevention (1991). *Faculty members' handbook: Strategies for preventing alcohol and other drug problems.* Washington DC: U.S. Department of Health and Human Services, p. 4.

30. Hersh, Richard H. (1994, September 26). The culture of neglect: Our colleges have to lead, not follow. *Newsweek,* pp. 12–13.

31. Johnston, Lloyd D., O'Malley, Patrick M., and Bachman, Jerald G. (1994). *National survey results on drug use from the Monitoring the Future study, 1975–1993* Vol. 1. Rockville MD: National Institute on Drug Abuse, Table 1.

32. Office of Substance Abuse Prevention. *Faculty members' handbook,* pp. 21–25.

Index

---

* Bold-faced terms are defined on the page number in bold-faced type.

415

Dexedrine (d-amphetamine), 103
Dextroamphetamine (d-amphetamine), 103, 104–5
Dextromethorphan, 162
Dextromethorphan hydrobromide, 162
Diagnostic and Statistical Manual, fourth edition (DSM-IV), 258–59
    criteria for substance dependence and abuse in, 40–41
Diarrhea, opiates for treatment of, 161–62
Diazepam, 34, **121,** 121–22, 124, 186, 363, 364, 387
    DAWN statistics on, 123
    for LSD panic, 186
    withdrawal, 127
Dibenzoxazepines, 381
Dickens, Charles, 286–87
Diethylbarbituric acid, 114
Diethylpropion, 107
Dihydroindolones, 381
Dilantin (phenytoin), 43, 243
Dilaudid (hydromorphone), 161, 347
Dimetane (brompheniramine), 362
Dimetapp (brompheniramine), 362
Dimetapp (phenylpropanolamine), 107
2, 5,-Dimethoxy-4-methylamphetamine (DOM or STP), 179, **191,** 191–92
Dimethyltryptamine (DMT), 179, **190**
Diphenhydramine, 362, 364, **369,** 369–70
Direct method of decaffeination, 323–24
Disease, alcoholism as, 272, 282
Disinhibition theory, 247
Dissociative anesthetic hallucinogens, 197
Dissociative disorders, 378
Distillation, 230, 230–31
Distilled spirits, 230, 230–31
Disulfiram, 243, **273**
Diuretic effects of alcohol, 241–42
Diuretics, 243, 345
    caffeine in, 323
Diuril, 243
Dr. Agnew's Catarrh Powder, 9
Dole, Vincent, 170
Dolorphine (methadone), 161
DOM, 179, **191,** 191–92
Domestic violence, alcoholism and, 257
Doors of Experience, The (Huxley), 181
Dopamine, 78, 79
    amphetamines and, 103
    cocaine and, 95
    mesotelencephalic dopamine pathway (MTDP), 82
Dopaminergic neurons, 383–85
Dopaminergic receptor, 80
Dope, 345
Doriden (glutethimide), 118, 169, 243

Dose, 29
    effective, 30
    lethal, 30, 30–31
    tolerance and, 35–37, **36**
Dose-response curve, 29, 29–30, 32
Double-blind procedures, **83**
Doxylamine succinate, 369, 369–70
D-propoxyphene, 34, 347
Drake, Sir Francis, 285
Drinking, symptomatic, 256. *See also entries related to alcohol*
Dristan (oxymetazoline), 107, 323
Drivers, designated, 405
Driving skills
    alcohol and, 245–46
    marijuana and, 211
Driving while intoxicated (DWI), 245, 246
Dronabinol, 218
Drug abuse, 5, **6**
    AIDS and, 42–44
    defined, 6
    dependence and, 38–41
    inhalant abuse as gateway to future, 141–42
    in pregnancy, 41–42, 43
Drug Abuse Resistance Education (DARE), 402
Drug Abuse Warning Network (DAWN), 32, 32–35, **36,** 363
Drug Abuse Warning Network (DAWN) reports, 119
    on alcohol, 243
    on benzodiazepines, 123
    on cocaine, 98
    on LSD, 184, 185
    on PCP, 198
"Drug automatism," 116
Drug combinations, 6
Drug Efficacy Study Investigation (DESI), 361, 362
Drug Enforcement Administration (DEA), 53, 192, 341
Drug-Free Workplace Act (1988), 406–7
Drug interactions, 66–67, 68
Drug laws, 50–54
    enforcement of, 50, 52–54
Drug misuse, 5, 5–6
Drugs, 4
    contradictory messages about, 2–3
    defining, 4–5
    factors determining physiological impact of, 66–68
    history of, 6–12, 19
    intent in use of, 4
    legality of, 5, 25–26
    regulation of, 48–52
    routes of administration, 61–65
    source of future, 19–21
    types of, 3
Drug selling, 47–48

Drug smuggling, international, 397
Drug-taking behavior, 3–4
    among American youth, 12–17
    attitude toward, 12
    behavioral tolerance and, 37
    cycle of dependence and, **4**
    DAWN statistics on, 34–35
    drug abuse, 5, **6**
    drug misuse, 5, 5–6
    factors influencing, 16–17
    gender differences in, 14
    through history, 6–12
    instrumental use, 5
    physiological aspects of, 78–82
    predictions of future, 17–21
    psychological factors in, 82–83
    racial and ethnic differences in, 14
    recreational use, 5
DSM-IV (*Diagnostic and Statistical Manual,* fourth edition), 258–59
DTs, 263
Dukakis, Michael and Kitty, 105
Duke, James B., 288
Dumas, Alexandre, 206
Durabolin (nandrolone phenproprionate), 336
Duragesic (fentanyl), 161
Duramorph (morphine), 161
DWI, 245, 246
Dycodan (hydrocodone), 161
Dylan, Bob, 182
Dynorphins, 164

EAPs (Employee Assistance Programs), 277
East India Company, 153
Ebers Papyrus, 7, 82, 152
Economically compulsive violence, 46, 46–47
Economics, tobacco and, 286
Ecstasy, 179, 192–93
Eden Express (Vonnegut), 382
Edison, Thomas, 90
Education
    affective, 399
    negative, 398
    smoking and, 302, 306
Educational intervention programs on AIDS and drug abuse, 42–44
Effective dose, 30
Effexor (venlafaxine), 387
EIA (Enzyme Immunoassay), 345, 345–36
Eighteenth Amendment to U.S. Constitution, 9, 261–62
800 numbers for professional help, 411
Elavil (amitriptyline), 34, 363–64, 386
Elderly, the
    alcohol abuse among, 269–70
    benzodiazepines for, 123
    drug responses of, 358
    prescription drugs and, 371